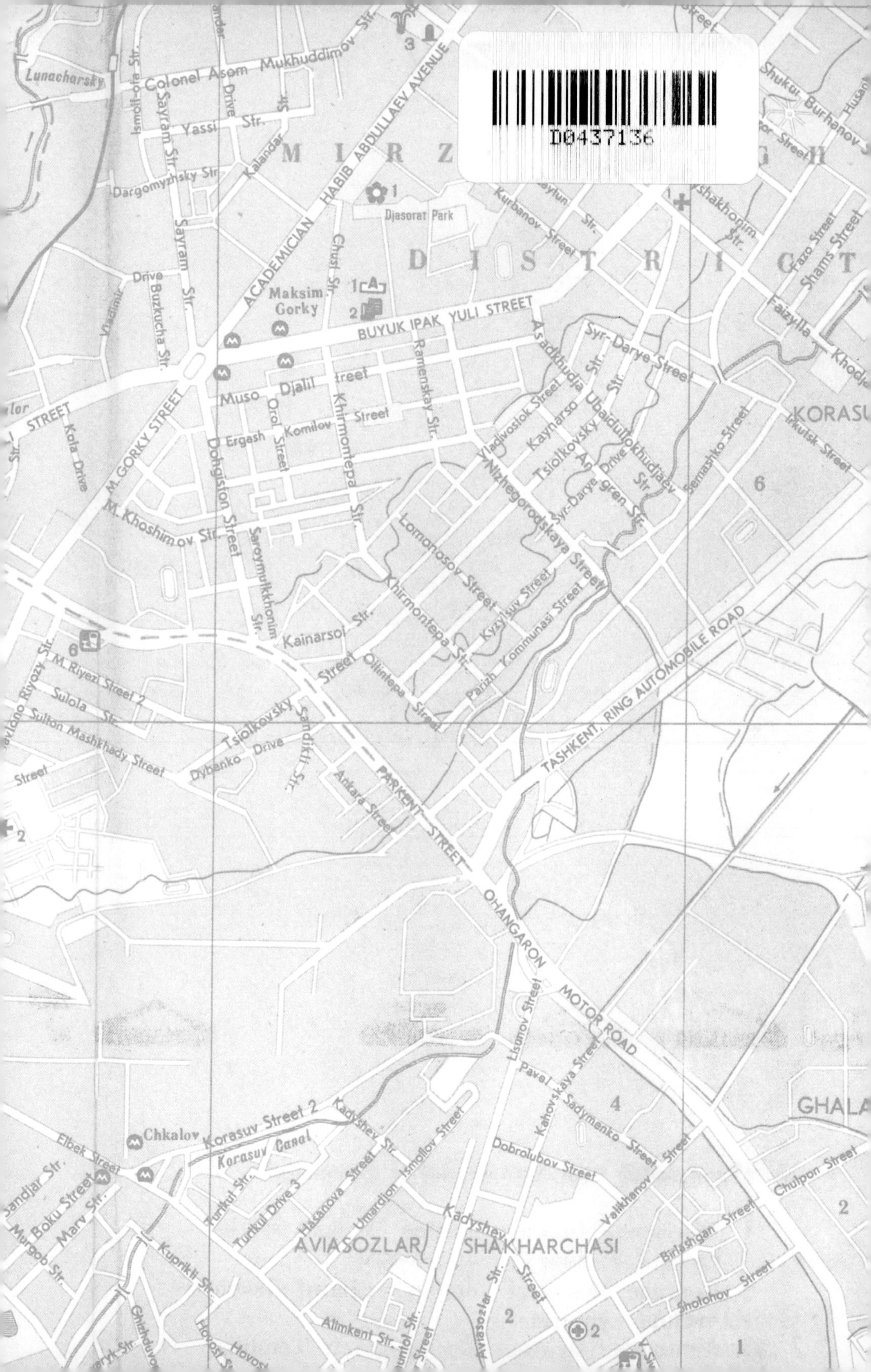
Lunacharsky
Colonel Asom Mukhuddimov Str.
Ismoil-ota Str.
Sayram Str.
Yassi Str.
Drive
Str.
Kalandar
Dargomyzhsky Str.
ACADEMICIAN HABIB ABDULLAEV AVENUE
M I R Z
Djasorat Park
Kurbanov Street
Shakhonim Str.
Shukur Burhanov Str.
D I S T R I C T
Chust Str.
Maksim Gorky
BUYUK IPAK YULI STREET
Vladimir
Drive
Buzkucha Str.
Sayram Str.
Faizylla Khodjaev
Fazo Street
Shams Street
Asadkhudja Str.
Syr-Darye Street
Ramenskay Str.
Muso Djalil Street
Orol Street
Komilov Street
Khirmontepa Str.
Ergash
Dohgiston Street
M. GORKY STREET
STREET
Kola Drive
Vladivostok Street
Kaynarso Str.
Tsiolkovsky Str.
Ubaidullokhudjaev Str.
Angren Str.
Syr-Darye Drive
Nizhegorodskaya Street
Semashko Street
Irkutsk Street
KORASU
6
M. Khoshimov Str.
Saroymulkkhonim Str.
Lomonosov Street
Khirmontepa Str.
Kyzylsuv Street
Kommunasi Street
Kainarsoi Str.
Street
Oltintepa Street
Parizh
TASHKENT RING AUTOMOBILE ROAD
6
M. Riyezi Street 2
Sulola Str.
Sulton Mashkhady Street
Tsiolkovsky
Dybenko Drive
Sandikli Str.
Ankara Street
PARKENT STREET
Street
2
OHANGARON MOTOR ROAD
Lisunov Street
Kahovskaya Street
Pavel Sadymenko Street
4
GHALA
Chkalov
Korasuv Street 2
Korasuv Canal
Kadyshev Str.
Elbek Street
Sandjar Str.
Boku Street
Marv Str.
Murgob Str.
Turkul Str.
Turkul Drive 3
Hasanova Street
Umardjon
Ismoilov Street
Dobrolubov Street
Valikhanov Street
Chulpon Street
2
Kadyshev
AVIASOZLAR SHAKHARCHASI
Birlashgan Street
Shotohov Street
Kuprikli Str.
Aviasozlar Str.
Street
2
2
Alimkent Str.
1

SILK ROAD TO RUIN

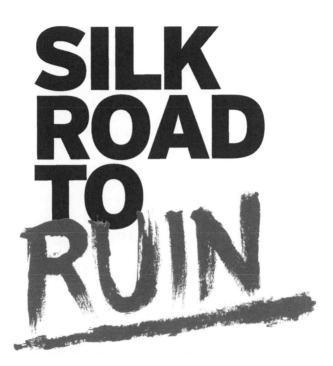

Also Available by Ted Rall from NBM:

My War With Brian, $8.95

2024, $16.95 hc., $9.95 pb.

To Afghanistan and Back, $15.95 hc., $9.95 pb.

Generalissimo El Busho, $19.95 hc., $13.95 pb.

Edited by Ted Rall:

Attitude: The New Subversive Political Cartoonists, $13.95

Attitude 2: The New Subversive Alternative Cartoonists, $13.95

Attitude 3: The New Subversive Online Cartoonists, $13.95

Other Books by Ted Rall:

Waking Up in America

All The Rules Have Changed

Revenge of the Latchkey Kids

Search and Destroy

Gas War

Wake Up, You're Liberal!

America Gone Wild

SILK ROAD TO RUIN

IS CENTRAL ASIA THE NEW MIDDLE EAST?

TED RALL

Acknowledgements:

As a child my mom encouraged me not to believe in limits; Yvonne Rall also bought the subscription to *National Geographic* that first brought Kazakhstan in particular and Central Asia in general to my attention. Randall Lane was editor of *P.O.V.* magazine, which sent me on my first two trips to the former Silk Road. Doug Simmons and Ted Keller at *The Village Voice* sent me to Afghanistan via Tajikistan in 2001 to cover the U.S. invasion. David G. Hall was the program director at KFI Radio, which both financed Stan Trek 2000 and my 2001 trip to Afghanistan. Tracy Aguilar, my producer at KFI, accompanied me on Stan Trek, where she helped keep the madness to a minimum. Bob Guccione, Jr. was the editor of *Gear* magazine, which commissioned me to travel to Tajikistan to cover *buzkashi* but folded before it could be published. (It ran in *Drill* magazine instead, thanks to Featurewell editor David Wallis.) Ted Rall's non-graphic novella cartoons originally appeared at EurasiaNet.org. Justin Burke edited the stand-alone cartoons that appeared at EurasiaNet. My wife traveled with me to Central Asia on three occasions and proofread this book.

Editor: J.P. Trostle

Front and Back Cover Design: Henry H. Owings
"Ruin" brush art by Firebreathing Media
Maps on pages 17 and 232 by J.P. Trostle.

"High Anxiety" and "A Good Day to Die" previously appeared in *P.O.V.* and *Drill* magazines, respectively.

Photographs on pages 96, 101 and 102 appear courtesy of the Library of Congress; page 160, courtesy of Human Rights Watch; page 161, courtesy of the Press-Service of the President of Uzbekistan; and page 238, courtesy of the Embassy of Kazakhstan to the U.S. and Canada. Images on pages xi, 16, 98, 100, 103 and 249 are in the public domain.

Ted Rall Online: www.RALL.com

Silk Road to Ruin
ISBN-10: 1-56163-454-9; ISBN-13: 978-1-56163-454-5

Library of Congress Cataloging-in-Publication Data

Rall, Ted.
  Silk road to ruin / Ted Rall.
    p. cm.
    ISBN 1-56163-454-9 (alk. paper) ~
    1. Graphic novels. I. Title.
PN 6727.R35S56 2006
741.5'973~dc22
                          2006042041

Contents

History tells us that the Soviet Union collapsed in 1991, but don't tell that to the people of Central Asia. The legacy of Russian influence and state socialism lives on in republics that declared independence only after they were evicted from the USSR. Former citizens of a superpower seethe as riches from newly tapped oil and gas wells pour into the pockets of their corrupt leaders.

In a region where autocratic police states are the standard form of government, Saparmurat Niyazov presides over the most extravagant cult of personality in the most highly developed totalitarian dictatorship. A comprehensive examination of the rule of the tiny man who calls himself the Thirteenth Prophet.

Whether it's a trip to the market or across the continent, Central Asia's corrupt militsia make travel so difficult and expensive that few citizens dare to attempt it. Bribery and extortion have replaced more traditional forms of economic activity as a result.

Nearly a century after Stalin carved a region of borderless mountain ranges and steppes into arbitrary nation-states, Central Asians are struggling to define themselves and their ethnicities.

How to lose forty-four pounds in six weeks, otherwise known as the shashlyk diet plan, a.k.a. why sustenance is a more brutal adversary than the militsia along the Silk Road.

A 2002 assassination attempt against the president of Uzbekistan and his subsequent crackdown on Muslims highlights the powderkeg of rising Islamism in Central Asia and how government attempts to counter radical movements strengthen them instead. Meanwhile, the United States and the West sabotages a nascent democracy in Kyrgyzstan and precipitates its plunge into anarchy.

MAPS & COUNTRY PROFILES

Who Lost Central Asia?
Introduction by Ahmed Rashid

After September 11, 2001, Central Asia embraced America. However, the regimes of the five Central Asian Republics—Kazakhstan, Kyrgyzstan, Uzbekistan, Tajikistan and Turkmenistan—did so for quite different reasons than the peoples of Central Asia. After a decade of stagnation and international isolation, the authoritarian regimes embraced the presence of U.S. bases and troops on their soil in the belief that this would further legitimize their personal grip on power, allow them to carry on conducting rigged elections, show disrespect for human rights and give them negotiating space with their overpowering neighbours Russia and China.

The people embraced America because they thought a U.S. presence would force their regimes to carry out much needed political and economic reforms and push them towards greater accountability and democracy. For the fifty million people of Central Asia, the majority of whom are Muslim, America was unknown territory. Most people had never met an American, but what they associated with Americans was greater freedom and democracy. In the military campaigns against Al Qaeda and later Iraq, Central Asia was the only Muslim region of the world where the image of America remained consistently high.

Yet America failed Central Asia, for the administration of President George W. Bush decided in its infinite wisdom to side with the regimes rather than the peoples. President Islam Karimov of Uzbekistan was so convinced of his invincibility because of the favours he was doing for the U.S. Defence Department and the CIA, not least by hosting "black prisons" for secret Al Qaeda detainees, that he thought it inconsequential to massacre between seven hundred and one thousand of his protesting citizens in Andijon in May 2005. The U.S. tolerated the cruel eccentricities of President Saparmurat Niyazov (or Turkmenbashi) of Turkmenistan as long as he gave U.S. military aircraft over-flight facilities to the war zones in Afghanistan.

When the U.S. was forced to side with outraged world public opinion after the Andijon massacre and condemn Uzbekistan, Karimov told the Americans to pack up and leave their bases and he turned towards Russia and China for support.

Nobody in Washington thought of asking the obvious question of the Bush administration: Who lost Uzbekistan ?

Now, as of this writing, it seems more than likely that the Kyrgyz regime is about to throw out the American bases or demand much more money from them.

Just five years after being welcomed with open arms, it seems the U.S. is being forced to abandon Central Asia. In Washington the question very quickly should become: Who lost Central Asia? But so far nobody is asking and the Bush administration is providing no accountability for its actions.

Indeed there is another new Great Game afoot in Central Asia between the U.S., China and Russia and smaller regional states such as Turkey, Iran, Pakistan and India. It's about influence and power politics and the best way to combat Islamic extremism, but above all it's about oil and gas and access to what may be the last major untapped energy reserves in the world. What happens in Central Asia will determine to a great extent the future for all the countries around it and ultimately the United States of America.

Ted Rall has captured all this and much more in a hysterically funny, deeply serious and sincere book. Rall has no qualms in pointing out the absurd within the deeply profound—surely the hallmark of a great writer and cartoonist. Yet it is also clear that he is personally involved, that he loves these people and the empty steppes, windy deserts and snowy mountains that they live in. Central Asia is a spectacular melange of all kinds of human faces and every type of natural scenery. Its politics conjure up misery, brutality and charm all at the same time, something that only Rall with his exquisite—sometimes excruciating—skills can convey.

If the truth be told, every part of our conflicted world needs an American interpreter of events and places such as Ted Rall. There should be a Ted Rall of the Middle East and a Ted Rall of Latin America—so that Americans and the rest of us can better understand the world we live in and try and make it a better place.

Ahmed Rashid
Lahore, April 2006

Ahmed Rashid, a Pakistani journalist, is the author of the best-selling books "Taliban: Militant Islam, Oil and Fundamentalism in Central Asia" and "Jihad: The Rise of Militant Islam in Central Asia." He is the Pakistan, Afghanistan and Central Asia correspondent for the Far Eastern Economic Review *and the* Daily Telegraph *of London.*

Foreword

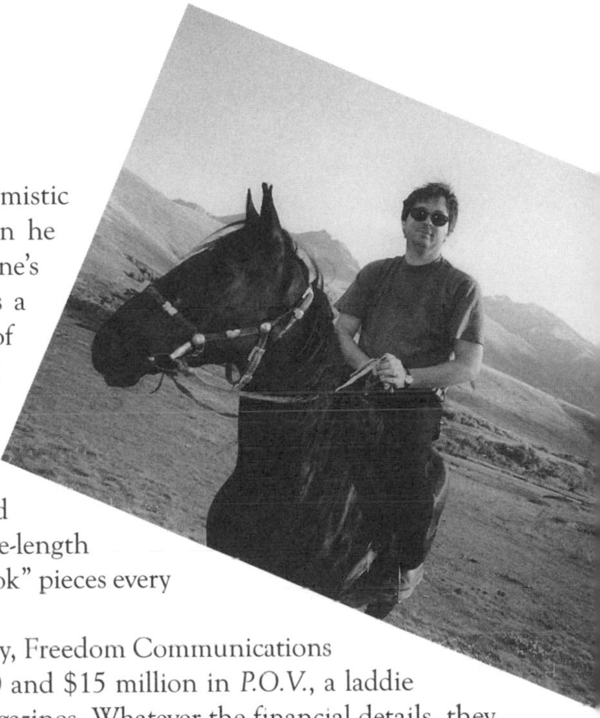

Randall was lubricated, optimistic and therefore exuberant when he welcomed me to *P.O.V.* magazine's 1996 year-end party. I had landed as a staff writer at *P.O.V.* after the collapse of *Might*, the snarky San Francisco-based glossy dedicated to the prospect that Generation X would inherit the earth but regret it, with an arrangement that Hunter S. Thompson would have gleefully abused: write two feature-length articles and two short "front of the book" pieces every year in return for a monthly retainer.

Depending on who told the story, Freedom Communications had invested somewhere between $10 and $15 million in *P.O.V.*, a laddie magazine before there were laddie magazines. Whatever the financial details, they felt flush. "Dude," Randall put his arm around me, "what's the wildest, craziest, most over-the-top story you've ever wanted to write but couldn't because you didn't have the money? You name it, we'll do it!" he promised.

I flicked the salt off my margarita and flashed back to the summer of 1975, or maybe 1976 or 1977. I was in junior high school, it was summer and I was lying in my mom's backyard reading *National Geographic*. I pulled out a fold-out photograph of a pair of horsemen riding across the steppe. Jagged mountains filled the horizon. The photo had been taken in the Kazakh Soviet Socialist Republic, which—as I remember it—the magazine described as "the most remote place on earth." The most remote place on earth! If anyone knew where that was, it was *National Geographic*. They went everywhere. They even went to Antarctica.

I remember sitting on my mom's white lawn chair, the kind with the big rubber bandy things that leave marks on your skin and pinch you, and looking up at the Ohio sky. "I will never, ever go to the most remote place on earth," I thought.

Randall, I knew, was a bit of a daredevil. He liked to test himself by throwing himself into stressful situations: skydiving, scuba, even driving a racecar in a long-distance high-speed rumble across the Southwest. So I pitched him something I knew would appeal to him: a reckless headlong plunge into the belly of post-Soviet Central Asia. "I'll drive the Silk Road from Beijing to Istanbul," I proposed, "via Kazakhstan, Kyrgyzstan, Uzbekistan, Turkmenistan, Iran and Turkey. I won't do research. I'll just show up and see what happens."

Of course I did *some* research. I read *The Lonely Planet Guide to Central Asia*. I talked to consuls at visa offices for the various countries I was planning to visit. I even plowed through a classic history of Central Asia, Peter Hopkirk's *The Great Game*. My overall plan, however, was not to plan. I would play things by ear. I would buy a car—or, even better, a motorcycle with sidecar—in Beijing and drive it across the biggest landmass on earth until I arrived in Istanbul. What if I broke down? I'd have to find someone to make repairs, or purchase a replacement vehicle. Things would go wrong; it would be disappointing if they didn't.

Revelation

Things went wrong. For one thing, it turned out to be difficult for a foreigner to buy a car in China and virtually impossible to transport it across the border to Kazakhstan. I called Randall from Beijing to tell him that I would take the train as far west as possible. He wasn't pleased. "But this is about *driving* the Silk Road. It isn't about taking the train like some ordinary tourist." He said "tourist" the way men sneer "pussy." I told him not to worry. "I'll buy the car in Kazakhstan," I said. "There's an *autobazaar* in Almaty where you can buy them for cash. Or a motorcycle, with sidecar."

He sounded relieved. "Motorcycle? OK, that'll be cool. Keep me posted."

In Ürümqi, the administrative capital of the Xinjiang Uyghur Autonomous Region and the railway terminus at the time, I forked over nearly ten times the standard bus fare for a "sleeper ticket" across the mountains to Almaty where my car, or motorcycle with sidecar, awaited. Estimated travel time: thirty hours. Indeed, when I boarded the bus, I saw two beds near the front. Sure, they were ratty mattress pads covered with stained blankets, but they looked a lot more comfortable than the hard wood benches the other poor sods were going to be stuck with as we humped the Tian Shan mountain range. My guilt evaporated, however, upon being made to understand that my expensive "sleeper" ticket had purchased me the same seats as the riff-raff. The cots belonged to the back-up drivers. But why, I wondered, would they need extra drivers for a trip of that length?

That became clear soon enough. The drivers stopped every twenty or thirty kilometers to pick up and drop off smuggled goods. Thirty hours? More like three days. It was a grueling experience, but at least I had the four-star luxury of the Hotel Ala Too to look forward to once I arrived in Almaty. Well, I might have if the joint

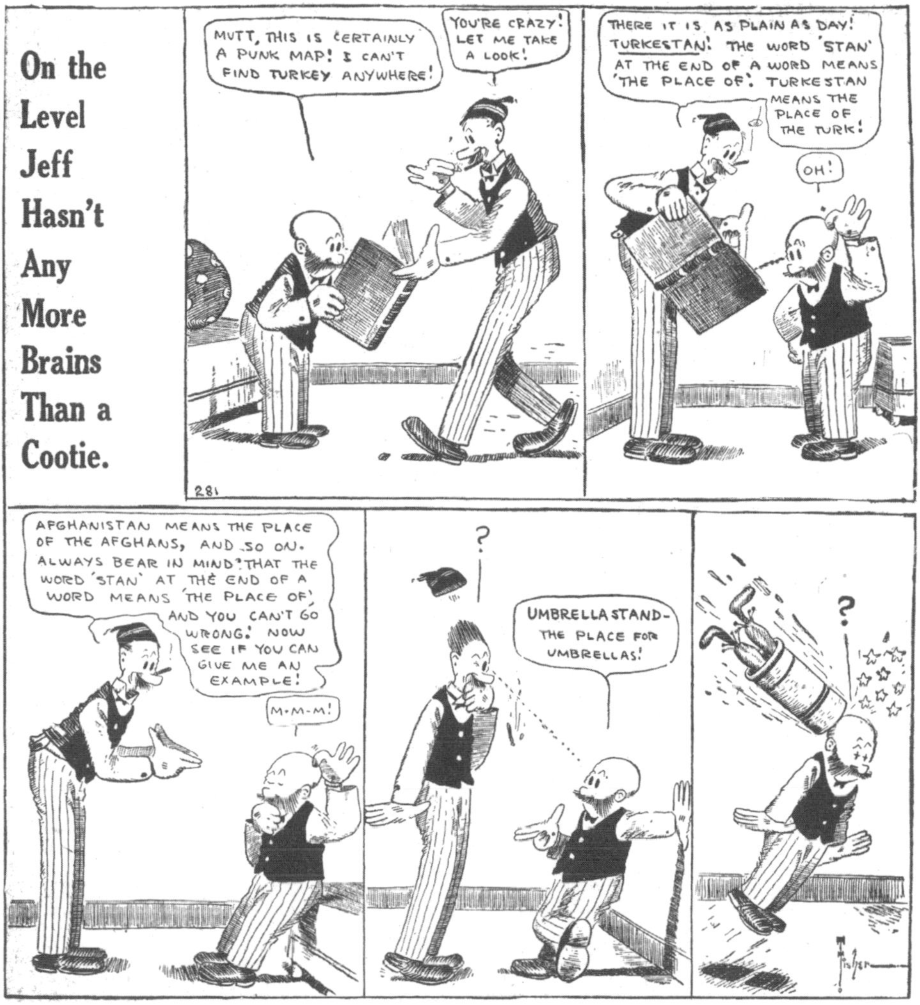
On the Level Jeff Hasn't Any More Brains Than a Cootie.
MUTT, THIS IS CERTAINLY A PUNK MAP! I CAN'T FIND TURKEY ANYWHERE!
YOU'RE CRAZY! LET ME TAKE A LOOK!
THERE IT IS AS PLAIN AS DAY! TURKESTAN! THE WORD 'STAN' AT THE END OF A WORD MEANS 'THE PLACE OF'. TURKESTAN MEANS THE PLACE OF THE TURK!
OH!
AFGHANISTAN MEANS THE PLACE OF THE AFGHANS, AND SO ON. ALWAYS BEAR IN MIND THAT THE WORD 'STAN' AT THE END OF A WORD MEANS 'THE PLACE OF', AND YOU CAN'T GO WRONG! NOW SEE IF YOU CAN GIVE ME AN EXAMPLE!
M-M-M!
?
UMBRELLA STAND- THE PLACE FOR UMBRELLAS!
?

A "Mutt and Jeff" cartoon from the World War I era.

hadn't been under renovation. Not all of it—but unknown miscreants had mortared it the evening before. (Fortunately I hadn't taken the three-day express bus.)

Almaty's *autobazaar*, along with just about everything else in town, turned out to be closed for a long Constitution Day weekend. As I trudged away I stopped to admire a beautiful old 1960s vintage Gaz-21 Volga sedan parked on the street. It was bulky, yet elegant, like an old Checker cab. "Hey!" its owner shouted from an open first-floor apartment window. "Want to buy my car?" I had a vision of pulling in front of Istanbul's Aya Sofia, dusty and triumphant, weeks thereafter in my marvel of Soviet engineering.

"*Skolke stoit?*" I asked.

"Never mind money," he replied. Let's go for a drive." The old man was a shark.

Camels near the ruins of Merv (modern-day Mary), Turkmenistan.

We got in. He primed the clutch. He turned the key. Nothing. More priming. More nothing. He looked chagrined. "But it *always* works," he swore. I said nothing.

"How about two thousand dollars?" he asked.

"It doesn't start," I pointed out.

"Price is four thousand if starts!" I got out.

No biggie, I thought. *Lonely Planet* said that there was an *autobazaar* in Bishkek, a mere one hundred twelve miles east. Well, there would have been: I pulled into town on Kyrgyz Independence Day. "Come back in two weeks," a guy selling bootleg parts for a Lada engine across a plaid blanket advised. So much for my plan to drive the Silk Road.

National holidays screwed up just about everything. When my long-promised Iranian visa wasn't waiting for me in Ashkhabat, I had to spend every morning for a week waiting to find a consular official willing to help me. Finally, I demanded the truth: "You tell me to come back every morning, but when I do I spend the whole time staring at the photograph of Ayatollah Kholmeini and watching children's cartoons in your waiting room. What's going on?"

"It is the Birthday of Imam Mahdi," the official admitted. Everyone is on vacation. We have not heard from Teheran in days."

Driving the Silk Road never happened, but I suffered enough ill health and *militsia* robbery misadventures to satisfy Randall and hopefully his readers. More important to me, my trip had prompted a revelation.

Five years after having been cut loose by the imploding Soviet Union the Central Asian republics—colloquially known as the Stans—were reeling from an identity crisis precipitated by economic collapse. Citizens of a great superpower had awoken to find themselves living in Third World anarchy. Closed societies were opening up to the West for the first time. Guards at the Chinese-Kazakh border detained me for hours at one checkpoint after another; the Kazakhs still faxed Moscow for advice on how to handle me because they had never seen an American passport.

Elderly people were starving to death in nations sitting atop the world's largest untapped reserves of oil and natural gas. Looters were cavalierly ambling around in flatbed trucks loaded with disinterred nuclear missiles. Statues of and slogans by crazy dictators were springing up as quickly as their corrupt military policemen could rob a passing motorist. And on the main drag in the capital city of each of these profoundly dysfunctional societies, a gleaming American embassy housed a staff that was quietly calling the shots in a new campaign to de-Russify access to those staggering energy resources.

CIA agents, oilmen and prostitutes mixed uneasily and awkwardly in ad hoc British-style pubs where beers cost a dollar—a day's pay and more than enough to keep the locals away. In an extreme case of the "oil curse," wealth was being pillaged by U.S.-backed autocrats while their subjects plunged into poverty. The official name of one government office building in Ashkhabat, engraved on a shiny Pier 1 Import-style brass plaque, was the Turkmen Ministry for the Benefit of the Account of the President. Meanwhile, Taliban-trained Islamic radicals were waiting to fill the leadership vacuum created by dictators who didn't make the slightest pretense of caring about ordinary people.

It was a combustible mix, one that made the Middle East look stable and calm in comparison. Clearly the United States would suffer consequences ("blowback" in CIA parlance) for its role in propping up hated despots. "If you people"—he

A bizarre, disused Soviet-era public park behind a hotel outside Bishkek, Kyrgyzstan.

meant Americans—"would just get out of our way, we could kill scum like [Uzbek president Islam] Karimov and liberate ourselves," a Muslim vendor of Pakistani knockoffs of cheap Iranian sweaters told me through gritted teeth in Samarkand's central bazaar. "You are helping our enemy, so you are becoming our enemy," he said. I couldn't argue. Rulers like Karimov were even worse than higher-profile dictators such as Iraq's Saddam Hussein and Moammar Khadafi in Libya, who at least invested a portion of their nations' wealth into necessary infrastructure. The U.S. was courting disaster by supporting them, and I wanted to raise the alarm. But how? And would anybody care?

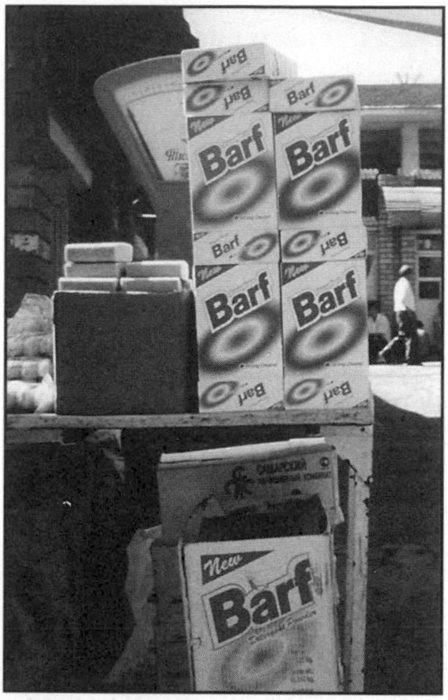
New
Barf

Barf detergent on offer in Tashkent, Uzbekistan. ("Barf" means "snow" in Farsi; it is manufactured in Iran.)

My magazine account of my 1997 trip through Central Asia, "Silk Road to Ruin," was soon followed by a feature I launched on my Los Angeles radio talk show. "Stan Watch: Breaking News from Central Asia" was conceived as a send-up of Americans' presumed disinterest in foreign affairs. Once again, the joke turned serious. "Stan Watch"'s obscure news stories from the world's most remote countries, which many Americans couldn't even pronounce, became wildly popular. NPR and the BBC simulcast it. A 1999 assassination attempt on President Karimov became a subject of intense speculation among my listeners. Americans, it turned out, *were* interested in the outside world. They just couldn't read much about it in their local newspaper.

When I returned from my 1997 trip I was forty-two pounds lighter and thrilled to be home. Nothing tasted sweeter than mustard vinaigrette sauce on a fresh endive salad at an Upper West Side bistro after endless weeks of mystery meat on a stick and bowls of botulism. Central Asia, I believed, was out of my system. But like the Vietnam veterans who kept dreaming about southeast Asia, many of whom have since returned to visit or live there permanently, I thought about it all the time. The steppes, the mountains, the region's anarchic beauty and its utterly pointless ongoing tragedy—Central Asia was a sort of secret that spoke to me the way a city speaks to you when you tell yourself for no reason in particular: "I could live here." I *had* to go back.

So I have. And I'll return again. No one understands my obsession with Central Asia. I don't blame them; the Kyzylkum desert isn't exactly the French Riviera. Travel is difficult and often menacing, tourist attractions are scarce and the food seriously sucks. But only a fool goes to Central Asia to relax. One travels there be-

Yurts beside Tianchi (Heavenly) Lake, sixty miles outside the gritty industrial city of Ürümqi, administrative capital of Xinjiang in western China.

cause it is always changing and because it is where everything that will matter to the world in the next few decades is happening or about to happen.

I returned in 1999, again for *P.O.V.*, to visit the region's rural mountain villages and test my vertigo on the world's highest-altitude and most dangerous highway. A year later I brought two dozen curious Americans, fans of "Stan Watch" on KFI, on a bus tour from hell that presaged the "Survivor" reality-television series. I traveled both as a rogue independent and as a guest of the U.S. State Department. I went back after 9/11 to cover the American invasion of Afghanistan, passing through Tajikistan, then went back again. (The Afghan portion of that journey is covered by my book *To Afghanistan and Back*.) Capitals moved, street names changed and the economic fortunes of entire nations turned on a dime from one year to the next, but those transformations merely reinforced my firm belief that Central Asia is the new Middle East: thrilling, terrifying, simultaneously hopeful and bleak, a battleground for proxy war and endless chaos. It is the world's ultimate tectonic, cultural and political collision zone. Far away from television cameras and Western reporters, Central Asia is poised to spawn some of the new century's worst nightmares.

Prequel

I would be remiss if I didn't provide you with some historical background.

Central Asia is arid and landlocked. Its dry climate makes agriculture largely impractical, which has led to the region's long dominance by nomadic horse cultures. Its distance from the sea restricts the number of trade routes. Steppe nomads, epitomized by the 13th century invasion of the west by Genghis Khan's

Handy Reference Atlas
Plate 34
CENTRAL ASIA
English Miles
AKMOLINSK
SEMIPOLATINSK
TURGAI
URALSK
SEMIRECHENSK
Ust Urt
Orenburg
Astrakhan
Khiva
Kashgar
Yarkand
EASTERN TURKESTAN
Takla Makan Desert
TEHERAN
PERSIA
AFGHANISTAN
BELUCHISTAN
ARABIA
INDIA
Delhi

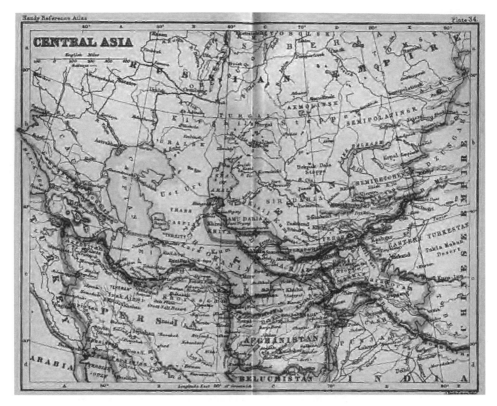

Mongols, frequently resorted to raids against settled villages and travelers—such attacks featuring varying degrees of violence—for sustenance.

Nomadic dominance faded with the 16th century spread of firearms. The Russian and Chinese empires invaded Central Asia, holding some sections outright while controlling others as vassal states. By the end of the 19th century czarist Russia controlled almost all of modern-day Uzbekistan, Kyrgyzstan and Kazakhstan while China had a tenuous hold on contemporary Xinjiang Province.

Alexander the Great was the first major Western influence on Central Asia, having spread Hellenism as far east as Tajikistan in 329 B.C.E. The Silk Road trading routes between China and Europe developed a few centuries later and, despite repeated interruptions caused by war, famine and even plague, continued well into the medieval period. Empires expanded and retracted: the Seleucids, Bactrians (who morphed into the Greco-Bactrians), Greco-Buddhists, Kushans, Sassanids and Parthians. The last of these were the Dzungars, who were decisively defeated by the Chinese Manchu Dynasty in 1758.

Russian General Mikhael Cherniaev captured Tashkent in 1865, sealing the fate of Turkestan until 1991 (and, by some measures, the present day). The city-states of Khojend, Djizak and Samarkand soon fell, followed by the Khokand Khanate and Emirate of Bukhara. Modern Turkmenistan was forcibly and bloodily annexed during the 1880s, and the communists inherited Russian Turkestan after

CENTRAL ASIA
Russia
ASTANA
Kazakhstan
Russia
Aral Sea
Caspian Sea
ÜRÜMQI
ALMATY
Uzbekistan
BISHKEK
KHIVA
Kyrgyzstan
Xinjiang Uyghur Autonomous Region
Azerbaijan
TASHKENT
OSH
BAKU
BUKHARA
KASHGAR
Turkmenistan
Tajikistan
Karakoram Highway
ASHKHABAT
DUSHANBE
MAZAR-E-SHARIF
KABUL
HERAT
Iran
Afghanistan
ISLAMABAD
KANDAHAR
China
Iraq
Pakistan
India
Nepal

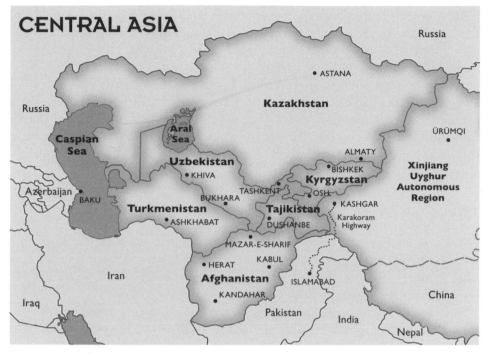

A map of 1900 (left) depicts a different Central Asia than today (above).

the 1918 Russian Revolution.

The Soviet period in Central Asia was characterized by large movements of populations from other parts of the Soviet Union to Central Asia. Forced collectivization led to the deaths by starvation and execution of a million Kazakhs and ethnic Russians in the Kazakh Soviet Socialist Republic; the 1954 Virgin Lands Campaign resettled more than three hundred thousand Ukrainians to the Kazakh SSR. Analogous colonization schemes had similar effects in Chinese Turkestan/Xinjiang.

Perestroika, the "openness" campaign launched by Mikhail Gorbachev during the last decade of Soviet rule, resulted in multi-party elections and loosened control on the press in the Central Asian republics starting in 1988. It didn't last long. Absolute dictatorship returned with independence in 1991, except in Kyrgyzstan.

Silk Road to Ruin

In a way, this is the book that I had hoped to write instead of *To Afghanistan and Back*. When I returned from Afghanistan in December of 2001, I intended to relate my experience there in an eventual book that would encompass all of my journeys to Central Asia, place the region into cultural and historical context and explain its geopolitical importance from an American point of view. The U.S. invasion of Afghanistan, after all, was part of the broader, modern story of Central Asia. But I wasn't ready to write that book at the time. I had already been financially compensated for my troubles by the radio station and newspaper that had funded my war correspondency, I told myself, and I didn't need to double-dip. Looking back now, I know the truth: I was still traumatized and depressed.

Nevertheless, my publisher encouraged me to share what I'd seen in Afghanistan with a broader public. He stressed the importance of publishing the book as quickly as possible, a judgment with which I concurred. By January 2002 a new Afghan government had been set up and the war appeared to be winding down. Early rumblings about an invasion of Iraq had appeared in the press. I banged out *To Afghanistan and Back* over the course of six weeks. It hit stores in late March, making history as both the first "instant" graphic novel and the first volume of reportage about the fall 2001 war against the Taliban.

Whatever benefit of hindsight was lost by my hasty authorship of *Afghanistan* was probably made up for by its sheer immediacy. Other works on the same subject feature tighter construction, consistent tone and academic footnotes, but none will give you as good a sense of what the war zone looked, felt and smelt like during the late fall of 2001. I tried to explain why the war had happened, what it meant and what its ramifications would likely be. I don't know whether or not I succeeded. My book did manage to create a sense of place.

Despite *Afghanistan*'s success I have since desired to fill out the broader picture about America's involvement, not only in Afghanistan but throughout Central Asia. I tackled oil politics in newspaper essays and my book *Gas War*. Is it perverse to take on Central Asia while the United States seems more obsessed than ever with its old 20th century hotspot the Middle East? Sure it is. That's part of the appeal.

The Samarkand bazaar in Uzbekistan.

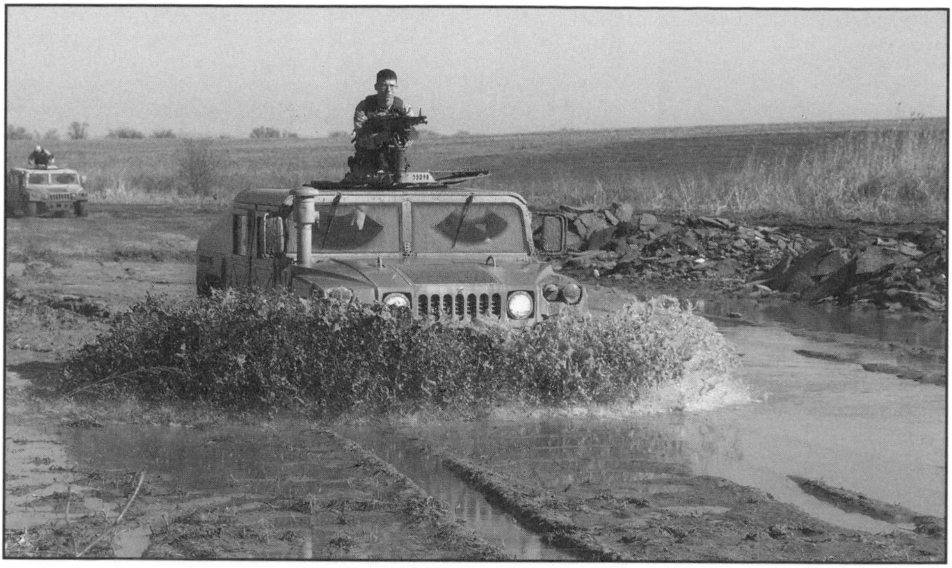

PHOTO COURTESY OF DEPARTMENT OF DEFENSE

Members of the U.S. Air Force patrol the perimeter of Manas Airbase in Kyrgyzstan. The U.S. has set up permanent military bases in strategic locations across Central Asia.

At this writing the United States has one hundred thirty-two thousand soldiers, forty-six thousand support personnel and twenty thousand private mercenaries stationed in occupied Iraq. The Bush Administration, having declared Iran a charter member of an "Axis of Evil," is considering the possibility of a preemptive attack that could even involve nuclear weapons—primarily to counter the threat posed by a nuclear-armed Iran to Israel. Saber-rattling against Syria comes and goes. And the United States has initiated economic sanctions against the Palestinian Authority in the occupied territories. The Middle East, one could be excused for assuming, remains the focus of American foreign policy concerns.

The American presence in Central Asia, on the other hand, is comparatively small. There are at most ten thousand troops at U.S. military bases in Kyrgyzstan and Tajikistan, plus another eighteen thousand in Afghanistan.

For now.

Despite assertions by some theorists that the United States now creates its own reality, the real reality is that it continues to react to developments initiated by others based elsewhere. A possible war against Iran may be "preemptive" but an attack wouldn't have been contemplated had the country's president not announced his intention to ramp up his uranium enrichment program. U.S. foreign policy planners are more like firefighters waiting for a call than arsonists plotting their next attack. In coming years, more alarms will be sounded in Uzbekistan, where a reviled dictator's hold on power must inevitably yield to ethnic and sectarian divisions suppressed for nearly a century, and Kazakhstan, where the U.S. is competing with Russia and China for control and influence over its oil reserves. A four-alarm blaze is consuming Kyrgyzstan, where a flawed but democratically-elected presiden-

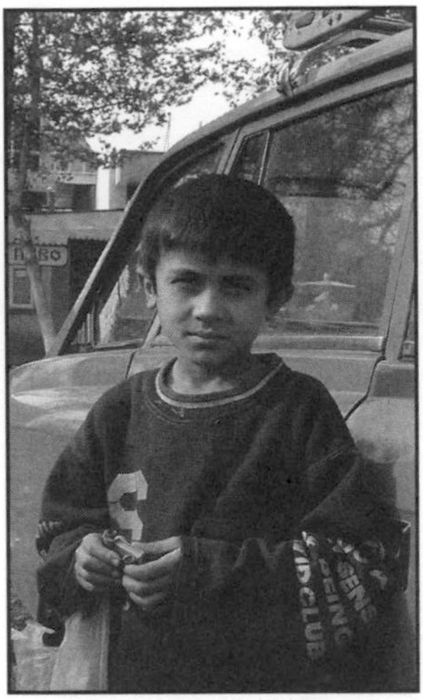

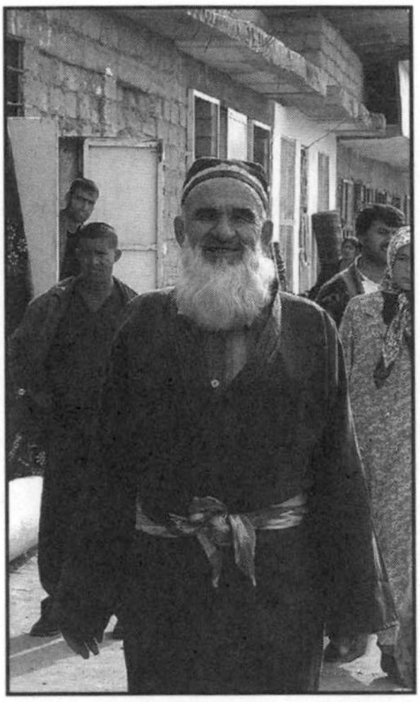

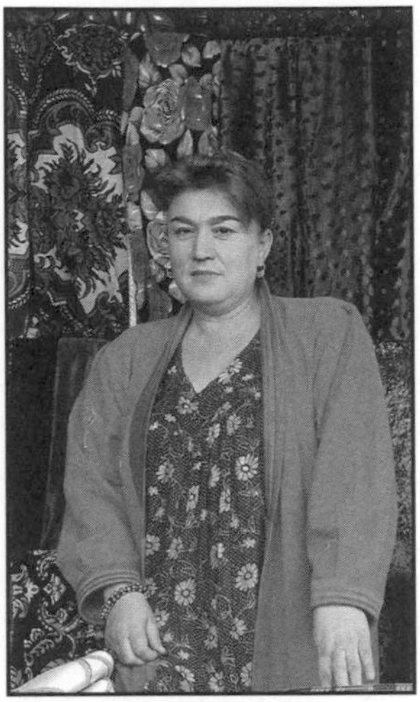

cy has been replaced by so much anarchic violence that international organizations are designating it a "failed state." True, no one is paying much attention—but that will only make the fallout that much more difficult to deal with down the road. Central Asia's importance as a source of energy (and proximity to the Middle East and South Asia) will make it impossible to ignore.

First and foremost, *Silk Road to Ruin* attempts to explain why Central Asia is the new Middle East. "Lenin Lives!" and "The Glory That is Turkmenbashi" explore the way the region's dictatorships, controlled by personalities who achieved power under the old USSR, blend the old regime's oppression with gangster capitalism minus the Soviet-era safety net. A chapter on the rise of Islamic fundamentalism discusses how religious groups, often on the ideological extreme, help fill a gap created by governments with little concern for the welfare of their alienated citizens. Chapters covering the disastrous environmental legacy of the Soviet Union and about how Central Asia may be the ultimate breeding ground for the "oil curse" expose the immense challenge faced by the governments of the Stans and the superpowers that are wooing them as their future client states.

Central Asia, however, is more than a political hot zone. It is a fascinating place rich with some of the human race's oldest history. That, not the strife, is why I keep going back. I need you to get a feel for what it's like. So *Silk Road to Ruin* is really two books, one about current affairs and the other a travelogue.

As I did for *Afghanistan* I've drawn graphic novellas (long cartoons) about each of five of the seven trips I've taken to Central Asia. The purpose of these is primarily to show what these places feel like when you visit. Prose chapters such as "Checkpoint Madness" and "High Anxiety" are included for the same reason. The chapter on *buzkashi*? Well, *buzkashi* is awesome. No book on Central Asia would be complete without one. You'll see.

Ted Rall
New York, May 2006

A note on spelling: The inherently subjective transliteration of words from their respective languages into spelling that is meaningful to English readers and respects their etymological history in English, particularly relevant here to names of people and places, is made more challenging by the fact that no such system has been developed for Central Asian languages and dialects. Where there are disagreements between American English ("Kazakh") and British English ("Kazak"), American usage is used in this book. Modern ("Kabul") is similarly preferred to archaic ("Cabool") transliterations. Where the jury is still out ("Ashkabat" versus "Ashkhabat") the author's preference prevails.

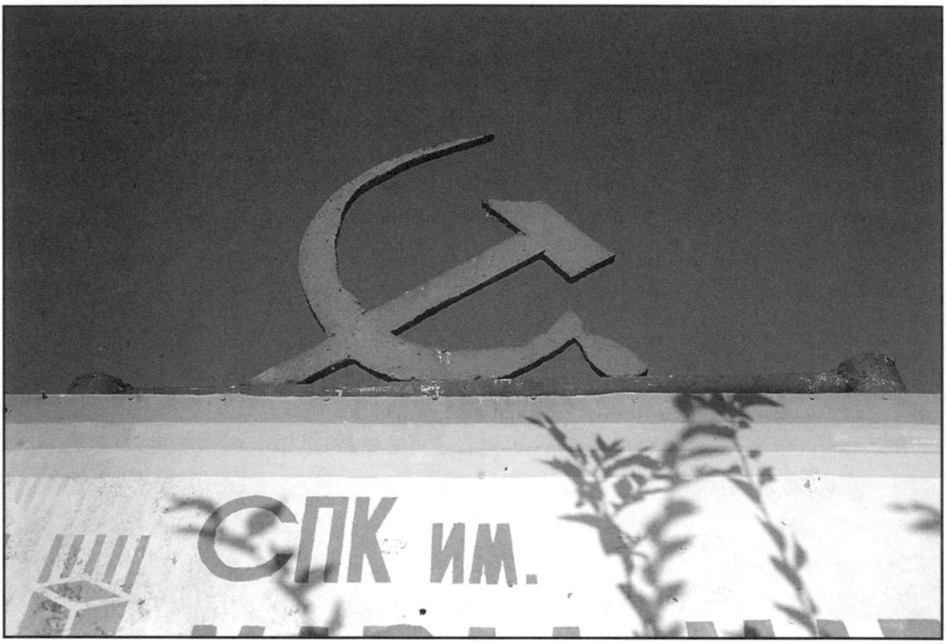
СПК им.

JEROEN NOOTER

Years after the collapse of the Union of Soviet Socialist Republics, symbols of the old order can still be found throughout Central Asia. A hammer and sickle (above) rusts on the roof of an abandoned building in Kazakhstan.

Lenin Lives!

Using psychological and other special methods, we will turn [the people of Central Asia] into zombies, obedient to the will of the secret [neo-Soviet] state and investing their money where the state tells them to.

– Maxim Kalashnikov, "Russia's Tom Clancy," in his Soviet revanchist manifesto *Forward to the USSR-2*

Collapsing regimes are optimistic. Among the most prized items in my personal collection of paper ephemera is a poster distributed in Normandy a few days after D-Day. Printed by the German occupation authorities as they fled the awesome power of the biggest armada ever assembled, it advises soon to be liberated Frenchmen that their law shall remain in force even in territories controlled by the Allies and that, upon their return, anyone who violates Nazi regulations after their withdrawal will be executed. Whether it stems from arrogance, denial or bluster one has to admire that never-say-die attitude. I similarly treasure a banknote, dated 1992, given to me by a Russian bureaucrat who stole a stack of them from his office amid the chaos of collapse, printed in advance by a Soviet central bank that would cease to exist on December 25, 1991. Poor guys. They really didn't see it coming.

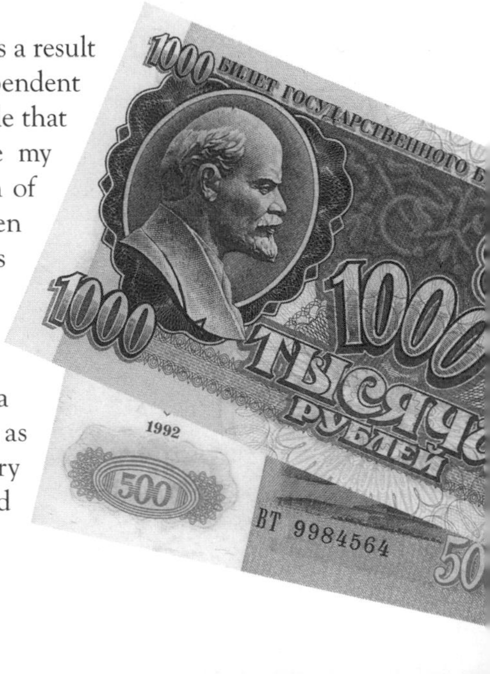
1000
1000
ТЫСЯЧ
РУБЛЕЙ
1992
500
ВТ 9984564

"Due to the situation which has evolved as a result of the formation of the Commonwealth of Independent states," Mikhael Gorbachev addressed his people that fateful Christmas Day, "I hereby discontinue my activities at the post of president of the Union of Soviet Socialist Republics." It was all over but even he wasn't sure that it was; his resignation came as a protest over obscure procedural violations of the soon-to-be null Soviet constitution. In any event, the system collapsed. The superpower dubbed the Evil Empire imploded, sending a quarter of the world's economy into a tailspin as state-controlled enterprises closed and factory managers replaced them with a mafia-based plutocracy cobbled together at the point of a gun. During 1992, the first year of what Western-advised Russian officials euphemistically called "market reform" and others dubbed "shock economics," retail prices rose a staggering two thousand five hundred twenty percent. The birth rate dropped for the first time since the 1930s famine, by thirteen percent in 1991. Deaths increased by seven percent, marking the start of a steady population decline that today continues unabated.

I met an old classmate for coffee in Manhattan during the summer of 1992. She brought along a Russian friend who, until our meeting, hadn't bothered to call home. Making conversation, I mentioned that I'd heard on the radio that morning that the ruble, which had recently become a free-floating currency, had plunged from about twelve rubles to more than one hundred fifty per dollar. "It's impossible!" the Russian woman shouted. "How dare you say such things!" my friend scolded me. The woman's life savings had been erased with the wave of a currency trader's hand.

The same harsh transformation from central planning to Darwinian anarchy jolted the post-Soviet hinterlands, among whom the most favored had been those in Central Asia. The five brand-new Central Asian nations of Turkmenistan, Uzbekistan, Kyrgyzstan, Kazakhstan and Tajikistan had enjoyed a positive net balance of trade and tax subsidies from Moscow for decades. Now the Soviet state, their largest employer, had gone out of business. Salaries, pensions, state welfare agencies, even schools, ceased.

Chaos dominated these societies. Aeroflot planes that happened to be parked at individual Central Asian airports on December 25, 1991, became the property of

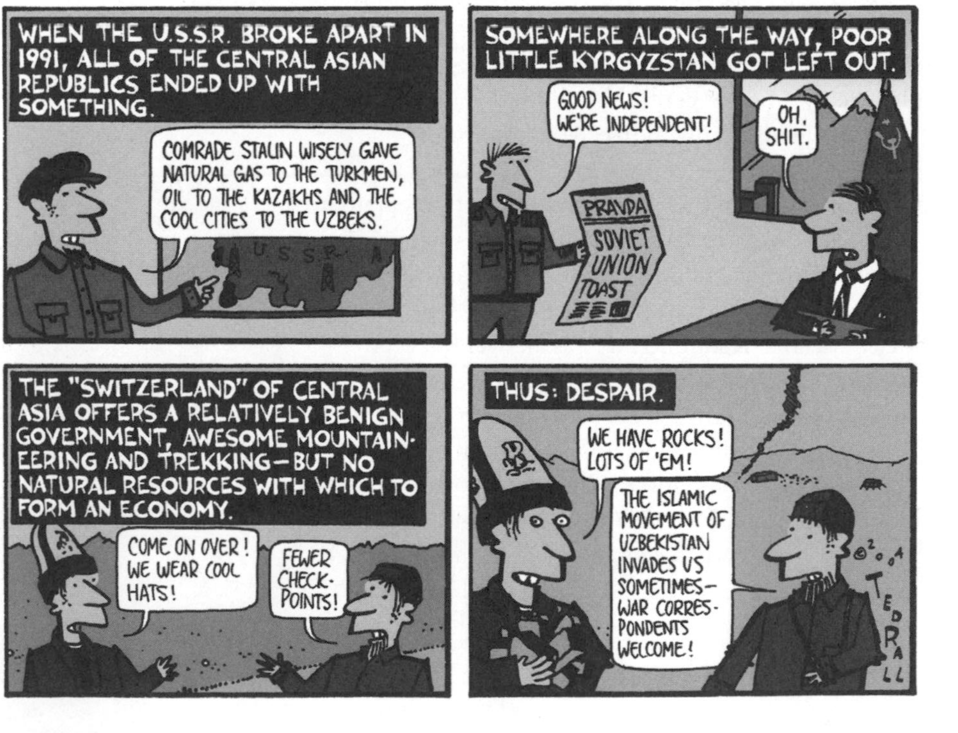
WHEN THE U.S.S.R. BROKE APART IN 1991, ALL OF THE CENTRAL ASIAN REPUBLICS ENDED UP WITH SOMETHING.
COMRADE STALIN WISELY GAVE NATURAL GAS TO THE TURKMEN, OIL TO THE KAZAKHS AND THE COOL CITIES TO THE UZBEKS.
U.S.S.R.
SOMEWHERE ALONG THE WAY, POOR LITTLE KYRGYZSTAN GOT LEFT OUT.
GOOD NEWS! WE'RE INDEPENDENT!
OH, SHIT.
PRAVDA
SOVIET UNION TOAST
THE "SWITZERLAND" OF CENTRAL ASIA OFFERS A RELATIVELY BENIGN GOVERNMENT, AWESOME MOUNTAINEERING AND TREKKING—BUT NO NATURAL RESOURCES WITH WHICH TO FORM AN ECONOMY.
COME ON OVER! WE WEAR COOL HATS!
FEWER CHECK-POINTS!
THUS: DESPAIR.
WE HAVE ROCKS! LOTS OF 'EM!
THE ISLAMIC MOVEMENT OF UZBEKISTAN INVADES US SOMETIMES—WAR CORRESPONDENTS WELCOME!
©2004 TED RALL

Ala Too Square, downtown Bishkek. A Soviet-era World War II memorial is in the background. In 1997, when this photo was taken, there was virtually no automobile traffic due to the collapse of the economy and fuel shortages. Even street lights ceased to function. During the 2005 "Tulip Revolution," this square would be filled with throngs of Kyrgyz.

their respective republic's new national carrier. These so-called "Baby Flots," reported *Travel and Leisure* magazine, "continued to use the name Aeroflot (even though they weren't supposed to), mainly because they couldn't afford to repaint the fuselages. Without formal regulation, the standard prerequisites for pilot certification and training, and money to repair deteriorating equipment, the safety record for many of the Baby Flots was appalling. (And when something bad happened, the press would often simply blame 'Aeroflot,' even though it had ceased to exist.) Conditions became so dire that in 1993 the International Airline Passenger Association, a watchdog group based in Dallas, recommended that no one fly over any part of the former Soviet Union, citing aging aircraft, pilot error, and a lack of cockpit discipline."

Hope I Die Before I Get Old

Times were still hard when I arrived at the Chinese-Kazakh border town of Dostyk in the late summer of 1997. After a day in Almaty I noticed something odd. "Hey, Alan," I asked my traveling companion, "Where are the old people?" The same question could have been asked about the very young. Of course there *were* kids, and every now and then I caught sight of some codger hawking his World War II medals in a pedestrian underpass in a pathetic attempt to earn enough to buy that night's dinner. Both the young and the old were shockingly scarce. Most people, when asked about the paucity of the non-mid-range age demographic, shook their heads and walked away. Others told variants of the same story. "The winter of 1992 killed them," a woman selling off her silverware on a dirty blanket told me. "They starved." Others made it through 1992, only to succumb in 1993.

Though the southern city of Almaty, overlooking the Kyrgyz Tian Shan Range, remains the economic and cultural center of Kazakhstan, President Nursultan Nazarbayev moved his country's capital north to the windswept steppe town of Astana later that year. Almaty was still the capital, however, and the city couldn't afford the electricity to power streetlamps or traffic signals. During the day the paucity of traffic (and red lights because of power outages) encouraged Kazakh drivers, always reckless, to zoom through intersections at breakneck speed. If you wanted to alleviate your boredom, all you had to do was stand on the corner of a major intersection to see someone die. Eventually two cars, at least one a 1970s or 1980s Lada (the Soviet analogy to a Toyota Corolla) would smash into each other at a ninety degree angle. If they spied any movement in a wreck, passersby would amble over, extract the poor sods unlucky enough to have survived and leave them on the sidewalk where the military police ambulance service would presumably pick them up.

At night you could enjoy a sound sleep in those same streets, provided you managed to avoid the notice of roving gangs of drunken young Russian men looking for trouble. No one ventured outdoors, much less by car. When the prostitute scene at the Mexican restaurant-bar in the basement of the Hotel Otrar turned tedious, I headed up to the lobby to find a rumored outdoor disco about a mile away. The hotel manager intercepted me on the way out.

"Where are you going?"

"Out," I replied, annoyed by what I presumed was his adherence to the common tendency among Third World pseudo-officialdom to intrude in the private affairs of foreigners.

"No, you're not," he warned. "I won't let you leave without these." The manager emerged from behind his desk with a box filled with automatic pistols, revolvers, knives and, my personal favorite, a hand grenade—which was a dud, he assured me. "Just to scare off."

I'd been a decent shot in Boy Scouts but I was long out of practice. On the other hand, the stiletto was appealing but too short to make the needed impression. I wanted something I could wave around. I picked out a flashlight and a butcher knife and headed into the night.

Trouble struck in under a minute. Four lumbering Russians, none older than twenty-five, spotted me from their hangout between two apartment blocks off ulitsa Gogolya and closed in on me across an empty lot. When they got close I turned off the flashlight and began swinging the knife. Cynical smiles flashed across their thin lips. They raised their arms in the international hey-whoa-dude-no-harm-no-foul motion and backed off. Catch you next time.

A pair of huge goons manned a folding table that marked the entrance to the renowned outdoor disco where a dozen couples swayed to the dance version of "The X-Files" theme song. "One dollar and give weapon," the "doorman" commanded. He didn't ask *if* I had one. I didn't bother to deny it. He placed my knife on a back table and indicated that I could retrieve it when I left. I counted three AK-47s and a small machine gun that I believe was an Uzi. The rest were Glocks.

Where the USSR Lingers On

Not everyone was happy about the new disorder in 1997. A decade later, because it reflects a society's longing for predictability, self-respect and even grandeur, the iconography of lapsed communism remains potent in this once formidable empire transformed into a dozen-plus grim narcostates run by dimwitted gangsters. Despite repeated proposals to evict him Lenin still lies in his famed tomb in Red Square, visited daily by throngs of visitors—some, no doubt, still admirers. And it's not just symbolism. The old state apparatus has outlived the state. In Russia the KGB briefly became the watered-down FSK (Federal Counterintelligence Service) and, in 1995 returned as the FSB (Federal Security Service of the Russian Federation), virtually indistinguishable from its Soviet predecessor. The hammer-and-sickle logo remains on a million doors and the iron gates of government offices throughout the former USSR; though capitalism has

Ala Too Hotel, Almaty, Kazakhstan. My plan to stay in this "luxury" hotel was scuttled upon discovering that it was under renovation. Also, it had been hit by mortar fire shortly before my arrival from western China.

brightened luxury shop windows most Russians live and work in buildings distinctive for their Soviet-era architecture and decaying infrastructure. In the Central Asian republics almost everything useful and accessible to ordinary people—public baths, parks, stadiums—was built thanks to Soviet funding. Now, even in the oil-boom city of Almaty, the Kazakh government is just breaking ground on a Metro system originally scheduled to open in 1997.

From East Berlin to Mongolia the Soviet hangover persists, yet nowhere has the Soviet legacy lingered longer or more overtly than in the Central Asian republics, where the activities of supposedly liberated peoples are monitored with the same fearsome zeal as before, by governments that rely on brute force and intimidation in order to remain in power. Military police checkpoints dot the landscape, clogging major arteries when negotiations over bribes for safe passage take longer than usual and making inter-republic trade, the lifeblood of economic life along the old and new Silk Roads alike, virtually impossible.

Although enforcement is erratic, foreign travelers are still legally required to register with the local Office of Visas and Registration (OVIR), the branch of

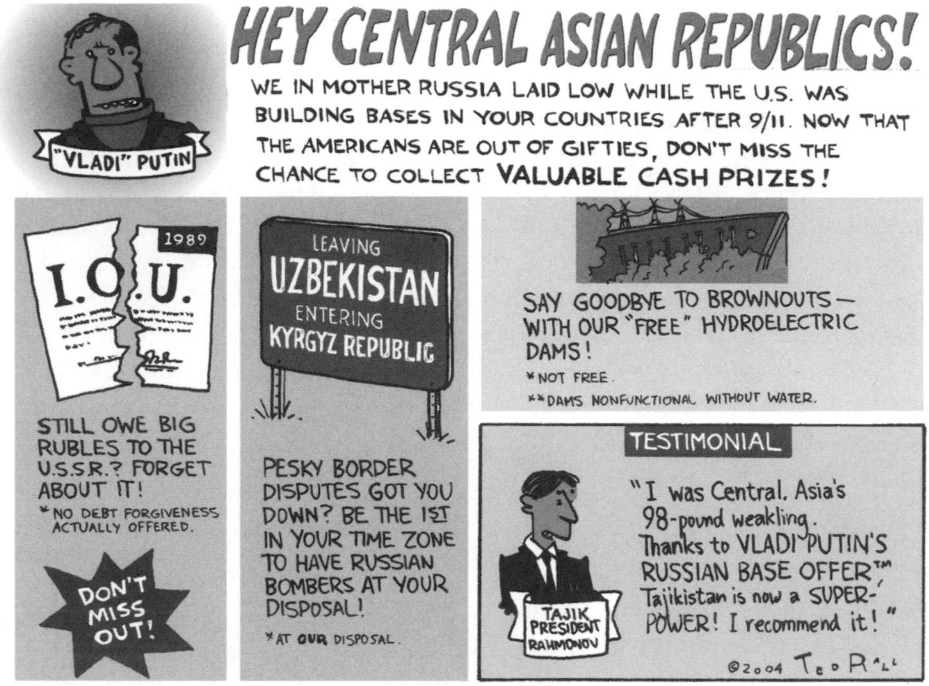
HEY CENTRAL ASIAN REPUBLICS!
WE IN MOTHER RUSSIA LAID LOW WHILE THE U.S. WAS BUILDING BASES IN YOUR COUNTRIES AFTER 9/11. NOW THAT THE AMERICANS ARE OUT OF GIFTIES, DON'T MISS THE CHANCE TO COLLECT VALUABLE CASH PRIZES!
"VLADI" PUTIN
1989
I.O.U.
STILL OWE BIG RUBLES TO THE U.S.S.R.? FORGET ABOUT IT!
*NO DEBT FORGIVENESS ACTUALLY OFFERED.
DON'T MISS OUT!
LEAVING UZBEKISTAN ENTERING KYRGYZ REPUBLIC
PESKY BORDER DISPUTES GOT YOU DOWN? BE THE 1ST IN YOUR TIME ZONE TO HAVE RUSSIAN BOMBERS AT YOUR DISPOSAL!
*AT OUR DISPOSAL.
SAY GOODBYE TO BROWNOUTS— WITH OUR "FREE" HYDROELECTRIC DAMS!
*NOT FREE.
**DAMS NONFUNCTIONAL WITHOUT WATER.
TESTIMONIAL
"I was Central Asia's 98-pound weakling. Thanks to VLADI PUTIN'S RUSSIAN BASE OFFER™ Tajikistan is now a SUPER-POWER! I recommend it!"
TAJIK PRESIDENT RAHMONOV
©2004 TED RALL

each Central Asian republic's security service assigned to monitor potential foreign subversives and limit their interaction with the local citizenry, upon arrival in a town. Uzbek station agents won't sell train tickets to foreigners; only OVIR's shadowy non-uniformed personnel may do so, provided one can be found before one's planned departure. Visitors, including locals, are proscribed from visiting areas classified as sensitive for security reasons: a hundred-kilometer buffer zone along Tajikistan's border with Afghanistan; the Uzbek military garrison town of Termiz; the Kazakh Cosmodrome that Russia still uses as launching and landing sites for its space program.

Pre-1991 "internal passports" prompted some of the loudest complaints about the Soviets' stifling of freedom of movement. They were a violation of the basic right to move about and an especially annoying irritant to Central Asians steeped in steppe culture's fungible borders, yet the citizens of the new autocracies still have to carry them to pass between provinces and, not infrequently, even to leave their city of residence. (This problem, like most others, is universally solved by the presentation of a few bank notes.)

No one knows whether stingy budgets or politics are to blame for the bizarre sight of Turkmen presenting leftover Soviet "foreign passports"—used for external travel—at the airport. When I quizzed an official of the Turkmen Foreign Affairs Ministry he confirmed that they were still being printed. Contemporary issue dates—2003, 2004, 2005—on a burgundy "CCCP" booklet add to the nation's already staggering surreality.

Politics certainly explain the Stans' reluctance to erase the Soviet legacy. Nations such as the Baltic republics of Latvia and Lithuania, chafing under communist rule equivalent to occupation, quickly seized the first chance they got to declare independence from Moscow when *perestroika* brought about the beginning of the end of the old regime. The Turkmen, Uzbek, Kyrgyz and Tajik Soviet Socialist Republics, on the other hand, were literally kicked out of the Soviet Union. It seems bizarre that the new Russian Federation would choose to expel nations sitting atop the world's largest untapped oil and natural gas reserves. Indeed, a regretful Russia has since become an eager competitor with China and the United States in what Pakistani journalist Ahmed Rashid has dubbed a New Great Game over Caspian Sea energy resources. During the late 1980s and early 1990s, however, the central government in Moscow was penniless. Lacking technology and manpower to effectively exploit the Caspian, Soviet-era Russia oddly found itself suffering a net outflow of financial subsidies to its outlying southern buffer states. In objective terms the cost of maintaining political control over an area possessing literally limitless wealth was nominal. At the time, however, with triple-digit inflation threatening anarchy and mass starvation, relatively tiny subsidies were more than they could afford.

Enterprising go-getters, Russian carpetbaggers and thugs of all political inclinations appropriated state assets to rise in the Nineties as Russia's plutocrats. This process was mirrored in the seizure of newly emerging political structures, but with a twist: those in control of state organs of oppression remained in the

The endless grey ribbon of the M37, the main highway connecting the Central Asian capitals of Ashkhabat, Tashkent, Bishkek and Almaty. Dushanbe, like Tajikistan itself, is off the grid.

best positions to enrich and empower themselves. "In Central Asia... communist leaders in Soviet republics took over when power fell like manna from heaven into their lap after the grandstand fight between Gorbachev and Yeltsin, which in effect destroyed the Soviet Union," K. Gajendra Singh recalled for a 2003 article for *Asia Times*, the essential source of Central Asian news and analysis. "To begin with, most Central Asian leaders felt like orphans and unhappy at the disintegration, but soon, gingerly following the lead from the Baltics and European Russia, Muslim majority republics from Central Asia and Azerbaijan first declared sovereignty, provided for in the Soviet Union's constitution, and then full independence. Since then most have ruled their fiefs with the communist style of an iron hand but based on political linkages of family, tribal, ethnic and regional ties. They have themselves reelected regularly with nearly one hundred percent of votes, after making opposition candidates ineffective or disappear."

Fifteen years after 1991, four of the five Central Asian republics are still ruled by their Soviet-era Communist Party bosses. Even Askar Akayev, whose actual electoral legitimacy qualified him as the sole exception to the rule (he was deposed during the spring of 2005), owed his fame and influence to his chairmanship of the Science Department of the USSR Central Committee of the Communist Party of Kyrgyzstan. New boss, same as the old boss, sang The Who. The clichéd song lyric is a dictionary definition of Central Asian governance.

It was probably inevitable that Central Asians would feel a tad wistful for their previous membership in one of the world's two superpowers, having by force of circumstance been downgraded to citizens of impoverished backwaters with an average income of twenty dollars per month. But the region's dictators have also exploited nationalist sentiment by rebranding their cultural signifiers. Turkmenistan and Uzbekistan in particular have aggressively harassed ethnic Russians in the hope, largely successful, of encouraging them to emigrate. Tajikistan recently became the last of the Central Asian states to rename the ruble—to the *sonomi*, after the 10th century Sogdian considered to have founded the first ethnic Tajik state and who is sometimes credited with inventing paper currency. A decade after independence Turkmenistan, so obsessed with Ataturk's concept of pan-Turkism that its buses and taxis are painted with Turkish and Turkmen flags side by side, abandoned its Soviet-imposed Cyrillic script in favor of Turkey's Latinized alphabet.

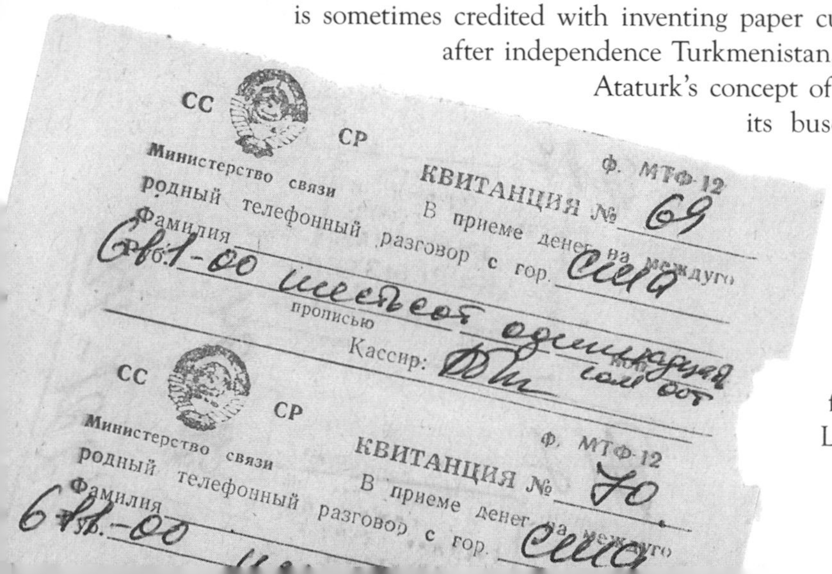
СССР
Министерство связи
ф. МТФ-12
КВИТАНЦИЯ № 69
В приеме денег на междугородный телефонный разговор с гор. США
Фамилия
прописью
Кассир:

СССР
Министерство связи
ф. МТФ-12
КВИТАНЦИЯ № 70
В приеме денег на междугородный телефонный разговор с гор. США
Фамилия

Twelve-year-old Johnny, left, was the youngest Stan Trekker on the August 2000 trip. Here he takes a Kyrgyz boy's donkey out for a spin, somewhere along the road south of Lake Issyk-Kul. His father had earlier purchased a policeman's hat.

Many communist-era street names (*ulitsa Lenini, ulitsa Marx*) have been renamed. But most people, and not just the old timers, continue to use the old names. Russian literary giants like Gorky have mostly survived on street signs, as have Soviet-era building plaques and memorials to the sacrifices made during the Great Patriotic War. And in Central Asia's polyglot bazaars, where mastery of Persian-rooted Tajik is as essential as Turkic languages like Uyghur and Kyrgyz, Russian is still the region's somewhat resented and eminently useful *lingua franca*.

Central Asian soldiers, ostensibly the face of sovereign nation-states, wear hammer-and-sickle belt buckles and hat badges. Though finally removed in 2003 from his perch in central Ala Too Square in front of the Historical Museum, Vladimir Lenin still looms over similar public spaces throughout Central Asian capitals. Tajikistan, whose twelve hundred-mile-long southern border with a perpetually disintegrating Afghanistan is still patrolled by the ten thousand Russian troops of the old Soviet 201st Motorized Infantry Division, is the most remote and thus Soviet-est of the former Soviet outposts. So out of touch with breaking developments is this mountainous cul de sac of transportation on the Chinese border that it held a meeting of the Executive Committee of the Kulab Regional Council of People's Deputies nearly a year after the dissolution of the USSR. The 16th session of the Supreme Soviet, 12th Convocation was called on November 19, 1992, where Imomali Rakhmonov was elected Chairman of the Supreme Soviet of the Republic of Tajikistan. Rakhmonov, the nation's current and sole president since independence, waited until 1994 before shedding his Soviet honorific. At 24,590 feet Ishmail Somoni Peak is Tajikistan's highest mountain; it is still depicted on official maps as Communism Peak, its pre-1998 name. Nostalgists still have Lenin Peak, the Soviet Union's second highest mountain (23,405 feet) on the Tajik-Kyrgyz border.

Infrastructure remains Sovietized, from a telephone system that treats inter-CIS calls (Tashkent to Moscow, for example) as regional rather than international to the Moscow-centric air transportation grid. Phones have improved since 1996, when Eric Johnson told EurasiaNet that only a thousand Turkmen could afford cellphones. He quoted a local source: "Our cities are so small that telephones aren't important enough to merit spending lots of money on a cellphone; if you can't get through, you just drive over with your question–it's only a couple minutes, and there's no hurry to do anything in Central Asia."

"International" travelers en route to Central Asia–those arriving from the West–arrive at Moscow's Sheremetyevo 2 airport. "Domestic" flights, whether within Russia via Aeroflot or to officially sovereign states like Azerbaijan or Kazakhstan, depart from Sheremetyevo 1 or Domodedovo, an hour away by taxi.

Soviet Repression Meets Gangster Capitalism

Nothing says Soviet like architecture or gulags. Central Asia has an ample supply of both. Government ministries and apartment blocks, many visibly con-

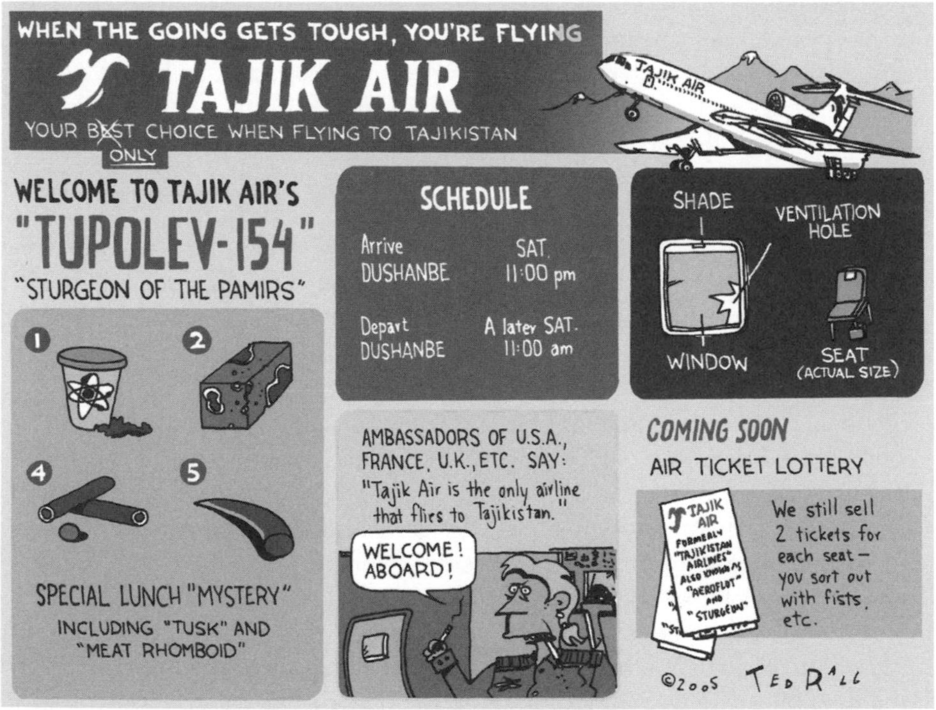
WHEN THE GOING GETS TOUGH, YOU'RE FLYING
TAJIK AIR
YOUR BEST CHOICE WHEN FLYING TO TAJIKISTAN
ONLY
TAJIK AIR
WELCOME TO TAJIK AIR'S
"TUPOLEV-154"
"STURGEON OF THE PAMIRS"
1
2
4
5
SPECIAL LUNCH "MYSTERY"
INCLUDING "TUSK" AND "MEAT RHOMBOID"
SCHEDULE
Arrive DUSHANBE SAT. 11:00 pm
Depart DUSHANBE A later SAT. 11:00 am
SHADE
VENTILATION HOLE
WINDOW
SEAT (ACTUAL SIZE)
AMBASSADORS OF U.S.A., FRANCE, U.K., ETC. SAY:
"Tajik Air is the only airline that flies to Tajikistan."
WELCOME! ABOARD!
COMING SOON
AIR TICKET LOTTERY
TAJIK AIR FORMERLY "TAJIKISTAN AIRLINES" ALSO KNOWN AS "AEROFLOT" AND "STURGEON"
We still sell 2 tickets for each seat – you sort out with fists, etc.
©2005 TED RALL

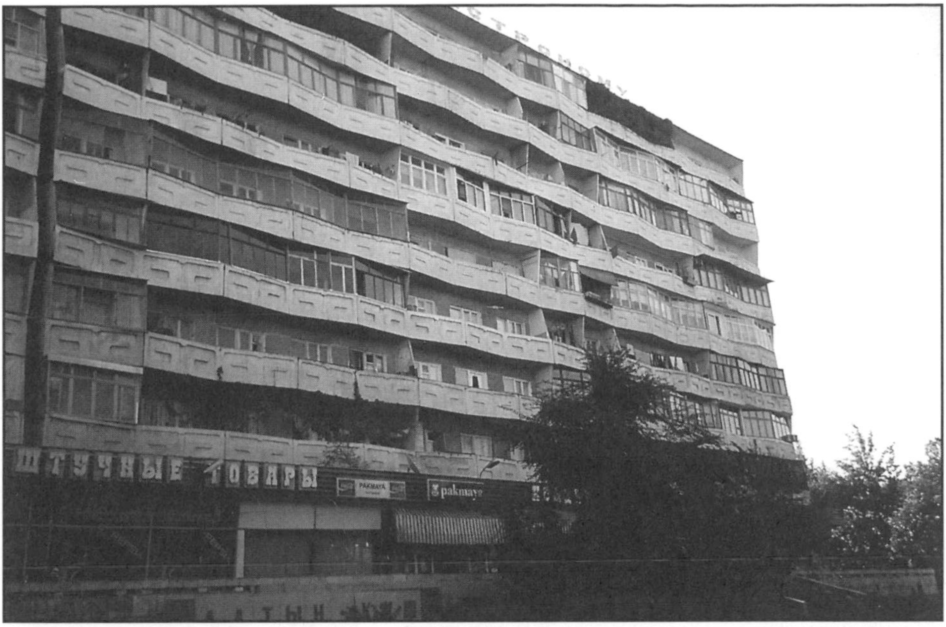
ШТУЧНЫЕ ТОВАРЫ

Soviet-era apartment building, Almaty.

structed from stacked pre-fabricated concrete cubes evocative of Legos, compose skylines from Ashkhabat to Dushanbe. Central Asians are sensitive to snide remarks by Westerners about the supposedly outdated style of their major buildings. "It does not have any bad influences of Soviet architecture, as some critics claim," a Kyrgyz government tourism website assures prospective visitors to Bishkek, most of whom will stay at the delightfully decrepit, prostitute-infested, Soviet-era Hotel Dostuk. Personally, I love Soviet aesthetics and wonder how residents of glass-and-plastic piles like Sydney and New York can summon the cajones to mock other cities. Moreover, the interior spaces are comfortable and brilliantly designed within their own paradigm. At the Dostuk, for example, hot water pipes in the bathrooms double as a towel rack so your towel is toasty and warm upon emerging from your rust-water bath. Rooms, even in government-subsidized apartments, are spacious and intelligently proportioned.

During the czarist and Soviet periods inmates of the Siberian gulag system who misbehaved were transferred to camps in modern-day Kazakhstan for even harsher treatment. Many of those gulags remain in operation, mainly to house the nation's soaring population of drug addicts, victims of their country's geography along the Afghanistan-to-Moscow narcotics trafficking corridor. The regime officially states that it has at least three hundred fifty thousand drug addicts and, by their its admission, cannot control the problem despite harsh legislation. Article 259 of the Kazakh penal code provides for penalties of fifteen years at hard labor for dealing and ten years for possession of drugs in quantities as small as a single seed of marijuana. But in a country where pot grows naturally along roadsides and even high-ranking officials

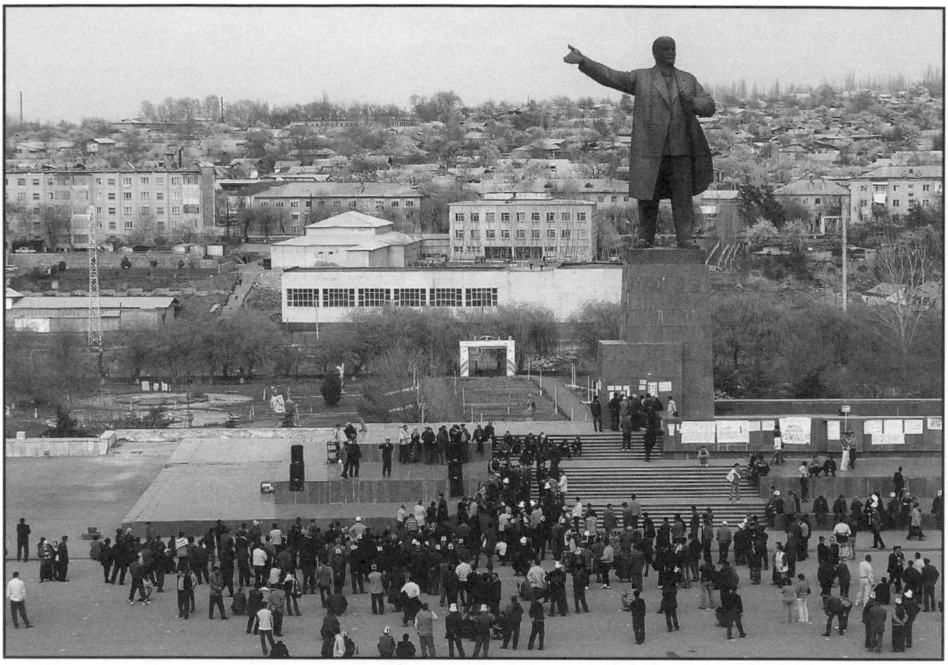

©IRIN

Protesters in Osh convene at a statue of Lenin in 2005.

are involved with drugs—in May 2000 Kazakh cops caught a top Tajik diplomat with eighty-six kilograms of heroin in his car—there's little hope of improvement. By most accounts few survive more than three or four years in a Kazakh gulag.

Drugs are a problem in Uzbekistan too, but the government headed by Islam Karimov worries more about suppressing internal dissent, which it blames on Islamic fundamentalists based in its conservative Ferghana Valley. Gulags come in handy there as well. After boiling her son Muzafar Avozov to death for belonging to the outlawed Muslim political opposition group Hizb-ut-Tahrir, in 2004 Karimov had sixty-two-year-old Fatima Mukhadirova convicted on dubious charges of "unsanctioned religious literature, membership in a banned religion organization, and attempted encroachment on the constitutional order." Mukhadirova was dispatched to six years in an Uzbek gulag, a de facto death sentence.

Perhaps the most pervasive vestige of post-Soviet oppression is the exit visa, which prevented Soviets from leaving and remained in force in all the Central Asian republics through 2002. Although officially eliminated since 2005, in practice border guards continue to demand exit visas for departure from airports and via international border crossings. Uzbeks were still required to obtain internal exit visas to travel to neighboring provinces as late as 2004.

The dictators of Central Asia have also retained the Soviet policy of regulating the opiate for the masses until outright suppression becomes politically feasible. From the standpoint of American policymakers engaged in a war against Islamic fundamentalists, requirements that churches and mosques be registered with the authorities and refrain from political activity cut in two directions. As a 2003 report of the International Crisis Group notes, "Seventy years of Soviet rule in Central Asia did not crush Islam but it had a profound effect in secularizing society and political elites. Nevertheless, after independence there was a surge of interest in Islam, including the emergence of political Islamist groups seeking to challenge the secular nature of these new states." Soviet-era secularization has its legacy in Central Asian cities whose urban culture is decidedly liberal. Long-legged women in miniskirts and tight blouses are a common sight in Bishkek and Almaty, a city famous for its nightlife. One rarely sees Muslims praying or going to mosque in Tashkent. Even self-identified devout Muslims smoke cigarettes and drink vodka. But the countryside—poor, more conservative, where central government control is considered distant—is changing. And the dictators are terrified.

It's difficult to reconcile America's cozy relationship with these regimes with their harsh treatment of religious people, whether their members belong to a minority or dominant majority. According to Felix Corley of the Keston News Service, which monitors stories relating to religious freedom, Uzbek President Islam Karimov hasn't limited his efforts to fending off the Taliban-trained Islamic Movement of Uzbekistan: "There's a lot of official pressure on people who belong to religious communities that the government does not like. And it extends far beyond Jehovah's Witnesses. It's extended especially to Protestant Christians [and] to Muslims that try to function outside the framework of the government-approved Muslim board." Karimov's neighbors share his hostility to religiosity: "In Turkmenistan, communities need to have five hundred members before they can register as an individual religious community. And the government has prevented any religious community—apart from those from the Muslim board and the Russian Orthodox Church—from registering officially. Which means in effect that their activity is treated as illegal although the religion law does not say that unregistered religious activity is illegal." In Kazakhstan, Corley continues, "the government uses a provision of the Administrative Code which punishes unregistered religious activity. A lot of Baptist churches have recently had their leaders fined. The Hare Krishna community also has problems running a farm near the commercial capital, Almaty. Protestant churches in country areas, which are mainly populated by ethnic Kazakhs of Muslim background, have had a lot of problems."

With the sole exception of Kyrgyzstan, every Central Asian republic is still ruled by the same Communist Party boss as ruled its Soviet counterpart before 1991. (Turkmenistan's Niyazov has been in power for more than two decades, since 1985.) Each nation maintains its original Soviet security apparatus, *militsia* military police system, jails and camps. Soviet postcards and stamps are still sold at post offices. Skylines, military uniforms, tax forms, street names—they're all the same. Complaining about the government can still get you executed. Life may have become a little harder on a day-to-day basis but, for the most part, Uzbekistan in 2006 feels pretty much the same as it did in 1986. Which is why, even today, you'll still hear people say: "Here in the Soviet Union..."

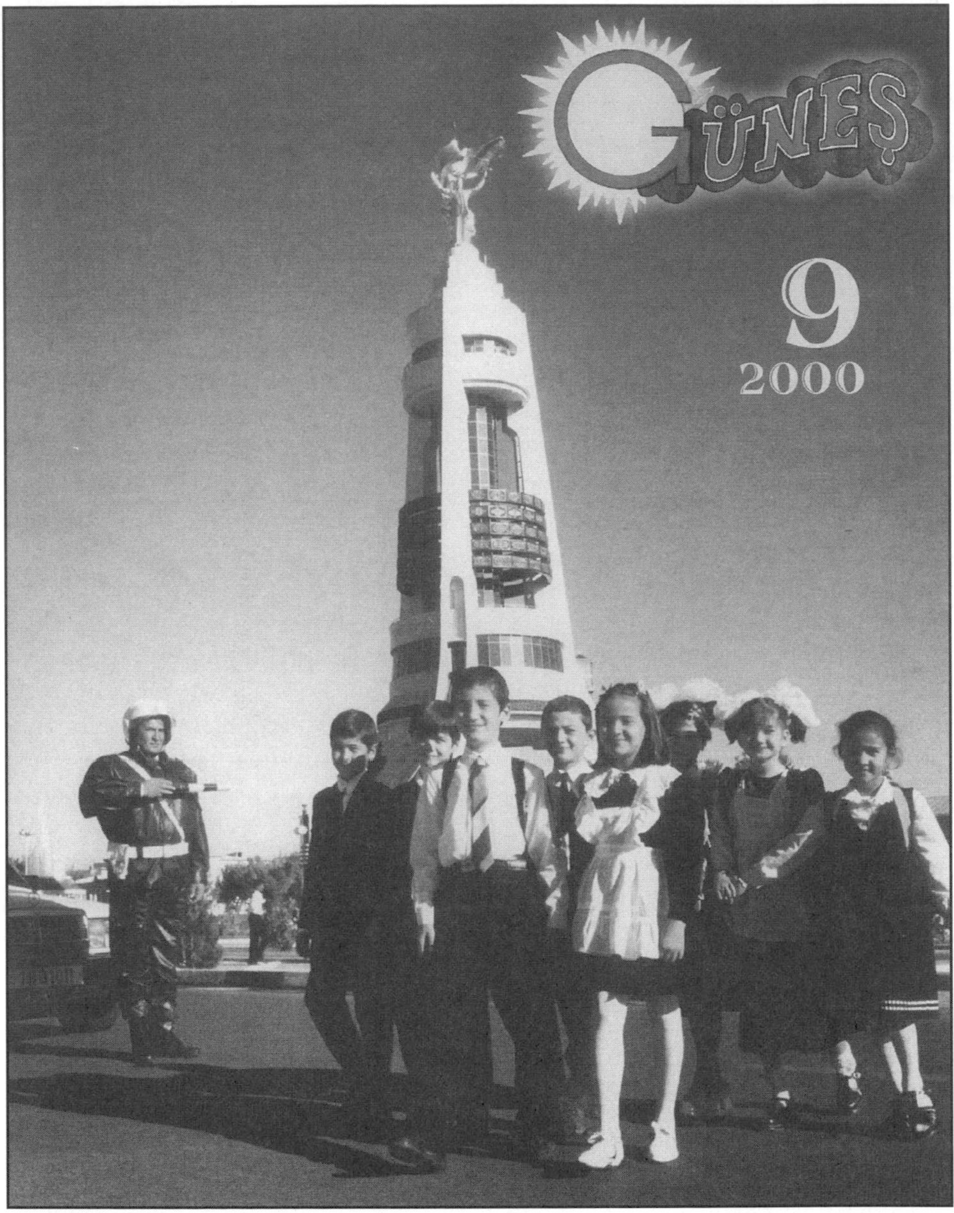
GÜNEŞ
9
2000

On the cover of a Turkmen children's magazine (above), schoolchildren pass in front of a gilt statue celebrating Turkmenistan's supreme ruler, Saparmurat Ataevich "Turkmenbashi" Niyazov. Propaganda bearing the dictator's image and advice are ubiquitous (right).

The Glory That Is Turkmenbashi

In a region still dominated by ex-Communist leaders, Niyazov stands out as the most bizarre and egotistical leader west of North Korea.

–*UK Telegraph*, February 5, 2004

In a region where no one can imagine a president who isn't an egotistical tyrant, posters of each country's beloved benevolent despot festoon every police checkpoint and corruption is merely an economical term to describe business as usual. Saying that Turkmenbashi's Turkmenistan sets the standard for autocracy is selling him short. Not only has the Central Asian dictator created the most elaborate and grotesquely comical personality cult since Ptolemy put the pharaohs out of business, his unique blending of naked greed and breathtakingly obvious stupidity has elevated autocracy to an art form. He has also reduced one of the world's potentially wealthiest nations into a showcase of despair and near universal poverty.

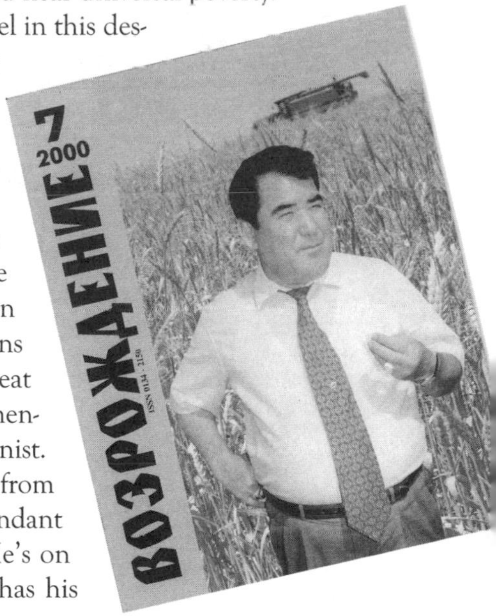
ВОЗРОЖДЕНИЕ
7
2000

Like American Express, wherever you travel in this desolate desert nation nestled between southwest Russia and Iran, Turkmenbashi is there. Giant posters bearing his face and his ubiquitous Nazi-inspired motto "Halk, Watan, Turkmenbashi!" ("One Nation, One People, One Leader") adorn every building, public and private, in a country that would otherwise be most notable for its geographic inhospitality to the five million people doomed to have been born there. Signs bearing quotes by and images of the not-so-great dictator's face are everywhere you turn. Turkmenbashi is on a painting behind the hotel receptionist. He's on the businessman's lapel pin, hanging from the taxi driver's rearview mirror, even on a pendant hanging around the casino prostitute's neck. He's on T-shirts, CDs, DVDs, groceries, mosques. He has his own line of cologne. No one can get away from Turkmenbashi—not even in the most remote stretches of desert.

Turkmenistan one of the few countries on earth to not have a river run through it. Its vast Karakum desert is home to animals—cobras, scorpions, giant monitor lizards called *zemzen* ("land crocodiles")—that bite and sting and claw with alarming ferocity and regularity. Temperature readings of more than one hundred fifty-five degrees Fahrenheit in the shade are not rare; heat exceeding one hundred is standard. There is, however, no shade in this, the westernmost nation of Central Asia. Water is processed and piped in from the oil-fouled Caspian Sea and the Amu Darya river (Alexander the Great knew it as the Oxus) running along the eastern border with Uzbekistan. Most Turkmen are nomads similar in culture and tradition to the Bedouin. Outside the capital of Ashkhabat and a few outlying provincial capitals, Turkmen set up their yurts wherever a few blades of grass poke out of the sand to feed their camels. City life, secularized by seven decades of Soviet rule, centers around grim mafia-run discos and thinly-patronized English-style pubs with CNN piped in on a time delay so that negative news about Turkmenistan and its Central Asian neighbors can be intercepted and blacked out. Even the U.S. embassy is isolated; Turkmenbashi cuts off international telephone and Internet service for days at a time. Out in the desert, old traditions live on. Women carry their family savings in clunky silver jewelry hollowed out to hold bank notes; touching, much less robbing, a woman, is just cause for murder. Nomadic hospitality, on the other hand, occasionally prompts men to loan their wives to sate the desires of

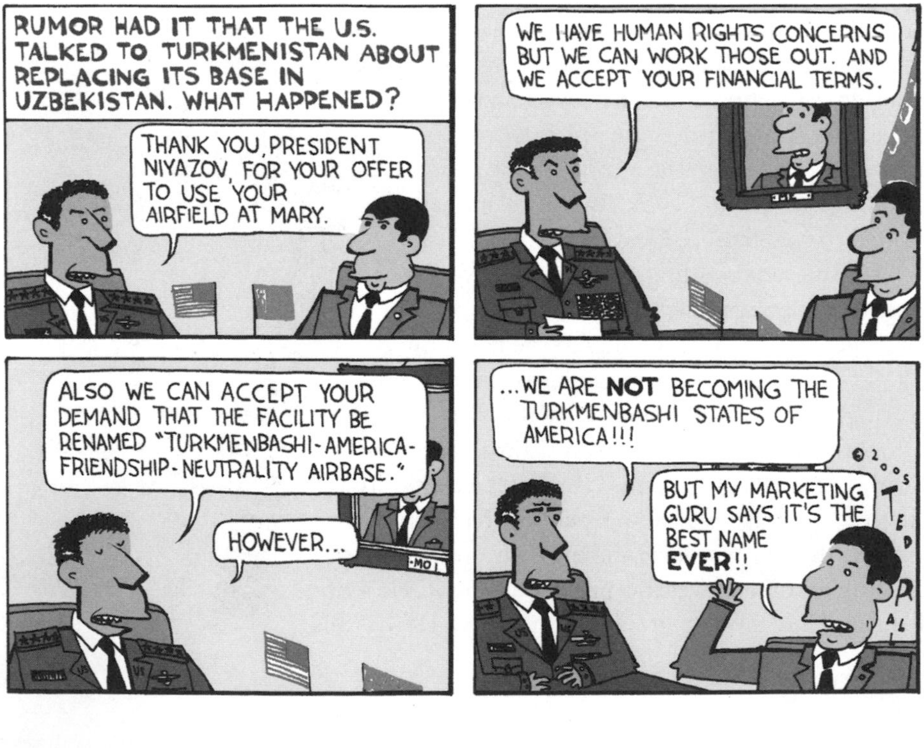
RUMOR HAD IT THAT THE U.S. TALKED TO TURKMENISTAN ABOUT REPLACING ITS BASE IN UZBEKISTAN. WHAT HAPPENED?
THANK YOU, PRESIDENT NIYAZOV, FOR YOUR OFFER TO USE YOUR AIRFIELD AT MARY.
WE HAVE HUMAN RIGHTS CONCERNS BUT WE CAN WORK THOSE OUT. AND WE ACCEPT YOUR FINANCIAL TERMS.
ALSO WE CAN ACCEPT YOUR DEMAND THAT THE FACILITY BE RENAMED "TURKMENBASHI-AMERICA-FRIENDSHIP-NEUTRALITY AIRBASE."
HOWEVER...
...WE ARE **NOT** BECOMING THE TURKMENBASHI STATES OF AMERICA!!!
BUT MY MARKETING GURU SAYS IT'S THE BEST NAME **EVER**!!
© 2005 TED RALL

passing visitors. They would, after all, do the same for you. Sometimes they sell women; the going rate for a tribal wife is two to five thousand dollars depending on age, appearance and personality.

It feels like the end of the world. But in the wind-blown desert, along remote stretches of road that see less than one vehicle daily, immense billboards have been erected to proclaim the glory that is Turkmenbashi. Halk! Watan! Turkmenbashi!

A dry mud mound of crumbled buildings at Nisa, capital of the long fallen Parthian empire, marks Turkmenistan's peak of political power twenty centuries ago. All that remains of the once impressive Silk Road city of Merv (renamed Mary) are a few walls and minarets Genghis Khan left behind during his westward depredations eight hundred years ago. Even Turkmen culture seems

The Ruins of Merv, in eastern Turkmenistan (above). The ancient Silk Road city, one of the world's most magnificent, was completely destroyed by Genghis Khan's Golden Horde. The mausoleum of Sultan Sanjar (1118-1157 AD) dominates the ruins of Merv and is one of its few relatively intact buildings (below). He ruled during the high point of the Seljuk empire.

cursed. The nomadic Turkmen never developed a written language before 1924, when the conquering Bolsheviks imposed a Cyrillic alphabet upon the local Turkic-derived dialect. Turkmen literature, poetry and even cartooning emerged during the 1990s post-independence period, but then Turkmenbashi banned Cyrillic in favor of the Latinized script used in modern post-Ataturk Turkey. This change effectively killed the nascent Turkmen written tongue and virtually eradicated non-official expression overnight. Opera and ballet performances, popular throughout the former Soviet Union, have been banned. "Unnecessary," Turkmenbashi calls such distractions. So have movies, which were hugely popular throughout the former Soviet Union. "Un-Turkmen," he spat. Turkmen sculptors, renowned during the Soviet era for their experimental approach to abstraction, have been ordered to produce just one kind of artwork—statues and busts of Turkmenbashi.

TURKMENBASHI IS A HARSH MISTRESS
TURKMEN PRESIDENT NIYAZOV HAS THE ULTIMATE HEALTHCARE REFORM PLAN:
NO MORE FREE CLINICS IN THE PROVINCES. IF YOU'RE SICK, COME TO ASHGABAT!
EYES JUST OPERATED UPON IN GERMANY
TURKMENISTAN IS, OF COURSE, A LARGE NATION FEATURING SOME OF THE WORLD'S HARSHEST LIVING CONDITIONS AND DIRE POVERTY—AVERAGE INCOME IS $100 A MONTH.
300 miles
500 miles
HERE BE SCORPIONS COBRAS AND BIG LIZARDS
ASHGABAT
DON'T EXPECT TO LIVE A LONG TIME IF YOU'RE POOR AND SICK AND LIVING IN THE TURKMEN DESERT.
NICE KNOWING YOU, PAL.
VISA
AS USUAL, TURKMENBASHI HAS AN ANSWER TO HIS CRITICS.
ALL THE REMEDIES YOU NEED CAN BE FOUND IN MY BOOK, THE *RUHNAMA*—IF YOU LIVE OUTSIDE ASHGABAT, ANYWAY.
©2005 TED RALL

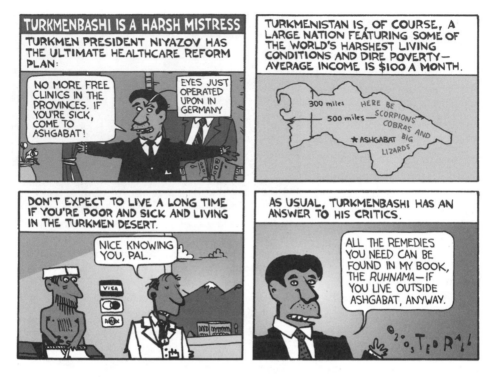

The World According to Turkmenbashi

Turkmenbashi owes everything he has to the U.S.S.R. He was an *apparatchik*, a Communist Party boss. But different times call for different propaganda. Now he decries the Soviet influence, saying that it crushed a Turkmen cultural patrimony that he is working hard to revive.

"I lived in the Soviet era and when I was young I recognized and felt my people's lack of trust in justice and their hopeless view of the future," the Turkmen leader remembered. "Our people were not only unable to understand what they were experiencing but also unable to judge their daily life. There was this kind of belief among our people: 'Day belongs to the powerful, and *kawurma* [mutton imbedded in fat] belongs to those who have canines.' They used to believe that whatever you do, you cannot prosper...The state was divided, tribes fought with each other, the nation lost its core, was almost led to forsake their religion, its language was simplified, culminating in the loss of their horse, costume, jewelry, and customs which had been gained through a thousand years' work. Nothing happens in this universe without a reason; whether it is a natural or man-made disaster which afflicts a nation, there is always a reason for it."

Like the other Central Asian breakaway republics, Turkmenistan had a large ethnic Russian population in 1991. Turkmenbashi has expelled most of them. Ethnic cleansing led to the loss of most of the educated class of technocrats.

Turkmenbashi's statues are as populous as the military police who can clear out a busy market merely by talking a stroll. But while every dictatorship features statues of its Dear Leader, Turkmenbashi makes guys like Saddam and Moammar Khadafi look modest and self-effacing. He has constructed the Mother of All Statues to himself: gilt, thirteen yards high atop a twenty-four-yard high pedestal he calls the Arch of Neutrality. ("Neutrality" is Turkmenbashi's simplistic yet effective take on a foreign policy that has left his nation just the way he likes it—isolated, with his people bound to his every whim.) The dominant feature on Ashkhabat's sprawling low-rise skyline revolves three hundred sixty degrees every day, precisely timed so that he faces the sun at any given moment. ("Actually, the sun turns to follow him," goes a local joke.)

His face is on every denomination of the inflation-ravaged *manat*. The highest, ten-thousand-manat denomination is worth about fifty cents. One of the three national news channels has been named "The Epoch of Turkmenbashi." Streets, airports, major cities, items considered newsworthy (a large meteorite that fell over the vast northern desert made the cut in 1998) and even the month of January have renamed in his honor. Turkmen calendar reform affected all twelve months as well as the seven days of the week. April is now "Gurbansoltan-edje," for Turkmenbashi's mother, who died in a 1948 earthquake that devastated Ashkhabat. (In 2002 the Turkmen word for bread, *chorek*, was scrapped in favor of Gurbansoltan-edje.) September is "*Rukhnama*," the title of a little green book of Turk-

The author "pays his respects" to the statue of Turkmenbashi, the focus of downtown Ashkhabat. City residents joke that the statue, which turns to face the sun as the day passes, actually works the other way around.

menbashi's aphorisms on ethics, culture, history and "the rebirth of the Turkmen nation" that has become required reading for Turkmen schoolchildren and, on Saturdays, for every adult. In 2006 Turkmenbashi promised that young people who read the book three times would be guaranteed entry to paradise. In the meantime, here on earth, they will "become intelligent and grasp the nature and laws of things and the worth of mankind." The year 2003 was named "The Year of the Mother" —Gurbansoltan-edje to be precise. There's Turkmenbashi tea and yogurt. And if all Turkmenbashi all the time begins to get on your nerves, you can numb your brain with a bottle of Turkmenbashi-brand national vodka.

Even the days of the week have been Turkmenbashized:
Monday – Major Day
Tuesday – Young Day
Wednesday – Favorable Day
Thursday – Blessed Day
Friday – Friday
Saturday – Spiritual Day
Sunday – Rest Day

Turkmenbashi ("Leader of All Ethnic Turkmens," an honorific he awarded himself) is Saparmurat Ataevich Niyazov, the sixty-six-year-old party boss of the Turkmen Soviet Socialist Republic since 1985 and the President for Life of the Republic of Turkmenistan since 1991. Signs bearing his slogans also refer to him as Saparmurat Turkmenbashi. The Soviets liked to groom orphans for top jobs because of their presumed loyalty to the state. The theory worked perfectly with Niyazov, whose father fell dead in the snow during the Great Patriotic War Against the Fascists, a.k.a. World War II. At age eight Niyazov's mother was killed along with his other relatives in a catastrophic 1948 earthquake that claimed more than four hundred thousand lives from Ashkhabat to Samarkand to Tashkent. One hundred ten thousand people died in Ashkhabat alone. The thoroughly indoctrinated Niyazov attended a technical college and rose through the ranks of the electrical engineering corps via a combination of self-described workaholicism and suckuppery. When Moscow pulled the plug on financial subsidies to its southern republics in 1991, effectively forcing them to declare independence, the dim but ambitious brown-noser who got his start running a power plant outside Ashkhabat had himself elected president. More titles followed: President, Prime Minister, Commander in Chief, Chairman of the Cabinet of Ministers, Chairman of the National Olympic Committee and Chairman of the Democratic Party of Turkmenistan, successor to the Communist Party—now the nation's only legal political party. In addition, reads his government biography, "Mr. Niyazov was awarded the Magtymguly International Prize for achieving the aim of Magtymguly, the great Turkmen poet and philosopher: the establishment of an independent state of Turkmenistan."

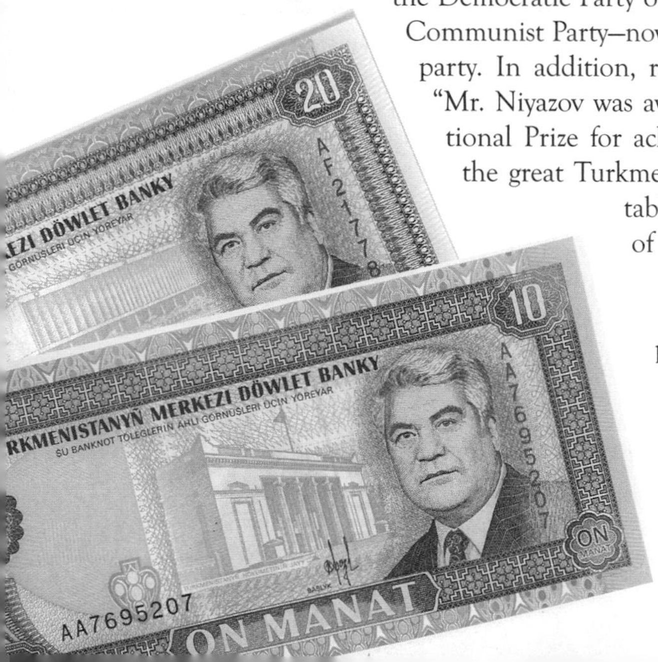
20
DÖWLET BANKY
10
RKMENISTANYŇ MERKEZI DÖWLET BANKY
AA7695207
ON MANAT

It only seems fair.

Reptiles and climate aside, post-Soviet Turkmenistan holds one ace in the hole: the U.S. Department of Energy estimates that the country may have reserves of as much as five hundred thirty-five trillion cubic

Camels are a common sight in Turkmenistan. Here, a new state-sponsored mosque can be seen in the distance.

feet of natural gas. At current production capacity Turkmenistan is ranked the world's fifth largest producer of natural gas, a status that will improve upon completion of pipelines now under construction. Turkmenistan also enjoys substantial oil and mineral resources.

In 1991, Turkmenbashi promised his worried subjects that their new country would enjoy the same gross domestic product as Kuwait within ten years. Thanks to the exploitation of oil and gas, he swore, every Turkmen household would own a house and a car. As of 2006, however, that promise remained unfulfilled. Although endemic corruption has stymied attempts to attract foreign investment, Turkmenistan's biggest problem is geography: it needs a reliable pipeline to get its refined oil and gas out to deep-sea ports. The shortest and most stable pipeline route would pass through Iran to the Persian Gulf, but trade sanctions against Iran prohibit oil companies interested in good relations with the United States from beginning construction. A long-planned Unocal-led pipeline project to carry Turkmen gas and Kazakh oil across Afghanistan has been revived but remains bogged down by logistical issues and continuing civil war. The Russian state oil company Gazprom maintains a Soviet-era pipeline heading north but refuses to pay market rates for Turkmen crude, so Turkmenbashi boycotts it.

The national average income was six hundred seventy dollars per year as of 2005, the same as the war-ravaged and oil-free Ivory Coast. While a tiny cabal of Turkmenbashi-connected elites reside in sumptuous palaces, survival for ordinary people is only possible because the government provides free water, housing and,

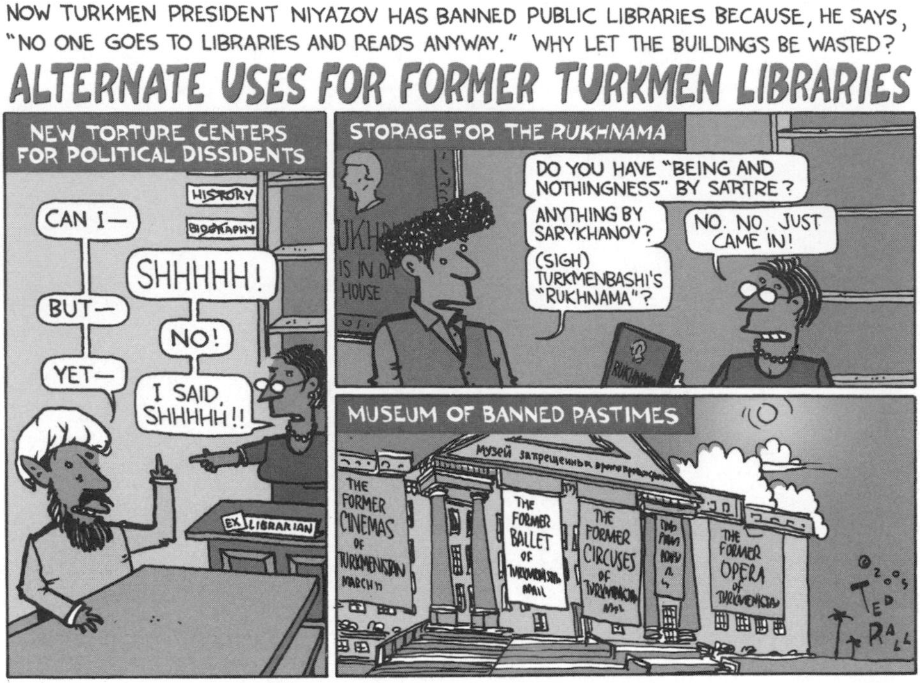
NOW TURKMEN PRESIDENT NIYAZOV HAS BANNED PUBLIC LIBRARIES BECAUSE, HE SAYS, "NO ONE GOES TO LIBRARIES AND READS ANYWAY." WHY LET THE BUILDINGS BE WASTED?
ALTERNATE USES FOR FORMER TURKMEN LIBRARIES
NEW TORTURE CENTERS FOR POLITICAL DISSIDENTS
HISTORY
CAN I—
SHHHHH!
BUT—
NO!
YET—
I SAID, SHHHHH!!
EX LIBRARIAN
STORAGE FOR THE RUKHNAMA
IS IN DA HOUSE
DO YOU HAVE "BEING AND NOTHINGNESS" BY SARTRE?
ANYTHING BY SARYKHANOV?
(SIGH) TURKMENBASHI'S "RUKHNAMA"?
NO. NO. JUST CAME IN!
MUSEUM OF BANNED PASTIMES
THE FORMER CINEMAS OF TURKMENISTAN
THE FORMER BALLET OF
THE FORMER CIRCUSES OF
THE FORMER OPERA OF
© 2005 TED RALL

of course, natural gas. Matches, however, are still so scarce that it is standard practice in Turkmen households to leave one's stove on twenty-four hours a day. At least most commodities are cheap. Fifty cents buys a meal for two and a beautiful Turkmen carpet runs two hundred bucks, the same price as a camel. Only in the projects that reflect Turkmenbashi's grandiose dreams of an energy-rich future are the prices sky-high. Four-star hotels built to accommodate an imaginary stream of foreign investors list rooms at five hundred dollars a night. They go out of business as quickly as they rise over the blazing desert.

In February 2003 Turkmenbashi launched a pilot program that he claimed would begin to fulfill his promise to put a car in every driveway. In practice, it will be more limited: it will put every cabinet minister, party boss and committee head behind the wheel. Each top official now receives a free Mercedes-Benz every year. He is then expected to pass his hand-me-downs to his seconds-in-command. "We have the right to have something to be proud of," he told his cabinet.

Who could argue?

In 1999 the Khalk Maslakhaty ("People's Council"), Niyazov's rubber-stamp parliament, passed a law authorizing him to remain President of the Republic while scheduling elections in the future should he feel so moved. He might want to run for "reelection," Turkmenbashi said at the time, around 2008 or 2010. After thinking things over for a few years, however, Niyazov decided that he could do without the election option. Emboldened by the attention focused on the region by the U.S.-led "war on terrorism" and increased overtures and incentives to a nation that borders both Afghanistan and Iran, Turkmenbashi got the Khalk Maslakhaty to declare him what everyone already knew he was: "With long and excited applause," read the government press release, "delegates to the supreme governmental body literally forced Niyazov to accept the title of President for Life."

During the same ebullient session, the body declared Niyazov "Hero of Turkmenistan" for the third time. This was apparently a promotion from 2001, when the parliament named him a mere "prophet."

False modesty is one key to Turkmenbashi's mystique. "If I was a worker and my president gave me all the things they have here in Turkmenistan," he told an interviewer on the CBS television news program "60 Minutes," I would not only paint his picture, I would have his picture on my shoulder, or on my clothing. I'm personally against seeing my pictures and statues in the streets—but it's what the people want." In February 2003 he ordered Turkmen state media to stop toadying to him. "As soon as one switches the TV set on," he said, "a program is in progress either about me or about my mother or my father. I beg you not to praise me so much, otherwise it is impossible for me to watch any of your programs." Surprisingly, his request has not been honored.

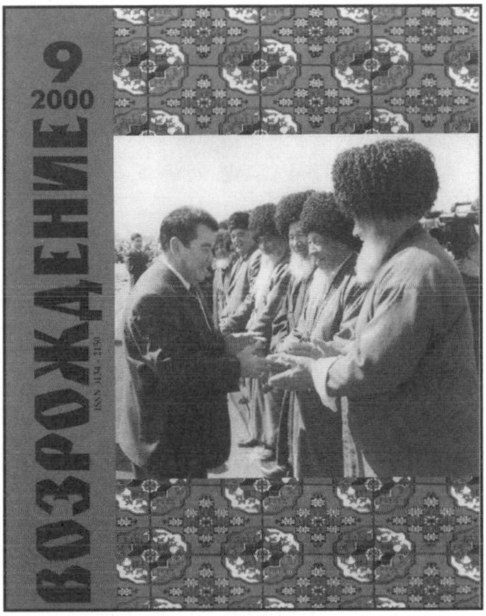
ВОЗРОЖДЕНИЕ
9
2000
Turkmenbashi works a crowd. From government propaganda (what else?)

Unlike other dictators, Turkmenbashi is a do-it-yourself tyrant. Turkmen high school students send their college applications directly to Turkmenbashi himself. The Hero of Turkmenistan decides whether or not to grant admission and what subject he or she should study. (Regardless of one's major, classes like "The Domestic and International Politics of Turkmenbashi" are part of the core curriculum.) Niyazov, rather than a personal secretary, decides whether or not the president—he—ought to grant an audience to foreign reporters. (His answer is usually in the negative.) Turkmenbashi personally approves the editorial content of newspapers and magazines, all of which are owned and published by a government ministry whose idea of an independent press is separate offices for each "editor." So much control, yet he still can't stop his image from springing up on lapel pins, taxis and T-shirts. Absolute dictatorship has fewer privileges than one would expect.

The personal touch extends to sartorial legislation that turns strictures of the Taliban, once and future rulers of Turkmenistan's destabilizing southern neighbor, on their head. Beards and long hair, which some secular Central Asians interpret

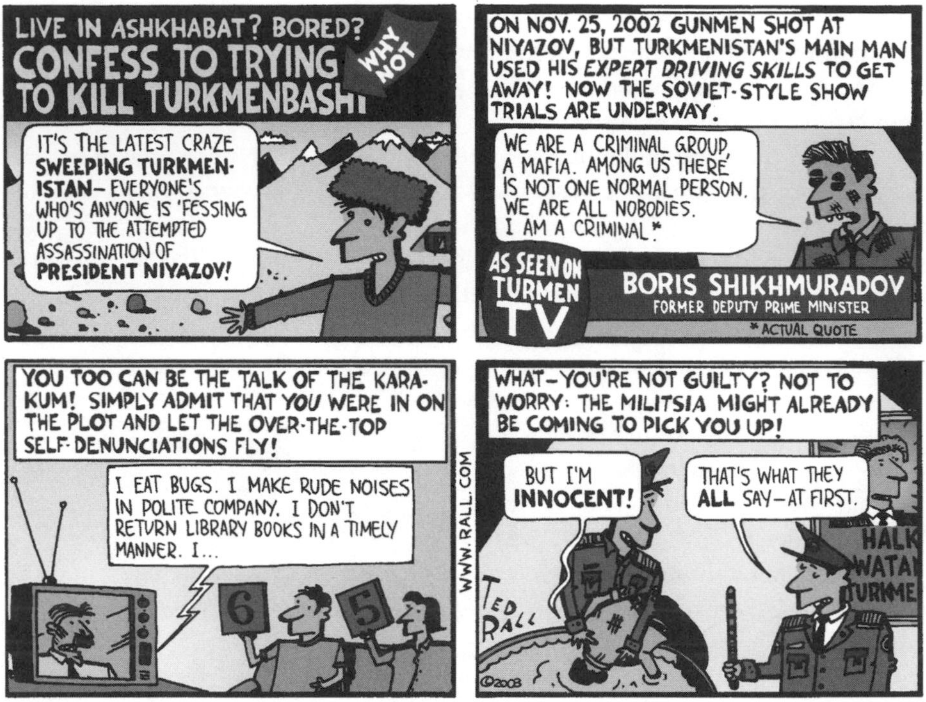
LIVE IN ASHKHABAT? BORED?
CONFESS TO TRYING TO KILL TURKMENBASHI
WHY NOT
IT'S THE LATEST CRAZE SWEEPING TURKMENISTAN— EVERYONE'S WHO'S ANYONE IS 'FESSING UP TO THE ATTEMPTED ASSASSINATION OF PRESIDENT NIYAZOV!
ON NOV. 25, 2002 GUNMEN SHOT AT NIYAZOV, BUT TURKMENISTAN'S MAIN MAN USED HIS EXPERT DRIVING SKILLS TO GET AWAY! NOW THE SOVIET-STYLE SHOW TRIALS ARE UNDERWAY.
WE ARE A CRIMINAL GROUP, A MAFIA. AMONG US THERE IS NOT ONE NORMAL PERSON. WE ARE ALL NOBODIES. I AM A CRIMINAL.*
AS SEEN ON TURMEN TV
BORIS SHIKHMURADOV
FORMER DEPUTY PRIME MINISTER
*ACTUAL QUOTE
YOU TOO CAN BE THE TALK OF THE KARA-KUM! SIMPLY ADMIT THAT YOU WERE IN ON THE PLOT AND LET THE OVER-THE-TOP SELF-DENUNCIATIONS FLY!
I EAT BUGS. I MAKE RUDE NOISES IN POLITE COMPANY. I DON'T RETURN LIBRARY BOOKS IN A TIMELY MANNER. I...
6
5
WWW.RALL.COM
WHAT—YOU'RE NOT GUILTY? NOT TO WORRY: THE MILITSIA MIGHT ALREADY BE COMING TO PICK YOU UP!
BUT I'M INNOCENT!
THAT'S WHAT THEY ALL SAY—AT FIRST.
HALK WATAN TURKME
TED RALL
©2003

as signs of excessive devotion to Islam, have not been legally banned but are nevertheless prohibited for young men. Why pass a law? Turkmenbashi had spoken! The day after Turkmenbashi went on television, shaggy young Turkmen lined up at barbers to request the clean-cut look. He has ordered girls to wear traditional braids and Turkmen fur hats. Gold teeth, the great legacy of Soviet dentistry, are also frowned upon. "I watched young dogs when I was young," amateur folk dentist Niyazov was quoted by the Interfax news agency upon the issuance of his anti-gold-tooth diktat. "They were given bones to gnaw. Those of you whose teeth have fallen out did not gnaw on bones. This is my advice." Turkmen news anchorpeople are proscribed from wearing lipstick because Turkmenbashi had trouble telling men and woman apart. A December 2005 decree banned video games because they encourage violence among young Turkmen. When Turkmenbashi hits the road—because he doesn't trust chauffeurs he drives himself—all of Ashkhabat's streets are closed to other motorists. (Turkmen drivers, proscribed from listening to their car radios because they're a distraction, are also required to pass a quiz about Turkmenbashi's *Rukhnama* in order to renew their licenses.)

When assassins armed with automatic weapons ambushed his bulletproof Mercedes on an Ashkhabat highway on November 25, 2002, Niyazov got a chance to show off his fearsome driving skills. With bullets flying and members of his entourage falling dead and wounded in the other vehicles in his motorcade, the intrepid Turkmenbashi skillfully maneuvered around a roadblock of vehicles, piloted his car down a steep embankment and up a hillside to another road from which he made his getaway. Even political opponents gave their sixty-two-year-old Niyazov thumbs-up for his panache under fire.

The assassination attempt ushered in a period of even harsher repression of would-be political opponents. Prominent Moscow-based opposition leader and ex-foreign minister Boris Shikhmuradov, discovered hiding in the Uzbek embassy a month after the incident, joined thirty-two alleged accomplices in a Stalin-style show trial broadcast on state television. Reading a confession that claimed that he had planned Niyazov's killing while under the influence of drugs, Shikhmuradov appeared with visible scars, obviously from a prison beatdown, on his face. As People's Council deputies stood and applauded while facing a giant screen televising the sentencing, he was dispatched to life in prison without chance for parole. "Forty-six people have been convicted," Niyazov told Turkmen television. "There were another five or ten people involved, but we're not going to keep on looking for them now."

He expelled the Uzbek ambassador in retaliation for harboring Shikhmuradov, closed the Turkmen-Uzbek border and ordered Turkmen consulates and embassies to stop issuing visas to journalists or representatives of human rights and other non-governmental organizations. As its quirky leader ratcheted up political repression and issued increasingly odd edicts Turkmenistan, always difficult to access from the West, became a closed society—and slid further into news oblivion.

Papa Niyazov

To be fair, Turkmenbashi's personality quirks include a soft, paternal side. He was the first Central Asian ruler to abolish the death penalty. And, in 1997, after heart surgery that his Russian doctors told him had been necessitated by his smoking habit, he issued a law slapping a five hundred thousand *manat* (thirty dollar) fine—about a month's average wage—on the sale, possession and consumption of tobacco products within the republic. Turkmenistan went from a country where nearly every adult male smoked to one in which few people claimed to miss the habit in a matter of months. "I hate Turkmenbashi," an Ashkhabat taxi driver told me in 1997, "I would kill him myself. But I thank him for making me stop smoking. It was a terrible habit."

Turkmenistan's First Jock again kicked indolence in its pudgy cheeks with his October 2000 "health walk" to celebrate the ninth anniversary of Turkmen independence. Ministers and other government officials were ordered to trek twenty-four miles out of town under the blazing sun. Turkmenbashi also used the occasion to announce a blanket amnesty for half his nation's twenty-two thousand prisoners. Nine thousand more were released to mark the end of Ramadan in November 2004.

If you believe his press, Turkmenbashi has become concerned about a growing trade in Central Asian women being forcibly shipped to the Gulf States to work as prostitutes. In an effort supposedly developed to protect Turkmen women against falling prey to white slavers, he enacted a November 2001 edict requiring foreigners wishing to marry a Turkmen woman to deposit fifty thousand U.S. dol-

The Wit and Wisdom of Saparmurat Niyazov

Turkmen President Saparmurat Niyazov, better known as Turkmenbashi, fancies himself a philosopher prince. By his own account he is busily engaged in the process of building the mythology of national statehood out of thin air in a nation whose borders couldn't possibly be more artificial. Niyazov personally penned the Turkmen Oath, equivalent to the U.S. Pledge of Allegiance. Take note of the personal loyalty aspect:

Turkmenistan,
My beloved motherland,
My beloved homeland!
You are always with me
In my thoughts and in my heart.
For the slightest evil against you
Let my hand be lost.
For the slightest slander about you
Let my tongue be lost.
At the moment of my betrayal
To my motherland,
To her sacred banner,
To Saparmurat Turkmenbashi the Great
Let my breath stop

Scary stuff. He means it, too: After an assassination attempt Niyazov enacted a new Betrayers of the Motherland Law that imposes life sentences in prison without the possibility of parole for a variety of forms of political dissent. In 2003 the chairman of the Turkmen supreme court issued a directive to the mayor of the capital of Ashkhabat to evict the wives and children of men accused of membership in the anti-Niyazov conspiracy from their homes.

Turkmenbashi's greatest achievement in the realm of state-building is the *Rukhnama*, his Not So Little Green Book. The *Rukhnama* relates his version of Turkmen history and culture, references the obligations and duties of Turkmen citizens and even provides guidance on how to live one's daily life. Following are quotes from this work, which the Turkmen government compares favorably to the Bible and Koran:

About the book: "*Rukhnama* is the veil of the Turkmen people's face and soul. It is the Turkmen's first and basic reference book. It is the total of the Turkmen mind, customs and traditions, intentions, doings and ideals. It will be our legacy to the future after drawing lessons from the past! One part of *Rukhnama* is our past that the existing knowledge at present could not enlighten and the other part is our future! One part of *Rukhnama* is sky, the other part is earth."

On the Soviets who looted the Turkmen treasury before *1991:* "Turkmenistan contributed revenue of ten to eighteen billion U.S. dollars from the production of oil, gas, cotton and chemicals to the Soviet Treasury, and less than one million came back. Because of this, moral values ceased to exist, and immorality, lack of trust, infidelity and fraud became widespread."

On generosity: "If you ask for a loan from someone, he will lend you money, even if the lender is a bad person. But if the lender is a good person and does not have money, he says, 'Come and relax, and have a cup of tea,' and then goes out secretly and borrows from his neighbor so that he can lend money to the asker. Even the bad person will reply to all requests for help, but the good one shares his bread too."

On a positive attitude: "When you meet a crowd of people, don't hurt anyone and pay compliments to everybody, and you will win everyone's heart. This way you will see that they smile not only on the face but in the heart and their hearts will blossom like roses. Both you and others will be pleased to see this."

On ethics: "When people with good ethics increase in number, life itself becomes more beautiful."

On equestrianism: "Listen to the advice of Gorkut Ata: 'Gain your reputation while your father is alive, and get ahead while you have your horse.'"

On wealth: "Proper wealth comes after honest deeds, and improper wealth follows from deceit."

On trashtalk: "Engaging in lies, gossip and slander lie at the source of all evils. For these are means that set a veil over sins and improper deeds."

On mortality: "Time is a mace. Hit or be hit!"

lars into the government's state insurance company—ostensibly to provide for the children in the event of a divorce. Although a bride price, or *kalym*, is traditional in Central Asian marriages, it is normally paid to the bride's family. Critics charged that Turkmenbashi was merely trying to add to his growing treasure—estimates of the loot he has spirited out of Turkmenistan and placed into his personally controlled foreign accounts range between $1.4 and $2.5 billion.

In an August 2002 decree Turkmenbashi declared war against aging. Dividing the lifespan of a Turkmen citizen into twelve-year cycles, Turkmenbashi extended adolescence to age twenty-five and postponed old age to eighty-five. Here, according to Turkmenbashi, are the official designations for each age group:

0-12: childhood
13-25: adolescence
25-37: youth
37-49: maturity
49-61: prophetic
61-73: inspirational
73-85: wisdom
85-97: old age
97-109: Oguzkhan (named for the mythical founder of the Turkmen nation)

Few Turkmen will ever live to see the age of wisdom, much less the coveted Oguzkhan. Average life expectancy is sixty for a Turkmen male and sixty-five for a female.

On other occasions Niyazov has boldly whistled past the meteorological graveyard. In 2001 he broke ground on a one-hundred-forty-yard deep, thirteen-hundred-square mile, artificial lake in the middle of the hottest place on earth, the Karakum desert; the water is to be drained from a river that feeds the Aral Sea, which has already been devastated by Soviet-era irrigation schemes. (The Aral Sea disaster is discussed at greater length in Chapter 10.) The twenty-year project, Turkmenbashi says without blinking either of his big round eyes, will inaugurate a Turkmen fishing industry. And in February 2006 he ordered each cabinet ministry to plant trees that will, according to a speech broadcast on state television, eventually form a cypress forest "stretching one thousand square kilometers." The idea is to "improve the Turkmen climate."

The Soviets built ice palaces in north Russia, above the snow line. Turkmenbashi's ambitions cannot be contained by mere feasibility studies. "Let us build a palace of ice," Niyazov ordered in August 2004, "big and grand enough for one thousand people. Our children can learn to ski. We can build cafes there, and restaurants." He has ordered a vast aquarium for the same site. A long cable-car run would carry heat-ravaged Ashkabatians from the capital to the project site in the nearby Kopet Dag mountains. "The Turkmen mountains are relatively high," noted the British Broadcasting Corporation, "but it is hard to imagine the palace remaining frozen without some sort of technical help."

CRITICS SAY TURKMEN PRESIDENT NIYAZOV'S RUHNAMA WAS PLAGIARIZED FROM A BRITISH HISTORY PROFESSOR. NOW OTHER SOURCES FOR TURKMENBASHI'S "LITTLE RED BOOK" ARE LEAKING OUT...
SAY IT AIN'T SO, SAPARMURAT!
NIYAZOV'S DECISION TO ELIMINATE DUAL CITIZENSHIP PROMPTED RUSSIAN-TURKMEN NATIONALS TO FLEE. COULD HE HAVE SPENT TOO MUCH TIME AT THE MOVIES?
THE RUSSIANS ARE COMING THE RUSSIANS ARE COMING
HMMM...
WHAT GIVES ONE MAN THE RIGHT TO LIVE IN OPULENCE WHILE MILLIONS SUFFER? MAYBE HE GOT THE IDEA FROM A DUSTIN HOFFMAN CLASSIC.
DUSTIN HOFFMAN
LITTLE BIG MAN
WWW.RALL.COM
HIS ADVICE FOR THE MASSES? IT CLEARLY COMES FROM THE BEST-SELLING SERIES OF "DON'T SWEAT THE SMALL STUFF" BOOKS.
WE'RE OUT OF FOOD.
"NOT TO SWEAT SMALL THINGS," HONEYCHEEKS!
TED RALL

Perhaps Turkmenbashi is hoping for intervention of another kind. "Turkmenistan is a secular state, in which religion is separated from bodies of power," he said in 2004. Whereas other rulers promise not to interfere in religious affairs, Turkmenbashi views the understanding in reverse. "The main task of clergymen is not to interfere in politics," he says. Nevertheless, calling himself "the thirteenth prophet," Turkmenbashi has leapt over another line his fellow Central Asian despots haven't dared cross, the divide between mosque and state. A hundred-million-dollar mosque in his home village of Kipchak, named for his mother and believed to be the largest mosque in Central Asia, features lines from his *Rukhnama* inscribed on the walls alongside verses from the Koran. "The *Holy Rukhnama*," says the official Turkmen Web site, is "on par with the Bible and the Koran, is to be used as a Spiritual Guide—to remove the complexities and anguishes from day-to-day living." He has banned future mosque construction and issued an edict requiring Russian Orthodox churches and mosques (other religions are prohibited as, you guessed it, un-Turkmen) to prominently display and read from the *Rukhnama* during services. Turkmenistan's grand mufti Nasrullah ibn Ibadullah was sentenced to twenty-two years in prison for opposing Turkmenbashi's interference with spiritual matters. For good measure, he was also accused of membership in the 2002 assassination plot. "There are few leaders in the world who can match his audacity," a former U.S. diplomat with experience in Turkmenistan told the *San Francisco Chronicle*. "There aren't many spheres of life left where Turkmenbashi doesn't dictate behavior."

Unsurprisingly, most conversations in Turkmenistan revolve around Saparmurat Niyazov. What will the mercurial leader do next? What's the status of the big desert lake? When will the *Rukhnama Volume II* be available? (Good news! It's out now!) What will happen should his heart finally give out? (Niyazov is estranged from both his son and his daughter, both of whom live abroad. No secondary official has been groomed to take over the country, whose culture is based on tribal and clan affiliations, after Turkmenbashi departs for the big pink pleasure palace in the sky. Despite the fact that, at eight-one percent Turkmen, the country is Central Asia's most ethnically homogenous, many Turkmenistan watchers expect the country to disintegrate into civil war fueled by inter-clan rivalries.) The obsession with Turkmenbashi reached dizzying heights with the Hair Crisis of 2000-2004.

Until the summer of 2000 Turkmenbashi's official portraits bore his dyed black mane, when an urge to go *au naturel* drove the President for Life to let his gray grow out to match Turkmen currency, designed during an earlier gray period. For several months the man who appeared day and night on state television looked starkly different from his widely disseminated images. Normally a color adjustment would have been in order, but Turkmen officials were cautious. "Maybe Turkmenbashi prefers to leave the posters as they are," the editor of a state-owned newspaper told me. "We won't change them until we hear differently." An official in the foreign ministry had a more prosaic explanation for the color gap. "Big posters are too expensive to change," he said. "We'll wait to see if he really means it."

The foreign ministry man proved prescient. After a few years passed and the

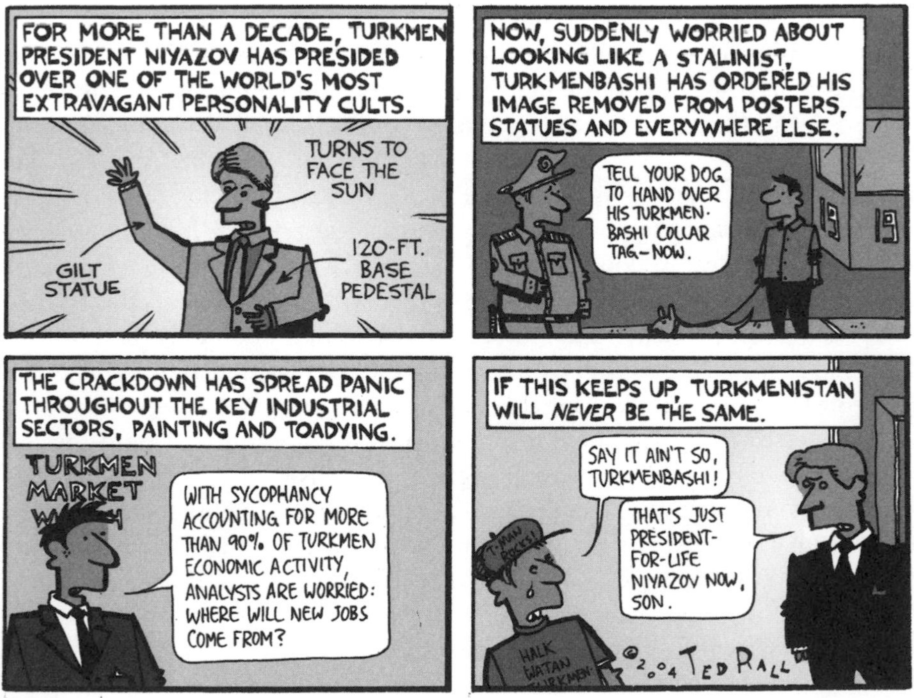
FOR MORE THAN A DECADE, TURKMEN PRESIDENT NIYAZOV HAS PRESIDED OVER ONE OF THE WORLD'S MOST EXTRAVAGANT PERSONALITY CULTS.
TURNS TO FACE THE SUN
GILT STATUE
120-FT. BASE PEDESTAL
NOW, SUDDENLY WORRIED ABOUT LOOKING LIKE A STALINIST, TURKMENBASHI HAS ORDERED HIS IMAGE REMOVED FROM POSTERS, STATUES AND EVERYWHERE ELSE.
TELL YOUR DOG TO HAND OVER HIS TURKMENBASHI COLLAR TAG—NOW.
THE CRACKDOWN HAS SPREAD PANIC THROUGHOUT THE KEY INDUSTRIAL SECTORS, PAINTING AND TOADYING.
TURKMEN MARKET WATCH
WITH SYCOPHANCY ACCOUNTING FOR MORE THAN 90% OF TURKMEN ECONOMIC ACTIVITY, ANALYSTS ARE WORRIED: WHERE WILL NEW JOBS COME FROM?
IF THIS KEEPS UP, TURKMENISTAN WILL *NEVER* BE THE SAME.
SAY IT AIN'T SO, TURKMENBASHI!
THAT'S JUST PRESIDENT-FOR-LIFE NIYAZOV NOW, SON.
T-MAN ROCKS!
©2004 TED RALL

Although Turkmenistan is the world's foremost manufacturer of hand-woven oriental carpets, exporting those rugs is nearly impossible thanks to draconian state restrictions. Disgusted dealers say that export fees and bribes far exceed the cost of the carpets themselves.

president's hair showed no sign of going back to black, the posters were switched out. Down came the giant portrait over the front of Saparmurat Turkmenbashi International Airport. So did the mural at the entrance to the port city of Turkmenbashi. Then, in 2004, Niyazov did the unthinkable: he dyed his hair again. This time officials put in requests for instructions through official channels. Update the posters, they were told, and so they did. Fortunately some wily propagandist had stored all of the 1990s-era posters in a government warehouse, supposedly for a future Turkmenbashi National Archive. Out came the old as the new, and everyone could breathe easier.

By far the most ludicrous yet rarely noted facet of the cult of Turkmenbashi is his complete absence of aesthetic charisma. Say what you will about Saddam Hussein's mass graves and unprovoked invasion of Iran, the deposed Iraqi dictator played up his original gangsta vibe to a fascinating extent. Who could doubt that, when he had himself videotaped firing a shotgun in the air with one hand while wearing a fedora worthy of a mobster in a 1940s film noir, that he was The Man? Hitler, Stalin, Idi Amin Dada, Moammar Khadafi, Fidel Castro—all the great dictators had style and panache. Niyazov, on the other hand, looks like a slightly overweight oil company executive stuffed into an off the rack suit after one too many three-martini lunches. Some have compared the pudgy ruler to a Mexican B-movie has-been. A vacant stare and facial features utterly devoid of character complete the overall impression of a man who just happens to Be There. A guy like that could easily become a high-level minister in a European technocracy, but how could he become the absolute ruler of a nation whose traditional Turkic culture is based on fealty to a charismatic chief?

As an Iranian, my friend Jay may not be the fairest judge of the Turkmen national character. "Look at all this stupidity," he spat sarcastically as we walked past yet another Turkmenbashi-festooned ministry building. "Turkmen people are stupid; they love this desert chief stuff. We Persians, we are civilized and cannot stand it." Iran is New York to Turkmenistan's New Jersey. Jay is wrong about the Turkmen being stupid. Still, you can't help wonder why people tolerate such ludicrous governance. One middle-aged Turkmen applied street-side psychoanalysis as he watched the tenth anniversary Soviet-style independence parade devoted to You Know Who. "He didn't get enough love as a child," he said. "That's why he needs all this attention now."

Niyazov worries about stupidity. "Guys, don't allow any wrong doings in your work and departments," he advised his cabinet on March 16, 2006. "Remove foolish people, and search for intelligent people [to replace the foolish ones]. If we don't do this, we will face misfortune sooner or later. If a foolish person comes [into authority], they could shake the foundations of our stable government."

That would be bad.

What's easy to forget amid all the pomp and frivolity is that Turkmenistan is a national tragedy, a place where the vast majority of people are living in abject poverty because their national patrimony is being stolen by a monster—a comical monster, perhaps, but a monster nevertheless. Twenty-five percent of Turkmenistan's adult population is estimated to be unemployed. Many more are underemployed or scraping by as subsistence farmers, petty thieves and drug smugglers. (The fall of the Taliban brought renewed opium smuggling through southern Turkmenistan en route to Amsterdam and other European capitals with a high demand for heroin.) Turkmenistan ought to export ten to fifty times more natural gas than it does at present, but since Turkmenbashi steals almost everything that comes out of the ground now he feels little urgency to explore alternative pipeline routes to improve the lives of his people. He has also failed to exploit his country's share of the Caspian Sea oil spoils.

One fairly viable alternative to both the Iranian and Afghan pipeline schemes would involve Azerbaijan, but Turkmenbashi has repeatedly picked idiotic fights with his neighbor across the Caspian. This do-nothing mentality pervades every sector of the Turkmen economy. For example, Turkmenistan is the world's foremost manufacturer of hand-woven oriental carpets but exporting those rugs is nearly impossible. Tourists may only purchase brand-new carpets (those made prior to 2001 are classified as "antique") if they take them to the culture ministry in Ashkhabat, which is only open two hours on alternating weekday afternoons. Disgusted dealers say that export fees and bribes usually exceed the cost of the carpets themselves. So the carpets remain in Turkmenistan, put on offer at local prices to

TURKMENISTAN

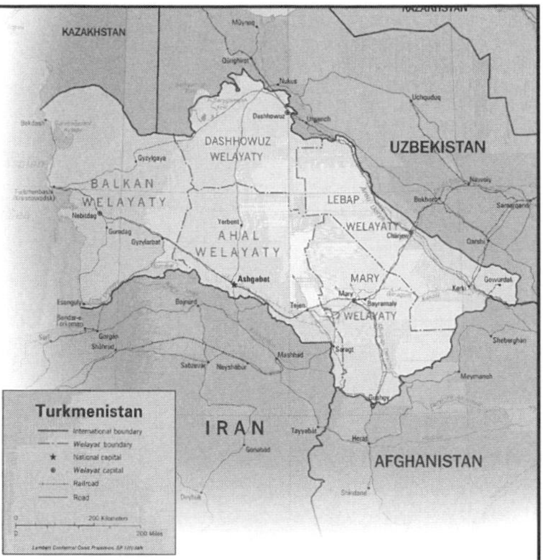
KAZAKHSTAN
UZBEKISTAN
DASHHOWUZ WELAYATY
BALKAN WELAYATY
AHAL WELAYATY
LEBAP WELAYATY
MARY WELAYATY
Ashgabat
IRAN
AFGHANISTAN
Turkmenistan

Capital: Ashkhabat
Form of Government: Dictatorship
Leader: President for Life Saparmurat Atayevich Niyazov (born 1940), aka Serdar Saparmurat Turkmenbashi the Great, or Turkmenbashi
Population (July 2005): 4,952,081
Major Ethnic Groups (2003):
Turkmen 85%
Uzbek 5%
Russian 4%
Area (square miles): 188,456 (slightly larger than California)
Terrain (as per CIA Factbook): "flat-to-rolling sandy desert with dunes rising to mountains in the south; low mountains along border with Iran; borders Caspian Sea in west"
Currency/Exchange Rate (April 2006): US $1 = 25,000 *manat* (officially 5,200)
Oil Reserves (proven): 546 million barrels
Natural Gas Reserves (proven): 2.9 trillion cubic meters
Coolest Thing About Turkmenistan: The Tolkuchka Bazaar outside Ashkhabat, the biggest and best outdoor marketplace in Central Asia, possibly the world
Worst Thing About Turkmenistan: The *militsia*
Best Way to Get Thrown Into Jail: Threaten or insult Turkmenbashi
Per Capita Annual Income: $1,440
Unemployment Rate: 60%
Life Expectancy: 61

Home to the world's hottest deserts, this blazing and dusty backwater is equal parts Middle East, Persia and Central Asia—adding to the surreality provided by its bizarre political situation. As citizens of likely pipeline conduit routes for Kazakhstan's vast untapped oil reserves and its own massive natural gas resources, Turkmen ought to enjoy one of the highest standards of living in Central Asia. Instead they suffer grinding poverty while their vainglorious dictator, Saparmurat Niyazov, who has renamed himself Turkmenbashi, Chief of the Turkmen, builds himself pink pleasure palaces and methodically transfers his country's wealth to secret overseas bank accounts. As "Halk! Watan! Turkmenbashi!" signs sprout across the countryside the Turkmen people somehow manage to struggle by and preserve their nomadic horse culture outside Ashkhabat's sleepy sprawl, a slumber that is broken only by the military police's closure of city streets whenever Turkmenbashi is on the move. Aside from the opportunity to gape at the madness of a dictatorship unmatched outside North Korea, Turkmenistan offers travelers such historical treasures such as the ruins of the Parthian capital at Nisa and the Silk Road oasis of Merv, as well as the chance for the foolhardy to hang-glide the rugged canyons of the country's northern provinces. At this writing, sadly, Turkmenistan has become a society nearly as completely closed as Afghanistan under the Taliban. Turkmenbashi, increasingly conscious of international ridicule and human rights complaints, has virtually ceased issuing visas.

people who can't afford them and confiscated by the airport police when visitors try to smuggle them out.

Turkmenistan's problem is simple: Turkmenbashi siphons off its oil and gas profits, the only hope to improve the living standards of its people, for his personal use. And whatever he doesn't embezzle he wastes on ludicrous projects that benefit no one. Months after he fired fifteen thousands nurses and doctors from his nation's beleaguered hospitals and medical clinics—citing fiscal shortfalls—Niyazov unveiled yet another over-the-top construction boondoggle. Reuters reported in April 2004: "Turkmenistan's autocratic president opened a gleaming new leisure center Monday, equipped with a swimming pool, air conditioning and even medical facilities—all of it for horses. President for Life Saparmurat Niyazov showed foreign diplomats around the vast fifteen-million-dollar complex which includes an operating theater, a hippodrome and stables kept cool from the desert heat."

Short of a successful assassination attempt or internal coup, it is difficult to imagine how change could come to Turkmenistan minus external military involvement—an unlikely development that has become even more improbable thanks to the September 11, 2001, terrorist attacks. As Rachel Dember of Human Rights Watch wrote in 2002: "Turkmenistan's massive natural gas reserves used to prevent the United States government from treating it like any other despotic regime. When Niyazov's destructive economic polices and the wild looting of state assets caused the United States to shelve large-scale gas pipeline projects, Turkmenistan fell into foreign policy oblivion. Then after September 11, the country became an ally in the global war on terrorism, allowing humanitarian aid to pass through its seven-hundred-forty-four kilometer border with Afghanistan, though not much more." The United States was content to let the Turkmen people suffer under Niyazov's oppressive rule.

Then, two weeks after an uprising toppled Kyrgyz president Askar Akayev, Turkmenbashi shocked the world.

"We will certainly hold presidential elections in 2008 on a broad democratic basis so that people themselves can make a choice," Niyazov announced to his cabinet on April 8, 2005. Rejecting suggestions that he had been spooked by the Kyrgyz events and announcing that Turkmenistan was finally ready for multiparty democracy, he said that "the country's destiny should not depend on one person. One must go sooner or later." Turkmenbashi, we hardly knew ye!

In an echo of 1999, however, Turkmen state media soon reported that elections would be held in 2009, not 2008. They also said that the People's Council had begged him to remain President for Life. Turkmenbashi has promised to carefully consider their request.

Checkpoint Madness

A series of suicide bombings...followed a series of explosions and attacks on police checkpoints in Tashkent and the city of Bukhara between 28 March and 1 April, which killed more than forty people—mostly police officers and alleged attackers.

—Amnesty International, 2004

As our bus was pulled over by military police for the umpteenth time along the highway somewhere between Bukhara and Samarkand, one of the twenty-three people I'd taken on KFI radio's proto-*Survivor* tour of Central Asia spoke up. "This is all going to change as these countries develop into democracies," he predicted. "The checkpoints will be gone and people will be allowed to drive wherever they want without getting hassled."

I disagreed. "I don't think Uzbekistan will become more like the United States. The United States will become more like Uzbekistan." Thirteen months after that kitchen-cabinet bus debate, nineteen men hijacked four commercial passenger jets and crashed three of them into the World Trade Center and Pentagon. Most people expected increased security at the airports. The checkpoints were the big surprise.

Southbound avenues in Manhattan were blocked at 14th Street by wet-behind-the-ears national guardsmen toting automatic rifles more than half their heights. Other weekend warriors began prowling airports and bus terminals. Only citizens who carried proof of their residency in what became known in my circle of media types as the Arachnid Quarantine Zone (a reference to the movie *Starship Troopers*) were allowed to pass. After a few weeks, the AQZ moved south to Canal Street—closer to, but still ridiculously far away from, Ground Zero. Entrances to bridges and tunnels became permanent outposts for highly armed policemen, guardsmen and officers of the newly created Homeland Security Department. The Transit Authority even built a special box in the first subway station in Brooklyn on the L line where an unlucky twenty-four-hour cop was assigned make sure that evil jihadis didn't enter the tunnel to plant bombs beneath the East River. (New York eliminated its "box cops" during a 2006 budget crunch.)

Checkpoints sprung up all over the country after 9/11, most having little to

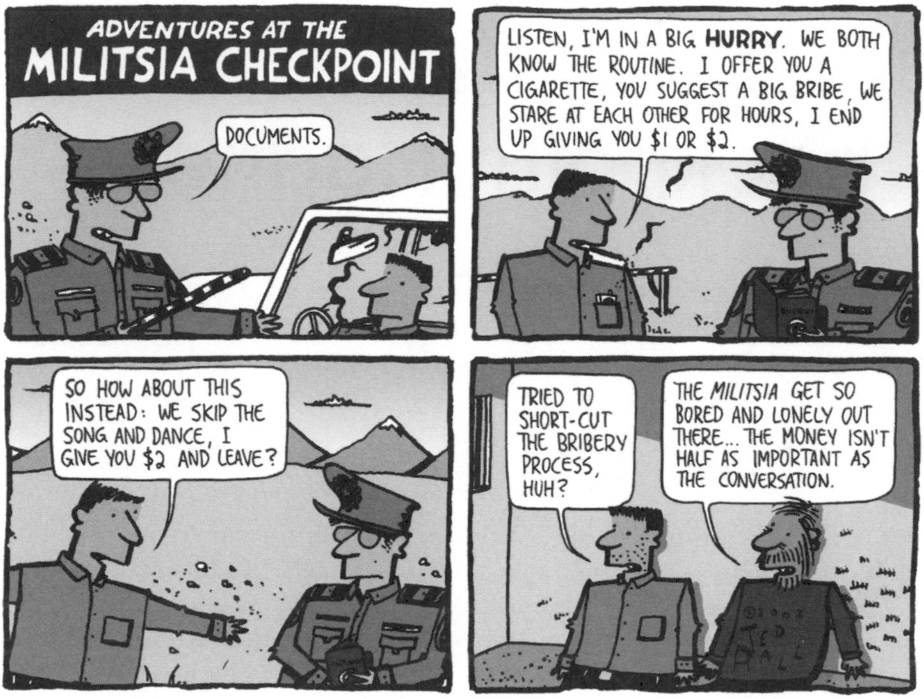
ADVENTURES AT THE MILITSIA CHECKPOINT
DOCUMENTS.
LISTEN, I'M IN A BIG HURRY. WE BOTH KNOW THE ROUTINE. I OFFER YOU A CIGARETTE, YOU SUGGEST A BIG BRIBE, WE STARE AT EACH OTHER FOR HOURS, I END UP GIVING YOU $1 OR $2.
SO HOW ABOUT THIS INSTEAD: WE SKIP THE SONG AND DANCE, I GIVE YOU $2 AND LEAVE?
TRIED TO SHORT-CUT THE BRIBERY PROCESS, HUH?
THE MILITSIA GET SO BORED AND LONELY OUT THERE... THE MONEY ISN'T HALF AS IMPORTANT AS THE CONVERSATION.

nothing to do with the global war on terror (GWOT, in guvspeak). Highways near the U.S. borders with Canada and Mexico were blocked to check for drug traffickers and illegal immigrants. Random sobriety checks had occurred before the terrorist attacks in New York and Washington; afterward they multiplied exponentially.

Checkpoints are a highly ineffective way to catch terrorists or other criminal masterminds; the smartest enemies of the state take roundabout routes, store incriminating evidence away from their homes and carry documents that withstand such routine scrutiny. Security is a ruse. Checkpoints serve two real purposes. In a democracy, they create a false sense of safety among skittish citizens, creating the calming illusion that their government is protecting them. Authoritarian regimes use them to control their citizenry, to remind them that movement is unpleasant and often costly, that the government is always there, watching. As democratic countries adopt authoritarian practices—random detentions, warrant-free searches and seizures, concentration camps—checkpoints begin to serve the second purpose more than the first.

As in most other former Soviet republics, you will encounter checkpoints in all of the Central Asian states. Uzbekistan has the most; it is rare to drive twenty kilometers on any highway in the country without being flagged down by a baton-waving *militsia*. Kyrgyzstan has the fewest. The authorities may stop cars to check documents, including the still-used Soviet "internal passport" outside major cities like Bishkek and Tokmak but usually only at night and often without demanding a bribe. Turkmenistan, Kazakhstan and Tajikistan station their *militsia* at provincial borders as well as on the outskirts of town. Additional checkpoints are manned near national parks and historic sites, as well as militarily sensitive regions such as the Uzbek base at Termiz where the Soviets built the Friendship Bridge to invade Afghanistan and the Baikonur Cosmodrome, a active space launch facility in western Kazakhstan. National frontiers between Central Asian republics typically require passing through a gauntlet of at least three or four outposts. Other borders can be even more of a chore; I counted nine checkpoints—five on the Kyrgyz side—when I crossed the Torugart Pass to China. (That frontier was only open on Friday mornings between nine a.m. and noon.)

The rise of the Taliban in Afghanistan owed much to public discontent over checkpoints. Regional warlords and local military commanders had set them up all over the country, even on small dirt tracks separating tiny hamlets. Drivers and pedestrians who tried to cross were robbed, raped and even murdered by rapacious soldiers. According to Taliban lore, Mullah Mohammad Omar led his *madrassa* students in a fatal attack on a checkpoint where one too many local women had been raped. His famous act of vigilantism inspired others to take back the night and led to the founding of the Taliban militia that ruled the country between 1996 and 2001—that, and millions of dollars in weapons and cash funneled into the country by the United States Central Intelligence Agency via Pakistan's Inter-Services Intelligence agency. The Taliban received some of their strongest support from Turkmen and Pakistani truckers who, for the first time in memory, could drive the full length of Afghanistan without encountering a single checkpoint or shakedown attempt.

Minefields and fortifications mark the border between China and the former Soviet republic of Kyrgyzstan.

Afghanistan's checkpoints, once again the site of numerous rapes and murders, were reestablished after the American invasion of October-December 2001.

Officially speaking, motorists and bus passengers with up-to-date documentation have nothing to fear but a few lost minutes at a checkpoint. One presents one's national identification card (or, for foreigners and locals crossing a national border, passport). These are checked for the any required visas and special permissions. In reality, each checkpoint offers hopelessly corrupt and belligerently drunk cops a chance to shake down passing travelers with the glee of great white sharks shredding a seal. A hundred-kilometer drive that would otherwise require a couple of hours can easily become an all-day, all-night ordeal as the police negotiate their "tolls" using every tactic from physical intimidation to a meaningful glance at a holding cell. Bus and truck drivers have the system down to a science; they carry a box with each bribe paperclipped in chronological order and pass each out the window without so much as a hello. (Bus passengers, sucking up unfiltered gas fumes in un-air-conditioned Soviet-era death traps, are generally assumed to be too poor to be worth robbing.) Foreign travelers and would-be entrepreneurs, on the other hand, are routinely asked for hundreds of dollars for the right to travel another few miles.

Nights, invariably fueled by dollar-a-plastic-bottle vodka, are especially bad times to deal with the *militsia*. Strangely, buses seem apparently timed to cross international borders in the middle of the night.

Each country's *militsia*, it should be noted, has its quirks. The Kyrgyz and

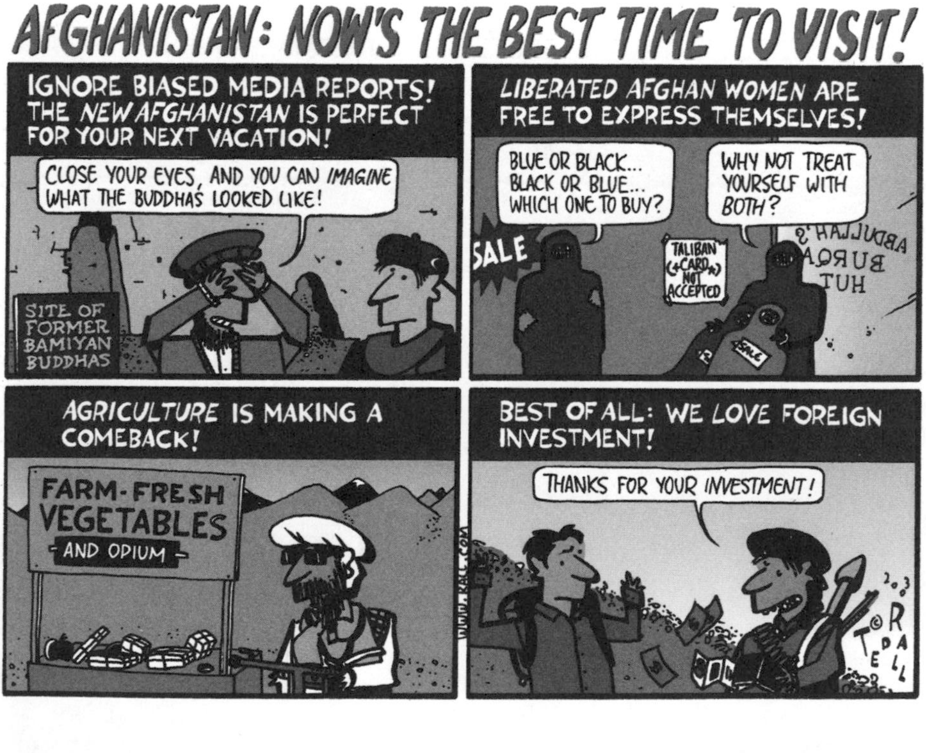
AFGHANISTAN: NOW'S THE BEST TIME TO VISIT!
IGNORE BIASED MEDIA REPORTS! THE NEW AFGHANISTAN IS PERFECT FOR YOUR NEXT VACATION!
CLOSE YOUR EYES, AND YOU CAN IMAGINE WHAT THE BUDDHAS LOOKED LIKE!
SITE OF FORMER BAMIYAN BUDDHAS
LIBERATED AFGHAN WOMEN ARE FREE TO EXPRESS THEMSELVES!
BLUE OR BLACK... BLACK OR BLUE... WHICH ONE TO BUY?
WHY NOT TREAT YOURSELF WITH BOTH?
SALE
TALIBAN CARD NOT ACCEPTED
AGRICULTURE IS MAKING A COMEBACK!
FARM-FRESH VEGETABLES
AND OPIUM
BEST OF ALL: WE LOVE FOREIGN INVESTMENT!
THANKS FOR YOUR INVESTMENT!

Journalists detained at a checkpoint marking the entrance to Tajikistan's special security zone along the Afghan border during the fall of 2001.

Tajiks are satisfied with minute "gifts"—a single cigarette or pen. Turkmen and Uzbek police are voracious to the point that they have made movement within both countries virtually impossible. Since trade is the biggest income source on the steppe, corruption has brought already shattered economies to a standstill. In 2004 desperate Uzbeks resorted to the most extreme possible form of political resistance: suicide bombings. After dozens of Uzbeks detonated themselves at *militsia* checkpoints, Ermer Islamov reported for EurasiaNet: "There is a growing belief among Uzbeks that the attacks constitute a reprisal against a rapacious police force. Fueling this view is the fact that most of the attacks to date have targeted police officers, while avoiding strikes at government buildings and other strategic installations. Many Uzbeks seethe over the arbitrary and corrupt action of agents of the state's security apparatus. At bazaars across Uzbekistan, police brutality is on display every day. This correspondent was at the Chorsu bazaar in Tashkent recently, observing numerous police shakedowns of vendors, many of whom operate illegally to evade punitive government taxation. These shakedowns were conducted in plain view. In one particularly troubling incident, a police officer viciously kicked an elderly woman who did not move out of the way fast enough. The Chorsu bazaar was the scene of two suicide bombings on March 29."

The Kazakhs deploy innocuous-looking standard poodles (don't be fooled, they're ferocious) to sniff for illegal drugs. Marijuana grows wild along roadsides, but the penalty for possession is a draconian ten years—almost always a de facto death sentence—at hard labor. They're also obsessed with accuracy on currency declaration forms.

Travelers entering former Soviet countries are required to declare how many Turkmen *manat*, Kazakh *tenge*, euros, U.S. dollars, etc. they are carrying. Customs keeps one copy; you keep another in your passport until you surrender it (with an update to allow for whatever you spent) when you leave. Predatory police officers prompt tourists to underdeclare their cash, but this is a bad idea in Kazakhstan. Whereas the Turkmen and Uzbeks will rarely resort to body searches, the Kazakhs will strip you bare and count every penny you're carrying. If the total conforms to your customs form, you're free to go—with your cash. If, however, you're off by the tiniest amount, even if you overdeclare, they will keep it all. Seasoned veterans of Kazakh border crossings count their money at least five times before crossing the border.

How do shakedowns work? It's a simple routine. Upon inspecting a prospective pigeon's documents, the policeman pronounces them unacceptable. A visa has expired; a special permission must be obtained from the Ministry of Foreign Affairs, where is it? Extra permissions obtained from well-connected government officials can get you off the hook. Journalist credentials help keep your money belt out of official hands. On one particularly desperate occasion when the Uzbek-Kazakh frontier was closed due to a border skirmish, I hired a *militsia* lieutenant to ride as my passenger past his greedy Uzbek subordinates. Don't have any tricks up your sleeve? Then it's time to negotiate.

You have a *problema*, the cop will say, not one that he can fix but one that he can ignore for the proper inducement. If you're like me the first time I was accosted in this way, you'll want to kill the bastard. Don't.

In fact, the best approach when first flagged down at a checkpoint is a wide smile. Get out of your vehicle, stride over to the cop and give the man a hearty handshake. Remember, he's been sitting out in the sun all day. He's bored shitless. A couple of jokes and the offer of a Marlboro cigarette—aw, heck, keep the pack!—indicates that you know the drill. It says that you're not easily intimidated and, worse from his point of view, not in much of a hurry. Being in a rush, or more to the point appearing to be in a rush, is the single biggest mistake Westerners make at checkpoints. So what if you miss a train that only runs twice a week? Time is all you have, certainly more than money. Hell, it's so nice out here with your new best friend that you might move right on in.

Hang out for twenty, thirty minutes and take in the view. Yawn ostentatiously. The approach of another vehicle marks a good time to dash for the exit. Put the local equivalent of twenty-five or fifty cents in the palm of your hand—dollars signal wealth and therefore vulnerability—and give him another friendly handshake. Then walk away. Odds are that, having scored a tithe from you, he'll turn his attention to his fresh prey, er, new arrivals. Your willingness to pay a small amount also shows that you know the going rate and don't intend to pay more than that.

Years ago, when I was a year out of college, my friend and I were mugged by four teenagers in a Harlem subway station. We were about to hand over our wallets

AFGHANISTAN

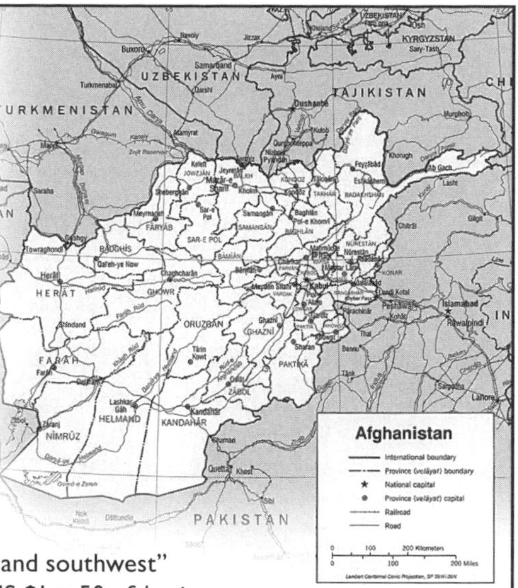

TURKMENISTAN
UZBEKISTAN
TAJIKISTAN
IRAN
PAKISTAN
HERAT
FARAH
HELMAND
KANDAHAR
NIMRUZ
ORUZGAN
GHOWR
Afghanistan

Capital: Kabul
Form of Government:
U.S. Occupation (Kabul and some provinces in north and east); Northern Alliance warlords (west); Taliban (south)
Nominal Leader: President Hamid Karzai (in Kabul et al.) (born 1957)
Population (July 2005): 29,928,987
Major Ethnic Groups (2003):
Pashtun 42%; Tajik 27%; Hazara 9%;
Uzbek 9%; Aimak 4%; Turkmen 3%; Baluch 2%
Area (square miles): 249,935
(slightly smaller than Texas)
Terrain (as per CIA Factbook):
"mostly rugged mountains; plains in north and southwest"
Currency/Exchange Rate (2005): US $1 = 50 *afghanis*
Oil Reserves (proven): 1.6 billion barrels
Natural Gas Reserves (proven): 15.7 trillion cubic meters
Coolest Thing About Afghanistan: Generous people who will give you the clothes off their backs and protect you with their lives
Worst Thing About Afghanistan: Murderous cutthroats
Best Way to Get Thrown Into Jail: Wave around a Bible
Per Capita Annual Income: 0 (yes, zero)
Unemployment Rate: 40% (official – actually closer to 95%)
Life Expectancy: 43

Afghanistan was originally envisioned as a buffer state between the British Raj in India and modern-day Pakistan and czarist Russia. That historical legacy has created a nation whose heterogeneous ethnic mix of tribes has only been united by the force of arms, most recently by the Taliban, who managed to control ninety-five percent of the country by appealing to cultural Islamism and brutal suppression of potential opponents. Afghanistan's history as a battleground and graveyard for invaders is currently being continued with the Taliban's resistance to American occupation. Northern Afghanistan is geologically, topographically and culturally part of Central Asia; the Pashtun-dominated south centered around Kandahar is more properly South Asian. The northern city of Mazar-e-Sharif is dominated by ethnic Uzbeks and the northeastern provinces of Takhar and Badakhshan are Tajik (also called Dari). The Northern Alliance received arms and other supplies from Russia during the civil war of the 1990s. An oil and natural gas pipeline, alternately called Turkmenistan-Afghanistan-Pakistan or Trans-Afghanistan Pipeline (either way, TAP), was conceived during the Taliban period by Western oil companies to run from Herat southeast toward Kandahar and the Pakistani border to a port on the Arabian Sea. The project was revived during the U.S. invasion of 2001 and is now under construction. On March 14, 2006, the U.S. Geological Survey announced that Afghanistan, previously believed to be important only as a conduit for Turkmen gas and Kazakh oil, has "eighteen times the oil and triple the natural gas resources previously thought" in the Afghan-Tajik Basin and Amu Darya Basin, respectively.

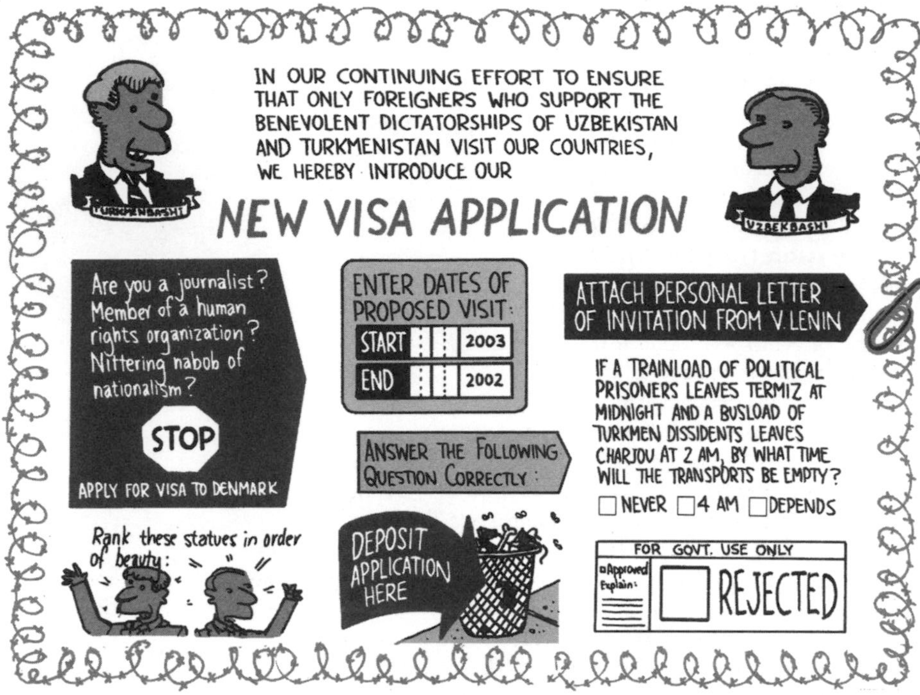
IN OUR CONTINUING EFFORT TO ENSURE THAT ONLY FOREIGNERS WHO SUPPORT THE BENEVOLENT DICTATORSHIPS OF UZBEKISTAN AND TURKMENISTAN VISIT OUR COUNTRIES, WE HEREBY INTRODUCE OUR
NEW VISA APPLICATION
TURKMENBASHI
UZBEKBASHI
Are you a journalist? Member of a human rights organization? Nittering nabob of nationalism?
STOP
APPLY FOR VISA TO DENMARK
ENTER DATES OF PROPOSED VISIT:
START 2003
END 2002
ATTACH PERSONAL LETTER OF INVITATION FROM V. LENIN
ANSWER THE FOLLOWING QUESTION CORRECTLY:
IF A TRAINLOAD OF POLITICAL PRISONERS LEAVES TERMIZ AT MIDNIGHT AND A BUSLOAD OF TURKMEN DISSIDENTS LEAVES CHARJOU AT 2 AM, BY WHAT TIME WILL THE TRANSPORTS BE EMPTY?
NEVER
4 AM
DEPENDS
Rank these statues in order of beauty:
DEPOSIT APPLICATION HERE
FOR GOVT. USE ONLY
Approved
Explain:
REJECTED

when we each looked down at our attackers' hands and realized they weren't holding any weapons. We punched them in their stomachs and made our getaway. Oppression is psychological: no one can oppress you without your cooperation. The micro-level mugging relies on surprise and intimidation more than brute force.

Cases of cops pulling guns on their prey and strip-searching them are not unheard of in Central Asia. They are, however, rare. In ninety-nine percent of shakedowns, the *militsia* will take you somewhere private—a guard shack or the back room of a police station. They'll demand your passport and refuse to give it back unless you fork over a "gift." They probably won't touch you, but things can turn ugly.

During my first trip to Central Asia in 1997 I was pulled out of the ticket line at a train station in the border town of Charjou (since renamed Turkmenabat), Turkmenistan by a *militsia* who took my passport, claimed there was a "problem" and made me wait on a bench while our train for Ashkhabat left without us. The next train wasn't due for another three days. That delay cost me a side trip to Iran which I had been looking forward to for years and forced me to shell out an extra seven hundred dollars for a plane ticket I wouldn't otherwise have needed. I struggled with my overwhelming desire to beat the fucker's brains in with my bare hands—an act that I could have carried off given our respective sizes even if it would have left me rotting in one of Saparmurat "Turkmenbashi" Niyazov's filthy prisons for the rest of my life.

§ § §

Caveat Porcor

Rich or poor, rural Islamist or secular apartment dweller, everyone in the former Soviet Union hates the *militsia*. "Fucking pigs" is the standard reply when the subject of the police comes up. Streets empty wherever they appear; people rejoice when one is killed. Everyone agrees that they're scum—even top government officials and their commanding officers. The reason for this universal contempt is simple: not only do the police refuse to find and arrest criminals, they *are* the criminals.

They man checkpoints whose sole purpose is to collect bribes from motorists and pedestrians. "*Problema*" is their battle cry, a grudging payoff their victims' sole resort. Shopkeepers, students and even religious leaders are pigeons to be plucked by these official government thugs. No one, except drivers of vehicles with government plates, is exempt. Days pass before the bodies of victims of Kazakhstan's Russian-affiliated gangs are removed from sidewalks. No one calls the *militsia* because they would arrest whoever called after robbing them and their neighbors.

Now a catchall phrase for a variety of (theoretical) law enforcement agencies, the *militsia* (or, alternatively, *politsia*) is a Soviet holdover created by the Bolsheviks after the 1917 revolution in order to distinguish it from its czarist predecessors. The USSR's Workers' and Peasants' Militia retained its *militsia* shorthand after a name change and subordinated it to the Ministry of Internal Affairs (MVD), which controls not only the official policing agency in each of the former Soviet republics but also such operations as the traffic police, customs and passport control. Whereas police in Western democracies are civil agencies headed by elected or appointed chiefs, the *militsia* is organized according to a military hierarchical structure headed by a general. The U.S. National Guard, as deployed domestically during emergencies, is a reasonable analogy. Policemen are technically called *militsioner*, or according to local argot, *ment* or *musor* ("trash," or "garbage").

Russia's *militsia* is so desperate to win hearts and minds that it hired the McCann Erickson and BBDO public relations firms to launch a "guerilla advertising campaign" to bolster its image. "The armed force has a reputation for violence and elaborate protection rackets which could be impossible to shake off," the British *Independent* newspaper reported in 2003. "Beatings in police cells are common and off-duty policemen are known to hire themselves out to mafia groups. Officers at metro stations and in the street often single out Russians from Caucasus regions like Chechnya for repeated questioning and document checks, leaving police open to accusations of racism. A survey earlier this year by the VTsIOMa polling agency found that only ten per cent of Russians polled thought the *militsia* deserved their trust."

"The *militsia's* image is one of bad behavior and corruption and all sorts of negative things," Alexander Mozhaev, managing director of McCann Erickson Russia, told the newspaper.

The sharpest Madison Avenue image maker would have even less to work with in Central Asia, where the *militsia* are corrupt to the last man, at least in part because their government outsources their salary. "A common practice" in Kazakh-stan, writes Robert Kangas, "is for *militsia* to occasionally flag motorists down and cite a violation. However, a modest 'fee' will generally satisfy the arresting officer, and the motorist is allowed to proceed. While motorists dislike this occurrence, some do see it as the only way in which street police actually get paid (wage arrears are major problems in government departments)." Uzbekistan, already home to Central Asia's most oppressive police presence, increased its force by as much as tenfold after the massacre at Andijon. Shakedowns have become so routine that the French government's website warns visitors to Uzbekistan against contact with the *militsia*. It's pretty much the same deal in Turkmenistan and Tajikistan. And Kyrgyzstan, on the verge of being formally declared a "failed state" on the pre-Tal-iban Afghanistan model of the early 1990s, is getting worse.

"It is a recognized fact, even by the government, that corruption has a system-ic character in Kazakhstan," says Sergey Zlotnikov of Transparency Kazakhstan, an anti-corruption group that estimates that eighty percent of the nation's eco-nomic activity occurs on the black market. Much of this is in the form of payoffs to government employees, particularly the *militsia*. "Nothing moves from province to province, much less in and out of any of these countries," a frustrated American entrepreneur told me a few years ago. "It's either pay them or you're out of business. Or you do pay them so much that you go bankrupt anyway."

The Kazakh government understands that systemic corruption as exemplified by *militsia* shakedowns of travelers is hobbling its attempt to capitalize on the coun-try's immense gas and oil resources. Although there have been attempted crack-downs—most famously carried out by top officials who drove around the country and fired the miscreants who shook them down—energy wealth attracts vultures who make the *militsia* look like amateurs by comparison. An American adviser to President Nazarbayev was indicted in the biggest violation of the Foreign Corrupt Practices Act in U.S. history for funneling sixty million dollars in kickbacks to the dictator's Swiss accounts. Prosecutors also accused him of giving thirty thousand dollars worth of mink coats, an eighty-thousand-dollar Donzi speedboat and a pair of fancy snowmobiles to the Nazarbayev family on behalf of ExxonMobil, Chev-ronTexaco, TotalFinaElf, Royal Dutch Shell, British Gas, BP and ConocoPhillips for access to the blockbuster Kashagan oilfield. "There is high corruption in the oil industry. Corruption is everywhere, from the bottom to the top [of society]," Zlotnikov adds.

Kazakhstan ranks number one hundred eight out of one hundred fifty-eight in Transparency International's 2005 Corruption Perception Index. Afghanistan (one hundred seventeen), Kyrgyzstan (one hundred thirty-six), Uzbekistan (one hundred thirty-seven), Tajikistan (one hundred forty-four) and Turkmenistan (one hundred fifty-five) bring up the rear.

§ § §

Dos and Don'ts

Because so much is at stake in a tourist's encounters with the *militsia* of the Stans, here are some vital dos and don'ts to make the best of a lousy experience.

Allow extra travel time. Western travelers quickly learn that nobody's time is valuable in the Third World, least of all yours. Buses leave when they're full, not at their scheduled departure times. Taxi drivers stop on the way to your destination—on your dime—to let their pals hitch a ride. Policemen are the worst offenders; telling them that you're running late provides additional inducement to give you the squeeze. When planning a journey, whether it's a year crisscrossing the steppe or a seemingly straightforward fifty kilometers between villages, always allow extra time for checkpoint shakedowns. I would have been more likely to catch my train in Turkmenistan had I not let the *militsia* know that I was eager to be on board.

Don't go anywhere private. It's an open secret that the police are the biggest thieves in every Central Asian republic. Oddly, they nevertheless prefer to carry out their *biznez* transactions in private. If a *militsia* motions you to follow him away from a busy bus terminal to a corner office under the stairs, refuse. First try feigning stupidity: an insipid grin isn't resisting arrest. If he insists, repeatedly say *nyet*. Don't move. These guys rarely carry guns and those who do aren't likely to pull one on a foreigner, especially not in public. They probably won't manhandle you; such unpleasantness could ruffle feathers after the news arrives at the Ministry of Foreign Affairs. Make them demand their bribes in public. Still better is to arrange for a local to carry your bags; he will make an unwelcome witness to police shenanigans.

No one can oppress you without your consent. Remember, shakedowns rely on psychology. However, if an official points a gun and threatens to shoot you unless you give him your valuables, for God's sake comply. Short of that, however, they're just talking. Stand your ground. Conversation can't hurt you. Keep your money and identification documents out of sight; don't even mention the possibility of paying a bribe. If you keep cool you'll probably get away without paying.

Yes, you have to turn over your passport. Many foreigners freak out at the fact that a corrupt police officer has their passport, but this too is a psychological gambit. Do not refuse to turn it over to any official who demands it; you're in their country, bound by their laws and they have that right. In the worst-case scenario, however, you can always go to your nation's embassy if the police refuse to give back your passport. If there is no consular representation in that nation, go directly the airport to explain your situation. Because *militsia* corruption is both frowned upon and widely known, your story will be believed. The policeman will get into trouble for causing an embarrassing international incident. At times, when bribe negotiations seemed to have broken down, I've stood up and announced that I was leaving and that, if I didn't get my passport back, I would report that the relevant officer had stolen it while trying to extort my money. It worked. Also, it's a good idea to keep color photocopies of your passport and its relevant visa pages buried in your luggage.

Pay bribes, but only tiny ones. With military police earning roughly half of the region's average twenty dollar per month salary, it should come to nobody's surprise that they supplement their incomes with bribes. Although the practice is deplorable and further undermines the legitimacy of the autocratic and malevolent regimes that employ them, avoiding the system altogether is sheer fantasy. Everybody pays. The question is: how much? As noted above, the going rate is less than a dollar to cross an international border and even less than that at regional and provincial roadblocks. Unfortunately there have been numerous instances of clueless foreigners shelling out hundreds of dollars at a time as they made their way across the former strategic underbelly of the Soviet Union. Such largess encourages bribe inflation that victimizes fellow foreigners as well as locals, empowers the police and generally makes everyone else's lives more miserable. Do yourself and future travelers a favor: carry small denomination currency in your pockets and rely on these local banknotes to pay off the fuzz.

Bribes can't fix problems. In the United States a well-placed bribe can make a ticket, even an arrest, vanish. Not so in the former Soviet republics, where the bureaucracy is so entrenched that even high-ranking functionaries don't possess the means of "disappearing" your difficulties. Pointing out this powerlessness is an effective means of lowering or eliminating a bribe; it's also a reminder to yourself that bribes require you to pay for a service you will not receive. One of my talking points at the Charjou train station was to ask whether the *militsia* could repair the "problem" for whether he simply wanted me to pay him off. "You need a new Turkmen visa," he insisted. "Give me money and I'll look the other way." "But if I give you my money," I said, "I'll have the same problem with another *militsia*. Can you issue me a new Turkmen visa?" "Oh, no," he said. "You must go to the Foreign Ministry in Ashkhabat." "So why should I pay you?" I asked. "There must be hundreds of policemen between here and there." He didn't have an answer for that.

Businesspeople have repeatedly advised Central Asian leaders that their nations will never attract large-scale foreign investment until their governments pursue policies of increased transparency. Police shakedowns, which routinely begin immediately upon arrival at the airport, are the most public face of corruption and as such are occasionally targeted by politicians genuinely interested in creating free-market economic systems.

Checkpoints will likely remain a part of life in Central Asia for the foreseeable future. For foreigners starting to adjust to their new post-9/11 police states back home, Central Asian checkpoint culture can rapidly become as tiresome as it is expensive. But look at the bright side. Unlike the citizens of Turkmenistan, you don't have to pay for an exit visa to return home.

In Tajikistan, on the other hand...

MUSCOVY
Moscow
Kostroma
Great Bulgaria
Bashkirs
SIBIR-SIBIR
Ugrians
Samoyedes
Obi R.
Irtish R.
Tobol R.
Volga R.
Ural R.
Aral Sea
Kharesm
CASPIAN SEA
KHORASAN
PERSIA
Herat
Kandahar
Sind
Multan
Lahore
Delhi
Agra
Oudh
Kanauj
HINDUKUSH MTS.
PAMIR
KASHMIR
Yarkand
KASHGAR
Tarim R.
T'IEN SHAN MTS.
KUEN-LUN MTS.
TIBET
Lhasa
HIMALAYA MTS.
ALTAI MTS.
Karakorum
Khalkas
Mongols
Great Desert (Desert of Gobi)
Lena R.
Yenisei R.
Lower Tunguska R.
Ormuz

Beijing to Istanbul
1997

Ceylon
Maldive Islands
Colombo
Adam's Peak
Pt. de Galle
Dundra Head
Nicobar Islands
Malacca
Singapore
G
70
H
80
Land routes
Sea "
Route of John of Pian de Carpine, 1245-1247
" " William of Rubruck (Rubruquis), 1253-1255

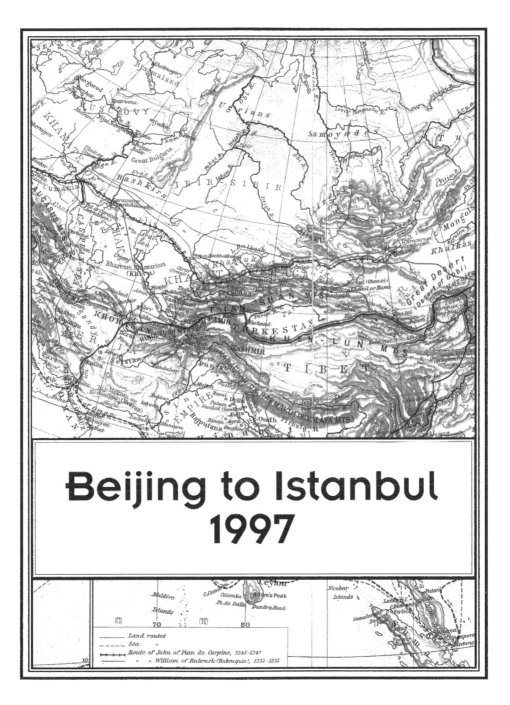

I went to China in the late summer of 1997 with the objective of driving from Beijing to Istanbul via the northern half of the old Silk Road. Accompanied by a friend who was also a journalist, I traveled overland through Kazakhstan, Kyrgyzstan, Uzbekistan and Turkmenistan. P.O.V. magazine, which funded my journey, published my article "Silk Road to Ruin" as a feature story. It was my first trip to Central Asia, and it changed my life.

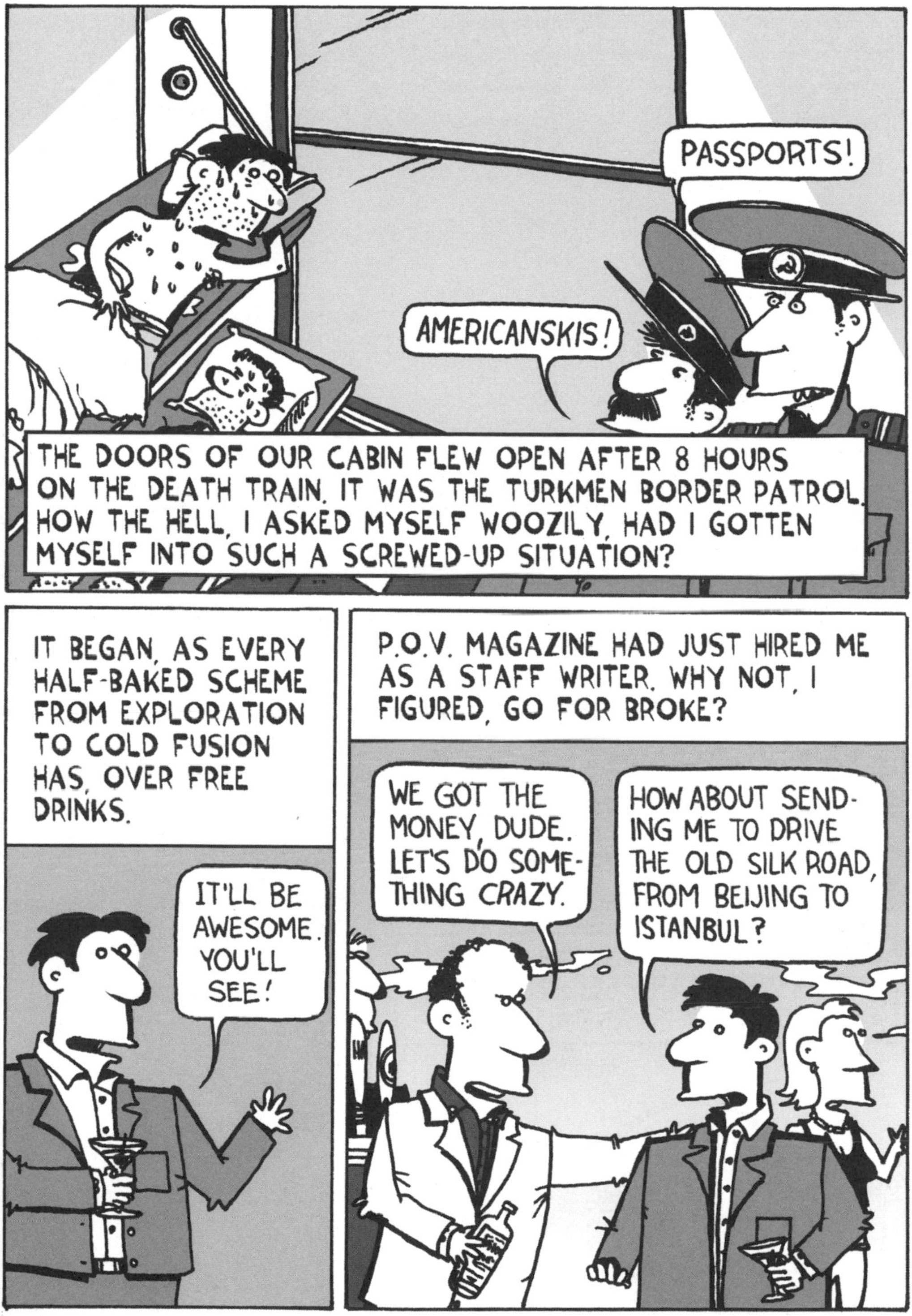
PASSPORTS!
AMERICANSKIS!
THE DOORS OF OUR CABIN FLEW OPEN AFTER 8 HOURS ON THE DEATH TRAIN. IT WAS THE TURKMEN BORDER PATROL. HOW THE HELL, I ASKED MYSELF WOOZILY, HAD I GOTTEN MYSELF INTO SUCH A SCREWED-UP SITUATION?
IT BEGAN, AS EVERY HALF-BAKED SCHEME FROM EXPLORATION TO COLD FUSION HAS, OVER FREE DRINKS.
IT'LL BE AWESOME. YOU'LL SEE!
P.O.V. MAGAZINE HAD JUST HIRED ME AS A STAFF WRITER. WHY NOT, I FIGURED, GO FOR BROKE?
WE GOT THE MONEY, DUDE. LET'S DO SOMETHING CRAZY.
HOW ABOUT SENDING ME TO DRIVE THE OLD SILK ROAD, FROM BEIJING TO ISTANBUL?

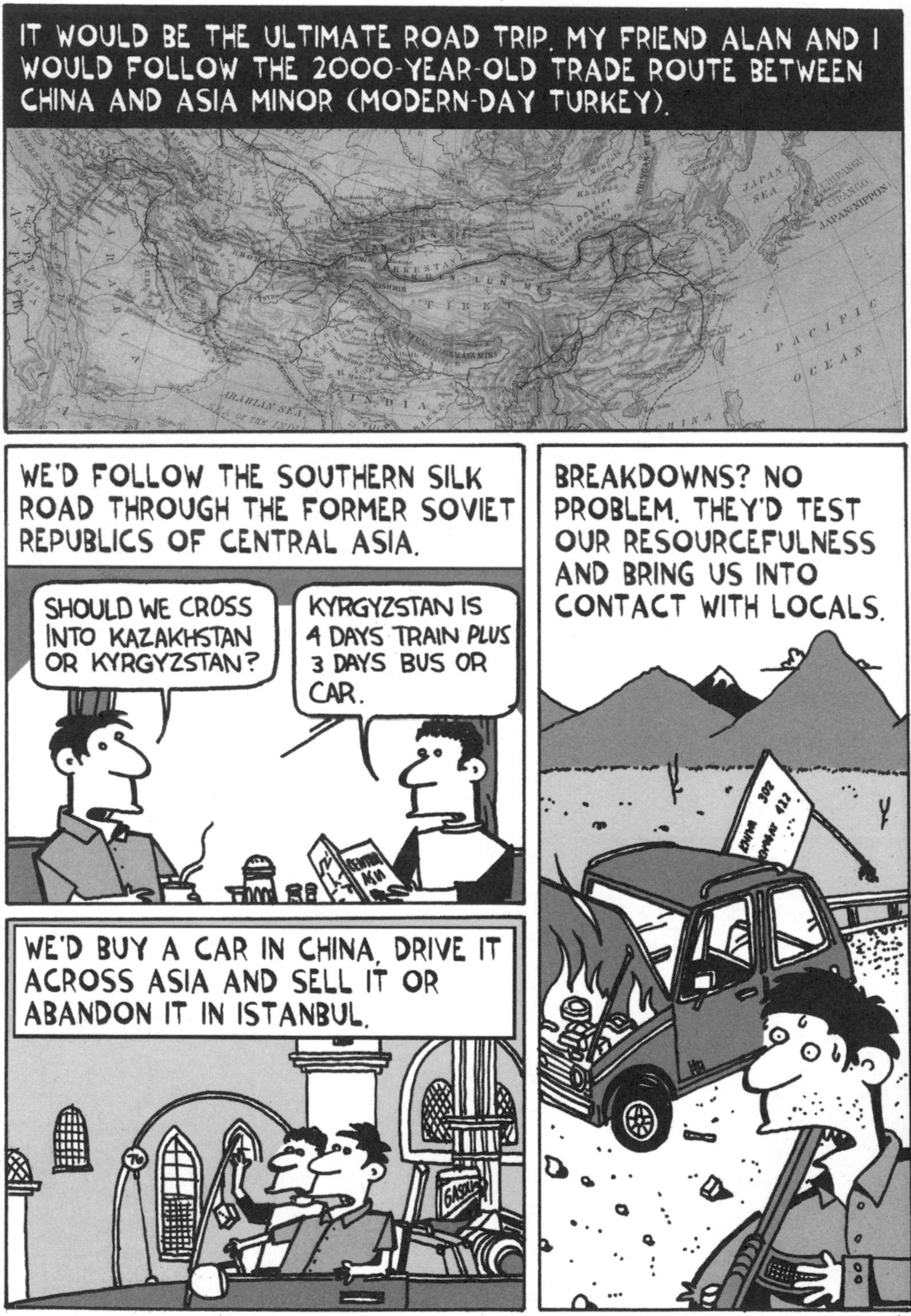
IT WOULD BE THE ULTIMATE ROAD TRIP. MY FRIEND ALAN AND I WOULD FOLLOW THE 2000-YEAR-OLD TRADE ROUTE BETWEEN CHINA AND ASIA MINOR (MODERN-DAY TURKEY).
JAPAN SEA
PACIFIC OCEAN
TIBET
INDIA
ARABIAN SEA
WE'D FOLLOW THE SOUTHERN SILK ROAD THROUGH THE FORMER SOVIET REPUBLICS OF CENTRAL ASIA.
SHOULD WE CROSS INTO KAZAKHSTAN OR KYRGYZSTAN?
KYRGYZSTAN IS 4 DAYS TRAIN *PLUS* 3 DAYS BUS OR CAR.
CENTRAL ASIA
WE'D BUY A CAR IN CHINA, DRIVE IT ACROSS ASIA AND SELL IT OR ABANDON IT IN ISTANBUL.
BREAKDOWNS? NO PROBLEM. THEY'D TEST OUR RESOURCEFULNESS AND BRING US INTO CONTACT WITH LOCALS.

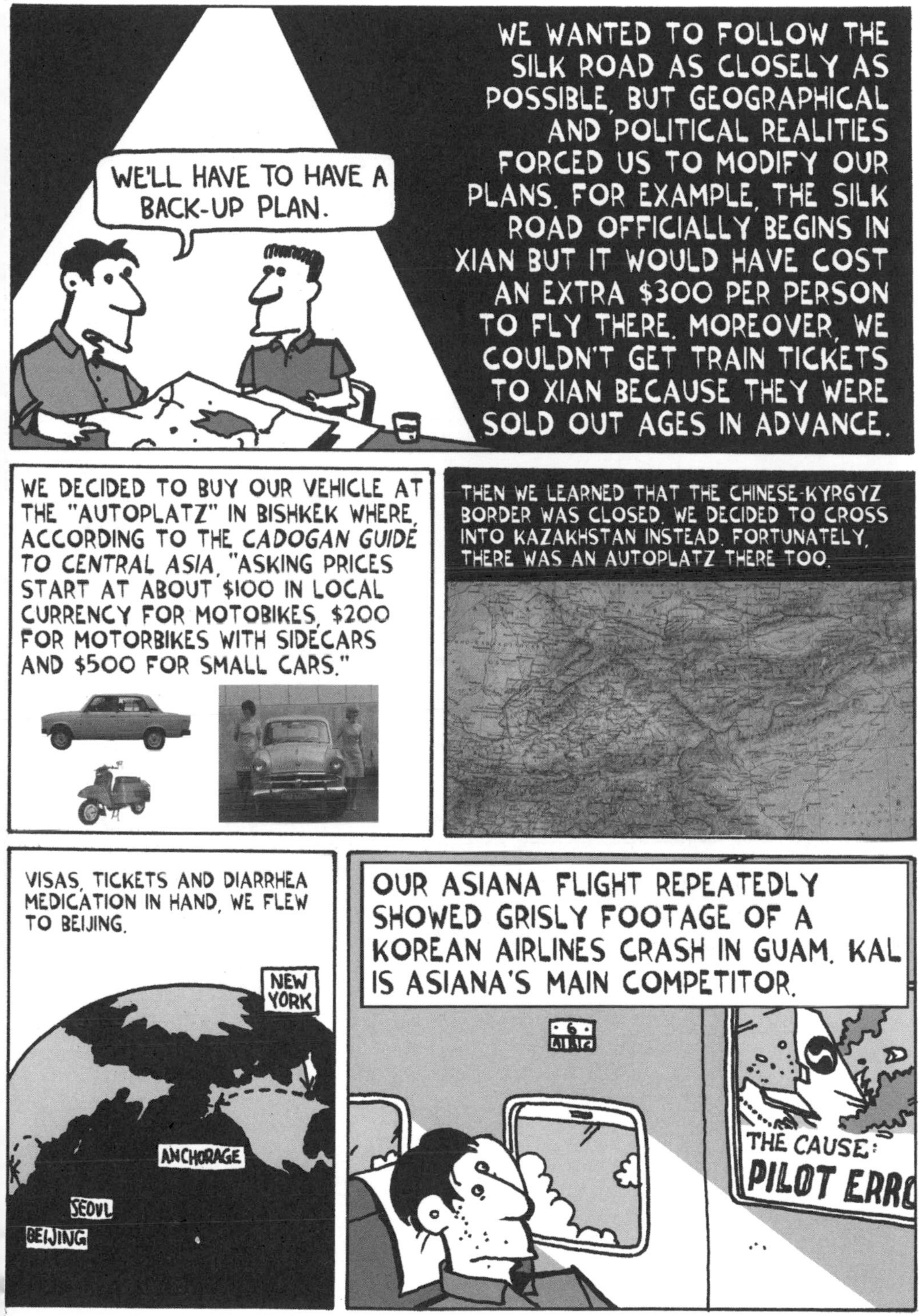
WE WANTED TO FOLLOW THE SILK ROAD AS CLOSELY AS POSSIBLE, BUT GEOGRAPHICAL AND POLITICAL REALITIES FORCED US TO MODIFY OUR PLANS. FOR EXAMPLE, THE SILK ROAD OFFICIALLY BEGINS IN XIAN BUT IT WOULD HAVE COST AN EXTRA $300 PER PERSON TO FLY THERE. MOREOVER, WE COULDN'T GET TRAIN TICKETS TO XIAN BECAUSE THEY WERE SOLD OUT AGES IN ADVANCE.
WE'LL HAVE TO HAVE A BACK-UP PLAN.
WE DECIDED TO BUY OUR VEHICLE AT THE "AUTOPLATZ" IN BISHKEK WHERE, ACCORDING TO THE *CADOGAN GUIDE TO CENTRAL ASIA*, "ASKING PRICES START AT ABOUT $100 IN LOCAL CURRENCY FOR MOTOBIKES, $200 FOR MOTORBIKES WITH SIDECARS AND $500 FOR SMALL CARS."
THEN WE LEARNED THAT THE CHINESE-KYRGYZ BORDER WAS CLOSED. WE DECIDED TO CROSS INTO KAZAKHSTAN INSTEAD. FORTUNATELY, THERE WAS AN AUTOPLATZ THERE TOO.
VISAS, TICKETS AND DIARRHEA MEDICATION IN HAND, WE FLEW TO BEIJING.
NEW YORK
ANCHORAGE
SEOUL
BEIJING
OUR ASIANA FLIGHT REPEATEDLY SHOWED GRISLY FOOTAGE OF A KOREAN AIRLINES CRASH IN GUAM. KAL IS ASIANA'S MAIN COMPETITOR.
THE CAUSE:
PILOT ERR

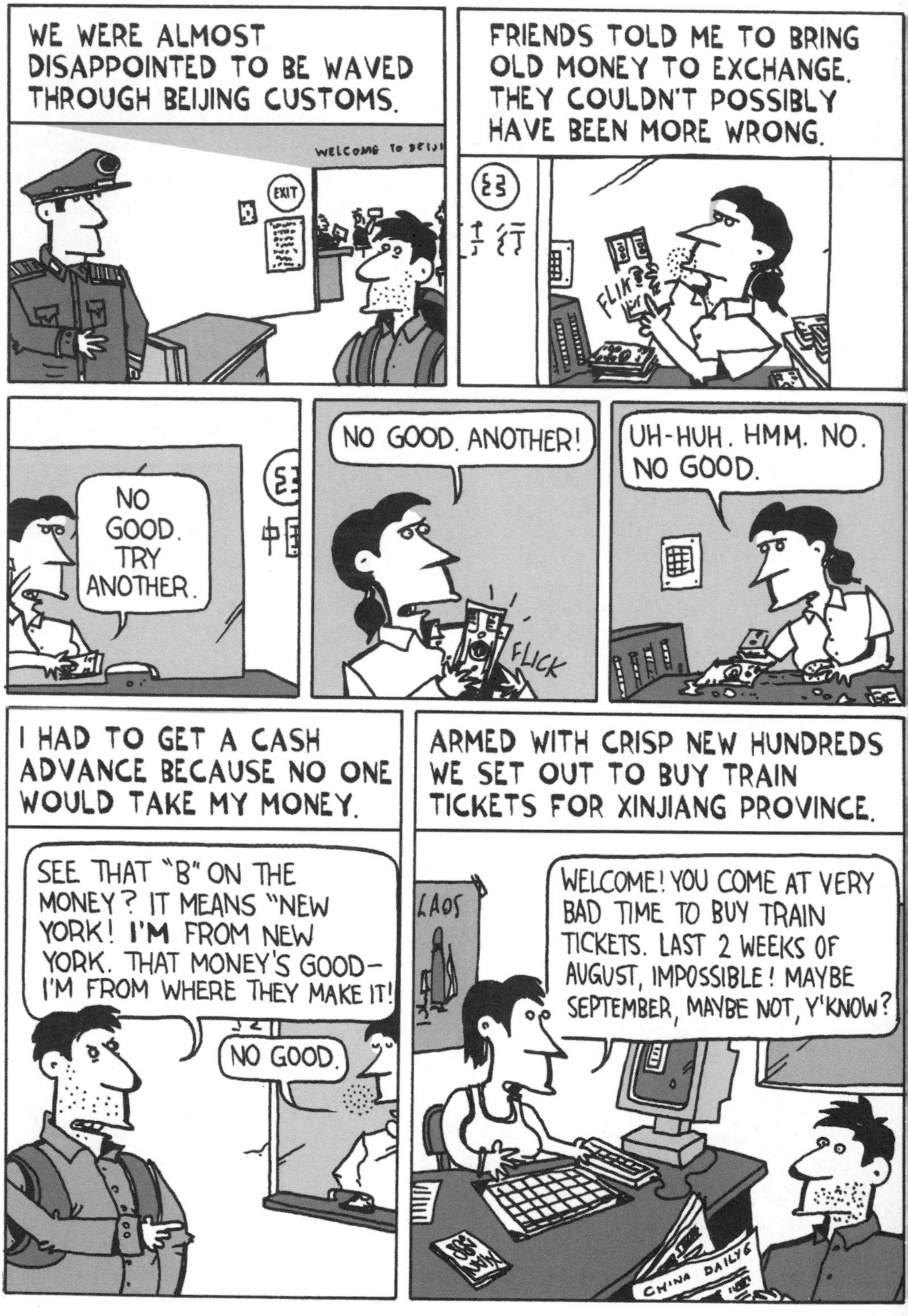
WE WERE ALMOST DISAPPOINTED TO BE WAVED THROUGH BEIJING CUSTOMS.
EXIT
FRIENDS TOLD ME TO BRING OLD MONEY TO EXCHANGE. THEY COULDN'T POSSIBLY HAVE BEEN MORE WRONG.
FLIK
NO GOOD. TRY ANOTHER.
NO GOOD. ANOTHER!
FLICK
UH-HUH. HMM. NO. NO GOOD.
I HAD TO GET A CASH ADVANCE BECAUSE NO ONE WOULD TAKE MY MONEY.
SEE THAT "B" ON THE MONEY? IT MEANS "NEW YORK! I'M FROM NEW YORK. THAT MONEY'S GOOD- I'M FROM WHERE THEY MAKE IT!
NO GOOD.
ARMED WITH CRISP NEW HUNDREDS WE SET OUT TO BUY TRAIN TICKETS FOR XINJIANG PROVINCE.
LAOS
WELCOME! YOU COME AT VERY BAD TIME TO BUY TRAIN TICKETS. LAST 2 WEEKS OF AUGUST, IMPOSSIBLE! MAYBE SEPTEMBER, MAYBE NOT, Y'KNOW?
CHINA DAILY

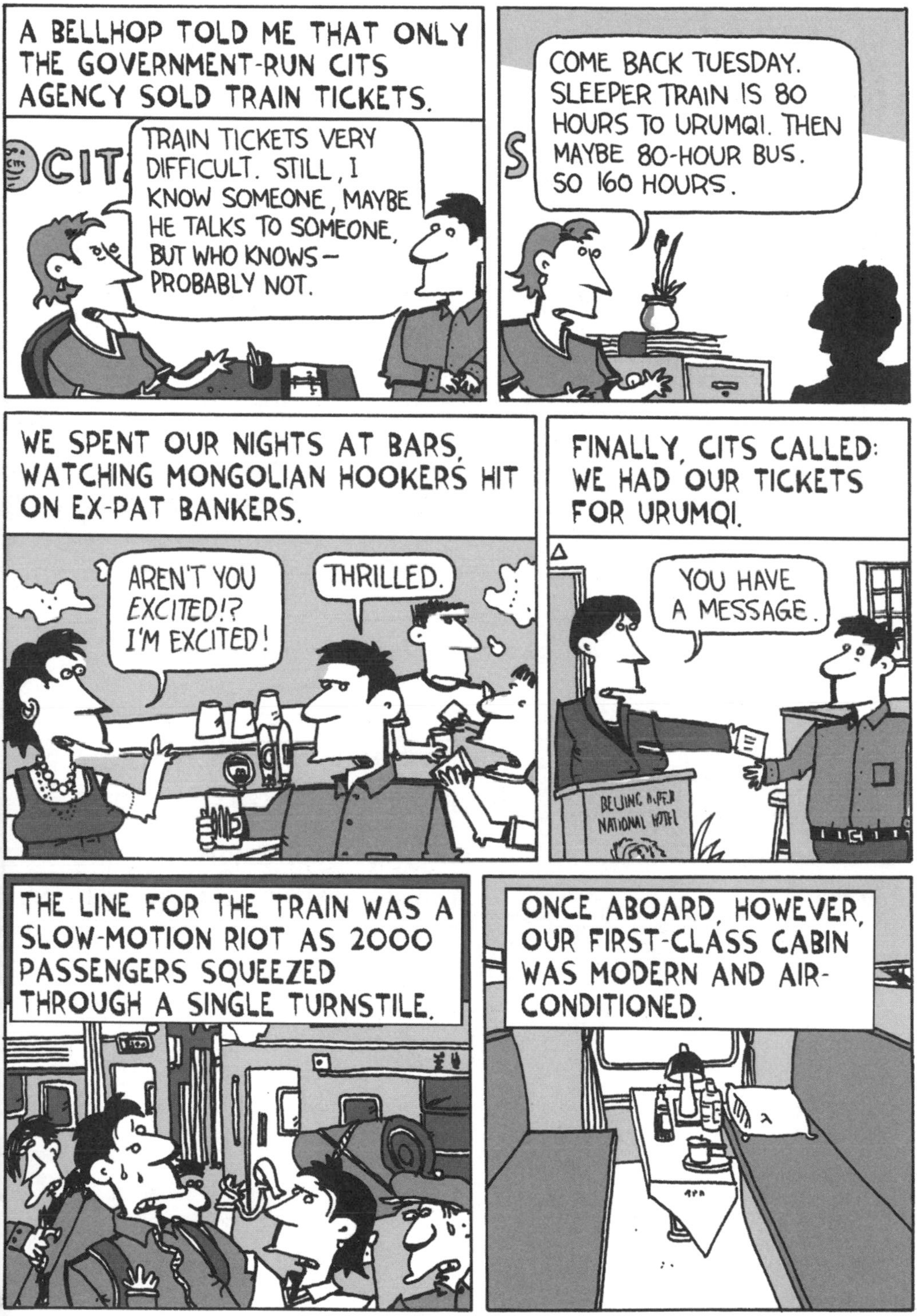
A BELLHOP TOLD ME THAT ONLY THE GOVERNMENT-RUN CITS AGENCY SOLD TRAIN TICKETS.
CITS
TRAIN TICKETS VERY DIFFICULT. STILL, I KNOW SOMEONE, MAYBE HE TALKS TO SOMEONE, BUT WHO KNOWS— PROBABLY NOT.
COME BACK TUESDAY. SLEEPER TRAIN IS 80 HOURS TO URUMQI. THEN MAYBE 80-HOUR BUS. SO 160 HOURS.
WE SPENT OUR NIGHTS AT BARS, WATCHING MONGOLIAN HOOKERS HIT ON EX-PAT BANKERS.
AREN'T YOU *EXCITED!?* I'M EXCITED!
THRILLED.
FINALLY, CITS CALLED: WE HAD OUR TICKETS FOR URUMQI.
YOU HAVE A MESSAGE.
THE LINE FOR THE TRAIN WAS A SLOW-MOTION RIOT AS 2000 PASSENGERS SQUEEZED THROUGH A SINGLE TURNSTILE.
ONCE ABOARD, HOWEVER, OUR FIRST-CLASS CABIN WAS MODERN AND AIR-CONDITIONED.

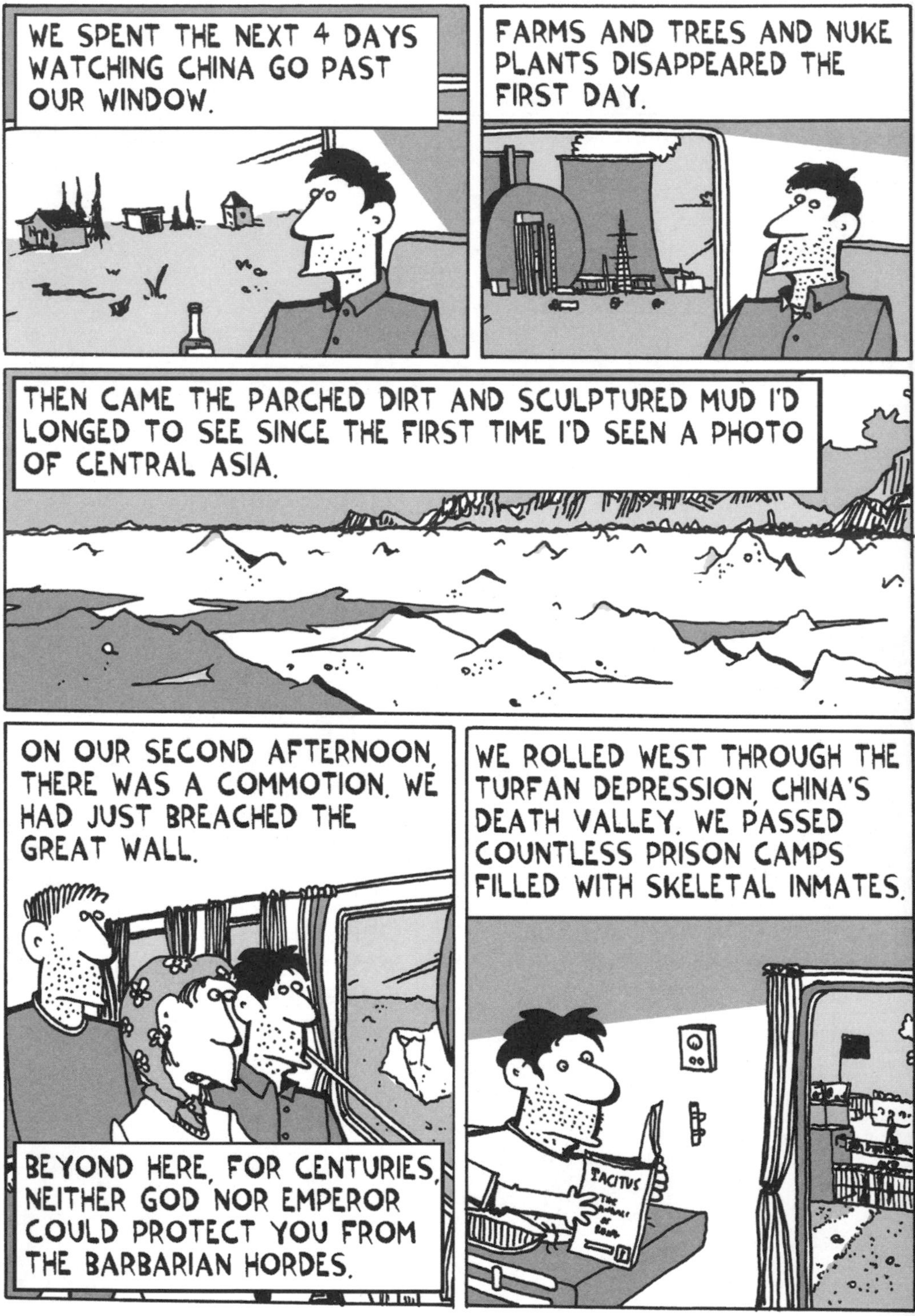
WE SPENT THE NEXT 4 DAYS WATCHING CHINA GO PAST OUR WINDOW.
FARMS AND TREES AND NUKE PLANTS DISAPPEARED THE FIRST DAY.
THEN CAME THE PARCHED DIRT AND SCULPTURED MUD I'D LONGED TO SEE SINCE THE FIRST TIME I'D SEEN A PHOTO OF CENTRAL ASIA.
ON OUR SECOND AFTERNOON, THERE WAS A COMMOTION. WE HAD JUST BREACHED THE GREAT WALL.
BEYOND HERE, FOR CENTURIES, NEITHER GOD NOR EMPEROR COULD PROTECT YOU FROM THE BARBARIAN HORDES.
WE ROLLED WEST THROUGH THE TURFAN DEPRESSION, CHINA'S DEATH VALLEY. WE PASSED COUNTLESS PRISON CAMPS FILLED WITH SKELETAL INMATES.
TACITUS

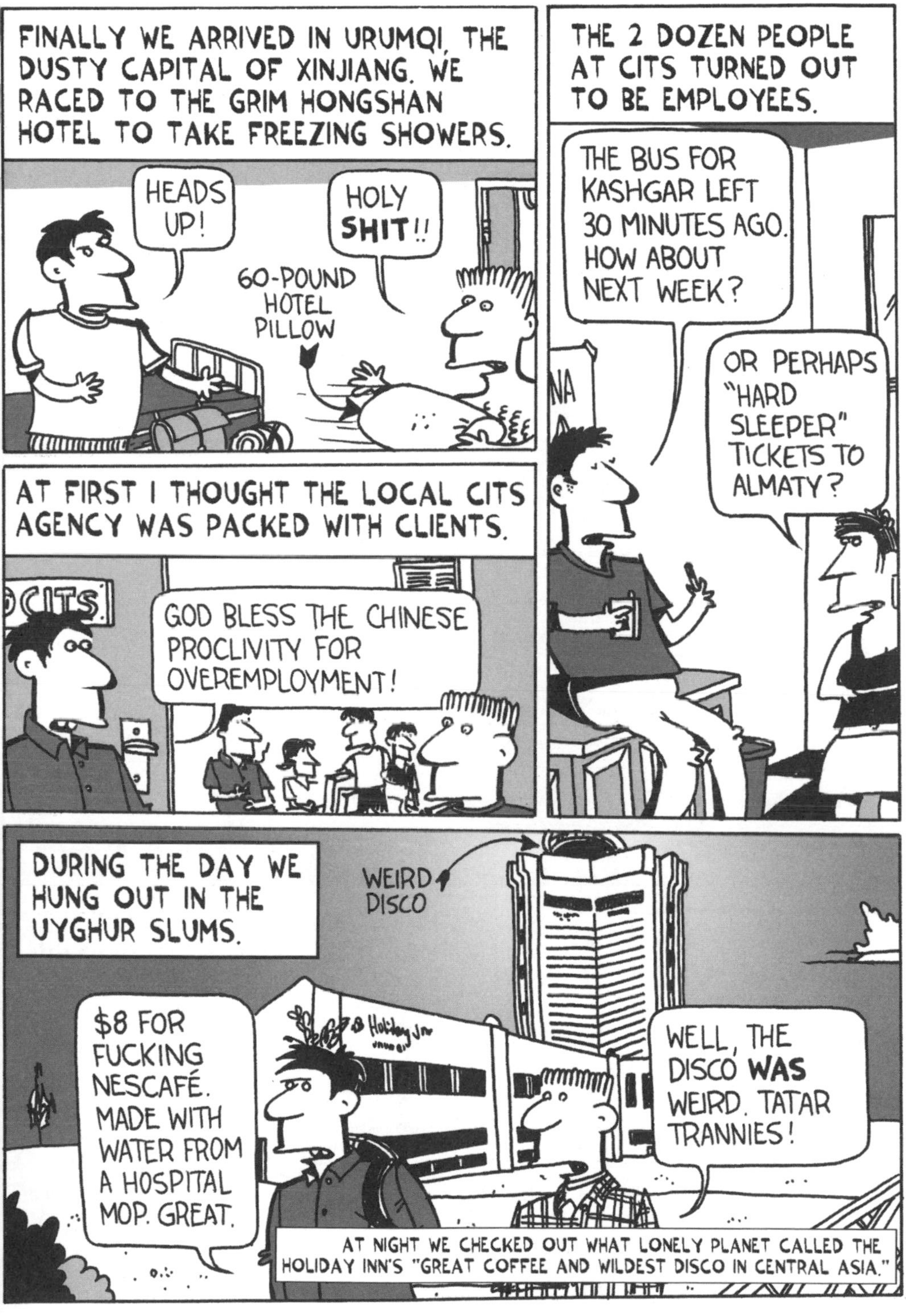
FINALLY WE ARRIVED IN URUMQI, THE DUSTY CAPITAL OF XINJIANG. WE RACED TO THE GRIM HONGSHAN HOTEL TO TAKE FREEZING SHOWERS.
HEADS UP!
HOLY SHIT!!
60-POUND HOTEL PILLOW
THE 2 DOZEN PEOPLE AT CITS TURNED OUT TO BE EMPLOYEES.
THE BUS FOR KASHGAR LEFT 30 MINUTES AGO. HOW ABOUT NEXT WEEK?
OR PERHAPS "HARD SLEEPER" TICKETS TO ALMATY?
AT FIRST I THOUGHT THE LOCAL CITS AGENCY WAS PACKED WITH CLIENTS.
CITS
GOD BLESS THE CHINESE PROCLIVITY FOR OVEREMPLOYMENT!
DURING THE DAY WE HUNG OUT IN THE UYGHUR SLUMS.
WEIRD DISCO
$8 FOR FUCKING NESCAFÉ. MADE WITH WATER FROM A HOSPITAL MOP. GREAT.
WELL, THE DISCO WAS WEIRD. TATAR TRANNIES!
AT NIGHT WE CHECKED OUT WHAT LONELY PLANET CALLED THE HOLIDAY INN'S "GREAT COFFEE AND WILDEST DISCO IN CENTRAL ASIA."

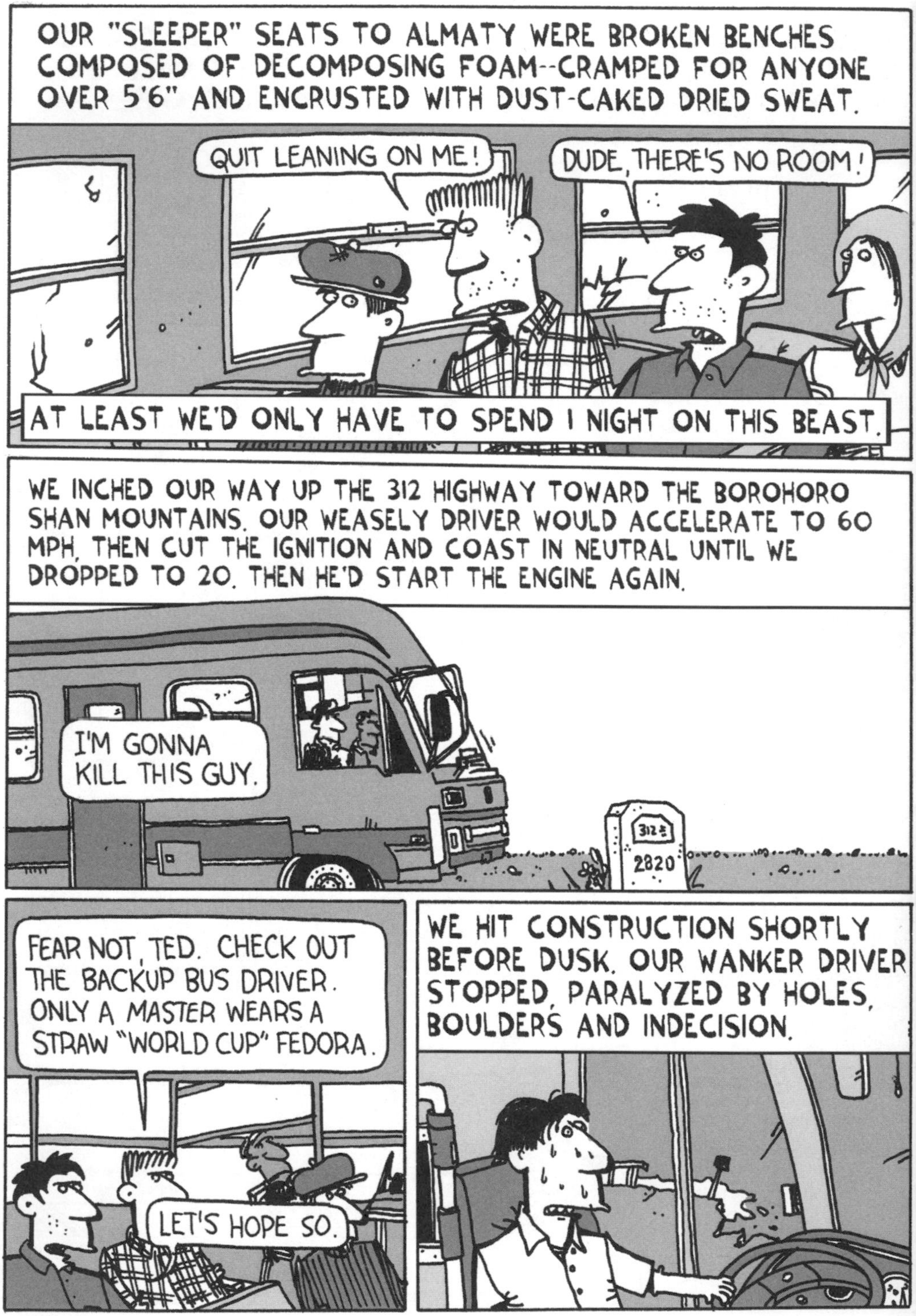
OUR "SLEEPER" SEATS TO ALMATY WERE BROKEN BENCHES COMPOSED OF DECOMPOSING FOAM--CRAMPED FOR ANYONE OVER 5'6" AND ENCRUSTED WITH DUST-CAKED DRIED SWEAT.
QUIT LEANING ON ME!
DUDE, THERE'S NO ROOM!
AT LEAST WE'D ONLY HAVE TO SPEND 1 NIGHT ON THIS BEAST.
WE INCHED OUR WAY UP THE 312 HIGHWAY TOWARD THE BOROHORO SHAN MOUNTAINS. OUR WEASELY DRIVER WOULD ACCELERATE TO 60 MPH, THEN CUT THE IGNITION AND COAST IN NEUTRAL UNTIL WE DROPPED TO 20. THEN HE'D START THE ENGINE AGAIN.
I'M GONNA KILL THIS GUY.
2820
FEAR NOT, TED. CHECK OUT THE BACKUP BUS DRIVER. ONLY A MASTER WEARS A STRAW "WORLD CUP" FEDORA.
LET'S HOPE SO.
WE HIT CONSTRUCTION SHORTLY BEFORE DUSK. OUR WANKER DRIVER STOPPED, PARALYZED BY HOLES, BOULDERS AND INDECISION.

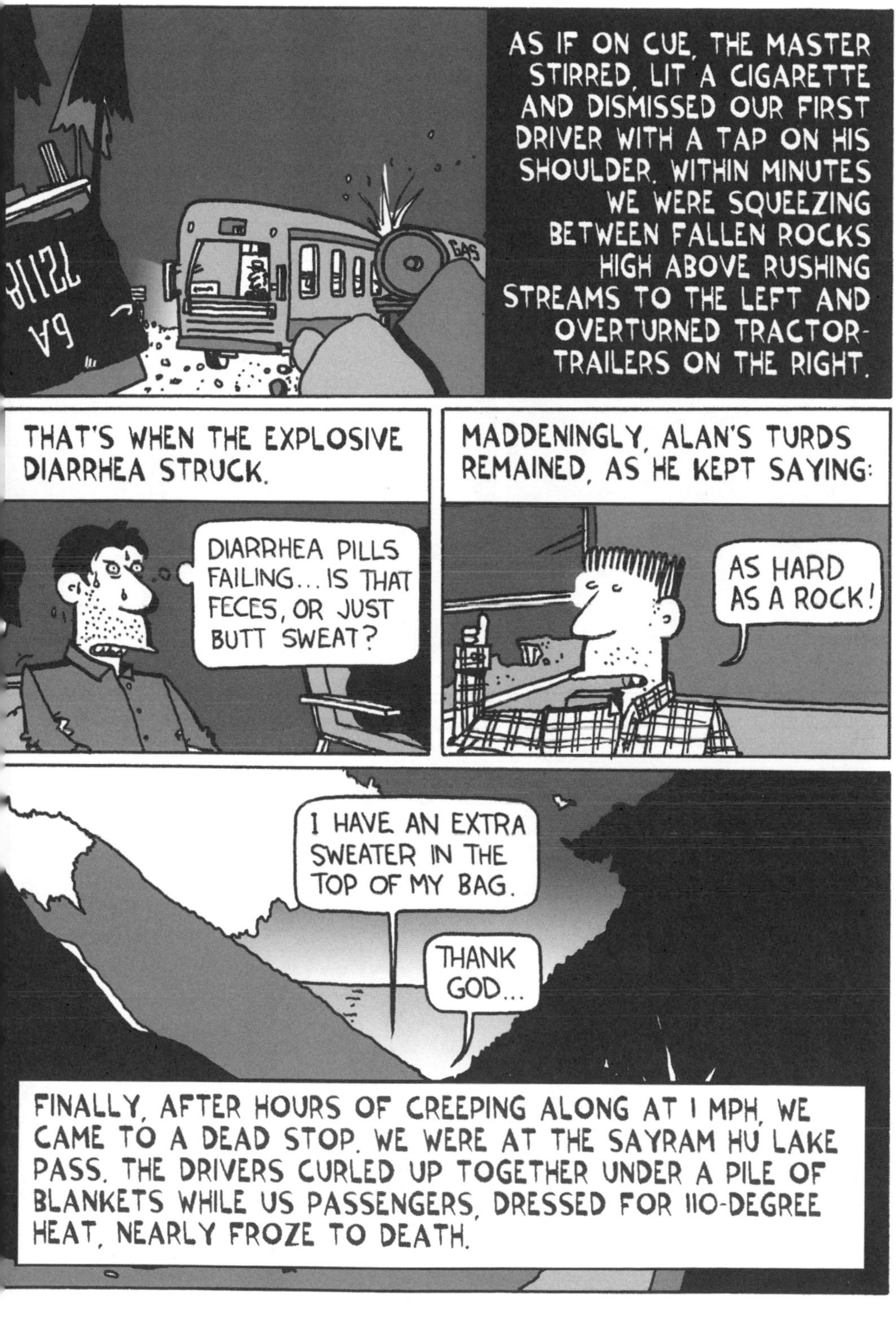
AS IF ON CUE, THE MASTER STIRRED, LIT A CIGARETTE AND DISMISSED OUR FIRST DRIVER WITH A TAP ON HIS SHOULDER. WITHIN MINUTES WE WERE SQUEEZING BETWEEN FALLEN ROCKS HIGH ABOVE RUSHING STREAMS TO THE LEFT AND OVERTURNED TRACTOR-TRAILERS ON THE RIGHT.
GAS
THAT'S WHEN THE EXPLOSIVE DIARRHEA STRUCK.
DIARRHEA PILLS FAILING... IS THAT FECES, OR JUST BUTT SWEAT?
MADDENINGLY, ALAN'S TURDS REMAINED, AS HE KEPT SAYING:
AS HARD AS A ROCK!
I HAVE AN EXTRA SWEATER IN THE TOP OF MY BAG.
THANK GOD...
FINALLY, AFTER HOURS OF CREEPING ALONG AT 1 MPH, WE CAME TO A DEAD STOP. WE WERE AT THE SAYRAM HU LAKE PASS. THE DRIVERS CURLED UP TOGETHER UNDER A PILE OF BLANKETS WHILE US PASSENGERS, DRESSED FOR 110-DEGREE HEAT, NEARLY FROZE TO DEATH.

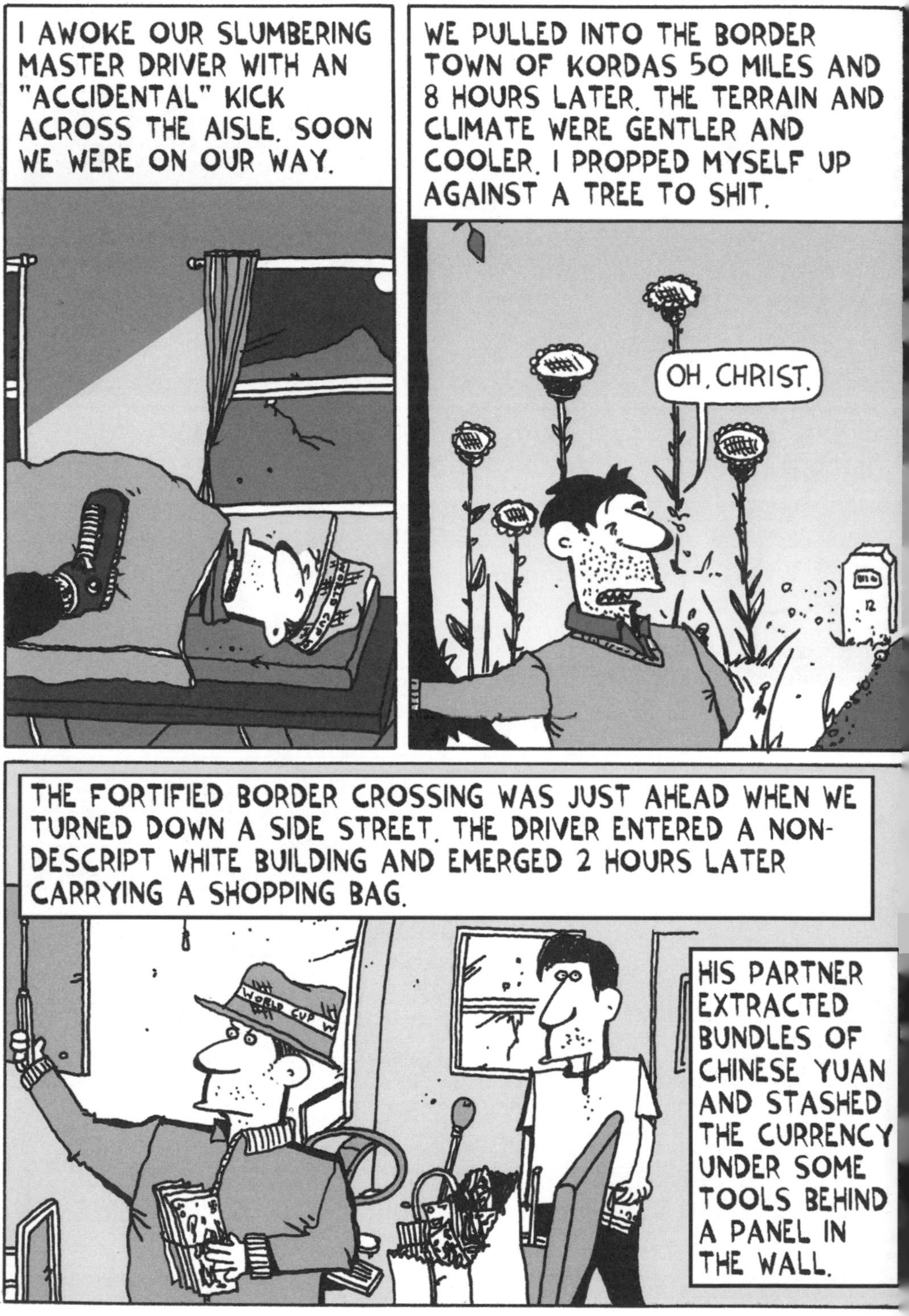
I AWOKE OUR SLUMBERING MASTER DRIVER WITH AN "ACCIDENTAL" KICK ACROSS THE AISLE. SOON WE WERE ON OUR WAY.
WE PULLED INTO THE BORDER TOWN OF KORDAS 50 MILES AND 8 HOURS LATER. THE TERRAIN AND CLIMATE WERE GENTLER AND COOLER. I PROPPED MYSELF UP AGAINST A TREE TO SHIT.
OH, CHRIST.
THE FORTIFIED BORDER CROSSING WAS JUST AHEAD WHEN WE TURNED DOWN A SIDE STREET. THE DRIVER ENTERED A NON-DESCRIPT WHITE BUILDING AND EMERGED 2 HOURS LATER CARRYING A SHOPPING BAG.
WORLD CUP
HIS PARTNER EXTRACTED BUNDLES OF CHINESE YUAN AND STASHED THE CURRENCY UNDER SOME TOOLS BEHIND A PANEL IN THE WALL.

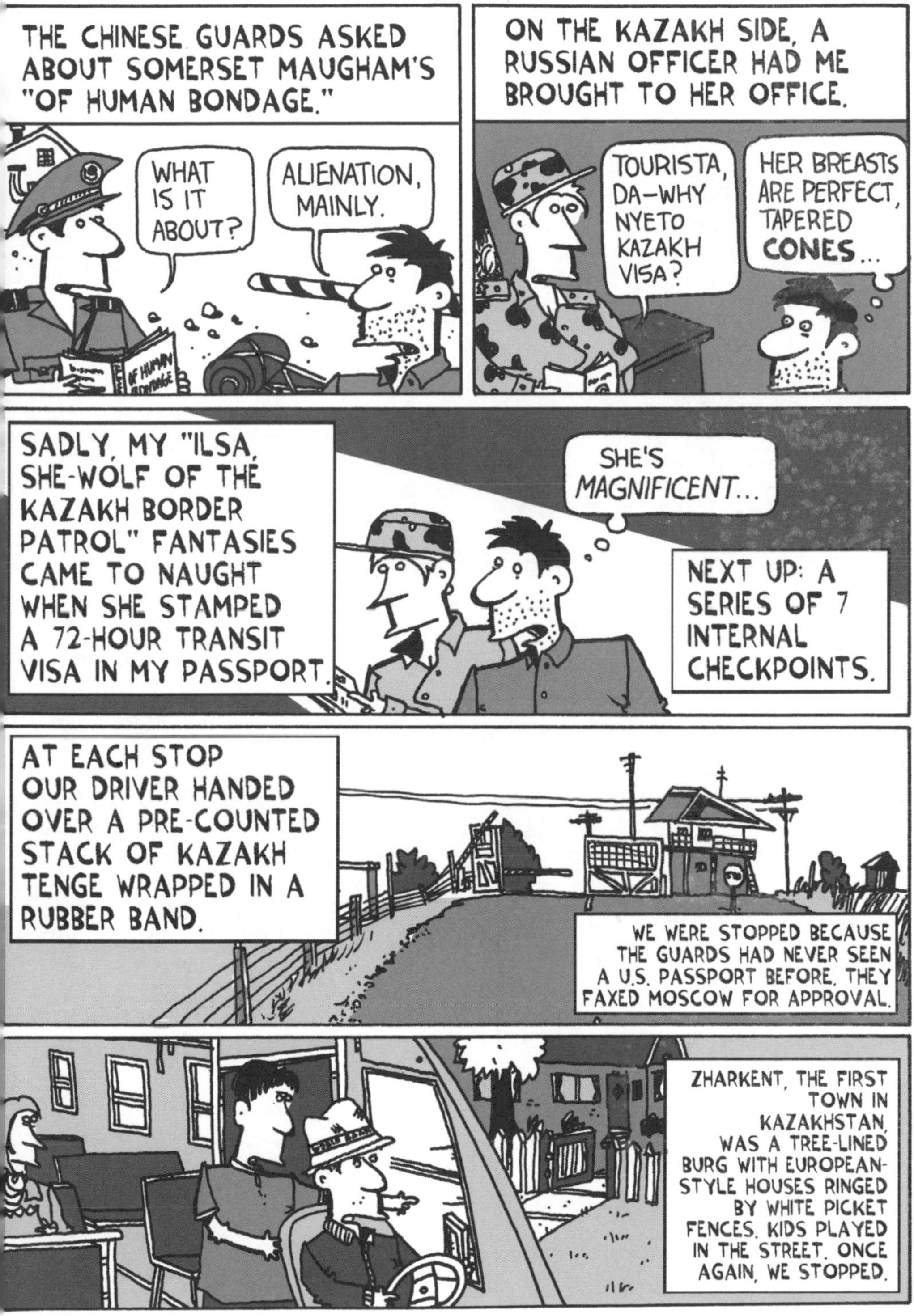
THE CHINESE GUARDS ASKED ABOUT SOMERSET MAUGHAM'S "OF HUMAN BONDAGE."
WHAT IS IT ABOUT?
ALIENATION, MAINLY.
OF HUMAN BONDAGE
ON THE KAZAKH SIDE, A RUSSIAN OFFICER HAD ME BROUGHT TO HER OFFICE.
TOURISTA, DA—WHY NYETO KAZAKH VISA?
HER BREASTS ARE PERFECT, TAPERED CONES...
SADLY, MY "ILSA, SHE-WOLF OF THE KAZAKH BORDER PATROL" FANTASIES CAME TO NAUGHT WHEN SHE STAMPED A 72-HOUR TRANSIT VISA IN MY PASSPORT.
SHE'S MAGNIFICENT...
NEXT UP: A SERIES OF 7 INTERNAL CHECKPOINTS.
AT EACH STOP OUR DRIVER HANDED OVER A PRE-COUNTED STACK OF KAZAKH TENGE WRAPPED IN A RUBBER BAND.
WE WERE STOPPED BECAUSE THE GUARDS HAD NEVER SEEN A U.S. PASSPORT BEFORE. THEY FAXED MOSCOW FOR APPROVAL.
ZHARKENT, THE FIRST TOWN IN KAZAKHSTAN, WAS A TREE-LINED BURG WITH EUROPEAN-STYLE HOUSES RINGED BY WHITE PICKET FENCES. KIDS PLAYED IN THE STREET. ONCE AGAIN, WE STOPPED.

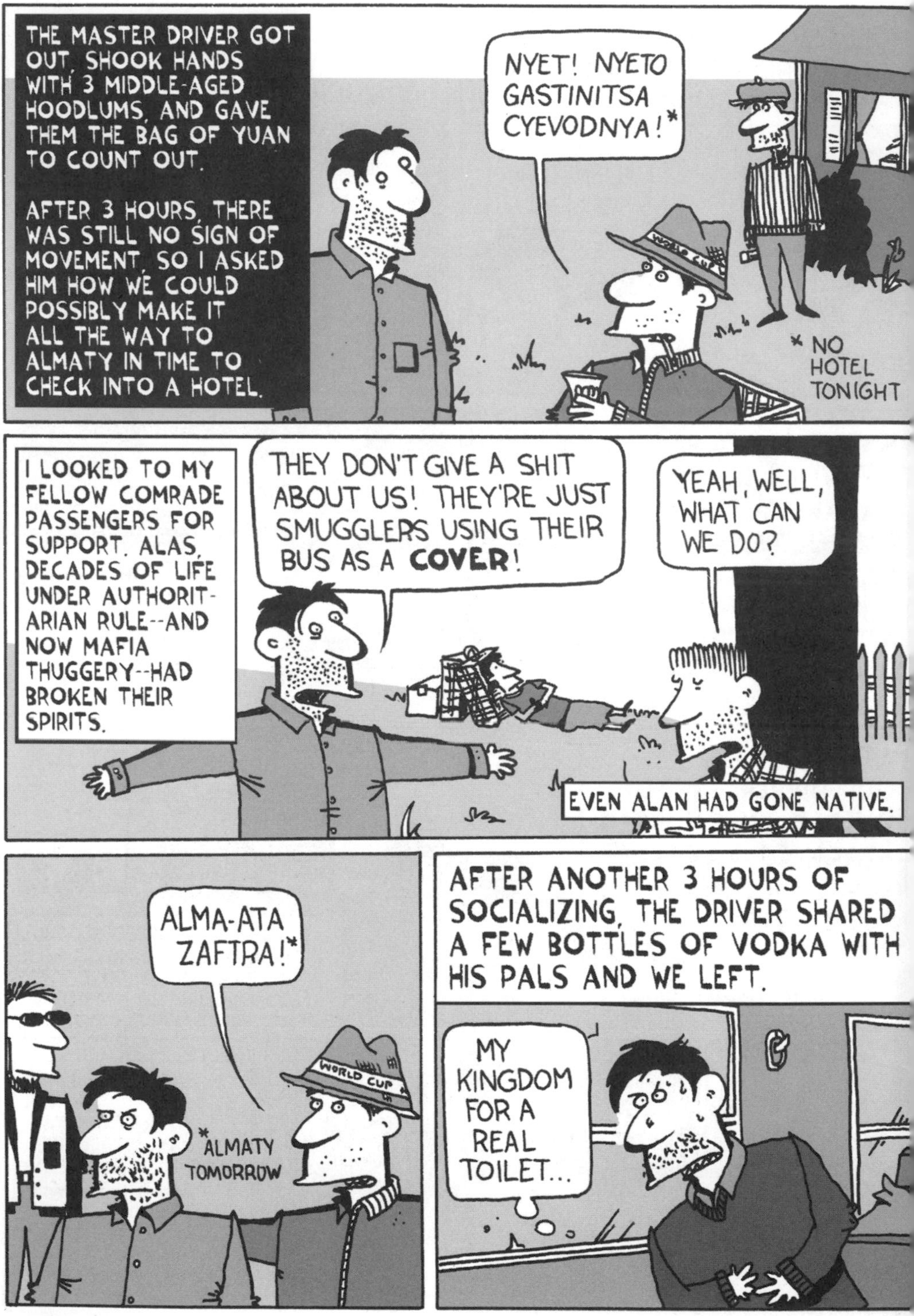
THE MASTER DRIVER GOT OUT, SHOOK HANDS WITH 3 MIDDLE-AGED HOODLUMS, AND GAVE THEM THE BAG OF YUAN TO COUNT OUT.
AFTER 3 HOURS, THERE WAS STILL NO SIGN OF MOVEMENT, SO I ASKED HIM HOW WE COULD POSSIBLY MAKE IT ALL THE WAY TO ALMATY IN TIME TO CHECK INTO A HOTEL.
NYET! NYETO GASTINITSA CYEVODNYA!*
* NO HOTEL TONIGHT
WORLD CUP
I LOOKED TO MY FELLOW COMRADE PASSENGERS FOR SUPPORT. ALAS, DECADES OF LIFE UNDER AUTHORITARIAN RULE--AND NOW MAFIA THUGGERY--HAD BROKEN THEIR SPIRITS.
THEY DON'T GIVE A SHIT ABOUT US! THEY'RE JUST SMUGGLERS USING THEIR BUS AS A **COVER**!
YEAH, WELL, WHAT CAN WE DO?
EVEN ALAN HAD GONE NATIVE.
ALMA-ATA ZAFTRA!*
*ALMATY TOMORROW
WORLD CUP
AFTER ANOTHER 3 HOURS OF SOCIALIZING, THE DRIVER SHARED A FEW BOTTLES OF VODKA WITH HIS PALS AND WE LEFT.
MY KINGDOM FOR A REAL TOILET...

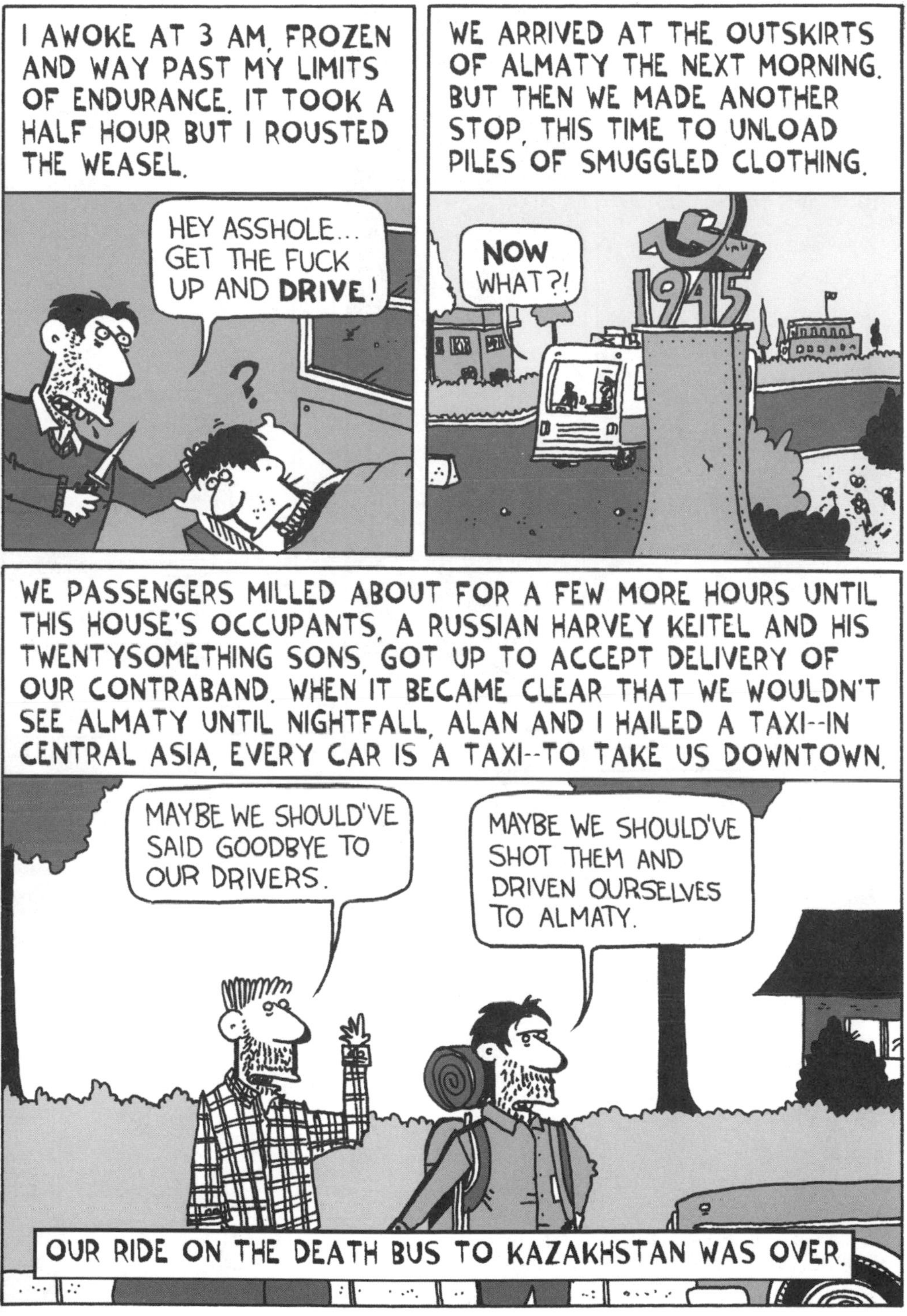
I AWOKE AT 3 AM, FROZEN AND WAY PAST MY LIMITS OF ENDURANCE. IT TOOK A HALF HOUR BUT I ROUSTED THE WEASEL.
HEY ASSHOLE... GET THE FUCK UP AND **DRIVE**!
?
WE ARRIVED AT THE OUTSKIRTS OF ALMATY THE NEXT MORNING. BUT THEN WE MADE ANOTHER STOP, THIS TIME TO UNLOAD PILES OF SMUGGLED CLOTHING.
NOW WHAT?!
1945
WE PASSENGERS MILLED ABOUT FOR A FEW MORE HOURS UNTIL THIS HOUSE'S OCCUPANTS, A RUSSIAN HARVEY KEITEL AND HIS TWENTYSOMETHING SONS, GOT UP TO ACCEPT DELIVERY OF OUR CONTRABAND. WHEN IT BECAME CLEAR THAT WE WOULDN'T SEE ALMATY UNTIL NIGHTFALL, ALAN AND I HAILED A TAXI--IN CENTRAL ASIA, EVERY CAR IS A TAXI--TO TAKE US DOWNTOWN.
MAYBE WE SHOULD'VE SAID GOODBYE TO OUR DRIVERS.
MAYBE WE SHOULD'VE SHOT THEM AND DRIVEN OURSELVES TO ALMATY.
OUR RIDE ON THE DEATH BUS TO KAZAKHSTAN WAS OVER.

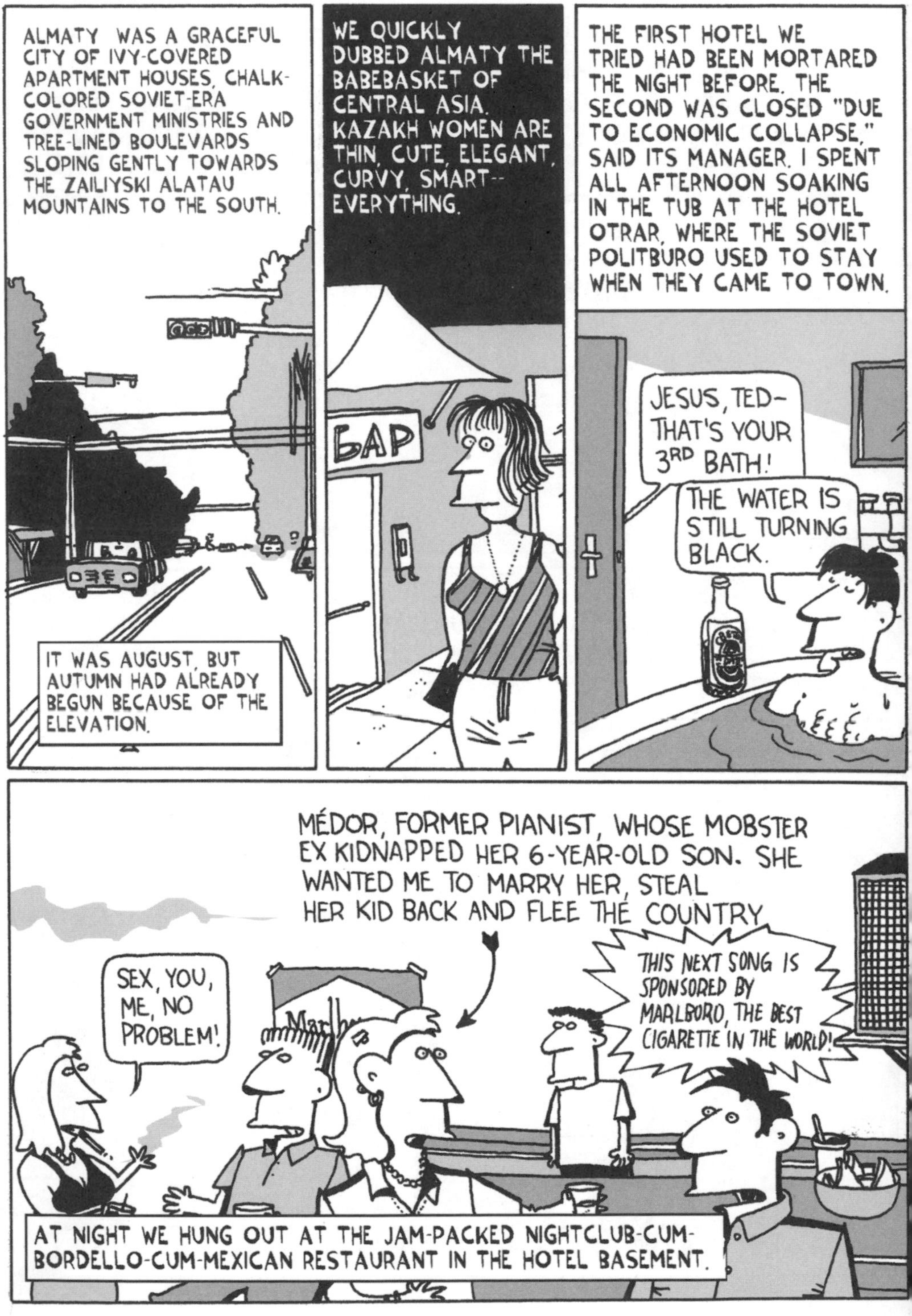
ALMATY WAS A GRACEFUL CITY OF IVY-COVERED APARTMENT HOUSES, CHALK-COLORED SOVIET-ERA GOVERNMENT MINISTRIES AND TREE-LINED BOULEVARDS SLOPING GENTLY TOWARDS THE ZAILIYSKI ALATAU MOUNTAINS TO THE SOUTH.
IT WAS AUGUST, BUT AUTUMN HAD ALREADY BEGUN BECAUSE OF THE ELEVATION.
WE QUICKLY DUBBED ALMATY THE BABEBASKET OF CENTRAL ASIA. KAZAKH WOMEN ARE THIN, CUTE, ELEGANT, CURVY, SMART--EVERYTHING.
БАР
THE FIRST HOTEL WE TRIED HAD BEEN MORTARED THE NIGHT BEFORE. THE SECOND WAS CLOSED "DUE TO ECONOMIC COLLAPSE," SAID ITS MANAGER. I SPENT ALL AFTERNOON SOAKING IN THE TUB AT THE HOTEL OTRAR, WHERE THE SOVIET POLITBURO USED TO STAY WHEN THEY CAME TO TOWN.
JESUS, TED-THAT'S YOUR 3RD BATH!
THE WATER IS STILL TURNING BLACK.
MÉDOR, FORMER PIANIST, WHOSE MOBSTER EX KIDNAPPED HER 6-YEAR-OLD SON. SHE WANTED ME TO MARRY HER, STEAL HER KID BACK AND FLEE THE COUNTRY
SEX, YOU, ME, NO PROBLEM!
THIS NEXT SONG IS SPONSORED BY MARLBORO, THE BEST CIGARETTE IN THE WORLD!
AT NIGHT WE HUNG OUT AT THE JAM-PACKED NIGHTCLUB-CUM-BORDELLO-CUM-MEXICAN RESTAURANT IN THE HOTEL BASEMENT.

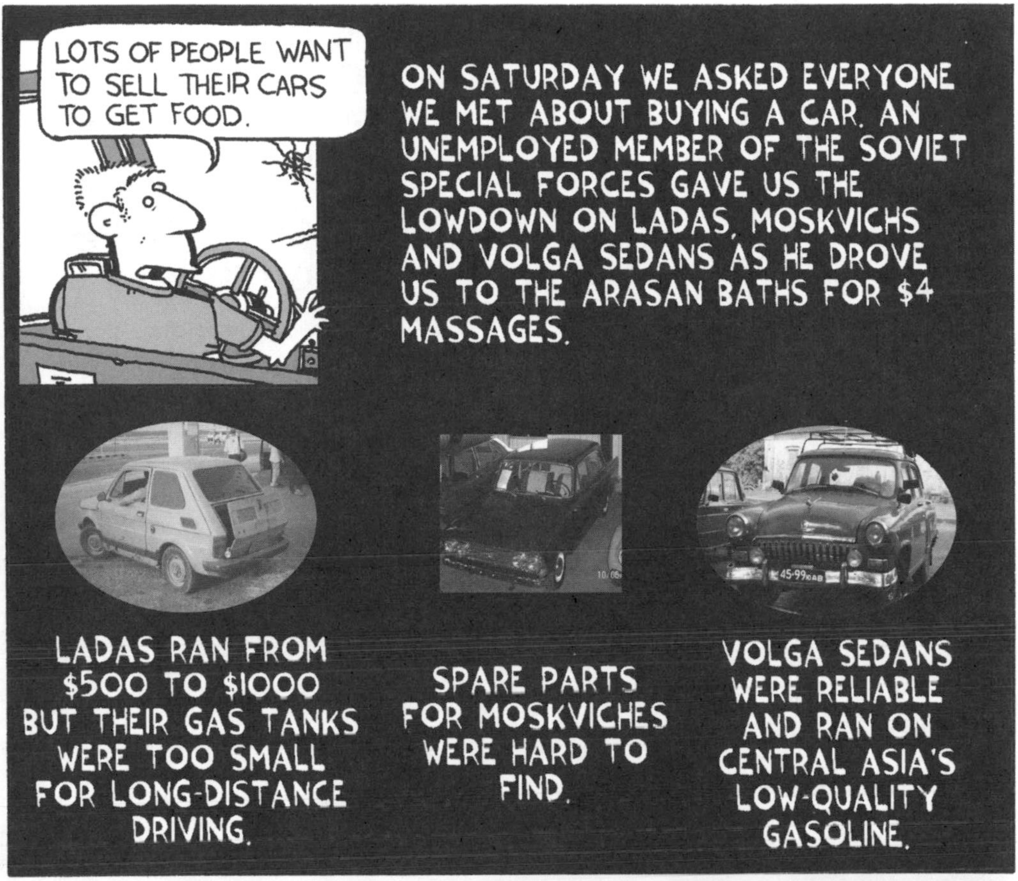
LOTS OF PEOPLE WANT TO SELL THEIR CARS TO GET FOOD.
ON SATURDAY WE ASKED EVERYONE WE MET ABOUT BUYING A CAR. AN UNEMPLOYED MEMBER OF THE SOVIET SPECIAL FORCES GAVE US THE LOWDOWN ON LADAS, MOSKVICHS AND VOLGA SEDANS AS HE DROVE US TO THE ARASAN BATHS FOR $4 MASSAGES.
LADAS RAN FROM $500 TO $1000 BUT THEIR GAS TANKS WERE TOO SMALL FOR LONG-DISTANCE DRIVING.
SPARE PARTS FOR MOSKVICHES WERE HARD TO FIND.
VOLGA SEDANS WERE RELIABLE AND RAN ON CENTRAL ASIA'S LOW-QUALITY GASOLINE.

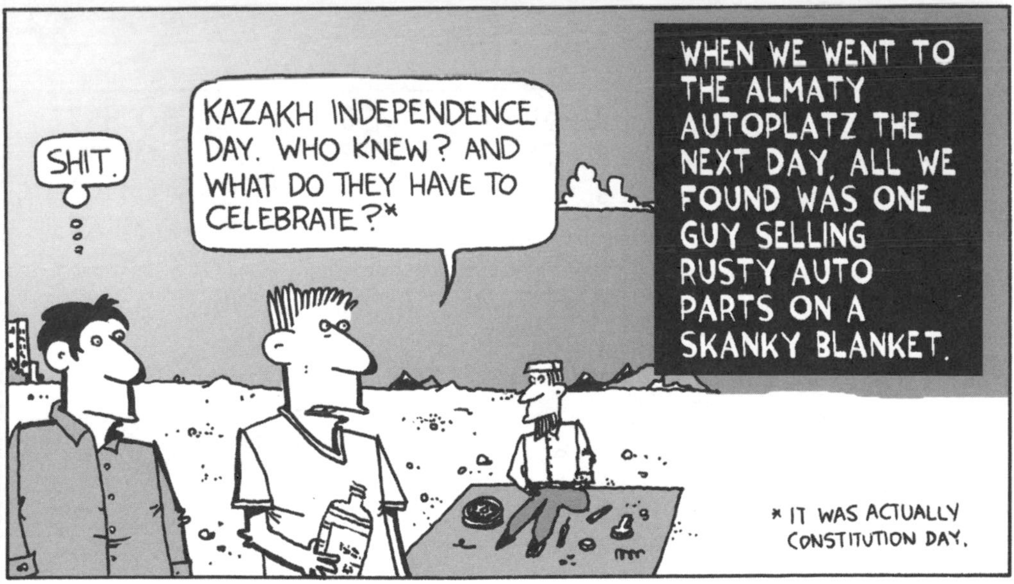
WHEN WE WENT TO THE ALMATY AUTOPLATZ THE NEXT DAY, ALL WE FOUND WAS ONE GUY SELLING RUSTY AUTO PARTS ON A SKANKY BLANKET.
SHIT.
KAZAKH INDEPENDENCE DAY. WHO KNEW? AND WHAT DO THEY HAVE TO CELEBRATE?*
* IT WAS ACTUALLY CONSTITUTION DAY.

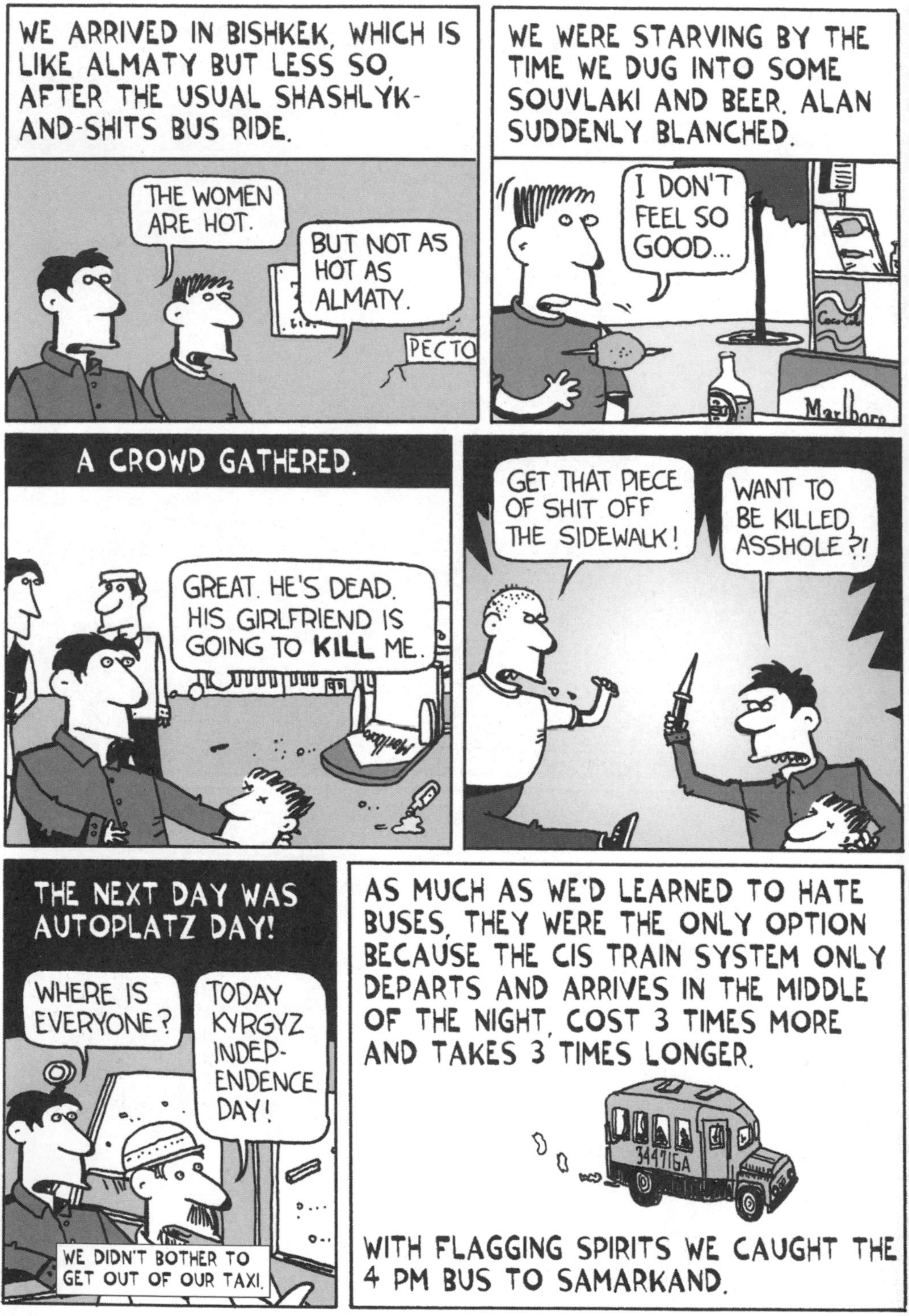
WE ARRIVED IN BISHKEK, WHICH IS LIKE ALMATY BUT LESS SO, AFTER THE USUAL SHASHLYK-AND-SHITS BUS RIDE.
THE WOMEN ARE HOT.
BUT NOT AS HOT AS ALMATY.
PECTO
WE WERE STARVING BY THE TIME WE DUG INTO SOME SOUVLAKI AND BEER. ALAN SUDDENLY BLANCHED.
I DON'T FEEL SO GOOD...
Marlboro
A CROWD GATHERED.
GREAT. HE'S DEAD. HIS GIRLFRIEND IS GOING TO KILL ME.
GET THAT PIECE OF SHIT OFF THE SIDEWALK!
WANT TO BE KILLED, ASSHOLE?!
THE NEXT DAY WAS AUTOPLATZ DAY!
WHERE IS EVERYONE?
TODAY KYRGYZ INDEP-ENDENCE DAY!
WE DIDN'T BOTHER TO GET OUT OF OUR TAXI.
AS MUCH AS WE'D LEARNED TO HATE BUSES, THEY WERE THE ONLY OPTION BECAUSE THE CIS TRAIN SYSTEM ONLY DEPARTS AND ARRIVES IN THE MIDDLE OF THE NIGHT, COST 3 TIMES MORE AND TAKES 3 TIMES LONGER.
WITH FLAGGING SPIRITS WE CAUGHT THE 4 PM BUS TO SAMARKAND.

SAMARKAND

NO ONE SHOULD DIE BEFORE SEEING SAMARKAND, A WORLD-CLASS TOURIST ATTRACTION ON PAR WITH PARIS. BUILT BY THE 15TH CENTURY WARRIOR TIMUR, ITS PERFECT GEOMETRY BALANCES WEIGHT AND GRACE IN JOYFUL ASYMMETRY. WE SPENT 2 DAYS TAKING IN THE SITES AND STUDYING THE MORBIDLY OBESE MAFIOSOS AT THE HOTEL AFROSIAB.

BIBI KHANYM MOSQUE

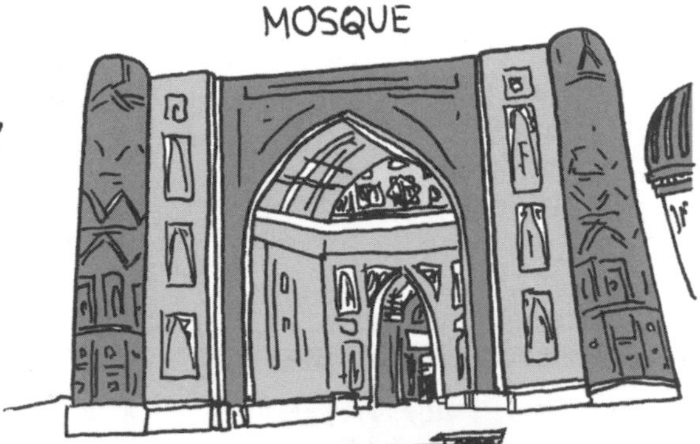

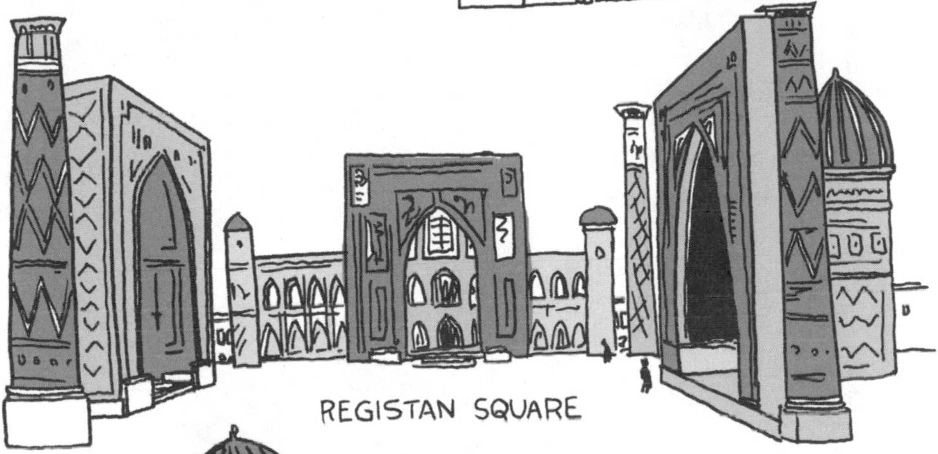

REGISTAN SQUARE

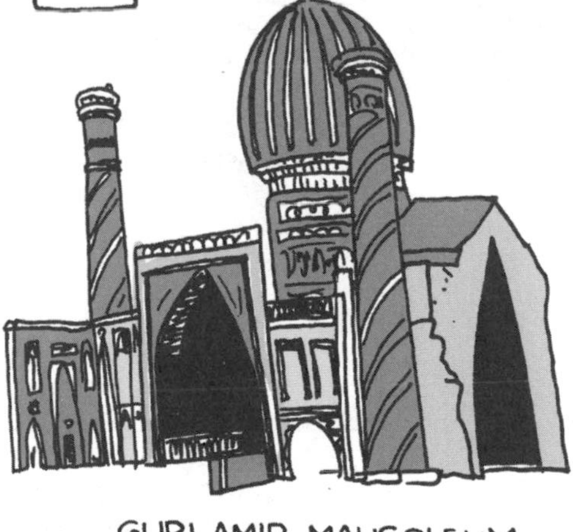

GURI AMIR MAUSOLEUM

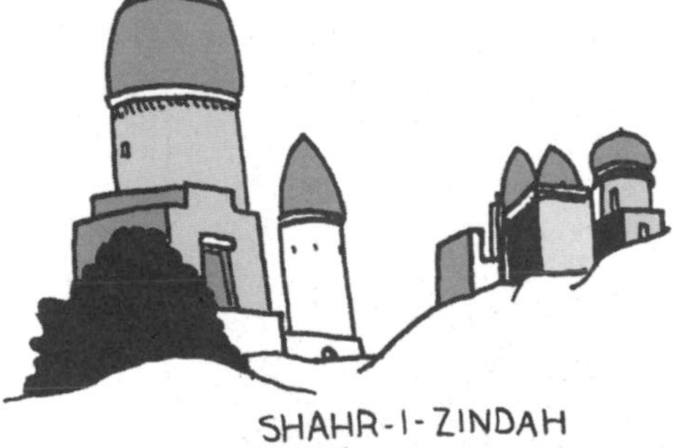

SHAHR-I-ZINDAH
TOMBS INCLUDE QUSAM IBN-ABBAS

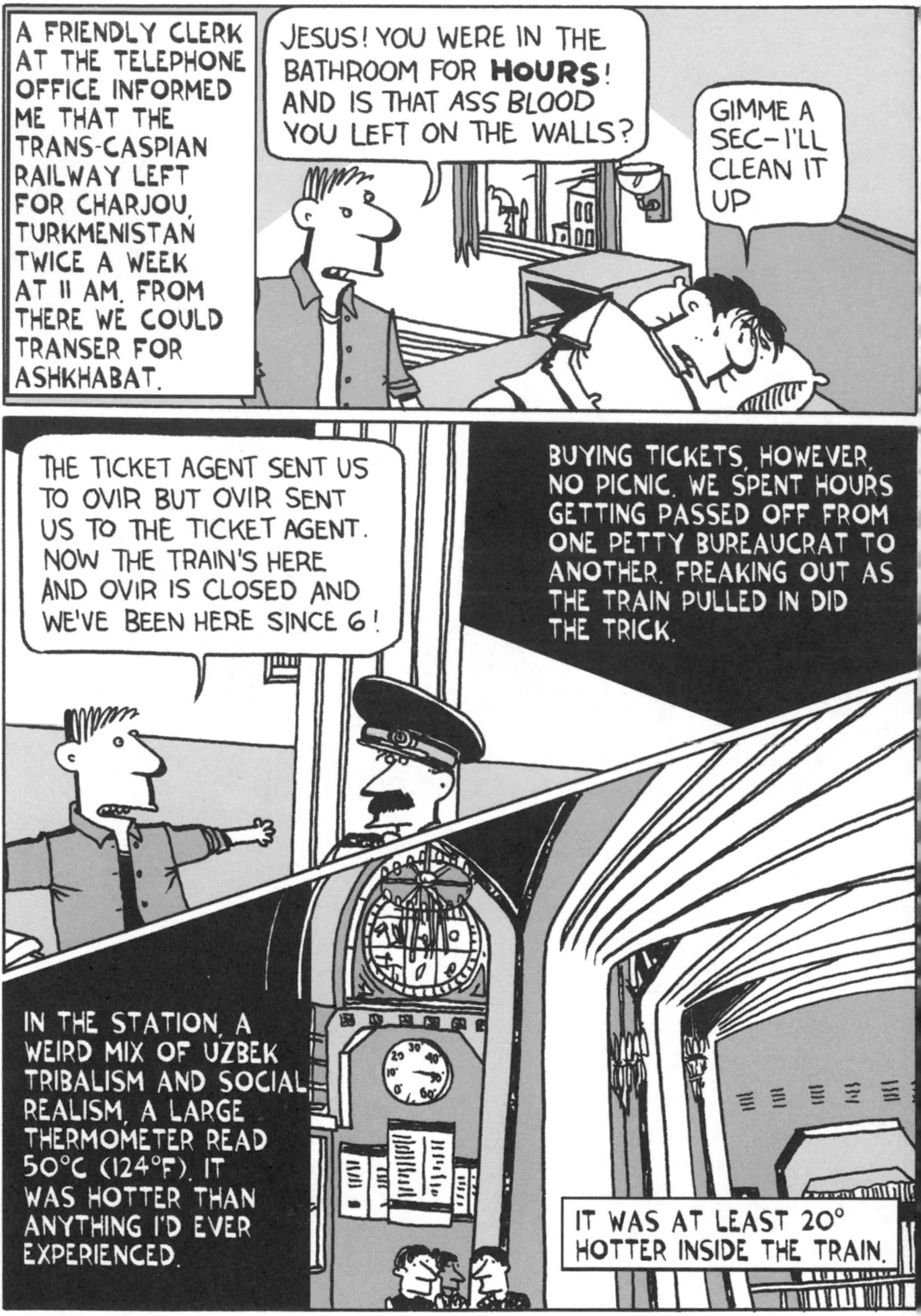
A FRIENDLY CLERK AT THE TELEPHONE OFFICE INFORMED ME THAT THE TRANS-CASPIAN RAILWAY LEFT FOR CHARJOU, TURKMENISTAN TWICE A WEEK AT 11 AM. FROM THERE WE COULD TRANSER FOR ASHKHABAT.
JESUS! YOU WERE IN THE BATHROOM FOR **HOURS**! AND IS THAT ASS BLOOD YOU LEFT ON THE WALLS?
GIMME A SEC—I'LL CLEAN IT UP
THE TICKET AGENT SENT US TO OVIR BUT OVIR SENT US TO THE TICKET AGENT. NOW THE TRAIN'S HERE AND OVIR IS CLOSED AND WE'VE BEEN HERE SINCE 6!
BUYING TICKETS, HOWEVER, NO PICNIC. WE SPENT HOURS GETTING PASSED OFF FROM ONE PETTY BUREAUCRAT TO ANOTHER. FREAKING OUT AS THE TRAIN PULLED IN DID THE TRICK.
IN THE STATION, A WEIRD MIX OF UZBEK TRIBALISM AND SOCIAL REALISM, A LARGE THERMOMETER READ 50°C (124°F). IT WAS HOTTER THAN ANYTHING I'D EVER EXPERIENCED.
IT WAS AT LEAST 20° HOTTER INSIDE THE TRAIN.

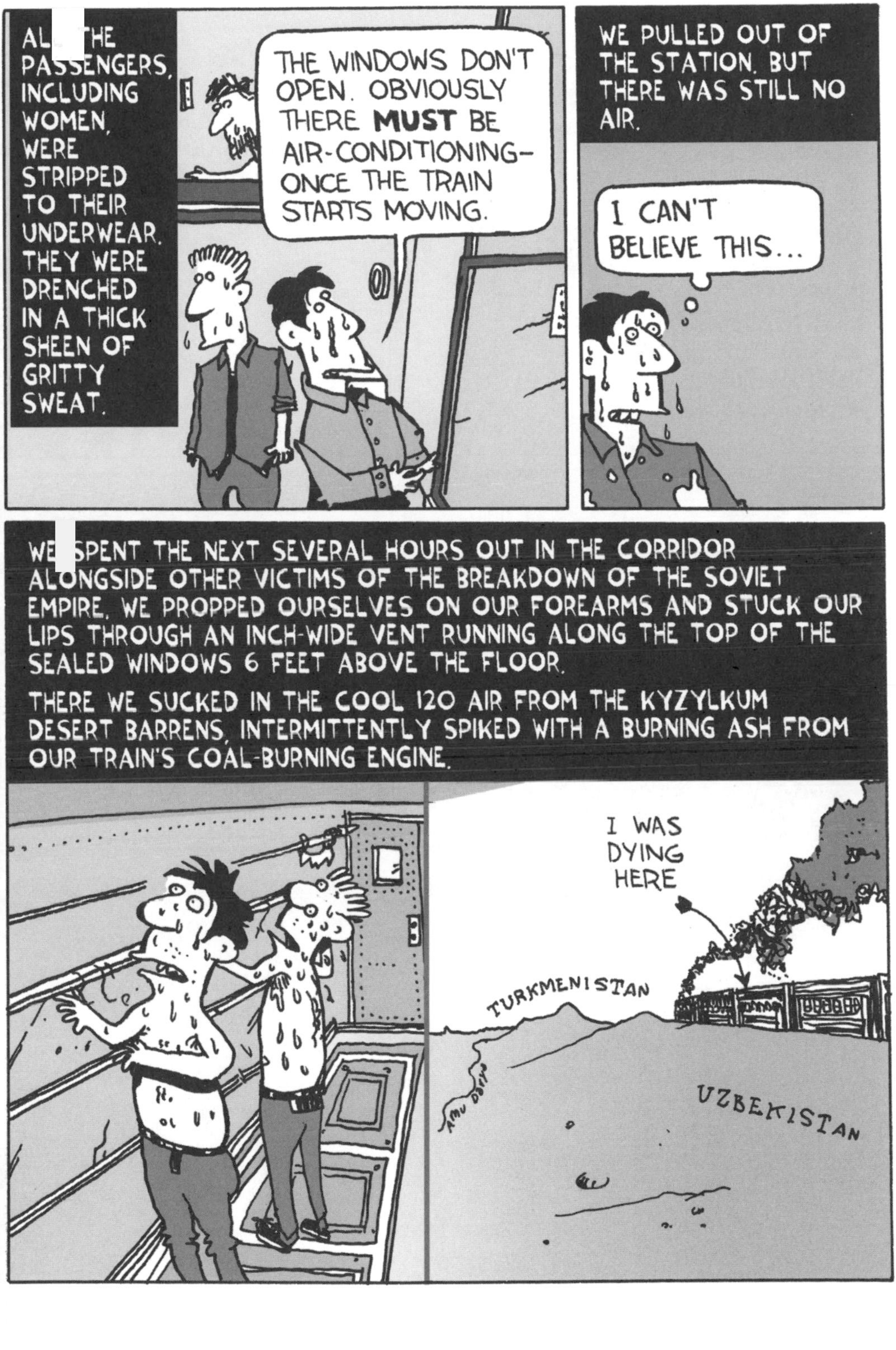
ALL THE PASSENGERS, INCLUDING WOMEN, WERE STRIPPED TO THEIR UNDERWEAR. THEY WERE DRENCHED IN A THICK SHEEN OF GRITTY SWEAT.
THE WINDOWS DON'T OPEN. OBVIOUSLY THERE **MUST** BE AIR-CONDITIONING— ONCE THE TRAIN STARTS MOVING.
WE PULLED OUT OF THE STATION. BUT THERE WAS STILL NO AIR.
I CAN'T BELIEVE THIS...
WE SPENT THE NEXT SEVERAL HOURS OUT IN THE CORRIDOR ALONGSIDE OTHER VICTIMS OF THE BREAKDOWN OF THE SOVIET EMPIRE. WE PROPPED OURSELVES ON OUR FOREARMS AND STUCK OUR LIPS THROUGH AN INCH-WIDE VENT RUNNING ALONG THE TOP OF THE SEALED WINDOWS 6 FEET ABOVE THE FLOOR.
THERE WE SUCKED IN THE COOL 120 AIR FROM THE KYZYLKUM DESERT BARRENS, INTERMITTENTLY SPIKED WITH A BURNING ASH FROM OUR TRAIN'S COAL-BURNING ENGINE.
I WAS DYING HERE
TURKMENISTAN
AMU DARYA
UZBEKISTAN

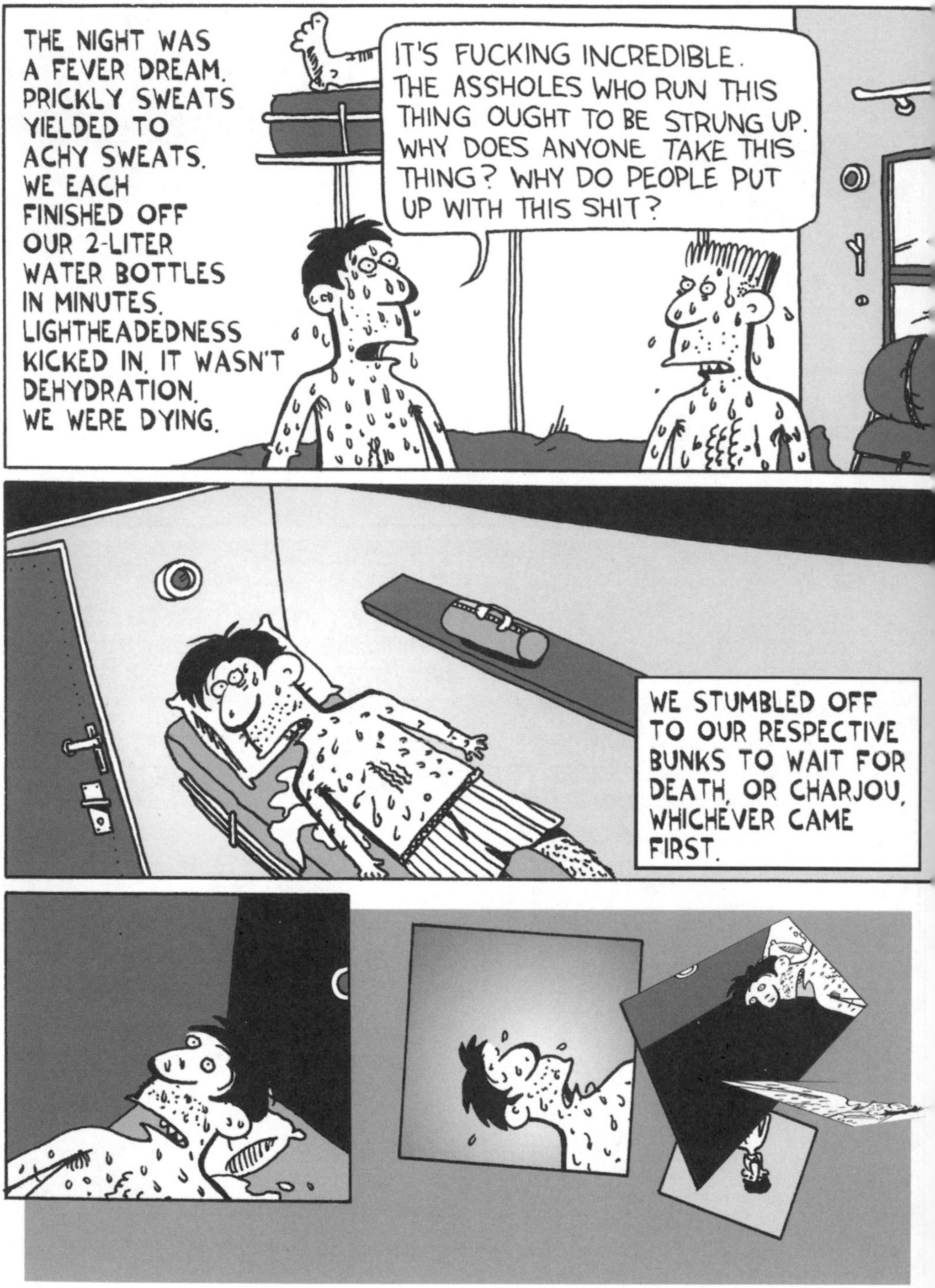
THE NIGHT WAS A FEVER DREAM. PRICKLY SWEATS YIELDED TO ACHY SWEATS. WE EACH FINISHED OFF OUR 2-LITER WATER BOTTLES IN MINUTES. LIGHTHEADEDNESS KICKED IN. IT WASN'T DEHYDRATION. WE WERE DYING.
IT'S FUCKING INCREDIBLE. THE ASSHOLES WHO RUN THIS THING OUGHT TO BE STRUNG UP. WHY DOES ANYONE TAKE THIS THING? WHY DO PEOPLE PUT UP WITH THIS SHIT?
WE STUMBLED OFF TO OUR RESPECTIVE BUNKS TO WAIT FOR DEATH, OR CHARJOU, WHICHEVER CAME FIRST.

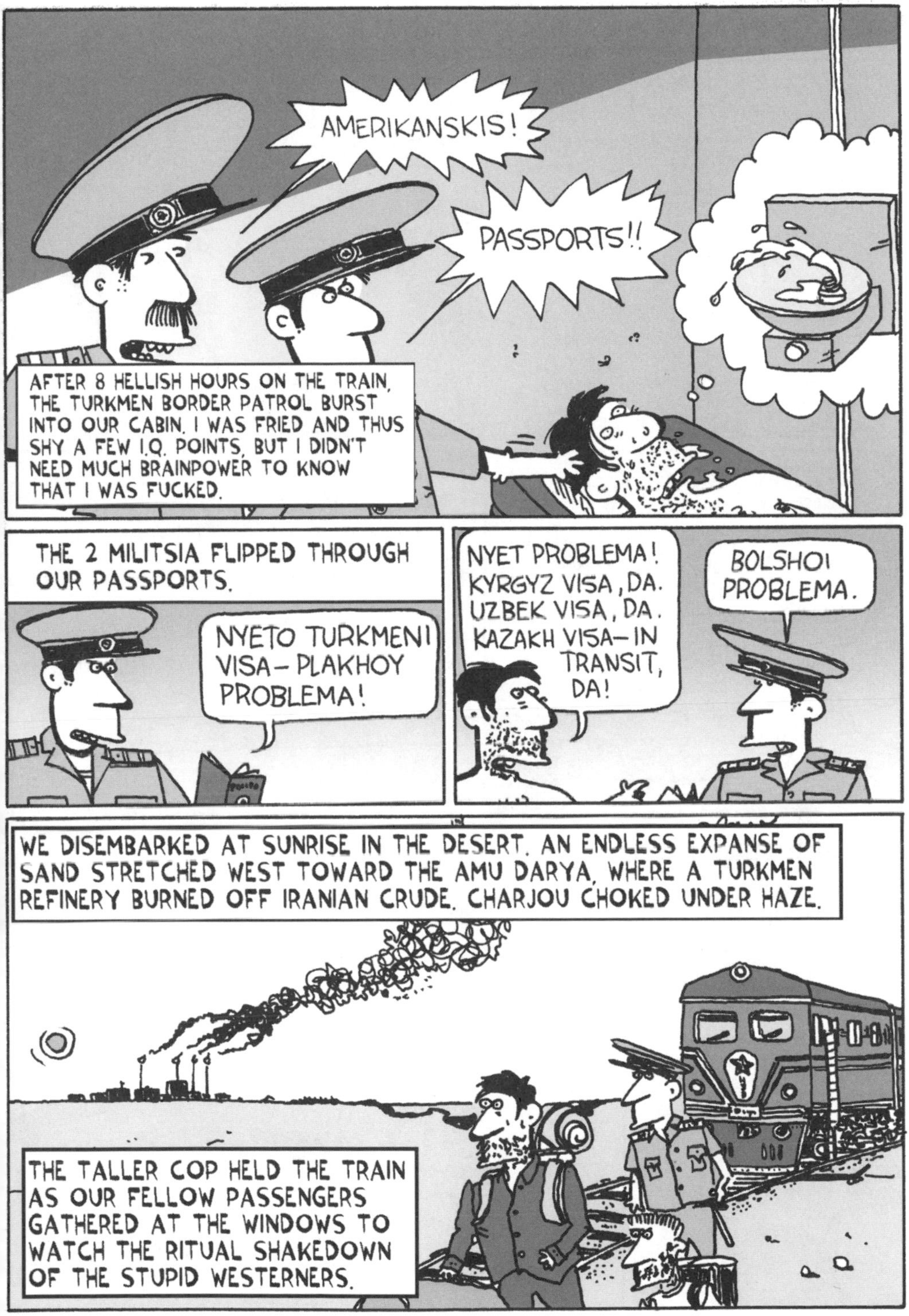
AMERIKANSKIS!
PASSPORTS!!
AFTER 8 HELLISH HOURS ON THE TRAIN, THE TURKMEN BORDER PATROL BURST INTO OUR CABIN. I WAS FRIED AND THUS SHY A FEW I.Q. POINTS, BUT I DIDN'T NEED MUCH BRAINPOWER TO KNOW THAT I WAS FUCKED.
THE 2 MILITSIA FLIPPED THROUGH OUR PASSPORTS.
NYETO TURKMENI VISA– PLAKHOY PROBLEMA!
NYET PROBLEMA! KYRGYZ VISA, DA. UZBEK VISA, DA. KAZAKH VISA– IN TRANSIT, DA!
BOLSHOI PROBLEMA.
WE DISEMBARKED AT SUNRISE IN THE DESERT. AN ENDLESS EXPANSE OF SAND STRETCHED WEST TOWARD THE AMU DARYA, WHERE A TURKMEN REFINERY BURNED OFF IRANIAN CRUDE. CHARJOU CHOKED UNDER HAZE.
THE TALLER COP HELD THE TRAIN AS OUR FELLOW PASSENGERS GATHERED AT THE WINDOWS TO WATCH THE RITUAL SHAKEDOWN OF THE STUPID WESTERNERS.

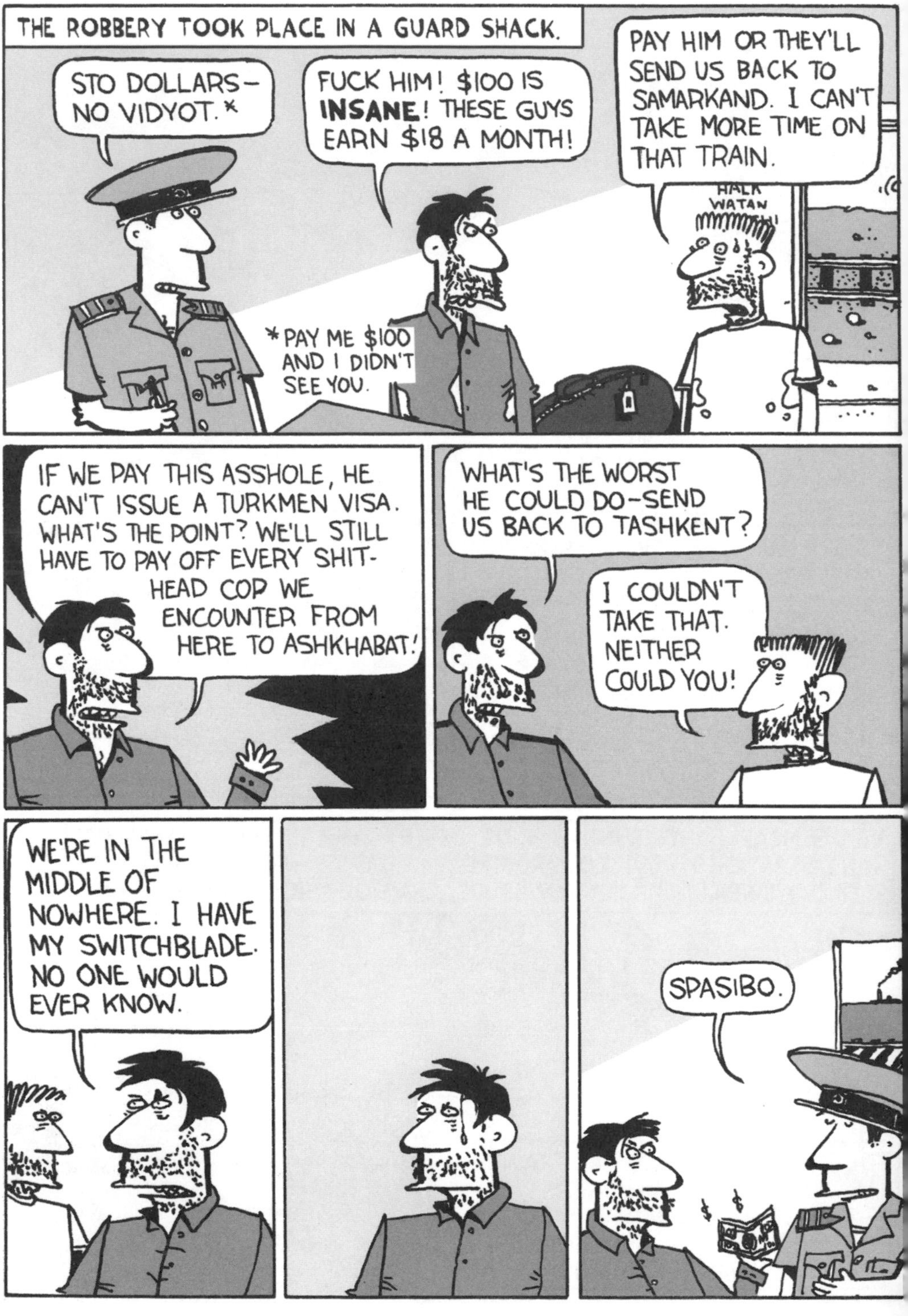
THE ROBBERY TOOK PLACE IN A GUARD SHACK.
STO DOLLARS— NO VIDYOT.*
FUCK HIM! $100 IS INSANE! THESE GUYS EARN $18 A MONTH!
PAY HIM OR THEY'LL SEND US BACK TO SAMARKAND. I CAN'T TAKE MORE TIME ON THAT TRAIN.
WATAN
*PAY ME $100 AND I DIDN'T SEE YOU.
IF WE PAY THIS ASSHOLE, HE CAN'T ISSUE A TURKMEN VISA. WHAT'S THE POINT? WE'LL STILL HAVE TO PAY OFF EVERY SHIT-HEAD COP WE ENCOUNTER FROM HERE TO ASHKHABAT!
WHAT'S THE WORST HE COULD DO—SEND US BACK TO TASHKENT?
I COULDN'T TAKE THAT. NEITHER COULD YOU!
WE'RE IN THE MIDDLE OF NOWHERE. I HAVE MY SWITCHBLADE. NO ONE WOULD EVER KNOW.
SPASIBO.

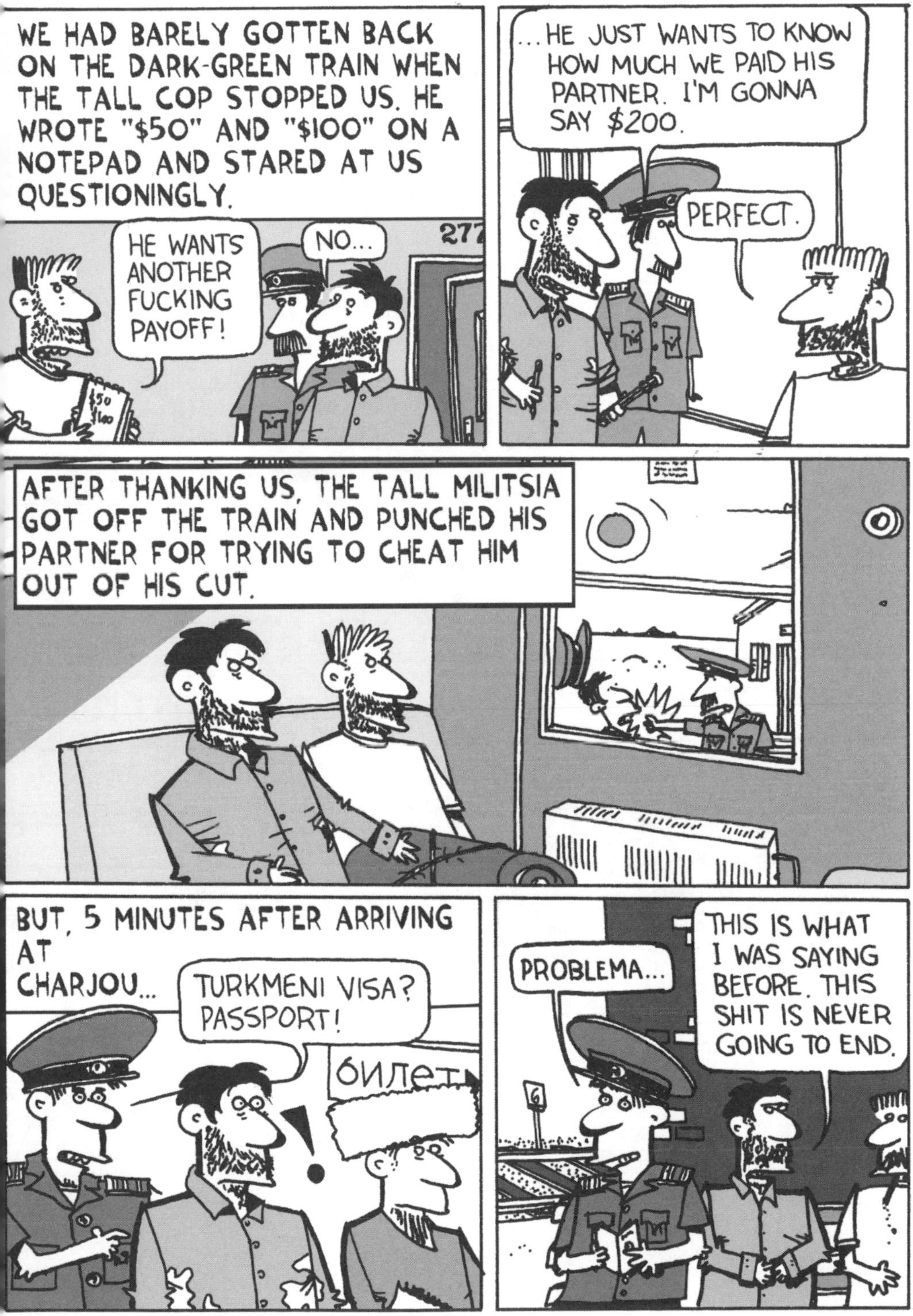
WE HAD BARELY GOTTEN BACK ON THE DARK-GREEN TRAIN WHEN THE TALL COP STOPPED US. HE WROTE "$50" AND "$100" ON A NOTEPAD AND STARED AT US QUESTIONINGLY.
HE WANTS ANOTHER FUCKING PAYOFF!
NO...
277
$50
$100
...HE JUST WANTS TO KNOW HOW MUCH WE PAID HIS PARTNER. I'M GONNA SAY $200.
PERFECT.
AFTER THANKING US, THE TALL MILITSIA GOT OFF THE TRAIN AND PUNCHED HIS PARTNER FOR TRYING TO CHEAT HIM OUT OF HIS CUT.
BUT, 5 MINUTES AFTER ARRIVING AT CHARJOU...
TURKMENI VISA? PASSPORT!
билет
PROBLEMA...
THIS IS WHAT I WAS SAYING BEFORE. THIS SHIT IS NEVER GOING TO END.

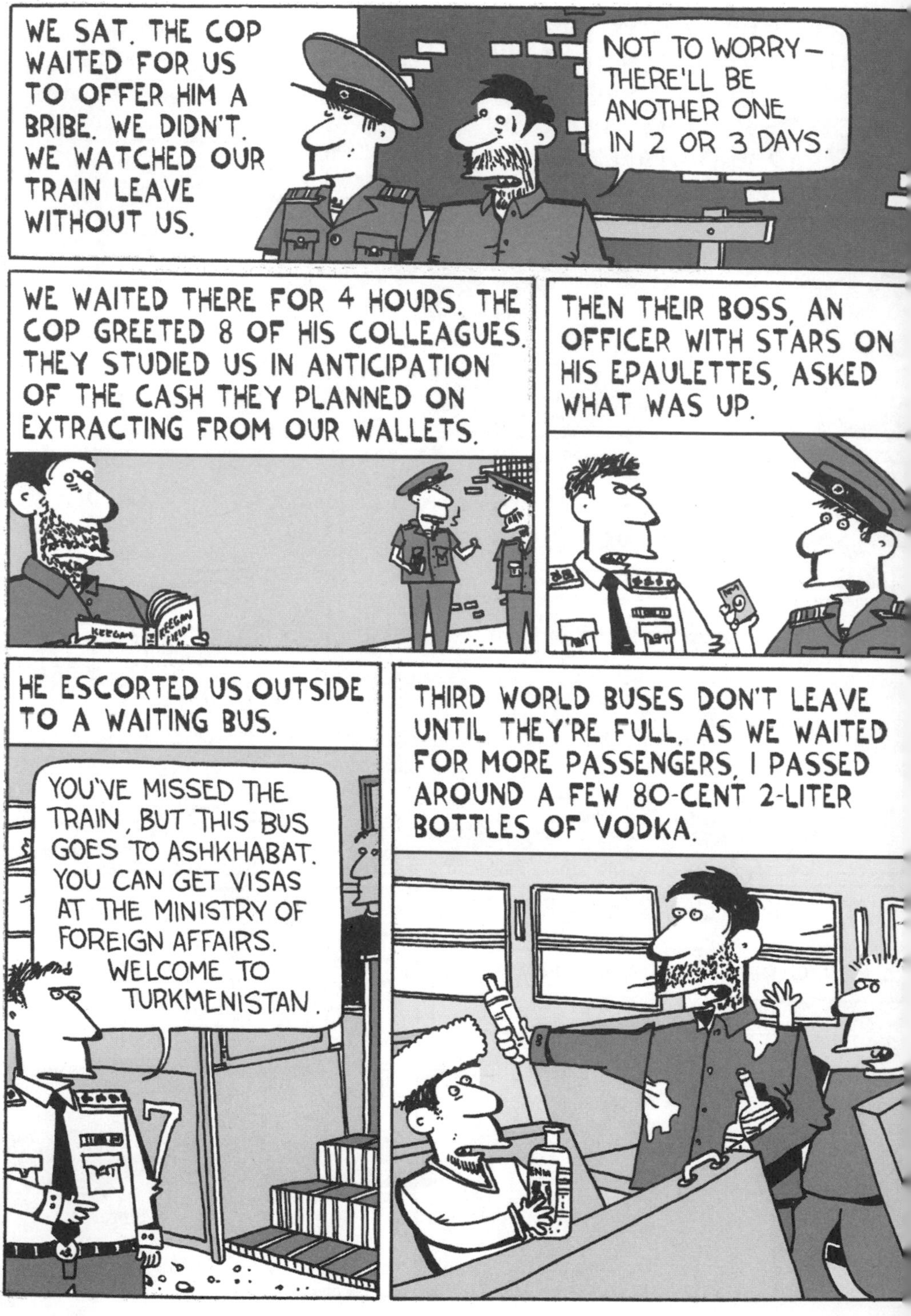
WE SAT. THE COP WAITED FOR US TO OFFER HIM A BRIBE. WE DIDN'T. WE WATCHED OUR TRAIN LEAVE WITHOUT US.
NOT TO WORRY— THERE'LL BE ANOTHER ONE IN 2 OR 3 DAYS.
WE WAITED THERE FOR 4 HOURS. THE COP GREETED 8 OF HIS COLLEAGUES. THEY STUDIED US IN ANTICIPATION OF THE CASH THEY PLANNED ON EXTRACTING FROM OUR WALLETS.
THEN THEIR BOSS, AN OFFICER WITH STARS ON HIS EPAULETTES, ASKED WHAT WAS UP.
HE ESCORTED US OUTSIDE TO A WAITING BUS.
YOU'VE MISSED THE TRAIN, BUT THIS BUS GOES TO ASHKHABAT. YOU CAN GET VISAS AT THE MINISTRY OF FOREIGN AFFAIRS. WELCOME TO TURKMENISTAN.
THIRD WORLD BUSES DON'T LEAVE UNTIL THEY'RE FULL. AS WE WAITED FOR MORE PASSENGERS, I PASSED AROUND A FEW 80-CENT 2-LITER BOTTLES OF VODKA.

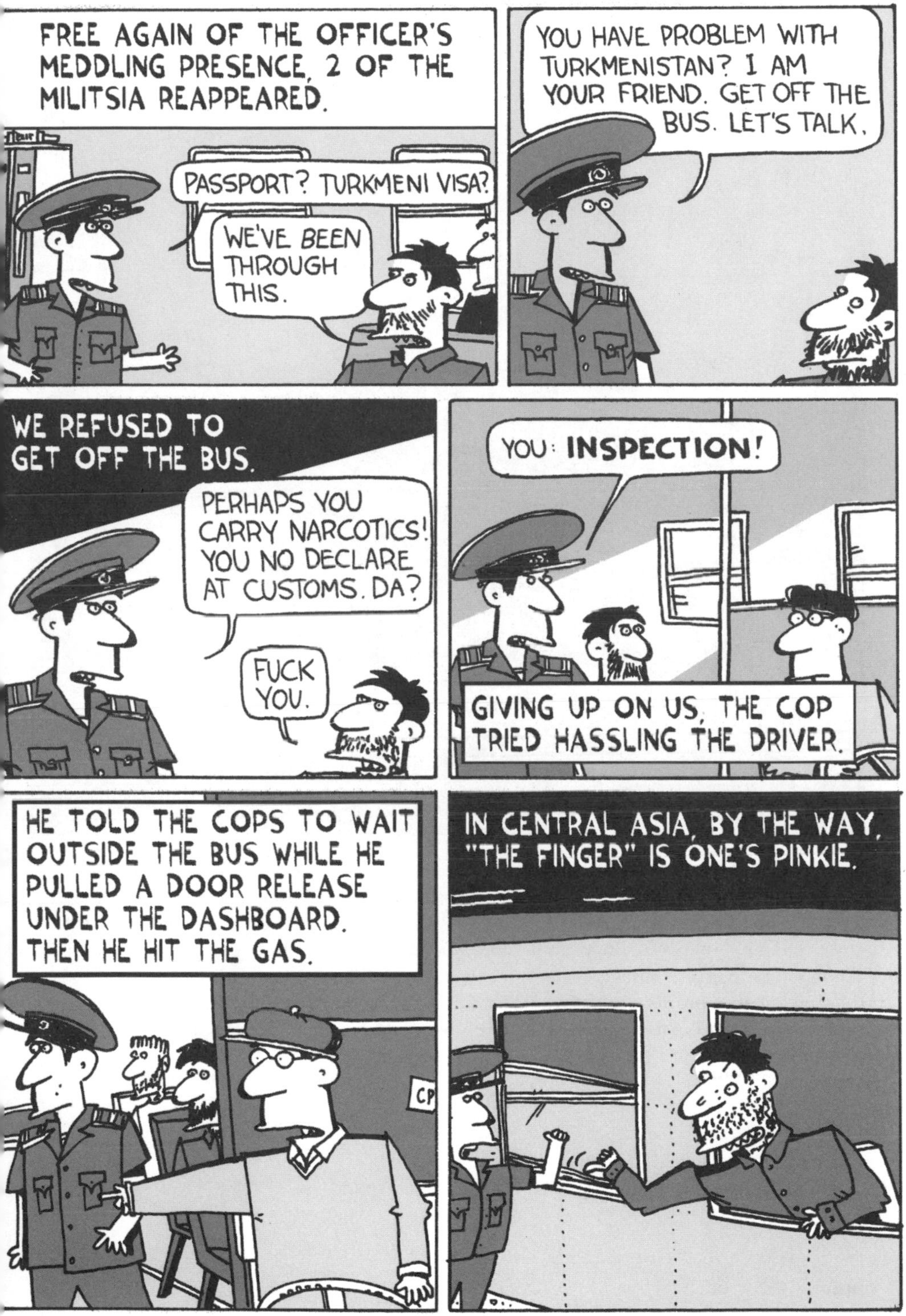
FREE AGAIN OF THE OFFICER'S MEDDLING PRESENCE, 2 OF THE MILITSIA REAPPEARED.
PASSPORT? TURKMENI VISA?
WE'VE BEEN THROUGH THIS.
YOU HAVE PROBLEM WITH TURKMENISTAN? I AM YOUR FRIEND. GET OFF THE BUS. LET'S TALK.
WE REFUSED TO GET OFF THE BUS.
PERHAPS YOU CARRY NARCOTICS! YOU NO DECLARE AT CUSTOMS. DA?
FUCK YOU.
YOU: INSPECTION!
GIVING UP ON US, THE COP TRIED HASSLING THE DRIVER.
HE TOLD THE COPS TO WAIT OUTSIDE THE BUS WHILE HE PULLED A DOOR RELEASE UNDER THE DASHBOARD. THEN HE HIT THE GAS.
IN CENTRAL ASIA, BY THE WAY, "THE FINGER" IS ONE'S PINKIE.

Alim Khan, the last Emir of Bukhara, shortly after his accession in 1911. The Emirate of Bukhara, now part of Uzbekistan, was an autonomous city-state in Islamic Central Asia and a major stop along the trade routes of the Silk Road. For centuries its emirs ruled over the city as absolute monarchs. (Bukhara became infamous at the height of the 19th century Great Game for its "bug pit," a thirty-feet-deep hole in the ground stocked with snakes, scorpions, rats and bones of previous prisoners.) By the mid-1800s, however, Bukhara had become a vassal state of the Russian Empire. After the Soviet takeover in 1920, the Emir fled to Afghanistan where he died in 1944.

Tajiks Don't Live in Tajikistan

According to official Soviet demographic information in the 1930s, there were about 300,000 Uyghurs living in the Soviet Union at that time. In 1937, during Stalin's campaign of purging "counter-revolutionaries" across the Soviet Union, many Uyghurs were forced to change their ethnic affiliation. Official Soviet statistics in 1979 put the Uyghur population at 29,104 and official statistics in 1989 put that number at 35,700.

—N.T. Tarimi, Asia Times

The French live in France. Japan is overwhelmingly Japanese. It's reasonable to assume that Uzbeks live in Uzbekistan, and they do, but only seventy-one percent of Uzbeks are *ethnically* Uzbek. There are also Tajiks (five percent, according to the government's nationalism-motivated lowball estimate), Kazakhs, Tatars, Karakalpaks and, as in all the Central Asian republics, a significant number of Russians (eight percent) left over from Soviet colonization schemes.

Most Tajiks, on the other hand, don't live in Tajikistan. Uzbeks, who despite their differing languages have a lot of cultural and ethnic similarities with Tajiks, were arbitrarily separated into distinct tribes during the 1920s by Soviet central planners who exaggerated their preexisting but relatively minor differences. The Soviets' scheme of assigning each of Central Asia's tribes to settled homelands within the Motherland actually worked; now most

A Tajik *buzkashi* player. The nomadic lifestyle continues to have a strong hold on the Central Asian imagination.

Uzbeks and Tajiks consider themselves separate tribes. Tajiks account for twenty-four percent of the population of Uzbekistan, whose most famous cities, Samarkand and Bukhara, are majority Tajik—although few Tajiks, worried about being considered disloyal to the Uzbek government, will publicly admit to being anything

97

Ottomon Turkish map of the Persian Empire by Ibrahim Mutafarrikah, possibly 18th century. It depicts the Caucasus, southern Russia, Transcaucasian Turkestan, Iraq, and part of Anatolia. Note the absence of political borders.

other than Uzbek. Other "Tajiks" include Kyrgyz, Turkmen and populations forcibly resettled or sentenced to gulags by Stalin: Ukrainians, Germans, Koreans, European and Bukharan Jews, Belorussians and Armenians. Confused? So are they.

Pre-Soviet Central Asia, under czarist influence during the late 19th and early 20th centuries, did not feature modern nation-states as we know them. West towards the Caspian Sea along the rough boundaries of contemporary Turkmenistan was a vaguely defined "Turkmen Country," a sandy waste crisscrossed by nomadic tribesmen who were among the last of Central Asians to succumb to rule from Moscow. Russian Turkestan, or simply Turkestan, similarly referred to areas where Turkic-speaking peoples traveled freely with their herds of goats, sheep and camels in search of food and, on occasion, unfortunate passersby to rob. Russian Turkestan included most of today's Uzbekistan and what Central Asian old-timers call Khirgizia: Kyrgyzstan and Kazakhstan. Last conquered were the remote Pamirs, fast against the border with the Indian Raj, Afghanistan and Chinese Turkestan, now modern-day Tajikistan. The Tajik language is an archaic form of Farsi, or Dari—a legacy of the nation's history as the eastern outpost of the Persian Empire.

All the other major tribes of Central Asia—the Turkmen, Uzbeks, Kyrgyz and Kazakhs—are Turkic peoples whose languages are considered dialects of Turkish by some linguists, and distinct but closely related tongues of the Indo-European language group by others.

The western section of Russian Turkestan that bordered Turkmen Country included the still-powerful yet fading emirates of Khiva and Bukhara, renowned for the capricious cruelty of their rulers as well as vibrant cultural and economic exchanges that characterized the Silk Road's contribution to culture. Chinese Turkestan referred to Central Asian city-states like Kashgaria—now Kashgar or Kashi—under nominal Chinese influence during periods of instability in Beijing and direct rule at other times. Today it is part of China's Xinjiang Province. Topographically and demographically, northern Afghanistan is also properly considered a part of Central Asia.

As far as everyday life was concerned, however, the average person knew no border. He rode his horse wherever he wanted, a state of affairs that has not entirely changed. The closely guarded frontiers between China and Kyrgyzstan, Afghanistan and Turkmenistan, and elsewhere are routinely crossed by tribesmen without passport controls by official and tacit consent. That, after all, is the way things have always been.

Russian Turkestan, under Soviet domination after the mid-1920s, was carved by Stalin into ethnic "homelands" where each major tribe was expected to settle as part of an industrializing and sedentary Soviet Union. A nation, Stalin wrote, is a "stable and historically constituted human community founded on its community of language, territory, economic life, and spiritual makeup, the last contained in the idea of community of national culture." Nomadism was in direct opposition to this Soviet vision. Most historians consider today's borders clumsy and arbitrary, the result of a misbegotten attempt to impose nationhood on peoples for whom the concept was cultural anathema. "The Soviet planners who redrew the map in the 1920s divided Central Asia broadly along linguistic lines, hoping to construct nations from the various nomadic and semi-nomadic tribes of desert and steppe by exaggerating the differences between their dialects," The Economist wrote in 1998. "These divisions, imperfect to start with, were subsequently blurred further by heavy Russian immigration and Stalin's eastward push in the 1930s of ethnic groups such as the Volga Germans and Tatars. More than a third of the inhabitants of Kazakhstan are Russian, and so are around eighteen percent of the people of Kyrgyzstan, despite a large exodus in recent years."

Other analysts detect a sinister strategy to pit ethnicities against one another in the ultimate gerrymander. According to a 2005 paper for an American intelligence think tank: "In creating the five republics, Stalin used the new borders to divide concentrations of single ethnic groups, isolate as many as possible from their ancestral homelands to create internal irredentist tensions, and break up ownership of natural resources to create economic interdependencies for Moscow to take advantage of. This divide-and-conquer strategy worked perfectly as the five republics set about competing with one another for Moscow's favor, and the need to balance tensions between clans and ethnic groups within the republics kept leaders too busy even to contemplate organizing resistance against Moscow."

Whatever Stalin's intentions, the result of his adventures in cartography is a mish-mash of tribal identities, some more imagined than real, in which nationhood is barely related to tribal affiliation. Here's a look at the major tribes of Central Asia:

Tajiks

Tajiks (from *taj* (crown) and *ik* (head), referring to anyone of Persian extraction, thus "one who wears a crown on his head") are mainly descendants of the Aryans, one of Central Asia's most ancient ethnic groups. Also descended from Bactrians, Sogdians, Parthians and Persians who fled to the Pamir mountain range during the Muslim expansion, Tajiks speak the sole Central Asian language not related to Turkish. Speakers of Farsi, Dari (the Afghan variant of Farsi) and Tajik can converse fairly easily.

Tajiks typically have dark hair and eyes and resemble modern-day Iranians, though many have lighter eyes and hair. There are at least five million Tajiks, of which three million live in Tajikistan, two million in Uzbekistan and between five hundred thousand and one million refugees from the Afghan civil war in Pakistan's Northwest Frontier Province.

Uzbeks

Although *Uzbeks* (the name refers either to Oz Beg, a historical tribal chieftain, or to the words *oz* (genuine) and *beg* (man)) trace their distinct cultural lineage to the Turkic-Mongol conqueror Tamerlane, now buried in the Tajik-majority Uzbek city of Samarkand, Uzbek identity coalesced in the 15th and 16th centuries when Mohammed Shaybani united the Kipchak, Nayman, Kanglis, Kungrat, Mangit and other steppe tribes and declared himself khan of the Uzbeks. The Uzbek language is closer to Uyghur, the language of the dominant Turkic tribe now living in western China, than Kazakh or Turkmen. Like all Central Asian tribes Uzbeks are ethnically and genetically heterogeneous thanks to intermarriage, repeated contact with others along the Silk Road and, most recently, Stalin's policy of forced exile and coloniza-

A woman in traditional Uzbek wedding garb, circa 1860.

tion of Europeanized peoples during the Soviet period. To Western eyes Uzbeks are Central Asia's quintessential Eurasian tribe, possessing facial features that seem to run roughly halfway between white European and Asian. The Central Asian stereotype of Uzbeks views them as them aggressive and sometimes hostile and arrogant. This owes more to Uzbek national foreign policy than observed reality.

Today there are twenty-six million Uzbeks, including twenty million in Uzbekistan, three million in Afghanistan and 1.5 million in Tajikistan. Uzbek can be written in Arabic, Latin and Cyrillic script; the latter has given way to Latinized script as the revival of Pan-Turkism has gathered steam.

Turkmen

Traditionally all Turkic peoples living West of the Amu Darya were called *Turkmen* (*Turk* plus the Farsi *manand*, thus meaning "pure Turk"). Now, however, these Oghuz Turks—who are genetically indistinguishable from actual Turks—are the only true Turkmen. Their language, a variant of the South Azerbaijani spoken directly on the opposite side of the Caspian Sea, emerged from the 9th and 10th century migrations from eastern Central Asia.

Turkmen camel driver, about 1915.

Turkmen became a written language only after the intervention of Soviet linguists, and no oral tradition of proto-literature survives. They were and remain the most fierce and nomadic of Central Asian tribes.

Many other Central Asians have a dim view of the seven million-strong Turkmen, of whom 4.3 million live in Turkmenistan, two million in Iran and five hundred thousand in Afghanistan, viewing them as violent, deceitful and (especially) dimwitted. Older men wear large fur hats (*telpeks*) to protect themselves from the sun, a unique cultural trait among Turkic peoples. The latter perception probably stems from the bizarre authoritarian regime in Turkmenistan.

Kyrgyz

The *Kyrgyz* ("forty girls," referring to the original number of unified tribes that repelled Mongol and Chinese expansion on two fronts as described in the *Manas* oral epic) are in many respects identical to their northern neighbors the Kazakhs. Older men often wear the distinctive white, peaked felt hats you'll see in Central Asian photographic exotica and a substantial minority of these mountain-dwelling people continue to practice shamanism.

Kyrgyzstan is frequently called the Switzerland of Central Asia for its mountains and low-key atmosphere; the Kyrgyz are known by their neighbors for their patience and generosity. Although some probably exist, I have never heard an anti-Kyrgyz slur.

Kazakhs

The *Kazakhs* ("free" in Turkish, related to "Cossacks") reflect the cultural tradition between the Mongol invasion led by Genghis Khan and the Turkic steppe peoples of the late Middle Ages. More Mongol than European, Kazakhs have a sophisticated tribal hierarchy in which most people belong to one of three *juz* (higher, middle, and junior), with *taypa* sub-tribes and *rw* (clans) in each sub-tribe. Current president of Kazakhstan Nursultan Nazarbayev belongs to a *tore* outside the *juz*; the *tore* refers to descendants of Genghis' Golden Horde. There are also *qoja* (descendants of Arabic warriors and missionaries) as well as *tolengit* (whose ancestors were *oirat*, or slaves).

Nomadic Kazakhs on the steppe, around 1911.

Traditional Kazakhs were expected to be able to recite their tribal affiliation and lineage for seven generations and were banned from marrying if they had a common ancestor for that period. Nevertheless Kazakhs do not feud between clans.

The world's eleven million Kazakhs are divided between Kazakhstan (eight and a half million), western China (one and a half million) and Uzbekistan (one million). Kazakh is written in a modified Cyrillic alphabet.

Karakalpak

With a small population of five hundred thousand, the *Karakalpak* (or *Qoraqalpog*, meaning "black hat") Turkic tribe comprises two and a half percent of the citizenry of Uzbekistan. Although even tinier numbers of these people live in Uzbekistan, Turkmenistan and Kazakhstan, the Karakalpaks are particularly beleaguered. Not only are they discriminated against by the central Uzbek government, they live in the growing wasteland formed by the evaporating Aral Sea—now called the Aral Kum desert—with nothing but the scorching Kyzylkum surrounding them. The Karakalpak language is considered close to Kazakh, a possible legacy of their 15th century affiliation with the Kazakh lower horde.

Tatars

Tatars (from the Ta-ta Gobi Desert Mongols of the 5th century), who account for one and a half percent of the population of Uzbekistan, is something of a generic term for Turkic tribes of Eastern Europe and Central Asia. Prior to the Russian Revolution "Tatar" referred to anyone living in southern czarist dominions. Today in Central Asia the term refers primarily to the so-called Volga Tatars, who were Bulgars conquered by Genghis in the 13th century but permitted to retain their tribal identity. This was probably a sign of respect for their fighting prowess.

Intermarriage and migration accounts for vast ethnic diversity within the Tatar designation, ranging from Mongoloid to Caucasoid appearances.

Uyghurs

Although their numbers are dwindling both in actual and proportional terms, the nine-million-strong *Uyghurs* remain the dominant ethnic group in the vast Xinjiang Uyghur Autonomous Region, the western province comprising one-sixth of the territory of China. The central government in Beijing is conducting a low-intensity war against the Uyghur presence in Xinjiang that is analogous to the situation in Tibet. This includes the importation of Han Chinese colonists to cities such as Ürümqi and Kashgar, the demolition of old Uyghur neighborhoods, systemic job and economic discrimination and, most recently, the arrest, execution and sometimes even deportation of Uyghur independence activists of the East Turkestan Independence Movement to the United States detention camp at Guantánamo Bay, Cuba as part of the "war on terror."

A Uyghur musician with a *satar*. The satar is usually played by the *muqamchi*, or lead singer, in the *muqam*, a highly structured set of melodies, poetry and folk songs that can take hours to complete. They have both spiritual and cultural significance for Uyghurs.

The Uyghur tribal federation was ruled by the Juan Juan during the late 5th and early 6th centuries before being absorbed by the Gokturk Khanate. Then, in 744, the Uyghurs successfully rebelled against the Turkic Empire and formed a new Uyghur Empire at Otuken that ruled southern Central Asia from the Caspian Sea to Manchuria. Independence was not to last. The Kyrgyz overran them in 840, pushing them to their present location in western China. Their Indiqut Kingdom similarly succumbed to Genghis Khan in 1209. Later Uyghur history has been informed by the ebb and flow of Chinese influence, depending on the relative strength of the empire at any given time, as well as the tribe's confluence of Mongol and Turkic heritage, which has prompted contempt on the part of the Han Chinese and repeated acts of rebellion against Chinese colonization.

They can also be found in neighboring Kyrgyzstan and Kazakhstan.

§ § §

The silk section of the Sunday Market in Kashgar, in southwest Xinjiang Province. Over a million people attend this bazaar.

Selling Out the Uyghurs, or, Why Even More of Them Hate Us

A four-day ride on the westbound express train from Beijing takes you to China's Wild West. Xinjiang Province, hundreds of miles beyond an eroded earthen mound that was once the Great Wall, lies southwest of Mongolia, east of Afghanistan and north of the Tibetan plateau. Full of dusty deserts, soaring mountains and eight million Muslims, Xinjiang is—like so many geopolitically sensitive places—the middle of nowhere but in between a lot. (Early 20th century British explorer Aurel Stein noted the region's "desolate wilderness, bearing everywhere the impress of death.") Today Chinese-occupied Central Asia is a case study in how American foreign policy turns pro-American Muslims into deadly enemies.

"From the pre-modern era until the mid-18th century, Xinjiang was either ruled from afar by Central Asian empires or not ruled at all," Joshua Kurlantzick writes in *Foreign Affairs*. During the 1950s Mao's Communist Party worked to consolidate its power by centralizing Chinese culture and politics in Beijing. That meant suppressing cultures and religions out of step with the majority ethnic Han Chinese, such as the Tibetans and Mongols. The jackboot came down hardest on Xinjiang, where in 1955 more than ninety percent of the population were Turkic Muslims—mostly Uyghurs along with smaller portions of such Central Asian tribes as Kazakhs, Kyrgyz, Uzbeks, Tajiks and Tatars. The Uyghurs, whose rich pre-Muslim Buddhist culture gave their language (which can be written in Arabic and Roman script) to Genghis Khan's Mongol Empire, were viewed by China's new government as a threat to national cohesion. They may have had a point. After all, they had revolted against pre-communist China forty-two times in two hundred years.

Repression of the Uyghurs has been primarily motivated by the Chinese government's simple desire to maintain control of its most remote border region. Their concern became more urgent after Xinjiang joined the rest of Central Asia as a major player in the energy sweepstakes, first as a transit conduit for a new pipeline carrying oil east from Kazakhstan to the Pacific Ocean and then as a major source of new oil reserves in its own right. "Xinjiang is going to become China's largest oil and gas production base with its oil and gas output predicted to reach sixty million tons by 2010 and one hundred million tons by 2020, according to Ismail Tiliwaldi, chairman of People's Government of the Xinjiang Uyghur Autonomous Region," the state-controlled *China Daily* reported in March 2006. Oil company geologists believe the Santanghu Basin holds one billion tons of oil.

The current anti-Uyghur campaign follows decades of similar abuses. "Thousands of mosques were shuttered, imams were jailed, Uyghurs who wore headscarves or other Muslim clothing were arrested, and during the Cultural Revolution, the Chinese Communist Party purposely defiled mosques with pigs," wrote Kurlantzick. "Many Muslim leaders were simply shot. The Uyghur language was purged from school curricula, and thousands of Uyghur writers were arrested for 'advocating separatism'—which often meant nothing more than writing in Uyghur."

Demographic manipulation at the hands of Chinese central planners has proven even more devastating to the Uyghur people. The Chinese imposed forced birth control on Uyghurs while shipping three hundred thousand Han settlers west every year where there had been only the same number to start. By 1997, there were more than six million Chinese "settlers" in Xinjiang. The Uyghurs had become a minority in their own homeland. But Xinjiang was far from pacified when I visited the provincial capital of Ürümqi that summer.

A few months earlier, on the eve of Ramadan, the police had arrested thirty imams in Ghulja. As about six hundred angry young Muslim men marched toward local government offices in order to demand their release, police broke up their demonstration with electrical clubs and tear gas. More Uyghurs returned the next day. Overwhelmed police opened fire, killing one hundred sixty-seven people and arresting five thousand. Then the Chinese unveiled a new tactic that would soon become a frequent occurrence: they drove around the bazaar district with seven Uyghurs in the back of a truck, executing them one by one. Nine outraged bystanders were also shot to death.

You couldn't miss the tension in the hot stinking air of the most landlocked city on earth. Uyghur separatists affiliated with the East Turkestan Independence Movement and other groups had set off bombs all across China, including three buses blown up in Ürümqi a few months earlier. The Chinese dispatched hundreds of suspected Uyghur dissidents to reeducation camps. Scores of others were put on trial and summarily shot. Good jobs in government and private business

XINJIANG UYGHUR AUTONOMOUS REGION

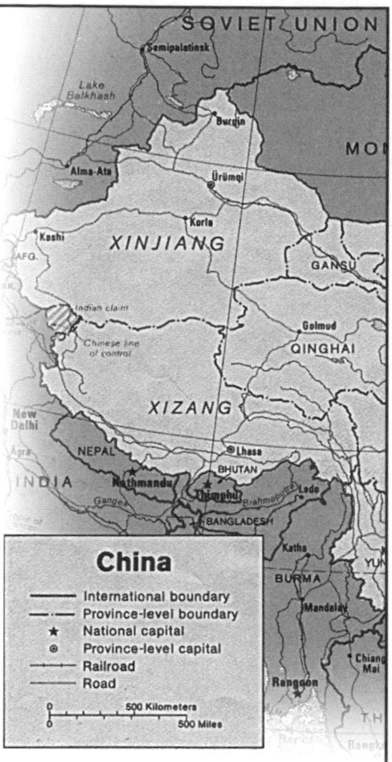
SOVIET UNION
Semipalatinsk
Lake Balkhash
Burqin
Alma-Ata
Ürümqi
Korla
Kashi
XINJIANG
AFG.
GANSU
Indian claim
Chinese line of control
Golmud
QINGHAI
New Delhi
XIZANG
NEPAL
Lhasa
BHUTAN
Agra
INDIA
Kathmandu
Thimphu
Brahmaputra
Ledo
Ganges
BANGLADESH
Katha
BURMA
Mandalay
Chiang Mai
Rangoon
China
International boundary
Province-level boundary
National capital
Province-level capital
Railroad
Road
0 500 Kilometers
0 500 Miles

Administrative Capital: Ürümqi
Form of Government: Province of China
Population (July 2005): 19,250,000
Major Ethnic Groups (2000):
Uyghur 45.2%; Han Chinese 40.6%; Kazakh 6.7%; Hui 4.6%; Kyrgyz 0.9%; Mongol 0.8%; Dongxiang 0.3%; Tajik 0.2%
Area (square miles): 640,760 (one sixth of China)
Terrain (as per *CIA Factbook*):
"mostly mountains, high plateaus, deserts"
Currency/Exchange Rate (2005):
US $1 = 8.19 *yuan (also RMB)*
Oil Reserves (proven): 20 billion barrels
Natural Gas Reserves (proven):
10.3 trillion cubic meters
Coolest Thing About Xinjiang:
laghman noodles, the mouth-watering delicacy you'll miss every day for the rest of your life
Worst Thing About Xinjiang:
Dust, so much dust
Best Way to Get Thrown Into Jail: Buy drugs
Per Capita Annual Income: $240
Unemployment Rate: 4%
Life Expectancy: 71

Xinjiang, the largest of China's provinces, is the nation's far west. It has a political situation analogous to that of Tibet. Both have distinctly non-Chinese cultures which the central government is trying to eradicate through direct oppression and colonization by Han Chinese from the east. Xinjiang looks, feels and sounds like Central Asia; its dominant Uyghurs are a Turkic people, similar to the Kazakhs, who have never willingly succumbed to Chinese rule. The 1862 Tungani Revolt led to an independent Kashgaria under Yakub Beg from 1865 until 1877, when the Qing Dynasty reconquered the west. During the Chinese civil war Uyghurs took advantage of the chaos to set up an independent Islamic Republic of East Turkestan in 1933 and 1944; both were suppressed by Soviet interference. When Mao came to power in 1949 he dispatched troops to put down the rebellious Uyghurs once and for all. In 1990 the Uyghurs, Kyrgyz and Kazakhs of Xinjiang began a full-fledged uprising which continues today. Bombings of government offices and assassinations of public officials, quickly followed by mass round-ups and summary public executions, have become commonplace. Political unrest aside, Xinjiang is a fascinating place to visit. The ancient Silk Road city of Kashgar (also called Kashi) is both the originating point of the high-altitude Karakoram Highway to Pakistani-occupied Kashmir as well as the southern terminus of the road connecting China to the Kyrgyz Republic. It is also the location of the Sunday Market, where a million people from everywhere from Afghanistan to Tajikistan to Tibet congregate to buy and sell food, camels, weapons and everything else—including silk.

are reserved exclusively for Han Chinese, adding sky-high unemployment to the ravages of cultural apartheid. Han policemen manning roadblocks surrounding the old Muslim quarter tried to discourage me from entering the quarantined zone. "There's nothing of interest there," a cop told me. I insisted. When I arrived at the square in front of a dilapidated mosque, Uyghur men wearing white skullcaps glared menacingly at Han colonists zooming by in shiny new Volvos. Fortunately, they brightened up when they learned that I was American.

"We love the United States!" one man told me. "They will come help us kick out China." The largest Uyghur independence group, the ETIM, seeks the recreation of the free Republic of East Turkestan declared by earlier Uyghur rebels. The Home of East Turkestan Youth, known as "Xinjiang's Hamas," has two thousand members.

"I listen to Radio Free Asia," added an older guy knowingly. Radio Free Asia aired broadcasts in the Uyghur language. "America is coming to give us our freedom, we know that, but when exactly?"

How could I tell these people that most Americans had never heard of Uyghurs, East Turkestan, or Xinjiang? That the cavalry wasn't coming? Given their status as non-entities, even being on the foreign policy backburner (like the Kurds) would be an improvement.

By the time of my 1999 trip to the Silk Road city of Kashgar in southern Xinjiang, what Western media call "a low level insurgency" had heated up. The Chinese had demolished all but a few blocks of the ancient old city in order to put up prefab apartment buildings. But the Uyghurs weren't taking it lying down. ETIM separatists, some of whom had trained at jihadi camps in Afghanistan, were blowing up a Chinese government office every few days. "Goodbye, Interior Ministry!" gloated my server at a sidewalk noodle joint after the sound of an explosion ricocheted down the boulevard. "We are fighting hard against China to show you Americans we are serious. The U.S. stands for freedom."

Then came 9/11. The Bush Administration, seeking to avert a Chinese veto of its invasions of Afghanistan and Iraq in the U.N. security council, drafted China into its "war on terrorism" by granting it a free pass to beat up its Tibetans and Uyghurs. Citing the fact that ETIM members had received arms and training from the Taliban in neighboring Afghanistan (but only to fight China), China convinced the U.S. State Department and the United Nations to declare the group a "terrorist organization" affiliated with al Qaeda. "This is an important step toward greater cooperation in Central Asia against common terrorist threats and the instability and horror that they sow," a State Department spokesman said, conflating the tactic of terrorism with the 9/11 attackers. In "Xinjiang: China's Muslim Borderland," Graham Fuller and Jonathan Lippman write that this "U.S. declaration [was] catastrophic" for the Uyghurs. The United States had given Beijing "carte blanche to designate all Uyghur nationalist...movements as 'terrorist.' " Brad Adams of Human Rights Watch added: "The worldwide campaign against terrorism has given

Beijing the perfect excuse to crack down harder than ever in Xinjiang. Other Chinese enjoy a growing freedom to worship, but the Uyghurs, like the Tibetans, find that their religion is being used as a tool of control."

Twenty-three Uyghurs have since joined the ranks of the "terrorists" incarcerated at Guantánamo concentration camp. Two Uyghur men, twenty-nine and thirty-one, faced a U.S. military tribunal on November 19, 2005, charged only with membership in ETIM and attending a Taliban training camp for anti-Chinese fighters. Even though a man named Mahmut initially pled guilty to avoid being sent back to China—"If I am sent back to China, they will torture me really bad," he told the tribunal, "they will use dogs...they will pull out my nails"—the three were cleared of enemy combatant status. The U.S. refused their application for political asylum. After a lengthy delay, Albania finally agreed to accept the former detainees. Military insiders say most of the Uyghurs will eventually be released, but not to China—our ally in the "war on terrorism"—because they would probably be tortured and/or executed.

Chinese officials have ordered Uyghur university students to spend more time studying ideological correctness and to report any classmates they notice observing the fast at Ramadan. "We have an agreement with the Chinese government that I am responsible for preventing students from fasting during Ramadan," a representative of the Kashgari religious affairs committee openly admitted in 2004. The same man, speaking to Radio Free Asia, is charged with ensuring Xinjiang's twelve-month-a-year nightlife: "I am responsible for making sure that the restaurants stay open as normal [during Ramadan]. I have to write a report every day for the officials higher up about the situation and also I have two people on duty at night to pass on information and report to higher up." Some officials even pressure employers to take their workers out to lunches during Ramadan. Cultural genocide is a strange business.

The crackdown swept up the editor of the *Kashgar Literature Journal* for publishing an original short story "Wild Pigeon," the author of which is already serving a ten-year-prison sentence for writing what the authorities saw as a thinly-veiled allegory criticizing harsh Chinese rule in Xinjiang. The editor, Korash Huseyin, will likely receive a harsher sentence if convicted. As if persecuting Uyghur activists within China isn't enough, the government also demands cooperation from neighboring states. Both the Kyrgyz and Kazakh governments, violating the international principle of "non-refoulement," have arrested and extradited Uyghur men wanted for political offenses.

Martial law remains in full force in Xinjiang. The post-9/11 crackdown began with hundreds of arrests and the executions of nine "religious extremists and terrorists." One of the dead, convicted of "contributing to disturbance by nationalist splittism forces," had been overheard joking that he hoped America would come to Xinjiang to free the Uyghurs from Chinese rule.

Good Eats

Of their food and victuals you must know that they eat all their dead animals without distinction, and with such flocks and herds it cannot be but that many animals die. Nevertheless, in summer, so long as lasts their kumis, *that is to say mare's milk, they care not for any other food. So then if it happens that an ox or a horse dies, they dry its flesh by cutting it into narrow strips and hanging it in the sun and the wind, where at once and without salt it becomes dry without any evil smell. With the intestines of horses they make sausages better than pork ones, and they eat them fresh.*

—William of Rubruck, emissary of French King
Louis IX to the Mongols, 1253-1255

Need to lose weight? Atkins not working? Try running five miles a day, every day. Stop eating potatoes. Give up beer. You might want to consider gastric bypass surgery. But if you're up for a truly radical slimming solution, there's only one place to go: your travel agency.

I'm six feet two inches tall. Six weeks during the late summer of 1997 brought me down forty-four pounds (from one hundred ninety-two). How'd I do it? Diarrhea. And giardia. The Central Asia Diet Plan isn't for weaklings, but unlike those schemes you see on daytime television, it's guaranteed to work.

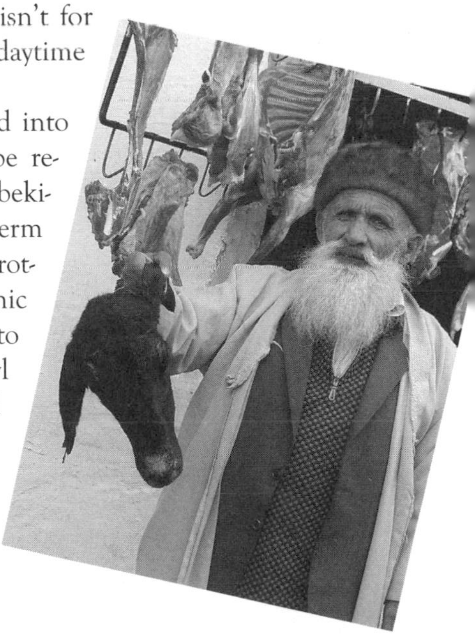

It was week three when Alan and I strolled into the Restaurant Dilshod, an event unlikely to be recorded in future histories of the Republic of Uzbekistan but one that will remain locked in my long-term memory long after other parts of my brain have rotted away. Thanks to the trip's previous gastronomic attacks I had already migrated from my loosest to tightest belt loop. (I subsequently borrowed an awl to punch new holes.) I had become accustomed to shitting at least once an hour, skipping two or three at night. Fortunately my anus, which had begun bleeding during a tortuous crossing by bus of the Tian Shan mountains separating

Chinese Turkestan and southeastern Kazakhstan, had crusted over by Uzbekistan. I considered this development a happy one as this scab acted as a sort of natural butt plug, mitigating the volume of diarrheic flow.

How much worse could things get?

Samarkand's Restaurant Dilshod was a prefab concrete heap, since closed by the personal intervention of Allah, set approximately one hundred feet back from Kommunistichestskaya Street. This arrangement permitted diners the pleasure of dining outdoors—where it was a mere one hundred degrees on a particularly cool August day, which compared favorably to the non-climatized furnace inside—while avoiding the fumes of passing cars. Traffic was nearly non-existent because no one

Calf's feet on offer at a market: One of many reasons obesity isn't a major problem in Central Asia.

could afford fuel during the mid-1990s economic collapse, but the setback nevertheless reflected the Uzbek proclivity for optimistic planning amid the bleakest of conditions.

Having spent most of the night slaughtering mosquitoes in our room at the Hotel Vatan, we had slept through the hotel's free cucumber, tomato slice and feta cheese breakfast and were hungry for lunch. As we were its only patrons, service at the Dilshod at least promised to be timely.

Alan, the kind of guy who bums a cigarette when his girlfriend isn't around, had become a chain smoker somewhere around the Kyrgyz-Kazakh border. "Get matches," I encouraged him. "I want Restaurant Dilshod matches." The waiter took Alan's Hollywood cigarette to the kitchen and returned with it lit.

As is customary in your classier Third World dining establishments, the waiter presented us with multi-page menus encased in Lucite-thick plastic. Entries were typed in Cyrillic with cryptic English translations: "some bird with pretty sauce, second type." I pointed to a set of characters that somewhat resembled a dish I'd previously ordered elsewhere that, since I had not yet died, must have been acceptably non-toxic. "No, sorry, not today, sir."

I forgot to mention that he was wearing a black vest, jacket and bow tie.

I tried something else. No luck, so I passed off to Alan.

Alan attempted three of four orders, none of which turned out to have been available that day.

Finally I asked what, if anything, there was to eat for lunch. Our waiter did not smile. "There is [unintelligible]," he said.

From Ashkhabat to Almaty it's *shashlyk*—and it's what for dinner! And lunch! And breakfast! Shashlyk is meat, typically mutton, on a stick. Greasy and spicily delicious upon first taste, the repetitive nature of Central Asian food soon wears on travelers' health and sanity.

"What is that?" I asked.

"[Unintelligible]," he repeated, louder.

Alan cupped his ear.

"[UNINTELLIGIBLE]!"

"Two," I said. I made a peace sign as a backup form of communication. The waiter disappeared with a hint of a bow.

We sprawled back in our white plastic chairs to take in the view. Left, right, no one to be seen. A pack of wild dogs frolicked among the disused cinderblocks, empty water bottles and rusted cables covering the "yard" between the restaurant and the street. The alpha male, his relative health superiority indicated by the presence of more than half of his matted fur clinging to his exposed ribs, nipped at his underlings to remind them of their place in the canine hierarchy.

Our waiter broke our dehydrated reverie with a flourish. "Voilà!" he announced, depositing two covered plates on the plastic checkered tablecloth covering our plastic table. (Okay, he didn't say "voilà" but he may as well have.) The covers, judging by the stone-cold food revealed within, were evidently designed to protect them from the searing heat.

But what stone-cold food it was!

"What is it?" I asked Alan, not expecting an answer.

"Maybe it's a kind of *shashlyk.*"

Shashlyk, Turkic for meat on a stick, is the ubiquitous street meal of Russia,

Stan Trekker Bill tastes *kumis*, fermented mare's milk. The salty drink, a staple among Kyrgyz and Kazakh nomads, is supposedly good for avoiding altitude sickness.

the Caucasus, Central Asia and much of the Middle East. Typically you get a kebab of greasy mutton cubes grilled over charcoal. Other meats are used as well, either lamb or—in rare cases—beef. Quality varies wildly, from nearly savory to gag-inducing. The problem is, there's usually nothing else. Behold the traveler's conundrum: you get sick unless you eat, but eating makes you sick.

Sometimes shashlyk is created from minced meats blended with spices and pasted to a skewer. Central Asians may disagree, but most Westerners consider these bastard creations even more repugnant than standard-issue shashlyk.

"Could be," I agreed. "But look at the shape. Those squished shashlyks usually taper to each edge. And they're much thinner in the middle."

"And the color looks more like meat," Alan added.

We'd seen a lot of shashlyk.

"These aren't shashlyks," I announced. "These are meatpods."

Alan picked up his and sniffed at it. "Sawdust, mixed with urine," he guessed.

My meatpod was tan. I found this disturbing because, though many foods are tan, I'd never encountered this shade of tan before—not in food, nor anything else. "There's also a vomit thing going on," I said.

"More like cat vomit," Alan corrected me. We both owned cats.

We looked at each other. Then we scanned the perimeter of the patio. "The waiter's still not here," Alan said, flinging his meatpod at the dogs a second before I did the same.

The ravenous beasts ran up to our offerings, tongues dangling, paws bleeding from glass cuts. Then something terrible happened.

Alpha Male took a small bite. A puzzled expression crossed his face. He let out a horrified yelp and ran off at full speed, his front paws swinging between his back ones as his comrades followed him.

Bear in mind that these animals were at death's door, scavenging for sustenance in blazing heat. Note that, even when physically robust, dogs aren't picky. They eat shit and like it. Yet whatever was in those meatpods repelled them to the point that they hightailed in terror. *And I almost ate one.*

Central Asia is a region ruled by corrupt despots presiding over stupid, vicious military police, where violence from border skirmishes to bombings and invasions can and does occur at random. It features the planet's most daunting mountains and its sketchiest transportation, its hottest deserts and coldest plateaus. Yet these inconveniences pale compared to the lousy food.

Funny travel stories are often based on food, and one of my favorites involves shashlyk. In 2000, while leading Stan Trek, I encouraged the drivers of my chartered bus to take us into eastern Kyrgyzstan, along the eastern bank of Lake Issyk-Kul, using a rarely-used border crossing from Kazakhstan. The *militsia*, who were close to blind drunk in mid-afternoon, were shocked to see us—to see anyone. I handed one fat cop, the buttons on his uniform shirt straining from the pressure of his belly, a stack of passports to process. He opened his logbook, then stopped.

"How many are there?"

"Twenty-four," I replied.

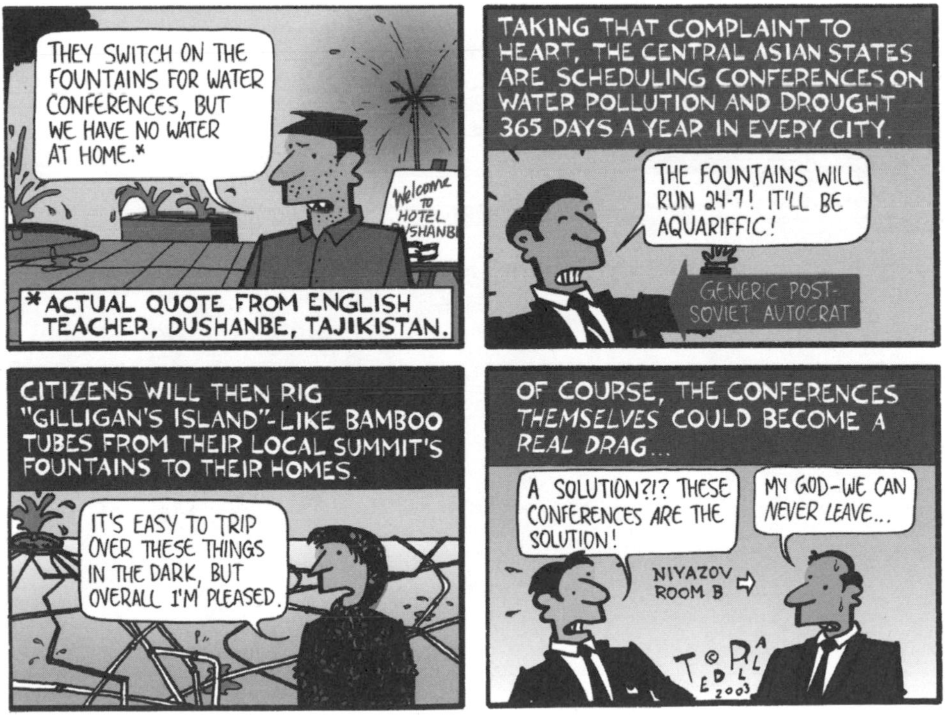
THEY SWITCH ON THE FOUNTAINS FOR WATER CONFERENCES, BUT WE HAVE NO WATER AT HOME.*
Welcome TO HOTEL
*ACTUAL QUOTE FROM ENGLISH TEACHER, DUSHANBE, TAJIKISTAN.
TAKING THAT COMPLAINT TO HEART, THE CENTRAL ASIAN STATES ARE SCHEDULING CONFERENCES ON WATER POLLUTION AND DROUGHT 365 DAYS A YEAR IN EVERY CITY.
THE FOUNTAINS WILL RUN 24-7! IT'LL BE AQUARIFFIC!
GENERIC POST-SOVIET AUTOCRAT
CITIZENS WILL THEN RIG "GILLIGAN'S ISLAND"-LIKE BAMBOO TUBES FROM THEIR LOCAL SUMMIT'S FOUNTAINS TO THEIR HOMES.
IT'S EASY TO TRIP OVER THESE THINGS IN THE DARK, BUT OVERALL I'M PLEASED.
OF COURSE, THE CONFERENCES THEMSELVES COULD BECOME A REAL DRAG...
A SOLUTION?!? THESE CONFERENCES ARE THE SOLUTION!
MY GOD—WE CAN NEVER LEAVE...
NIYAZOV ROOM B
TED RALL © 2003

He paused. "Too much work," he said, handing them back to me. He waved his thick hand. "Just go!" he ordered, disgusted.

The Stan Trekkers, who had left Almaty the morning the day before, had finished off their Powerbars and were now famished. "The next time you see a shashlyk stand," I asked the bus driver, "please stop." Central Asian bus drivers are an indolent bunch who would rather do just about anything than drive, so I assumed that he would welcome yet another opportunity to take a nap. Yet we kept passing one shashlyk outfit after another, never stopping. Finally, I demanded an explanation. "The shashlyk," he said, "is not good here."

"Shashlyk is never good. Just stop!" He floored it.

I don't know whether his refusal to pull over was the result of passive-aggressiveness or something even more frightening: shashlyk that's *even worse than the norm.*

Oh, there are culinary delights. Melons come in infinite varieties and taste so exquisite that you'll shun supermarket melons forevermore. Laghman noodles, the wide fat pasta of Xinjiang, eastern Afghanistan and Tajikistan, form the base of a soup so delicious you'll never understand why they're not sold on every street corner in the world. Southeastern Kazakhstan is a cultural collision zone so close to China that they eat with chopsticks, where Chinese and Turkic cuisines combine in a perfect synthesis of east and west. But even these foods, prepared in insect-infested squalor and served in bowls rinsed with cold dirty water, will make you ill. And their tastiness is the exception.

The only tasty alternative to *shashlyk*: Central Asia's huge variety of delicious melons.

Uzbek vegetable vendors at a typical Soviet-built market.

From one time zone to the next, from Azerbaijan to the west of the Caspian Sea to Almaty in southern Kazakhstan, dubious shashlyk is the norm. Occasionally you'll score some stray radishes and cucumbers, and perhaps a small tomato, but that's about it for vegetables.

Beer, on the other hand, is cheap, tasty and plentiful. And, since beer calories are the only ones you'll keep more than an hour at a time, they're essential to human sustenance.

Creature comforts are in short supply throughout the former Soviet republics. Rural toilets are holes in the ground. The urban version is a squat previously used by drunk, inaccurate patrons. None have toilet paper. Seasoned Central Asia hands import packs of paper handkerchiefs and wet wipes to soothe incipient hemorrhoids. Worst of all, for women in particular, the most common bathroom is the great outdoors.

Because nearly everyone, including the locals, suffers from permanent diarrhea, long bus rides are punctuated by frequent urination and defecation breaks. No one talks much in between. Men pull their belts away from their aching stomachs. Both sexes moan gently, working through the stabbing pains in their intestines while hoping not to soil themselves. The driver pulls over, everyone jumps off in search of tall grass or a tree and does it right there, on the spot. The urge for privacy can drive people to extreme measures. It also prompts some odd pit stops.

On one mountain road in southeastern Kazakhstan in 1997, our bus stopped in front of a summer dacha in the Tian Shan foothills. As the front door had been pried open, we went inside—I assumed, mistakenly, to use the absentee owner's bathroom. We walked into the Russified version of a suburban living room: sofa, coffee table, end tables, lamps, curtains. But something was very, very wrong:

Scattered across the floor, in every room and even up the stairs, were crumbled pieces of thin pink tissue I immediately recognized as the restaurant napkins people in every Third World country steal in order to use as toilet paper. And next to each pink ball was a piece, or two, of shit.

A lot of the shit was hardened due to age. Some appeared to be fairly recent, possibly a week old. My fellow passengers milled about in search of a few vacant square feet to take a dump. I found Alan outside. "It's the *maison de merde!*" I exclaimed. "Literally a shithouse!" he replied. We cracked up laughing. But why the hell had we stopped there? Who would deserve to have this happen to his home? Why didn't the bus passengers hesitate to take a dump in someone's dining room? It was one of the great mysteries of my life, and one I was determined to solve. Finally, after repeated prodding, the bus driver allowed that the house belonged to a man he said had stolen and married his wife.

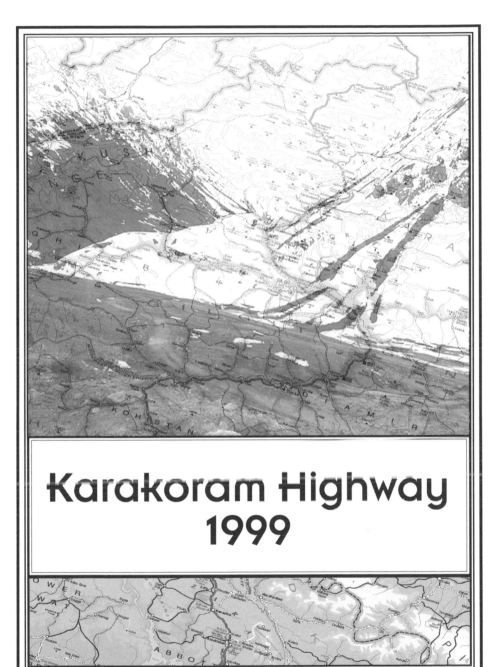

Karakoram Highway
1999

In 1999 P.O.V. sent me back to Central Asia, this time to write about "The World's Most Dangerous Highway," the Karakoram Highway linking Kashgar in China's Xinjiang Uyghur Autonomous Region to the Pakistani capital of Islamabad. My best friend and I flew to Tashkent, spent a few days in Almaty and then crossed Kyrgyzstan to the high-altitude Torugart Pass to China, officially off-limits to foreigners at the time, to access the road to Kashgar. As our bus wound its way up the Karakoram mountain range to the Khunjerab Pass marking the frontier of Pakistani-occupied Kashmir, General Pervez Musharraf seized power in a coup and opened the Kashmiri border to Taliban insurgents.

MY SECOND TRIP TO CENTRAL ASIA BEGAN INAUSPICIOUSLY. DAYS AFTER HUNDREDS OF ISLAMIC MOVEMENT OF UZBEKISTAN GUERILLA FIGHTERS HAD CROSSED FROM THEIR BASES IN TAJIKISTAN INTO SOUTHERN KYRGYZSTAN, UZBEK PRESIDENT ISLAM KARIMOV HAD BOMBED 4 KYRGYZ VILLAGES UNDER IMU CONTROL. VILLAGES ACROSS THE BORDER IN TAJIKISTAN WERE STRUCK BY UZBEK BOMBS AS WELL.

THE KYRGYZ AND TAJIK GOVERNMENTS RECALLED THEIR AMBASSADORS AND CLOSED THEIR FRONTIERS WITH UZBEKISTAN. COLE AND I NEEDED TO GET TO BISHKEK, WHICH REQUIRES FIRST ENTERING KAZAKHSTAN, BUT THE KAZAKHS HAD SEALED THEIR BORDER AS WELL.

FIGHTING WAS RAGING A FEW MILES EAST OF TASHKENT: CENTRAL ASIA HUNG IN THE BALANCE. ALL I COULD THINK ABOUT, HOWEVER, WAS THE PAIN IN MY GROIN. I HAD UNDERGONE A HERNIA OPERATION A MONTH EARLIER.

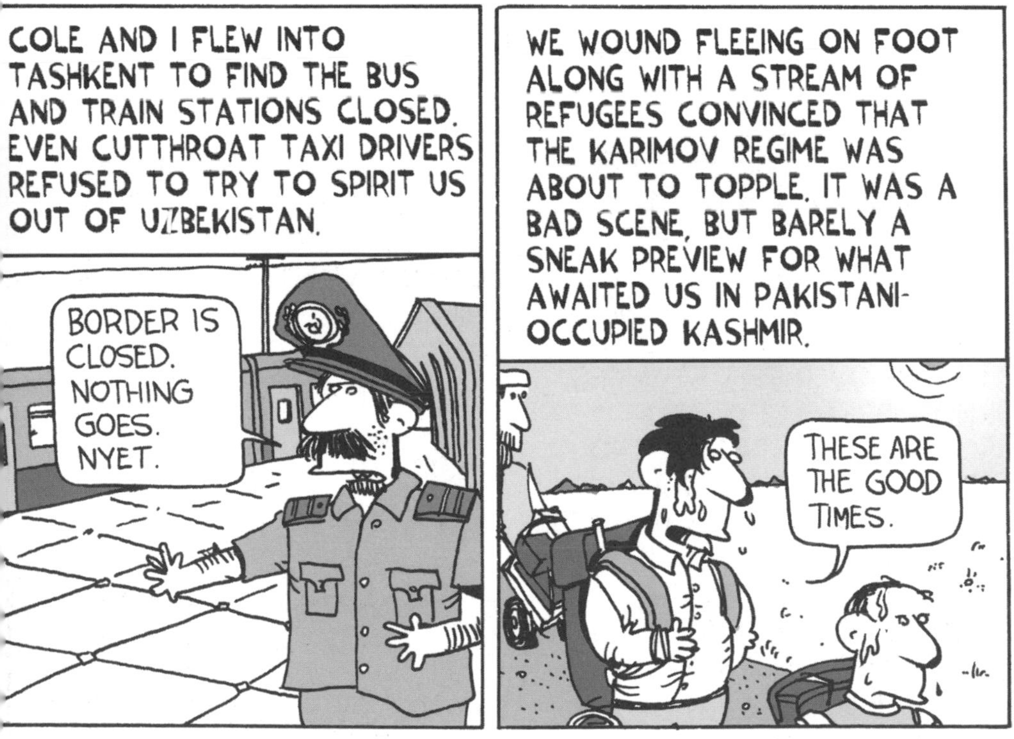
COLE AND I FLEW INTO TASHKENT TO FIND THE BUS AND TRAIN STATIONS CLOSED. EVEN CUTTHROAT TAXI DRIVERS REFUSED TO TRY TO SPIRIT US OUT OF UZBEKISTAN.
BORDER IS CLOSED. NOTHING GOES. NYET.
WE WOUND FLEEING ON FOOT ALONG WITH A STREAM OF REFUGEES CONVINCED THAT THE KARIMOV REGIME WAS ABOUT TO TOPPLE. IT WAS A BAD SCENE, BUT BARELY A SNEAK PREVIEW FOR WHAT AWAITED US IN PAKISTANI-OCCUPIED KASHMIR.
THESE ARE THE GOOD TIMES.

BUT I'M GETTING AHEAD OF MYSELF. FIRST YOU NEED TO KNOW ABOUT

KASHMIR

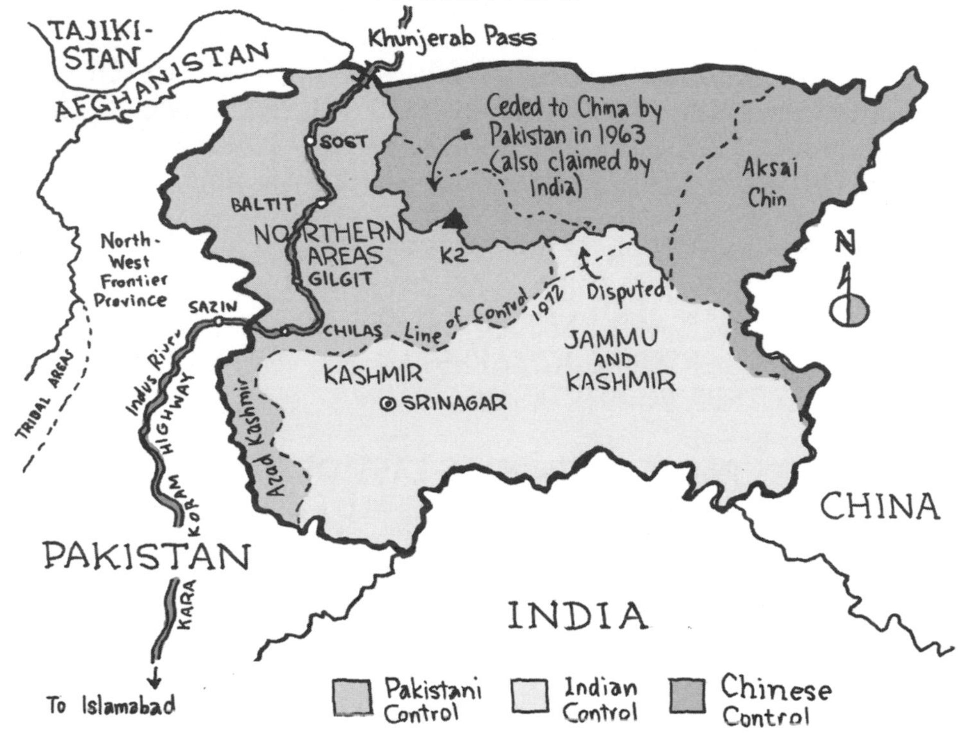
TAJIKI-STAN
AFGHANISTAN
Khunjerab Pass
SOST
Ceded to China by Pakistan in 1963 (also claimed by India)
Aksai Chin
BALTIT
NORTHERN AREAS
GILGIT
K2
N
North-West Frontier Province
SAZIN
CHILAS
Line of Control 1972
Disputed
JAMMU AND KASHMIR
KASHMIR
SRINAGAR
TRIBAL AREAS
Indus River
KARAKORAM HIGHWAY
Azad Kashmir
CHINA
PAKISTAN
INDIA
To Islamabad
Pakistani Control
Indian Control
Chinese Control

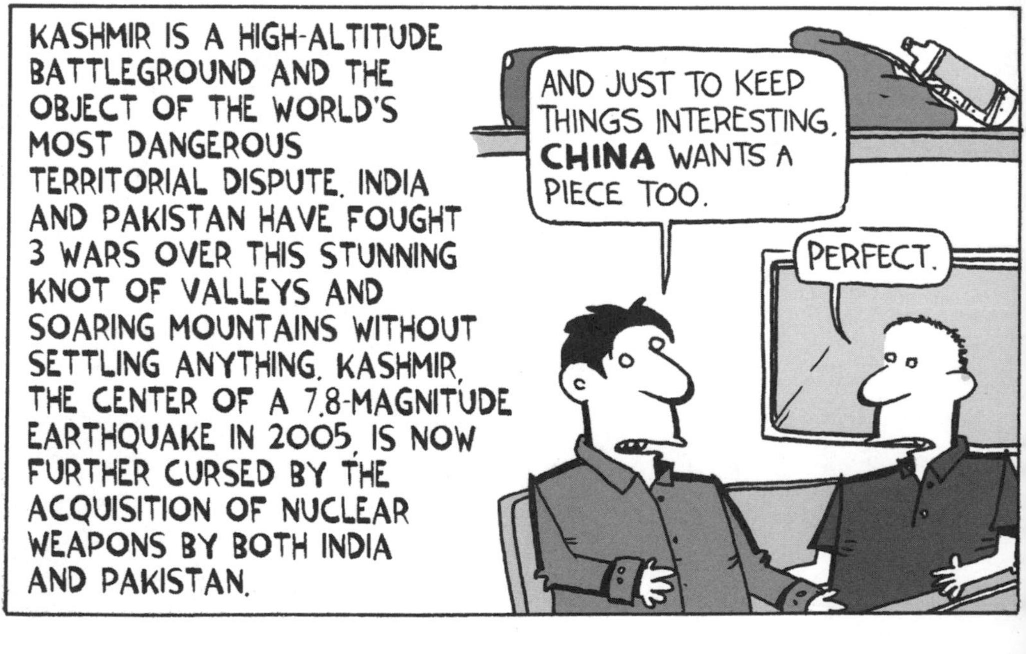
KASHMIR IS A HIGH-ALTITUDE BATTLEGROUND AND THE OBJECT OF THE WORLD'S MOST DANGEROUS TERRITORIAL DISPUTE. INDIA AND PAKISTAN HAVE FOUGHT 3 WARS OVER THIS STUNNING KNOT OF VALLEYS AND SOARING MOUNTAINS WITHOUT SETTLING ANYTHING. KASHMIR, THE CENTER OF A 7.8-MAGNITUDE EARTHQUAKE IN 2005, IS NOW FURTHER CURSED BY THE ACQUISITION OF NUCLEAR WEAPONS BY BOTH INDIA AND PAKISTAN.
AND JUST TO KEEP THINGS INTERESTING, CHINA WANTS A PIECE TOO.
PERFECT.

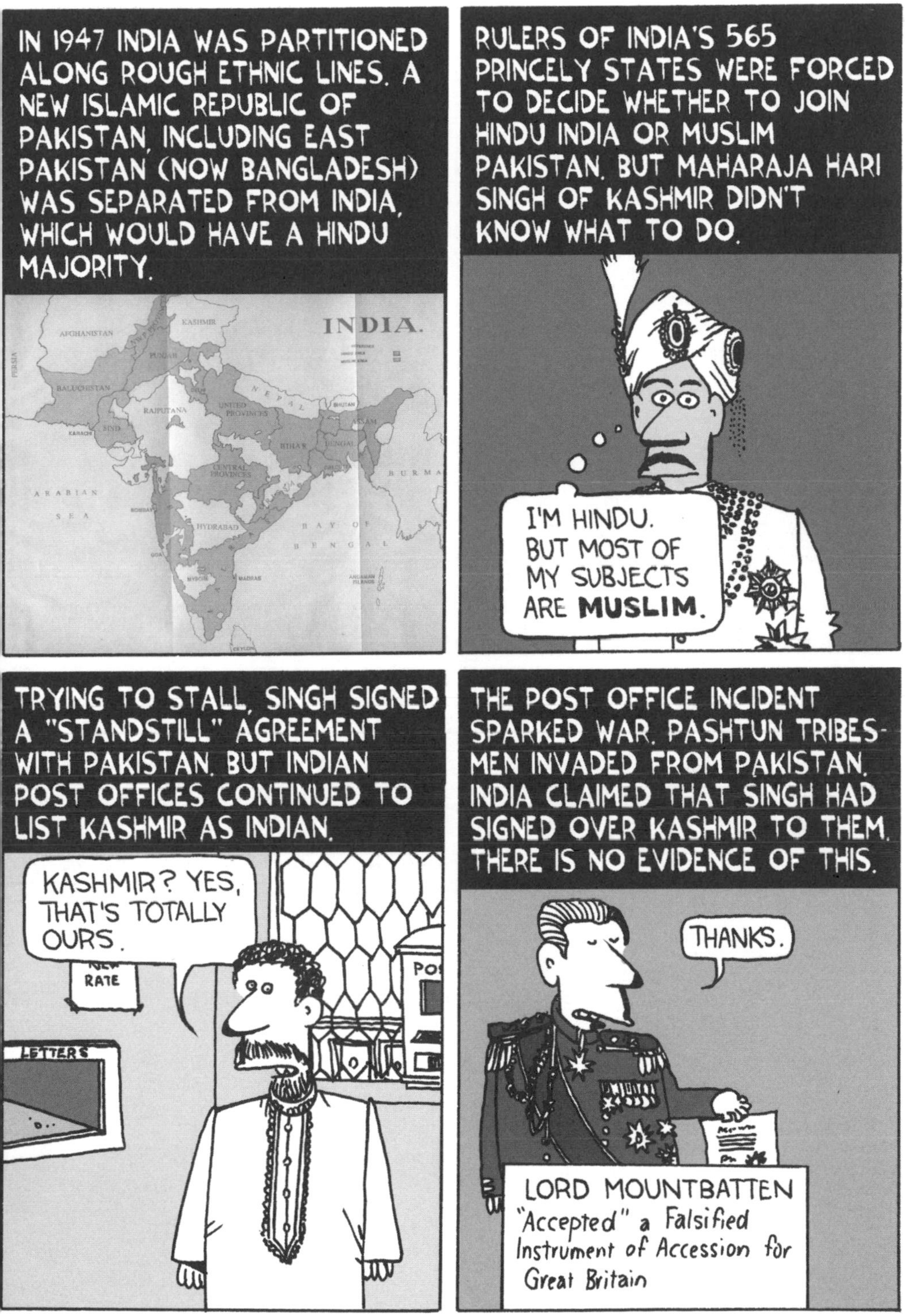
IN 1947 INDIA WAS PARTITIONED ALONG ROUGH ETHNIC LINES. A NEW ISLAMIC REPUBLIC OF PAKISTAN, INCLUDING EAST PAKISTAN (NOW BANGLADESH) WAS SEPARATED FROM INDIA, WHICH WOULD HAVE A HINDU MAJORITY.
INDIA.
AFGHANISTAN
KASHMIR
PUNJAB
BALUCHISTAN
NEPAL
RAJPUTANA
UNITED PROVINCES
SIND
BIHAR
BENGAL
CENTRAL PROVINCES
BURMA
ARABIAN SEA
HYDRABAD
BAY OF BENGAL
RULERS OF INDIA'S 565 PRINCELY STATES WERE FORCED TO DECIDE WHETHER TO JOIN HINDU INDIA OR MUSLIM PAKISTAN. BUT MAHARAJA HARI SINGH OF KASHMIR DIDN'T KNOW WHAT TO DO.
I'M HINDU. BUT MOST OF MY SUBJECTS ARE **MUSLIM**.
TRYING TO STALL, SINGH SIGNED A "STANDSTILL" AGREEMENT WITH PAKISTAN. BUT INDIAN POST OFFICES CONTINUED TO LIST KASHMIR AS INDIAN.
KASHMIR? YES, THAT'S TOTALLY OURS.
RATE
LETTERS
THE POST OFFICE INCIDENT SPARKED WAR. PASHTUN TRIBESMEN INVADED FROM PAKISTAN. INDIA CLAIMED THAT SINGH HAD SIGNED OVER KASHMIR TO THEM. THERE IS NO EVIDENCE OF THIS.
THANKS.
LORD MOUNTBATTEN
"Accepted" a Falsified Instrument of Accession for Great Britain

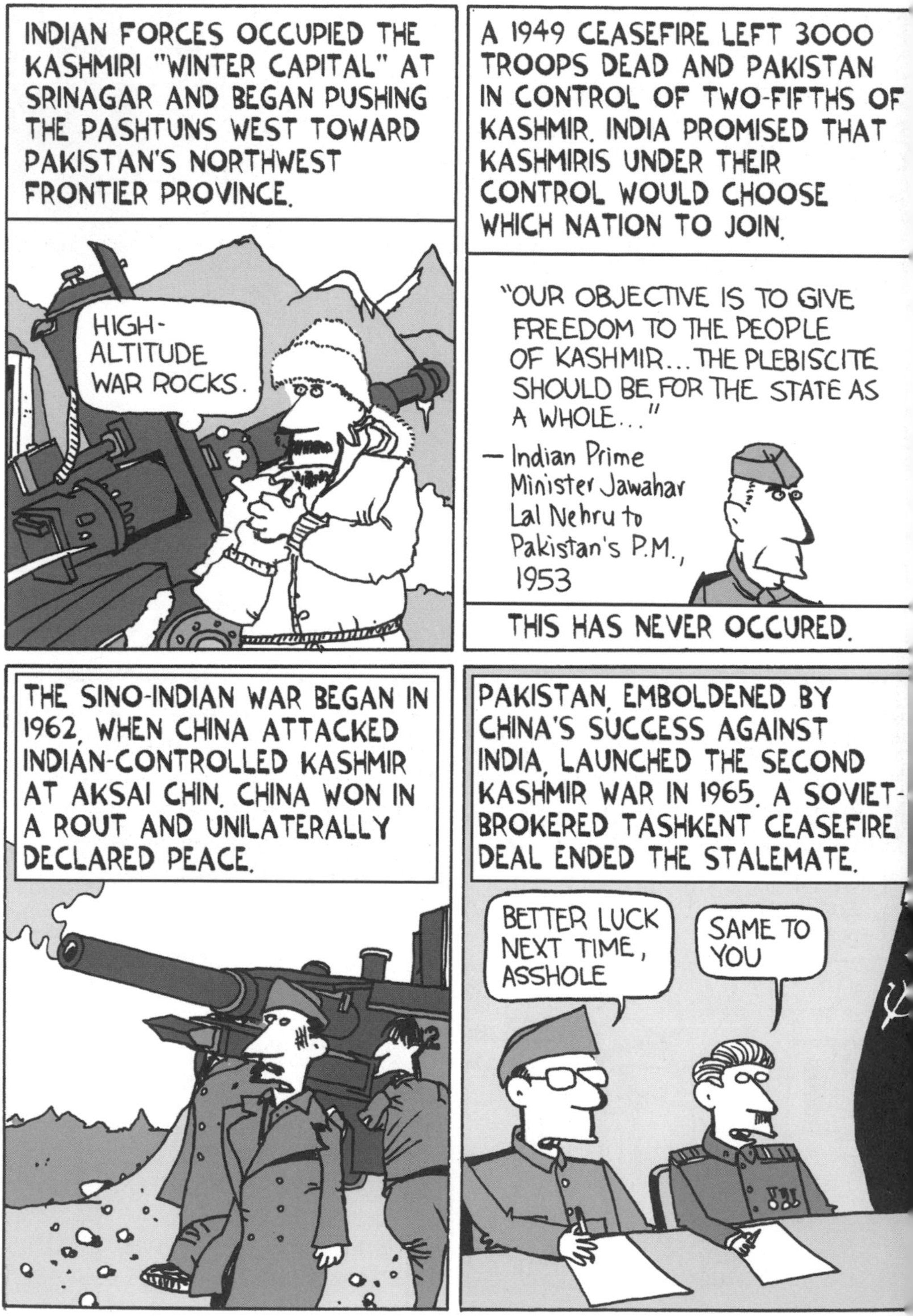
INDIAN FORCES OCCUPIED THE KASHMIRI "WINTER CAPITAL" AT SRINAGAR AND BEGAN PUSHING THE PASHTUNS WEST TOWARD PAKISTAN'S NORTHWEST FRONTIER PROVINCE.
HIGH-ALTITUDE WAR ROCKS.
A 1949 CEASEFIRE LEFT 3000 TROOPS DEAD AND PAKISTAN IN CONTROL OF TWO-FIFTHS OF KASHMIR. INDIA PROMISED THAT KASHMIRIS UNDER THEIR CONTROL WOULD CHOOSE WHICH NATION TO JOIN.
"OUR OBJECTIVE IS TO GIVE FREEDOM TO THE PEOPLE OF KASHMIR... THE PLEBISCITE SHOULD BE FOR THE STATE AS A WHOLE..."
— Indian Prime Minister Jawahar Lal Nehru to Pakistan's P.M., 1953
THIS HAS NEVER OCCURED.
THE SINO-INDIAN WAR BEGAN IN 1962, WHEN CHINA ATTACKED INDIAN-CONTROLLED KASHMIR AT AKSAI CHIN. CHINA WON IN A ROUT AND UNILATERALLY DECLARED PEACE.
PAKISTAN, EMBOLDENED BY CHINA'S SUCCESS AGAINST INDIA, LAUNCHED THE SECOND KASHMIR WAR IN 1965. A SOVIET-BROKERED TASHKENT CEASEFIRE DEAL ENDED THE STALEMATE.
BETTER LUCK NEXT TIME, ASSHOLE
SAME TO YOU

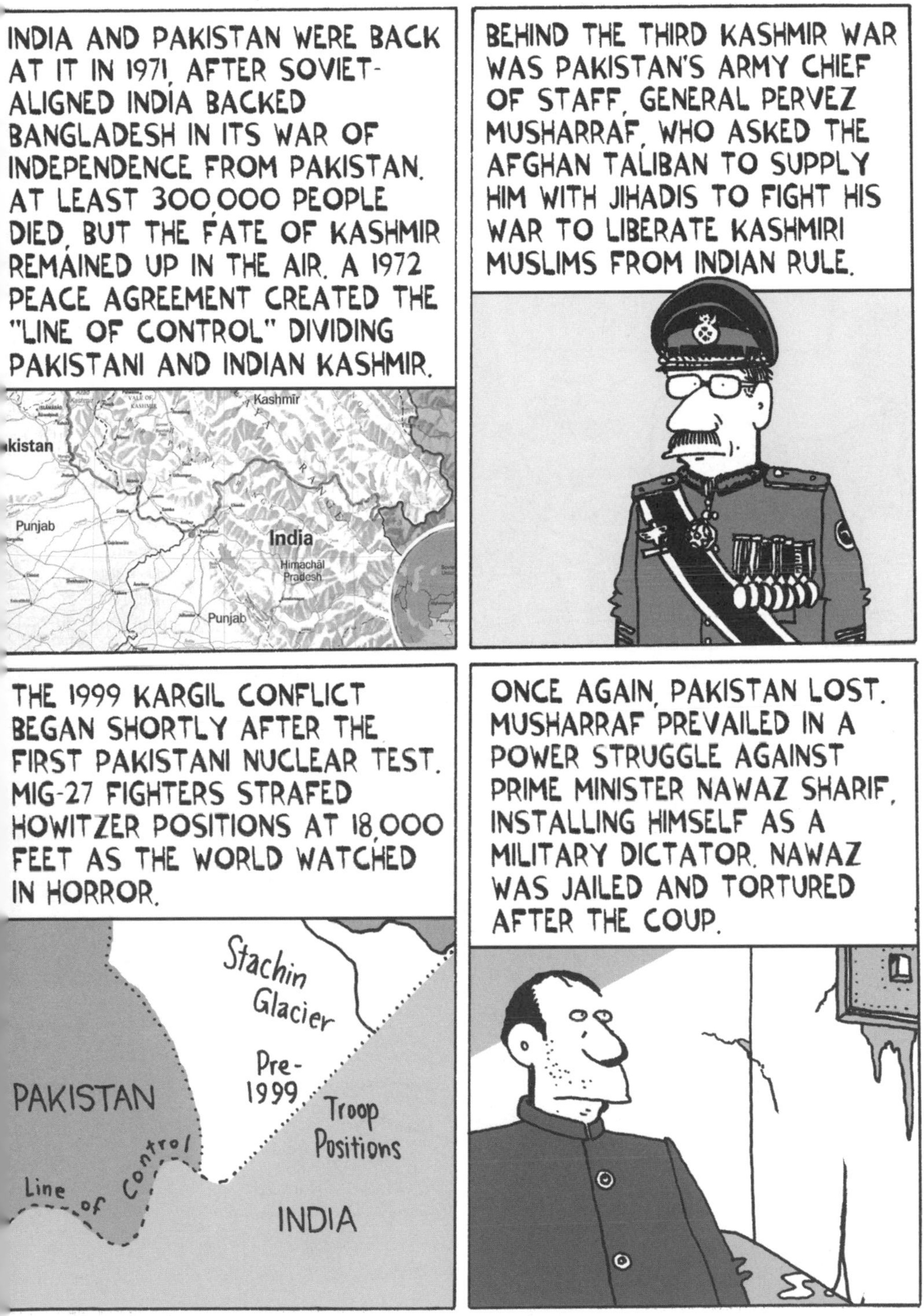
INDIA AND PAKISTAN WERE BACK AT IT IN 1971, AFTER SOVIET-ALIGNED INDIA BACKED BANGLADESH IN ITS WAR OF INDEPENDENCE FROM PAKISTAN. AT LEAST 300,000 PEOPLE DIED, BUT THE FATE OF KASHMIR REMAINED UP IN THE AIR. A 1972 PEACE AGREEMENT CREATED THE "LINE OF CONTROL" DIVIDING PAKISTANI AND INDIAN KASHMIR.
Kashmīr
kistan
Punjab
India
Himachal Pradesh
Punjab
BEHIND THE THIRD KASHMIR WAR WAS PAKISTAN'S ARMY CHIEF OF STAFF, GENERAL PERVEZ MUSHARRAF, WHO ASKED THE AFGHAN TALIBAN TO SUPPLY HIM WITH JIHADIS TO FIGHT HIS WAR TO LIBERATE KASHMIRI MUSLIMS FROM INDIAN RULE.
THE 1999 KARGIL CONFLICT BEGAN SHORTLY AFTER THE FIRST PAKISTANI NUCLEAR TEST. MIG-27 FIGHTERS STRAFED HOWITZER POSITIONS AT 18,000 FEET AS THE WORLD WATCHED IN HORROR.
Stachin Glacier
Pre-1999 Troop Positions
PAKISTAN
Line of Control
INDIA
ONCE AGAIN, PAKISTAN LOST. MUSHARRAF PREVAILED IN A POWER STRUGGLE AGAINST PRIME MINISTER NAWAZ SHARIF, INSTALLING HIMSELF AS A MILITARY DICTATOR. NAWAZ WAS JAILED AND TORTURED AFTER THE COUP.

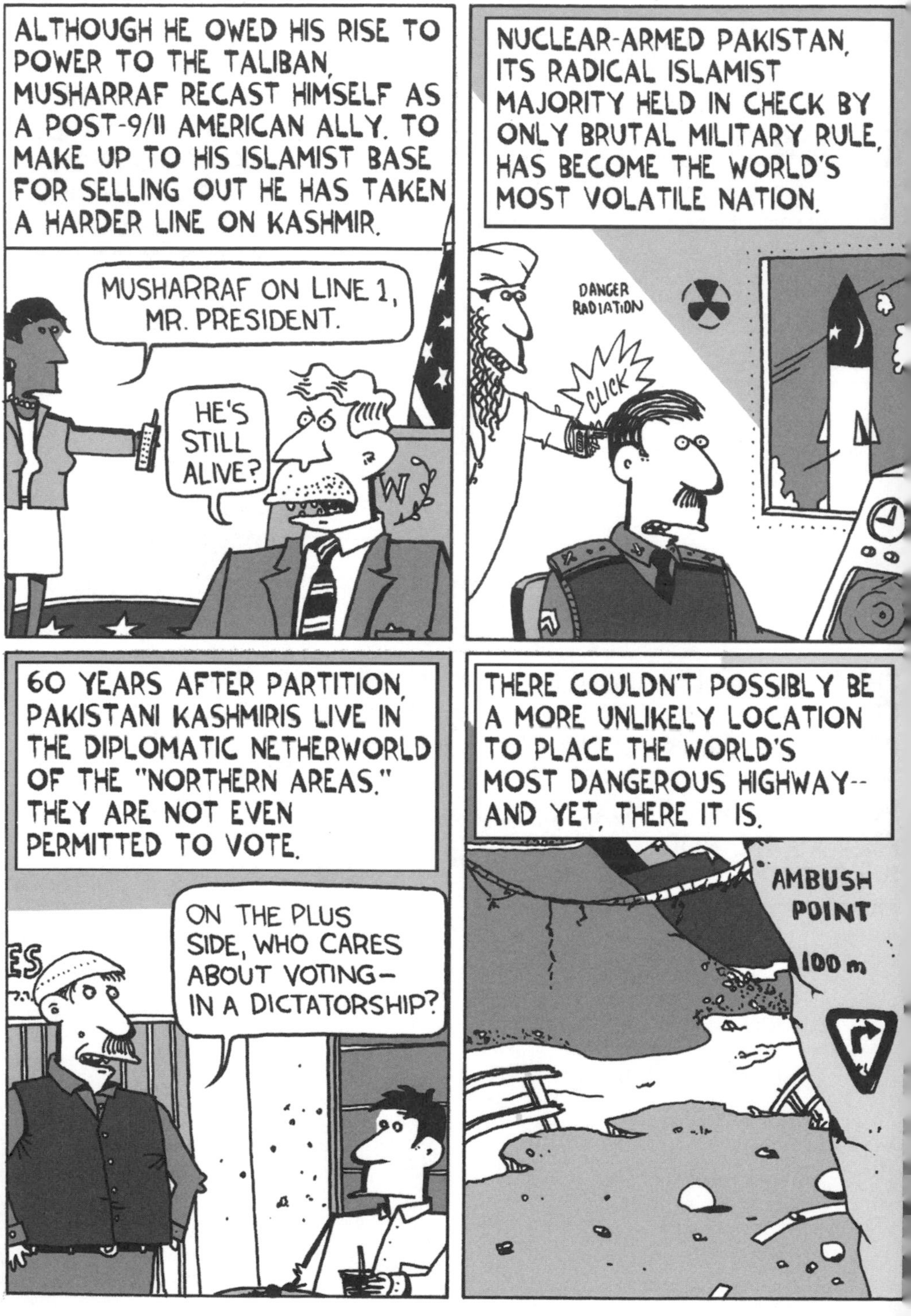
ALTHOUGH HE OWED HIS RISE TO POWER TO THE TALIBAN, MUSHARRAF RECAST HIMSELF AS A POST-9/11 AMERICAN ALLY. TO MAKE UP TO HIS ISLAMIST BASE FOR SELLING OUT HE HAS TAKEN A HARDER LINE ON KASHMIR.
MUSHARRAF ON LINE 1, MR. PRESIDENT.
HE'S STILL ALIVE?
W
NUCLEAR-ARMED PAKISTAN, ITS RADICAL ISLAMIST MAJORITY HELD IN CHECK BY ONLY BRUTAL MILITARY RULE, HAS BECOME THE WORLD'S MOST VOLATILE NATION.
DANGER RADIATION
CLICK
60 YEARS AFTER PARTITION, PAKISTANI KASHMIRIS LIVE IN THE DIPLOMATIC NETHERWORLD OF THE "NORTHERN AREAS." THEY ARE NOT EVEN PERMITTED TO VOTE.
ON THE PLUS SIDE, WHO CARES ABOUT VOTING— IN A DICTATORSHIP?
THERE COULDN'T POSSIBLY BE A MORE UNLIKELY LOCATION TO PLACE THE WORLD'S MOST DANGEROUS HIGHWAY-- AND YET, THERE IT IS.
AMBUSH POINT
100 m

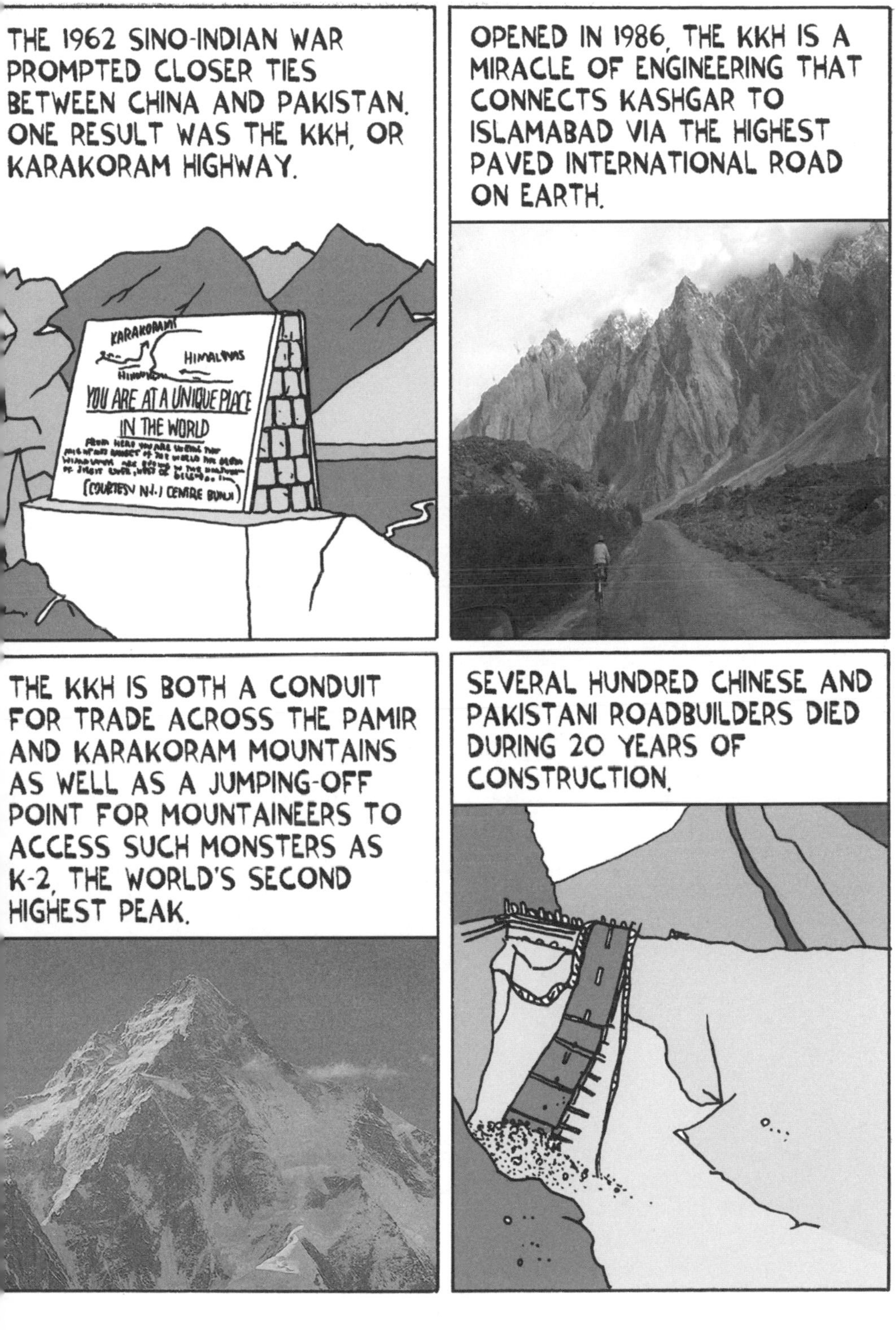
THE 1962 SINO-INDIAN WAR PROMPTED CLOSER TIES BETWEEN CHINA AND PAKISTAN. ONE RESULT WAS THE KKH, OR KARAKORAM HIGHWAY.
KARAKORAMS
HIMALAYAS
YOU ARE AT A UNIQUE PLACE
IN THE WORLD
OPENED IN 1986, THE KKH IS A MIRACLE OF ENGINEERING THAT CONNECTS KASHGAR TO ISLAMABAD VIA THE HIGHEST PAVED INTERNATIONAL ROAD ON EARTH.
THE KKH IS BOTH A CONDUIT FOR TRADE ACROSS THE PAMIR AND KARAKORAM MOUNTAINS AS WELL AS A JUMPING-OFF POINT FOR MOUNTAINEERS TO ACCESS SUCH MONSTERS AS K-2, THE WORLD'S SECOND HIGHEST PEAK.
SEVERAL HUNDRED CHINESE AND PAKISTANI ROADBUILDERS DIED DURING 20 YEARS OF CONSTRUCTION.

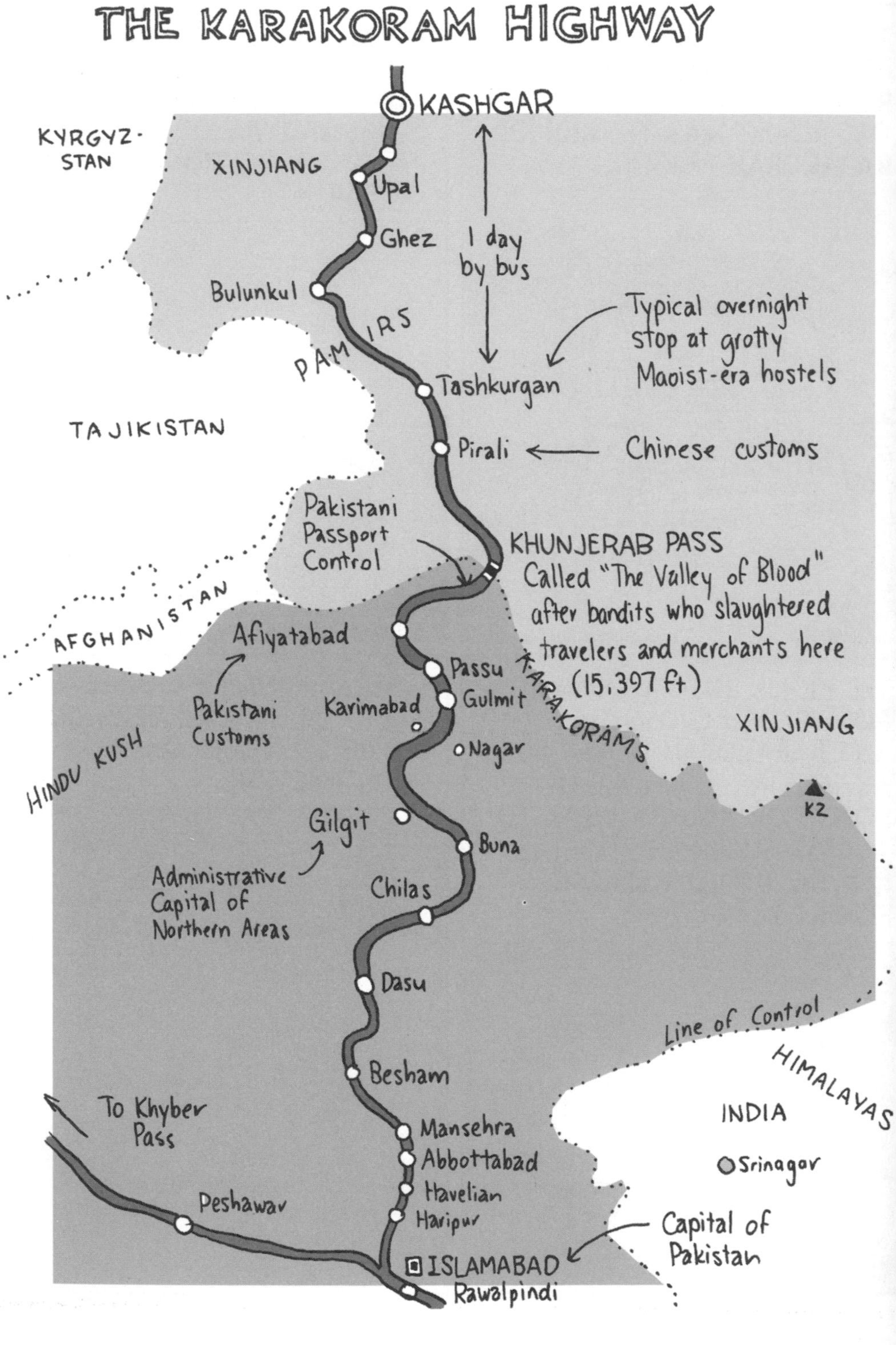
THE KARAKORAM HIGHWAY
KASHGAR
KYRGYZSTAN
XINJIANG
Upal
Ghez
1 day by bus
Bulunkul
PAMIRS
Typical overnight stop at grotty Maoist-era hostels
Tashkurgan
TAJIKISTAN
Pirali
Chinese customs
Pakistani Passport Control
KHUNJERAB PASS
Called "The Valley of Blood" after bandits who slaughtered travelers and merchants here (15,397 ft)
AFGHANISTAN
Afiyatabad
Pakistani Customs
Passu
Gulmit
Karimabad
KARAKORAMS
Nagar
XINJIANG
HINDU KUSH
K2
Gilgit
Administrative Capital of Northern Areas
Buna
Chilas
Dasu
Line of Control
Besham
HIMALAYAS
To Khyber Pass
Mansehra
INDIA
Abbottabad
Srinagar
Havelian
Peshawar
Haripur
Capital of Pakistan
ISLAMABAD
Rawalpindi

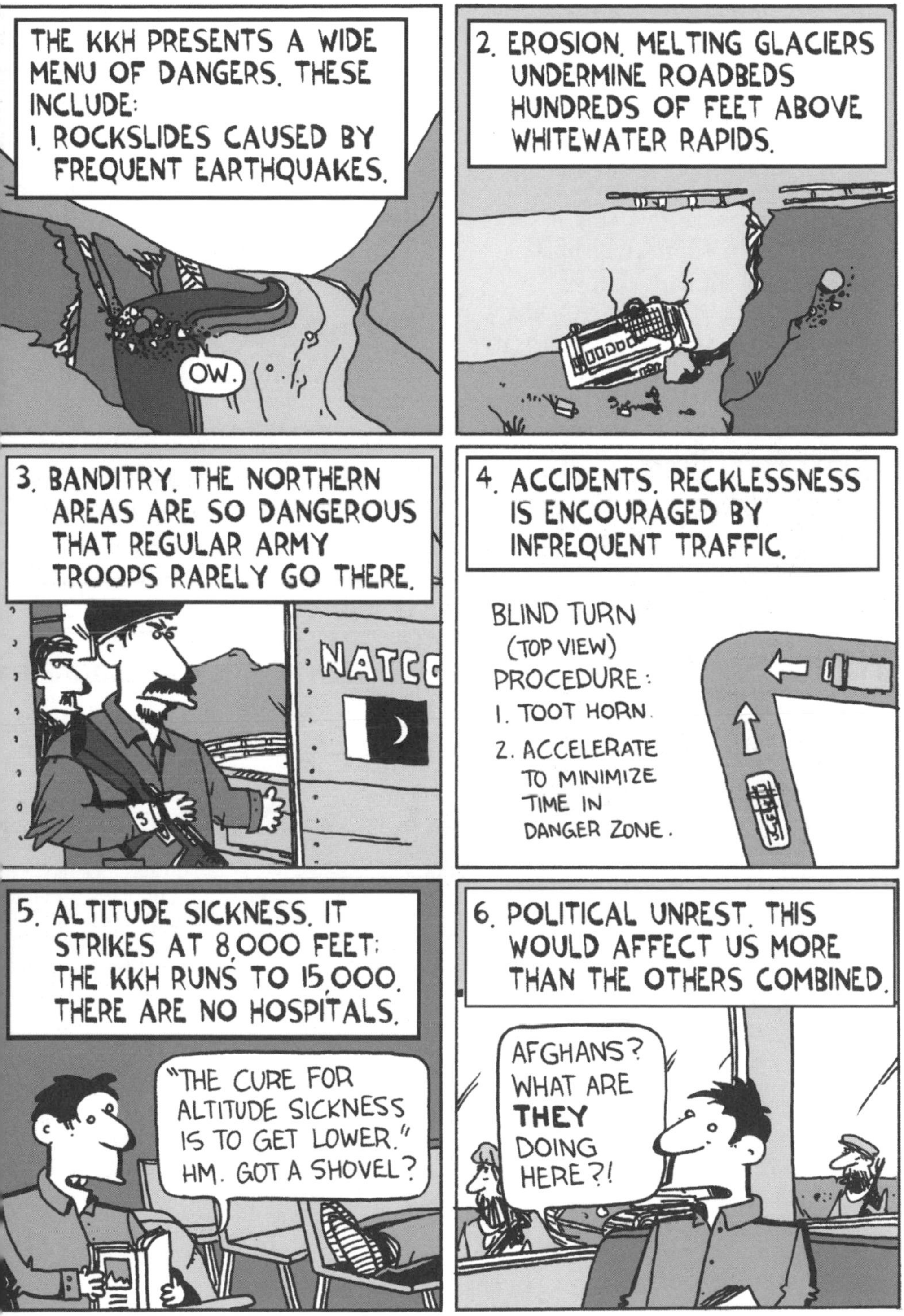
THE KKH PRESENTS A WIDE MENU OF DANGERS. THESE INCLUDE:
1. ROCKSLIDES CAUSED BY FREQUENT EARTHQUAKES.
OW.
2. EROSION. MELTING GLACIERS UNDERMINE ROADBEDS HUNDREDS OF FEET ABOVE WHITEWATER RAPIDS.
3. BANDITRY. THE NORTHERN AREAS ARE SO DANGEROUS THAT REGULAR ARMY TROOPS RARELY GO THERE.
NATCO
4. ACCIDENTS. RECKLESSNESS IS ENCOURAGED BY INFREQUENT TRAFFIC.
BLIND TURN
(TOP VIEW)
PROCEDURE:
1. TOOT HORN.
2. ACCELERATE TO MINIMIZE TIME IN DANGER ZONE.
5. ALTITUDE SICKNESS. IT STRIKES AT 8,000 FEET; THE KKH RUNS TO 15,000. THERE ARE NO HOSPITALS.
"THE CURE FOR ALTITUDE SICKNESS IS TO GET LOWER." HM. GOT A SHOVEL?
6. POLITICAL UNREST. THIS WOULD AFFECT US MORE THAN THE OTHERS COMBINED.
AFGHANS? WHAT ARE **THEY** DOING HERE?!

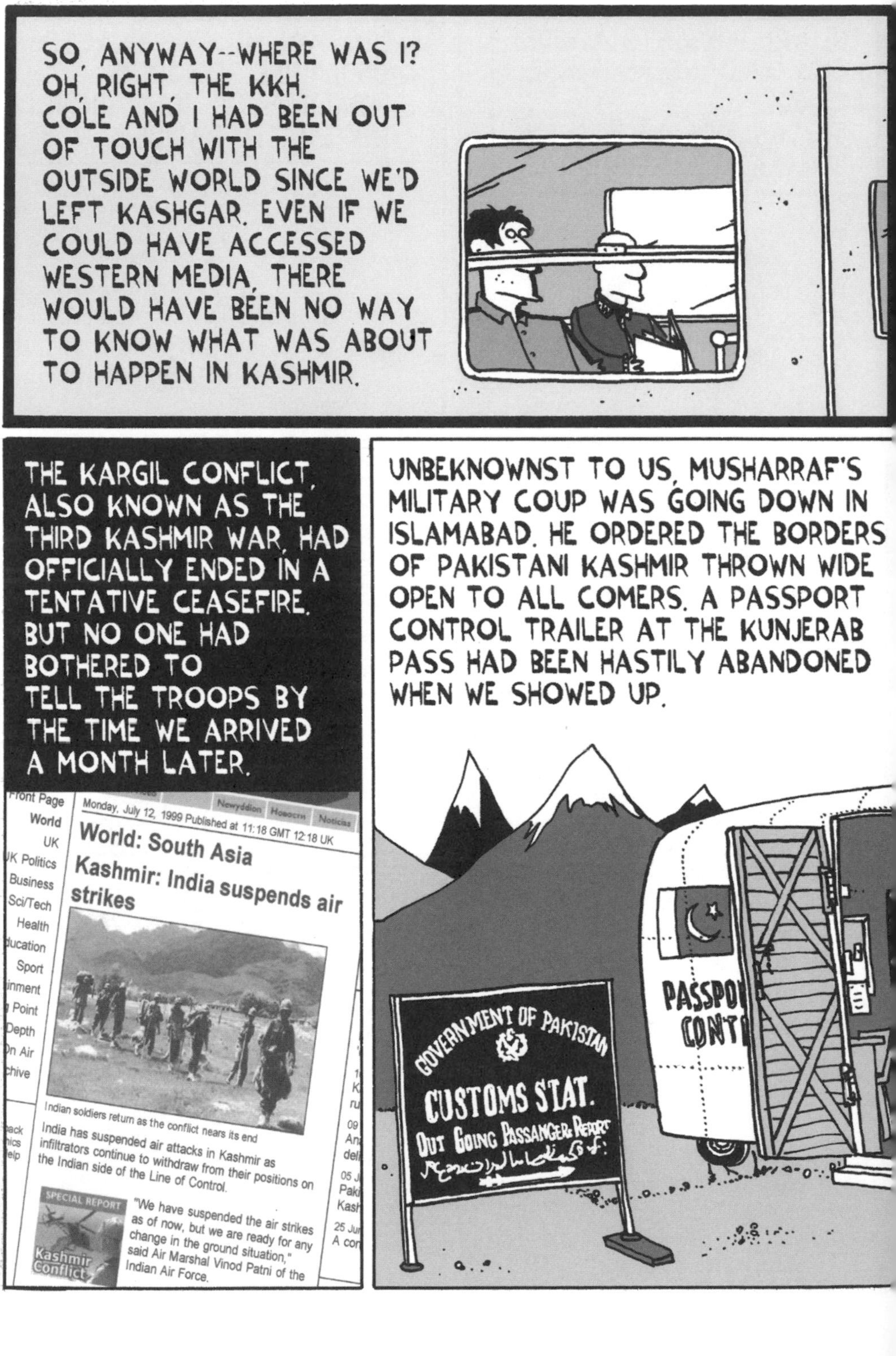
SO, ANYWAY--WHERE WAS I? OH, RIGHT, THE KKH. COLE AND I HAD BEEN OUT OF TOUCH WITH THE OUTSIDE WORLD SINCE WE'D LEFT KASHGAR. EVEN IF WE COULD HAVE ACCESSED WESTERN MEDIA, THERE WOULD HAVE BEEN NO WAY TO KNOW WHAT WAS ABOUT TO HAPPEN IN KASHMIR.
THE KARGIL CONFLICT, ALSO KNOWN AS THE THIRD KASHMIR WAR, HAD OFFICIALLY ENDED IN A TENTATIVE CEASEFIRE. BUT NO ONE HAD BOTHERED TO TELL THE TROOPS BY THE TIME WE ARRIVED A MONTH LATER.
Front Page
World
UK
UK Politics
Business
Sci/Tech
Health
Sport
Monday, July 12, 1999 Published at 11:18 GMT 12:18 UK
World: South Asia
Kashmir: India suspends air strikes
Indian soldiers return as the conflict nears its end
India has suspended air attacks in Kashmir as infiltrators continue to withdraw from their positions on the Indian side of the Line of Control.
SPECIAL REPORT
Kashmir Conflict
"We have suspended the air strikes as of now, but we are ready for any change in the ground situation," said Air Marshal Vinod Patni of the Indian Air Force.
UNBEKNOWNST TO US, MUSHARRAF'S MILITARY COUP WAS GOING DOWN IN ISLAMABAD. HE ORDERED THE BORDERS OF PAKISTANI KASHMIR THROWN WIDE OPEN TO ALL COMERS. A PASSPORT CONTROL TRAILER AT THE KUNJERAB PASS HAD BEEN HASTILY ABANDONED WHEN WE SHOWED UP.
GOVERNMENT OF PAKISTAN
CUSTOMS STAT.
OUT GOING PASSANGER REPORT

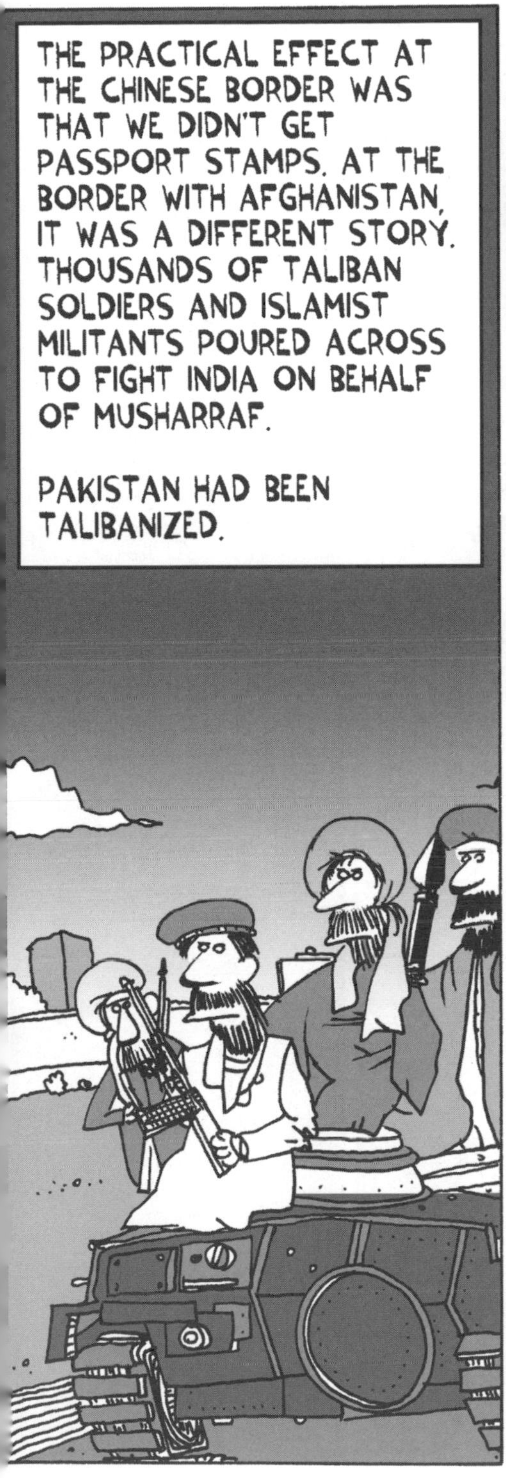
THE PRACTICAL EFFECT AT THE CHINESE BORDER WAS THAT WE DIDN'T GET PASSPORT STAMPS. AT THE BORDER WITH AFGHANISTAN, IT WAS A DIFFERENT STORY. THOUSANDS OF TALIBAN SOLDIERS AND ISLAMIST MILITANTS POURED ACROSS TO FIGHT INDIA ON BEHALF OF MUSHARRAF.
PAKISTAN HAD BEEN TALIBANIZED.

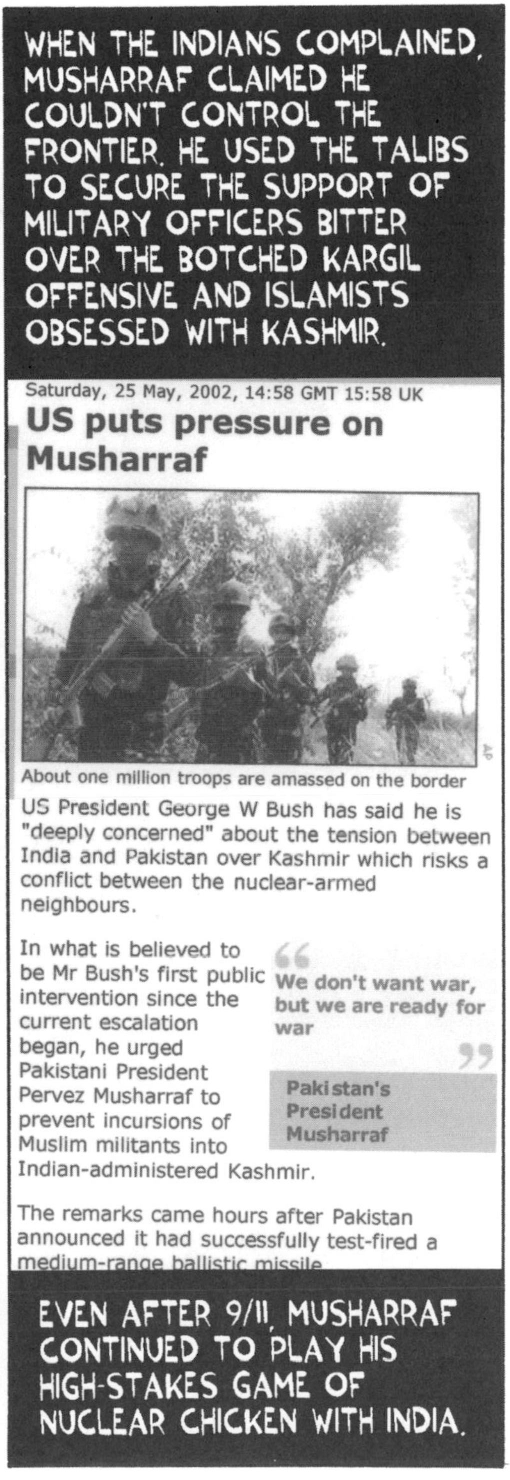
WHEN THE INDIANS COMPLAINED, MUSHARRAF CLAIMED HE COULDN'T CONTROL THE FRONTIER. HE USED THE TALIBS TO SECURE THE SUPPORT OF MILITARY OFFICERS BITTER OVER THE BOTCHED KARGIL OFFENSIVE AND ISLAMISTS OBSESSED WITH KASHMIR.
EVEN AFTER 9/11, MUSHARRAF CONTINUED TO PLAY HIS HIGH-STAKES GAME OF NUCLEAR CHICKEN WITH INDIA.

Saturday, 25 May, 2002, 14:58 GMT 15:58 UK

US puts pressure on Musharraf

About one million troops are amassed on the border

US President George W Bush has said he is "deeply concerned" about the tension between India and Pakistan over Kashmir which risks a conflict between the nuclear-armed neighbours.

In what is believed to be Mr Bush's first public intervention since the current escalation began, he urged Pakistani President Pervez Musharraf to prevent incursions of Muslim militants into Indian-administered Kashmir.

> **"We don't want war, but we are ready for war"**
> **Pakistan's President Musharraf**

The remarks came hours after Pakistan announced it had successfully test-fired a medium-range ballistic missile

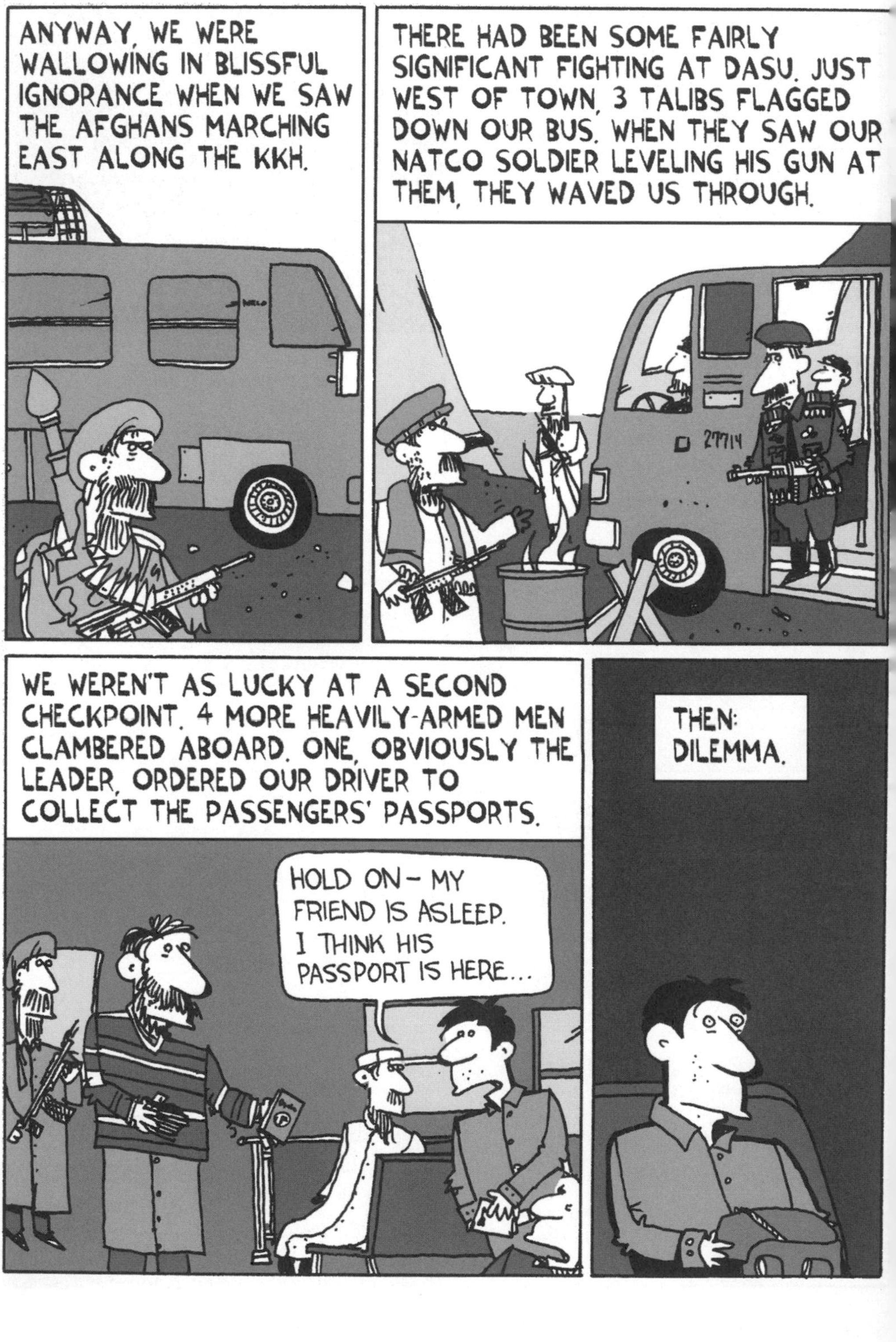
ANYWAY, WE WERE WALLOWING IN BLISSFUL IGNORANCE WHEN WE SAW THE AFGHANS MARCHING EAST ALONG THE KKH.
THERE HAD BEEN SOME FAIRLY SIGNIFICANT FIGHTING AT DASU. JUST WEST OF TOWN, 3 TALIBS FLAGGED DOWN OUR BUS. WHEN THEY SAW OUR NATCO SOLDIER LEVELING HIS GUN AT THEM, THEY WAVED US THROUGH.
WE WEREN'T AS LUCKY AT A SECOND CHECKPOINT. 4 MORE HEAVILY-ARMED MEN CLAMBERED ABOARD. ONE, OBVIOUSLY THE LEADER, ORDERED OUR DRIVER TO COLLECT THE PASSENGERS' PASSPORTS.
HOLD ON – MY FRIEND IS ASLEEP. I THINK HIS PASSPORT IS HERE...
THEN: DILEMMA.

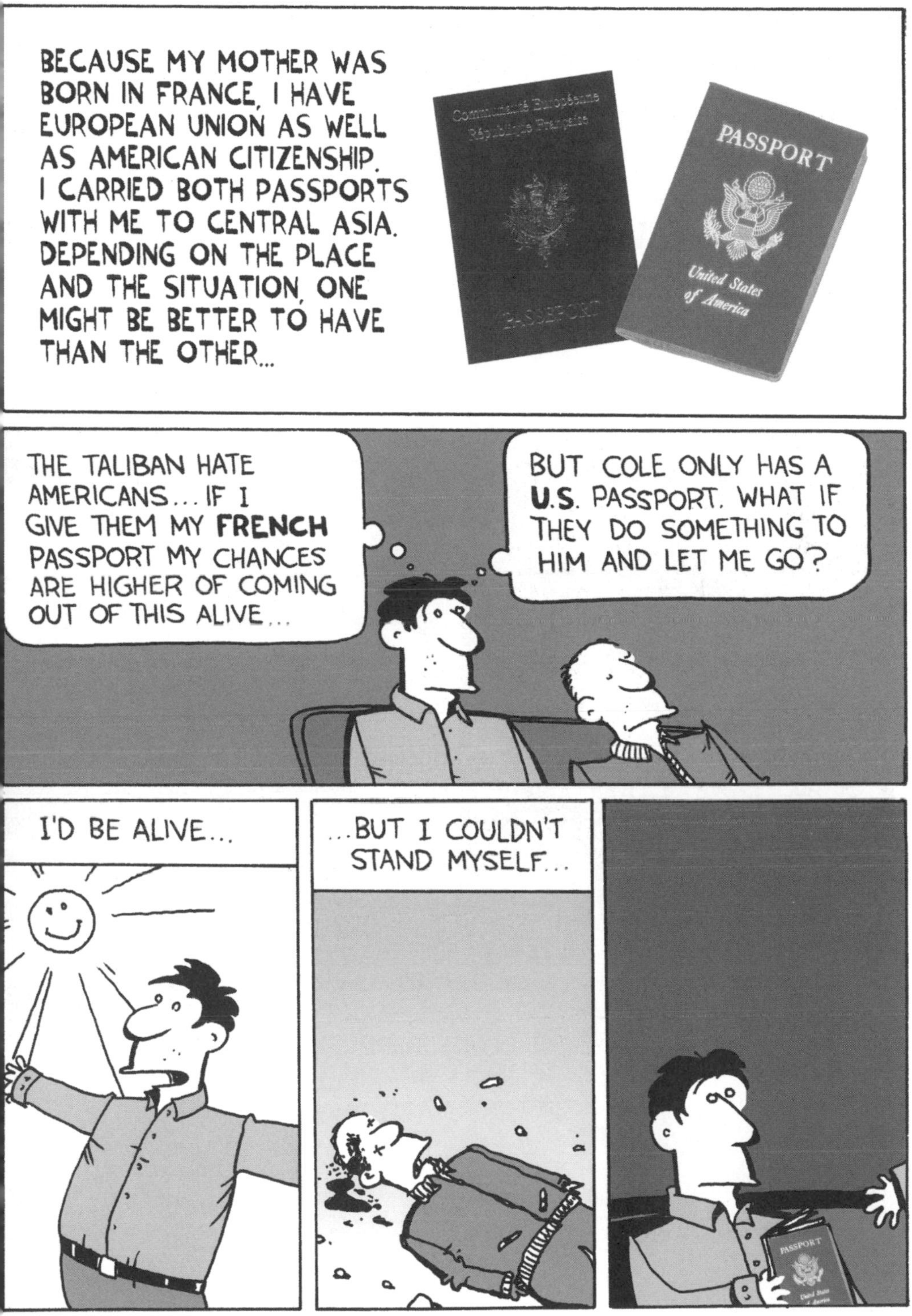
BECAUSE MY MOTHER WAS BORN IN FRANCE, I HAVE EUROPEAN UNION AS WELL AS AMERICAN CITIZENSHIP. I CARRIED BOTH PASSPORTS WITH ME TO CENTRAL ASIA. DEPENDING ON THE PLACE AND THE SITUATION, ONE MIGHT BE BETTER TO HAVE THAN THE OTHER...
Communauté Européenne
République Française
PASSPORT
PASSPORT
United States of America
THE TALIBAN HATE AMERICANS... IF I GIVE THEM MY FRENCH PASSPORT MY CHANCES ARE HIGHER OF COMING OUT OF THIS ALIVE...
BUT COLE ONLY HAS A U.S. PASSPORT. WHAT IF THEY DO SOMETHING TO HIM AND LET ME GO?
I'D BE ALIVE...
...BUT I COULDN'T STAND MYSELF...
PASSPORT

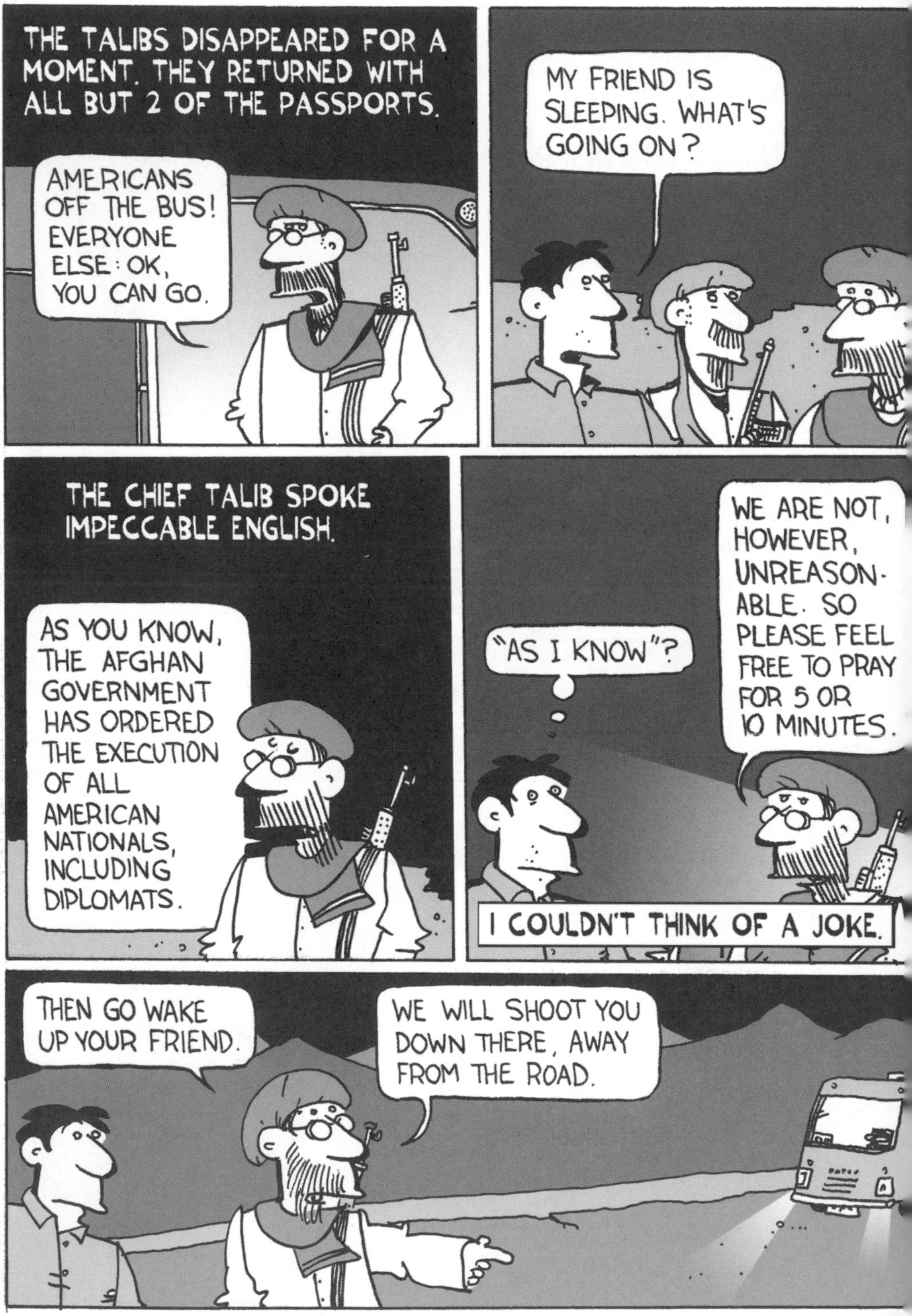
THE TALIBS DISAPPEARED FOR A MOMENT. THEY RETURNED WITH ALL BUT 2 OF THE PASSPORTS.
AMERICANS OFF THE BUS! EVERYONE ELSE: OK, YOU CAN GO.
MY FRIEND IS SLEEPING. WHAT'S GOING ON?
THE CHIEF TALIB SPOKE IMPECCABLE ENGLISH.
AS YOU KNOW, THE AFGHAN GOVERNMENT HAS ORDERED THE EXECUTION OF ALL AMERICAN NATIONALS, INCLUDING DIPLOMATS.
"AS I KNOW"?
WE ARE NOT, HOWEVER, UNREASON-ABLE. SO PLEASE FEEL FREE TO PRAY FOR 5 OR 10 MINUTES.
I COULDN'T THINK OF A JOKE.
THEN GO WAKE UP YOUR FRIEND.
WE WILL SHOOT YOU DOWN THERE, AWAY FROM THE ROAD.

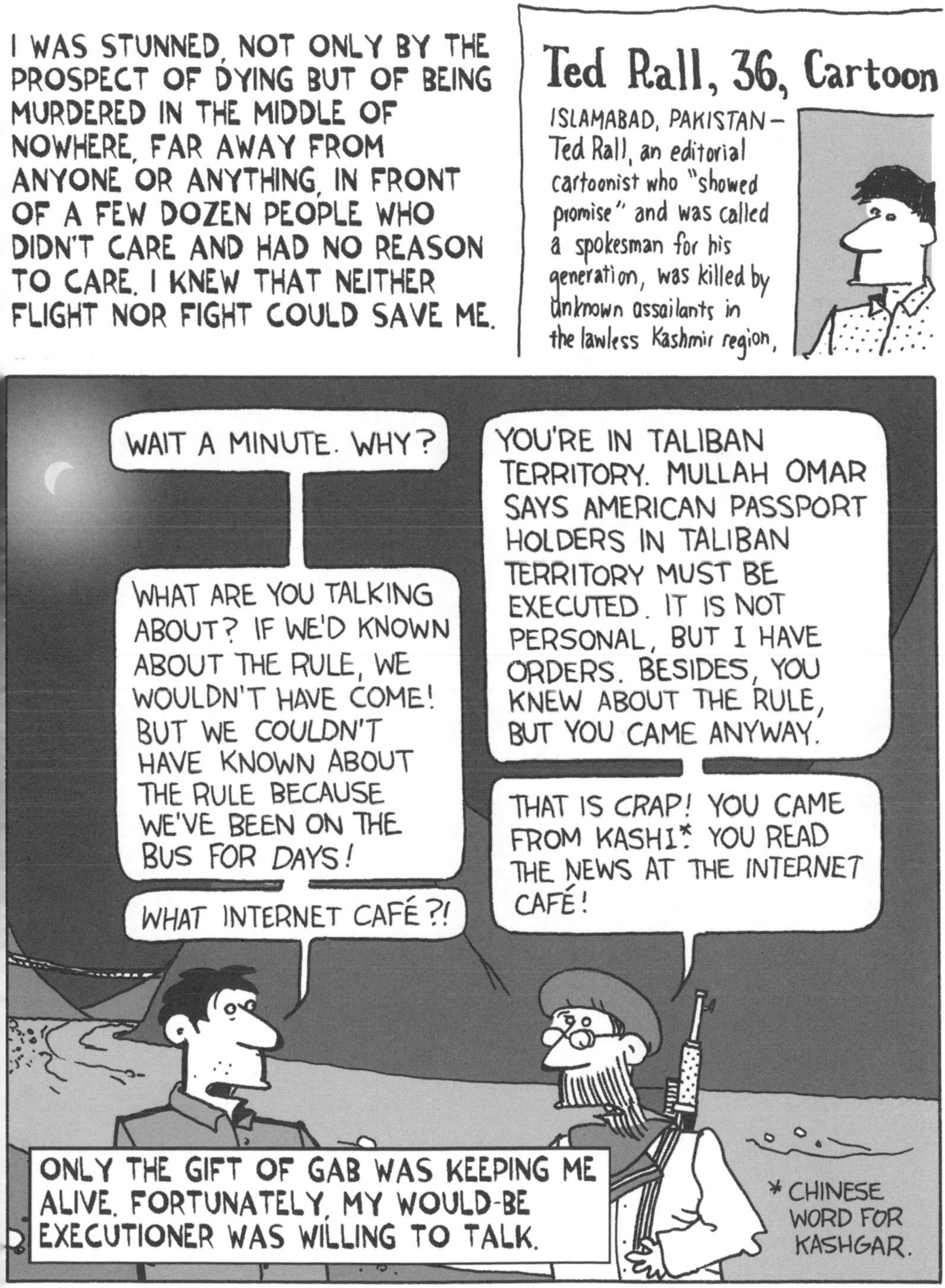
I WAS STUNNED, NOT ONLY BY THE PROSPECT OF DYING BUT OF BEING MURDERED IN THE MIDDLE OF NOWHERE, FAR AWAY FROM ANYONE OR ANYTHING, IN FRONT OF A FEW DOZEN PEOPLE WHO DIDN'T CARE AND HAD NO REASON TO CARE. I KNEW THAT NEITHER FLIGHT NOR FIGHT COULD SAVE ME.
Ted Rall, 36, Cartoon
ISLAMABAD, PAKISTAN— Ted Rall, an editorial cartoonist who "showed promise" and was called a spokesman for his generation, was killed by unknown assailants in the lawless Kashmir region,
WAIT A MINUTE. WHY?
YOU'RE IN TALIBAN TERRITORY. MULLAH OMAR SAYS AMERICAN PASSPORT HOLDERS IN TALIBAN TERRITORY MUST BE EXECUTED. IT IS NOT PERSONAL, BUT I HAVE ORDERS. BESIDES, YOU KNEW ABOUT THE RULE, BUT YOU CAME ANYWAY.
WHAT ARE YOU TALKING ABOUT? IF WE'D KNOWN ABOUT THE RULE, WE WOULDN'T HAVE COME! BUT WE COULDN'T HAVE KNOWN ABOUT THE RULE BECAUSE WE'VE BEEN ON THE BUS FOR DAYS!
THAT IS CRAP! YOU CAME FROM KASHI.* YOU READ THE NEWS AT THE INTERNET CAFÉ!
WHAT INTERNET CAFÉ?!
ONLY THE GIFT OF GAB WAS KEEPING ME ALIVE. FORTUNATELY, MY WOULD-BE EXECUTIONER WAS WILLING TO TALK.
* CHINESE WORD FOR KASHGAR.

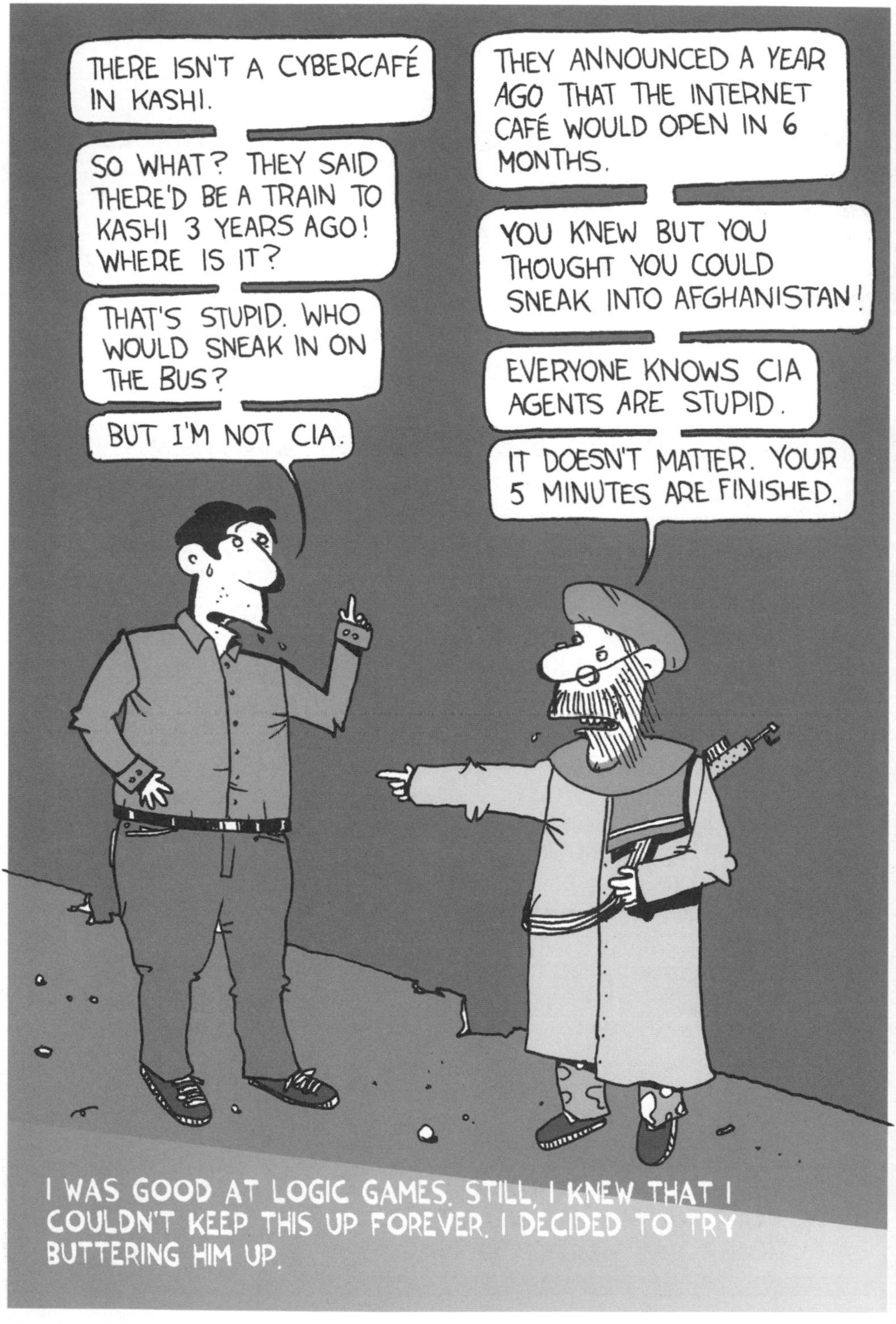
THERE ISN'T A CYBERCAFÉ IN KASHI.
THEY ANNOUNCED A YEAR AGO THAT THE INTERNET CAFÉ WOULD OPEN IN 6 MONTHS.
SO WHAT? THEY SAID THERE'D BE A TRAIN TO KASHI 3 YEARS AGO! WHERE IS IT?
YOU KNEW BUT YOU THOUGHT YOU COULD SNEAK INTO AFGHANISTAN!
THAT'S STUPID. WHO WOULD SNEAK IN ON THE BUS?
EVERYONE KNOWS CIA AGENTS ARE STUPID.
BUT I'M NOT CIA.
IT DOESN'T MATTER. YOUR 5 MINUTES ARE FINISHED.
I WAS GOOD AT LOGIC GAMES. STILL, I KNEW THAT I COULDN'T KEEP THIS UP FOREVER. I DECIDED TO TRY BUTTERING HIM UP.

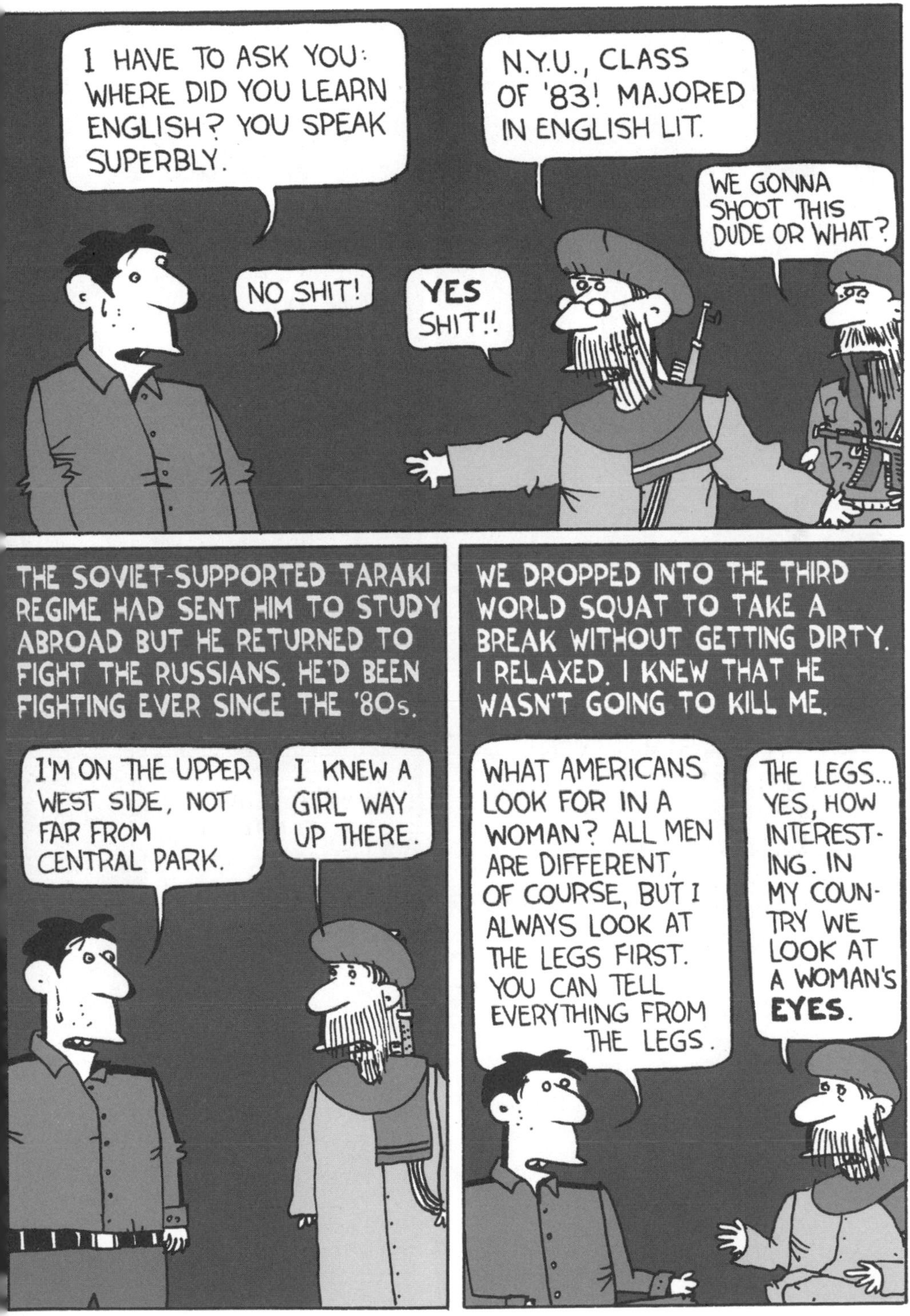
I HAVE TO ASK YOU: WHERE DID YOU LEARN ENGLISH? YOU SPEAK SUPERBLY.
N.Y.U., CLASS OF '83! MAJORED IN ENGLISH LIT.
WE GONNA SHOOT THIS DUDE OR WHAT?
NO SHIT!
YES SHIT!!
THE SOVIET-SUPPORTED TARAKI REGIME HAD SENT HIM TO STUDY ABROAD BUT HE RETURNED TO FIGHT THE RUSSIANS. HE'D BEEN FIGHTING EVER SINCE THE '80s.
I'M ON THE UPPER WEST SIDE, NOT FAR FROM CENTRAL PARK.
I KNEW A GIRL WAY UP THERE.
WE DROPPED INTO THE THIRD WORLD SQUAT TO TAKE A BREAK WITHOUT GETTING DIRTY. I RELAXED. I KNEW THAT HE WASN'T GOING TO KILL ME.
WHAT AMERICANS LOOK FOR IN A WOMAN? ALL MEN ARE DIFFERENT, OF COURSE, BUT I ALWAYS LOOK AT THE LEGS FIRST. YOU CAN TELL EVERYTHING FROM THE LEGS.
THE LEGS... YES, HOW INTEREST-ING. IN MY COUN-TRY WE LOOK AT A WOMAN'S EYES.

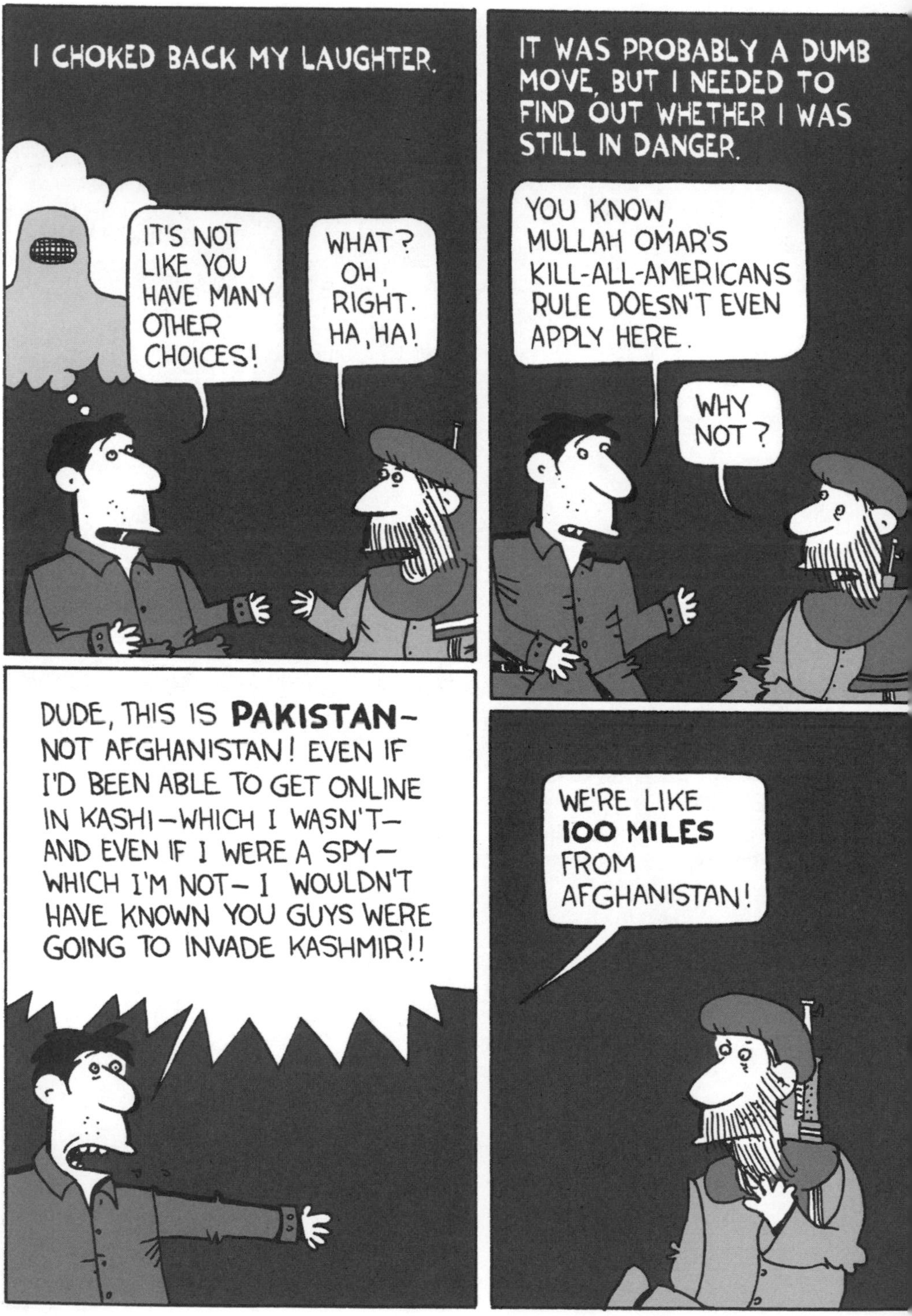
I CHOKED BACK MY LAUGHTER.
IT'S NOT LIKE YOU HAVE MANY OTHER CHOICES!
WHAT? OH, RIGHT. HA, HA!
IT WAS PROBABLY A DUMB MOVE, BUT I NEEDED TO FIND OUT WHETHER I WAS STILL IN DANGER.
YOU KNOW, MULLAH OMAR'S KILL-ALL-AMERICANS RULE DOESN'T EVEN APPLY HERE.
WHY NOT?
DUDE, THIS IS **PAKISTAN**—NOT AFGHANISTAN! EVEN IF I'D BEEN ABLE TO GET ONLINE IN KASHI—WHICH I WASN'T—AND EVEN IF I WERE A SPY—WHICH I'M NOT—I WOULDN'T HAVE KNOWN YOU GUYS WERE GOING TO INVADE KASHMIR!!
WE'RE LIKE **100 MILES** FROM AFGHANISTAN!

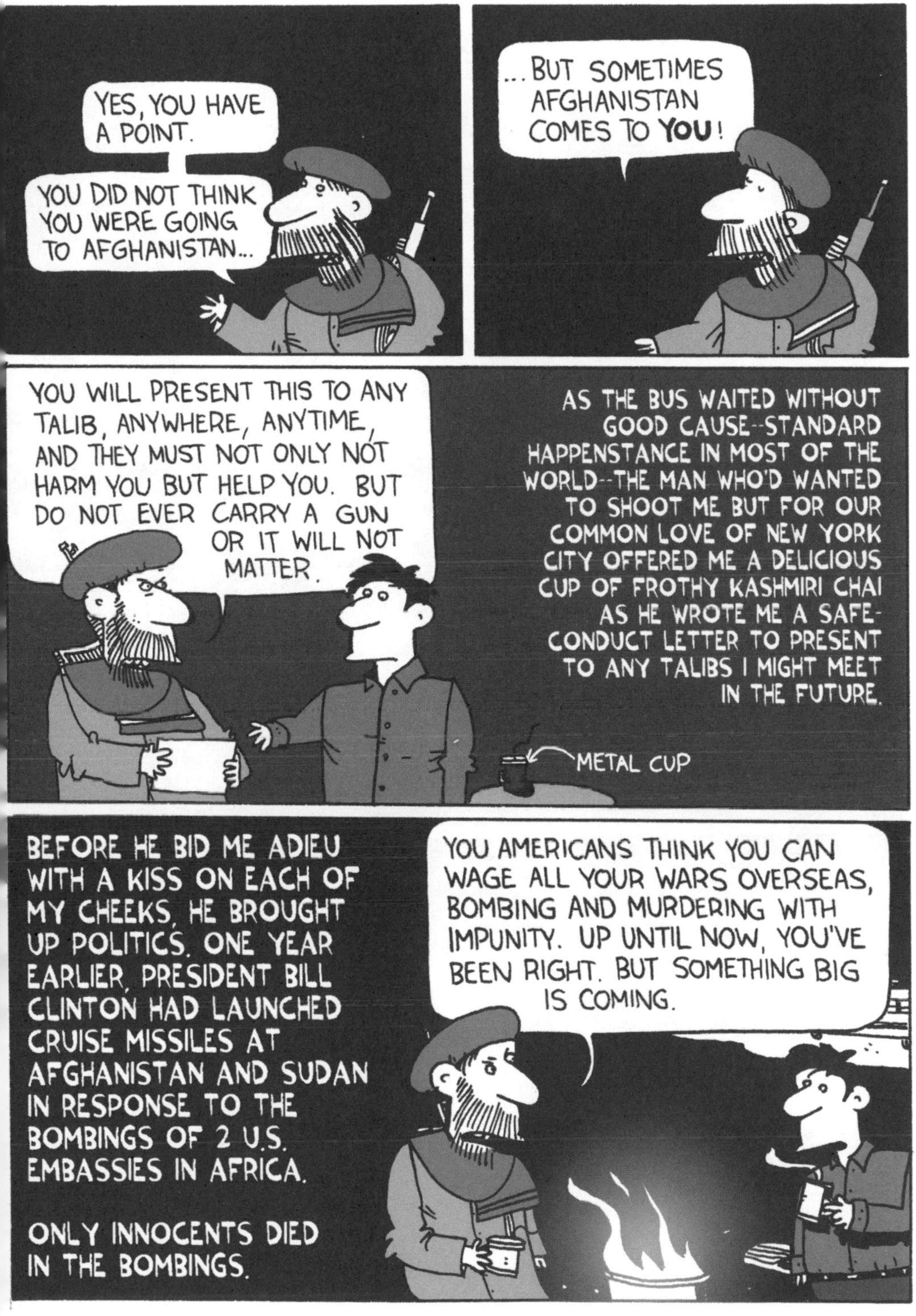
YES, YOU HAVE A POINT.
YOU DID NOT THINK YOU WERE GOING TO AFGHANISTAN...
...BUT SOMETIMES AFGHANISTAN COMES TO YOU!
YOU WILL PRESENT THIS TO ANY TALIB, ANYWHERE, ANYTIME, AND THEY MUST NOT ONLY NOT HARM YOU BUT HELP YOU. BUT DO NOT EVER CARRY A GUN OR IT WILL NOT MATTER.
AS THE BUS WAITED WITHOUT GOOD CAUSE--STANDARD HAPPENSTANCE IN MOST OF THE WORLD--THE MAN WHO'D WANTED TO SHOOT ME BUT FOR OUR COMMON LOVE OF NEW YORK CITY OFFERED ME A DELICIOUS CUP OF FROTHY KASHMIRI CHAI AS HE WROTE ME A SAFE-CONDUCT LETTER TO PRESENT TO ANY TALIBS I MIGHT MEET IN THE FUTURE.
METAL CUP
BEFORE HE BID ME ADIEU WITH A KISS ON EACH OF MY CHEEKS, HE BROUGHT UP POLITICS. ONE YEAR EARLIER, PRESIDENT BILL CLINTON HAD LAUNCHED CRUISE MISSILES AT AFGHANISTAN AND SUDAN IN RESPONSE TO THE BOMBINGS OF 2 U.S. EMBASSIES IN AFRICA.
ONLY INNOCENTS DIED IN THE BOMBINGS.
YOU AMERICANS THINK YOU CAN WAGE ALL YOUR WARS OVERSEAS, BOMBING AND MURDERING WITH IMPUNITY. UP UNTIL NOW, YOU'VE BEEN RIGHT. BUT SOMETHING BIG IS COMING.

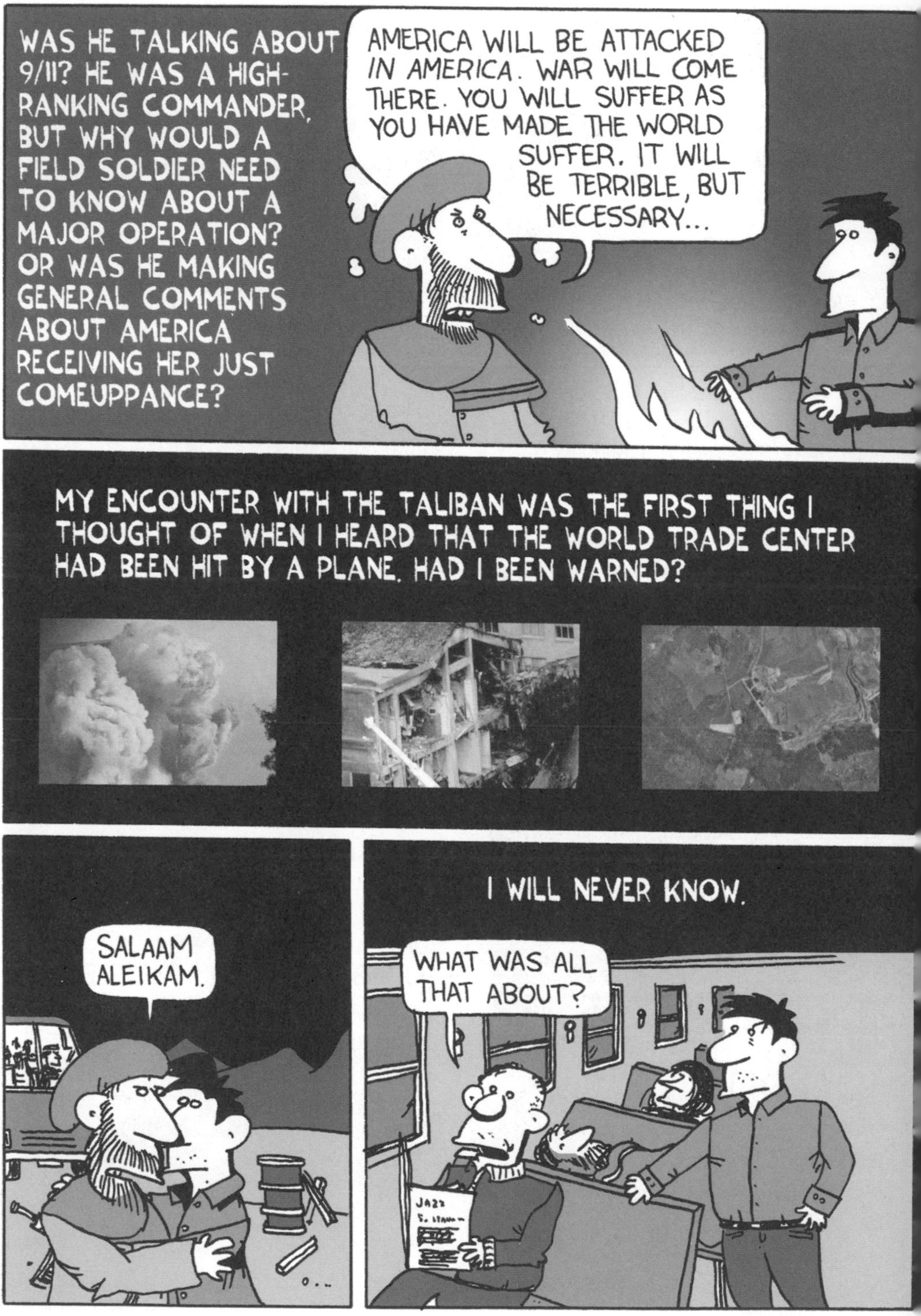
WAS HE TALKING ABOUT 9/11? HE WAS A HIGH-RANKING COMMANDER, BUT WHY WOULD A FIELD SOLDIER NEED TO KNOW ABOUT A MAJOR OPERATION? OR WAS HE MAKING GENERAL COMMENTS ABOUT AMERICA RECEIVING HER JUST COMEUPPANCE?
AMERICA WILL BE ATTACKED IN AMERICA. WAR WILL COME THERE. YOU WILL SUFFER AS YOU HAVE MADE THE WORLD SUFFER. IT WILL BE TERRIBLE, BUT NECESSARY...
MY ENCOUNTER WITH THE TALIBAN WAS THE FIRST THING I THOUGHT OF WHEN I HEARD THAT THE WORLD TRADE CENTER HAD BEEN HIT BY A PLANE. HAD I BEEN WARNED?
SALAAM ALEIKAM.
I WILL NEVER KNOW.
WHAT WAS ALL THAT ABOUT?

Radicals, Repression & Revolution

At the heart of Central Asia lies a cultural vacuum, which cannot be filled with imitations of Western culture.

—Ahmed Rashid, *Jihad: The Rise of Militant Islam in Central Asia*

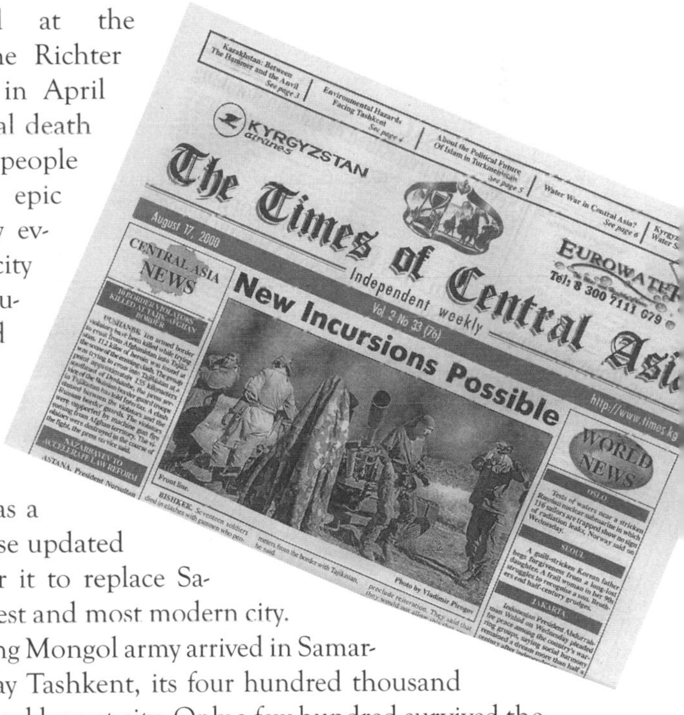

Kyrgyzstan airlines
The Times of Central Asia
Independent weekly
August 17, 2000
Central Asia News
New Incursions Possible
World News
Eurowatch

A earthquake estimated at the strength of 6.5 on the Richter scale struck Tashkent in April 1966. The relatively low official death toll—about two hundred people died—belies the earthquake's epic and catastrophic scale. Nearly every significant building in the city was destroyed, including Timurid mosques that had survived six centuries, setting the stage for one of the biggest reconstruction projects in Soviet history. The resulting new capital of the Uzbek S.S.R. was a rationally planned sprawl whose updated infrastructure set the stage for it to replace Samarkand as Central Asia's largest and most modern city. (When Genghis Khan's invading Mongol army arrived in Samarkand, just south of modern-day Tashkent, its four hundred thousand people lived in the world's second largest city. Only a few hundred survived the slaughter.) Unlike comparative backwaters such as Dushanbe and Bishkek, most international airlines serve Tashkent several times daily; you can even fly direct from New York. It's impossible to score a Tajik visa in neighboring Kyrgyzstan, but not in Tashkent—perhaps because Uzbekistan is the only Central Asian republic to border all the others, most of the world's nations supply consular representation to Tashkent's two million souls. Tashkent even has Central Asia's only subway system, one that rivals Moscow's for its design and efficiency.

Presiding over this relative jewel of Westernized civility is Uzbek President Islam Karimov, age sixty-eight, the militantly secular dictator who rules the region's most militarily aggressive and pervasive police state. If Turkmenbashi's personality cult tolerates no dissent, at least most of his political opponents rot in jail. Turkmen dissidents are even released on occasion. Uzbeks, on the other hand, know that it's smart to make funeral arrangements before badmouthing Karimov. Uzbek *militsia* have recently become renowned for boiling their prisoners to death. State television's hottest programming is its latest Stalinist-style show trial, wherein arrested unfortunates confess over-the-top crimes against the motherland and common decency before vanishing forevermore. Turkmen cops shake down travelers with the best of them but only in Uzbekistan can you rent a uniformed military police officer to drive you through checkpoints—and the checkpoints just keep coming, and coming—and coming.

The regime's foreign policy resembles America's. If it happens near Uzbekistan or it might be said to concern it in some unfathomable way, Karimov considers it Uzbekistan's business. Lately that's meant going after Islamic militants he views a threat, even taking a page from the doctrine of preemptive warfare by bombing Kyrgyz villages occupied by Tajikistan-based militants he judges to be a threat. Neighboring countries lodge protests and close their borders after such incidents, but everyone knows there isn't much they can do about it. "Uzbeks are our United

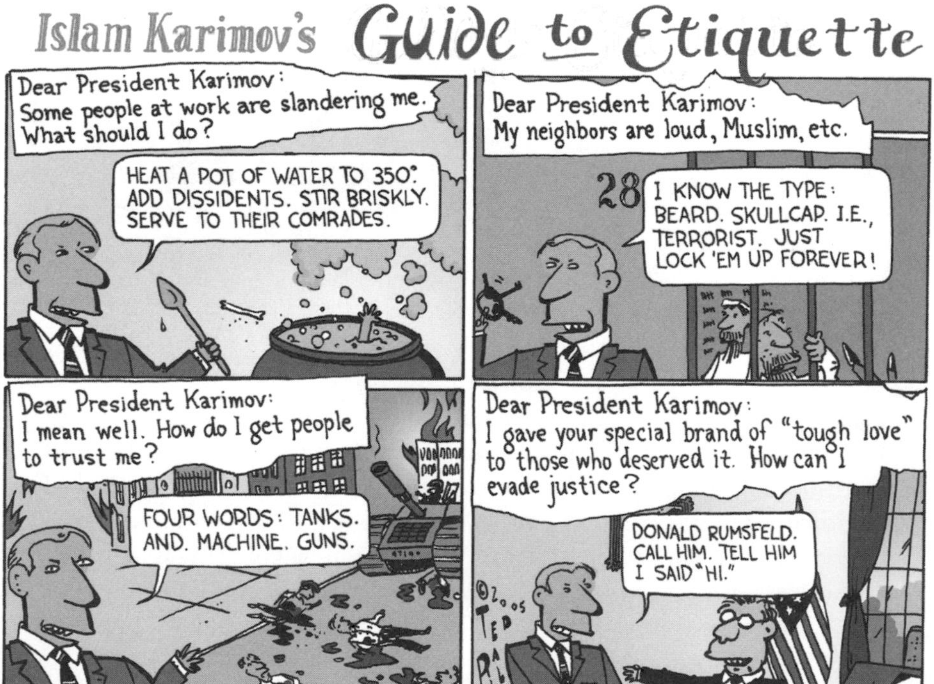
Islam Karimov's Guide to Etiquette
Dear President Karimov: Some people at work are slandering me. What should I do?
HEAT A POT OF WATER TO 350°. ADD DISSIDENTS. STIR BRISKLY. SERVE TO THEIR COMRADES.
Dear President Karimov: My neighbors are loud, Muslim, etc.
28
I KNOW THE TYPE: BEARD. SKULLCAP. I.E., TERRORIST. JUST LOCK 'EM UP FOREVER!
Dear President Karimov: I mean well. How do I get people to trust me?
FOUR WORDS: TANKS. AND. MACHINE. GUNS.
Dear President Karimov: I gave your special brand of "tough love" to those who deserved it. How can I evade justice?
DONALD RUMSFELD. CALL HIM. TELL HIM I SAID "HI."
©2005 TED RALL

The Miri Arab Madrassa in Bukhara. This 500-year-old Islamic theological school —one of the few in Central Asia to continue operating throughout Soviet rule—has been extensively restored and repaired during the last few decades.

States," a Tajik official sighed over tea one sunny spring day in Dushanbe. "They think they're the policemen of Central Asia." Uzbekistan is, after all, the proud proprietor of the blockbuster Silk Road cities of Khiva, Bukhara and Samarkand, which double as centers of commercial trade and sources of tourist revenues. It also has the region's largest standing army, presided over by a commander-in-chief who rarely hesitates to use it.

Karimov symbolizes the clash between post-Soviet authoritarianism and rising Islamic fundamentalism that appears destined to shape Central Asia for the foreseeable future.

Islam is a complicated subject in Central Asia. Ninety-five percent of the region's population self-identifies as Muslim. "Al-hamdulillah [praise be to Allah], I am a Muslim," most people will tell you when asked. Though it dates to the sweeping Turkic invasions of the eighth century, Central Asian Islam's historical roots—not only as Sunni but as part of the liberal Hanafi madhab subgenre of Sunniism—have made it a far more moderate strain than one finds in Saudi Arabia or Pakistan. Mountain shepherds traditionally consume *kumis*, fermented mare's milk. City dwellers don't shy away from vodka and other alcohol. The nomadic Kazakhs and Kyrgyz, while considering themselves Muslims, also view women as equals. Not only do they ride horses and dress as uncovered as men, they sometimes enjoy a sort of cultural superiority over men. In the traditional game "kiss the girl," for example, a woman of marrying age tests her suitors' ability to plant a kiss on her from horseback. She may refuse his advances using any means at her disposal, including unbelievable brutality. At a "kiss the girl" match in Almaty in 1997, I watched a one hundred forty-seven-time undefeated would-be bride slash a young man's eyes with her riding crop with the grim efficiency of a garbage collector. Likely blinded for life, the poor bastard had lasted fewer than thirty seconds. Alas, the yurt of love alongside the field of battle, reserved for consummation in the unlikely event of marriage following victory, remained empty another night.

All of Almaty was talking about her. "She is so beautiful and strong," a twenty-one-year-old swooned at an outdoor bar near a casino. "To be with such a woman is even worth one's eyes." Stupid, yes, but not spoken like a Wahhabiist.

Soviet Suppression, Post-Soviet Confusion

When Central Asia fell under Soviet domination during the 1910s and 1920s communist leaders banned many religious practices outright and did everything possible to discourage the remainder. Mosques became museums and public buildings, and Islam, a fairly relaxed affair to begin with, waned. "National and religious institutions sustained big blows and losses during the expeditions of Russia into the region and following the creation of the Bolshevik state," says Abdul Hakim Juzjani, professor of law at Tashkent Islamic University. "Large [collections detailing] achievements in the arts and science were looted, books were closely monitored, the people who had [religious books] used to be taken to court, or sent to exile in Siberia or, if the book was about religious doctrine the owner used to face even harder punishments."

The end of Soviet rule has led to a resurgence in long-suppressed public expressions of faith, especially in rural areas such as the Ferghana Valley, where the borders of Kyrgyzstan, Uzbekistan and Tajikistan intertwine. "To be sure, there has been a surge of Islamic activity among Uzbeks in Osh since Kyrgyzstan's independence in 1991," wrote Morgan Liu for EurasiaNet in 2000. "Literally hundreds of small neighborhood mosques, which were utilized as warehouses and shops during the Soviet era, have been restored and reopened. Formerly banned religious holidays are communally celebrated. Every year hundreds of pilgrims go on the Haj from Osh, enduring an arduous weeklong bus ride to Mecca. In addition, Islamic study groups have spontaneously formed within Osh's Uzbek neighborhoods in the past ten years. These self-run home groups of about fifteen, called *ziyofats*, gather weekly to study Islam over tea and food....At the same time, most Osh Uzbeks express horror and disgust at 'Wahhabism,' drawing a sharp distinction between it and the Islam of their ancestors. They oppose movements that aim to overthrow current governments and administer Islamic law."

"There is no doubt that the people of this region connected to Islam by their historical roots and their big contributions to Islamic culture and their thoughts are well-known," says Magda Makhloof, professor of Turkish and Persian Studies at Ain Shams University in Cairo. "However, the region was left under communist rule for a century, or about three-fourths of a century. And there is no doubt that this period affected the true knowledge of Islamic religion in the region. At

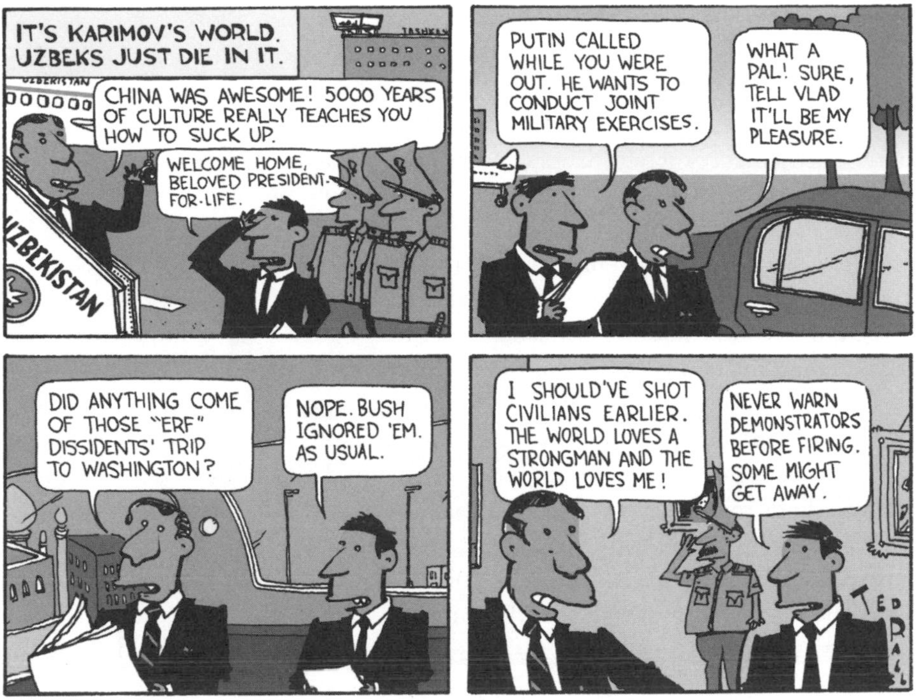
IT'S KARIMOV'S WORLD. UZBEKS JUST DIE IN IT.
CHINA WAS AWESOME! 5000 YEARS OF CULTURE REALLY TEACHES YOU HOW TO SUCK UP.
WELCOME HOME, BELOVED PRESIDENT-FOR-LIFE.
UZBEKISTAN
PUTIN CALLED WHILE YOU WERE OUT. HE WANTS TO CONDUCT JOINT MILITARY EXERCISES.
WHAT A PAL! SURE, TELL VLAD IT'LL BE MY PLEASURE.
DID ANYTHING COME OF THOSE "ERF" DISSIDENTS' TRIP TO WASHINGTON?
NOPE. BUSH IGNORED 'EM. AS USUAL.
I SHOULD'VE SHOT CIVILIANS EARLIER. THE WORLD LOVES A STRONGMAN AND THE WORLD LOVES ME!
NEVER WARN DEMONSTRATORS BEFORE FIRING. SOME MIGHT GET AWAY.
TED RALL

present, there are Islamic sentiments and feelings, but they lack true knowledge." That ignorance has permitted bizarre bastardizations of religion. Turkmen dictator Saparmurat "Turkmenbashi" Niyazov, for example, has even managed to expand his personality cult by mixing quotes from his *Rukhnama* "little green book" of whimsical political observations with those from the Koran on the walls of the nation's new mosque, which was built in his hometown of Kipchak. "Imams in Turkmenistan are forced to quote from the *Rukhnama* and hold *Rukhnama* classes in the mosques and have copies of the *Rukhnama* on the shelf in the mosque, on the same shelf with the Koran," said Felix Corley, chief editor of Forum-18, a Norwegian news agency that reports on religion.

Every Central Asian republic carefully monitors religious fervor within its borders. Every mosque and *madrassa* is required to be registered with its respective government. Clerics are hired and fired by politicians. It's an arrangement favored by insecure dictators worried about the threat of revolution, as well as parts of the population who came of age during the Soviet period.

"If Islam Abduganievich [Karimov] were removed from power," an Uzbek in Tashkent told a writer for *The New Yorker*, "there would be a fundamentalist government here within six months." A businessman added: "I would happily show my documents ten times a day if that would guarantee peace and stability here." That degree of police control is well underway, though neither peace nor stability are in large supply. Moreover, Karimov's approach has been widely imitated throughout the region.

Uzbekistan's 9/11

On February 16, 1999 Karimov was running fifteen minutes late for an eleven a.m. meeting at the Cabinet of Ministers Building in central Tashkent. As he arrived a car smashed through barricades surrounding Independence Square and a shootout ensued between its drivers and police. At that moment the first of six huge bombs went off in the square, demolishing the building's facade along with the Uzbek National Bank for Foreign Economic Affairs. Karimov was reported to have escaped death by a hundred meters. Two bombs took out the Interior Ministry. Another went off forty-five minutes later near the airport. Fifteen people were killed.

A furious Karimov went on state television, pledging to "eliminate the scoundrels" behind the bombings. It was not an idle threat.

Karimov's first instinct told him to respond with repression. "Uzbekistan remained the center of attempts by Central Asian Islamic militants based in Afghanistan to destabilize Central Asia," reported Dilip Hiro in *Asia Times*. "President Islam Karimov responded by a massive crackdown in the country imprisoning over fifteen hundred people, who were alleged to sympathize with the rebels." Within weeks Uzbekistan was in the throes of a brutal purge of its already beleaguered religious Muslims. That month a presidential decree authorized the punitive arrest of a suspect's father if his extremist sons could not be found. "If my child chose such a path," Karimov said, "I myself would rip off his head." Head-ripping was a recurring theme of Karimov's rhetoric. He added a promise to "tear off the heads of two hundred people in order to protect Uzbekistan's freedom and stability." It is un-

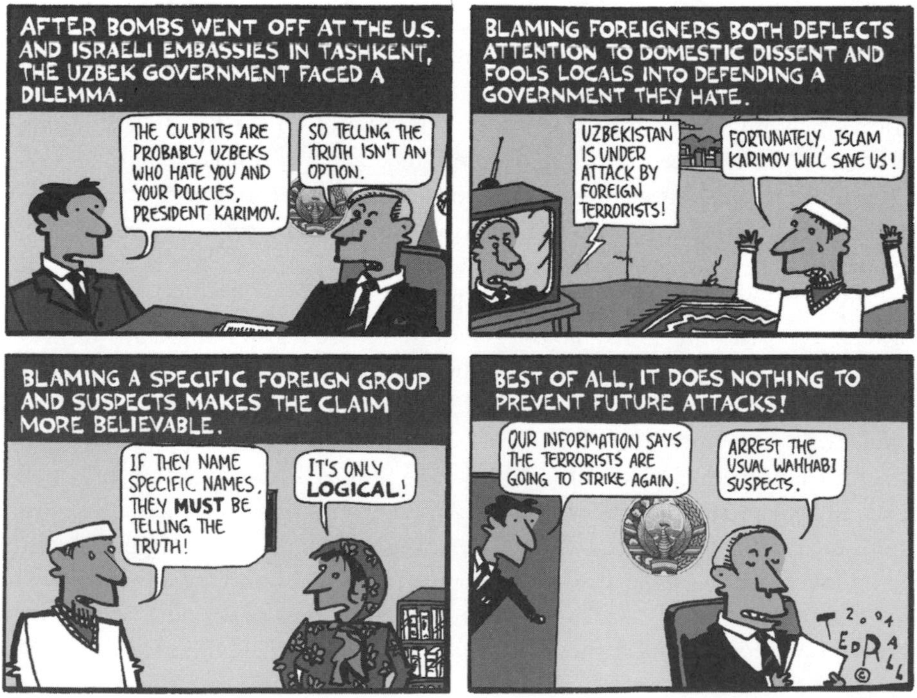
AFTER BOMBS WENT OFF AT THE U.S. AND ISRAELI EMBASSIES IN TASHKENT, THE UZBEK GOVERNMENT FACED A DILEMMA.
THE CULPRITS ARE PROBABLY UZBEKS WHO HATE YOU AND YOUR POLICIES, PRESIDENT KARIMOV.
SO TELLING THE TRUTH ISN'T AN OPTION.
BLAMING FOREIGNERS BOTH DEFLECTS ATTENTION TO DOMESTIC DISSENT AND FOOLS LOCALS INTO DEFENDING A GOVERNMENT THEY HATE.
UZBEKISTAN IS UNDER ATTACK BY FOREIGN TERRORISTS!
FORTUNATELY, ISLAM KARIMOV WILL SAVE US!
BLAMING A SPECIFIC FOREIGN GROUP AND SUSPECTS MAKES THE CLAIM MORE BELIEVABLE.
IF THEY NAME SPECIFIC NAMES, THEY MUST BE TELLING THE TRUTH!
IT'S ONLY LOGICAL!
BEST OF ALL, IT DOES NOTHING TO PREVENT FUTURE ATTACKS!
OUR INFORMATION SAYS THE TERRORISTS ARE GOING TO STRIKE AGAIN.
ARREST THE USUAL WAHHABI SUSPECTS.
TED RALL 2004 ©

UZBEKISTAN

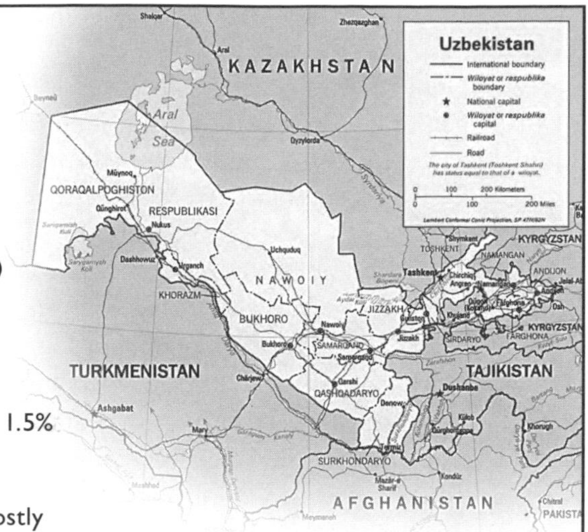

Uzbekistan
International boundary
National capital
Railroad
Road
KAZAKHSTAN
Aral Sea
QORAQALPOGHISTON
RESPUBLIKASI
KHORAZM
NAWOIY
BUKHORO
JIZZAKH
SAMARQAND
QASHQADARYO
SURKHONDARYO
TOSHKENT
NAMANGAN
ANDIJON
FARGHONA
SIRDARYO
TURKMENISTAN
TAJIKISTAN
KYRGYZSTAN
AFGHANISTAN
Ashgabat
Tashkent
Dushanbe

Capital: Tashkent
Form of Government:
Dictatorship
Leader: Head of the State Islam Abduganievich Karimov (born 1938)
Population (July 2005):
26,851,195
Major Ethnic Groups (2003):
Uzbek 80%; Russian 5.5%; Tajik 5%; Kazakh 3%; Karakalpak 2.5%; Tatar 1.5%
Area (square miles): 172,696
(slightly larger than California)
Terrain (as per *CIA Factbook*): "mostly flat-to-rolling sandy desert with dunes; broad, flat intensely irrigated river valleys along course of Amu Darya, Syr Darya (Sirdaryo), and Zarafshon; Ferghana Valley in east surrounded by mountainous Tajikistan and Kyrgyzstan; shrinking Aral Sea in west"
Currency/Exchange Rate (2005): US $1 = 1,114 *som*
Oil Reserves (proven): 600 million barrels
Natural Gas Reserves (proven): 1.9 trillion cubic meters
Coolest Thing About Uzbekistan: Registan complex of Timurid mosques and madrassas in the old city section of Samarkand, where grandiosity intersects with grace in a glorious celebration of asymmetry and architectural divinity
Worst Thing About Uzbekistan: Frequent *militsia* checkpoints make it nearly impossible to travel in, into, or out of the country
Best Way to Get Thrown Into Jail: Grow a beard
Per Capita Annual Income: $440
Unemployment Rate: Regime hilariously claims 0.6%; experts estimate 80%
Life Expectancy: 64

The only Central Asian nation to border all the others also has, as Uzbeks boast, all the best cities—Bukhara, Khiva, Samarkand and Tashkent, the only genuine metropolis in the region. Uzbekistan's location as the center of Central Asia and aggressive foreign policy make it "Central Asia's United States"—a nation that rarely shies away from the chance to lean on its neighbors, up to and including the occasional border incursion. Elevation rises from west to east in Uzbekistan, marking the transition between the sandblasted wastes of the Kyzyl Kum and Kara Kum deserts spreading into Turkmenistan and the gentler, colder mountainous climates prevalent in Kyrgyzstan and Kazakhstan. Home to a wide variety of ethnic groups including Bukharan Jews, Uzbekistan has become a boiling point for political and ethnic tensions, from rioting and suicide bombings in the conservative Muslim Ferghana Valley to frequent attempts to overthrow the regime of Islam Karimov, who has earned the distinction of murdering more of his subjects than any of his fellow dictators. Along with Uzbekistan's other great Silk Road cities, Samarkand ranks as a tourist attraction on par with Paris and Istanbul. Also worth seeing is the environmental nightmare created by the draining of the Aral Sea. Of all the Central Asian republics Uzbekistan is the most likely to disintegrate into civil war should anything happen to Karimov.

known whether Karimov personally supervises such reprisals; however, published reports claim that exactly that number of bodies of "Muslim extremists"—often the victims are identified as radicals simply because they wear long beards—were strung up from Tashkent lampposts in May. Exceptionally violent and corrupt even by Central Asian standards, the government of Uzbekistan is proof that a ruler can remain in power despite the near-universal contempt of his subjects. Two years later Karimov would be rehabilitated by American president George W. Bush as a key ally in his "war on terror," then cut loose after committing yet another massacre—then wooed again. Meanwhile, Uzbekistan staggers through convulsions of crackdowns followed by, most recently, suicide bombers who blow themselves up at *militsia* checkpoints. The attacks are coordinated but no one knows for certain whether they're motivated by Muslim fervor, generalized oppression or economic despair, or if any organization is responsible. There is so much systemic failure in Uzbek society that it's impossible to distill the dissidents' motivations. Every Uzbek is a potential enemy of the regime.

"The [Tashkent] bombings were Uzbekistan's equivalent of the World Trade Center attack, albeit much smaller in scale," said *The New Yorker*. "People were outraged and scared. In this country, where Muslims make up nearly ninety per cent of the population, Islamic extremists were blamed, accused of trying to turn Karimov's secular state into another Iran or Afghanistan. Human-rights activists estimate that forty thousand policemen now patrol the streets of Tashkent; ten years ago, that number patrolled the entire country. Roadblocks and document checks are common. In the fight against fundamentalism, mosques have been stripped of loudspeakers to mute the public broadcast of the call to prayer, and thousands of Muslims have been jailed for professing their religion in a manner not sanctioned by the state. These measures augment the preexisting authoritarian order, in which a free press and political opposition were stifled. (In Uzbekistan, the law prohibits public insults of the President.) As for democracy, in the most recent presidential election, last year, Karimov's nominal rival [Abdulhasiz Dzhalalov, the only other candidate permitted to run] announced that he had voted for Karimov."

The IMU's 800 Club

Karimov blamed the 2/16 attacks on the Islamic Movement of Uzbekistan, a Taliban-trained Islamist organization that earned international headlines due to its daring border incursions, kidnappings of foreigners and charismatic ethnic Uzbek leader, Juma Namangani. The IMU was the ideological heir of the United Tajik Opposition, one of the major Muslim factions that vied for power during the Tajik Civil War of the Nineties. The conflict, which at its height saw the Beirut-style partitioning of Dushanbe into rival governments, ended like Lebanon's, in stalemate begotten of mutual exhaustion.

As I arrived in Tashkent in August of 1999, an eight hundred-man-strong IMU incursion had swept across the knot of Ferghana Valley borders where Uzbekistan

One of the few known images of Tahir Yuldash, leader of the Islamic Movement of Uzbekistan (pictured second from right in this captured video frame). He is seen here in the summer of 2001, with Ayman al-Zawahiri—Al Qaeda's number two—standing to his right.

meets Kyrgyzstan and Tajikistan, capturing at least four Kyrgyz villages along the way. The kidnapping of four Japanese energy company geologists, one of whom was murdered, prompted the Uzbek air force to bomb Kyrgyzstan, which retaliated by closing its borders and using its army to expel the IMU force—towards Uzbekistan.

Namangani, influenced by the Afghan practice of seasonal warfare as much as by a multi-million-dollar ransom paid by the Japanese government, withdrew to his bases in southern Tajikistan along the wide and remote border with Afghanistan. Border controls remained so tense, however, that taxis, buses, trains or private cars were barred. Barely a month after I underwent a hernia operation, my travel mate and I found ourselves lugging our bags on rented wheelbarrows on foot along with hundreds of refugees across the dusty Uzbek-Kazakh border. But Namangani had absorbed a lesson from his 1999 campaign: the Kyrgyz were more inclined to push his forces towards his real enemies, the Uzbeks, than back to Tajikistan.

I brushed up against the IMU again the following year. I was sitting with some of the twenty-three travelers I had led on Stan Trek 2000, a KFI Radio-sponsored bus trip of Central Asia, in a hotel bar in Osh, the administrative capital of the Ferghana Valley, when a panicked Kyrgyz army officer ran in to order us to evacuate.

"The road is wide open," he panted, "the city will fall tomorrow."

I took him aside to avoid panicking the Stan Trekkers.

"I lost thirty men," he went on. "They're coming."

Americans accustomed to Vietnam-, or now Iraq-era, casualty counts might be inclined to dismiss the loss of thirty soldiers as relatively inconsequential. In a rural province of a poor region's second-poorest nation, however, an entire garrison may house just forty or fifty troops, many of them unarmed except for nightsticks. I asked my local fixer to get us on the next, last and only Kyrgyzstan Airlines flight to Bishkek. "Normal fare is forty dollars," he said, drolly pronouncing it *dole-arse*, "but I will need another forty dollars to ensure the reservations." We both knew what this meant. The flight was full but the airport manager would turn away reserved passengers in order to let us fly in their place. I handed him two thousand dollars. "Do it," I ordered, after obtaining his solemn assurance that the canceled passengers were local *biznezmen*. They would be inconvenienced by being stuck in Osh under IMU occupation. Americans might be killed.

The streets were deserted as we drove to the airport early the next morning. Except for eighteen angry Kyrgyz screaming at the police as seventeen American and one Mexican national were led via the VIP lounge past a series of disused baggage scanning machines to the tarmac, nothing seemed amiss. We boarded the mid-sized Soviet-era Yak-40, which started its engines and began taxiing down the runway the instant the doors were closed.

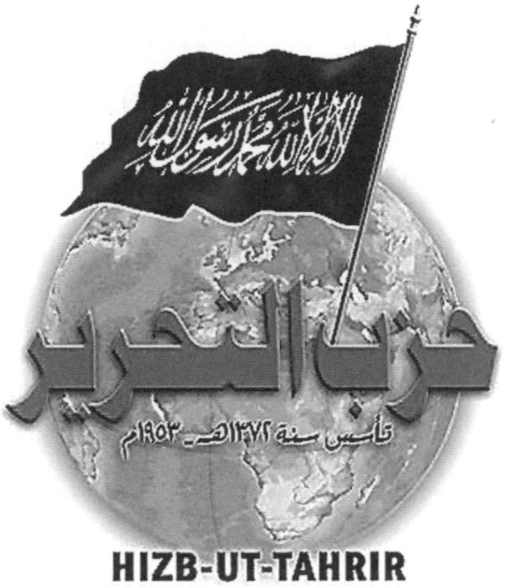
حزب التحرير
HIZB-UT-TAHRIR
Logo of the Party of Islamic Liberation, an organization which shares the goals of an Uzbek group accused of terrorism, but which hopes to achieve their ends without resorting to violence.

The view of the Tian Shan was picture-perfect—snow all around, breathtaking peaks, glistening clouds. As we corkscrewed a few hundred feet up, I looked down to catch the smoke rising from buildings in the eastern part of town, where the front had collapsed the night before. Men jumped out of jeeps and scattered down side streets. Two vehicles stopped below us where our plane had been parked. A man in military fatigues disembarked, shouldered a weapon and pointed it at us. There were a few muzzle flashes, but nothing happened. Those of us on the left side of the plane looked at each other, eyes widened. As far as I know no one told the others how close they had come to falling into the hands of the rebels, who days earlier had famously taken hostage a group of American mountain climbers.

Osh fell, but it didn't stick. The IMU departed days later, soon crossing the Uzbek border and advancing within ten miles of its goal of seizing Tashkent, where Namangani hoped to base his new Uzbek caliphate. But the brief taking of Osh in 2000 had broader implications. The IMU left behind enough agents and sympathizers to successfully start focusing the generalized discontent of young Muslim men into an organized revolutionary force. That seed planted in 2000, coupled with funding supplied by the American Central Intelligence Agency in an effort to undermine a Kyrgyz president who was judged uncooperative in the post-9/11 "war on terror," would bring down Central Asia's only democratically-elected ruler in the so-called Tulip Revolution of 2005.

The U.S. State Department ultimately declared the Taliban-trained, CIA-funded IMU a terrorist organization. In a pattern that American policy planners have since seen repeated, that increased IMU recruitment and pushed its leaders toward more ambitious goals. In the summer of 2001, for example, it tried to capture a Kyrgyz television relay station that broadcasts in Uzbekistan as well as Kyrgyzstan. Later the same year the IMU renamed itself the Islamic Movement of Turkestan, with the broader mission of uniting Turkmenistan, Uzbekistan, Kyrgyzstan, Kazakhstan, Tajikistan and China's Xinjiang province under an Islamic caliphate. Turkestan is the traditional umbrella name for Central Asia.

Namangani is rumored to have been killed while fighting with U.S.-allied forces in the Tribal Areas of western Pakistan during the immediate aftermath of the 2001 invasion of Afghanistan. Whatever the case, the former IMU (present IMT) maintains a "forward base of operations" in the Kyrgyz town of Batken near the Tajik border.

One of Namangani's last known activities was his campaign to unite his guerilla army with previously unarmed political opposition groups and parties, most notably the Hizb-ut-Tahrir al-Islami (Party of Islamic Liberation). The HUT shares the IMT's goal of a Central Asian caliphate but, at least until 2002, hoped to achieve it without resorting to violence.

"Previously, Hizb-ut-Tahrir used to say that they wanted to create an Islamic caliphate through peaceful policy," said Nikolai Tanayev, Kyrgyz prime minister under Askar Akayev, said in a 2002 interview. "We can [now] see the revival of radical members of Hizb-ut-Tahrir. We must take adequate measures, increase vigilance and increase the methods of influence." Moreover, not everyone is convinced that the charismatic Namangani is dead. "According to our information, Namangani survived after he was wounded in Afghanistan [during the anti-terror blitz]," Kyrgyz minister Misir Ashirkulov said a year later. Human rights groups with contacts in Uzbekistan estimate that at least seven thousand Hizb-ut-Tahrir al-Islami members are in prisons or gulags.

Has HUT morphed into a terrorist group? Uzbek authorities blamed them for a wave of explosions and suicide bombings at *militsia* checkpoints between March 28 and April 1, 2004 that killed more than forty people, including police and attackers. Among them were the attempted bombing of the Chorvak Reservoir in the Bostanlik District; had the dam breached Tashkent could have been flooded. A second wave of attacks struck in Tashkent with the July 30 bombing of the American and Israeli embassies as well as the state prosecutor's office. Six died and at least nine were injured. A new group said to be an ideological spinoff of HUT, Zhaomoat (Society) was also blamed. HUT supporters deny involvement, saying the attacks were a spontaneous expression of disgust for the regime and its military police enforcers. "Virtually everyone interviewed...expressed little sympathy for the police, and said government policies were driving people to revolt," wrote Esmer Islamov for EurasiaNet.

When Reality Becomes Irrelevant

In some respects, it doesn't really matter whether the Islamist challenge to the Central Asian dictatorships is real. "Promoting the IMU threat can serve a useful purpose for Central Asian leaders," noted a EurasiaNet analysis on the first anniversary of the September 11, 2001 attacks on New York and Washington. "The specter of a revived IMU helps to ensure long term U.S.-economic and military assistance. Long before September 11, Uzbek leader Islam Karimov used the threat of Islamic terrorism as justification for maintaining tight control over individual liberties. If anything, Karimov's stance has toughened over the last year...Kazakh and Kyrgyz leaders have emulated Karimov, trying to establish a link between the terrorist threat and opposition political activity."

The autocrats exploit the threats, both real and imagined, posed by the IMT, HUT and similar organizations, to justify harsh measures of repression: internal passports, preemptive imprisonment, torture, even mass executions. But, whether tensions caused by the rising popularity of Islamic fundamentalism simply cannot be kept bottled up or because oppressive regimes require external as well as internal scapegoats, Islam has become a subject of contention regionally as well. Not only did Karimov order the Uzbek bombings in Kyrgyzstan in response to what he called the incompetent response of Kyrgyz officials to the 1999 IMU incursion, he unilaterally declared new borders drawn in the Ferghana Valley. In July 2002 Kyrgyz Security Minister Misir Ashirkulov declared something of an open secret, that IMU fighters were in Tajikistan. Tajik officials angrily responded by closing the border and recalling their ambassador. In September an unknown assailant tried to assassinate Ashirkulov with a hand grenade.

Increased political repression and the post-Soviet economic collapse are driving more Central Asians to increased religiosity. Farkhad Iliassov of the Russian think tank Vlast told the Voice of America that Islamic fundamentalism is appealing because it's all there is: "In the absence of democratic alternatives with mostly liquidated socialistic values, the only remaining hope and ideology for the poor, destitute, and oppressed is Islam. [People] can't expect help from, or appeal to, any other alternative ideology." Ahmed Rashid says: "The enormous repression of the [Central Asian] regimes and the lack of any kind of political expression naturally forces politically oriented people to go underground and to become radicalized, and then join these Islamist groups." But it wasn't until 2005 that radical political Islam helped topple a government.

"It's the victory of the people," a Kyrgyz opposition party leader said as the nation's democratically-elected president for fourteen years, Askar Akayev, fled to Kazakhstan and then to exile in Russia. "But now we don't know how to stop these young guys."

The "young guys" were a mix of unemployed opportunists and IMT- and HUT-affiliated Islamists who had convoyed to Osh in a half-hearted attempt to topple the Akayev regime, long staggering into political irrelevance and economic bankruptcy. They gathered in Ala Too Square in the city center of Bishkek, set fires and threw rocks at riot police. When the cops retreated, the rebels seized their opportunity. They stormed government buildings and Akayev, having refused his security forces' entreaties to fire upon them, fled to Kazakhstan, from which he left for exile in Moscow.

Uzbekistan's Tiananmen Square

No single event better reflects the explosive nature of the clash between Islam and Soviet-style authoritarianism than the 2005 massacre of hundreds of anti-government protesters by Uzbek forces at Andijon, a Ferghana town of three hundred thousand souls in southeastern Uzbekistan within walking distance of the Kyrgyz frontier. Ed Vulliamy of *The UK Guardian* called it "one of the worst atrocities of recent times, a massacre which the perpetrators have tried to keep secret, and with whom the international diplomatic community cooperates through a conspiracy of silence."

The roots of the Andijon tragedy date to June 2004, when twenty-three local

VIKTOR KOROTAYEV, REUTERS

Residents of Andijon wait for news about relatives after hundreds of protesters, including women and children, were gunned down by Uzbek security forces in May 2005.

businessmen were arrested, tried for "religious extremism" and thrown into prison. Prosecutors accused them of membership in an HUT offshoot group called Akramiya, named after Akram Yuldoshev, that was formed in 1992. Yuldoshev is serving a seventeen-year prison term for his supposed role in the February 1999 Tashkent bombings. The businessmen's supporters and employees, who said the dissidents' real crime was their refusal to pay bribes to corrupt police and politicians, stormed a local *militsia* station on the night of May 12, 2005, three months into their imprisonment, where they seized weapons which they used to break the men out of prison. Townsfolk began gathering alongside the businessmen's supporters in the central square at about seven the next morning, May 13. "Unfortunately for the regime," wrote Vulliamy, "a correspondent for the London-based Institute for War and Peace Reporting, Galima Bukharbaeva, was present in Bobur Square as the state militia descended on a crowd of ten thousand to thirty thousand demonstrators and began to shoot indiscriminately. Otherwise, news of the ensuing massacre might never have reached the West. Bukharbaeva's notebook and press card now carry a bullet hole as a souvenir from the day."

Survivors, some of whom ended up as refugees in Romania, say the protest was driven by economics rather than religion. "We hoped the local government would come to hear our grievances. People said even Karimov himself would come," a man named Dolim told *The Guardian*. Indeed, Karimov did come to Andijon—to personally supervise the ensuing bloodbath.

The protesters issued two demands: that the prisoners remain free and that Akram Yuldoshev join them. People with other grievances tagged along. "We went because of unemployment, low salaries not paid, pensions not received. We had gone expecting speeches, not bullets." But the ensuing turkey shoot, in which an estimated one thousand people were murdered by government forces in direct contact with Karimov, strengthened the hand of the Islamists. "The [column of soldiers and paramilitary troops] opened fire directly at us," said a survivor named Yuldash. "I saw people falling around me, women and children too; screaming and blood everywhere. I saw at least five small children killed."

Most eyewitness accounts say the killing continued for about ninety minutes. "The dead were lying in front of me piled three-thick," said one man. "At one point, I passed out. When I regained consciousness, it was raining—on the ground, I could see water running with blood." As did others, Baltabai survived by hiding under piles of corpses for hours. "Then I crawled behind a tree and stood, looking at what I saw. Dead people everywhere, and some alive, just moving. I felt sick, because of all the things splattered on my clothes. I went into the college and saw the armored personnel carriers moving over the bodies. They wanted to kill anyone who was wounded. Soldiers walked down the sidewalk, firing single shots at anyone moving. It was a scene from hell, but I saw it, just a hundred days ago." Baltabai and the other survivors ran toward the Kyrgyz border along a thirty-mile road turned into a gauntlet of government snipers and American-supplied helicopter gunships. Shocked bor-

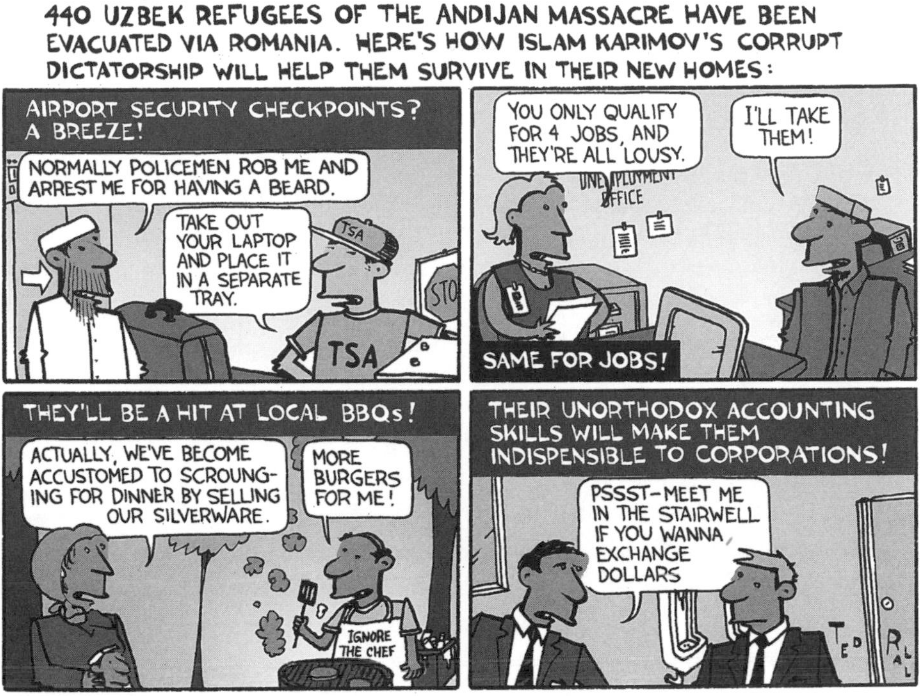
440 UZBEK REFUGEES OF THE ANDIJAN MASSACRE HAVE BEEN EVACUATED VIA ROMANIA. HERE'S HOW ISLAM KARIMOV'S CORRUPT DICTATORSHIP WILL HELP THEM SURVIVE IN THEIR NEW HOMES:
AIRPORT SECURITY CHECKPOINTS? A BREEZE!
NORMALLY POLICEMEN ROB ME AND ARREST ME FOR HAVING A BEARD.
TAKE OUT YOUR LAPTOP AND PLACE IT IN A SEPARATE TRAY.
TSA
YOU ONLY QUALIFY FOR 4 JOBS, AND THEY'RE ALL LOUSY.
I'LL TAKE THEM!
SAME FOR JOBS!
THEY'LL BE A HIT AT LOCAL BBQs!
ACTUALLY, WE'VE BECOME ACCUSTOMED TO SCROUNGING FOR DINNER BY SELLING OUR SILVERWARE.
MORE BURGERS FOR ME!
IGNORE THE CHEF
THEIR UNORTHODOX ACCOUNTING SKILLS WILL MAKE THEM INDISPENSIBLE TO CORPORATIONS!
PSSST—MEET ME IN THE STAIRWELL IF YOU WANNA EXCHANGE DOLLARS
TED RALL

der guards threw open the checkpoint upon seeing them soaked in blood.

The Karimov regime later admitted to killing one hundred eighty-seven "terrorists and extremists" launching "a terrorist action" orchestrated by unnamed "foreign forces." Conservative Western estimates, based on local coroners' log books, start at seven hundred fifty dead.

In a scene unthinkable to anyone familiar with the tense multiple exit and entry checkpoints at Central Asian border crossings, Uzbek policemen drove into Kyrgyzstan in hot pursuit, threatening to execute the families of those who chose to remain. "One man's son decided to go [back]," Yuldash said, "and they broke his arms and legs at the border. It was clear what was waiting for anyone who went back: prison and torture." Pulat said: "One man who went back had been taken for interrogation with needles in his nails. Later, they killed him, took the body to his parents and said: 'Here is your child. Let that be an example.'" At this writing Uzbek security forces continue to raid Kyrgyz territory, an easier feat in the continuing unrest following the Tulip Revolution, in search of the survivors of what has come to be known there as Uzbekistan's Tiananmen Square—and not as anything at all in most of the world, which remains oblivious.

The governments of Uzbekistan and other Central Asian nations at war with political Islam hope to crush it through the brand of brute force exhibited at Andijon, but are learning what Israeli occupation authorities in Palestine have experienced the hard way: repression radicalizes moderates. Suhrob Sharifov, head of the Center for International Relationships in Dushanbe, says: "Many experts believe that the Uzbek regime is to blame for the spread of religious extremism in the country because they arrest and insult both guilty and innocent people. People join extremist groups to express their protest to the regime."

Hikmatulloh Saifullohzoda, spokesman for the only "official" Muslim party in Central Asia, the Islamic Renaissance Party of Tajikistan, agrees: "When authorities put pressure on religious people, they sometimes respond with anger against the authorities' violent behavior. In other words, they are forced to react this way. If you treat these religious people by moderate means, I don't think they would behave in violent, extremist, or radical ways." Nothing indicates that the current regimes in power in Ashkhabat, Tashkent and other Central Asian capitals understand this simple but hard-learned truth.

§ § §

Kyrgyzstan's Tulip Revolution

When you think "Jockey," you think "tighty whities." But a few years back, far from the prying eyes of Western business writers, in the dusty capital of the remote former Soviet republic of Kyrgyzstan, Jockey tried to reinvent itself as a high-end men's formalwear designer.

Electricity was spotty and civil war was raging in neighboring Tajikistan, but Kyrgyzstan was flush with loans by Western banks beguiled by its unique status as a relatively benign republic ruled by a democratically-elected president. The mere existence of the Jockey store, overstaffed with supermodel-quality Kyrgyz women wearing uniforms of black microminis, testified to the optimism infecting Bishkek during the giddy summer of 1997. ("Does anybody shop here?" I asked a salesgirl. She assured me that people did. "Do they ever buy anything?" She giggled nervously. An average Kyrgyz worker would have needed a decade's salary to take home a styling Jockey suit.)

Alone among the Central Asian republics that emerged after the 1991 Soviet collapse, Kyrgyzstan was governed by a genuine parliament with political opposition groups allowed to campaign and win elected office. While his neighbors suppressed the news media, created ludicrous Stalinesque personality cults and presided over corrupt, violent police states, Askar Akayev created the "Switzerland of Central Asia," a calm and friendly mountain oasis in a region typically infamous for its misery and oppression. Absent were the ubiquitous checkpoints, political prisons and KGB-OVIR spies typical of Central Asian republics. The Kyrgyz didn't have much oil or gas, but who knew? European mountaineers and whitewater rafting aficionados might attract some tourist money.

The American-run IMF soon realized that rocks, the country's only natural resource, don't make for the best collateral. They pulled the fiscal feeding tube and burst the Kyrgyz economic bubble.

By 1999 the Jockey store was gone, replaced by a café that had evidently fol-

PHOTO BY VLADISLAV USHAKOV, EURASIANET

In March 2005, thousands of protesters filled Ala Too Square in Bishkek, eventually driving Kyrgyzstan's democratically-elected president into exile. This coup d'état became known as the Tulip Revolution.

lowed it into retail oblivion in the middle of a half-eaten lunch. You could have taken a nap in the middle of previously traffic-clogged streets without fear of being disturbed. The nights, however, were punctuated with gunshots.

As unemployment rose, the IMU crossed the southern Kyrgyz frontier from its camps in Tajikistan in an ongoing campaign to overthrow Uzbek dictator Islam Karimov. The impoverished Kyrgyz army, unable to afford heavy artillery, was overrun by both the invasion and the retreat. IMU fighters found sanctuary in the Ferghana Valley, the conservative Muslim heartland of Central Asia centered around the ancient southern Kyrgyz city of Osh.

Akayev also took note of the IMU incursion. With foreign aid cut off and half the country slipping out of his government's control, he resorted to watered-down versions of the tactics used by his neighboring Central Asian strongmen such as jailing former Soviet general Felix Kulov of the opposition movement and stuffing ballots in the March 13 parliamentary elections. That sparked demonstrations by Ferghana-based southerners, who seized Osh and Tokmak before trekking over the Tian Shan mountains to the capital.

Although the quest for freedom is understandable and laudable, recent events in Kyrgyzstan were less of a revolution than a looting raid on the capital by impetuous southerners. And the post-Akayev era forces the Kyrgyz to choose between two unpleasant options, autocratic former regime figures like Kulov (who became the Tulip Revolution's Acting Prime Minister) and the Taliban-influenced Islamists who drove the president from power.

Cynical regional experts detect the hand of American-inspired—and financed—regime change in many of the so-called "color revolutions" that swept the former Soviet Union beginning in 2003. First came Georgia's "Rose Revolution" in November 2003, which led to the ouster of Edvard Shevardnadze by crowds of tens of thousands of marchers. Long-time opposition leader Mikhail Saakashvili won a presidential election, only to be roundly defeated in parliamentary elections two years later by Georgians who charged that he betrayed promises for greater transparency. In December 2004 millions of demonstrators seized the streets of Kiev, bringing the Orange Revolution to Ukraine. In November 2005, thousands of people unsuccessfully attempted to topple the authoritarian regime of Ilham Aliev in Azerbaijan. A similar aborted coup took place in Belarus in March 2006; it ended when Alexander Lukashenko's *militsia* arrested protesters and destroyed their encampment.

The Tulip Revolution followed parliamentary elections in February and March 2005 that southern-based conservative political opposition parties claimed to have been rigged. In hindsight it's a wonder that the Akayev regime, whose *militsia* didn't carry guns, lasted as long as it did.

In March 2005 demonstrators seized the governor's offices in Jalalabad and Osh, where a few days passed before one thousand protesters took over government

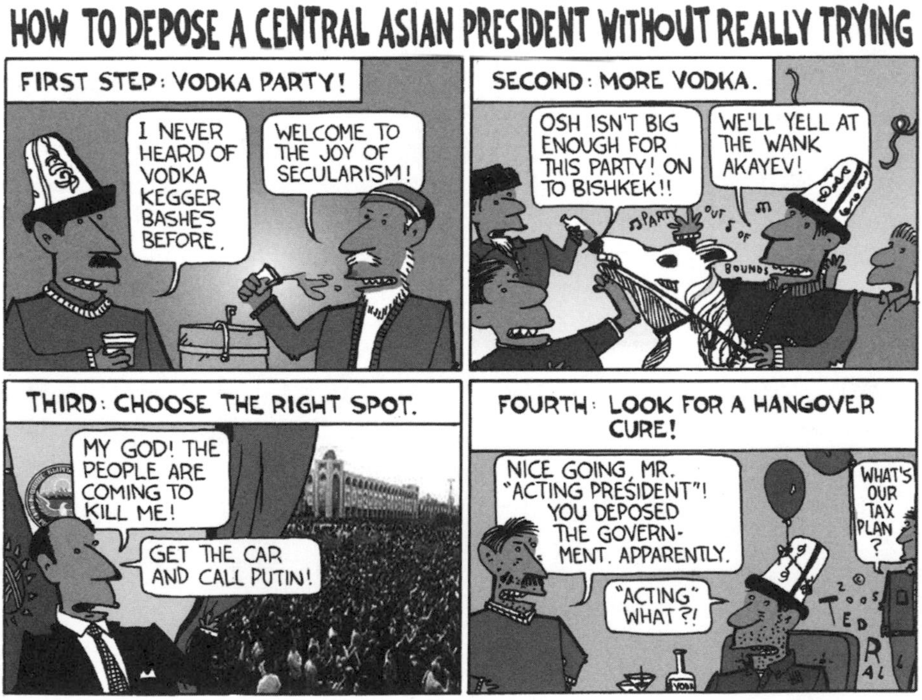
HOW TO DEPOSE A CENTRAL ASIAN PRESIDENT WITHOUT REALLY TRYING
FIRST STEP: VODKA PARTY!
I NEVER HEARD OF VODKA KEGGER BASHES BEFORE.
WELCOME TO THE JOY OF SECULARISM!
SECOND: MORE VODKA.
OSH ISN'T BIG ENOUGH FOR THIS PARTY! ON TO BISHKEK!!
WE'LL YELL AT THE WANK AKAYEV!
THIRD: CHOOSE THE RIGHT SPOT.
MY GOD! THE PEOPLE ARE COMING TO KILL ME!
GET THE CAR AND CALL PUTIN!
FOURTH: LOOK FOR A HANGOVER CURE!
NICE GOING, MR. "ACTING PRESIDENT"! YOU DEPOSED THE GOVERNMENT. APPARENTLY.
WHAT'S OUR TAX PLAN?
"ACTING" WHAT?!

KYRGYZSTAN

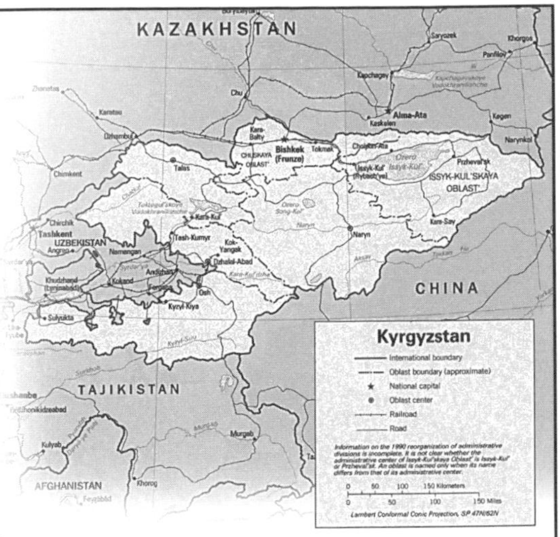
KAZAKHSTAN
CHINA
TAJIKISTAN
AFGHANISTAN
UZBEKISTAN
Bishkek (Frunze)
Alma-Ata
Naryn
Osh
Tashkent
Kyrgyzstan
International boundary
Oblast boundary (approximate)
National capital
Oblast center
Railroad
Road
Information on the 1990 reorganization of administrative divisions is incomplete. It is not clear whether the administrative center of Issyk-Kul'skaya Oblast' is Issyk-Kul' or Przheval'sk. An oblast is named only when its name differs from that of its administrative center.
0 50 100 150 Kilometers
0 50 100 150 Miles
Lambert Conformal Conic Projection, SP 47N/62N

Capital: Bishkek
Form of Government:
Interim (Leaders of 2005 Coup d'état)
Leader: Acting President
Kurmanbek Bakiev (born 1949)
Population (July 2005): 5,146,281
Major Ethnic Groups (2003):
Kyrgyz 64.9%; Uzbek 13.8%; Russian 12.5%; Dungan 1.1%; Ukrainian 1%; Uyghur 1%
Area (square miles): 76,621
(slightly smaller than South Dakota)
Terrain (as per *CIA Factbook*): "peaks of Tian Shan and associated valleys and basins encompass entire nation"
Currency/Exchange Rate (2005): US $1 = 40 *sum*
Oil Reserves (proven): 40 million barrels
Natural Gas Reserves (proven): 20 billion cubic meters
Coolest Thing About Kyrgyzstan: High-altitude "great lake" Issyk-Kul, where you can swim at reasonably warm temperatures all year long
Worst Thing About Kyrgyzstan: Scary nights on city streets
Best Way to Get Thrown Into Jail: Be Tajik
Per Capita Annual Income: $1,150
Unemployment Rate: 28%
Life Expectancy: 68

During the first decade after independence, the Kyrgyz Republic was an international darling. Under the liberal leadership of Askar Akayev, the only democratically elected president in the region, Kyrgyzstan became renowned as the Switzerland of Central Asia: mountainous, peaceful, relaxed. The *militsia* weren't merely honest, they were helpful. Funding from the International Monetary Fund, World Bank and other Western-backed financiers dried up in 1999 after the Kazakh oil strike turned neighboring Kazakhstan into the object of endearment. Energy-poor Kyrgyzstan, whose tiny gas and oil reserves are all but impossible to exploit, went broke. Economic collapse led to political disintegration, with high inflation and unemployment driving southerners centered around Osh, the historical capital of Ferghana, into the arms of the Islamic Movement of Uzbekistan and other extremist organizations that entered the country from Tajikistan. By early 2005 Akayev was already under siege by restive southerners. Then he made a fatal mistake: He requested that the Bush Administration close the "temporary" post-9/11 airbase it had established in 2001 to conduct operations against the Taliban. Rumors of CIA arms and cash shipments to IMU guerillas began circulating and, within weeks, a caravan of armed young men drove across the Tian Shan from Osh to Bishkek to topple Akayev. The Kyrgyz Republic hopes to attract international tourism, especially from Europe, with Silk Road-era ruins and ancient archeological sites, as well as outdoor sports like white-water rafting and hang-gliding but it's not the best place for a Westerner to be these days. The country is on the verge of becoming a "failed state" in the wake of the 2005 Tulip Revolution.

PHOTO BY VLADISLAV USHAKOV, EURASIANET

After clashing with *militsia* and storming government buildings in Bishkek during the Tulip Revolution, opposition demonstrators celebrate.

offices and the airport. A wave of anti-government demonstrators staged a sit-in in a central square in Bishkek while southern cities began falling one by one. On Thursday, March 24, a crowd estimated to have numbered in the tens of thousands, mostly composed of ethnic Uzbeks from the Ferghana Valley, massed near the main government buildings in downtown Bishkek. When *militsia* tried to beat back young people at the front of the crowd, those in the rear pushed forward, propelling a surge of humanity up the stairs and into history.

In May, the exiled Akayev accused the U.S. of being the real force behind the Tulip Revolution. The Bush Administration, he claimed, had ousted him in retaliation for allowing Russia to build an airbase and in questioning whether and why the United States required a military presence indefinitely. The chill in U.S.-Kyrgyz relations began when Akayev asked U.S. forces not to use Manas airbase for operations in the March 2003 invasion of Iraq. At the time Kulov's Ar-Namys Party pointedly criticized Akayev's stance and argued in favor of the U.S. presence.

"The regime that has come now certainly was backed from without. The revolution surely had U.S. financial and technical support. The United States apparently decided that [the Russian base at Kant] hurt its interests," Akayev said. "That marked the start of the preparation of plans for my ouster." It soon came to light that the United States had deliberately destabilized the Akayev government. Among other covert activities, an opposition party newspaper published photos of a new presidential palace being built for the president shortly before the disputed parliamentary elections. The publication was financed by Freedom House, whose president is former CIA director James Woolsey. Lorne Craner, U.S. Assistant Secretary of State for Democracy, Human Rights and Labor conceded: "The U.S. has been financing pro-democracy programs in Kyrgyzstan under the Freedom Support Act of 1992. We did a project recently...in Kyrgyzstan where there had only ever been one printing press. We funded the operation of another printing press there so that newspapers that were once unable to print day by day—due to censorship and lack of facilities—are now able to print much more often, basically every day now." And the Kyrgyz media had published a memo signed by U.S. ambassador Stephen Young calling for regime change. (Young claims that the document was forged.)

Kyrgyzstan's new leaders may want to heed Akayev's warnings about America's willingness to resort to regime change in order to defend its military interests. In August 2005 Valentin Bogatyryov, director of the official Kyrgyz International Institute of Strategic Studies told the Interfax news agency that his government wants the U.S. base closed: "As political life in Afghanistan is brought back to normal, it means that legitimate bodies of power, among them the president and parliament, should be established there...It will be necessary to raise the issue of completing the mission of the anti-terrorist coalition's military bases [in Central Asia]."

Acting president Bakiev may want to ask whether Akayev needs a roomie.

§ § §

A Vicious Partner in the War on Terror

So who is more brutal, Saddam Hussein or Islam Karimov? Reasonable people disagree. Saddam's goons electrocuted his political dissidents. Karimov, on the other hand, loots so much of his country's oil wealth that his state torturers don't have an electrical grid to draw upon. So his police torturers are forced to resort to medieval methods. They boil their "terrorist extremists"—businessmen who refuse to pay bribes—to death.

There's no question about which tyrant is more reviled. Saddam stole millions from the Iraqi treasury, yet he also spread around enough dough to build both a second-world infrastructure and an economic base of power among the Sunnis who amount to about forty percent of the population. Karimov, absolute ruler of Uzbekistan since the 1991 Soviet collapse, is a glutton whose personal motto echoes David Bowie's old promos for MTV: too much is never enough.

Uzbekistan, a major player in the Caspian Sea energy sweepstakes, is theoretically poised to become an economic success story. It is one of the world's largest producers of natural gas and possesses large untapped reserves of crude oil. Uzbekistan's strategic importance extends beyond the fact that it has common borders with all of the other Stans. But, unlike Saddam's Iraq, every cent generated by Uzbekistan's vast resources goes straight into Islam Karimov's pocket. His parsimony extends even to his thuggish *militsia* (military police): rather than pay them a realistic salary,

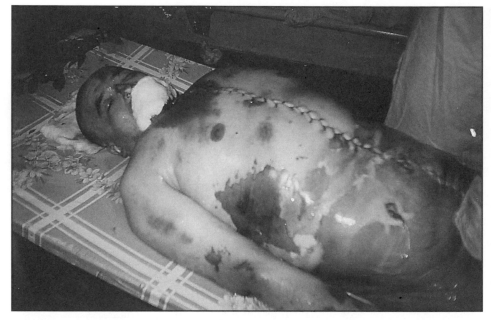

In 2002, the burned and mutilated body of Muzafar Avazov, a 35-year-old father of four, was returned to his family for burial. Avazov had been a prisoner at Uzbekistan's Jaslyk Prison which, according to Human Rights Watch, is infamous for its harsh conditions and torture of religious prisoners. Doctors examining Avazov's body reported that he had been badly beaten, his fingernails had been pulled, and sixty to seventy percent of his body was covered with burns, indicating that he had been boiled to death.

he grants them free reign to coerce, rob, jail and even murder at will. Not only do the *militsia* pay for themselves, their lawless behavior ensures loyalty. Every cop knows that his neighbors would kill him were Karimov to disappear.

Uzbekistan has a politically and ethnically diverse population comprising Uzbeks, Tajiks, Kazakhs and even Bukharan Jews. While it's common to see women wearing miniskirts on the streets of such secular urban centers as Khiva and Samarkand, the rural Ferghana Valley is home to a fundamentalist strain of Islamism reminiscent of the Taliban. But all Uzbeks have something in common. It doesn't matter whether you talk to a guerilla fighter for the radical Islamic Movement of Uzbekistan, a prostitute plying the bar at the Tashkent Sheraton or a kid hawking sodas at a bazaar: everyone hates Karimov and his *militsia*.

The full force of Uzbekistan's outlaw police fell upon anti-government rioters shouting "freedom" and demanding free elections and an end to official corruption in the Ferghana Valley city of Andijon on May 13, 2005. Although Karimov now claims that police acted independently, the *UK Independent* reports, "He was in command of the situation having flown to Andijon from the capital Tashkent and almost certainly personally authorized the use of...deadly force."

The paper reported: "The crowds, it has been established, were mown down by powerful coaxial 7.62mm machine guns mounted on two Russian-built BTR-

80 armored personnel carriers. Such cannons can unleash two thousand rounds, barely pausing for breath before they need to be reloaded. A military helicopter was used for reconnaissance purposes and Uzbek troops armed with Kalashnikov assault rifles opened fire on the demonstrators creating a deadly field of fire with the BTR-80s from which there was no escape. The soldiers made sure they had done their work well. After the shooting had finished they went from body to body delivering 'control shots' to the back of people's heads and scoured the town's streets for survivors to finish off."

The bloodletting followed Karimov's observation that ex-president Askar Akayev's order not to fire on demonstrators was the fatal error that led to his ouster in Kyrgyzstan.

Bush Administration officials, so strident when promoting liberation through regime change in Iraq, Ukraine and, ironically, when Islamists overthrew the democratically-elected Kyrgyz president—have downplayed the Uzbek massacre. "After 9/11," explains *Newsweek*, "the Bush administration established a strategic partnership with Karimov, plunking down

Karimov meets Bush at the White House during his first official visit in 2001.

five hundred million dollars for a military base in southern Uzbekistan in preparation for operations in Afghanistan and paying sixty million dollars or more a year in military aid and training."

The Bushies were well aware of Karimov's horrific record. Human Rights Watch's 2001 report on Uzbekistan put its "conservative estimate" of Uzbek political prisoners at seven thousand. According to HRW: "Prison guards systematically beat prisoners with wooden and rubber truncheons and exacted particularly harsh punishment on those convicted on religious charges, subjecting them to additional beatings...Torture remained endemic in pretrial custody as well." George W. Bush didn't mind. He accorded Karimov all the honors of a full state visit to the White House shortly afterwards.

Pressure by human rights organizations prompted the United States to temporarily suspend short-term subsidies and joint military training exercises. Never one to understand *realpolitik*, Karimov—no doubt unaware that such gestures are standard procedure for hypocritical Western nations mouthing politely about human rights while coddling brutal dictators—canceled America's lease on its post-9/11 air base at Karshi-Khanabad, also known as K-2, effective at the close of 2005. But another dirty deal remained in force.

Two weeks before Andijon *The New York Times* reported that there was "growing evidence that the United States has sent terror suspects to Uzbekistan for detention and interrogation, even as Uzbekistan's treatment of its own prisoners continues to earn it admonishments from around the world, including from the State Department. Uzbekistan's role as a surrogate jailer for the United States was confirmed by a half-dozen current and former intelligence officials working in Europe, the Middle East and the United States. The CIA declined to comment on the prisoner transfer program, but an intelligence official estimated that the number of terrorism suspects sent by the United States to Tashkent was in the dozens."

The United States continues to outsource torture to Uzbekistan.

Nevertheless Russian officials are using the Uzbek eviction to lobby the Kyrgyz to follow suit and the Uzbek regime is cozying back up to its former Motherland. The state-controlled *Novosti Uzbekistana* newspaper wrote in July 2005 that "enthusiasm for 'color revolutions' is declining across the Commonwealth of Independent States, noting that "those who wanted democracy [in Kyrgyzstan] [presumably the United States] got complete anarchy."

Chris Patten wrote in the *International Herald-Tribune*: "The Andijon shockwave continues to reverberate across Central Asia. In the immediate aftermath, hundreds of people tried to escape persecution by fleeing over the border to Kyrgyzstan, which, already close to becoming a failed state itself, was shaken very nearly to its breaking point. Weak and struggling, Kyrgyzstan and Tajikistan are essentially dependent on Uzbekistan for energy and transport. Even relatively prosperous Kazakhstan could be seriously troubled if violence were to drive Uzbeks across its border."

Alexei Malashenko, a Central Asia expert at the Carnegie Moscow Center, said that the Uzbek government believed that their close cooperation with the United States would inoculate them against paying a price for abusing political dissidents. Karimov, was "very astonished" at even the mild criticism he read in the media. "They were showing everybody, the West and especially America, that they were the final frontier against terrorism. Now they're disoriented, because all the time they believed America is an ally, and the fight against terrorism is a very good pretext to do anything in Uzbekistan as far as human rights are concerned and dealing with the opposition."

So the rift between Washington and Tashkent seems to have resulted from a terrible misunderstanding, one that the U.S. would like to resolve. More than five months after the Andijon massacre, Daniel Fried, assistant secretary of State for Europe and Eurasia, told Congress that he had delivered the American government's stance on Uzbekistan: "My message was we want to have better relations with you but there is a serious problem." Asked about possible sanctions, he replied: "I don't want to go further right now." As of this writing, no one has.

Irgiz
Sary su
Perovsk
Syr-darya
Chu
Turkestan
Chimkent
Tashkent

Stan Trek 2000

Amu-darya
AFGHANISTAN
200
250

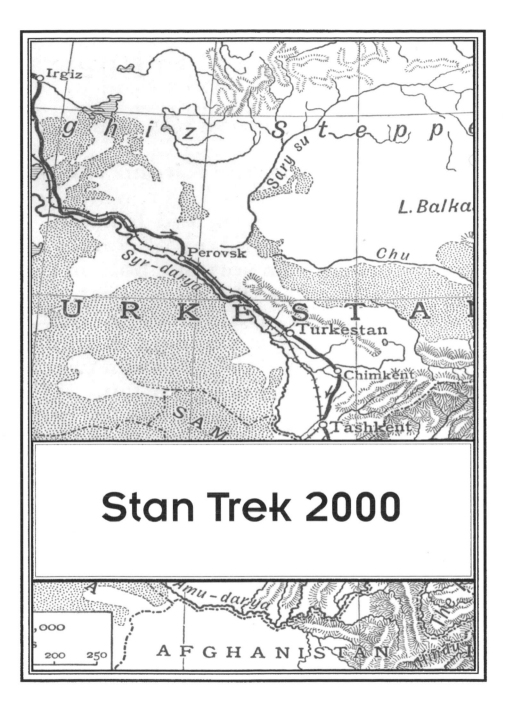

One of the most popular features on a talk show I hosted on KFI radio in Los Angeles was "Stan Trek: Breaking News from Central Asia." As both an experiment and a joke, I invited a group of listeners on the ultimate bus tour from hell: Stan Trek 2000. In August we flew from Los Angeles to Moscow to Baku to Ashkhabat, then picked up a series of buses across Turkmenistan, Uzbekistan, Kazakhstan and Kyrgyzstan. Our plan to drive the Pamir Highway to Dushanbe and enter Afghanistan via military helicopter was stymied when the militants of the Islamic Movement of Uzbekistan laid siege to Osh—where we were staying.

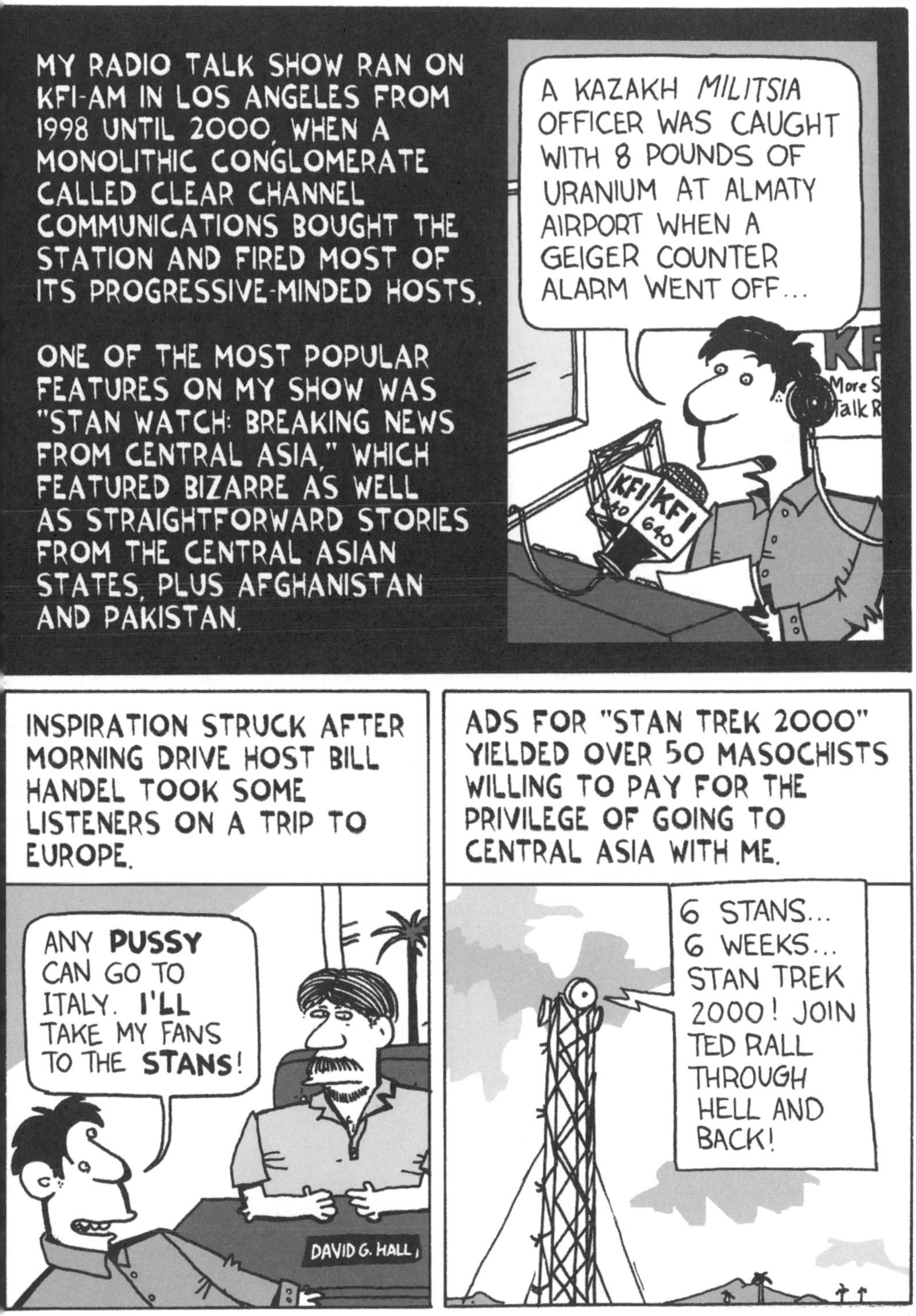
MY RADIO TALK SHOW RAN ON KFI-AM IN LOS ANGELES FROM 1998 UNTIL 2000, WHEN A MONOLITHIC CONGLOMERATE CALLED CLEAR CHANNEL COMMUNICATIONS BOUGHT THE STATION AND FIRED MOST OF ITS PROGRESSIVE-MINDED HOSTS.
ONE OF THE MOST POPULAR FEATURES ON MY SHOW WAS "STAN WATCH: BREAKING NEWS FROM CENTRAL ASIA," WHICH FEATURED BIZARRE AS WELL AS STRAIGHTFORWARD STORIES FROM THE CENTRAL ASIAN STATES, PLUS AFGHANISTAN AND PAKISTAN.
A KAZAKH *MILITSIA* OFFICER WAS CAUGHT WITH 8 POUNDS OF URANIUM AT ALMATY AIRPORT WHEN A GEIGER COUNTER ALARM WENT OFF...
KFI 640
INSPIRATION STRUCK AFTER MORNING DRIVE HOST BILL HANDEL TOOK SOME LISTENERS ON A TRIP TO EUROPE.
ANY **PUSSY** CAN GO TO ITALY. **I'LL** TAKE MY FANS TO THE **STANS**!
DAVID G. HALL
ADS FOR "STAN TREK 2000" YIELDED OVER 50 MASOCHISTS WILLING TO PAY FOR THE PRIVILEGE OF GOING TO CENTRAL ASIA WITH ME.
6 STANS... 6 WEEKS... STAN TREK 2000! JOIN TED RALL THROUGH HELL AND BACK!

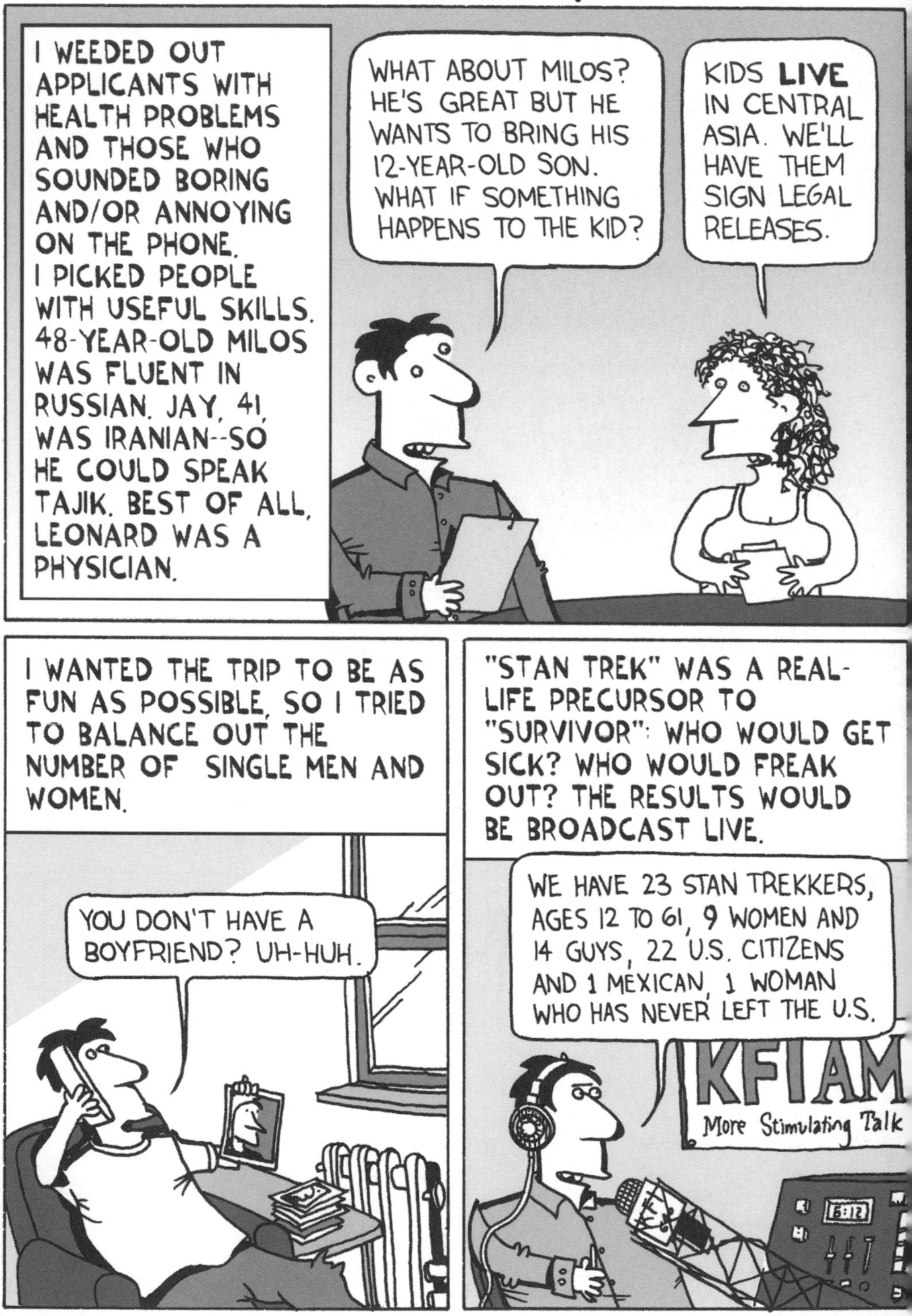
I WEEDED OUT APPLICANTS WITH HEALTH PROBLEMS AND THOSE WHO SOUNDED BORING AND/OR ANNOYING ON THE PHONE. I PICKED PEOPLE WITH USEFUL SKILLS. 48-YEAR-OLD MILOS WAS FLUENT IN RUSSIAN. JAY, 41, WAS IRANIAN--SO HE COULD SPEAK TAJIK. BEST OF ALL, LEONARD WAS A PHYSICIAN.
WHAT ABOUT MILOS? HE'S GREAT BUT HE WANTS TO BRING HIS 12-YEAR-OLD SON. WHAT IF SOMETHING HAPPENS TO THE KID?
KIDS **LIVE** IN CENTRAL ASIA. WE'LL HAVE THEM SIGN LEGAL RELEASES.
I WANTED THE TRIP TO BE AS FUN AS POSSIBLE, SO I TRIED TO BALANCE OUT THE NUMBER OF SINGLE MEN AND WOMEN.
YOU DON'T HAVE A BOYFRIEND? UH-HUH.
"STAN TREK" WAS A REAL-LIFE PRECURSOR TO "SURVIVOR": WHO WOULD GET SICK? WHO WOULD FREAK OUT? THE RESULTS WOULD BE BROADCAST LIVE.
WE HAVE 23 STAN TREKKERS, AGES 12 TO 61, 9 WOMEN AND 14 GUYS, 22 U.S. CITIZENS AND 1 MEXICAN, 1 WOMAN WHO HAS NEVER LEFT THE U.S.
KFIAM
More Stimulating Talk
6:12

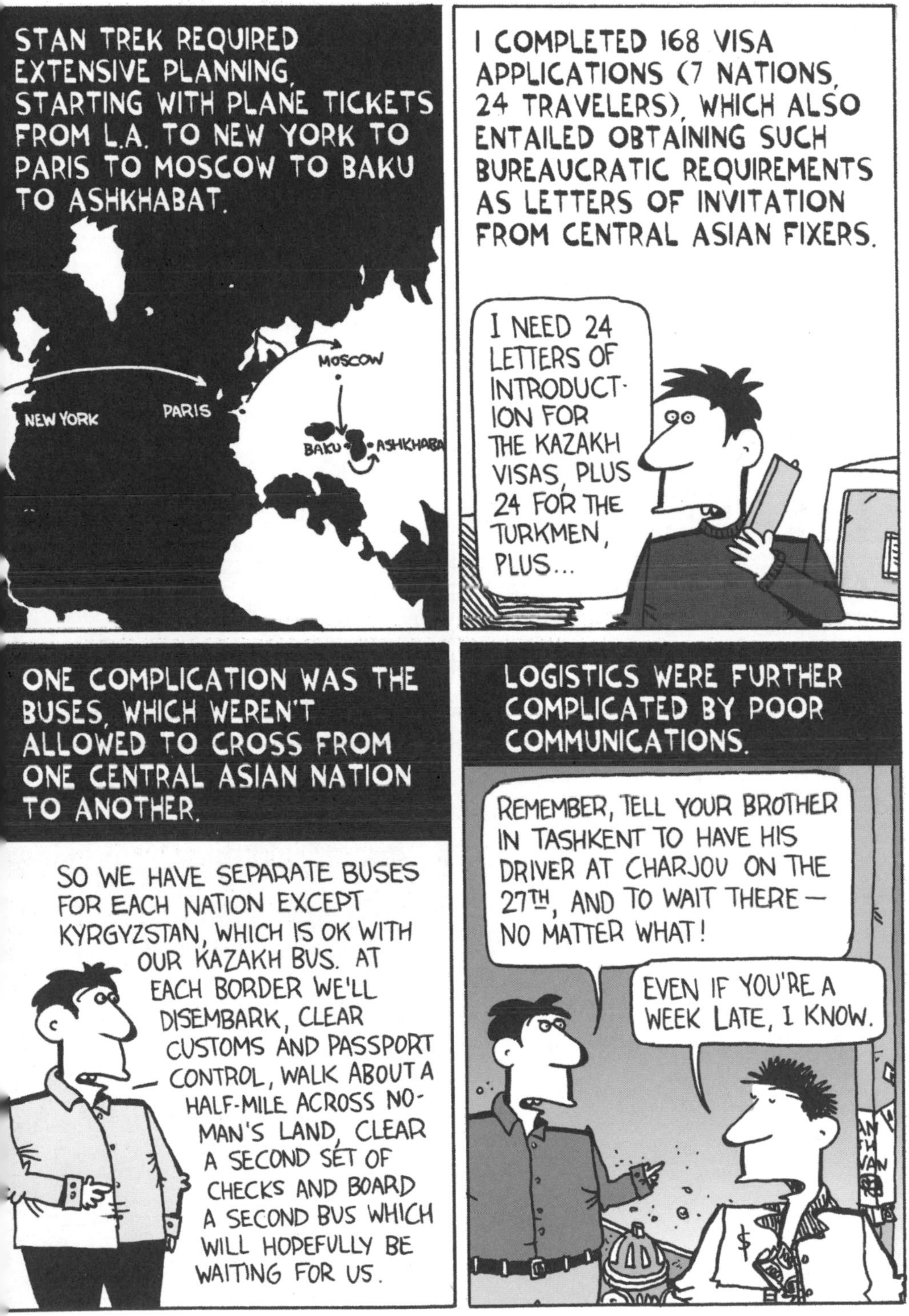
STAN TREK REQUIRED EXTENSIVE PLANNING, STARTING WITH PLANE TICKETS FROM L.A. TO NEW YORK TO PARIS TO MOSCOW TO BAKU TO ASHKHABAT.
MOSCOW
NEW YORK
PARIS
BAKU
I COMPLETED 168 VISA APPLICATIONS (7 NATIONS, 24 TRAVELERS), WHICH ALSO ENTAILED OBTAINING SUCH BUREAUCRATIC REQUIREMENTS AS LETTERS OF INVITATION FROM CENTRAL ASIAN FIXERS.
I NEED 24 LETTERS OF INTRODUCT-ION FOR THE KAZAKH VISAS, PLUS 24 FOR THE TURKMEN, PLUS...
ONE COMPLICATION WAS THE BUSES, WHICH WEREN'T ALLOWED TO CROSS FROM ONE CENTRAL ASIAN NATION TO ANOTHER.
SO WE HAVE SEPARATE BUSES FOR EACH NATION EXCEPT KYRGYZSTAN, WHICH IS OK WITH OUR KAZAKH BUS. AT EACH BORDER WE'LL DISEMBARK, CLEAR CUSTOMS AND PASSPORT CONTROL, WALK ABOUT A HALF-MILE ACROSS NO-MAN'S LAND, CLEAR A SECOND SET OF CHECKS AND BOARD A SECOND BUS WHICH WILL HOPEFULLY BE WAITING FOR US.
LOGISTICS WERE FURTHER COMPLICATED BY POOR COMMUNICATIONS.
REMEMBER, TELL YOUR BROTHER IN TASHKENT TO HAVE HIS DRIVER AT CHARJOU ON THE 27TH, AND TO WAIT THERE— NO MATTER WHAT!
EVEN IF YOU'RE A WEEK LATE, I KNOW.

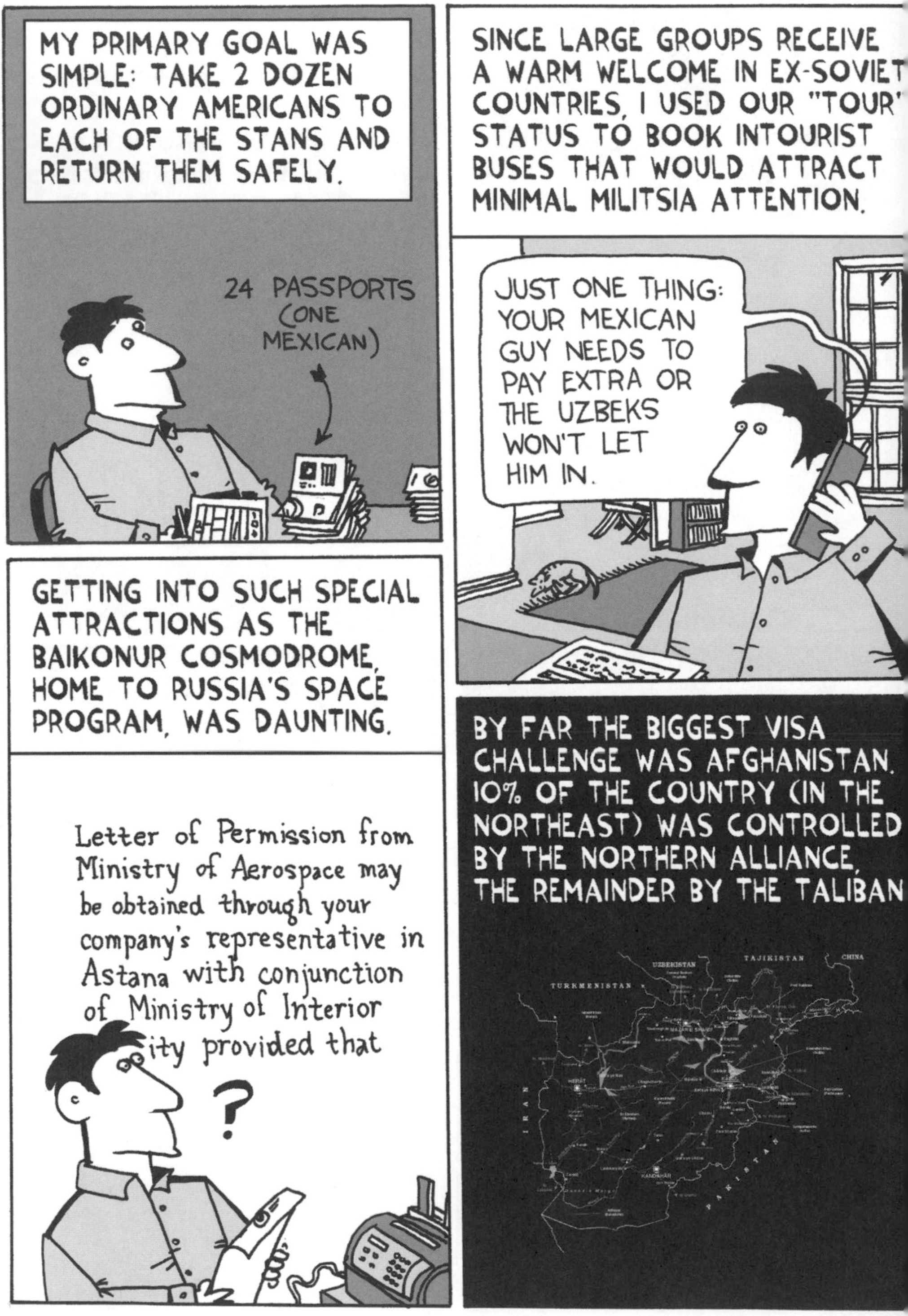
MY PRIMARY GOAL WAS SIMPLE: TAKE 2 DOZEN ORDINARY AMERICANS TO EACH OF THE STANS AND RETURN THEM SAFELY.
24 PASSPORTS (ONE MEXICAN)
SINCE LARGE GROUPS RECEIVE A WARM WELCOME IN EX-SOVIET COUNTRIES, I USED OUR "TOUR" STATUS TO BOOK INTOURIST BUSES THAT WOULD ATTRACT MINIMAL MILITSIA ATTENTION.
JUST ONE THING: YOUR MEXICAN GUY NEEDS TO PAY EXTRA OR THE UZBEKS WON'T LET HIM IN.
GETTING INTO SUCH SPECIAL ATTRACTIONS AS THE BAIKONUR COSMODROME, HOME TO RUSSIA'S SPACE PROGRAM, WAS DAUNTING.
Letter of Permission from Ministry of Aerospace may be obtained through your company's representative in Astana with conjunction of Ministry of Interior
ity provided that
?
BY FAR THE BIGGEST VISA CHALLENGE WAS AFGHANISTAN. 10% OF THE COUNTRY (IN THE NORTHEAST) WAS CONTROLLED BY THE NORTHERN ALLIANCE, THE REMAINDER BY THE TALIBAN.
UZBEKISTAN
TAJIKISTAN
CHINA
TURKMENISTAN
IRAN
PAKISTAN
HERAT
KANDAHAR

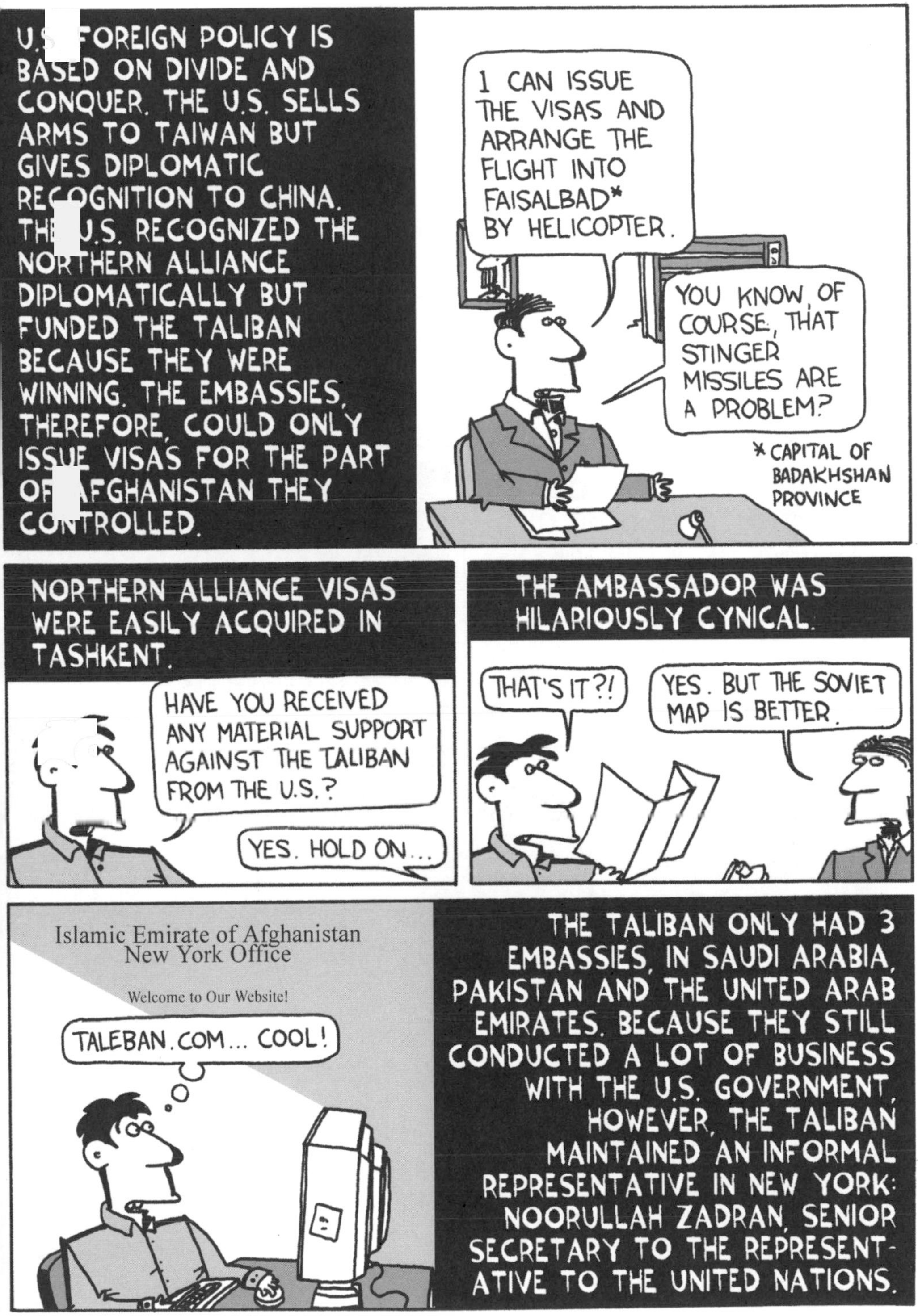
U.S. FOREIGN POLICY IS BASED ON DIVIDE AND CONQUER. THE U.S. SELLS ARMS TO TAIWAN BUT GIVES DIPLOMATIC RECOGNITION TO CHINA. THE U.S. RECOGNIZED THE NORTHERN ALLIANCE DIPLOMATICALLY BUT FUNDED THE TALIBAN BECAUSE THEY WERE WINNING. THE EMBASSIES, THEREFORE, COULD ONLY ISSUE VISAS FOR THE PART OF AFGHANISTAN THEY CONTROLLED.
I CAN ISSUE THE VISAS AND ARRANGE THE FLIGHT INTO FAISALBAD* BY HELICOPTER.
YOU KNOW, OF COURSE, THAT STINGER MISSILES ARE A PROBLEM?
* CAPITAL OF BADAKHSHAN PROVINCE
NORTHERN ALLIANCE VISAS WERE EASILY ACQUIRED IN TASHKENT.
HAVE YOU RECEIVED ANY MATERIAL SUPPORT AGAINST THE TALIBAN FROM THE U.S.?
YES. HOLD ON...
THE AMBASSADOR WAS HILARIOUSLY CYNICAL.
THAT'S IT?!
YES. BUT THE SOVIET MAP IS BETTER.
Islamic Emirate of Afghanistan
New York Office
Welcome to Our Website!
TALEBAN.COM... COOL!
THE TALIBAN ONLY HAD 3 EMBASSIES, IN SAUDI ARABIA, PAKISTAN AND THE UNITED ARAB EMIRATES. BECAUSE THEY STILL CONDUCTED A LOT OF BUSINESS WITH THE U.S. GOVERNMENT. HOWEVER, THE TALIBAN MAINTAINED AN INFORMAL REPRESENTATIVE IN NEW YORK: NOORULLAH ZADRAN, SENIOR SECRETARY TO THE REPRESENTATIVE TO THE UNITED NATIONS.

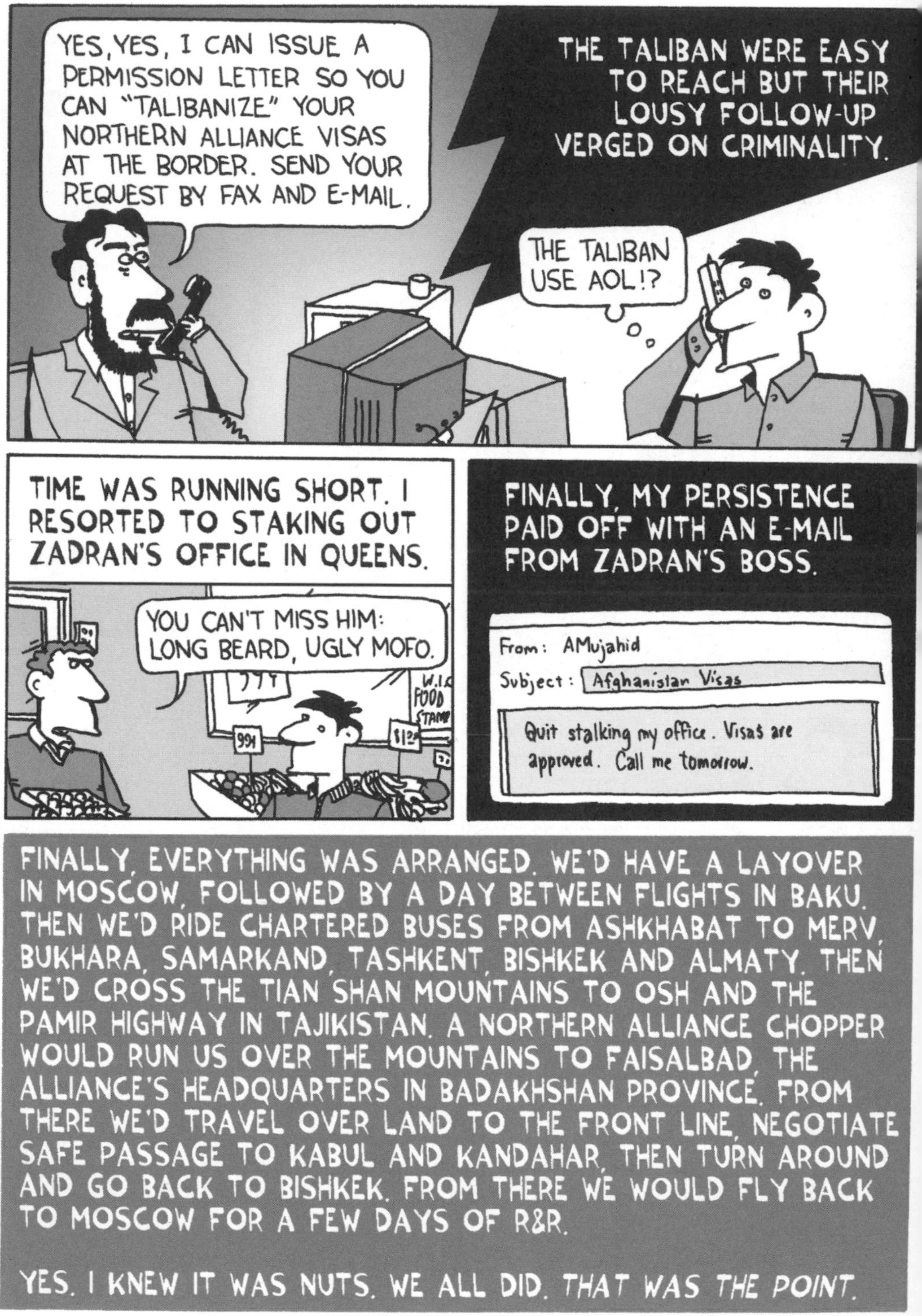
YES, YES, I CAN ISSUE A PERMISSION LETTER SO YOU CAN "TALIBANIZE" YOUR NORTHERN ALLIANCE VISAS AT THE BORDER. SEND YOUR REQUEST BY FAX AND E-MAIL.
THE TALIBAN WERE EASY TO REACH BUT THEIR LOUSY FOLLOW-UP VERGED ON CRIMINALITY.
THE TALIBAN USE AOL!?
TIME WAS RUNNING SHORT. I RESORTED TO STAKING OUT ZADRAN'S OFFICE IN QUEENS.
YOU CAN'T MISS HIM: LONG BEARD, UGLY MOFO.
FINALLY, MY PERSISTENCE PAID OFF WITH AN E-MAIL FROM ZADRAN'S BOSS.
From: AMujahid
Subject: Afghanistan Visas
Quit stalking my office. Visas are approved. Call me tomorrow.
FINALLY, EVERYTHING WAS ARRANGED. WE'D HAVE A LAYOVER IN MOSCOW, FOLLOWED BY A DAY BETWEEN FLIGHTS IN BAKU. THEN WE'D RIDE CHARTERED BUSES FROM ASHKHABAT TO MERV, BUKHARA, SAMARKAND, TASHKENT, BISHKEK AND ALMATY. THEN WE'D CROSS THE TIAN SHAN MOUNTAINS TO OSH AND THE PAMIR HIGHWAY IN TAJIKISTAN. A NORTHERN ALLIANCE CHOPPER WOULD RUN US OVER THE MOUNTAINS TO FAISALBAD, THE ALLIANCE'S HEADQUARTERS IN BADAKHSHAN PROVINCE. FROM THERE WE'D TRAVEL OVER LAND TO THE FRONT LINE, NEGOTIATE SAFE PASSAGE TO KABUL AND KANDAHAR, THEN TURN AROUND AND GO BACK TO BISHKEK. FROM THERE WE WOULD FLY BACK TO MOSCOW FOR A FEW DAYS OF R&R.
YES, I KNEW IT WAS NUTS. WE ALL DID. THAT WAS THE POINT.

FOR ME, THE WORST PART ABOUT STAN TREK--THE PAPERWORK--WAS OVER. FOR 23 OTHER UNSUSPECTING PEOPLE, HOWEVER, THIS MISADVENTURE OF A LIFETIME WAS ABOUT TO BEGIN.

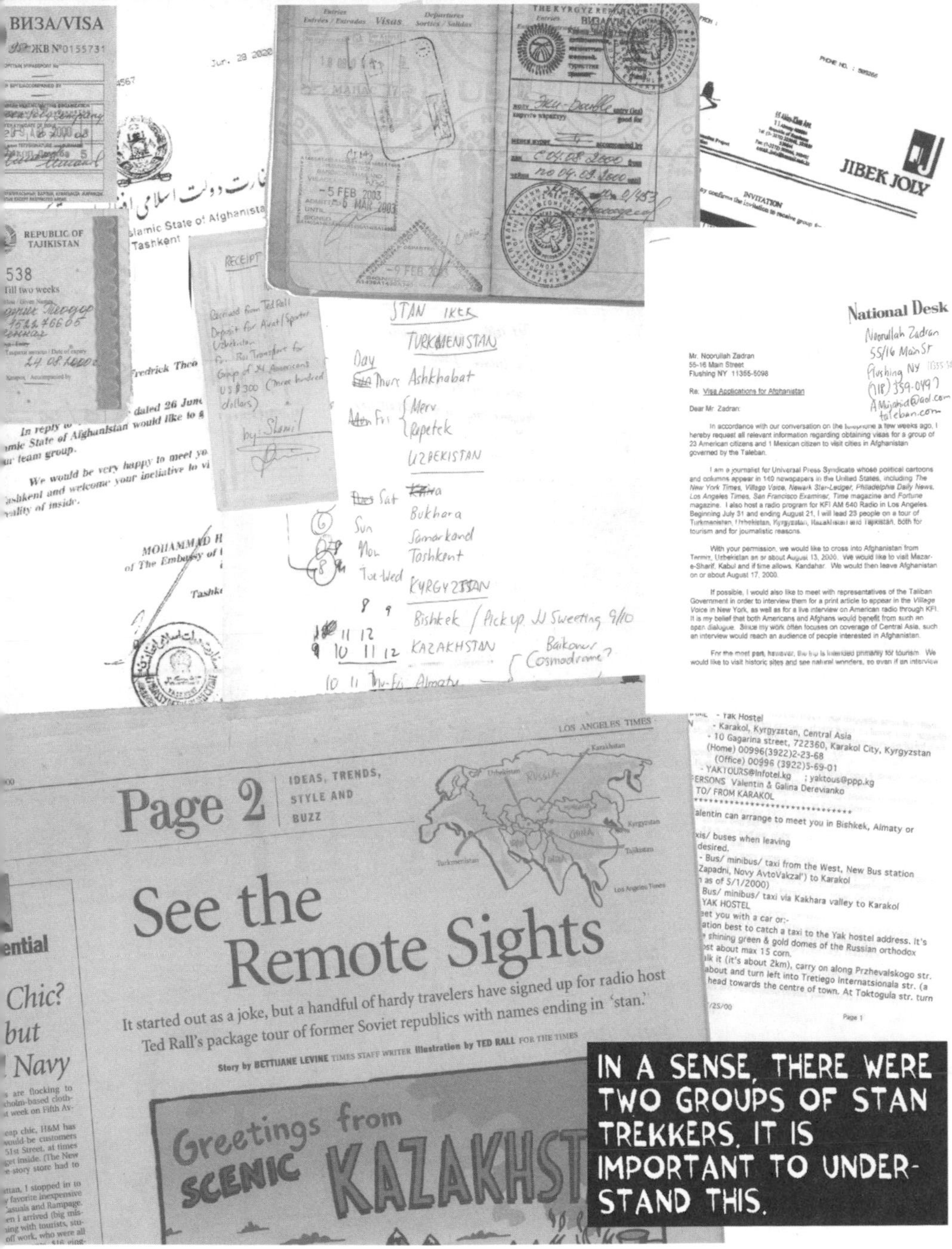
ВИЗА/VISA
REPUBLIC OF TAJIKISTAN
Islamic State of Afghanistan
Tashkent
RECEIPT
JIBEK JOLY
INVITATION
STAN TREK
TURKMENISTAN
Ashkhabat
Merv
Repetek
UZBEKISTAN
Bukhara
Samarkand
Tashkent
KYRGYZSTAN
Bishkek
KAZAKHSTAN
Baikonur Cosmodrome?
National Desk
Re: Visa Applications for Afghanistan
Dear Mr. Zadran:
Yak Hostel
Karakol, Kyrgyzstan, Central Asia
LOS ANGELES TIMES
Page 2
IDEAS, TRENDS, STYLE AND BUZZ
See the Remote Sights
It started out as a joke, but a handful of hardy travelers have signed up for radio host Ted Rall's package tour of former Soviet republics with names ending in 'stan.'
Story by BETTIJANE LEVINE TIMES STAFF WRITER Illustration by TED RALL FOR THE TIMES
Greetings from SCENIC KAZAKHST
Chic?
but
Navy
IN A SENSE, THERE WERE TWO GROUPS OF STAN TREKKERS. IT IS IMPORTANT TO UNDERSTAND THIS.

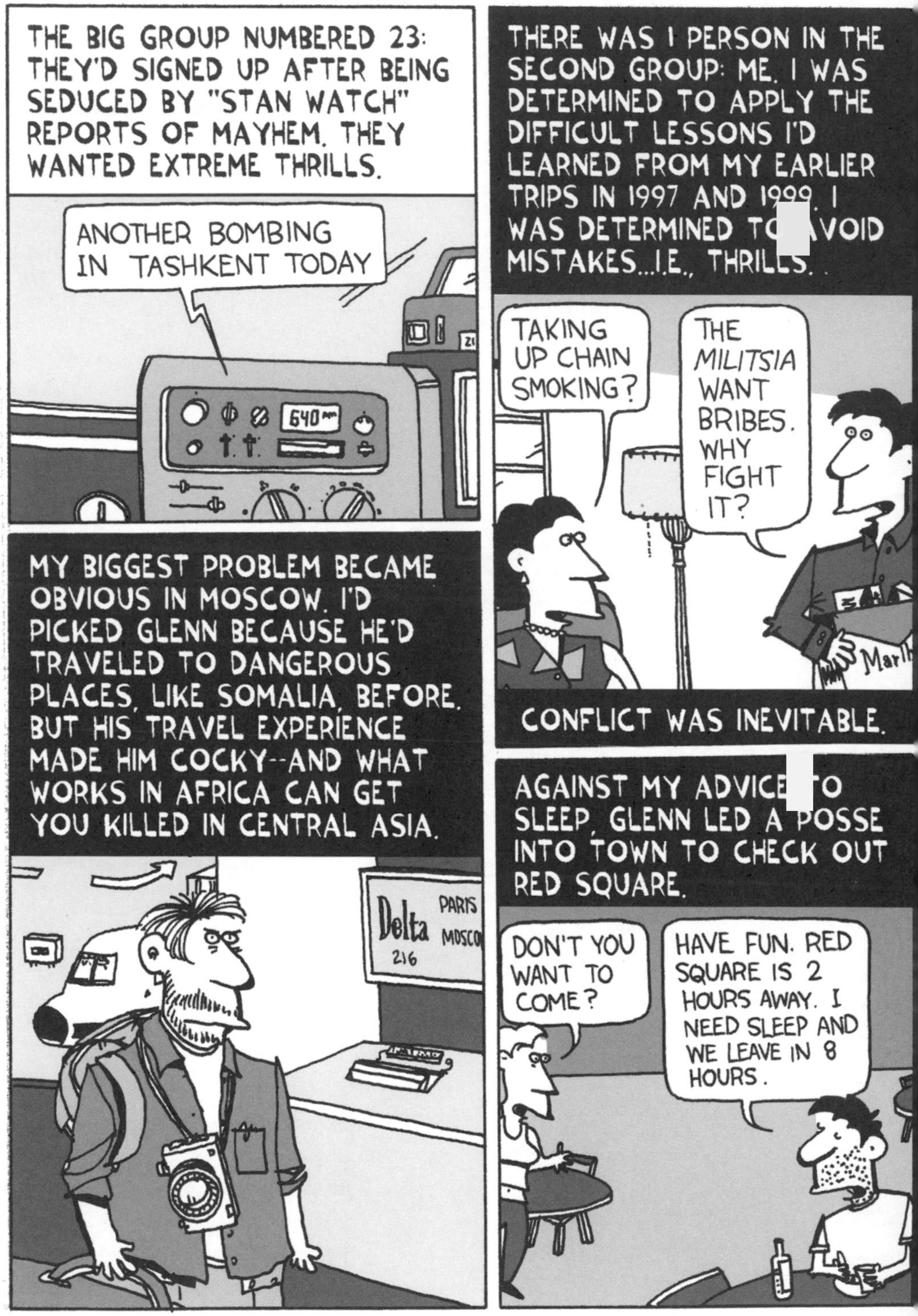
THE BIG GROUP NUMBERED 23: THEY'D SIGNED UP AFTER BEING SEDUCED BY "STAN WATCH" REPORTS OF MAYHEM. THEY WANTED EXTREME THRILLS.
ANOTHER BOMBING IN TASHKENT TODAY
THERE WAS 1 PERSON IN THE SECOND GROUP: ME. I WAS DETERMINED TO APPLY THE DIFFICULT LESSONS I'D LEARNED FROM MY EARLIER TRIPS IN 1997 AND 1999. I WAS DETERMINED TO AVOID MISTAKES...I.E., THRILLS.
TAKING UP CHAIN SMOKING?
THE MILITSIA WANT BRIBES. WHY FIGHT IT?
CONFLICT WAS INEVITABLE.
MY BIGGEST PROBLEM BECAME OBVIOUS IN MOSCOW. I'D PICKED GLENN BECAUSE HE'D TRAVELED TO DANGEROUS PLACES, LIKE SOMALIA, BEFORE. BUT HIS TRAVEL EXPERIENCE MADE HIM COCKY--AND WHAT WORKS IN AFRICA CAN GET YOU KILLED IN CENTRAL ASIA.
Delta
PARIS
216
AGAINST MY ADVICE TO SLEEP, GLENN LED A POSSE INTO TOWN TO CHECK OUT RED SQUARE.
DON'T YOU WANT TO COME?
HAVE FUN. RED SQUARE IS 2 HOURS AWAY. I NEED SLEEP AND WE LEAVE IN 8 HOURS.

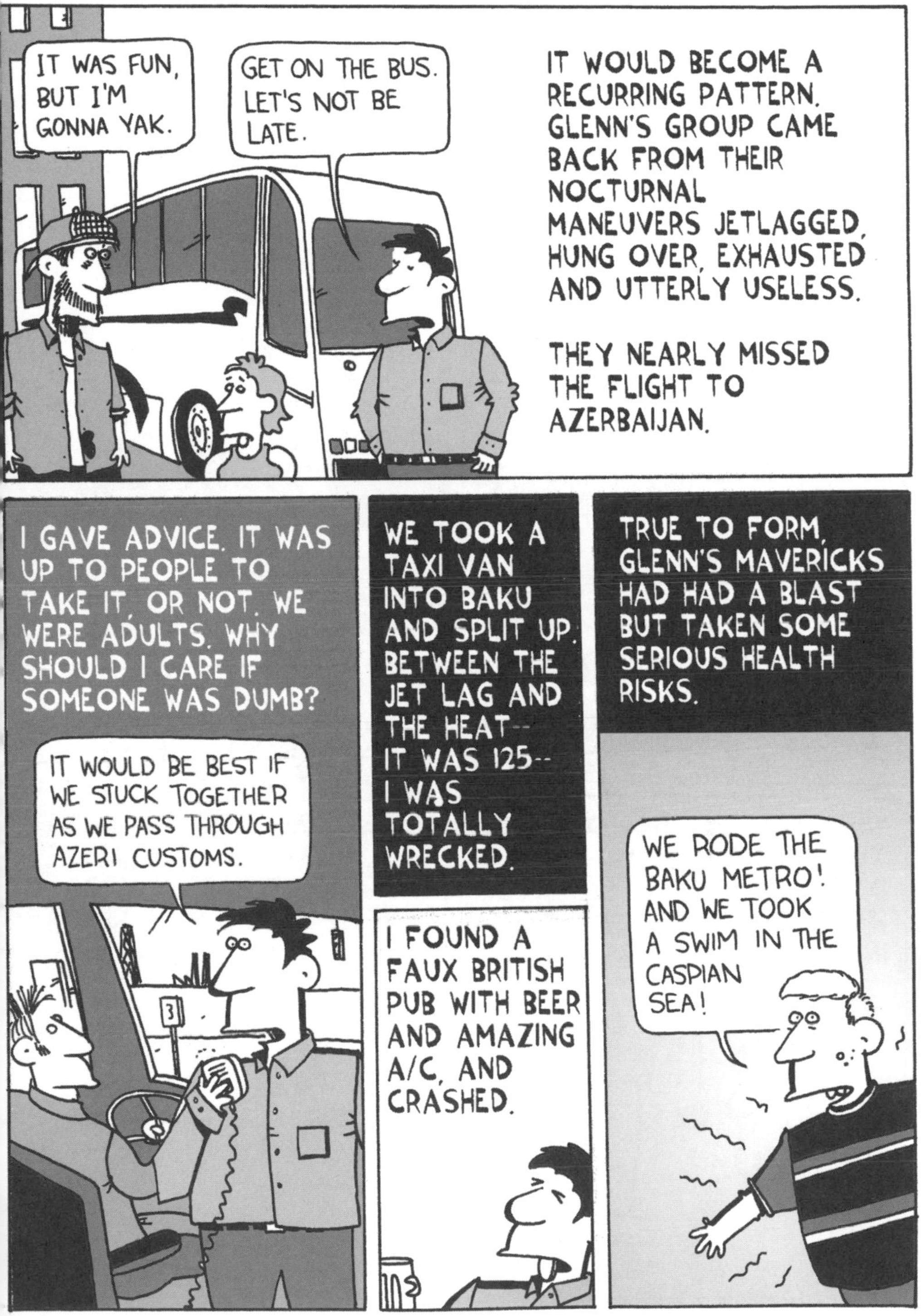
IT WAS FUN, BUT I'M GONNA YAK.
GET ON THE BUS. LET'S NOT BE LATE.
IT WOULD BECOME A RECURRING PATTERN. GLENN'S GROUP CAME BACK FROM THEIR NOCTURNAL MANEUVERS JETLAGGED, HUNG OVER, EXHAUSTED AND UTTERLY USELESS.
THEY NEARLY MISSED THE FLIGHT TO AZERBAIJAN.
I GAVE ADVICE. IT WAS UP TO PEOPLE TO TAKE IT, OR NOT. WE WERE ADULTS. WHY SHOULD I CARE IF SOMEONE WAS DUMB?
IT WOULD BE BEST IF WE STUCK TOGETHER AS WE PASS THROUGH AZERI CUSTOMS.
WE TOOK A TAXI VAN INTO BAKU AND SPLIT UP. BETWEEN THE JET LAG AND THE HEAT-- IT WAS 125-- I WAS TOTALLY WRECKED.
I FOUND A FAUX BRITISH PUB WITH BEER AND AMAZING A/C, AND CRASHED.
TRUE TO FORM, GLENN'S MAVERICKS HAD HAD A BLAST BUT TAKEN SOME SERIOUS HEALTH RISKS.
WE RODE THE BAKU METRO! AND WE TOOK A SWIM IN THE CASPIAN SEA!

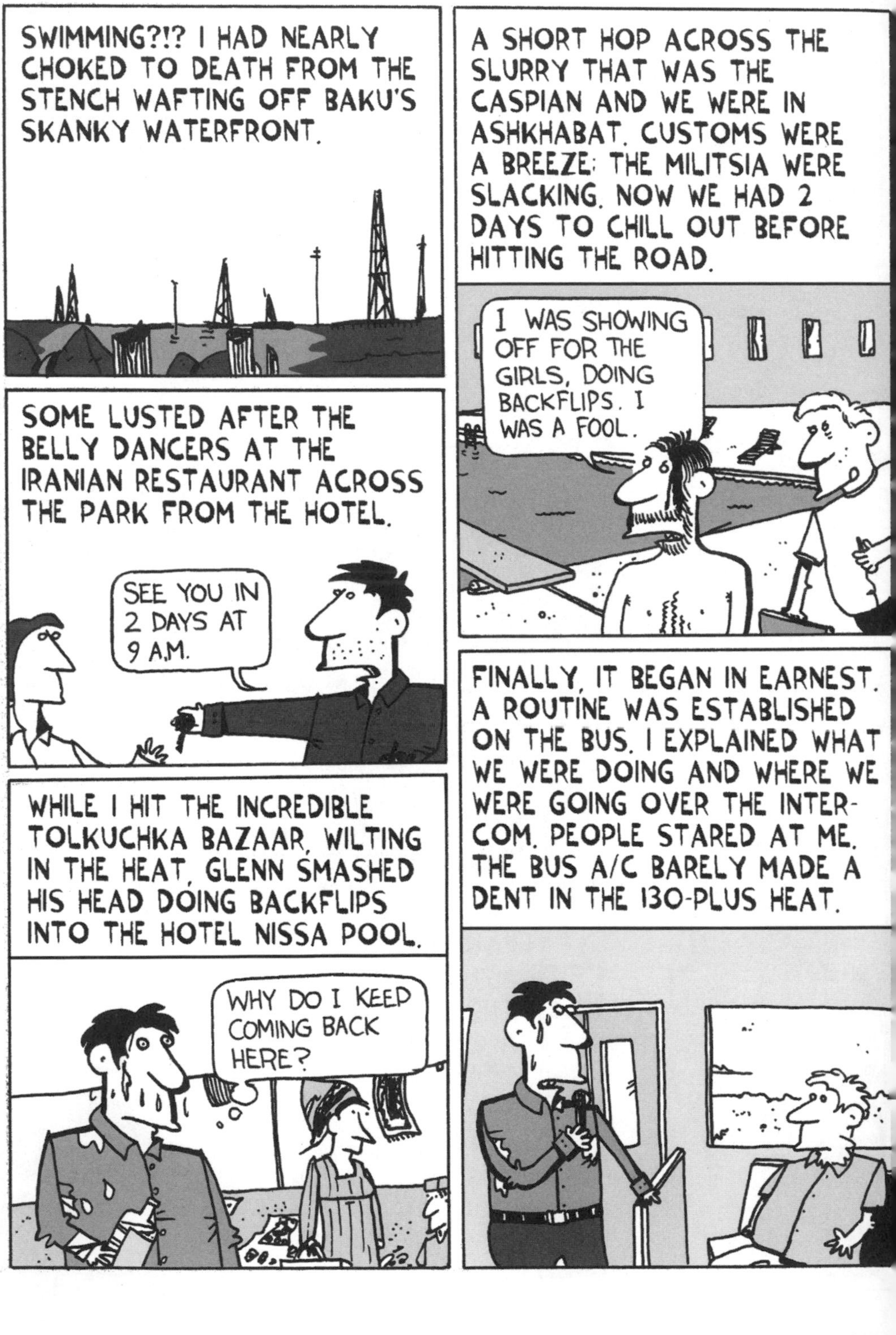
SWIMMING?!? I HAD NEARLY CHOKED TO DEATH FROM THE STENCH WAFTING OFF BAKU'S SKANKY WATERFRONT.
A SHORT HOP ACROSS THE SLURRY THAT WAS THE CASPIAN AND WE WERE IN ASHKHABAT. CUSTOMS WERE A BREEZE; THE MILITSIA WERE SLACKING. NOW WE HAD 2 DAYS TO CHILL OUT BEFORE HITTING THE ROAD.
SOME LUSTED AFTER THE BELLY DANCERS AT THE IRANIAN RESTAURANT ACROSS THE PARK FROM THE HOTEL.
SEE YOU IN 2 DAYS AT 9 A.M.
I WAS SHOWING OFF FOR THE GIRLS, DOING BACKFLIPS. I WAS A FOOL.
WHILE I HIT THE INCREDIBLE TOLKUCHKA BAZAAR, WILTING IN THE HEAT, GLENN SMASHED HIS HEAD DOING BACKFLIPS INTO THE HOTEL NISSA POOL.
WHY DO I KEEP COMING BACK HERE?
FINALLY, IT BEGAN IN EARNEST. A ROUTINE WAS ESTABLISHED ON THE BUS. I EXPLAINED WHAT WE WERE DOING AND WHERE WE WERE GOING OVER THE INTER-COM. PEOPLE STARED AT ME. THE BUS A/C BARELY MADE A DENT IN THE 130-PLUS HEAT.

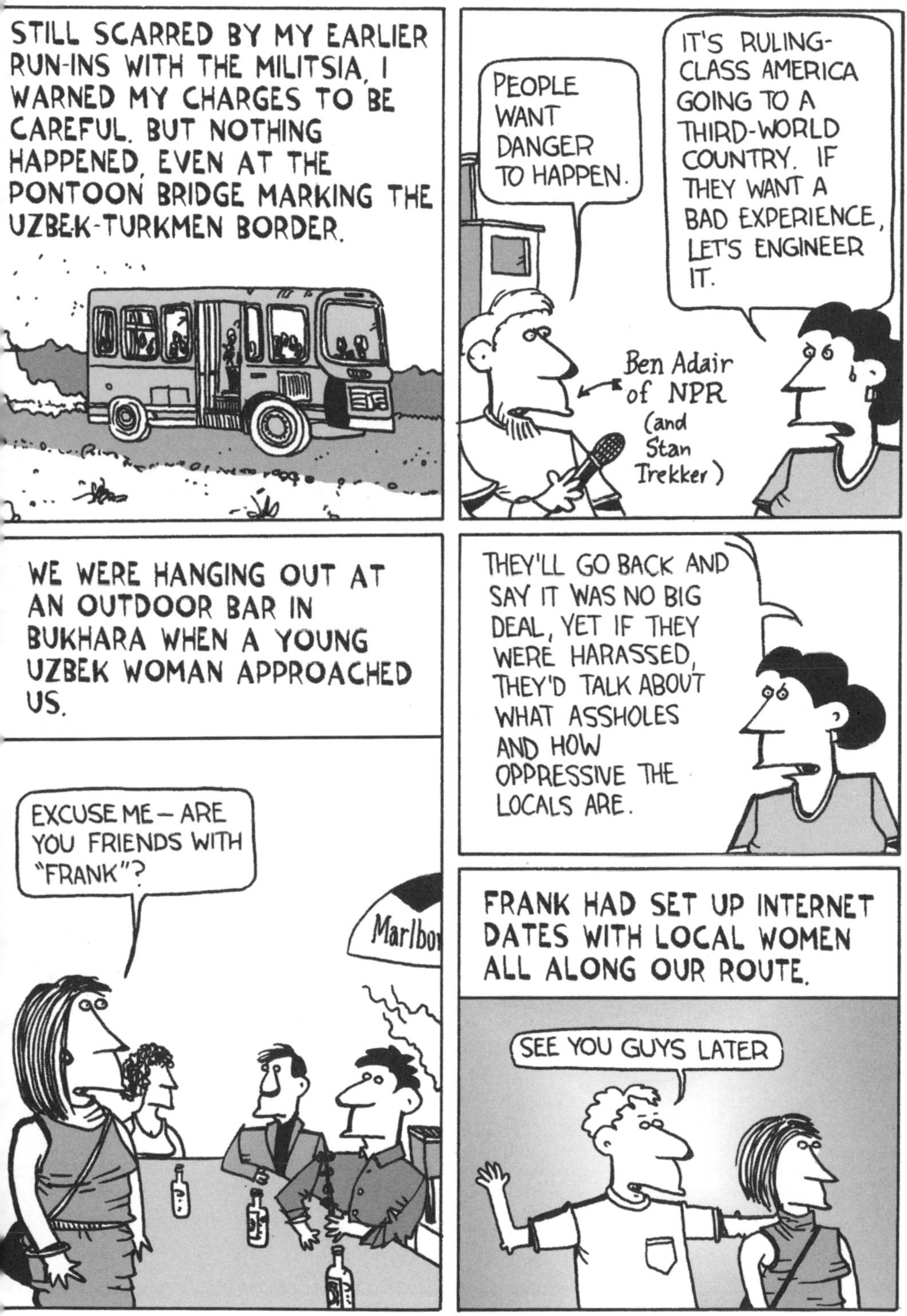
STILL SCARRED BY MY EARLIER RUN-INS WITH THE MILITSIA, I WARNED MY CHARGES TO BE CAREFUL. BUT NOTHING HAPPENED, EVEN AT THE PONTOON BRIDGE MARKING THE UZBEK-TURKMEN BORDER.
PEOPLE WANT DANGER TO HAPPEN.
IT'S RULING-CLASS AMERICA GOING TO A THIRD-WORLD COUNTRY. IF THEY WANT A BAD EXPERIENCE, LET'S ENGINEER IT.
Ben Adair of NPR (and Stan Trekker)
THEY'LL GO BACK AND SAY IT WAS NO BIG DEAL, YET IF THEY WERE HARASSED, THEY'D TALK ABOUT WHAT ASSHOLES AND HOW OPPRESSIVE THE LOCALS ARE.
WE WERE HANGING OUT AT AN OUTDOOR BAR IN BUKHARA WHEN A YOUNG UZBEK WOMAN APPROACHED US.
EXCUSE ME—ARE YOU FRIENDS WITH "FRANK"?
Marlbor
FRANK HAD SET UP INTERNET DATES WITH LOCAL WOMEN ALL ALONG OUR ROUTE.
SEE YOU GUYS LATER

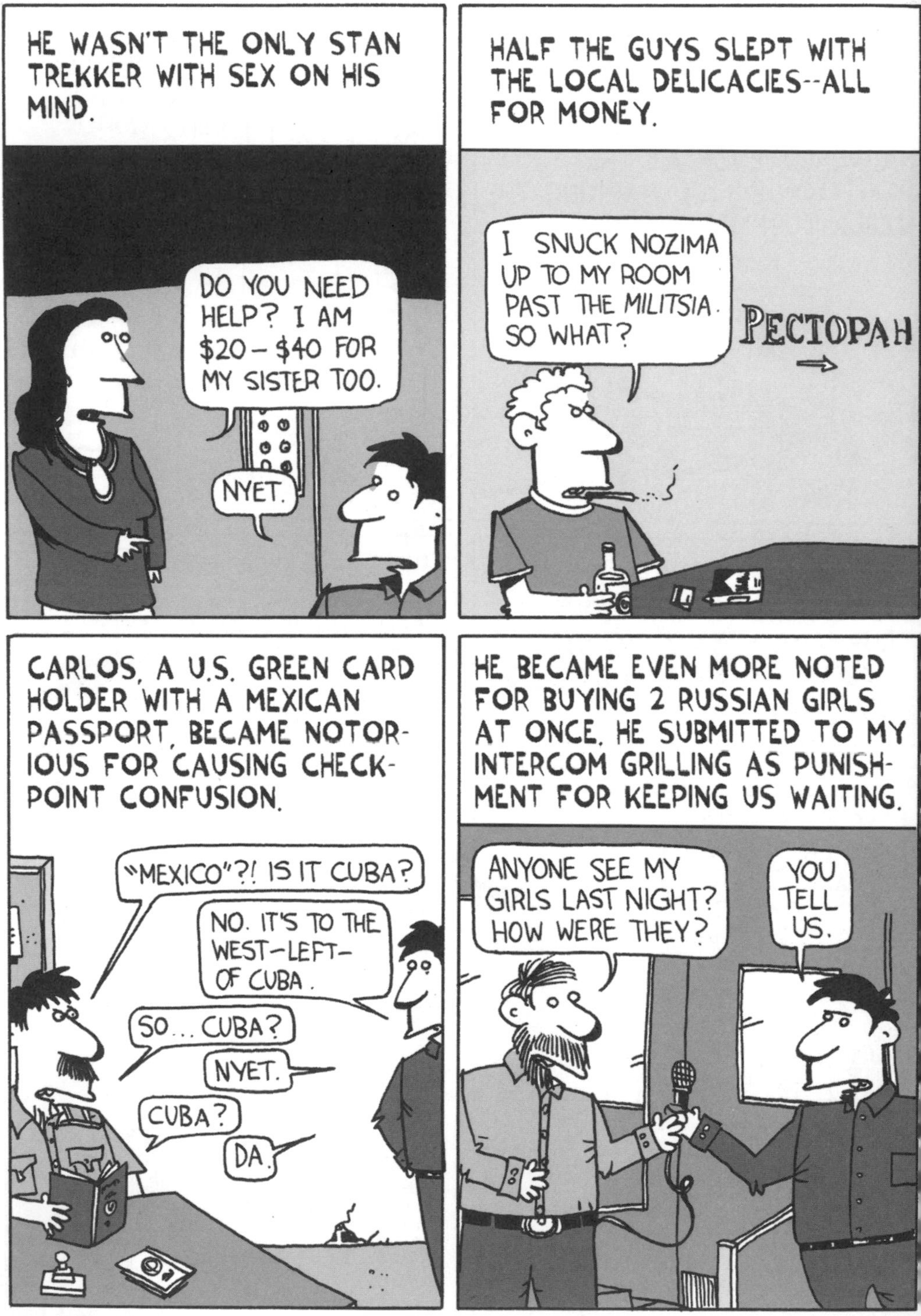
HE WASN'T THE ONLY STAN TREKKER WITH SEX ON HIS MIND.
DO YOU NEED HELP? I AM $20 – $40 FOR MY SISTER TOO.
NYET.
HALF THE GUYS SLEPT WITH THE LOCAL DELICACIES--ALL FOR MONEY.
I SNUCK NOZIMA UP TO MY ROOM PAST THE MILITSIA. SO WHAT?
PECTOPAH
CARLOS, A U.S. GREEN CARD HOLDER WITH A MEXICAN PASSPORT, BECAME NOTORIOUS FOR CAUSING CHECKPOINT CONFUSION.
"MEXICO"?! IS IT CUBA?
NO. IT'S TO THE WEST—LEFT—OF CUBA.
SO... CUBA?
NYET.
CUBA?
DA.
HE BECAME EVEN MORE NOTED FOR BUYING 2 RUSSIAN GIRLS AT ONCE. HE SUBMITTED TO MY INTERCOM GRILLING AS PUNISHMENT FOR KEEPING US WAITING.
ANYONE SEE MY GIRLS LAST NIGHT? HOW WERE THEY?
YOU TELL US.

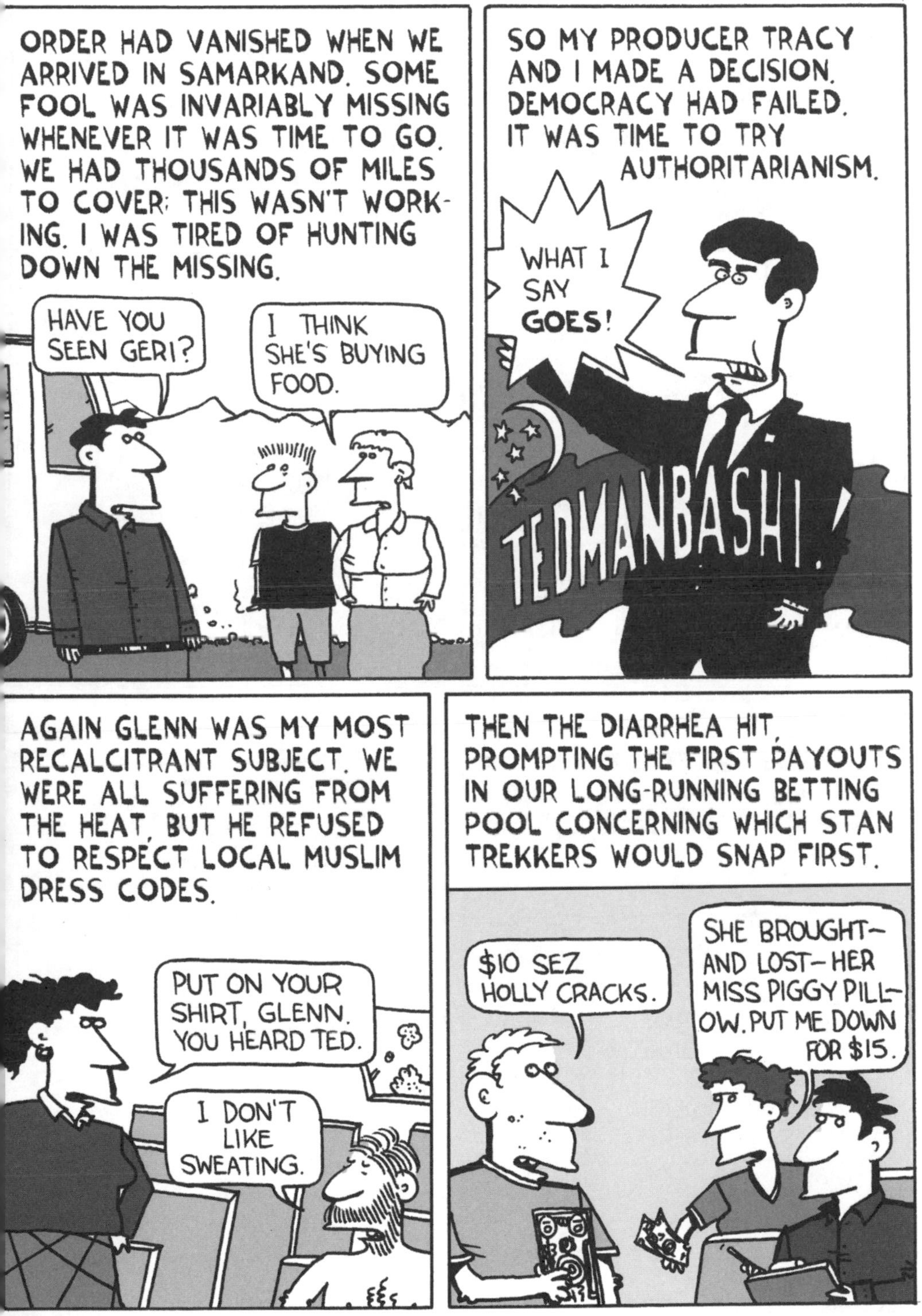
ORDER HAD VANISHED WHEN WE ARRIVED IN SAMARKAND. SOME FOOL WAS INVARIABLY MISSING WHENEVER IT WAS TIME TO GO. WE HAD THOUSANDS OF MILES TO COVER; THIS WASN'T WORKING. I WAS TIRED OF HUNTING DOWN THE MISSING.
HAVE YOU SEEN GERI?
I THINK SHE'S BUYING FOOD.
SO MY PRODUCER TRACY AND I MADE A DECISION. DEMOCRACY HAD FAILED. IT WAS TIME TO TRY AUTHORITARIANISM.
WHAT I SAY GOES!
TEDMANBASHI
AGAIN GLENN WAS MY MOST RECALCITRANT SUBJECT. WE WERE ALL SUFFERING FROM THE HEAT, BUT HE REFUSED TO RESPECT LOCAL MUSLIM DRESS CODES.
PUT ON YOUR SHIRT, GLENN. YOU HEARD TED.
I DON'T LIKE SWEATING.
THEN THE DIARRHEA HIT, PROMPTING THE FIRST PAYOUTS IN OUR LONG-RUNNING BETTING POOL CONCERNING WHICH STAN TREKKERS WOULD SNAP FIRST.
$10 SEZ HOLLY CRACKS.
SHE BROUGHT—AND LOST—HER MISS PIGGY PILLOW. PUT ME DOWN FOR $15.

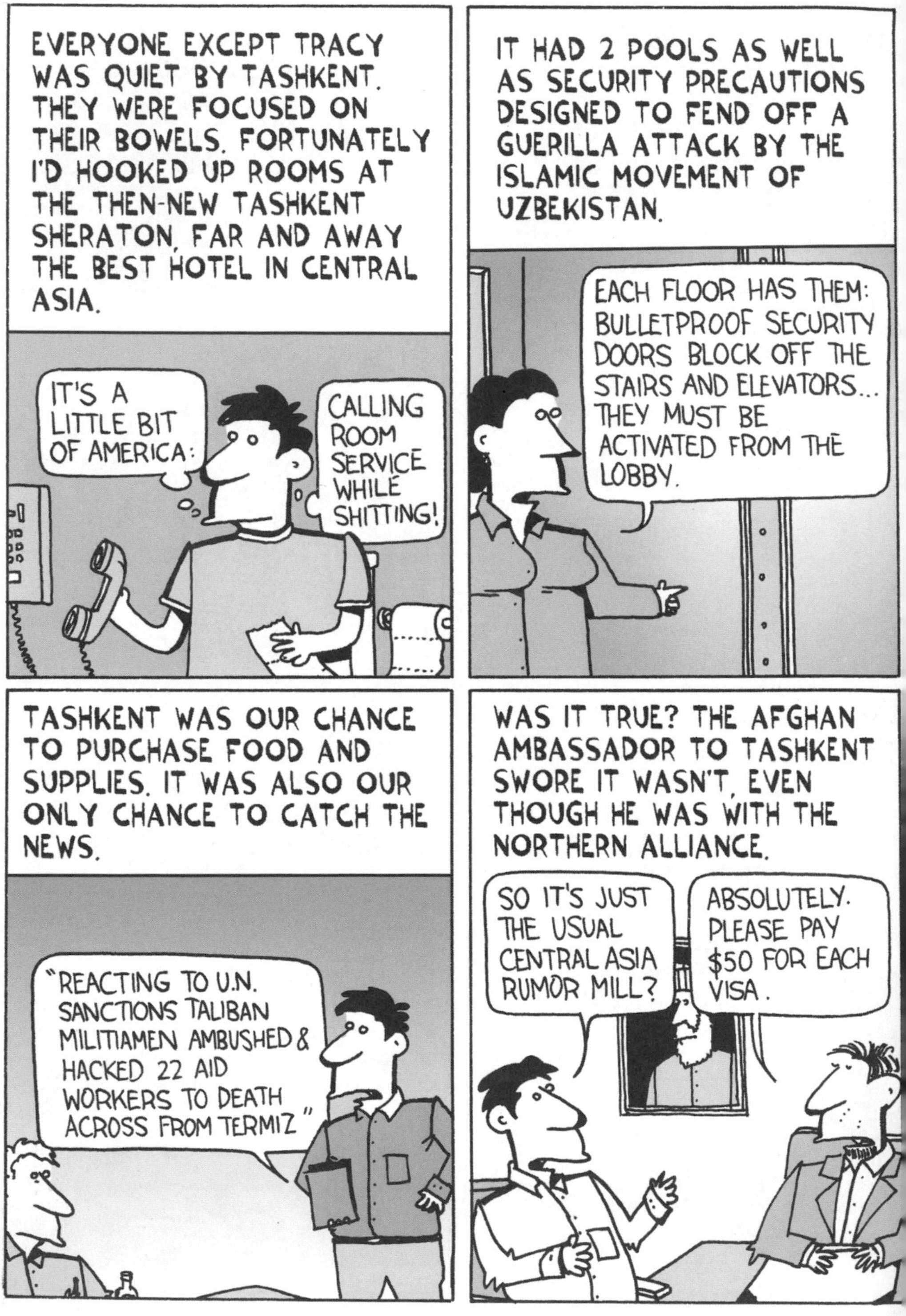
EVERYONE EXCEPT TRACY WAS QUIET BY TASHKENT. THEY WERE FOCUSED ON THEIR BOWELS. FORTUNATELY I'D HOOKED UP ROOMS AT THE THEN-NEW TASHKENT SHERATON, FAR AND AWAY THE BEST HOTEL IN CENTRAL ASIA.
IT'S A LITTLE BIT OF AMERICA:
CALLING ROOM SERVICE WHILE SHITTING!
IT HAD 2 POOLS AS WELL AS SECURITY PRECAUTIONS DESIGNED TO FEND OFF A GUERILLA ATTACK BY THE ISLAMIC MOVEMENT OF UZBEKISTAN.
EACH FLOOR HAS THEM: BULLETPROOF SECURITY DOORS BLOCK OFF THE STAIRS AND ELEVATORS... THEY MUST BE ACTIVATED FROM THE LOBBY.
TASHKENT WAS OUR CHANCE TO PURCHASE FOOD AND SUPPLIES. IT WAS ALSO OUR ONLY CHANCE TO CATCH THE NEWS.
"REACTING TO U.N. SANCTIONS TALIBAN MILITIAMEN AMBUSHED & HACKED 22 AID WORKERS TO DEATH ACROSS FROM TERMIZ"
WAS IT TRUE? THE AFGHAN AMBASSADOR TO TASHKENT SWORE IT WASN'T, EVEN THOUGH HE WAS WITH THE NORTHERN ALLIANCE.
SO IT'S JUST THE USUAL CENTRAL ASIA RUMOR MILL?
ABSOLUTELY. PLEASE PAY $50 FOR EACH VISA.

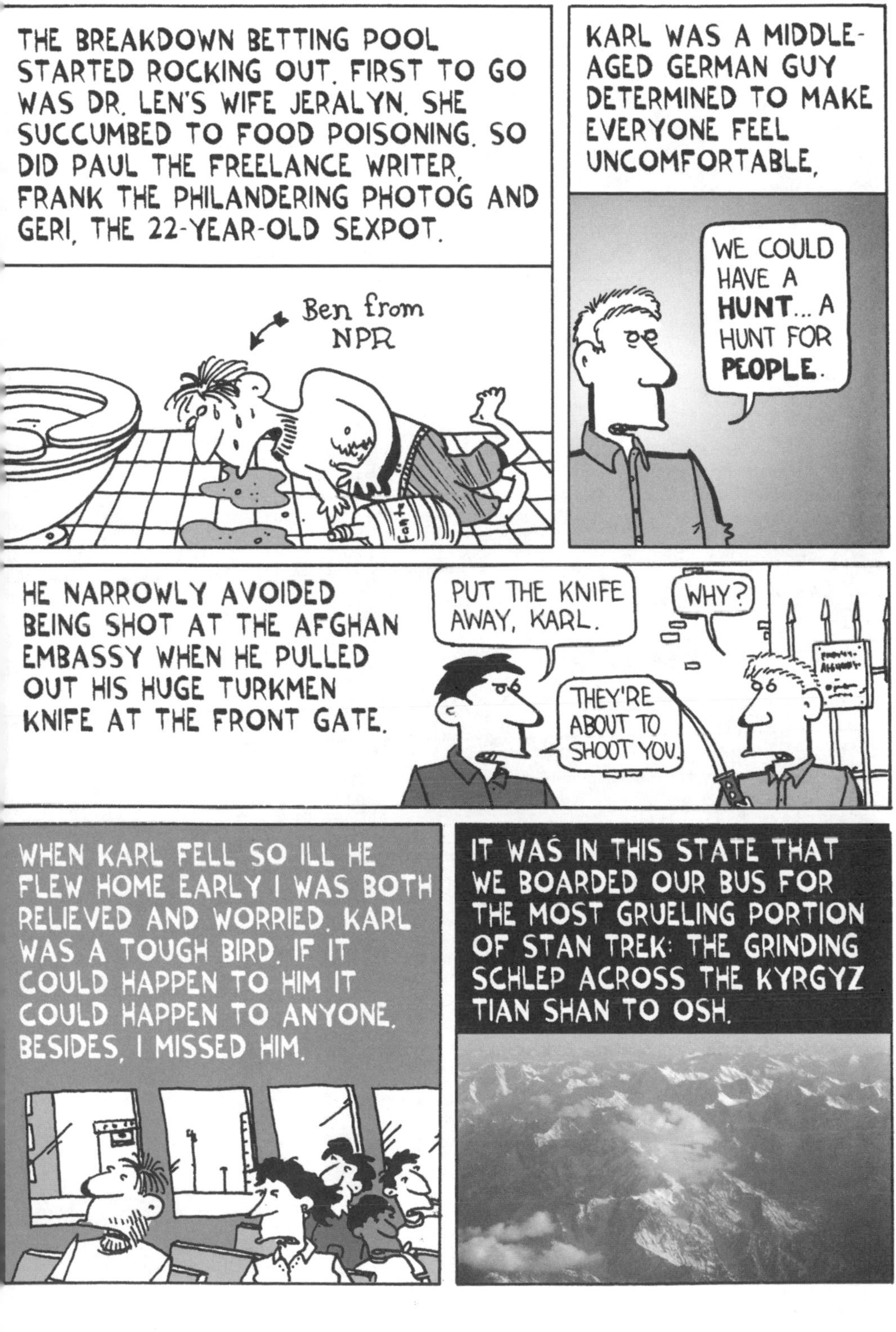
THE BREAKDOWN BETTING POOL STARTED ROCKING OUT. FIRST TO GO WAS DR. LEN'S WIFE JERALYN. SHE SUCCUMBED TO FOOD POISONING. SO DID PAUL THE FREELANCE WRITER, FRANK THE PHILANDERING PHOTOG AND GERI, THE 22-YEAR-OLD SEXPOT.
Ben from NPR
KARL WAS A MIDDLE-AGED GERMAN GUY DETERMINED TO MAKE EVERYONE FEEL UNCOMFORTABLE.
WE COULD HAVE A **HUNT**... A HUNT FOR **PEOPLE**.
HE NARROWLY AVOIDED BEING SHOT AT THE AFGHAN EMBASSY WHEN HE PULLED OUT HIS HUGE TURKMEN KNIFE AT THE FRONT GATE.
PUT THE KNIFE AWAY, KARL.
WHY?
THEY'RE ABOUT TO SHOOT YOU.
WHEN KARL FELL SO ILL HE FLEW HOME EARLY I WAS BOTH RELIEVED AND WORRIED. KARL WAS A TOUGH BIRD. IF IT COULD HAPPEN TO HIM IT COULD HAPPEN TO ANYONE. BESIDES, I MISSED HIM.
IT WAS IN THIS STATE THAT WE BOARDED OUR BUS FOR THE MOST GRUELING PORTION OF STAN TREK: THE GRINDING SCHLEP ACROSS THE KYRGYZ TIAN SHAN TO OSH.

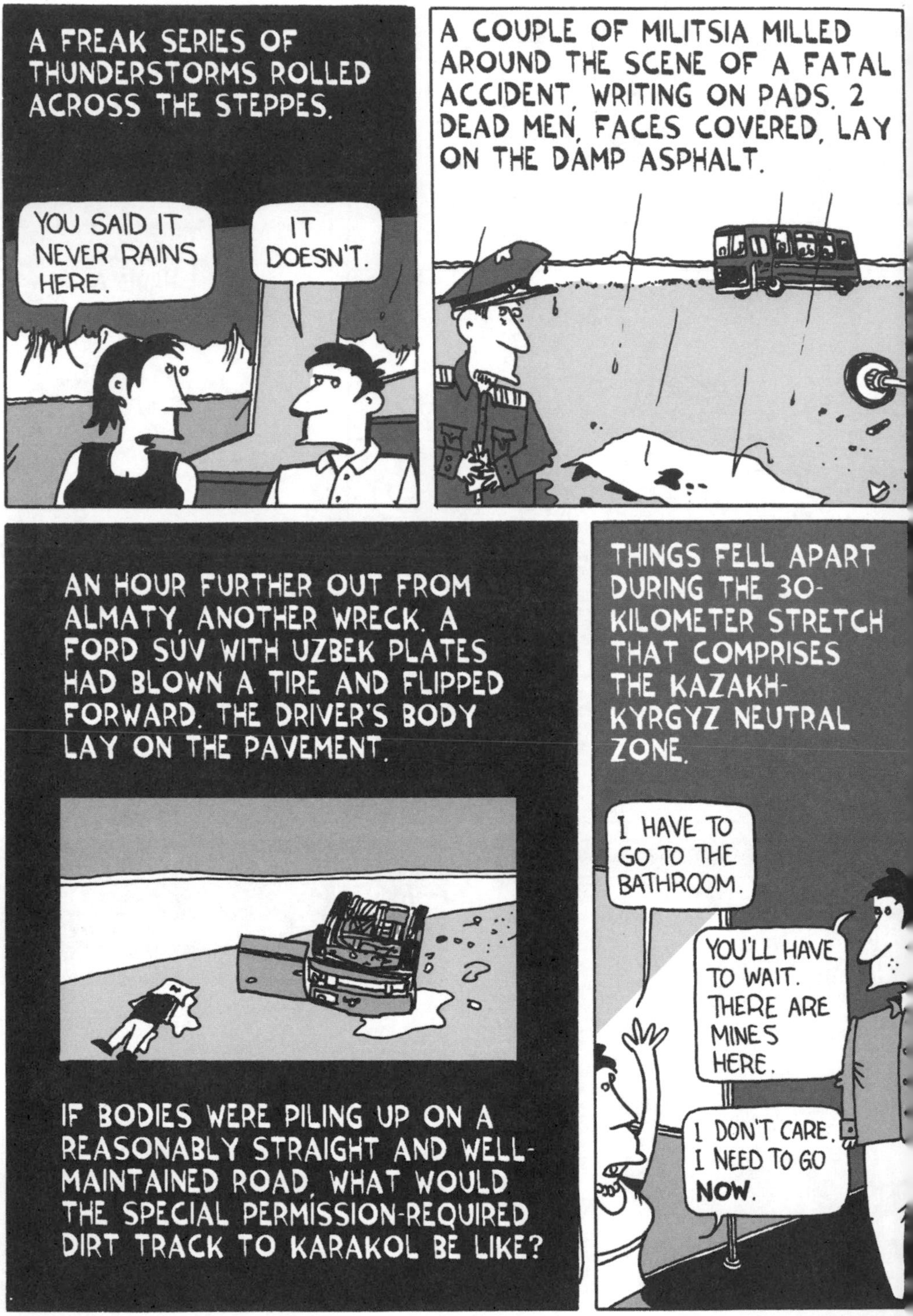
A FREAK SERIES OF THUNDERSTORMS ROLLED ACROSS THE STEPPES.
YOU SAID IT NEVER RAINS HERE.
IT DOESN'T.
A COUPLE OF MILITSIA MILLED AROUND THE SCENE OF A FATAL ACCIDENT, WRITING ON PADS. 2 DEAD MEN, FACES COVERED, LAY ON THE DAMP ASPHALT.
AN HOUR FURTHER OUT FROM ALMATY, ANOTHER WRECK. A FORD SUV WITH UZBEK PLATES HAD BLOWN A TIRE AND FLIPPED FORWARD. THE DRIVER'S BODY LAY ON THE PAVEMENT.
IF BODIES WERE PILING UP ON A REASONABLY STRAIGHT AND WELL-MAINTAINED ROAD, WHAT WOULD THE SPECIAL PERMISSION-REQUIRED DIRT TRACK TO KARAKOL BE LIKE?
THINGS FELL APART DURING THE 30-KILOMETER STRETCH THAT COMPRISES THE KAZAKH-KYRGYZ NEUTRAL ZONE.
I HAVE TO GO TO THE BATHROOM.
YOU'LL HAVE TO WAIT. THERE ARE MINES HERE.
I DON'T CARE. I NEED TO GO NOW.

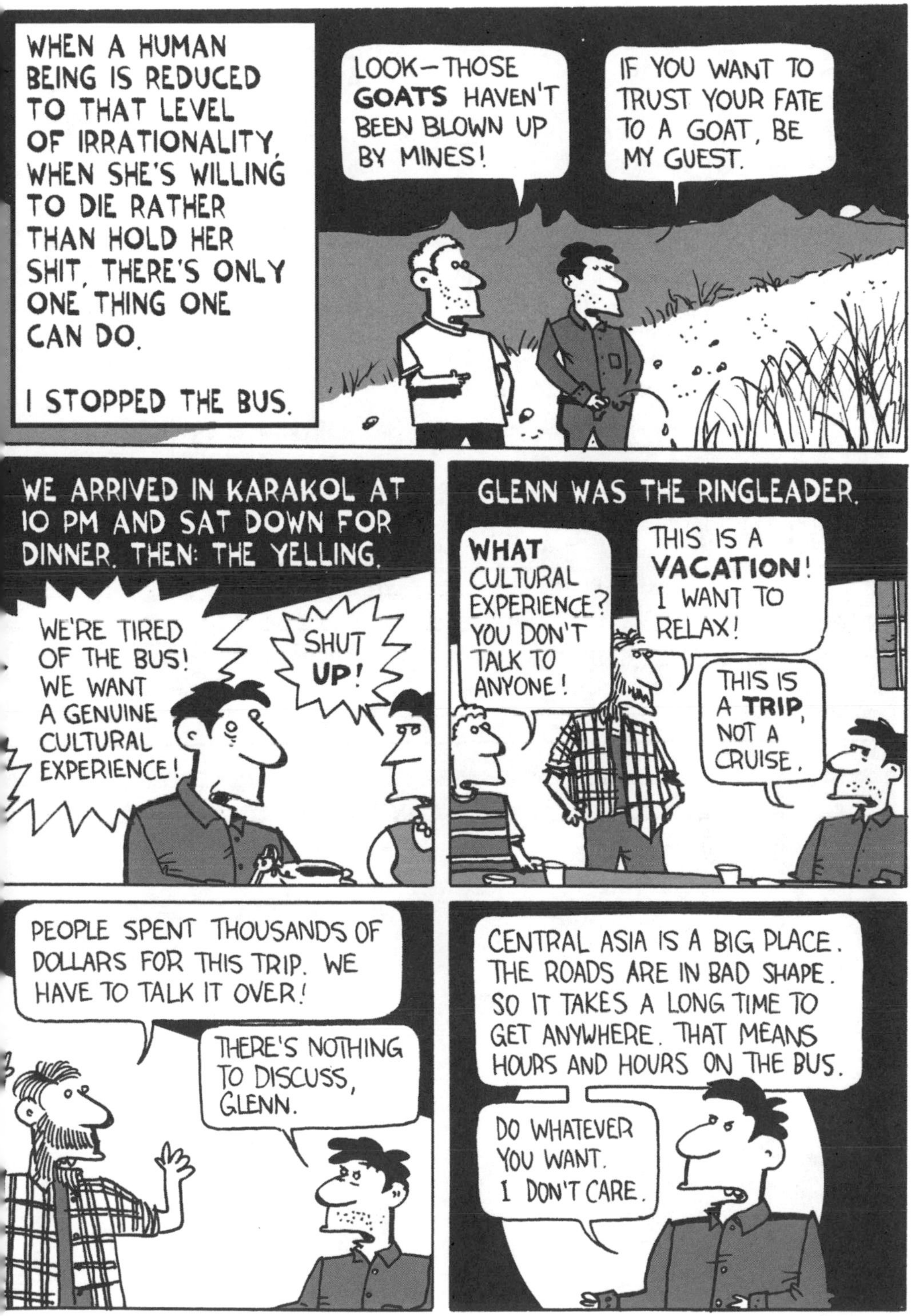
WHEN A HUMAN BEING IS REDUCED TO THAT LEVEL OF IRRATIONALITY, WHEN SHE'S WILLING TO DIE RATHER THAN HOLD HER SHIT, THERE'S ONLY ONE THING ONE CAN DO.
I STOPPED THE BUS.
LOOK—THOSE **GOATS** HAVEN'T BEEN BLOWN UP BY MINES!
IF YOU WANT TO TRUST YOUR FATE TO A GOAT, BE MY GUEST.
WE ARRIVED IN KARAKOL AT 10 PM AND SAT DOWN FOR DINNER. THEN: THE YELLING.
WE'RE TIRED OF THE BUS! WE WANT A GENUINE CULTURAL EXPERIENCE!
SHUT **UP**!
GLENN WAS THE RINGLEADER.
WHAT CULTURAL EXPERIENCE? YOU DON'T TALK TO ANYONE!
THIS IS A **VACATION**! I WANT TO RELAX!
THIS IS A **TRIP**, NOT A CRUISE.
PEOPLE SPENT THOUSANDS OF DOLLARS FOR THIS TRIP. WE HAVE TO TALK IT OVER!
THERE'S NOTHING TO DISCUSS, GLENN.
CENTRAL ASIA IS A BIG PLACE. THE ROADS ARE IN BAD SHAPE. SO IT TAKES A LONG TIME TO GET ANYWHERE. THAT MEANS HOURS AND HOURS ON THE BUS.
DO WHATEVER YOU WANT. I DON'T CARE.

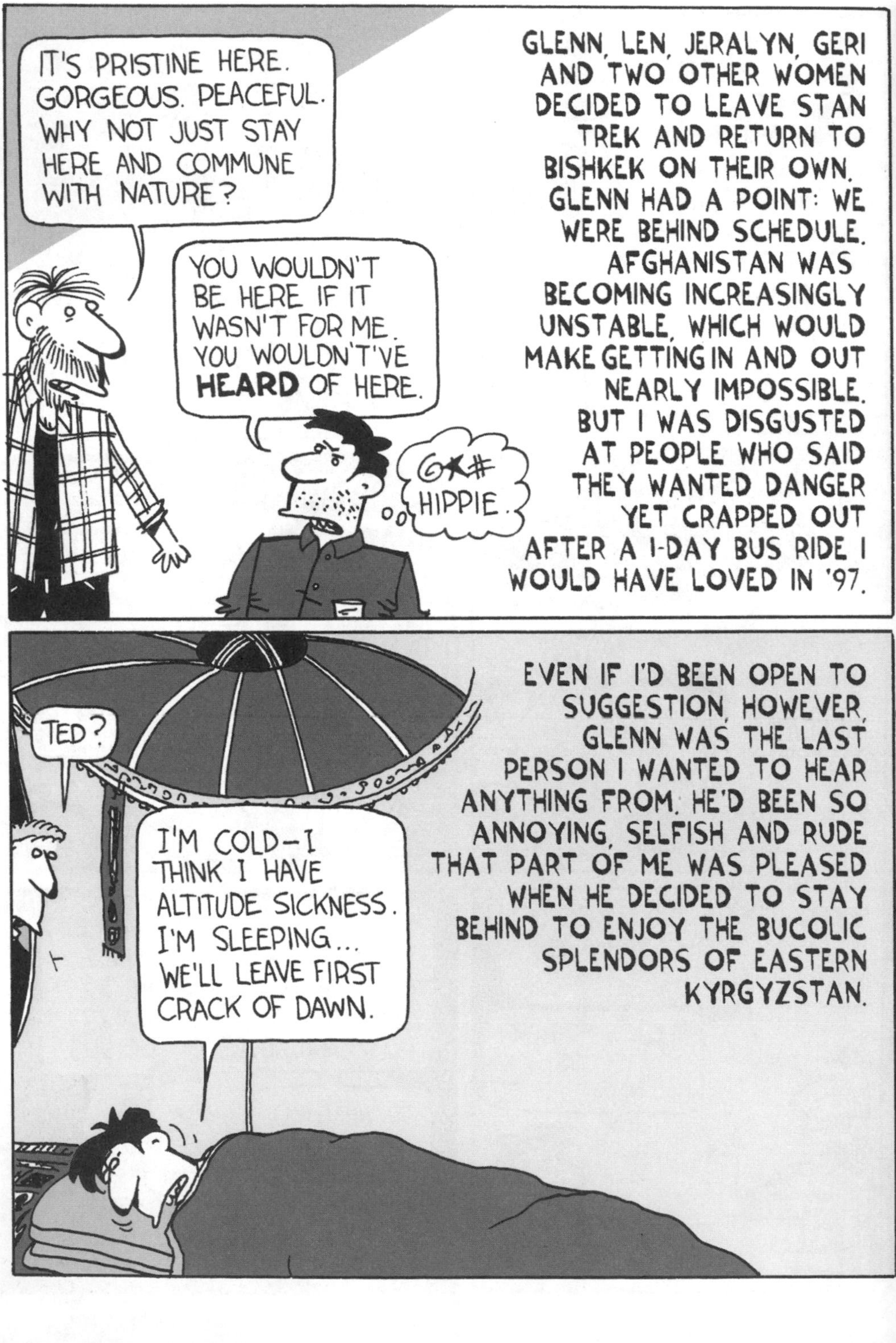
GLENN, LEN, JERALYN, GERI AND TWO OTHER WOMEN DECIDED TO LEAVE STAN TREK AND RETURN TO BISHKEK ON THEIR OWN. GLENN HAD A POINT: WE WERE BEHIND SCHEDULE. AFGHANISTAN WAS BECOMING INCREASINGLY UNSTABLE, WHICH WOULD MAKE GETTING IN AND OUT NEARLY IMPOSSIBLE. BUT I WAS DISGUSTED AT PEOPLE WHO SAID THEY WANTED DANGER YET CRAPPED OUT AFTER A 1-DAY BUS RIDE I WOULD HAVE LOVED IN '97.
IT'S PRISTINE HERE. GORGEOUS. PEACEFUL. WHY NOT JUST STAY HERE AND COMMUNE WITH NATURE?
YOU WOULDN'T BE HERE IF IT WASN'T FOR ME. YOU WOULDN'T'VE **HEARD** OF HERE.
G*# HIPPIE.
EVEN IF I'D BEEN OPEN TO SUGGESTION, HOWEVER, GLENN WAS THE LAST PERSON I WANTED TO HEAR ANYTHING FROM. HE'D BEEN SO ANNOYING, SELFISH AND RUDE THAT PART OF ME WAS PLEASED WHEN HE DECIDED TO STAY BEHIND TO ENJOY THE BUCOLIC SPLENDORS OF EASTERN KYRGYZSTAN.
TED?
I'M COLD—I THINK I HAVE ALTITUDE SICKNESS. I'M SLEEPING... WE'LL LEAVE FIRST CRACK OF DAWN.

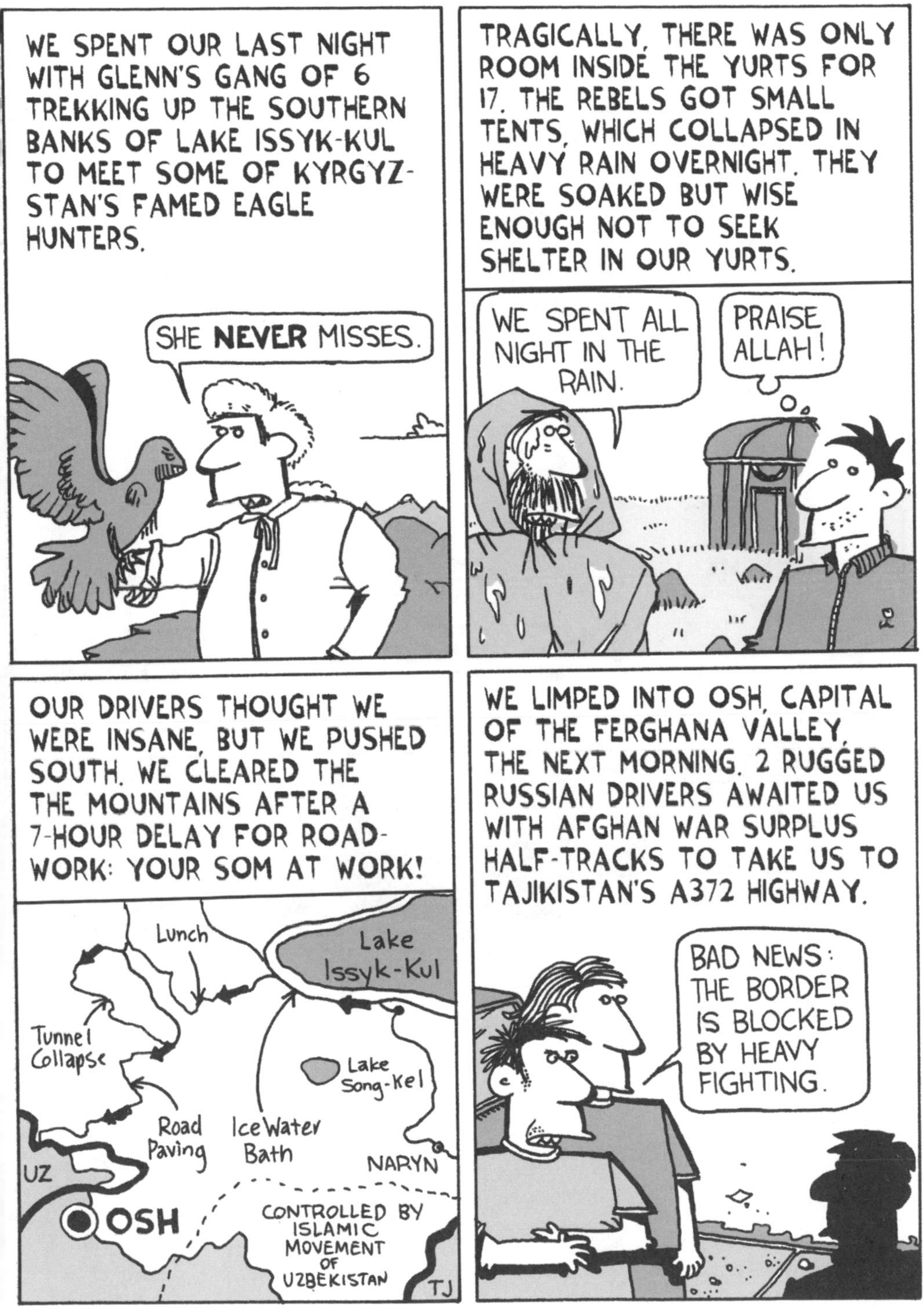
WE SPENT OUR LAST NIGHT WITH GLENN'S GANG OF 6 TREKKING UP THE SOUTHERN BANKS OF LAKE ISSYK-KUL TO MEET SOME OF KYRGYZ-STAN'S FAMED EAGLE HUNTERS.
SHE **NEVER** MISSES.
TRAGICALLY, THERE WAS ONLY ROOM INSIDE THE YURTS FOR 17. THE REBELS GOT SMALL TENTS, WHICH COLLAPSED IN HEAVY RAIN OVERNIGHT. THEY WERE SOAKED BUT WISE ENOUGH NOT TO SEEK SHELTER IN OUR YURTS.
WE SPENT ALL NIGHT IN THE RAIN.
PRAISE ALLAH!
OUR DRIVERS THOUGHT WE WERE INSANE, BUT WE PUSHED SOUTH. WE CLEARED THE THE MOUNTAINS AFTER A 7-HOUR DELAY FOR ROAD-WORK: YOUR SOM AT WORK!
Lunch
Lake Issyk-Kul
Tunnel Collapse
Lake Song-Kel
Road Paving
Ice Water Bath
NARYN
UZ
OSH
CONTROLLED BY ISLAMIC MOVEMENT OF UZBEKISTAN
TJ
WE LIMPED INTO OSH, CAPITAL OF THE FERGHANA VALLEY, THE NEXT MORNING. 2 RUGGED RUSSIAN DRIVERS AWAITED US WITH AFGHAN WAR SURPLUS HALF-TRACKS TO TAKE US TO TAJIKISTAN'S A372 HIGHWAY.
BAD NEWS: THE BORDER IS BLOCKED BY HEAVY FIGHTING.

I STUDIED THE MAP. OSH IS A CUL-DE-SAC.
THERE WERE ONLY 4 WAYS OUT:

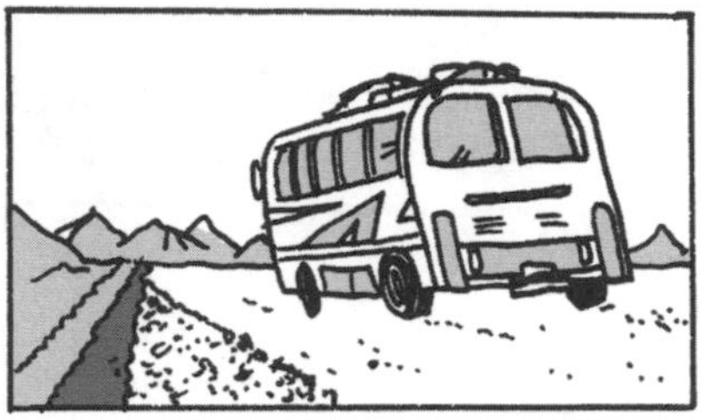

NORTH, BACK THE WAY WE CAME, TOWARDS BISHKEK. BUT WHAT WOULD BE THE POINT OF THAT?

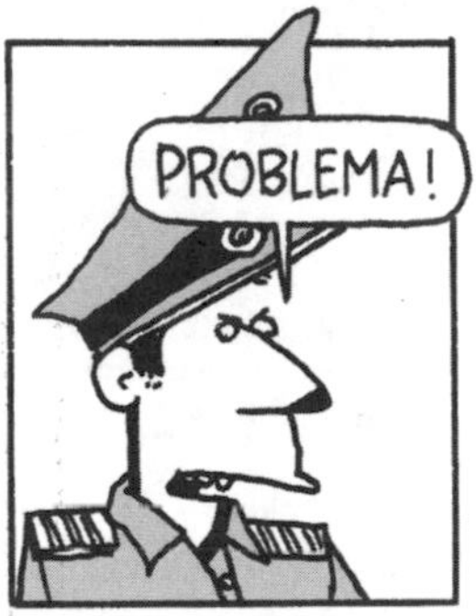
PROBLEMA!

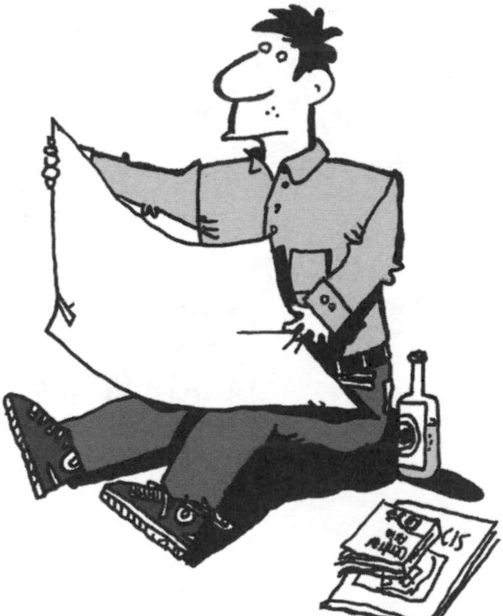
CIS

WEST, TO THE UZBEK BORDER. BUT WE'D USED UP OUR UZBEK VISAS AND COULDN'T GET NEW ONES IN OSH.

SOUTHEAST, AS WE'D PLANNED ORIGINALLY. BUT SOUTHERN KYRGYZSTAN NORTHERN TAJIKISTAN WERE BEING INVADED BY THE IMU. IT WAS THEIR BIG 2000 OFFENSIVE.

Kidnapped mountain climbers recount dramatic es

DAVIS, California (AP) -- American climbers held hostage for six days by Islar
militants in Kyrgyzstan say they escaped by pushing a guard off a cliff before
making a harrowing 18-mile trek to freedom.
"It is so hard to think of that now, but we were afraid we would not survive,"
Beth Rodden, 20, said Thursday.

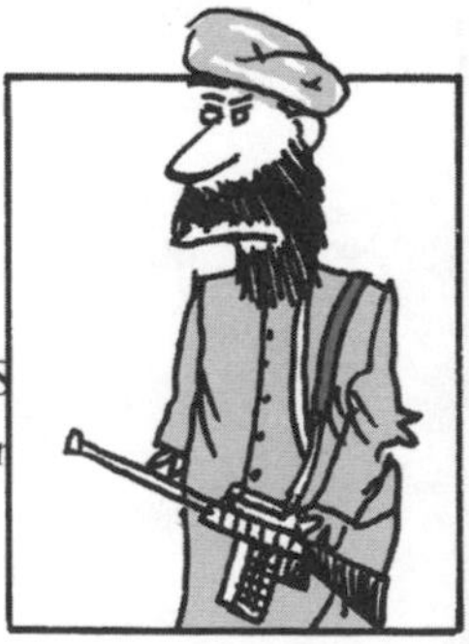

[FOUR YOUNG AMERICAN MOUNTAIN CLIMBERS WERE KIDNAPPED BY THE IMU NOT FAR FROM OSH. THEIR SIX DAYS OF CAPTIVITY WERE RECOUNTED IN "OVER THE EDGE," A 2001 BOOK BY GREG CHILD. CONTROVERSY HAS DOGGED THE CLIMBERS' ACCOUNT OF THE INCIDENT AND THEIR ESCAPE, PARTICULARLY AFTER THE IMU GUARD THEY CLAIMED TO HAVE SHOVED OFF A CLIFF TO HIS DEATH TURNED UP ALIVE AND WELL.]

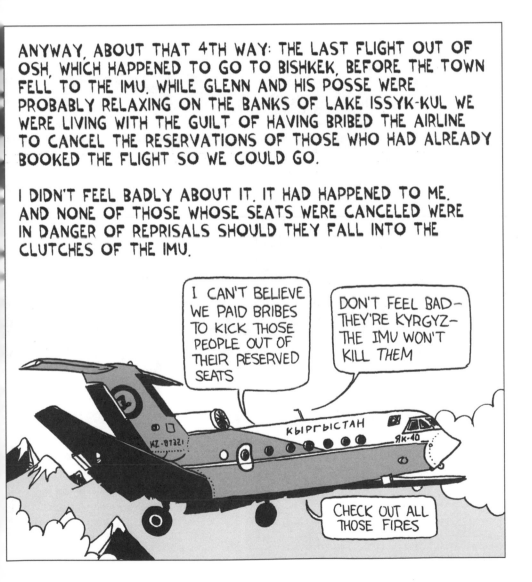

ANYWAY, ABOUT THAT 4TH WAY: THE LAST FLIGHT OUT OF OSH, WHICH HAPPENED TO GO TO BISHKEK, BEFORE THE TOWN FELL TO THE IMU. WHILE GLENN AND HIS POSSE WERE PROBABLY RELAXING ON THE BANKS OF LAKE ISSYK-KUL WE WERE LIVING WITH THE GUILT OF HAVING BRIBED THE AIRLINE TO CANCEL THE RESERVATIONS OF THOSE WHO HAD ALREADY BOOKED THE FLIGHT SO WE COULD GO.

I DIDN'T FEEL BADLY ABOUT IT. IT HAD HAPPENED TO ME. AND NONE OF THOSE WHOSE SEATS WERE CANCELED WERE IN DANGER OF REPRISALS SHOULD THEY FALL INTO THE CLUTCHES OF THE IMU.

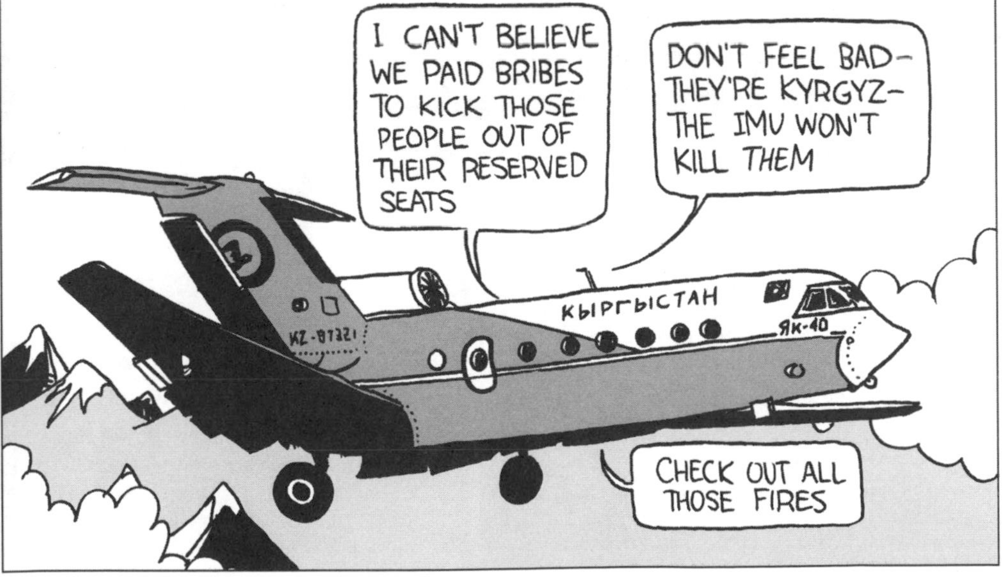
I CAN'T BELIEVE WE PAID BRIBES TO KICK THOSE PEOPLE OUT OF THEIR RESERVED SEATS
DON'T FEEL BAD– THEY'RE KYRGYZ– THE IMU WON'T KILL *THEM*
КЫРГЫСТАН
ЯК-40
CHECK OUT ALL THOSE FIRES

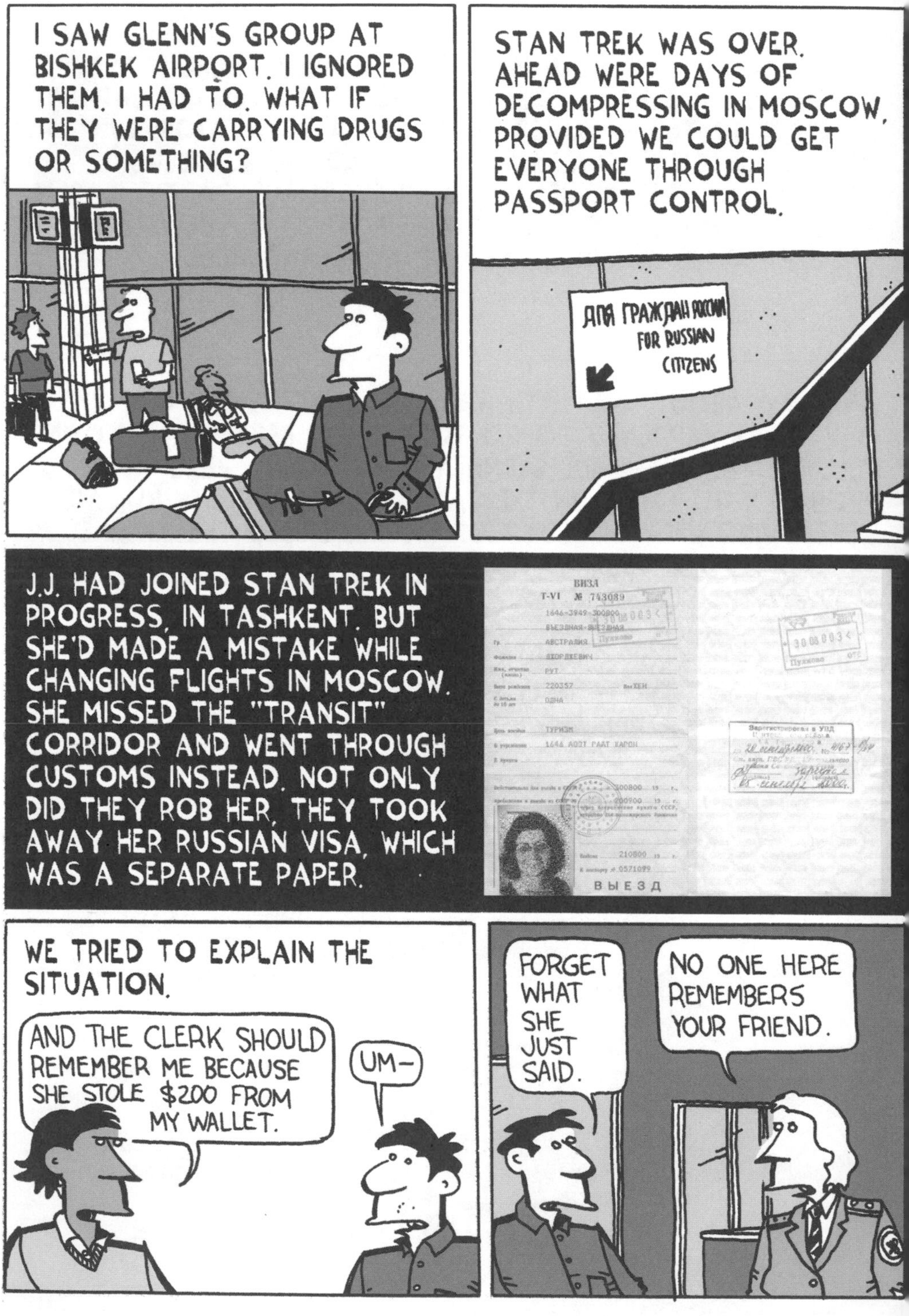
I SAW GLENN'S GROUP AT BISHKEK AIRPORT. I IGNORED THEM. I HAD TO. WHAT IF THEY WERE CARRYING DRUGS OR SOMETHING?
STAN TREK WAS OVER. AHEAD WERE DAYS OF DECOMPRESSING IN MOSCOW, PROVIDED WE COULD GET EVERYONE THROUGH PASSPORT CONTROL.
ДЛЯ ГРАЖДАН РОССИИ
FOR RUSSIAN CITIZENS
J.J. HAD JOINED STAN TREK IN PROGRESS, IN TASHKENT. BUT SHE'D MADE A MISTAKE WHILE CHANGING FLIGHTS IN MOSCOW. SHE MISSED THE "TRANSIT" CORRIDOR AND WENT THROUGH CUSTOMS INSTEAD. NOT ONLY DID THEY ROB HER, THEY TOOK AWAY HER RUSSIAN VISA, WHICH WAS A SEPARATE PAPER.
ВИЗА
ВЫЕЗД
WE TRIED TO EXPLAIN THE SITUATION.
AND THE CLERK SHOULD REMEMBER ME BECAUSE SHE STOLE $200 FROM MY WALLET.
UM—
FORGET WHAT SHE JUST SAID.
NO ONE HERE REMEMBERS YOUR FRIEND.

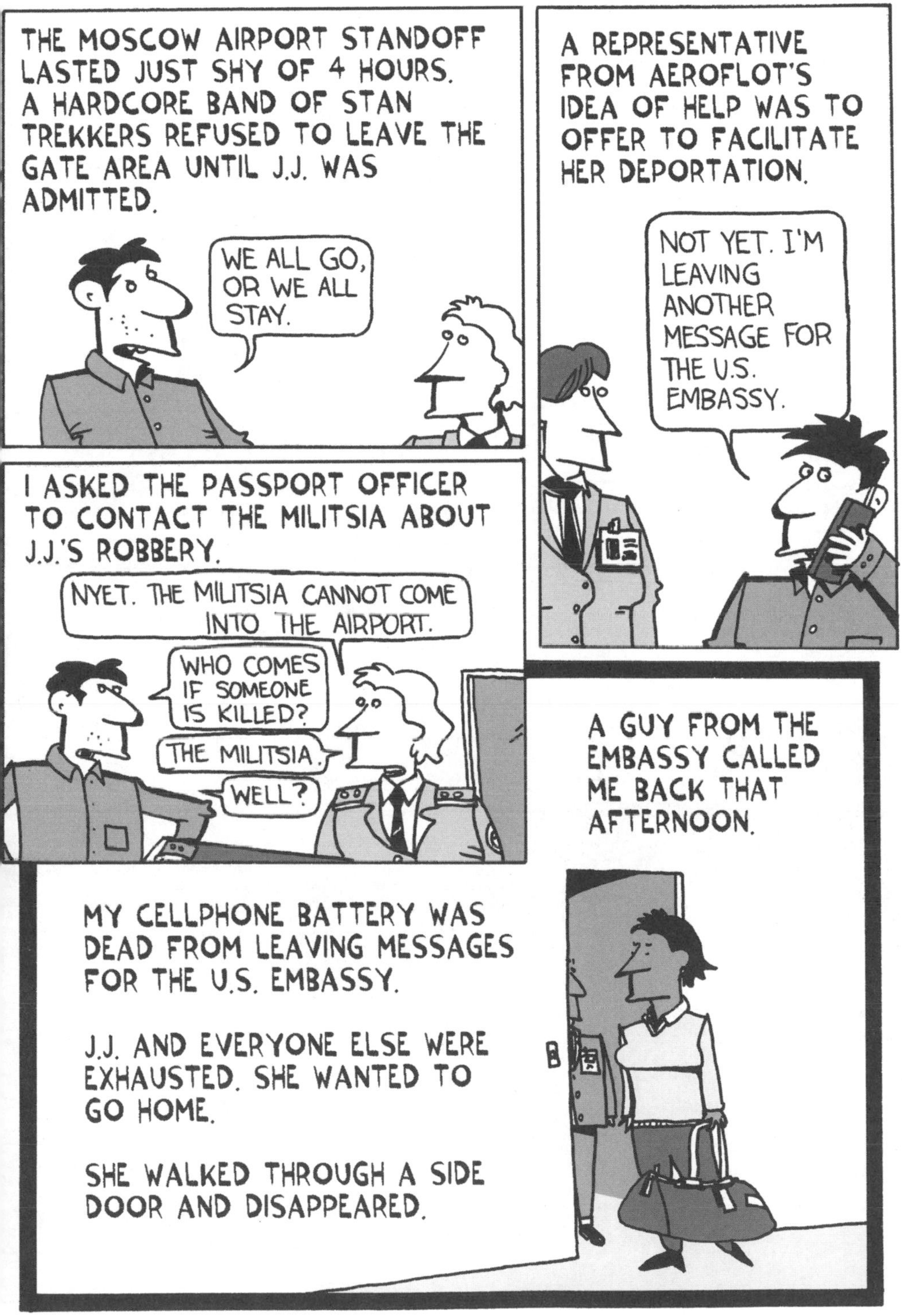
THE MOSCOW AIRPORT STANDOFF LASTED JUST SHY OF 4 HOURS. A HARDCORE BAND OF STAN TREKKERS REFUSED TO LEAVE THE GATE AREA UNTIL J.J. WAS ADMITTED.
WE ALL GO, OR WE ALL STAY.
A REPRESENTATIVE FROM AEROFLOT'S IDEA OF HELP WAS TO OFFER TO FACILITATE HER DEPORTATION.
NOT YET. I'M LEAVING ANOTHER MESSAGE FOR THE U.S. EMBASSY.
I ASKED THE PASSPORT OFFICER TO CONTACT THE MILITSIA ABOUT J.J.'S ROBBERY.
NYET. THE MILITSIA CANNOT COME INTO THE AIRPORT.
WHO COMES IF SOMEONE IS KILLED?
THE MILITSIA.
WELL?
MY CELLPHONE BATTERY WAS DEAD FROM LEAVING MESSAGES FOR THE U.S. EMBASSY.
J.J. AND EVERYONE ELSE WERE EXHAUSTED. SHE WANTED TO GO HOME.
SHE WALKED THROUGH A SIDE DOOR AND DISAPPEARED.
A GUY FROM THE EMBASSY CALLED ME BACK THAT AFTERNOON.

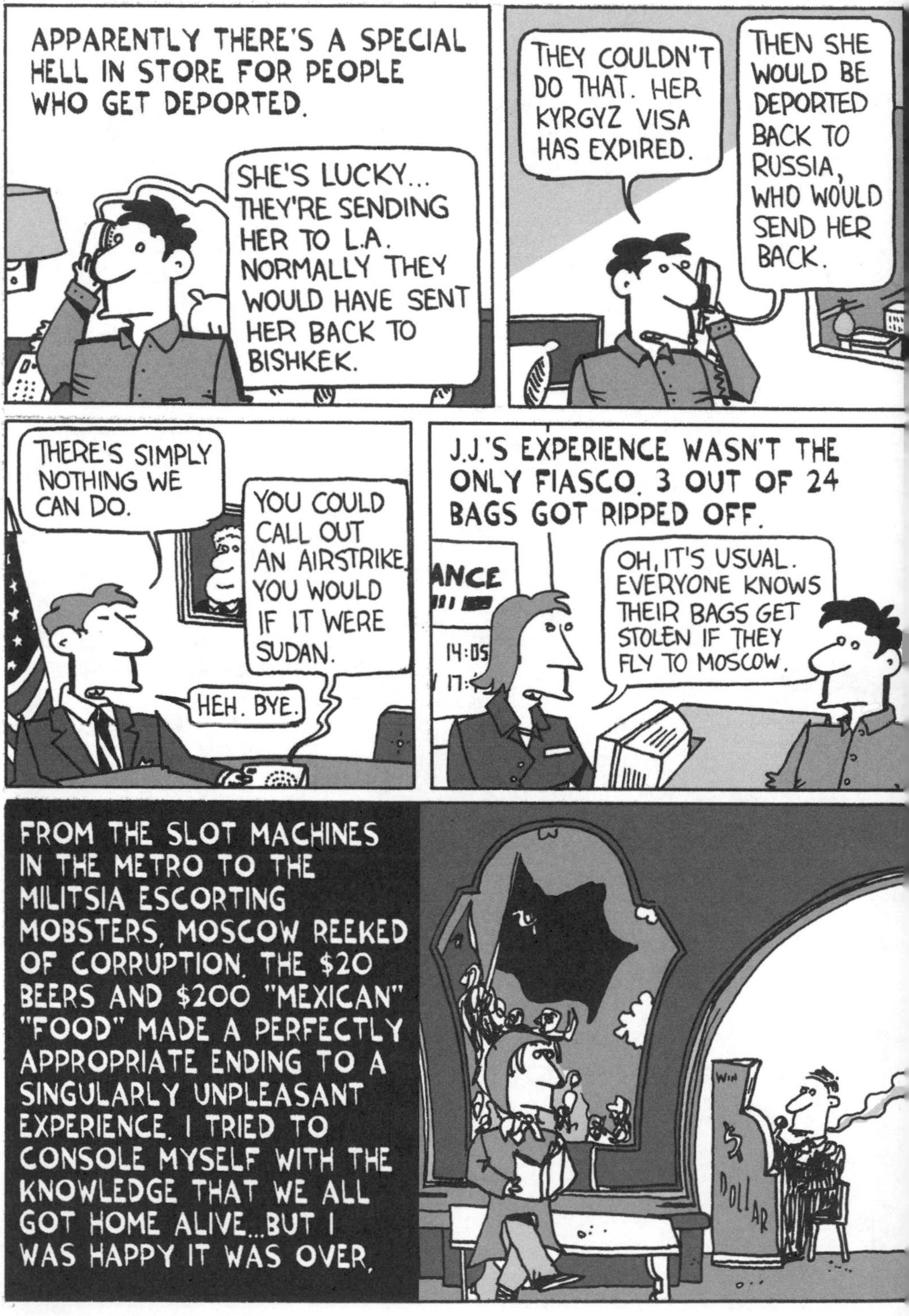

APPARENTLY THERE'S A SPECIAL HELL IN STORE FOR PEOPLE WHO GET DEPORTED.
SHE'S LUCKY... THEY'RE SENDING HER TO L.A. NORMALLY THEY WOULD HAVE SENT HER BACK TO BISHKEK.
THEY COULDN'T DO THAT. HER KYRGYZ VISA HAS EXPIRED.
THEN SHE WOULD BE DEPORTED BACK TO RUSSIA, WHO WOULD SEND HER BACK.
THERE'S SIMPLY NOTHING WE CAN DO.
YOU COULD CALL OUT AN AIRSTRIKE. YOU WOULD IF IT WERE SUDAN.
HEH. BYE.
J.J.'S EXPERIENCE WASN'T THE ONLY FIASCO. 3 OUT OF 24 BAGS GOT RIPPED OFF.
OH, IT'S USUAL. EVERYONE KNOWS THEIR BAGS GET STOLEN IF THEY FLY TO MOSCOW.
FROM THE SLOT MACHINES IN THE METRO TO THE MILITSIA ESCORTING MOBSTERS, MOSCOW REEKED OF CORRUPTION. THE $20 BEERS AND $200 "MEXICAN" "FOOD" MADE A PERFECTLY APPROPRIATE ENDING TO A SINGULARLY UNPLEASANT EXPERIENCE. I TRIED TO CONSOLE MYSELF WITH THE KNOWLEDGE THAT WE ALL GOT HOME ALIVE...BUT I WAS HAPPY IT WAS OVER.
DOLLAR

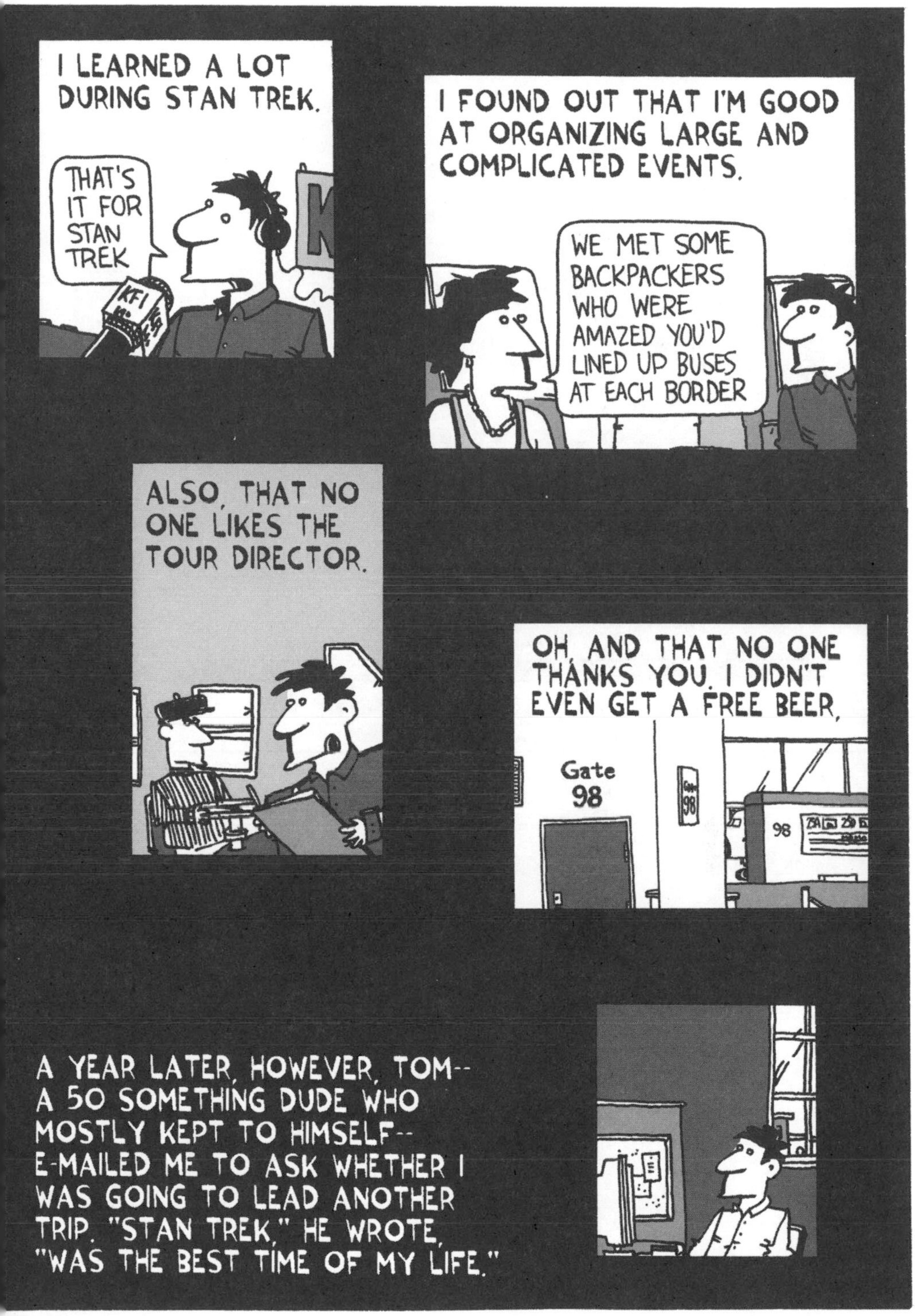
I LEARNED A LOT DURING STAN TREK.
THAT'S IT FOR STAN TREK
KFI
I FOUND OUT THAT I'M GOOD AT ORGANIZING LARGE AND COMPLICATED EVENTS.
WE MET SOME BACKPACKERS WHO WERE AMAZED YOU'D LINED UP BUSES AT EACH BORDER
ALSO, THAT NO ONE LIKES THE TOUR DIRECTOR.
OH, AND THAT NO ONE THANKS YOU. I DIDN'T EVEN GET A FREE BEER.
Gate 98
98
A YEAR LATER, HOWEVER, TOM--
A 50 SOMETHING DUDE WHO
MOSTLY KEPT TO HIMSELF--
E-MAILED ME TO ASK WHETHER I
WAS GOING TO LEAD ANOTHER
TRIP. "STAN TREK," HE WROTE,
"WAS THE BEST TIME OF MY LIFE."

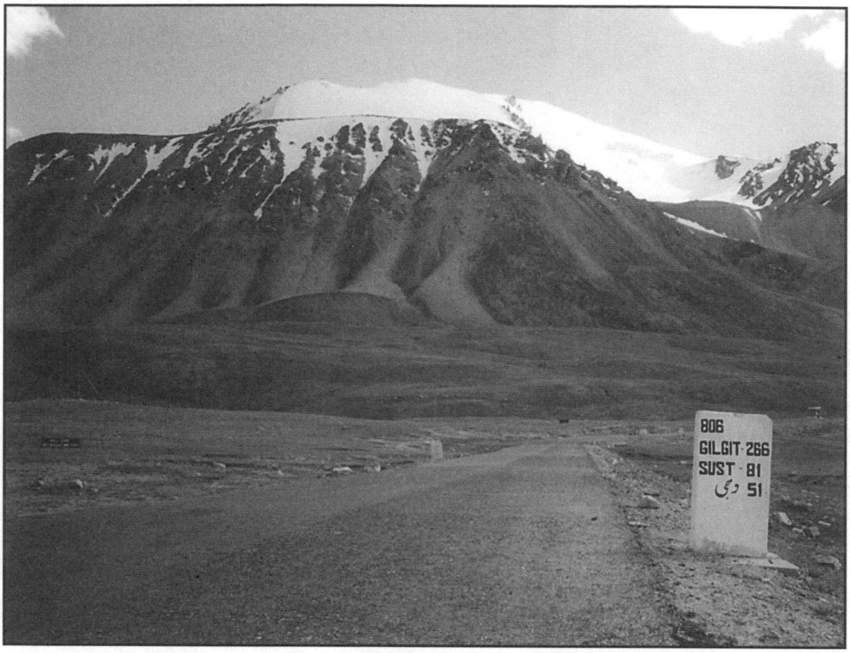
806
GILGIT 266
SUST 81

Entering Pakistani Kashmir from China via the Khunjerab Pass on the Karakoram Highway, the highest-altitude paved road in the world.

High Anxiety

GILGIT, Kashmir: The Karakoram Highway (KKH), blocked on Saturday evening following heavy landslides at various places and cleared for one-way traffic on Sunday morning, has been blocked again by a massive rockslide. The Frontier Works Organization said that huge boulders had hit the highway and damaged a 135-metre portion in Kohistan district, suspending traffic between Gilgit and Rawalpindi. The FWO has moved heavy machinery to various points along the KKH to clear the blockade. FWO sources said that blasting technique might be used to remove boulders from the road. Shopkeepers said the closure of the highway for two days had created a shortage of food and other essential items in the Northern Areas.

—DAWN newspaper, Pakistan, February 27, 2006

On your standard map it's a thousand miles of pavement connecting China to Pakistan. Of course, by the same measure New York City is just a black circle with a big fat dot in the middle. What the Karakoram Highway *is* is a nexus of madness in a place already chock full of every conceivable lunacy. Understanding that psychosis requires experiencing it firsthand. In the course of traveling over those thousand miles along with my friend Cole, I braved wild animals, a Pakistani military coup and an invasion by the Taliban—all par for the course for a road trip on the world's most dangerous highway.

The first thing you need to understand about the KKH (its name on the Pakistani side of the border) is that this expanse of asphalt may well be the most staggering engineering achievement since the Great Wall: fourteen hundred kilometers of two-lane roadway clinging to the side of immense, crumbling mountains, running alongside racing white water rivers prone to flooding and constant erosion, soaring through elevations from ten to eighteen thousand feet through areas so politically unstable that it's impossible to find two maps dated a year apart depicting the same borders. If Germany's autobahn represents the ultimate triumph of man over nature, on the KKH it's still up in the air as to which side will win in the end.

The KKH twists and turns through the Pamir, Kunlun, Karakoram, Hindu Kush and Himalayan mountain ranges; this clash of tectonic plates makes this junction between Asia and the subcontinent the world's most seismically active place.

Crossing into China from Kyrgyzstan via the Torugart Pass, 12,310 feet. Snowstorms in June are not uncommon.

Immense earthquakes that would flatten American cities in seconds are routine; fortunately, there's nothing much here except animals, a lot of amazing history and the highway itself. (Even these, however, were devastated by a 7.6-strength earthquake in October 2005. At least one hundred thousand Kashmiris were killed.) The mountains are constantly falling apart, and down upon, the KKH; rock slides frequently force the closure of this crucial artery.

At many points the highway, built from 1966 to 1986 as the part of the diplomatic resolution of a border dispute between Pakistan and China, runs alongside rivers that range from dry washes in late summer to vast, wide torrents during the spring. Water from the rivers eat under the pavement, opening lethal sinkholes. Authorities often close the narrow roadway until they're repaired—and that can take weeks or even months.

An extension of the Tibetan plateau, nowhere on earth is it so high for so long as it is in the Karakoram range. This fact allows for blizzards in June and forces the closure of the road from October through April to as late as May. Even in the middle of summer the KKH can be closed for weeks or longer. Altitude sickness starts to kill people at nine thousand feet above sea level; you're rarely ever that *low* on the KKH. In short, the Karakoram Highway is a doomed, psychotic proposition that may no longer exist as a viable transportation link by the time you read this. But if it does, and you can survive the landslides, Islamist terrorists and shortsighted snow leopards, the Karakoram Highway offers a cat's-eye view to some of the world's most dazzling scenery.

Being There

The KKH originates at the Silk Road trading town of Kashgar in western China and ends in Islamabad, the capital that locals joke is a fifteen-minute drive from Pakistan because its groomed antiseptic appearance is so unlike the rest of the country. Because we went there in August and September of 1999, we traveled south (from Kashgar to Islamabad) in order to minimize the effects of the already incipient Himalayan winter; in May one would choose to go the other direction. You'll need visas for China and Pakistan, but these can be hard to obtain because the KKH passes through the heart of Kashmir Province, where a war that began in 1947 over a Hindu raja's decision to attach his Muslim region to India seems destined to continue forever.

Getting to Kashgar by air requires so many changes of plane through shitty airstrips that it's virtually impossible; the most direct overland route from an international airport is the two-days-plus journey from Bishkek, Kyrgyzstan (which requires a third visa). But there's a catch—in Central Asia, there's *always* a catch—the border crossing between Kyrgyzstan and China, through the Torugart Pass, is permanently closed to foreigners. That means *you*, Americano.

The good thing about Central Asia, on the other hand, is that as it has for millennia along this ancient road between the Western and Eastern worlds, cash opens officially sealed frontiers. Conversely, the budget-traveler approach is extremely risky; we met a trio of Dutch backpackers who took the bus to the border,

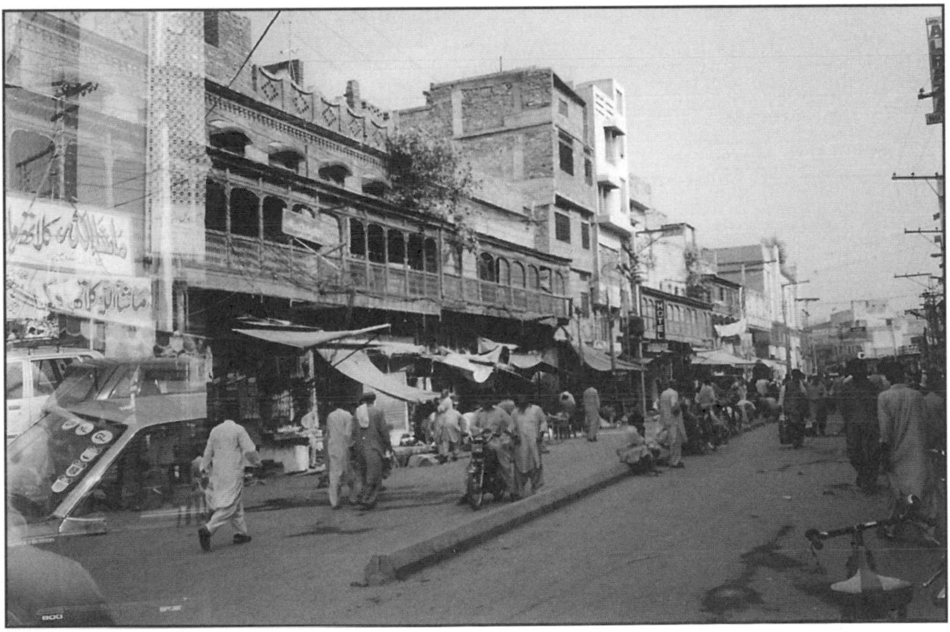
HOTEL

Old City, Kashgar. This street has since been demolished to be replaced by Chinese-style apartment houses, which were in turn bombed by Uyghur separatists of the East Turkestan Independence Movement. Kashgar has remained under martial law since 2001.

The Arch marking the tense high-altitude border crossing at the Torugart Pass between Kyrgyzstan—prior to 1991 the southern border of the USSR—and China. The three Dutch backpackers at left were stranded in no-man's land when their ride into China failed to materialize.

were released by Kyrgyz customs police but had failed to arrange for transportation to pick them up on the Chinese side of the old Soviet triumphal arch that's still standing, riddled with bullet holes. The Chinese won't let you in unless someone meets you at the political boundary and going back to Kyrgyzstan isn't allowed. The woman and two men we encountered were in bad shape; they'd been trapped in the windswept no-man's land between minefields at the roof of the world for twenty-nine days with no hope in sight. Severely sunburned, without tents or sleeping bags and out of food, they'd been reduced to eating grass and whatever leftovers passing Kyrgyz troops deigned to give them. Without official papers we couldn't take them with us. For all I know, they may still be up there.

It took three days and cost about six hundred dollars for the two of us to travel to Kashgar from Bishkek; we hired a pair of Ukrainian guides who knew which guards to bribe and how to bypass the worst police checkpoints on back roads.

Kashgar's history is remote and romantic, but only the first remains—now it's a monument to how efficiently architects and urban planners can fuck up a beautiful place. This legendary trading city still draws hundreds of thousands of people from Afghanistan, Tajikistan, Kyrgyzstan and western China each and every Sunday to sell everything from camels to silk cushions to Soviet-made missile detonators in the Muslim Uyghur neighborhood downtown, but the Chinese government has decimated the city's glorious past with vile concrete apartment blocks and factories that produce a putrid dusty haze that would clog the lungs of the most hardened Angeleno. Moreover, Taliban-trained Uyghur militants of the East Turkestan Independence Movement have spent the last few years bombing public buildings and assassinating Chinese officials, leading to a continuous state of martial law.

Try as we did to enjoy Kashgar, Cole was still suffering from altitude sickness acquired at the Torugart Pass. I spent most of the time there doubled over with stomach cramps and a cruel variety of diarrhea that's impossible to explain to the uninitiated. The food was so putrid—they wash bowls with filthy cold water and nothing else, namely not soap—that I sometimes had to skip the mouth-watering local *laghman* noodles.

Cole and I caught the faux-lux "International" bus bound for Sost, Pakistan, the next day, so named because it departs from a storied "Great Game"-era British embassy compound whose glory days ended with the 1949 Communist revolution. Trouble began within minutes: A Pakistani smuggler with an astonishing resemblance to Ted Danson ordered me to move my six-foot-two frame to the back of the bus so that he and his brother could enjoy my front-seat view. "But I need to stretch my—" I began to reason.

"Hey asshole—what part of 'no' do you not understand?" Cole barked from the other side of the aisle at the guy. Danson backed off, but the conflict set the tone for our journey. Here we were on a bus full of pissed-off Pakistanis and Afghans, some of them visibly armed, heading straight into the Kashmir war zone.

Like a hot chick who talks dirty but never puts out, the KKH (the Chinese call it the China-Pakistan Highway, or just the G314) teases drivers with perfectly-maintained pavement—complete with painted markers every tenth of a kilometer—the first few hours out of Kashgar. Then the road enters the immense Ghez Darya River canyon. That's where road maintenance ends for good, and the KKH really begins.

River Madness

High-altitude roads frequently follow riverbeds because they offer the straightest path through mountains; thus the KKH runs alongside massive flows of snowmelt. Rockslides occur frequently; our bus repeatedly had to squeeze past immense boulders that had tumbled thousands of feet down the side of the Pamir range within the previous few days. On the left side of the bus, the road vanished wherever the Ghez made a turn—in a monumental testimony to shortsighted stupidity, the Chinese side of the KKH has no levies to hold back the water. Washouts are indicated by rocks lined up at a forty-five-degree angle by road workers; rocks are the one thing that aren't in short supply along the KKH. In a scene out of the classic film "The Wages of Fear," the bus was forced to go off-road, rocking at wild angles over three-foot rocks at a fraction of a mile per hour, sections of shattered asphalt cracking and falling off into the torrent below. It's just the water, the mountain and you, and you're in the middle the whole way.

Judging from their green faces, even grizzled locals seemed not to take these side jaunts very well. But I was suffering particularly badly, having undergone a hernia operation a month before. You just haven't lived until you become fully aware of your large intestine.

A twenty-hour-long traffic jam on the Karakoram Highway connecting western China to Pakistan. The chickens in the foreground slowly wilted before succumbing to the heat.

Passing a vehicle coming from the opposite direction involves a perverse game of Central Asian chicken; both drivers seize the middle of the road and floor the gas. It doesn't matter if you were both all the way to the right to begin with—you move left as soon as you see the other bastard. At the last second before collision (and, according to locals, sometimes afterwards) the smaller vehicle of the two scoots over; it's not rare for one tire to slip momentarily off the road over nothingness. At blind curves, it's customary to speed up while honking ferociously at whatever might be coming around the other side. Despite its low volume of traffic—it's not unusual to go hours without seeing anything else—the authorities say that cars and trucks still tumble off the KKH every few days.

I didn't ask about the buses: I didn't have to. Evidence of their fate can be seen hundreds of feet down along side of the river's bank. There, along the curves, are the rusted carcasses of countless destroyed vehicles, rags that used to be clothes, and luggage.

Aside from sheer rock faces and incredibly bleak vistas, the mountains are home to some of the world's most endangered species, including the long-horned ibex, Marco Polo sheep and snow leopards. Man and nature collide in spectacular ways here, as demonstrated by the snow leopard that leapt from its perch on to the top of a passing car a few weeks before our arrival. The animal died on impact, lying splayed across the roof like a Wile E. Coyote. The car was totaled, but there was no word on the driver. A pair of Kyrgyz men lost no time gutting and skinning the animal, which soon began to stink up the bus. But while car and beast routinely mix it up on rural roads throughout the Third World, nothing beats the KKH for sheer volume of animal traffic. You pass herds of goats or sheep every few hundred meters; I lost count of how many suicidal yaks and bulls jumped out in front of us. There are Bactrian camels (the double-humped variety) too, but they're smart enough to edge off the roadway when a double-tractor-trailer piled thirty-feet high with God-knows-what passes them doing seventy.

The Ugly Americans Reach Out

About five hours out of Kashgar, about two hundred miles from the nearest village, we rounded a turn to find a line of trucks at a dead stop. The driver of the one in front of us was fast asleep on a red blanket on the ground. I took this as a bad sign.

We got out and walked forward; we found that someone had abandoned a fully loaded fuel tanker in the middle of the road on an incline up ahead. As men have since time immemorial, we carefully examined the situation and pondered how to resolve it.

More accurately, a hundred guys yelled at each other in Mandarin, Uyghur, Urdu and Tajik, languages that don't sound anything alike. Inexplicably, the Chinese men saw the rocks *in front of* the tires as the main problem—never mind that the contraption was parked uphill. The Uyghurs seemed to agree with Cole's plan, which was to remove the rocks from *behind* the tires, thus allowing the truck to go over the edge of the cliff into the Ghez Darya. And the Pakistanis turned to Allah, praying at wildly divergent angles towards Mecca.

After several hours, during which the Chinese occupied themselves by moving the same huge rocks back and forth with great enthusiasm, a truck appeared from the opposite direction. Its driver backed up and parked just far enough away from the gas truck to make it impossible to hook up a single cable. Then the guys began arguing about how to tie the cable. In all, the arguing process took four hours. Cole and I shouted and pointed to our watches, which was, I realize now, futile: In Central Asia, nobody's time is valuable, much less yours.

"This is *China!*" one guy in a business suit yelled at us while lugging a dusty hundred-pound boulder to the side of the road, evidently to imply that we ugly Americans would do well to mind our own national business. The Chinese gave out an exaggerated guffaw. The Uyghurs, who chafe under Chinese military occupation, grumbled ominously, but I couldn't tell if they were siding with us or merely expressing a general disgust with the situation. Tired, humiliated, and certain that these idiots were going to blow the KKH into nearby Tajikistan, Cole and I returned to the bus. Somehow the gas truck got moved. This would have made for a better story had it exploded, but life often fails to deliver on desired drama.

Anyway, our depressingly low powered bus rumbled on, dodging goats, boulders, holes and gaudy Pakistani trucks in a furious attempt to make up time. Just before nightfall the Ghez valley opened up into a lush, green plain containing the idyllic ethnic Kyrgyz enclave of Karakul. Karakul features a few hundred people, thousands of yaks and cattle and a few stone houses. Cole passed the two hours we waited there—Chinese army troops were filling in a spot where twenty feet of

road had been sucked into the sandy ground—passing out dozens of those free postcards they leave by the restrooms in American restaurants downstairs by the restroom to local kids. They featured the cover of the previous month's *Playboy*.

Five hours late, exhausted and covered with soot, we slouched into our freezing cold seats as an exquisite blackness enveloped the bus. Suddenly, to the right of the bus over a row of snow-capped mountains, a huge, dazzling flash brought

A fuel tanker truck abandoned hundreds of miles down the Karakoram Highway, south of Kashgar. Traffic was frozen for a full day while travelers argued in Uyghur, Mandarin, Kyrgyz, Pashtun and English about what to do. Ultimately the driver, who had gone to get a part, returned.

back daylight. A bright yellow ball streaked across the sky perhaps a mile away, a trail of light behind it. Then the meteor was gone, smashed into the countryside in an explosion of fire. OK, so you could see that in Wisconsin, but you could also live your entire life without ever seeing a meteor hit the ground—and I saw mine in the Xinjiang Uyghur Autonomous Region from my seat on the KKH.

The Rooster Crows For Thee

Everyone has a rooster with his name on it. It's only a matter of time before you and that rooster meet, and when you do, it's rarely beautiful.

I met my cock at 4:30 in the morning after barely four hours of fitful sleep in a dismal Orwellian dump of a hotel (we actually stayed in Room 101) in the backwater hamlet of Tashkurgan, the last town before the border. My rooster kept up the audio entertainment portion of the program until 5:30, when patriotic Communist songs and news updates, announced by an earnest young woman with an astonishingly grating voice, began blasting from loudspeakers outside.

The bus picked us up first thing in the morning, and drove us to the Chinese customs office, where every single book, bottle of aspirin and banana on the bus was carefully inspected while every gun and fat wad of cash was duly ignored. This took three hours, during which our driver got loaded out of a brown paper bag. Then we set off across an empty scrub of desert along the bed of the then-dry Tashkurgan River—the bus overheated twice—and climbed slowly up into the Pamir mountains, well past the snow line—and finally, majestically, inevitably—we arrived at the magnificent, wind-blasted Khunjerab Pass. By this point our driver was thoroughly shitfaced, a fact which with I had no problem. I don't think I could have navigated that bus up those mountains without a little help either.

Breathing becomes an exhilarating, triumphant act at sixteen thousand feet. The pass marks a change from crumbling Pamirs to stony Karakoram mountains, as well as to superior road maintenance. The Pakistani side of the KKH features better levies and walls to keep rocks and water at bay, but the flip side of sturdier engineering is greater risk: Here the highway runs anywhere from five hundred to a thousand feet above the river. Glaciers turn the mountains wet and slick, releasing saturated buildups occasionally in the form of mudslides. Downed power lines crisscross the road; our bus drove right over sparking high-tension wires. I lifted my feet off the floor. Missing guardrails and telephone poles—and small Muslim tomb markers topped with a crescent moon—offer mute testimony to those who came before but never left. Nonetheless, crossing the border into Pakistani-held Kashmir was far more frightening for what was missing.

No one was guarding the Pakistani-Chinese border.

The Khunjerab Security Force outpost, supposedly controlled by the Pakistani army as the main passport control checkpoint between the two nations, was unmanned. We continued about sixty miles down the road before we encountered a

Just north of the Torugart Pass in southern Kyrgyzstan, the Tash Rabat fortress lies on one of the branches of the Silk Road. Believed to date to the 10th century, this edifice was originally either a monastery used by Nestorian Christians prior to the Mongol invasion that spread Islam across the Tian Shan Range, a resting lodge for wary travelers, or a sort of early customs station where fees were collected for the right to passage.

The "dragon's teeth," mountains between China and southern Kyrgyzstan.

small shack where the bus' passengers were asked to sign a register book full of phony entries like "Joe Blow, the Lover Man." The sleepy guard didn't even bother to look at our passports. We soon found out why all semblance of authority was absent. The bus dropped us off at Sost, from which we caught a taxi to the Kashmiri village of Passu. Surrounded by three magnificent glaciers, rope suspension bridges crossing the legendary Hunza River and clouds so close you can actually touch them, our stay at the Passu Inn was a case study in low-tech life. Electricity came and went every few minutes; phones actually used a crank! (The phone number for our hotel was 7.) We spent the next morning trekking and negotiated with a surly local jeep driver to take us to Gilgit for thirty dollars. But you can't go back: Six years later Passu was nearly totally destroyed by the October 2005 earthquake, and its famous glaciers have almost all melted due to global warming.

The Passu-to-Gilgit bus ride requires eight hours, but if you use the same jeep driver as we did, you can do it in three. Convinced that he was being underpaid—although our hotel owner said twenty dollars was a fair price, he kept claiming that some Japanese dude had paid a hundred a week before—he drove wildly back and forth like a madman, intentionally skimming the edge of the abyss even when there wasn't any other traffic. To add to the sense of menace, local children and young men threw stones at us whenever we passed through a village. Cole read a film book (he's a movie critic); I attempted to look bored while I checked out Rakaposhi Peak (twenty-six thousand feet) and the Hunza Valley's terraced agriculture and stone-lined irrigation canals. Looking for the lost kingdom of Shangri-la? The myth places it squarely in the Hunza Valley, though its hard to envision.

From the perspective of scenery that you simply can't see anywhere else, this section of the KKH is the highlight. Europeans with months of vacation to spare spend weeks on side trips to villages off the highway in this region. We drove through a canyon that makes the Grand Canyon look like landfill and limped across roped suspension bridges where half the boards were missing (Cole: "So this is it, Ted. It's been nice knowing you") across a massive, primordial flow of white-water as impressive as the Mississippi and the Nile combined. Every few hundred feet signs advise: "Relax—Landslide Area Ends," but that's hard to do considering that no one has bothered to post where they *begin*. Because the Hunza is lined with farming communities, animals become a more frequent driving problem—and because the Pakistanis don't neuter their cattle the bulls are both huge and fierce.

Talking to the Taliban

Located at the southern bank of the Gilgit River, Gilgit is the spiritual and political center of disputed Kashmir province and a key stop on the KKH. Violence has been a part of life here since the partition of India in 1947, and the signs of the cheapness of life are everywhere—starving children and maimed old men line the sidewalks. More than ten thousand people were shot, bombed and lynched in Gilgit during the 1990s alone, which is more than live there now. A stone's throw from the Line of Control between Pakistani- and Indian-held Kashmir, that rumbling in the distance is just as likely to be mortar fire as thunder.

Gilgit is "The Wild Bunch" meets the bar scene in "Star Wars" set in a jihadi training camp. Like Kashgar, it's a dusty town where Pakistani, Afghan, Tajik, Kyrgyz and Chinese traders can get you anything for the right price. There's dodgy electricity and no sewage system; even getting a postcard out requires greasing the proper palms. I loved it. Where else can you get your old Doc Martens resoled for a buck, munching a *roti* while watching wild dogs chew off each other's limbs in the middle of rush-hour donkey-cart traffic? Still, our objective was the end of the KKH. After a few days of relaxation, we boarded a Northern Areas Transport Corporation (NATCO) bus for the sixteen-hour trip to the capital city of Islamabad.

The first thing we noticed as we assumed our customary spots at the front of the vehicle (we booked early) was the uniformed NATCO soldier riding shotgun—literally. He carried the shotgun right on his lap, occasionally pointing it right at me while chatting distractedly with the driver. He sat at the very front in a special seat, intentionally visible from the road. Then we checked out our fellow passengers. I hadn't seen such a motley collection of smugglers and scoundrels since, well, the bus from Kashgar. Just outside Chilas I saw the first of several official signs stenciled on the rocky face of the mountain: "Ambush Point: 600 meters." I asked the soldier about this.

"There are many, many bandits," he explained apologetically. "Sometimes it's not enough for them just to steal everything. Sometimes they kill everyone on the bus."

"That would be a problem," I tried to say blandly.

"Yes, it is," he agreed. "Then no one wants to take the bus anymore."

The Gilgit next becomes the Indus River, home to one of the planet's great ancient civilizations, and the views alternate wildly between lush green valleys and bleak chalky rocks tumbling off canyon after canyon into oblivion. It's breathtaking, but after a while sensory overload sets in; it's the kind of experience best digested after the fact.

The bus blew through one switchback after another until, just as darkness began to fall, things started getting weird. Hundreds of turbaned men carrying rocket launchers, automatic rifles and grenades walked along the side of the highway, dragging ammo behind them on the ground. I recognized their outfits from TV news footage.

"Holy shit," I realized aloud to Cole. "It's the *mujahedeen*."

Unbeknownst to us a week before we'd left for Kyrgyzstan the Taliban had declared Kashmir an "American-free zone." They had reserved for themselves the right to shoot any holder of a U.S. passport on sight, including diplomats. No one had taken the declaration seriously, especially since the KKH was at least a hundred miles from the Khyber Pass into Afghanistan. We learned that that night, in the interim, what had formerly been Pakistani-held Kashmir was now occupied by Taliban militants. Now I understood why the Pakistan-China border had been unguarded; under a new Taliban-backed regime (which, also unbeknownst to us, was seizing power in Islamabad that very moment) the Pakistanis had allowed themselves to be "invaded" so that the Afghans could fight their war with India on their behalf without provoking a nuclear confrontation. The Taliban, however, were far less interested in taking on the Indians over territory so barren that fighting has to be suspended every winter than their real goal: turning Pakistan into another Islamic fundamentalist state. They'd earned a rep as the Khmer Rouge of the 1990s for stoning adulterers to death and denying medical care to women. Now, working in conjunction with Pakistani General Pervez Musharraf in Islamabad (his coup d'état finally succeeded a few weeks later) they were in position to enforce their previous threats.

The bus pressed on into the hamlet of Dasu, the northern section of which had obviously been the scene of a recent skirmish. Fires crackled in brand-new ruins. Broken glass, from God knows what, was everywhere. An orange glow lit up the windows to the left side of the bus; something big had exploded there. Unattended horses wandered aimlessly through the streets, some bleeding from bullet wounds. A woman walked crazily in a semicircle—shock? The body of a man, in the generic *shalwar kameez* brown frocks worn by Pakistani Muslims, leaned against a storefront. There was no blood. Burned-out cars lined the KKH as we passed through what had been the bazaar district. On the outskirts of town, three Taliban soldiers flagged us down by making circles on the road with a flashlight.

In the Third World military checkpoints are a frequent nuisance, sort of like

The governments of China, Kyrgyzstan and Tajikistan allow nomads to cross borders freely. Here we encountered Afghans in China, just a few miles from Tajikistan.

bridge tolls manned by unstable gunmen. With a full-fledged war going on, two holders of American passports that the Pakistani authorities hadn't bothered to stamp weren't going to last long under Taliban occupation; such checkpoints were bound to spring up everywhere. The bus stopped and the front door opened. The soldiers gave the driver a big grin. My fellow passengers, who'd been glaring at Cole and I for hundreds of miles, looked entirely too pleased about this development for my taste. The NATCO soldier got up, looked at Cole and I, and walked to the door. Would we be taken off the bus and shot by the side of the road? It was entirely possible; certainly no one on this vehicle would miss us. I seriously doubted that anyone would ever be punished, or that there'd ever be an investigation. I remembered the European Community passport in my backpack (I'm a dual French-U.S. citizen); that red booklet would get me off the hook but, unlike me, Cole didn't have a backup nationality. I thought about the best arguments I could employ to try to save my life. Finally, I was angry at myself for not preparing properly—we could easily have bought guns in Gilgit.

Then the soldier did something for which I will always be grateful. Wearing a bored expression on his face, he nonchalantly pointed his gun straight at the lead *mujahedeen* and said something to the driver in Urdu. The bus moved forward, and

More than ten thousand monuments (nicknamed "bubbles") at Cholpon-Ata, Kyrgyzstan. The stone images, which date to the second millennium B.C.E., feature petroglyphs of ibex, horses, camels and snow leopards.

that was it—until the next checkpoint, when we had to talk our way out of being executed. (See the graphic novella starting on page 117 for the details.)

The stretch of the KKH between Dasu and Pattan is notoriously violent even in "peacetime"—a number of Western travelers have been beaten, robbed and raped there. But the military situation was relatively static; *mujahedeen* trudged along, too dog-tired to care about anything beyond their next footstep. Civilian vehicles, including small cars and trucks, shared the road with hundreds of refugees fleeing south into Pakistan proper and Afghan soldiers walking towards the Line of Control. Finally, at four in the morning, the road made a sharp southern turn, and the KKH became dark and empty. A farmer's mule darted out into the street; we hit the sucker doing about fifty. Our driver never slowed down.

We had three more hours ahead of us, and I figured that it was OK to try to catch some sleep. I was weak, hungry and still processing my brushes with death. The last section of KKH is notable for nothing in particular. The road leaves the mountains, goes straight and flat and the chances of getting killed by another vehicle or a terrorist or a beast of burden become relatively minimal. If it hadn't been for the Pakistani film music blaring from the speakers directly above our heads, it might even have been peaceful.

Fortunately, Cole had wire cutters.

A Good Day to Die

Buzkashi has two main forms: the traditional, grassroots game, known as tudabaray *(Persian [Dari]: "coming out of the crowd"), and the modern government-sponsored version,* qarajay *("black place"). Both feature mounted competitors who struggle for control of a decapitated, dehoofed, and, sometimes, gutted carcass weighing anywhere from forty to one hundred pounds, the eviscerated body being lighter. Neither style has many formal rules, but common etiquette prohibits a player from biting or pulling the hair of an opponent, grabbing the reins of an opponent's mount, or using weapons.*

—Encyclopedia Britannica

A few seconds ago, you were just another dirty face in a crowd of sweaty wannabes gussied up like Han Solo in an old Soviet tank helmet. Now you're the center of attention. This, you know now, is a very bad thing. Two or three hundred pumped-up, pissed-off horsemen—who can count all these lunatics?—are chasing you at full gallop. You're dragging a hundred pounds of dead goat with your left hand and pounding the crap out of your panicked horse with your right as you charge through a storm of dust in a mad dash for glory and survival.

Suddenly two guys catch up, one on each side. One smacks you hard across the face with his riding crop; a blot of blood splashes across an eye. His dirtbag friend lets out a spine-tingling rebel yell as he gleefully wraps his whip under your stallion's testes. You've trained your animal to keep running through such shocking pain, but one hoof nonetheless catches a rut in the fog of distraction. You both go down. Something feels broken; anyway, it doesn't matter since you're trapped under your impossibly heavy horse. A thousand pounding hoofs pass overhead as you tumble down a well of unconsciousness.

Victory or death is the choice when you sign up for *buzkashi*. Today, regrettably, victory belongs to another man.

Forget Thai kickboxing, NASCAR and skydiving; buzkashi (*buz* is Turkic for "goat" and *kashi* means "bashing") is the bloodiest and most anarchic sport currently played by the human race. There are buzkashi meets at local, regional and national gatherings throughout Central Asia, but the biggest, most violent, tournament in the world takes place on two dusty fields on the outskirts of Dushanbe, the hardscrabble capital of the Republic of Tajikistan. It all goes down during the

205

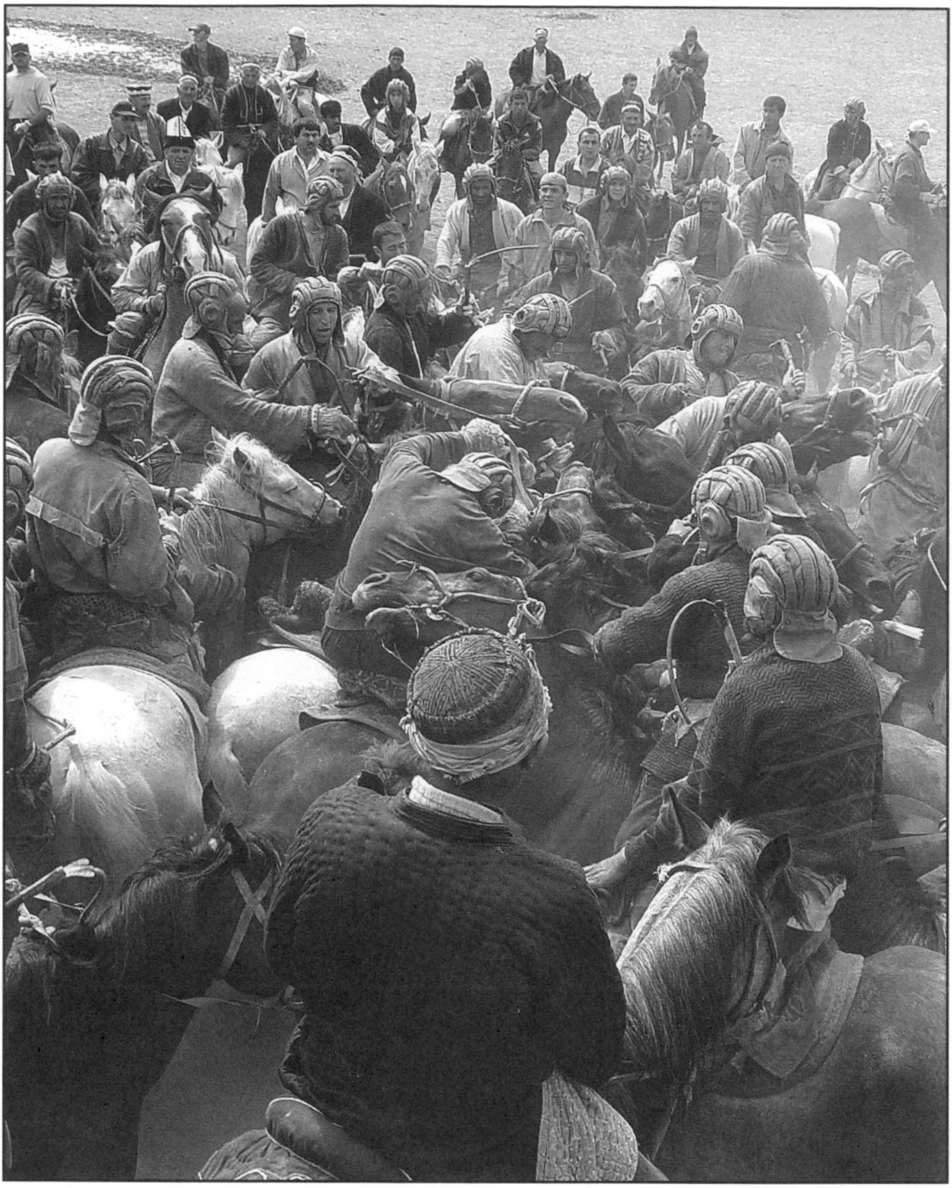

Up close and personal in a game of *buzkashi* (literally "goat bashing" in Turkic), the bloodiest and most anarchic sport currently played by the human race.

first two days of spring, first at a sort of semi-final at the ancient garrison town of Hissar and then at a final event at the Dushanbe Hippodrome. Officially these flamboyantly-dressed brutes risk life and limb for carpets and cheap televisions and the occasional car, but everyone knows the truth: buzkashi is about pride—national and personal—fueled by the foolhardy bravery that only testosterone can provide.

Thousands turned out for the two-day championship during the vernal festival of Navruz in March of 2002; the streets of this mountainous former Soviet republic's cities and villages had been emptied of men and boys. (A though a few brave souls attend, females are deemed too delicate for the brutal spectacle about to ensue.)

Live from Hissar

Anticipation is particularly keen this year for several reasons. The uptight Taliban, who had banned buzkashi as pre-Muslim and thus pagan in neighboring Afghanistan, are finally out of power, toppled by an American-led invasion force. The Afghans are fondly remembered from the early Nineties as inept, but insanely vicious, players—everyone wants to see what they'll do this year. And last year, in 2001, twenty-two buzkashi players met death. Hundreds more lost limbs or assorted motor functions. Most of all, though, this year is all about an old-fashioned grudge match.

"From the 1970s on, we Tajiks were the best buzkashi players in the world," notes Buzkashi Federation of Tajikistan president Mousso Ahyoev as we walk together in the shadow of the snow-capped Pamir mountains. 1998 marked the beginning of a long and humiliating string of victories by horsemen from neighboring Kyrgyzstan. "The Kyrgyz are best now," the forty-three-year-old native of the Tajik-ibadi village of Karatigen allows grudgingly, "but it is not right."

What went wrong in 1998? Some fans think doping has resulted in Mark Mc-Guiresque equines. "The Kyrgyz horses somehow became stronger," Ahyoev glares insinuatingly. "Kyrgyz horses and Tajik horses used to be basically the same in size and strength. Who knows what those people feed their horses?" A fierce expression of disgust darkens his face at the phrase *those people*.

Buzkashi connoisseurs agree that a horse's overall strength—a combination of agility, speed and brute force—is the most important, if not the sole, predictor of success in this no-holds-barred, high-speed rumble on horseback. Everything boils down to two essential objectives: securing the *buz* and dragging it through the goal—gambits in which a powerful horse often means the difference between victory and death. Whether the Kyrgyz have stooped to pumping up the equine side of the equation with steroids remains an open question.

The Rules (This Won't Take Long)

Experts agree that the history of buzkashi dates back thousands of years, but because most Central Asian cultures didn't have written languages until the 1920s its exact history is unknown. Genghis Khan's armies spread the game across Central Asia; the Golden Horde, however, preferred to use the headless body of an executed—or sometimes pre-executed—enemy soldier as the *buz*. This gory practice continued in some corners of Central Asia until the 19th century, and according to some reports made a comeback last fall in northern Afghanistan when thousands of captured Talibs mysteriously vanished from the Northern Alliance's prisoner-of-war rosters. Nowadays, the body of a goat is decapitated, drained of blood and

Crowds pack the boundaries of a *buzkashi* playing field. The gap to the left is the goal through which the carcass—the *buz*—must be dragged or carried.

soaked in salt water the night before a game. (A sheep or calf carcass may serve as acceptable substitutes.)

In every other respect buzkashi remains the same festival of orgiastic ultra-violence that broke up Mongol monotony during the 13ᵗʰ century. The playing field on the Hissar plain is a standard two hundred-by-two hundred-yard square surrounded by fifteen-foot walls sloped at a forty-five-degree angle. Hundreds of horsemen congregate on the opposite corner of the field from the goal, which is indicated by a ten-yard gap in the crowd of spectators. An official chucks the *buz* onto the field. A circle of contestants forms instantly.

Should you ever find yourself playing buzkashi, never take an early lead. Who-ever first gets to the *buz* must do so by half-dismounting, keeping his special knee-high high-heeled boot hanging from one stirrup while yanking a *buz* leg halfway off the ground with one hand. Immediately surrounding that brave sap are dozens of men rearing their horses onto their hind legs in an attempt to push forward through the crowd; the idea is to prod your horse to drop down hard, using his chest as a battering ram to create a gap between the animals to your left and right, like an icebreaker. Everyone rains their whips down frenetically, over and over again—on their steeds, on their neighbor's heads, and most of all, on the guy with the *buz* to try to make him drop it. And surrounding them, forming a perfect circle of rearing horses and whip-flailing men fifty feet in diameter, is an outer ring of frustrated contestants. No one gets out of there alive—not carrying the *buz*, anyway.

Buzkashi is primarily an every-man-for-himself game, but horseman can and occasionally do form ad hoc alliances. Sometimes one man will defend another from those trying to separate him from the *buz*; alternatively, others will work together to attack another.

Watching the harrowing proceedings from a viewing stand at the hundred-yard line are two dozen local dignitaries led by Abdurohid Karimov, Hissar's Tajik tribal chieftain. Theoretically, Karimov's deputies are supposed to prevent outbreaks of violence. "They are only allowed to grab the corpse," Karimov intones solemnly. "No kicking and no fighting, or the game will be stopped." In practice, buzkashi stops for no man. Karimov awards the highest prizes to the most bloodthirsty players while an official brandishing a megaphone barks at a mob of horsemen bogged down in one spot while they pound the stubborn *buz*-holder for ten minutes: "Quit messing around! Come on! Get it! Don't grab your dick—grab the *buz*!"

Later this afternoon a man will lose both of his eyes to a guy infamous for his two-fingered poking technique; the Pokerizer, as I call him in homage to a Stephen King story, will be rewarded a minute later with a new green carpet. There are no rules in buzkashi. Whatever it takes to get the *buz*—punching, whipping, biting, stabbing—is acceptable. Afghans are famous for packing AK-47s; though gunfire is considered poor form, it doesn't automatically result in disqualification.

A scrum forms around the *buz*. Many players wear Soviet-era tank helmets for protection—for all the good that does. Death and maiming are not uncommon among players.

Winning is everything in this Central Asian blend of polo, demolition derby and mosh pit from hell. A row of ambulances waiting behind the crowd sends a clear message; by the end of the day they will all have plenty of customers.

Suddenly, incredibly, someone breaks out of the circular mob. Leaning slightly

backward in his ornately-stitched saddle to balance himself against the weight of the *buz* and frantically whipping his horse, he heads for a wall to shake off his pursuers. Fans run for their lives as hundreds of thundering horses shoot up the ramp after the escapee, through a gap in the crowd and back down to the field. Sometimes the breakaway is intercepted and the circle of death descends upon him, but ultimately a new rider steals the *buz* and

Tribal dignitaries "officiate" over the game—although penalties are rarely, if ever, called.

makes it across the goal. After the *buz* is recovered, everyone returns to the other side of the field and the game begins anew.

Minimum prize at Hissar, for dragging a *buz* across the goal line once, is a green synthetic rug. Exceptional performances, as determined by the panel of slightly tipsy judges, score a hand-made wool carpet from Turkmenistan or Afghanistan. Repeat winners vie for various major appliances such as televisions and washing machines made by local Soviet-era factories. Champions go home with live calves and donkeys. A shiny new Volga sedan awaits the grand-prize winner.

What It Is; What It Was

In many respects, the world is becoming increasingly homogenous. Whether you're hanging out in Istanbul, Beijing or Chicago, you can eat a Big Mac, listen to the Backstreet Boys and catch the latest Mel Gibson flick at a strip mall indistinguishable from its twin in any suburb in America. The flipside of globalization is entropy; there have never been as many countries on the planet at one time as there are now. In Asia, the collapse of the Soviet Union freed up two dozen new nations to explore their traditional cultures. Nowhere has this transition from Soviet oppression to anarchic independence been more chaotic than in the southern breakaway republics of Central Asia. From that chaos have reemerged ancient spectacles that had long laid dormant under communism—like buzkashi.

In western Central Asia near the Caspian Sea are despotic Turkmenistan and Uzbekistan, each dominated by scorching deserts. In the middle are the grassy

TAJIKISTAN

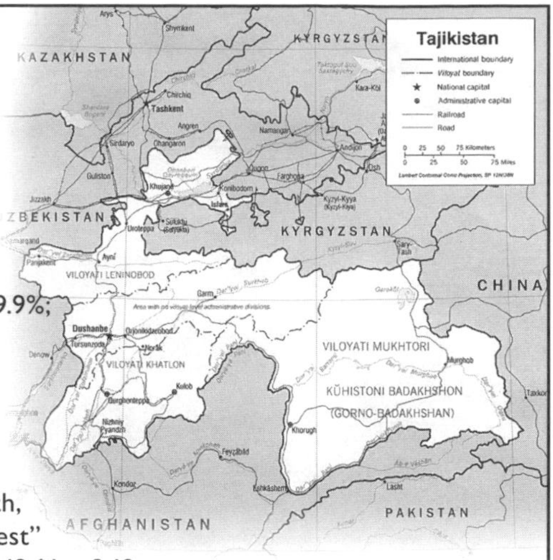
Tajikistan
KAZAKHSTAN
KYRGYZSTAN
CHINA
AFGHANISTAN
PAKISTAN
Tashkent
Dushanbe
VILOYATI LENINOBOD
VILOYATI KHATLON
VILOYATI MUKHTORI
KŪHISTONI BADAKHSHON
(GORNO-BADAKHSHAN)

Capital: Dushanbe
Form of Government: Dictatorship
Leader: President Emomali Sharipovich Rakhmonov (born 1952)
Population (July 2005): 7,163,506
Major Ethnic Groups (2000): Tajik 79.9%; Uzbek 15.3%; Russian 1.1%; Kyrgyz 1.1%
Area (square miles): 55,237 (slightly smaller than Wisconsin)
Terrain (as per *CIA Factbook*): "Pamir and Alay Mountains dominate landscape; western Fergana Valley in north, Kofarnihon and Vakhsh Valleys in southwest"
Currency/Exchange Rate (2005): US $1 = 3.12 *somoni*
Oil Reserves (proven): 12 million barrels
Natural Gas Reserves (proven): 124.3 billion cubic meters
Coolest Thing About Tajikistan: Stunning Pamir mountains
Worst Thing About Tajikistan: Tajik Air, its fleet composed of rotting Tupolev-154s flown by inebriated pilots, is the only way in and out
Best Way to Get Thrown Into Jail: Make friends with Afghan drug runners
Per Capita Annual Income: $280
Unemployment Rate: 50%
Life Expectancy: 65

Tajikistan, ninety-three percent covered by jagged mountains, is the most desperately poor and remote of the Central Asian republics and a classic case of international neglect. The country, beset by widespread starvation, was ravaged by a ferocious civil war between the post-Soviet communist regime and Afghan-trained *mujahedeen* based in the Tajik section of the Ferghana Valley that ended when the warring factions, exhausted and demoralized, finally quit the fight in 1997 and agreed to a power-sharing deal. At least Fifty thousand Tajiks were killed and eight hundred thousand forced into refugee camps. Much of the country is still mined. Militants of the Islamic Movement of Turkestan (formerly the Islamic Movement of Uzbekistan) are based in the south and launch periodic raids into Kyrgyzstan and Uzbekistan. Famine-racked Tajiks watched helplessly as Afghan-bound trucks containing food aid passed them by during the fall 2001 U.S. invasion. "It's the speed of the collapse that's so frightening, the transformation from being part of a superpower than can put men in space to being a scene of abject poverty," a BBC reporter observed at the time. Tajikistan is exceedingly difficult to access, even from neighboring Kyrgyzstan and Uzbekistan, and only has consular representation in seventeen countries. Tajikistan's misery may soon be alleviated, however, by its control over fifty-five percent of Central Asia's water. The Pyanj, Amu Darya and other important rivers originate in the Pamirs. Sooner rather than later, the Tajik government may be able to force concessions and even payment in return for keeping the water flowing. The Chinese government is courting Tajikistan, emphasizing ethnic and historical ties dating to the Silk Road. Russia, whose soldiers guard Tajikistan's borders, maintains a large military presence matched by the United States and France, which opened a secret military base as a staging area for attacks against Afghanistan after 9/11.

Players charge onto the field at the start of a match.

steppes of Kyrgyzstan and Kazakhstan—familiar terrain if you've driven across Montana and Idaho. And tucked away in steep snowy mountains adjacent to the Himalayas are Tajikistan and Afghanistan. Dozens of languages and religions are spoken and practiced in these countries, but most have something in common: they're horse peoples. Outside major cities horses remain the basic mode of transportation. In Afghanistan, horses are still so vital that a 2001 battle over control of the strategic center of Mazar-e-Sharif was won by a Northern Alliance cavalry charge against Taliban tanks.

The first order of business for rulers of the Stans after their 1991 independence was the creation of distinct nationalities: money, postage stamps and mythic historical figures meant as much to these new entities as borders, armies and new passports. Now it's on to phase two: the new nations are defining themselves by comparing themselves to and competing with their neighbors. This is, as it turns out, where the ancient sport of buzkashi is becoming a barometer of national identity.

Tajikistan and the other Central Asian republics celebrate the ancient Zoroastrian festival of Navruz to mark the arrival of spring on March 21-22. With the exception of Afghanistan, Tajikistan is the poorest Stan—and a civil war between the old Soviet regime and a radical Taliban-backed Islamist movement during the 1990s ruined what little infrastructure the place had to begin with.

Since independence, the region's status as a Fourth World backwater has increased its already remote isolation. Only one carrier, the Aeroflot-breakaway Tajikistan Airlines, flies to Dushanbe. You can catch the single flight a week from Istanbul, on Saturdays, or fly daily from Moscow, as I did. Because Tajik Air flies out of a different airport than Moscow's international Sheremetyevo 2, however,

you have to spring for a six hundred dollar Russian transit visa merely to change planes in Moscow. Tajik Air's 1950s-vintage Tupolev 154s have pioneered the art of negative leg room; anyone over five feet tall must sit with his legs on his own seat to avoid suffering a broken knee. Most seats are broken. Ice forms on the windows. Upon arrival in Dushanbe, the hotels are squalid Soviet shitholes. Unsurprisingly, few tourists are willing to make the trek to the Navruz buzkashi festivities, but that's their loss: buzkashi is more than worth the fleas and diarrhea.

The eternally broke Tajiks always manage to scare up enough donations from wealthy fans to host the biggest buzkashi event in Asia. Buzkashi horses are pricey; you can't find a horse worth its name for under ten thousand dollars. Organizers sponsor players, maintain and replace horses and come up with prizes good enough to lure players across war zones, fifteen-thousand-feet mountain passes and one-hundred-thirty-five-degree deserts. We may not have Kazakhstan or Uzbekistan's massive oil reserves, the Tajik message seems to be, but we

Age is no barrier to playing *buzkashi*. In fact, the older and more experienced the player, the more dangerous he tends to be.

can still raise the one hundred thousand *somoni* (thirty-five thousand dollars) it takes to put on a buzkashi meet—and kick your ass in the bargain.

Until 1998, anyway.

Ethnic stereotypes are front and center in discussions among buzkashi players and fans. Kazakhs and Mongols are renowned horsemen but tend to come in third or fourth at international match-ups because their approach is considered pedestrian next to the lyrical Tajiks and Kyrgyz. The Uyghurs of China's Muslim West are well-respected—because they ride baby camels back home, the lighter Tajik *buz* is relatively easy for them to handle—but few made it across the heavily-guarded Xinjiang-Tajik border (since opened) to compete. "Turkmen have the best horses, their Akhal-Tekes are second only to Arabians," smirks Junadulo Telove, a twenty-two-year-old Uzbek who with his small horse Zaychik (Kyrgyz for "rabbit") has won

A small pack breaks loose from the melee and makes a run for the goal, with the rest of the players in pursuit.

Dushanbe's city-wide competition every year since he turned fifteen, "but Turkmen are too dull and dimwitted to ride them correctly." Perhaps the Turkmen are simply tired because they travel the greatest distance to Dushanbe, I suggest. "The Kyrgyz have a shorter, but much harder, ride across the Tian Shan mountains," he counters, "but they are still OK." The highest compliment members of any tribe can muster for their rivals is grudging respect.

This year the man to beat is Ahmon Khalimov, a homely sixty-two-year-old Kyrgyz who claims to have won thirty-six national buzkashi championships. Buzkashi is a young man's game—most of those trampled to death last year were over age thirty—but the four-feet-ten Khalimov has brought cars and horses home to Kyrgyzstan every year since the 1998 sea-change. He has spent so much of his life riding horses that he can hardly walk. Khalimov could easily pass for ninety.

And he's a natural.

Khalimov hovers between the inner and outer rings when the *buz* first hits the ground, conserving his horse's strength for the combat to follow. Other riders avoid him. "That old man, he looks like nothing. Last year his horse killed three guys," shudders newbie Yormakhmat Yonosov, twenty-one, from a backwater called Nagorne.

Khalimov hangs back, waiting for an opportunity to strike. He's a thief; rather than beating his opponents senseless, he opportunistically waits for someone to break out; it's easier to pound a single *buz*-laden individual than a hundred.

Suddenly he swoops alongside like an avenging angel, nips off an ear or nose with savage precision and snatches the *buz* away from his bleeding victim as his horse dashes away with a prancing sidestep. Now and then he crosses the goal line before his prey realizes he's lost a hundred pounds of dragging carcass. Khalimov holds his whip in his teeth to free a fist for fending off would-be usurpers as he dashes into the screaming crowd. He's graceful, playful and a bad sport to the point of cruelty. Genghis would have loved this guy.

Stakes are high in *buzkashi*. Beyond the coveted tribal bragging rights, prizes include cars, goats (above) and carpets (below). It should be noted: the goats are worth more than carpets.

"I have fallen from my horse many times, but I have never been hurt in twenty-two years of playing buzkashi," Ahyoev, the Tajik official, claims. Not so Khalimov. "I break my leg almost every year," he grins, "always along the same place, just above the knee." Taking those extra risks makes the difference: Ahyoev lost the 2001 championship to

Khalimov by a single *buz*; this year, the Kyrgyz drives the Volga sedan home from Hissar.

No one dies, and except for the dude double-blinded by the Pokerizer, no one gets maimed. Twentysomething Hissar native son Homid Lugayev cites this year's picture-perfect weather for the disappointingly rock-bottom casualty rate. "It rained so much that all the horses were slipping and falling. That's why twenty-two people died last year. Now it's dry, and there is no wind storm." He delivers this observation devoid of emotional investment.

But Hissar is a mere PSAT next to the main event, held the following day. Even more horsemen—an estimated five hundred—gather at the Hippodrome in Dushanbe proper. President Emomali Rakhmonov will personally supervise the internationally televised must-see event of the year.

A player bravely reaches for a loose *buz* before a mob of horsemen closes in.

The Tajiks Strike Back

Rumors abound that a radical Islamist group, the Islamic Movement of Uz-bekistan, famous for launching daring incursions from southern Tajikistan through Kyrgyzstan as far as the suburbs of Tashkent, is planning a terrorist attack and/or assassination attempt at the Hippodrome for buzkashi day two. The atmosphere is tense. Fire engines line the running track surrounding the field. Each spectator is subjected to a documents check and a thorough pat-down, and more than a thousand heavily-armed military police are on hand to separate the ninety-nine percent male crowd from the playing field. (Bleachers remain half-finished, construction equipment rusting away, from Soviet days.)

Anyone on horseback, however, is waved through the checkpoint. Even a Tatar woman wearing lipstick and make-up is approved for play. It never occurs to anyone that even ruthless IMU terrorists would defile the sport of buzkashi by posing as a player.

Light intermittent rain and a long wait to get in makes the crowd edgy. The layout sucks; unlike the ideal buzkashi set-up at Hissar, the Hippodrome's terrain is flat. There's no ramp separating the horses and no height to permit good visibility. To make matters worse, the police keep people so far back that they can barely see the field or their president, who sits at a reviewing stand on the far end of the field. Every few minutes the crowd surges against the line of *militsia*, who respond by pounding heads with rubber truncheons.

Then the action shifts from the other side where most of the players had been showing off for President Rakhmonov. One man—it's Ahyoev!—breaks free of a circle that had been bogged down for nearly fifteen minutes. His ally pokes at an immense Kazakh with his whip to keep him at bay. The earth pounds as hundreds of horsemen head straight for where I'm standing. There's no place to run, so I stand perfectly still.

The crowd lets out a roar as the horses pass through us, between us, on top of us. Buzkashi has left the field, the police are in disarray, the crowd is running along with the horses. The crowd turns brazen—one man steals an officer's cap and runs. A few men lie injured in the field of battle, but even they're smiling: in this one-party dictatorship run by the same guy who ruled here under the Soviets, where the KGB still exists and the police are forever checking up on you and hitting you up for bribes, where there are no jobs to speak of and you'll likely die before you make it to age sixty, people have breathed the freedom that comes with rules being broken. Two kids find a loose *buz* leg and swing it around, spraying blood on police and civilians alike. The cops try to restore order, but it's no use—it's anarchy.

Ultimately, the day belongs to the people, but the grand prize belongs to a newcomer, Farydun Zangynov. His approach is workaday, methodical, almost

Tournaments take place over several days and are an occasion for tribes and families to gather, Here, next to the stadium, Tajik women sit in a booth at an adjoining fair.

More Fun And Games
In Central Asia

Heirs to tribesmen who survived perennial scarcity by raiding agrarian settlements and robbing hapless travelers, modern-day Central Asians continue to find pleasure in traditional pastimes involving risk and gratuitous violence. In addition to the startling blend of Mongol *bezerker* and Persian martial spirit of *buzkashi* one can find the following games and activities throughout the Central Asian republics, particularly in rural areas:

Kyzku (also *kesh-kumay*, or "Kiss the Girl") is, like *buzkashi*, a steppe horseman's game played for high stakes on a large open field. A woman of marriageable age starts a match by striking a male suitor, also on horseback, and racing across the field toward a goalpost on the oppose side of the field. If he catches up to her before the finish, he earns the right to kiss her while riding. If the girl is amenable to the young man's advances, she slows down enough to allow him to plant a wet one. Marriage follows soon—often immediately. At some matches a yurt (traditional nomad's tent) is set up on the side of the playing field to host the ensuing consummation of the blessed event. If the girl decides to play hard to get, she may use any means necessary—including lethal force—to repel his advances. *Kyzku* is generally played in what was known in czarist times as Khirgizia—modern-day Kyrgyzstan, Kazakhstan and parts of Mongolia and Tajikistan.

While female *buzkashi* players are rare, women do participate in a number of other steppe sports.

Other Kazakh horse games include the WWE-meets-Kentucky-Derby madness of *Audaryspak* (or *Kurosh*, "Wrestling on Horseback"), in which contestants beat the crap out of each other until one of them falls off their mount, and *Kumis Alu* (or *Tyiyn Enmei*, "Pick up the Coin") in which a rider is required to scoop a coin off the ground at a full gallop. In keeping with post-Soviet austerity the coin has been replaced by a handkerchief.

It's neither an organized sport nor much fun for some of the participants but the Kyrgyz practice of *Ala-Kachuu* ("Grab and Run"), a ritual form of bride-kidnapping in which *The New York Times* says "more than half of Kyrgyzstan's married women were snatched from the street by their husbands," is clearly a cultural cousin of *kyzku*. (*Ala-kachuu* is also practiced in other Central Asian countries, although to a significantly lesser extent.) "Recent surveys suggest that the rate of abductions has steadily grown in the last fifty years and that at least a third of Kyrgyzstan's brides are now taken against their will," reports the paper. "Kyrgyz men say they snatch women because it is easier than courtship and cheaper than paying the standard 'bride price,' which can be as much as eight hundred dollars plus a cow. Family or friends often press a reluctant groom, lubricated with vodka and beer, into carrying out an abduction... Once a woman has been taken to a man's home, her future in-laws try to calm her down and get a white wedding shawl onto her head. The shawl, called a *jooluk*, is a symbol of her submission. Many women fight fiercely, but about eighty percent of those kidnapped eventually relent, often at the urging of their own parents." There's a Kyrgyz saying: "Every good marriage begins in tears." Some Kyrgyz women commit suicide rather than submit to their kidnappers-in-law.

Another pastime not for the faint of heart is *eagle hunting*. Most common in the mountains where western Mongolia meets southeastern Kazakhstan and northeastern Kyrgyzstan, the *berkutchi* (eagle hunters) use full-grown golden eagles—which have a wing span of up to seven feet—to hunt for prey as small as a foxes and badgers and as large as wolves and Marco Polo sheep. As a young man a prospective eagle hunter steals an eagle chick while its mother is away from its aerie. He covers it with a cloth and starves it for a week in order to break its will, then nurses it back to health to create a bond. Eagle hunters, who consider falconry a mere child's

One of the golden eagles used by the *berkutchi* of Kyrgyzstan.

game, typically spend their entire lives with a single eagle. Such is the commitment required that some refuse to marry. Mukhamed Isabekov, deputy head of Kazakhstan's Association of Hunting Bird Owners, claims that his group's numbers are small and dwindling for lack of courage: "A person has to be wise to deal with a large, wild animal like an eagle. You have be tough and patient. That's why there are so few eagle-hunters. Many people want to be, but then realize it's not for them."

The joyous—and bloody—anarchy that is *buzkashi*.

boringly thuggish, but it's effective. Time after time, he wades into the mob, beats the crap out of whoever has the *buz*, and drags it across the goal line. "I played to win," Zangynov, twenty, says from atop his perfectly-proportioned Arabian Malesh ("baby"), "so I won." Something is bleeding under his white shirt, but I shut up. Why ruin the moment? People gather around as he guides Malesh to the reviewing stand to collect the chit for his car. "Where are you from?" the president's aide asks this year's champion. "I'm from Dushanbe!" A triumphant cry goes up as the word spreads.

The long and humiliating losing streak is over. A Tajik has reclaimed the long-stolen buzkashi title. Ahmon Khalimov, the ancient Kyrgyz champion, looks on: "That boy, he played well, but I will be ready for him next year," he promises.

Blood gushes down Khalimov's scalp as they load him into an ambulance.

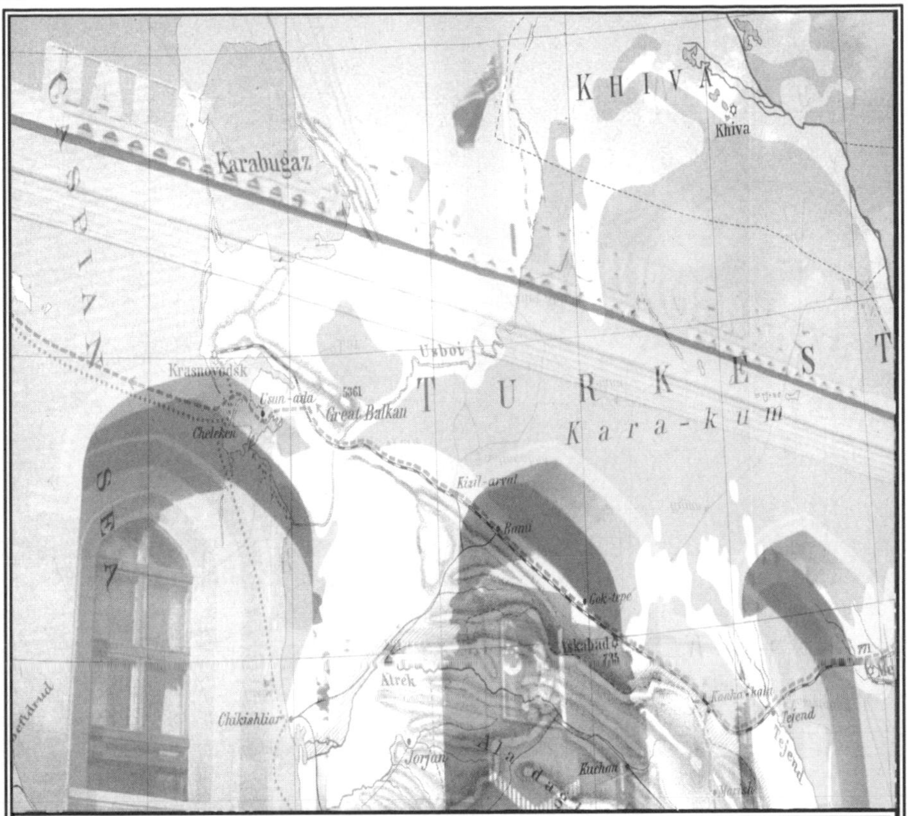
KHIVA
Khiva
Karabugaz
Usboi
Krasnovodsk
Great Balkan
Cheleken
TURKEST
Kara-kum
Kizil-arvat
Gok-tepe
Atrek
Chikishliar
Jorjan
Kuchan
Tejend

Turkmenistan 2000

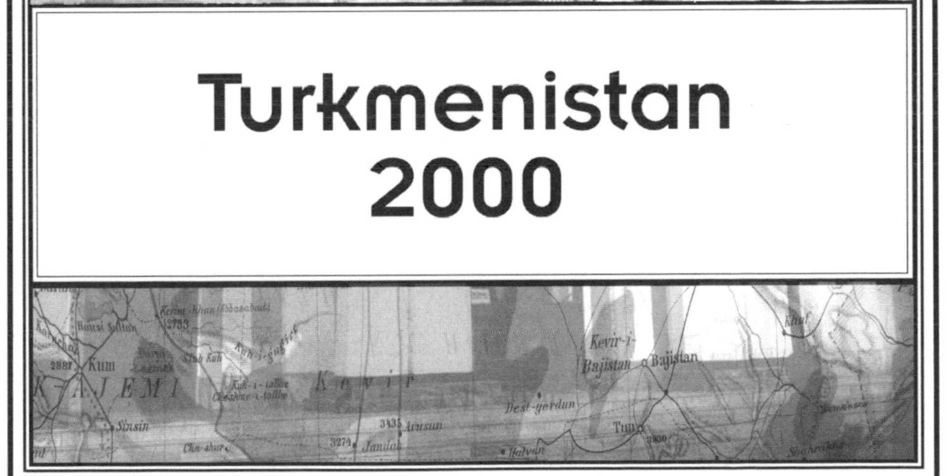
Kum
Kevir
Bajistan
Sinsin
Arusun
Jandak
Dest-gerdun

The State Department invited me to Turkmenistan in September 2000 to meet with Turkmen dissidents and to explain the nature of freedom of the press as it functioned in the United States. It was my only trip to the region through official channels. As such, it offered a unique set of revelations.

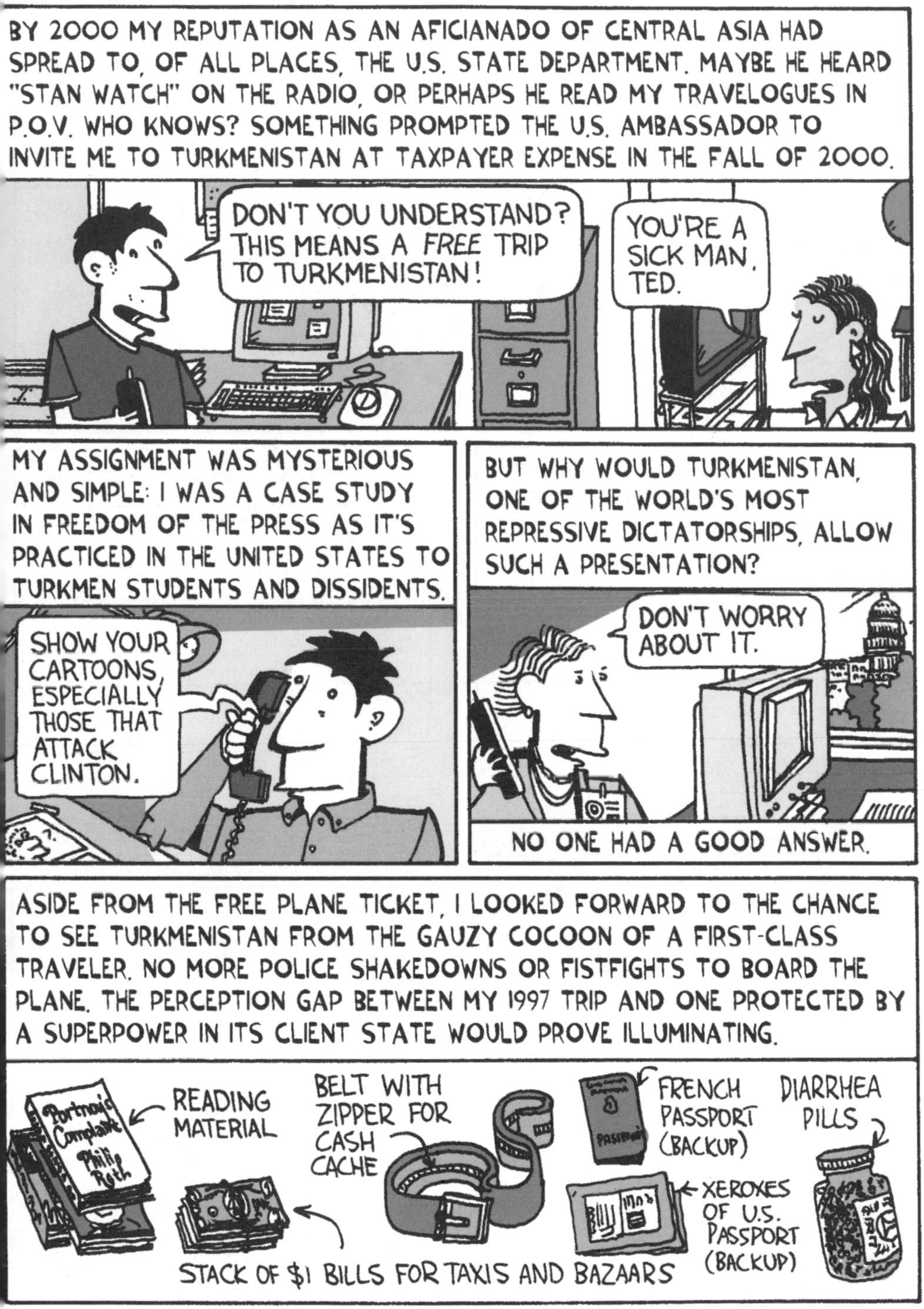
BY 2000 MY REPUTATION AS AN AFICIANADO OF CENTRAL ASIA HAD SPREAD TO, OF ALL PLACES, THE U.S. STATE DEPARTMENT. MAYBE HE HEARD "STAN WATCH" ON THE RADIO, OR PERHAPS HE READ MY TRAVELOGUES IN P.O.V. WHO KNOWS? SOMETHING PROMPTED THE U.S. AMBASSADOR TO INVITE ME TO TURKMENISTAN AT TAXPAYER EXPENSE IN THE FALL OF 2000.
DON'T YOU UNDERSTAND? THIS MEANS A *FREE* TRIP TO TURKMENISTAN!
YOU'RE A SICK MAN, TED.
MY ASSIGNMENT WAS MYSTERIOUS AND SIMPLE: I WAS A CASE STUDY IN FREEDOM OF THE PRESS AS IT'S PRACTICED IN THE UNITED STATES TO TURKMEN STUDENTS AND DISSIDENTS.
SHOW YOUR CARTOONS, ESPECIALLY THOSE THAT ATTACK CLINTON.
BUT WHY WOULD TURKMENISTAN, ONE OF THE WORLD'S MOST REPRESSIVE DICTATORSHIPS, ALLOW SUCH A PRESENTATION?
DON'T WORRY ABOUT IT.
NO ONE HAD A GOOD ANSWER.
ASIDE FROM THE FREE PLANE TICKET, I LOOKED FORWARD TO THE CHANCE TO SEE TURKMENISTAN FROM THE GAUZY COCOON OF A FIRST-CLASS TRAVELER. NO MORE POLICE SHAKEDOWNS OR FISTFIGHTS TO BOARD THE PLANE. THE PERCEPTION GAP BETWEEN MY 1997 TRIP AND ONE PROTECTED BY A SUPERPOWER IN ITS CLIENT STATE WOULD PROVE ILLUMINATING.
READING MATERIAL
BELT WITH ZIPPER FOR CASH CACHE
FRENCH PASSPORT (BACKUP)
DIARRHEA PILLS
XEROXES OF U.S. PASSPORT (BACKUP)
STACK OF $1 BILLS FOR TAXIS AND BAZAARS

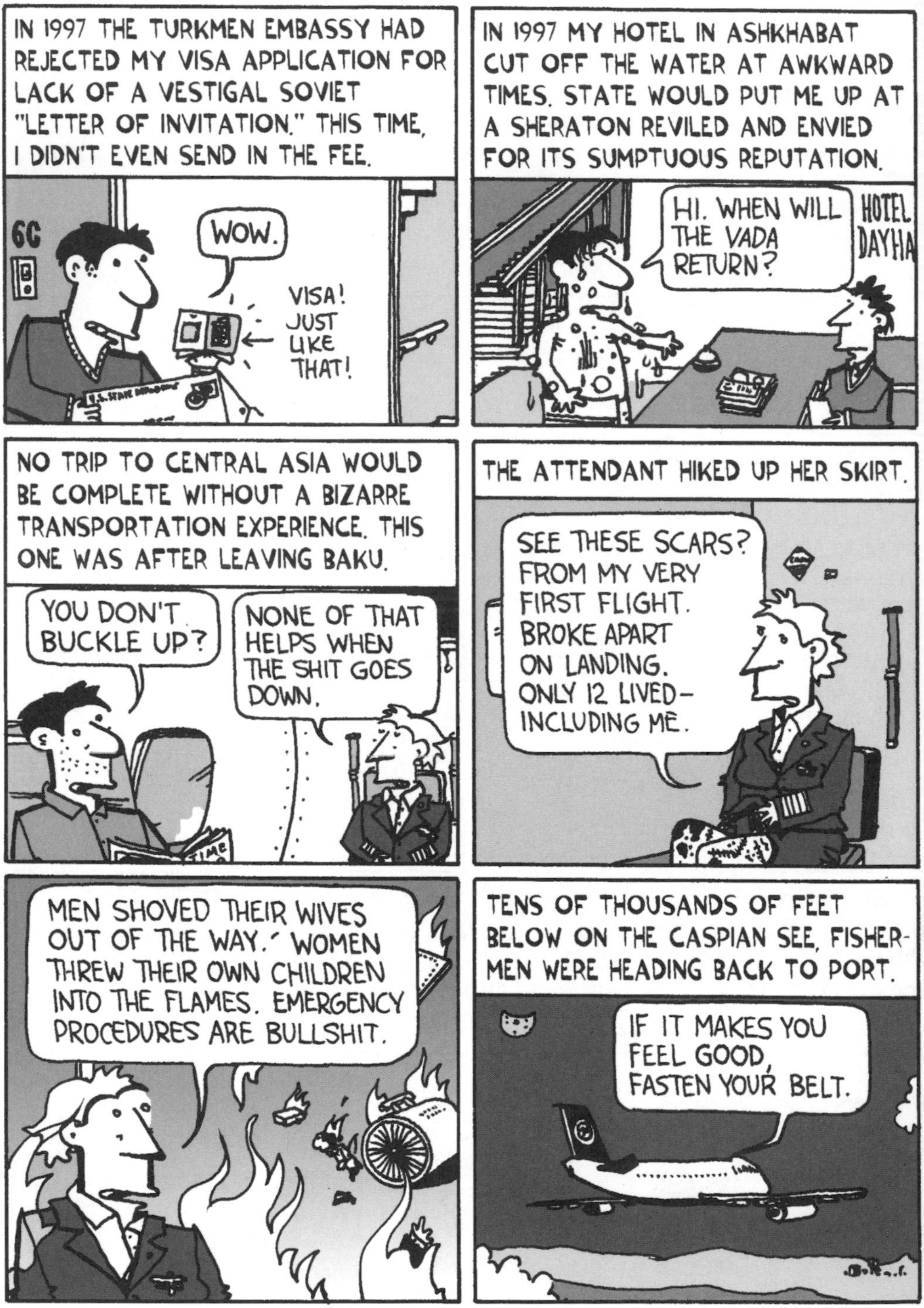
IN 1997 THE TURKMEN EMBASSY HAD REJECTED MY VISA APPLICATION FOR LACK OF A VESTIGAL SOVIET "LETTER OF INVITATION." THIS TIME, I DIDN'T EVEN SEND IN THE FEE.
6C
WOW.
VISA! JUST LIKE THAT!
IN 1997 MY HOTEL IN ASHKHABAT CUT OFF THE WATER AT AWKWARD TIMES. STATE WOULD PUT ME UP AT A SHERATON REVILED AND ENVIED FOR ITS SUMPTUOUS REPUTATION.
HI. WHEN WILL THE VADA RETURN?
HOTEL DAYHA
NO TRIP TO CENTRAL ASIA WOULD BE COMPLETE WITHOUT A BIZARRE TRANSPORTATION EXPERIENCE. THIS ONE WAS AFTER LEAVING BAKU.
YOU DON'T BUCKLE UP?
NONE OF THAT HELPS WHEN THE SHIT GOES DOWN.
TIME
THE ATTENDANT HIKED UP HER SKIRT.
SEE THESE SCARS? FROM MY VERY FIRST FLIGHT. BROKE APART ON LANDING. ONLY 12 LIVED— INCLUDING ME.
MEN SHOVED THEIR WIVES OUT OF THE WAY. WOMEN THREW THEIR OWN CHILDREN INTO THE FLAMES. EMERGENCY PROCEDURES ARE BULLSHIT.
TENS OF THOUSANDS OF FEET BELOW ON THE CASPIAN SEE, FISHERMEN WERE HEADING BACK TO PORT.
IF IT MAKES YOU FEEL GOOD, FASTEN YOUR BELT.

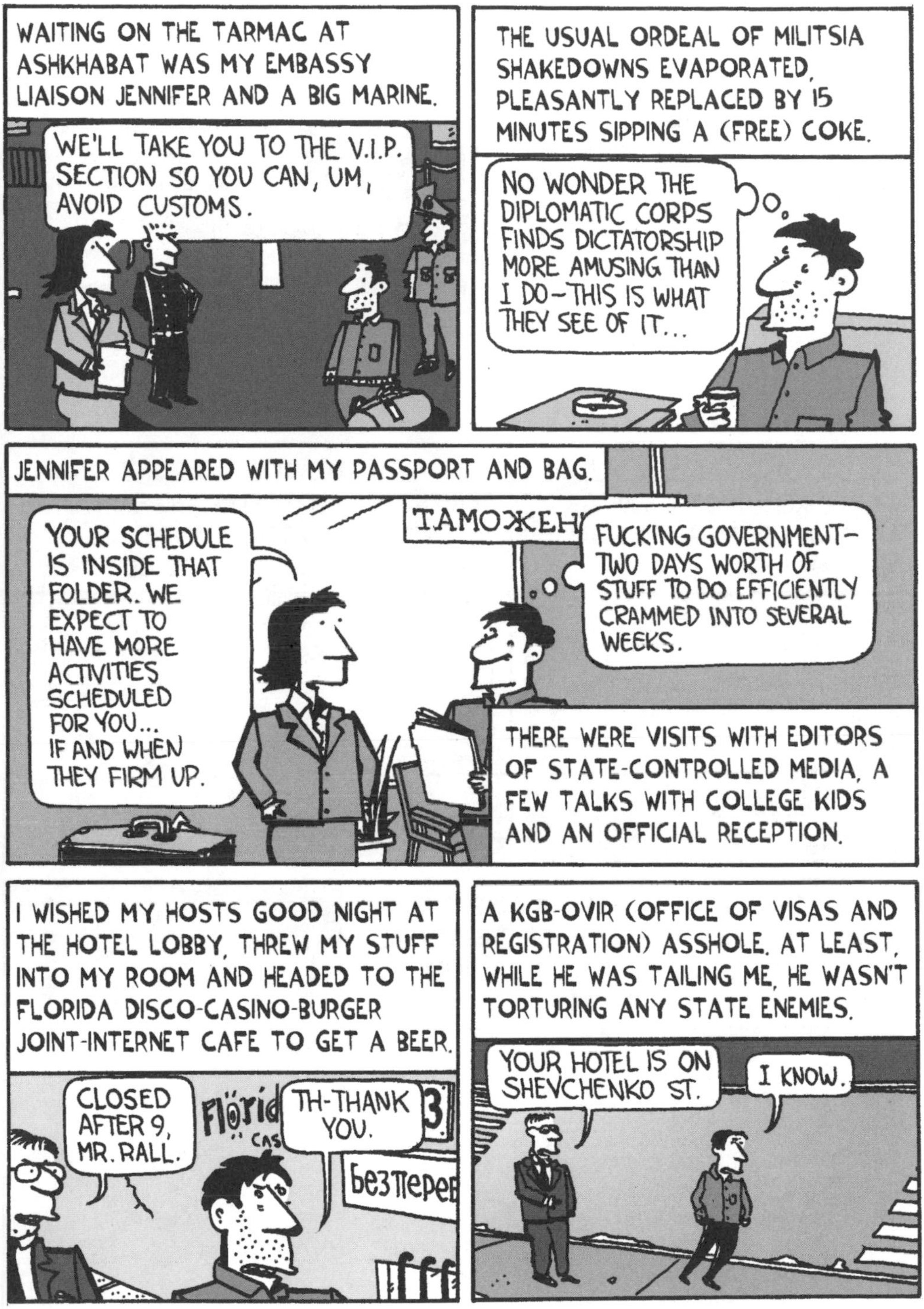
WAITING ON THE TARMAC AT ASHKHABAT WAS MY EMBASSY LIAISON JENNIFER AND A BIG MARINE.
WE'LL TAKE YOU TO THE V.I.P. SECTION SO YOU CAN, UM, AVOID CUSTOMS.
THE USUAL ORDEAL OF MILITSIA SHAKEDOWNS EVAPORATED, PLEASANTLY REPLACED BY 15 MINUTES SIPPING A (FREE) COKE.
NO WONDER THE DIPLOMATIC CORPS FINDS DICTATORSHIP MORE AMUSING THAN I DO—THIS IS WHAT THEY SEE OF IT...
JENNIFER APPEARED WITH MY PASSPORT AND BAG.
ТАМОЖЕН
YOUR SCHEDULE IS INSIDE THAT FOLDER. WE EXPECT TO HAVE MORE ACTIVITIES SCHEDULED FOR YOU... IF AND WHEN THEY FIRM UP.
FUCKING GOVERNMENT—TWO DAYS WORTH OF STUFF TO DO EFFICIENTLY CRAMMED INTO SEVERAL WEEKS.
THERE WERE VISITS WITH EDITORS OF STATE-CONTROLLED MEDIA, A FEW TALKS WITH COLLEGE KIDS AND AN OFFICIAL RECEPTION.
I WISHED MY HOSTS GOOD NIGHT AT THE HOTEL LOBBY, THREW MY STUFF INTO MY ROOM AND HEADED TO THE FLORIDA DISCO-CASINO-BURGER JOINT-INTERNET CAFE TO GET A BEER.
CLOSED AFTER 9, MR. RALL.
TH-THANK YOU.
A KGB-OVIR (OFFICE OF VISAS AND REGISTRATION) ASSHOLE. AT LEAST, WHILE HE WAS TAILING ME, HE WASN'T TORTURING ANY STATE ENEMIES.
YOUR HOTEL IS ON SHEVCHENKO ST.
I KNOW.

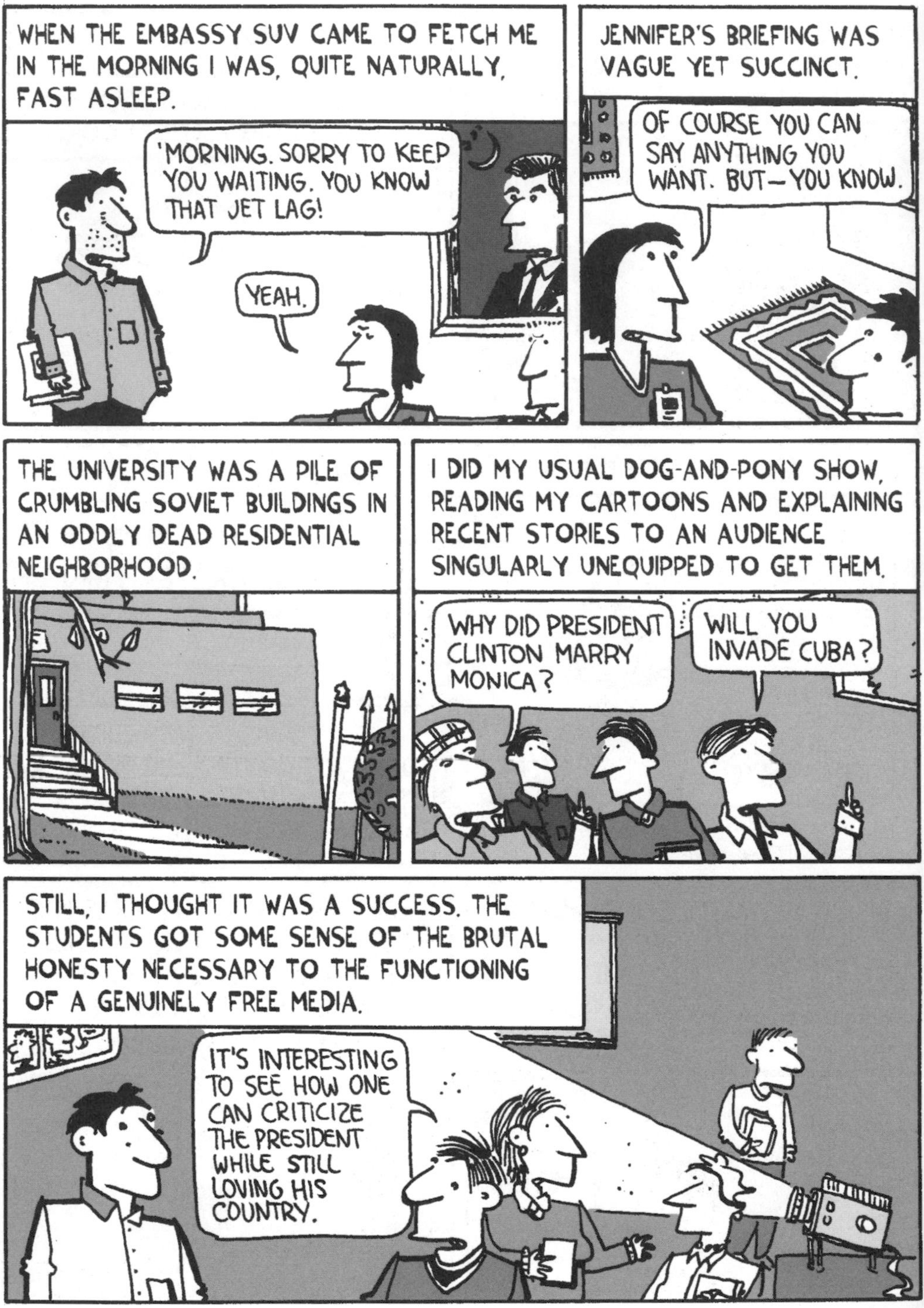
WHEN THE EMBASSY SUV CAME TO FETCH ME IN THE MORNING I WAS, QUITE NATURALLY, FAST ASLEEP.
'MORNING. SORRY TO KEEP YOU WAITING. YOU KNOW THAT JET LAG!
YEAH.
JENNIFER'S BRIEFING WAS VAGUE YET SUCCINCT.
OF COURSE YOU CAN SAY ANYTHING YOU WANT. BUT—YOU KNOW.
THE UNIVERSITY WAS A PILE OF CRUMBLING SOVIET BUILDINGS IN AN ODDLY DEAD RESIDENTIAL NEIGHBORHOOD.
I DID MY USUAL DOG-AND-PONY SHOW, READING MY CARTOONS AND EXPLAINING RECENT STORIES TO AN AUDIENCE SINGULARLY UNEQUIPPED TO GET THEM.
WHY DID PRESIDENT CLINTON MARRY MONICA?
WILL YOU INVADE CUBA?
STILL, I THOUGHT IT WAS A SUCCESS. THE STUDENTS GOT SOME SENSE OF THE BRUTAL HONESTY NECESSARY TO THE FUNCTIONING OF A GENUINELY FREE MEDIA.
IT'S INTERESTING TO SEE HOW ONE CAN CRITICIZE THE PRESIDENT WHILE STILL LOVING HIS COUNTRY.

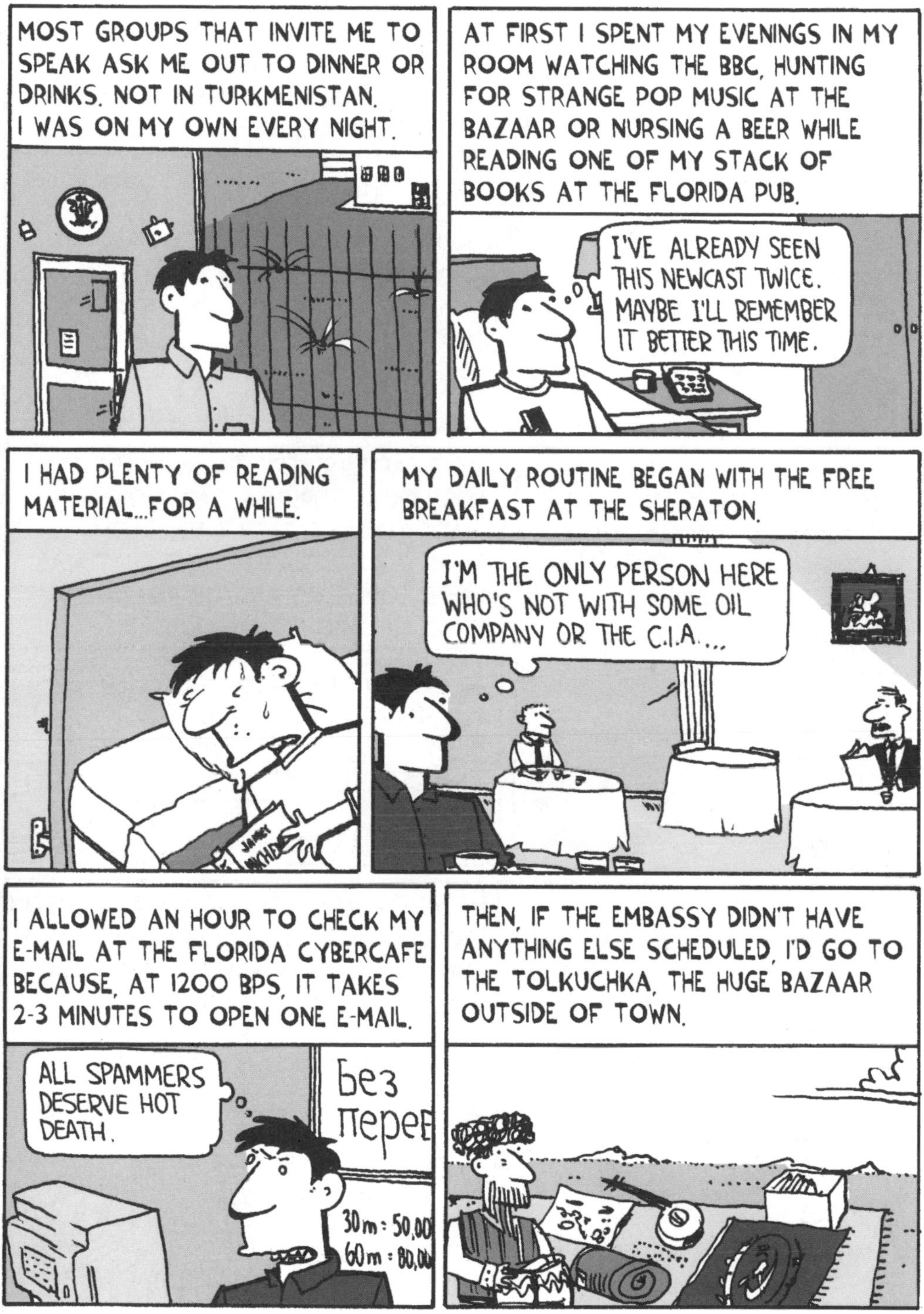
MOST GROUPS THAT INVITE ME TO SPEAK ASK ME OUT TO DINNER OR DRINKS. NOT IN TURKMENISTAN. I WAS ON MY OWN EVERY NIGHT.
AT FIRST I SPENT MY EVENINGS IN MY ROOM WATCHING THE BBC, HUNTING FOR STRANGE POP MUSIC AT THE BAZAAR OR NURSING A BEER WHILE READING ONE OF MY STACK OF BOOKS AT THE FLORIDA PUB.
I'VE ALREADY SEEN THIS NEWCAST TWICE. MAYBE I'LL REMEMBER IT BETTER THIS TIME.
I HAD PLENTY OF READING MATERIAL...FOR A WHILE.
MY DAILY ROUTINE BEGAN WITH THE FREE BREAKFAST AT THE SHERATON.
I'M THE ONLY PERSON HERE WHO'S NOT WITH SOME OIL COMPANY OR THE C.I.A. ...
I ALLOWED AN HOUR TO CHECK MY E-MAIL AT THE FLORIDA CYBERCAFE BECAUSE, AT 1200 BPS, IT TAKES 2-3 MINUTES TO OPEN ONE E-MAIL.
ALL SPAMMERS DESERVE HOT DEATH.
Без
THEN, IF THE EMBASSY DIDN'T HAVE ANYTHING ELSE SCHEDULED, I'D GO TO THE TOLKUCHKA, THE HUGE BAZAAR OUTSIDE OF TOWN.

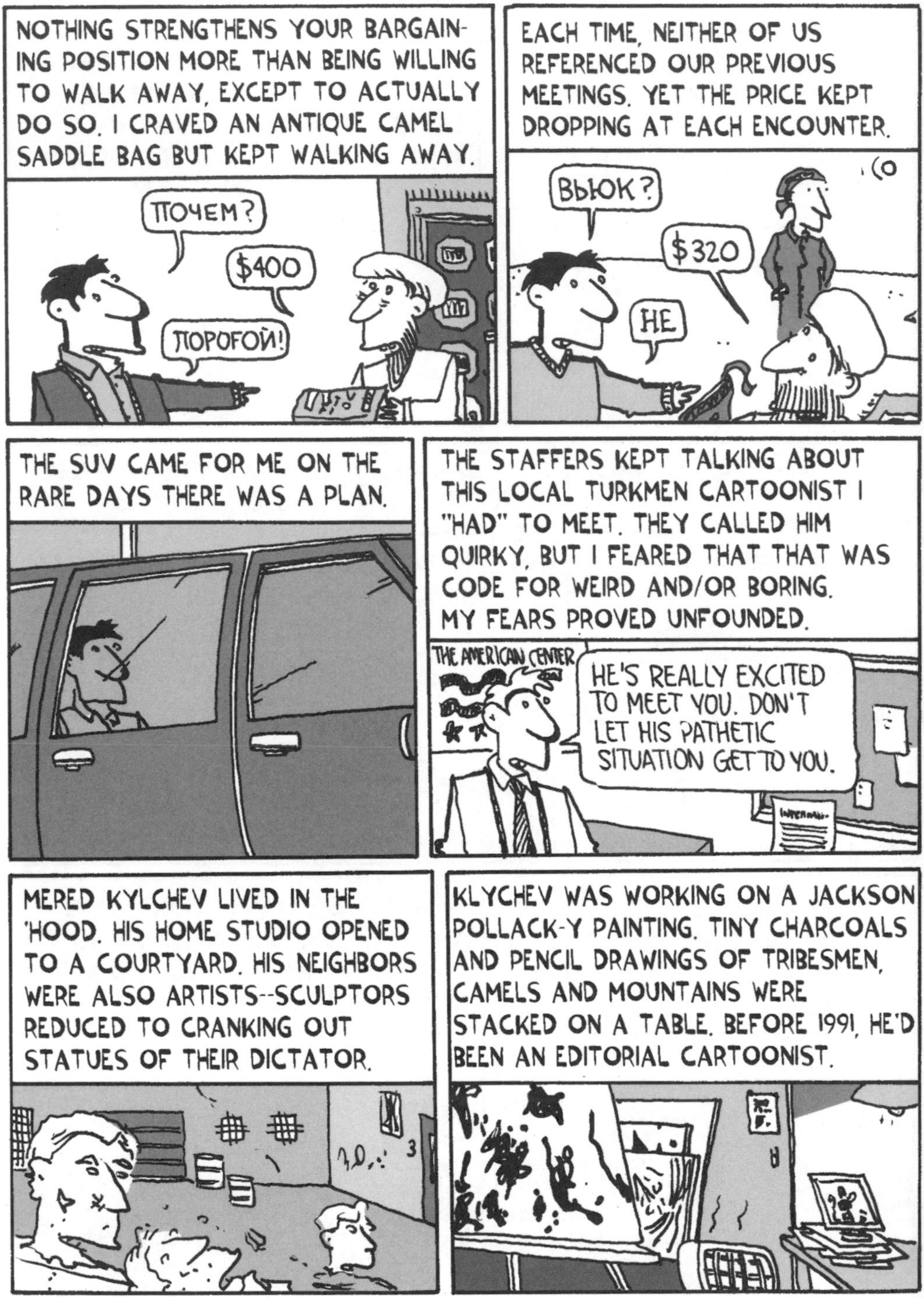
NOTHING STRENGTHENS YOUR BARGAINING POSITION MORE THAN BEING WILLING TO WALK AWAY, EXCEPT TO ACTUALLY DO SO. I CRAVED AN ANTIQUE CAMEL SADDLE BAG BUT KEPT WALKING AWAY.
ПОЧЕМ?
$400
ПОРОГОЙ!
EACH TIME, NEITHER OF US REFERENCED OUR PREVIOUS MEETINGS. YET THE PRICE KEPT DROPPING AT EACH ENCOUNTER.
ВЬЮК?
$320
НЕ
THE SUV CAME FOR ME ON THE RARE DAYS THERE WAS A PLAN.
THE STAFFERS KEPT TALKING ABOUT THIS LOCAL TURKMEN CARTOONIST I "HAD" TO MEET. THEY CALLED HIM QUIRKY, BUT I FEARED THAT THAT WAS CODE FOR WEIRD AND/OR BORING. MY FEARS PROVED UNFOUNDED.
THE AMERICAN CENTER
HE'S REALLY EXCITED TO MEET YOU. DON'T LET HIS PATHETIC SITUATION GET TO YOU.
MERED KYLCHEV LIVED IN THE 'HOOD. HIS HOME STUDIO OPENED TO A COURTYARD. HIS NEIGHBORS WERE ALSO ARTISTS--SCULPTORS REDUCED TO CRANKING OUT STATUES OF THEIR DICTATOR.
KLYCHEV WAS WORKING ON A JACKSON POLLACK-Y PAINTING. TINY CHARCOALS AND PENCIL DRAWINGS OF TRIBESMEN, CAMELS AND MOUNTAINS WERE STACKED ON A TABLE. BEFORE 1991, HE'D BEEN AN EDITORIAL CARTOONIST.

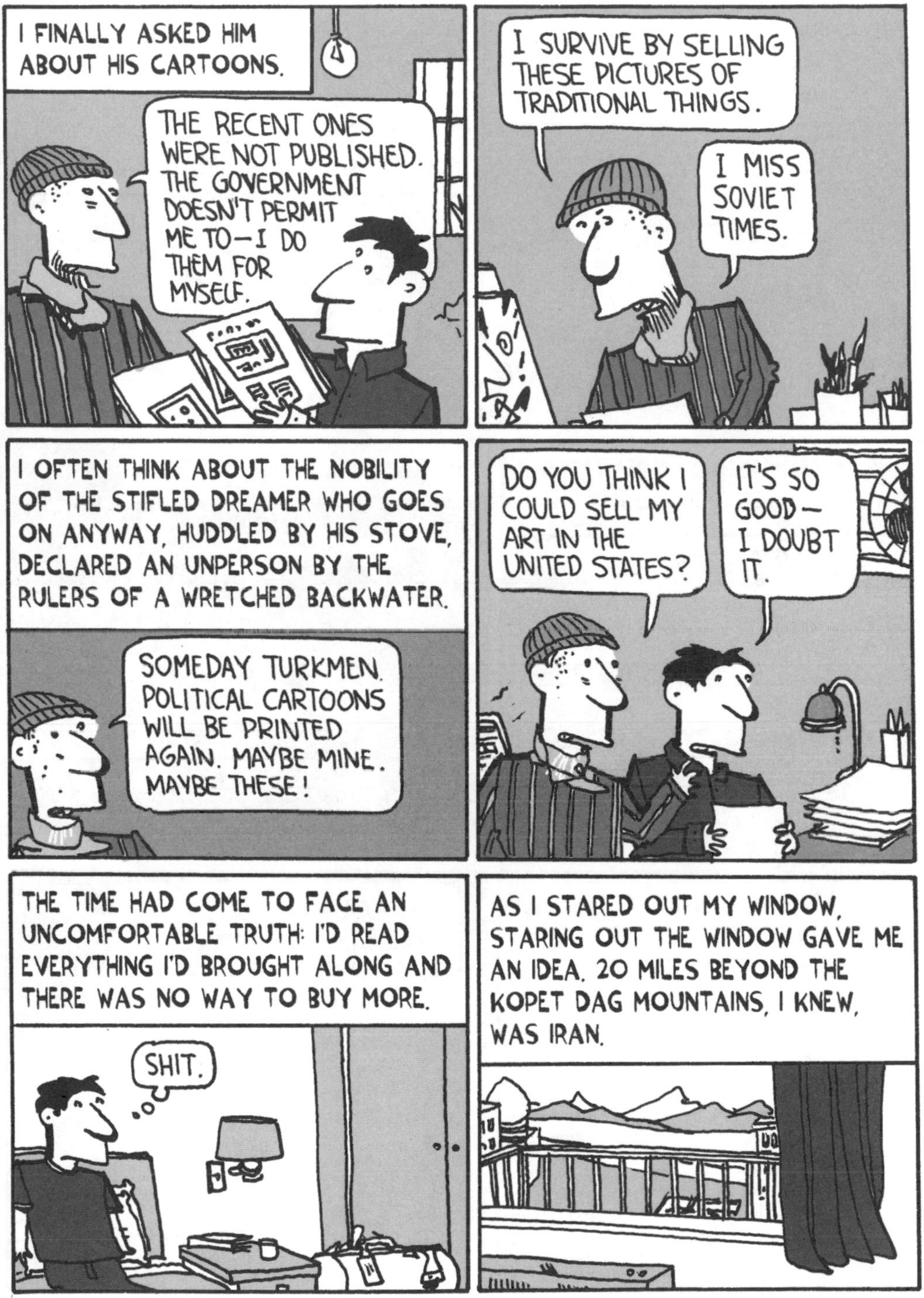
I FINALLY ASKED HIM ABOUT HIS CARTOONS.
THE RECENT ONES WERE NOT PUBLISHED. THE GOVERNMENT DOESN'T PERMIT ME TO—I DO THEM FOR MYSELF.
I SURVIVE BY SELLING THESE PICTURES OF TRADITIONAL THINGS.
I MISS SOVIET TIMES.
I OFTEN THINK ABOUT THE NOBILITY OF THE STIFLED DREAMER WHO GOES ON ANYWAY, HUDDLED BY HIS STOVE, DECLARED AN UNPERSON BY THE RULERS OF A WRETCHED BACKWATER.
SOMEDAY TURKMEN POLITICAL CARTOONS WILL BE PRINTED AGAIN. MAYBE MINE. MAYBE THESE!
DO YOU THINK I COULD SELL MY ART IN THE UNITED STATES?
IT'S SO GOOD—I DOUBT IT.
THE TIME HAD COME TO FACE AN UNCOMFORTABLE TRUTH: I'D READ EVERYTHING I'D BROUGHT ALONG AND THERE WAS NO WAY TO BUY MORE.
SHIT.
AS I STARED OUT MY WINDOW, STARING OUT THE WINDOW GAVE ME AN IDEA. 20 MILES BEYOND THE KOPET DAG MOUNTAINS, I KNEW, WAS IRAN.

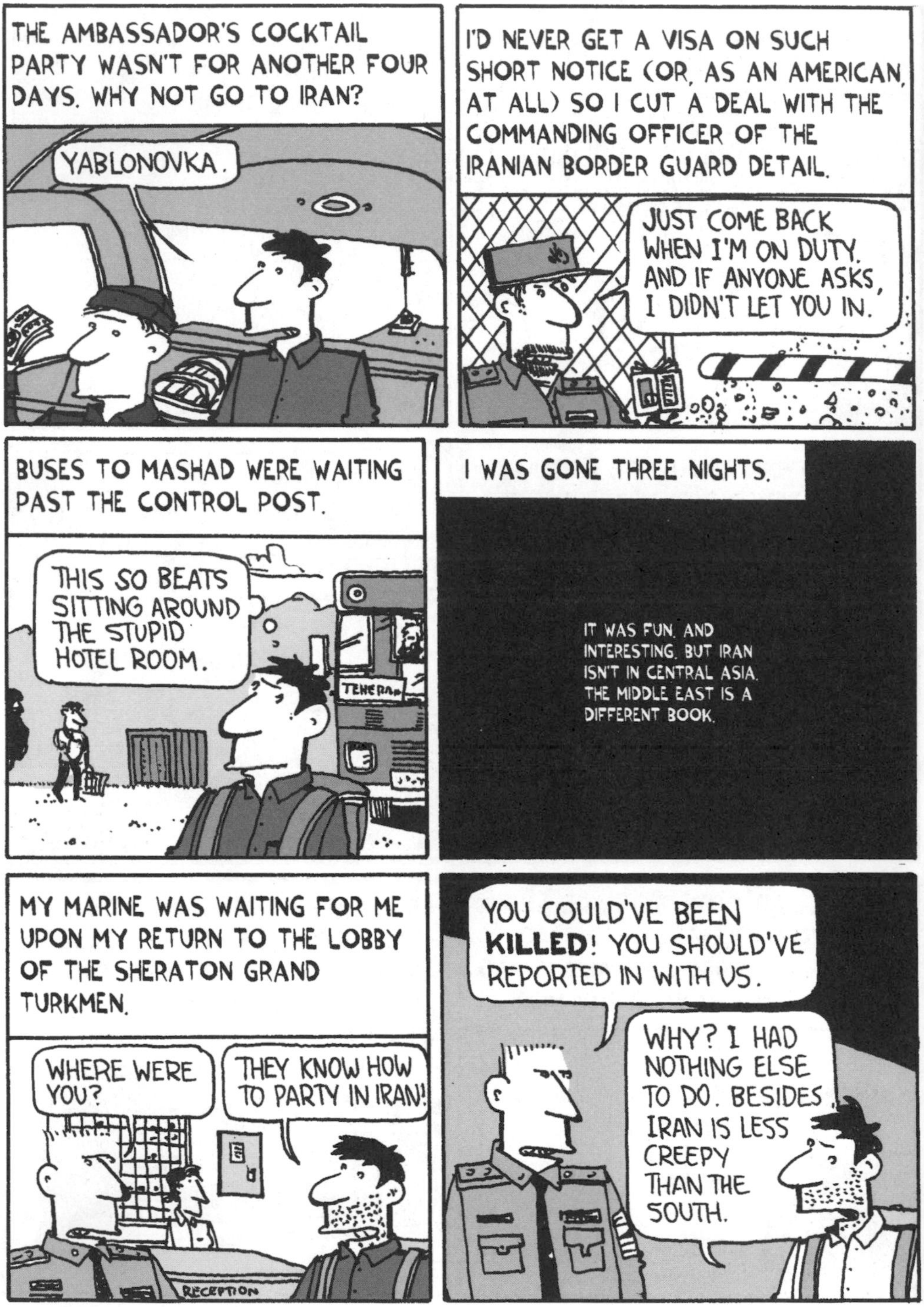
THE AMBASSADOR'S COCKTAIL PARTY WASN'T FOR ANOTHER FOUR DAYS. WHY NOT GO TO IRAN?
YABLONOVKA.
I'D NEVER GET A VISA ON SUCH SHORT NOTICE (OR, AS AN AMERICAN, AT ALL) SO I CUT A DEAL WITH THE COMMANDING OFFICER OF THE IRANIAN BORDER GUARD DETAIL.
JUST COME BACK WHEN I'M ON DUTY. AND IF ANYONE ASKS, I DIDN'T LET YOU IN.
BUSES TO MASHAD WERE WAITING PAST THE CONTROL POST.
THIS SO BEATS SITTING AROUND THE STUPID HOTEL ROOM.
I WAS GONE THREE NIGHTS.
IT WAS FUN. AND INTERESTING. BUT IRAN ISN'T IN CENTRAL ASIA. THE MIDDLE EAST IS A DIFFERENT BOOK.
MY MARINE WAS WAITING FOR ME UPON MY RETURN TO THE LOBBY OF THE SHERATON GRAND TURKMEN.
WHERE WERE YOU?
THEY KNOW HOW TO PARTY IN IRAN!
RECEPTION
YOU COULD'VE BEEN **KILLED**! YOU SHOULD'VE REPORTED IN WITH US.
WHY? I HAD NOTHING ELSE TO DO. BESIDES, IRAN IS LESS CREEPY THAN THE SOUTH.

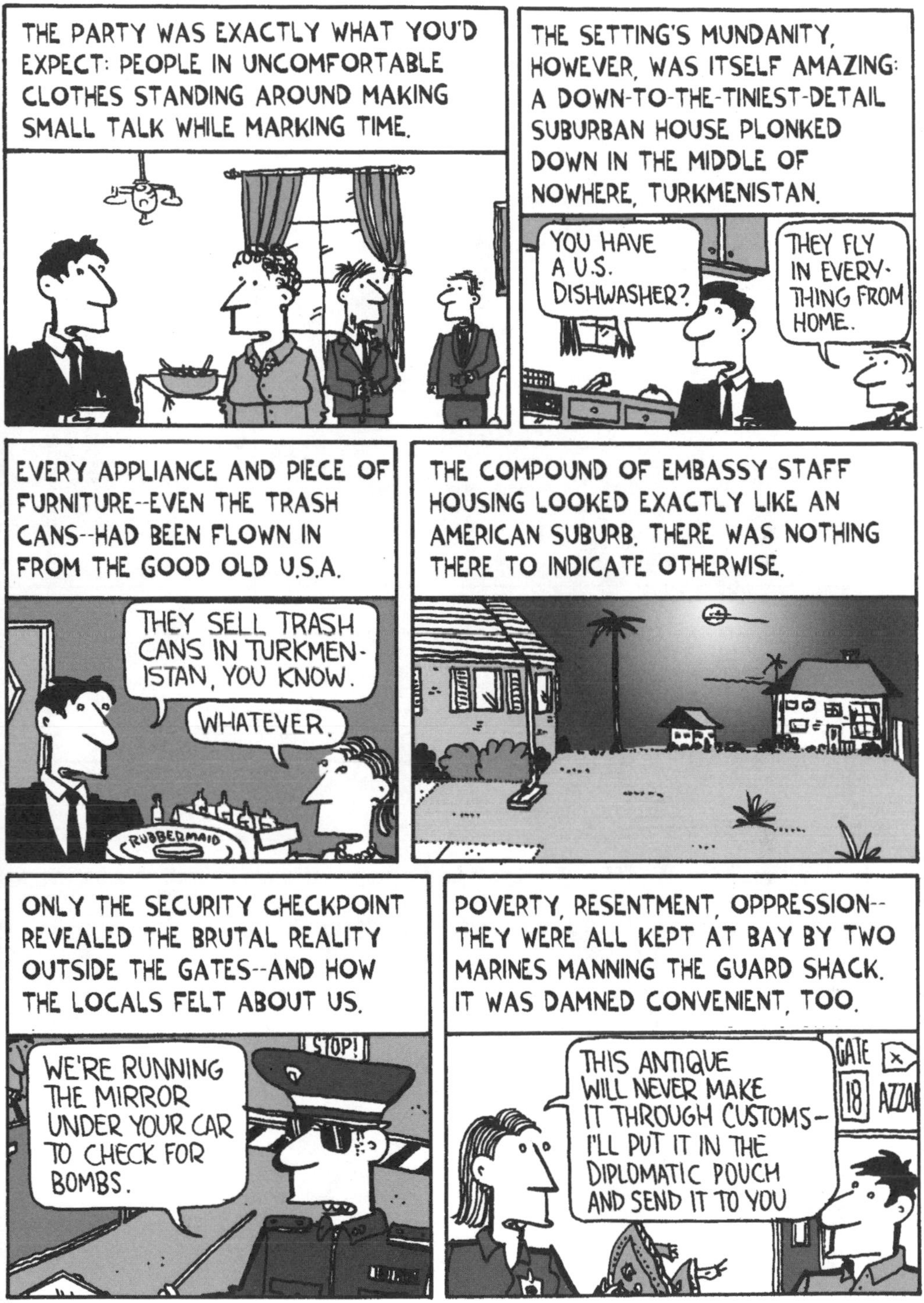
THE PARTY WAS EXACTLY WHAT YOU'D EXPECT: PEOPLE IN UNCOMFORTABLE CLOTHES STANDING AROUND MAKING SMALL TALK WHILE MARKING TIME.
THE SETTING'S MUNDANITY, HOWEVER, WAS ITSELF AMAZING: A DOWN-TO-THE-TINIEST-DETAIL SUBURBAN HOUSE PLONKED DOWN IN THE MIDDLE OF NOWHERE, TURKMENISTAN.
YOU HAVE A U.S. DISHWASHER?
THEY FLY IN EVERY-THING FROM HOME.
EVERY APPLIANCE AND PIECE OF FURNITURE--EVEN THE TRASH CANS--HAD BEEN FLOWN IN FROM THE GOOD OLD U.S.A.
THEY SELL TRASH CANS IN TURKMEN-ISTAN, YOU KNOW.
WHATEVER.
RUBBERMAID
THE COMPOUND OF EMBASSY STAFF HOUSING LOOKED EXACTLY LIKE AN AMERICAN SUBURB. THERE WAS NOTHING THERE TO INDICATE OTHERWISE.
ONLY THE SECURITY CHECKPOINT REVEALED THE BRUTAL REALITY OUTSIDE THE GATES--AND HOW THE LOCALS FELT ABOUT US.
STOP!
WE'RE RUNNING THE MIRROR UNDER YOUR CAR TO CHECK FOR BOMBS.
POVERTY, RESENTMENT, OPPRESSION--THEY WERE ALL KEPT AT BAY BY TWO MARINES MANNING THE GUARD SHACK. IT WAS DAMNED CONVENIENT, TOO.
GATE
18
THIS ANTIQUE WILL NEVER MAKE IT THROUGH CUSTOMS-I'LL PUT IT IN THE DIPLOMATIC POUCH AND SEND IT TO YOU

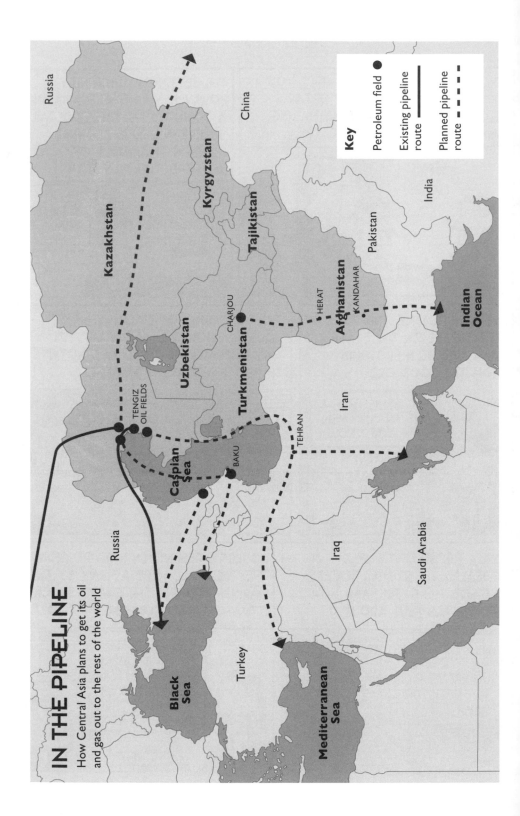

IN THE PIPELINE

How Central Asia plans to get its oil and gas out to the rest of the world

Key

Petroleum field ●

Existing pipeline route ——

Planned pipeline route ▪ ▪ ▪

Russia

China

Kazakhstan

Kyrgyzstan

Tajikistan

Uzbekistan

Turkmenistan

CHARJOU

HERAT

KANDAHAR

Afghanistan

Pakistan

India

Indian Ocean

TENGIZ OIL FIELDS

Caspian Sea

BAKU

TEHRAN

Iran

Russia

Iraq

Saudi Arabia

Black Sea

Turkey

Mediterranean Sea

Clash of the Titans

For most of the Middle East, this oil gift has been more of a curse than a blessing. Oil has fuelled tyrannical regimes and prevented the development of diversified economies producing wide ranges of goods and services. In the Middle East, oil is the tyrant's currency.

–Leon deWinter, Die Welt

The main spoils in today's Great Game are Caspian oil and gas. On its shores, and at the bottom of the Caspian Sea, lie the world's largest untapped fossil fuel reserves. Estimates range from 110 to 243 billion barrels of crude, worth up to $4 trillion.

–Lutz Kleveman, The UK Guardian, October 2003

The Caspian Sea basin, bordered by Azerbaijan, Iran, Turkmenistan, Kazakhstan and Russia, has long been exploited for its oil and natural gas. In his classic study of oil politics *The Prize*, Daniel Yergin wrote that "oil seepages were first discovered on the Aspheron peninsula, a dry, rocky extension of the Caucasus mountains projecting into the landlocked Caspian Sea. In the 13th century, Marco Polo recorded rumors of a spring that produced oil, which, though not edible, was 'good to burn,' and useful for cleaning the mange off camels. Baku was the home of the 'eternal pillars of fire' worshipped by the Zoroastrians. Phrased more prosaically, these pillars were the result of flammable gas escaping from cracks in limestone." Drilling began in earnest a century ago along the western coast of the Caspian near Baku; those Azeri oil fields were Hitler's primary objective in invading the Soviet Union during World War II. But geologists' suspicions that much more than merely a significant amount of oil–a vast, virtually limitless ocean of the stuff–remained untapped were confirmed in 1999 when a consortium of Kazakh

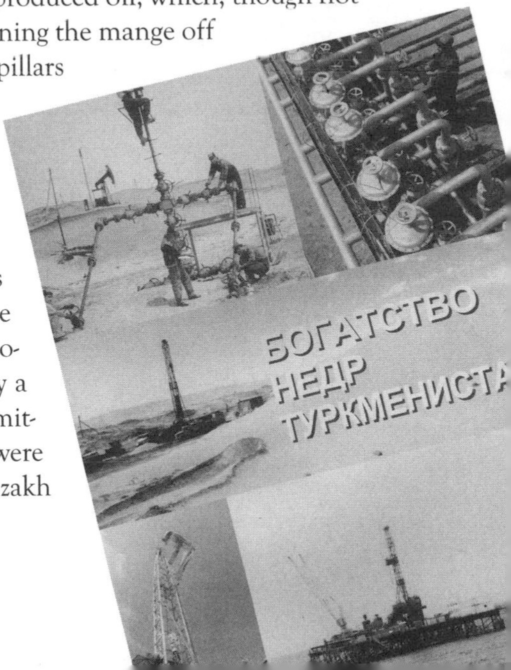
БОГАТСТВО
НЕДР

drillers hit black gold in its section of the Caspian. Overnight Kazakhstan became the proud owner of the world's largest untapped oil reserves.

"The size of the newly discovered petroleum reserve, a four hundred eighty square mile deposit known as the Kashagan field, is reportedly so large as to even surpass the size of the North Sea oil reserves," Richard Giragosian of the Central Asia-Caucasus Institute wrote breathlessly. "Such a find would enhance Kazakhstan to the position of the region's prime energy producer, overtaking oil-rich Azerbaijan and accelerating the international haggling over the selection and construction of pipeline export routes. With estimated reserves of anywhere between eight and fifty billion barrels of oil, this discovery returns the region to the top of the geopolitical agenda for the world's major powers." Geologists soon confirmed Kashagan's status as the world's second largest oil field—and that was before huge new strikes were discovered in 2002 and 2003.

The Western media failed to cover the story, but the world of oil exploration had been turned upside down. And Kazakhstan's new oil wealth soon became a central concern of policy makers in the United States, its allies and rivals. "Kashagan," wrote Paul Brown in *The Guardian*, "in which British Gas and Shell have 16.6 percent stakes, is poised to bring an end to the dominance in oil supply held by OPEC and the Middle East."

Now President Nursultan Nazarbayev isn't the only Kazakh dreaming of transforming his country into Central Asia's first oil emirate. The problem faced by the landlocked nation is how to get its oil and natural gas—many analysts believe that gas will play an even greater role in the Caspian Sea energy sweepstakes than oil in the long run—out to market via a deep-water port where it then can be loaded onto tankers for export to the big oil-consuming countries. Nazarbayev has an enviable problem, but a problem nevertheless: Whichever country builds a pipeline through its territory for Kazakh crude will control its flow and thus exert political and economic pressure on him.

"Kazakhstan has four [pipeline] options," posits energy consultant Ariel Cohen. "First—to Russia, where it already has an oil pipe to Orenburg and gas pipe links with the Russian system." But the Russian Federation screwed Turkmenistan during the early 1990s, diverting oil and gas, destined for export via the Black Seas for internal consumption—and then failing to pay for it. Central Asian governments can't trust that an economically unstable Russia won't pull a similar stunt in the future. There's also the new Baku-Tbilisi-Ceyhan pipeline, currently the second longest in the world. It originates at the Soviet-era oil refinery port in the Azeri capital and debouches on the Turkish coast of the Mediterranean. Nazarbayev has announced the imminent construction of a trans-Caspian pipeline to connect Kashagan to Baku. But he can't depend entirely upon Baku-Tbilisi-Ceyhan because it passes through wild sections of Georgia ravaged by two separatist guerilla armies as well as through Turkish-controlled Kurdistan, where a low-level civil war heated up in the wake of the U.S. invasion of Iraq. Moreover, the project is financed by and therefore indirectly controlled by the United States.

KAZAKHSTAN

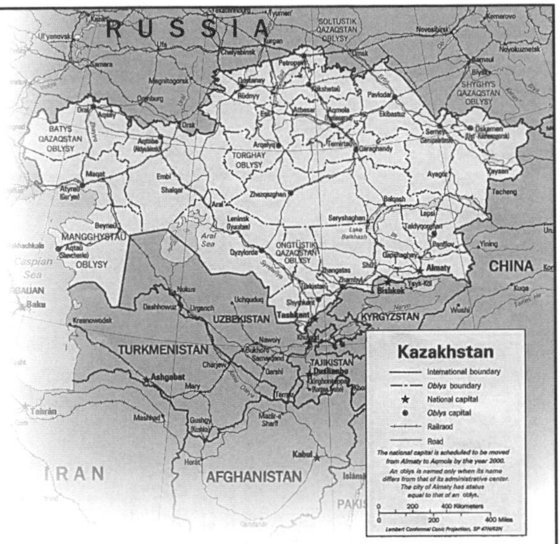
RUSSIA
CHINA
KYRGYZSTAN
UZBEKISTAN
TURKMENISTAN
TAJIKISTAN
AFGHANISTAN
IRAN
Almaty
Bishkek
Tashkent
Ashgabat
Kabul
Kazakhstan
International boundary
Oblys boundary
National capital
Oblys capital
Railroad
Road

Capital: Astana
Form of Government: Dictatorship
Leader: President Nursultan Abishuly Nazarbayev (born 1940)
Population (July 2005): 15,185,844
Major Ethnic Groups (2003):
Kazakh 53.4%
Russian 30%
Ukrainian 3.7%
Uzbek 2.5%
German 2.4%
Tatar 1.7%
Uyghur 1.4%
Area (square miles): 1,048,877 – same as the United States east of the Mississippi
Terrain (as per *CIA Factbook*): "extends from the Volga to the Altai Mountains and from the plains in western Siberia to oases and desert in Central Asia"
Currency/Exchange Rate (2005): US $1 = 133 *tenge*
Oil Reserves (proven): 26 billion barrels
Natural Gas Reserves (proven): 3 trillion cubic meters
Coolest Thing About Kazakhstan: The biggest open spaces you ever dreamed of
Worst Thing About Kazakhstan: Grim disco-casinos
Best Way to Get Thrown Into Jail: Lie to a customs agent
Per Capita Annual Income: $2,260
Unemployment Rate: 8% (official, probably closer to 30%)
Life Expectancy: 67

Should Kazakhstan transform itself into a civil society whose government represents its people, it is poised to become of the world's wealthiest countries. A 1999 strike made Kazakhstan, the largest republic in the former Soviet Union, the big winner in the Caspian Sea oil sweepstakes. Geologists believe that it has possible reserves exceeding those of Saudi Arabia—currently the biggest producer—by several times. This vast nation of windswept steppe and, to the north, the beginning of the tundra, is defined by its Mongol-derived horse culture, its legacy as a dumping ground for nuclear waste and testing and an autocratic president whose glib style belies his practice of having political opponents tortured and murdered. Kazakhstan is the belle of the New Great Game. The United States invaded Afghanistan at least partly to provide a conduit for Kazakh crude from the Caspian to deepwater ports, China is building the longest pipeline in history to accommodate it, and Russia wants to lure Nazarbayev back into the old Soviet energy grid. Official corruption is on the wane after the start of a genuine crackdown spurred by the realization that foreign investors had been staying away. The steppe, which is basically a whole lot of nothing, is the main reason to see Kazakhstan. An added attraction is the former capital city of Almaty, just east of Bishkek in Kyrgyzstan, a liberal and free-wheeling oasis of hot nightlife and decent food.

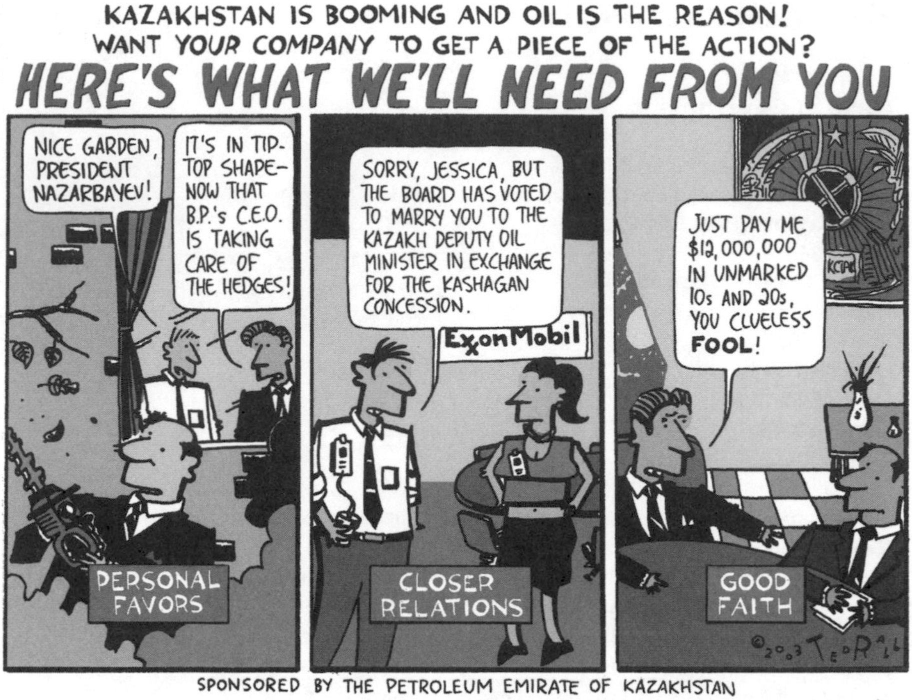
KAZAKHSTAN IS BOOMING AND OIL IS THE REASON!
WANT YOUR COMPANY TO GET A PIECE OF THE ACTION?
HERE'S WHAT WE'LL NEED FROM YOU
NICE GARDEN, PRESIDENT NAZARBAYEV!
IT'S IN TIP-TOP SHAPE–NOW THAT B.P.'s C.E.O. IS TAKING CARE OF THE HEDGES!
PERSONAL FAVORS
SORRY, JESSICA, BUT THE BOARD HAS VOTED TO MARRY YOU TO THE KAZAKH DEPUTY OIL MINISTER IN EXCHANGE FOR THE KASHAGAN CONCESSION.
ExxonMobil
CLOSER RELATIONS
JUST PAY ME $12,000,000 IN UNMARKED 10s AND 20s, YOU CLUELESS FOOL!
GOOD FAITH
©2003 TED RALL
SPONSORED BY THE PETROLEUM EMIRATE OF KAZAKHSTAN

"The third option," says Cohen, "is China. First they launched a pipeline to export two hundred fifty thousand barrels a day from western Kazakhstan to China. They built it quickly, they spent a lot on it–which shows China's strategy on Kazakh oil. Second, Kazakhstan and China have agreed to lay a gas pipeline to be coupled with Uzbekistan and later, probably, with Turkmenistan. This will make China an even bigger strategic player in Central Asian gas developments."

By far the most logical pipeline route runs from the Caspian port at Neka through Iran to the Persian Gulf. An Iranian conduit would be much shorter and therefore entail cheaper transit fees; unlike, say, Afghanistan, Iran enjoys relatively strong internal political stability. But the Americans are maintaining a post-1979 revolution policy of freezing out the country's Islamic leadership via economic sanctions: "[The Iranians] are already taking oil by barge from Kazakhstan and are planning to expand this... They are taking oil from the Kazakhs, selling it in the Persian Gulf and giving back the money. The U.S. is doing its best to prevent the project with Iran," says Cohen.

Remarkably, a pipeline across Afghanistan–one of the reasons that country was invaded in 2001–remains a viable alternative.

Turkmenistan and Uzbekistan, respectively the second and third Caspian Sea energy players, face the same pipeline transit options as Kazakhstan. Nazarbayev has lifted a page from Niyazov's "neutral" foreign policy by encouraging as many pipeline routes as possible in order to play rivals against one another and increase his options in case one or more outlets shut down. Presidents Niyazov and Karimov will likely pursue a similar approach.

Playing suitors against one another is working. Four days after American bombs began falling on Kabul during the fall 2001 invasion of Afghanistan, U.S. ambassador to Pakistan Wendy Chamberlain presided over a summit with Turkmenistan and Pakistan to revive Unocal's controversial Trans-Afghanistan Pipeline (TAP) scheme from the 1990s. After the three countries signed a series of formal pledges to arrange financing, the Asian Development Bank—the Eastern equivalent of the International Monetary Fund—green-lighted TAP (which now stands for Turkmenistan-Afghanistan-Pakistan), calling it "economically and financially a viable project." Meanwhile the first leg of the China-Kazakh pipeline project, geographically the most daunting but politically feasible thanks to China's autocratic command of resources and manpower, opened in late 2005. And, in April 2006, Turkmenbashi flew to Beijing to sign an accord for a Turkmenistan-China gas pipeline. Soon Kazakhstan and its neighbors will enjoy a choice of at least three major outlet conduits.

The New Great Game

The jockeying over pipeline transit rights for Central Asian oil has become so frenzied that it has spilled over into South Asia. In 2006 President George W. Bush ordered the Indian and Pakistani governments to reject a proposed pipeline from Iran via Pakistan. "Our beef with Iran is not the pipeline," Bush claimed in Islamabad before threatening sanctions if Pakistani and/or India went ahead anyway. "Our beef with Iran is the fact that they want to develop a nuclear weapon." The real reason for Washington's concern, however, appeared to be that the Iran-Pakistan-India proposal might render TAP redundant. "Other pipeline projects," added U.S. Energy Secretary Samuel Bodman with a wink, "are very good and we are ready to help." Afghan president Hamid Karzai, the former Talib-turned-Unocal consultant installed by the United States after 2001, quickly offered to turn TAP into TAPI—adding an Indian spur to the original debouchement proposal at the Pakistani port of Multan on the Arabian Sea.

Asia Times summed up the situation in 2005: "When and if this Unocal project [the U.S.-backed TAP]—intended to transport as many hydrocarbons from Turkmenistan, Uzbekistan, Kyrgyzstan and Kazakhstan as possible—succeeds, the U.S. may have attained its objective of acquiring access to most of the oil from the former Soviet republics in Central Asia, which is considered to be more secure than Middle Eastern oil and does not involve an implicit subsidy to Islamic fanatics. The pipeline projects illustrate the geopolitical rivalry between the world's hyper-power and the two giants of Asia: Russia and China."

The 19th century "Great Game" refers to the diplomatic derring-do and backwater hijinx that defined the fierce competition between czarist Russia and Great Britain (and to a lesser extent China). The Brits launched proxy incursions through their Indian Raj while Russia tried to insinuate itself into South Asia by pulling strings in Teheran. As Russia conquered the khanates of Khiva and Bukhara, and

Kazakh President Nursultan Nazarbayev meets with George W. Bush in 2001. The two nations have opened a new relationship based on a "long-term strategic partnership."

Britain invaded Afghanistan in 1839, a Central Asia that had been perceived as a two thousand-mile-wide buffer zone began to look more like a staging ground for possible invasion—whether north- or south-bound, depending on whose point of view was being considered. (The first Afghan War ended in 1842 with the massacre of the entire twenty thousand-strong British army and its camp followers as they attempted a retreat. Only one man survived, presumably allowed to live so he would tell the rest.)

The New Great Game for control of and influence over Central Asia involves the same rivals, with China playing a more aggressive role, but for a very different objective. This time around, Central Asia is strategically vital not for what it lies between, but for what lies beneath it.

United States foreign policy planners adhere to a strategy of "total energy dominance" developed in reaction to the OPEC oil crisis of 1973-74. Because the U.S. and global economies are heavily dependent on reliable access to cheap oil and gas, their thinking goes, the deployment of military, economic and diplomatic influence to ensure that continued access is essential to America's survival. At one extreme "total energy dominance" manifests itself in the wholesale invasion of energy-rich countries like Iraq and prospective pipeline routes like Afghanistan. On the other are indirect subsidies and low-interest IMF loans to nations such as Kazakhstan. In the middle of this scale of involvement is a huge range of initiatives, ranging from President Bill Clinton's 1993 Somalia "peace-keeping" operation (to control shipping through the Gulf of Aden) to George W. Bush's attempt to depose President Hugo Chávez of Venezuela (the Western hemisphere's largest oil producer) to the wrangling over the Iran-Pakistan-India pipeline proposal to the establishment of American military bases in or around countries that possess oil fields, pipelines or ports.

Central Asia is poised to surpass the Middle East as the focus of the United States' quest for total energy dominance. As then-future Vice President Dick Cheney told fellow oilmen in 1998, "I cannot think of a time when we have had a region emerge as suddenly to become as strategically significant as the Caspian." Costly direct military intervention on the level of the 2003 invasion of Iraq or even the 2001 overthrow of the Taliban in Afghanistan are unnecessary in Central Asia as long as pliant dictators keep things in order and sign over favorable concessions for their oil and gas, yet American planners want to be prepared for possible future interventions. Thus military bases, which put "boots on the ground" inside or in close proximity to potentially volatile—and vital—trouble spots have become the latest battleground over the control of Central Asia.

American Military Bases After 9/11

During the early post-Soviet independence period of the 1990s the United States hardly had to lift a finger in its overt campaign to de-Russify Central Asia. The Russian Federation, suffering convulsions from shock economic reform, a bloody civil war in Chechnya and the rise of the most fearsome mafia in history, had turned inward, washing its hands of the Stans. The communist leadership of China didn't see why they should care about the barbarians on the other side of the Tian Shan. Aside from a few secret deployments of U.S. forces to defend the region's dictators from Islamists and other dissident types, America assured its dominance by turning a blind eye to human rights abuses and the occasional World Bank sweetheart deal.

But much had changed by 2000. Although the average Russian was still living in misery, the Russian government had reasserted its control over the economy. Kashagan and the other big Caspian Sea oil strikes prompted Russian president Vladimir Putin and other post-Soviet nationalists to regret the loss of Central Asia. China's economy was booming; its manufacturing base required new and bigger sources of power.

The New Great Game, inevitable when terrorists bombed New York and Washington using passenger jets on September 11, 2001, heated up when Washington exploited the attacks—first to occupy Afghanistan, then to build military bases there and in neighboring countries.

At first the United States demanded that the Central Asian states grant it staging grounds and fly-over rights to wage an air war against the Taliban in Afghanistan. But, as Chalmers Johnson elegantly documented in his book *The Sorrows of Empire*, a "temporary" American military presence usually turns out to be anything but. Hamid Karzai was appointed as Afghanistan's first post-Taliban leader in December 2001. Afghanistan was officially free and sovereign, yet by February 2002, Secretary of State Colin Powell was still testifying to Congress that "America will have a continuing interest and presence in Central Asia of a kind that we could not have dreamed of

PHOTO COURTESY OF DEPARTMENT OF DEFENSE

U.S. soldiers inspect a fuel storage unit on the Karshi-Khanabdad base in Uzbekistan.

before" for the foreseeable future.

The U.S. had already begun construction of its airbase at Manas International Airport, nineteen miles outside of the Kyrgyz capital of Bishkek, where three thousand soldiers and two dozen aircraft would be permanently stationed. "I think it's fair to say there will be a long-term presence here well beyond the end of hostilities," Air Force Colonel Billy Montgomery dryly advised *The Washington Post*, which noted the "construction of a tent city, surgical ward, gym, hot showers and kitchen facilities at the airport." Kazakh foreign minister Kassymzhomart Tokaev admitted that his government was talking to the U.S. about a base there as well, but pressure from Russia tabled have since those discussions for the foreseeable future.

September 11th also prompted the deployment of two hundred French troops to Tajikistan who, despite ensuing Franco-American tensions over Iraq, functionally acted as American proxies under NATO command. The Tajiks also granted the U.S. direct landing rights at their airfields. Three sites were offered outright as permanent bases but rejected as unsuitable. Permissions were granted by "neutral" Turkmenistan for flyovers by American bombers. September 11th also precipitated the construction of another large new military base in Central Asia at Karshi-Khanabad in Uzbekistan (also known as K-2, or Camp Stronghold Freedom). According to Global Security.org, "The air-conditioned tents at the base, named K-2, are laid out on a grid, along streets named for the thoroughfares of New York: Fifth Avenue, Long Island Expressway, Wall Street. About one thousand U.S. troops worked at the facility as of August 2002, handling tons of supplies for the war in Afghanistan." By 2004 the U.S.-Uzbek relationship had become so cozy by that the Karimov regime told the

Bush Administration that it wanted to make Karshi-Khanabad a permanent base. (But then, in a rare move even for a Third World dictator, Uzbek president Islam Karimov retaliated for U.S. criticism of the massacre at Andijon and, perhaps more importantly, for receiving less than a third of the rent Kyrgyzstan received for its U.S. base of equivalent size. He formally evicted the U.S. from Karshi-Khanabad, to take effect in January 2006.)

Eighteen thousand soldiers were stationed at increasingly permanent-looking facilities at Bagram airbase, Kandahar and Mazar-e-Sharif in U.S.-occupied Afghanistan. In 2005, *Asia Times* broke the news that the U.S. had broken ground in Herat—the strategically vital border city where the Trans-Afghanistan pipeline is scheduled to enter the country from Turkmenistan—on a new central NATO military base for operations against Central and South Asia.

"The imperial perimeter is expanding into Central Asia," gushed Thomas Donnelly of the Project for a New American Century, the neoconservative think tank that authored the Bush Administration's "regime change" policy in Iraq. The New Great Game was on. At that point, the neocons believed that they had Central Asia all to themselves.

Russia Reacts

That the Russian Federation would have reasserted itself in its former Central Asian territories, even without the geopolitical threat posed by the United States, was a historical inevitability. The permanent U.S. bases in Kyrgyzstan, Afghanistan and, until recently, Uzbekistan, greatly accelerated an anti-American reaction that culminated with a joint Russian-Chinese declaration in 2005 that "considering that the active phase of the military anti-terrorist operation in Afghanistan has finished, [we] consider it essential that the relevant participants in the anti-terrorist coalition set deadlines for the temporary use [of Central Asian military bases]." Sergei Prikhodko, an aide to Russian President Vladimir Putin, put it simply: Russia, he said, wants "to know when [U.S.] troops will go home."

Whether it's Russia prior to 1991 or the United States afterward, weak countries fare better when great powers are fighting over them than they do under the hegemony of a single superpower. Just after 9/11 the Uzbek and Kyrgyz governments permitted the U.S. presence as a counterbalance to their historic master, Russia. Then, after the pendulum was deemed to have swung too far in favor of American dominance, they invited the Russians back in.

On 9/11 Russia had between six and seven thousand members of its Soviet 201st Motorized Rifle Division stationed in Dushanbe, as well as twenty thousand members of its Federal Border Service in the Special Zone along Tajikistan's border with Afghanistan. Tajikistan's post-independence history had been defined before 1997 by civil war and after 1998 as an arms depot where Russian weapons were funneled to the rump Northern Alliance government just across the Pyanj River in northeastern Afghanistan. Aside from these forces in Tajikistan there was no direct

Russian military presence throughout the former Soviet Union.

Alarmed by the waning of their influence symbolized by the permanent U.S. facility at Manas, the Russians pressured the Kyrgyz government to lease them a parallel airbase at Kant in exchange for cash and direct shipments of arms and equipment. Like the Americans, the Russians had no plans to leave. "We have invested big money in the Kant base and see it as a long-term project," Russian defense minister Sergei Ivanov told Acting Kyrgyz President Kurmanbek Bakiev after the 2005 Tulip Revolution. "Our base is here forever," affirmed General Vladimir Mikhailov, head of the Russian air force.

Kant emboldened Bakiev to demand a hundred-fold increase in rent for Manas, from two to two hundred seven million dollars per year, from the Americans. Did he really want the money? Or did he want to pressure the Americans into leaving? No one knows, but either way the Russians were putting the squeeze on the U.S.

Russia cannily miirrored the United States' rhetoric in fighting its own "war on terror." Russia's presence in Tajikistan, previously anticipated to decline and eventually vanish, was instead formalized and expanded. Russia's largest military base on foreign soil—for "neutralizing terrorist extremist attacks," according to Russian President Putin—opened there in 2004. "Here now, we legally have a military unit that is big enough. If we speak about size, there are more than five thousand Russian military personnel who will be located in Dushanbe, Kurgan-Tube, and Kulob. All the buildings have been given to the Russian state free of charge," noted Ivanov at the opening ceremony.

Russian diplomats rushed to court Islam Karimov after he announced the closure of America's K-2 military base in Uzbekistan. "This turning against the U.S. started before the Andijon events," said former Karimov intimate Farkod Inogombaev. "But this trend obviously climaxed after the Andijon events." Seigei Mikheev of the Moscow-based think tank Center for Political Technologies, said that "Russia is the only country [Karimov] can appeal to [after Andijon and the K-2 eviction]. And it's absolutely obvious that Russia has no interest in [seeing] the presence of the U.S. in Central Asia."

The result of this realignment was a staggering defeat for the U.S.: a full-fledged mutual defense treaty between Russia and the most influential state in Central Asia. If the United States were to lead a "regime change" operation against Karimov now, it would mean World War III against Russia. "Russia," Karimov said pointedly at a signing held less than two years after singing the same siren song to America, "is our most reliable partner and ally."

A Russian overreach that took place in late 2005, when it waged what now appears to have been a calculated campaign of disinformation about U.S. intentions in Turkmenistan, illustrates how seriously the Kremlin takes the Central Asian military base issue. On September 6 *Pravda* reported that "several construction companies from the United Arab Emirates have repaired the Mary-2 airbase" in Turkmenistan. The U.S. would use the facility, the newspaper claimed falsely, to replace the loss

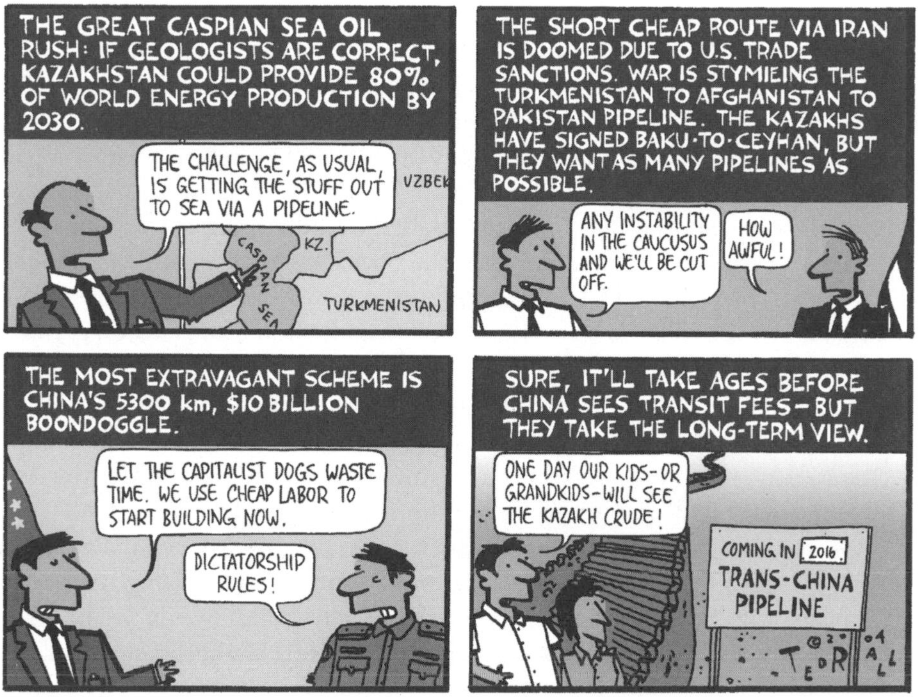
THE GREAT CASPIAN SEA OIL RUSH: IF GEOLOGISTS ARE CORRECT, KAZAKHSTAN COULD PROVIDE 80% OF WORLD ENERGY PRODUCTION BY 2030.
THE CHALLENGE, AS USUAL, IS GETTING THE STUFF OUT TO SEA VIA A PIPELINE.
UZBEK
KZ.
CASPIAN SEA
TURKMENISTAN
THE SHORT CHEAP ROUTE VIA IRAN IS DOOMED DUE TO U.S. TRADE SANCTIONS. WAR IS STYMIEING THE TURKMENISTAN TO AFGHANISTAN TO PAKISTAN PIPELINE. THE KAZAKHS HAVE SIGNED BAKU-TO-CEYHAN, BUT THEY WANT AS MANY PIPELINES AS POSSIBLE.
ANY INSTABILITY IN THE CAUCUSUS AND WE'LL BE CUT OFF.
HOW AWFUL!
THE MOST EXTRAVAGANT SCHEME IS CHINA'S 5300 km, $10 BILLION BOONDOGGLE.
LET THE CAPITALIST DOGS WASTE TIME. WE USE CHEAP LABOR TO START BUILDING NOW.
DICTATORSHIP RULES!
SURE, IT'LL TAKE AGES BEFORE CHINA SEES TRANSIT FEES—BUT THEY TAKE THE LONG-TERM VIEW.
ONE DAY OUR KIDS-OR GRANDKIDS-WILL SEE THE KAZAKH CRUDE!
COMING IN 2016 TRANS-CHINA PIPELINE
TED RALL ©2004

of K-2. Why the dissembling? "Moscow is likely upset over Niyazov's decision to downgrade Turkmenistan's Commonwealth of Independent States status, and Russian officials are orchestrating a media and diplomatic campaign aimed at compelling Turkmenbashi to reconsider," U.S. Army War College professor Stephen Blank theorized in EurasiaNet.

Russia has adopted a holistic approach to closer ties with its former southern republics. It formally joined the regional economic trade group the Central Asian Cooperation Organization, as well as the Collective Security Treaty Organization and Shanghai Cooperation Organization (SCO), then quickly moved to transform the two groups into counterbalances to American and Chinese power. It renewed its lease on the Baikonur Cosmodrome for fifty years. Finally, it convinced the SCO—Uzbekistan, Kyrgyzstan, Tajikistan, Kazakhstan and China—to issue a formal demand for the United States to close its bases in Central Asia. The message was clear: Russia, not America, is in Central Asia to stay.

The New Player: China

Spend a few hours in the Tajik capital and you'll notice something startling: the city's public buses have Chinese writing and flags on the side. Dushanbe's bus fleet was a gift from the People's Republic and the People's Republic wants Tajiks to know that. Chinese officials conduct shuttle diplomacy between Bishkek and Beijing. And in Almaty, not far from a Kazakh border province where people eat with chopsticks, the Ya-Lian Chinese bazaar is one of the biggest and most vibrant street markets.

China has been increasingly asserting its influence throughout the region by flexing its economic rather than military muscle. (The exception proves the rule: China's new military cooperation agreement with Tajikistan authorizes little more than training Tajik officers at Chinese military colleges.) After the Republican-controlled American Congress blocked the sale of Unocal—the lead company on the Trans-Afghanistan Pipeline project—to China in 2005, the China National Petroleum Corporation (CNPC) instead spent $4.2 billion on Petrokazakhstan, a Canadian-run corporation that had been the Soviet Union's biggest independent oil company. That followed China's seven hundred million dollar construction of the Kazakh-China pipeline to carry Kazakh oil from the Karaganda region to northwest Xinjiang, which will cover eight percent of China's energy needs. "China is being increasingly dependent on Middle East oil and it wants a supply that would be blockade- proof in case of a conflict over Taiwan," explained Thierry Kellner of the Free University of Brussels, who specializes in Chinese relations with Central Asia. "This is the new Silk Road," exulted Zhou Jiping, vice president of the CNPC.

On the new Silk Road cash flows west while oil goes east. China is issuing cheap IMF-style loans to any and all Central Asian takers, splitting the cost of power plants with Kazakhstan and promising a fiscally absurd twenty-five hundred-mile pipeline to help Turkmenbashi get around his vexing landlock dilemma. It has also pledged to invest four billion dollars in Central Asian infrastructure—half the gross domestic product of Tajikistan. In 2004 it reopened the long-disused border crossing between Tajikistan's Gorno-Badakhshan Autonomous Oblast, the remotest part of the remotest former Soviet republic, and the wild west of Xinjiang. The Chinese are also building a $1.5 billion highway across the Tian Shan to connect Kyrgyzstan and Tajikistan to Xinjiang, as well as a Xinjiang-Kyrgyzstan-Uzbekistan railway. In a place dependent on trade, the promise of improved transportation builds up a lot of good will.

Niklas Swanstrom of Uppsala University in Sweden explains the Chinese strategy. "China is rapidly emerging as a world power," he says. "In a decade or two, it might directly challenge the United States, Japan, and Europe. But before this happens, Beijing's leaders are trying to create a zone of friendly and stable countries around China's borders that will give them political support, as well as economic leverage in the future."

China's sparsely populated neighbors in Kyrgyzstan, Tajikistan and Kazakhstan remain suspicious of the true intentions of the world's most populous nation. But the threat of territorial expansion is remote, at least for the time being. For now, as Swanstrom says, China is a welcome player in a New Great Game whose main rule is the more the merrier: "From the Central Asian [states' perspective], there's also interest in decreasing the Russian influence and to have Chinese influence—maybe even Indian influence and American influence and European influence. They have realized over the years that it's not good to have one dominant power in the region."

Eco Hell

Execution of this genuine grandiose and fateful project will not only have tremendous socioeconomic and ecological impact on the citizens of independent and neutral Turkmenistan but also creates a reliable foundation for our country's future, as designed by the great inspirer of this miracle of Golden Age, Saparmurat Turkmenbashi the Great, our president for life.

—Turkmen State Television, July 24, 2002

Some historians point to the meltdown at the Ukrainian nuclear power plant at Chernobyl, and specifically Mikhail Gorbachev's eventual decision to reveal the full extent of the catastrophe to the international media, as the signal event that brought down the Soviet Union. The long-term historical pressures that led to 1991 might have been averted or indefinitely delayed, these scholars argue, had the communist system not been exposed as inept and dishonest and therefore unworthy of either respect or fear—which is especially ironic considering that the government's own policy reversal caused this last revelation.

It soon came to light, however, that the Chernobyl disaster was not the only ecological mess Soviet rule left behind. A dozen freshly independent nations, aided by foreign environmental groups, tabulated a grim tally: World War II-grade factory smokestacks belching a witches' brew of airborne toxins above major cities, abandoned mines whose hazardous waste by-products had seeped into the groundwater, secret military research facilities where fuel and components of weapons of mass destruction had been left to rust and decay. A hundred of the biggest Soviet cities had air pollution levels times ten times greater than internationally accepted standards.

Particularly during the Stalinist period of the 1930s and 1940s Soviet officials viewed, with some justification, their territory as so vast as to be virtually limitless. Nowhere was that sense of space greater than on the steppes of Central Asia. Coupled with the political reality that what goes on in Central Asia wasn't likely to get back to Moscow, the profligate mentality of Soviet leaders led to disastrous policies whose price is just beginning to become apparent—and which continued after independence. On May 20, 1998, for example, a truck owned by the Canadian mining company Cameco crashed into the Barskoon River, which feeds the great Kyrgyz inland sea Lake Issyk-Kul. Twenty tons of sodium cyanide spilled into the river. Bleaching powder was dumped into the Barskoon in order to try to neutralize the cyanide. Nevertheless, nine days later, some two hundred forty residents had fallen ill. Such mishaps are routine in countries where environmental regulations and enforcement are virtually nonexistent.

As Americans have seen in such ecological disasters as the draining of the Colorado River, the attitude that land, water and other natural resources were essentially valueless and therefore disposable led to grandiose irrigation and agricultural schemes, such as a decades-long attempt to transform Central Asia into the wheat-basket of the USSR—against the advice of local farmers who warned that the topsoil was too thin and prone to erosion to sustain such crops.

The Vanishing Aral Sea

In defiance of logic and repeated warnings by agricultural scientists the Soviets regularly diverted the Aral and Caspian Seas to irrigate cotton and rice fields in Turkmenistan, Uzbekistan and Kazakhstan, via projects such as the Karakum Canal. In addition, between thirty and seventy percent of the Karakum's water went to waste due to leaks and evaporation. The Aral Sea, once so big that it would have been the second largest of the Great Lakes in the United States, saw its water levels drop precipitously, leaving seaports that had been active as recently as 1973 some thirty to fifty miles away from the shoreline. Now they're desert towns blasted by the dust storms of the new "Aral Kum." (Kum means "desert" in Turkic.) The water kept dropping. A new island formed in the remaining sea, dividing it into the North Aral Sea and South Aral Sea in 1987. More water loss. Even the canal built to connect the two halves dried up. By 1999 the Aral had been effectively destroyed.

In 1959 Soviet fishermen pulled some fifty thousand tons of fish from the Aral Sea, celebrating a way of life that their government knew was doomed. Soviet scientists told officials, some of whom considered the Aral "nature's error," that they fully expected it to dry up. "It is obvious to everyone that the evaporation of the Aral Sea is inevitable," an engineer reported in 1968. The Uzbek port of Moynaq, which had once employed sixty thousand fishermen, now lies many miles from shore. Trawlers and even larger tankers rust in the middle of the desert; they have become the iconic symbol of the Aral Sea nightmare. Shipping and commercial fishing, the primary source of jobs for three million people including the impoverished Karakalpak minority of Uzbekistan, came to an end in 1987, which prompted the Gorbachev government to formally declare the Aral Sea an ecological disaster area. The secretary general's plan to reverse the water flow and abandon cotton cultivation became unaffordable and politically unfeasible after the demise of the USSR. "The Amu Darya and Syr Darya rivers [feeding the Aral] go through the territories of six Central Asian nations (Afghanistan, Kazakhstan, Kyrgyzstan, Tajikistan, Turkmenistan and Uzbekistan) and every nation tries to

PHOTOS COURTESY OF THE U.S. GEOLOGICAL SURVEY AND UNIVERSITY OF MARYLAND GLOBAL LAND COVER FACILITY

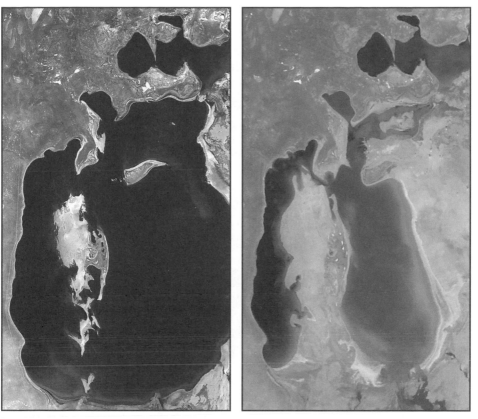

The satellite image at left is of the Aral Sea in the summer of 1989; the one on the right was taken only fourteen years later, in August 2003.

draw as much water from them as it wants," noted Rafael Matevosyan, an eighty-two-year-old Uzbek painter who has dedicated his work to chronicling the tragedy. "If everyone takes a bucket of water from a barrel, there will not be water in it. We cannot save the Aral and soon you will be able to see it only in pictures." He has dedicated his career to chronicling the death of the Aral.

In 1917 the Aral Sea was the world's fourth-largest inland body of water. After the two rivers that served as its principal sources, the Amu Darya and Syr Darya, were diverted for Central Asian irrigation, the water level began dropping at a rate of between three and four feet per year. Overall surface area had fallen by about seventy percent by the 1990s; its volume shrank by eighty percent between 1960 and 2000, reducing it at the turn of the millennium to the world's sixth-largest lake. Uzbekistan remains one of the world's largest producers of "white gold" (cotton) thanks to its exploitation of the Aral, but the environmental consequences have been grave. Not only are sediments blowing away from the former lake bed, destroying crops via soil salinization and melting mountain glaciers thousands of miles away, agricultural run-off pollution including pesticides and fertilizers have become airborne. Lakebed pollutants are contaminating the local population, whose infant mortality rate has skyrocketed to the highest in the former USSR. Even the weather has changed; a smaller Aral Sea means less evaporation.

"What appears to be snow on the seabed is really salt. The winds blow this as far as the Himalayas," Paul Welsh told BBC viewers in 2000.

Soviet-era naturalists once identified five hundred species of birds, two hundred mammals and one hundred fishes, as well as thousands of insects and invertebrates unique to the Aral Sea region. All are now extinct. Of the seventy types of mammals and three hundred nineteen bird species native to the Darya deltas, fewer than half remain. Environmentalists widely consider the Aral Sea to be the worst ecological disaster in human history. Until a few years ago, however, no one had done anything about it.

The Kazakh government has recently begun building dams to increase the flow of fresh water into the North Aral Sea. Kokarai Island will become a permanent dam as the South Aral Sea, also known as the "Big Aral," is consigned to oblivion, a victim of fiscal and environmental triage. At the current rate of evaporation the South Aral Sea is projected to disappear by the year 2020. Even if the North Aral Sea can be saved, however, the disaster is irreversible. "[They are] allowing more Syr Darya water to flow in and diking off that northern sea from the southern sea so the small Aral would get more water and have an opportunity to restore some of the ecological benefits that were there for the entire sea before," says Sandra Postel of the Global Water Policy Project. Early indications are promising—a new eight-mile-long dam raised the level of the North Aral Sea by twelve feet its first year—but the epic scale of the disaster remains daunting. Contributing to the challenge is the fact that the Uzbek government refuses to cooperate with the Kazakh project. "I think it's an attempt to salvage something, but certainly we're not going to see the Aral Sea as we once knew it."

Incredibly, not everyone believes that the Aral Sea deserves a break. In February 2006 the Uzbek state energy company Uzbekneftegaz announced its intention to prospect for oil and natural gas in what remains of the tenth, and soon-to-be eleventh, largest lake in the world. And as if that wasn't bad enough, the Aral Sea is also home to "Voz."

Vozrozhdeniye Island

The Soviet Union's main biological weapons test site, Vozrozhdeniye (Renaissance) Island, was originally chosen for its dry, hot climate and sandy soil. It was abandoned in 1992. The border between Uzbekistan and Kazakhstan splits the Aral Sea island as well as "Voz" Island, which lies in the middle of the Aral. Years of furtive tests on biological and chemical weapons have made Vozrozhdeniye one hell of a mess—most notably as the result of a 1988 operation in which, reported *The New York Times*, "Russian germ scientists transferred hundreds of tons of anthrax bacteria—enough to destroy the world's people many times over—into giant stainless steel canisters. Then they poured in bleach to decontaminate the deadly pink powder, packed the canisters onto a train two dozen cars long and sent the

The USSR detonated its first atomic bomb in 1947. Over the next four decades hundreds more would be exploded at the Semipalatinsk Nuclear Testing Grounds in Kazakhstan. The resulting radioactive contamination will remain for thousands of years.

cargo [to Vozrozhdeniye]. Here Russian soldiers dug huge pits and poured the sludge into the ground, burying the germs."

Other nasty bugs, including an experimental form of bubonic plague resistant to modern antibiotics, were tested in 1986 and 1987.

Many of the spores are still alive. To add to the fun, because of the shrinking of the Aral Sea "this deserted, isolated island has grown from seventy-seven square miles to seven hundred seventy and will soon be connected to the mainland. As a result, Uzbek and Kazakh experts fear, the buried anthrax spores could escape their sandy tomb, stirred up by carriers like gophers and other rodents, lizards and birds, and brought to Uzbek and Kazakh territory...In some of the pits, anthrax sludge is beginning to leach up through the sand." The Uzbek and Kazakh governments say they can't afford the expense of cleaning up Vozrozhdeniye; the United States canceled its already miniscule funding for such a project after George W. Bush became president in 2001.

Ten cases of plague (which is believed to have originated along the Silk Road) were reported in Turkmenistan in 2004, as were three confirmed infections in Kazakhstan's Mangistauskaya province. Mangistauskaya *oblast* lies between the Caspian and Aral Seas.

Semipalatinsk Nuclear Testing Grounds

Kazakhstan was the Soviet Union's Nevada and, due to Russia's continued operation of its space program, the Baikonur Cosmodrome in the southwestern section, still is. Awareness of the environmental hazards posed by the Cosmodrome spread after a Russian Proton rocket exploded and crashed near the town of Atasu in 1999, spraying fuel over a wide area. In 2005 the Russian Federation admitted that its rocket launches are causing children in the Altai region to contract endocrine and blood diseases and paid the government—rather than the victims—two hundred seventy thousand dollars in compensation. As frightening as they are, however, the hazards of Baikonur pale next to the legacy of Semipalatinsk.

Above-ground and subterranean atomic testing at Semipalatinsk spanned the length of the Cold War, from 1947 through the late 1980s, and included such ethically dubious experiments as deliberately exposing native Kazakhs to radiation from some of the four hundred fifty-six blasts recorded to have taken place there. Additional exposure has occurred as a result of the continuing use of the Semipalatinsk test range as a pasture by herders of sheep, cattle and other domesticated livestock by people who can no longer earn a living after the closure of the nuclear testing facility. Semipalatinsk, named after the nearby city of Semij in the remote nation's even more remote northeastern steppe near its frontier with Siberia, has left ten thousand square miles of uninhabitable land that is nevertheless inhabited.

Locals sell irradiated scrap metal and fish taken from Atomkul Lake, the weird result of a two-hundred-megaton nuclear detonation that dammed the Shagan River in 1965. Kazakhs living in the Semipalatinsk region suffer seven times the average rate of human birth defects in the former Soviet Union.

Kaisha Atakhanova, a Kazakh research biologist who received a 1994 MacArthur Foundation grant to study the aftermath of Soviet nuclear testing, adds: "Along with everything else, our nuclear monster, while devouring billions of rubles, also created a region of seismic danger. According to an ecological study of forty-five bomb craters located close to coal deposits, ten were found to be dangerously radioactive and three were releasing radioactive gases. Further more the loosened soil in the region is carried far and wide area by strong prevailing winds, introducing radioactive particulates into the air. Five percent of the region has been found to be contaminated by alpha and beta radiation."

Incredibly, the Kazakh regime is seriously contemplating a hair-of-the-dog solution: funding the clean-up by turning Semipalatinsk a global dumping ground for nuclear waste. "Scientists believe waste imports are necessary for Kazakhstan in order to raise money for the national program to bury its own radioactive waste and rehabilitate polluted areas," Kazakhstan Today state television announced in 2001.

In a region whose many problems were created by human folly, however, only divine retribution or the height of irony can explain the fact that its worst-case scenario was created by a purely random series of natural events: an outcropping of rock, an active earthquake zone, and high altitude.

Central Asia's Worst Fear

...is Lake Sarez, formed when the Margab River, one of the tributaries of the Amu Darya marking the border between Tajikistan and Afghanistan, was blocked by a huge landslide triggered in 1911 by a powerful earthquake high in the Tajik Pamirs. Lake Sarez, named for a nearby town, the result of that event, is thirty-seven miles long and growing. "If the dam were to break," the trade journal *U.S. Water News* reported in 1998, "experts say a wall of water would threaten parts of Tajikistan, Afghanistan, Uzbekistan, and Turkmenistan. The U.N. Department of Humanitarian Affairs, a Geneva-based group that coordinates U.N. relief operations, says such an event could easily become the deadliest natural disaster in history."

Lake Sarez (above), created in 1911 when an earthquake triggered a landslide that dammed the Murgab River. Authorities worry that a breach of the dam (below, seen in the lower left) would cause flooding that would threaten hundreds of thousands of people across four countries.

The Usoi natural dam created by the rockslide is the world's tallest: five hundred yards high and over a mile long. The fact that it holds back so much water (seventeen cubic kilometers) at such an extravagant altitude (10,700 feet

PHOTOS COURTESY OF H.R. WERNLI

above sea level) represents an enormous potential of released energy in the event of a breach. Dr. Arkady Sheko of the Russian Academy of Science and head of geology at the All-Russian Institute for Geology and Engineering Technologies explained: "If the dam were destroyed, the whole lake could spill out and threaten a twenty-thousand-square-mile area inhabited by five million people... Some fifteen hundred people live directly below the lake in the Murgab gorge. With the nearest villages nineteen miles from Sarez, a flood wave moving about sixteen feet per second would reach them in less than an hour." A one-hundred-yard-high torrent would inundate the Bartang, Pyanj and Amu Darya valleys, rushing hundreds of miles before petering out into the sands of the Uzbek desert or, the BBC reported in 2003, "as far down as the Aral Sea, more than one thousand kilometres (six hundred twenty-one miles) away."

Аральское море
-100км 0 100км 200км
- 1
- 2
НУКУС
ТАШКЕНТ
ТУРКМЕНИЯ
КИРГИЗИЯ
КИТАЙ
БАКАРДЕН
АШГАБАД
МАРЫ канал
ДУШАНБЕ
ТЕРМЕЗ
ХОРОГ
РУШАН

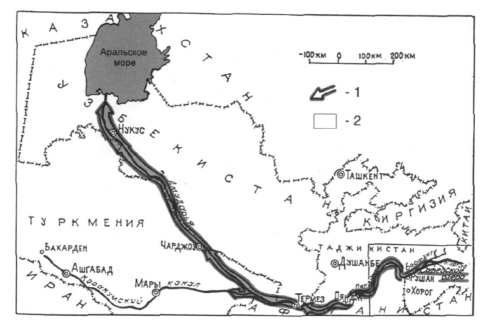

A map shows the projected flood path if the Usoi dam fails. The worst-case scenario predicts a wall of water eight hundred feet high traveling over six hundred miles inland.

Even if a proposed warning system were installed, it would be impossible to evacuate the flood zone. "They would all be killed. Everything would be swept away; everything standing in the way of a flood," said Dr. Sheko.

Large earthquakes occur frequently in the Pamirs. There are several possible scenarios for events that could cause the Usoi dam to burst. The one considered most likely by experts using computer projections concerns a large outcropping of rock currently jutting over the lake. If the formation were to fall in, the rock could trigger a huge wave that crests over the top of Usoi dam—a phenomenon that led to the levy break and flooding in New Orleans after Hurricane Katrina in 2005, but on an infinitely greater scale.

Geologists worry about the problem some call Central Asia's Sword of Damocles, but some doubt that a disaster will reach an epic scale. "The latest surveys indicate that only the upper part of the dam could possibly wash away...possible consequences could be dangerous but not on the scale that some newspapers or other sources claim," World Bank coordinator Rustam Bobojonov said in 2004. But pressure on the dam is building. The lake surface is rising by eight inches per year. And the rate is accelerating.

If Usoi dam bursts, the Lake Sarez Risk Mitigation Project projects the deaths of one hundred thirty thousand people in Tajikistan alone—the most sparsely populated area in the flood zone. An expedition launched by the Tajik Emergencies Ministry and Russia's International Mountaineering Federation "found that an earthquake with an epicentre in Afghanistan could send mudslides and avalanches crashing into the lake," reported Tajik state television. "The resulting wave would be up to two hundred fifty meters (eight hundred twenty feet) high and would force water through the lake's natural barrier...the torrent would cause further landslides in the valley below [and] could result in the largest flood ever seen."

Tajik President Emomali Rahmonov asked the United Nations for help with Lake Sarez in 2000. So far a mere $1.5 million has been allocated for a project that would require hundreds of millions due to the difficulties of transporting construction equipment thousands of feet up the Pamirs. Yet the threat posed by Tajikistan's water has a upside: years after oil and natural gas become obsolete Central Asia's demand for Tajikistan's water supply will only grow. Tajikistan and to a lesser extent Kyrgyzstan were desperately poor nations throughout the 1990s. Mountainous, remote and coming up empty in the Caspian Sea energy sweepstakes, many observers wrote them off as doomed. Now, although the Tajiks know that Uzbek president Islam Karimov would go to war if they did, they're aware of their ability to turn off the tap. Water is becoming clear gold, and the balance of power is starting to shift.

Turkmenbashi

As the Aral Sea recedes and the Aral Kum spreads, northern Uzbekistan and western Kazakhstan are drying up. Meanwhile, in an act of mindboggling nationalism, selfishness and obliviousness to ecological common sense, Turkmen dictator Saparmurat Niyazov is trying to turn his desert nation, by some measures the world's hottest, into a temperate zone.

Temperatures in Turkmenistan's Karakum ("black sand desert") soar over one hundred thirty-five degrees Fahrenheit for months at a time, yet this natural furnace, hundreds of miles from major population centers, is where the country's egomaniacal autocrat is building his one thousand three hundred square mile Turkmen Lake. It will, naturally, open at the same time as his new twelve-by-thirty-one-mile artificial forest near Ashkhabat.

"I am building the Turkmen Lake," Niyazov boasted. "I am building it for future generations. It will cost eight billion dollars. Hopefully, already a part has begun flowing. The salty waters from Dashoguz are flowing into the lake. It will join with waters from here. This lake is like a big sea. It will solve the water problem for the next generations. If we do not solve this problem, we will face water shortages."

Radio Free Europe described official Turkmen ambitions: "Planners say the lake will help create four thousand square kilometers of new farmland, more than twenty percent more arable land for the country, on which four hundred fifty thousand tons of cotton and three hundred thousand tons of grain can be grown."

Turkmen and foreign scientists worry that the project would pollute a vast area, setting the stage for a smaller-scale Aral Sea-like event. "The lake could pollute massive swathes of land with salt, and most of the water would evaporate from an open-air lake anyway," Michael Wilson of the European Union's Tacis support program predicts.

It's difficult to know how far the project, announced in 2000, has come along because Turkmenistan has been largely shut off to outsiders since 2004, when tourist and journalist visas became virtually impossible to obtain. Turkmen Lake, announced in 2000, had apparently been fully funded the time a report was broadcast on the state television station Watan on April 3, 2004: "Turkmen lake construction enterprise of Lebap Water Administration Production Association constructed the drainage channel going to the Turkmen lake and carry out final stages of work in Sedarabat additional branch of main drainage channels and thirteen kilometers out of fifteen kilometers of the channel was completed. By the completion of construction of the drainage channel, conditions of crop fields of Garashsyzlyk and Galkynysh districts of Lebap *welayat* (province) will be fundamentally improved. Along with excavation works, construction of bridges along the river is also under way. Excavation works should be carried out in another two kilometers. Drainage channel is further extending to the heart of Karakum River."

Moreover, in March 2006, Niyazov purchased thirty million dollars of construction equipment in order to accelerate the project: "We need to finish the construction of the Turkmen Lake and start filling it with water. This will change the flora, nature and boost livestock breeding."

The Karakum "River" expected to become the source of Turkmenbashi's new lake is actually the Soviet-era canal running from the Amu Darya south towards Turkmenistan's arid south and its increasingly thirsty capital, Ashkhabat. Every drop of water in the Karakum Canal hastens the destruction of the South Aral Sea and impedes efforts to save the North Aral Sea.

An eight-mile-long artificial river was opened in downtown Ashkhabat on the occasion of Turkmenbashi's sixty-sixth birthday in February 2006. The water was drawn from the Karakum Canal.

Ground Zero for Global Warming

Ecologically fragile Central Asian grasslands were virtually destroyed, reduced in many places to drifting desert dunes, as the result of five million horses that grazed their way west during the 13th century Mongol invasions. Neither the climate nor local populations have ever recovered. Seven hundred years later, areas that survived Genghis Khan are under siege by the internal combustion engine.

As an article by the Environmental Literacy Council explains: "If a region's climate is influenced directly by the ocean, the region tends to experience fewer extremes of hot and cold weather than regions with less oceanic influence." Nowhere is this less true than the "sharp continental" extremes of Central Asia, the largest and most landlocked landmass on the planet and home to its greatest temperature fluctuations. (Ürümqi, in Chinese Xinjiang, is the world's most landlocked city.) Kazakhstan's lowest recorded temperature is minus forty-nine Fahrenheit; its record high is one hundred thirteen.

As the world climate continues to suffer the effects of global warming, places

Factories belch toxins into the atmosphere on the outskirts of Ürümqi—the administrative capital of the Xinjiang Muslim Autonomous Region and the world's most landlocked city. Already home to the planet's greatest temperature fluctuations, Central Asia is facing even more extreme climate changes due to global warming.

with highly variable temperature face its most extreme consequences. According to the U.S. Geological Survey: "Over the past century, human activities such as the burning of fossil fuels, deforestation, grassland conversion, and other land-use changes have contributed to a large increase in the amounts of carbon dioxide and other greenhouse gases in the atmosphere. [Computer] models indicate that some parts of the world will probably be more severely affected than others. Parts of Africa and Central Asia, for example, are recognized as being particularly vulnerable to adverse climate change brought about by global warming. In particular, these areas likely will face higher inter-annual variability of rainfall, more extreme climate events such as floods and droughts, and—in dryland areas already severely afflicted by land degradation—irreversible desertification."

Temperatures are projected to rise forty percent faster in Central Asia than the global average. Scientists predict that the bubonic plague bacteria, which periodically breaks out in Kazakhstan, could benefit from warmer and wetter weather to spread more quickly to humans, leading to another Middle Ages-type pandemic. Amankul Bikenov of the Almaty Institute of Zoology believes that warming may be contributing to the decline in population of the famous snow leopard. "In our territory there are only two hundred fifty to three hundred [snow leopards]," he says. "It can be explained by the decrease of other species they use as food, such as Marco Polo sheep, wild goats, and others."

The tectonic collision zones of Kashmir, Afghanistan and the Tajik Pamirs, as well as the Issyk-Ata Fault below the Kyrgyz Tian Shan will see more frequent and more severe earthquakes because of higher and more extreme temperature variations. High-altitude glaciers are melting and increasing the risk of large floods.

The effects of global warming, noticeable though not yet disastrous in the West at this writing, have already killed thousands in a Central Asia that heated up between 0.8 and 3.6 degrees during the 20th century. The unusually severe drought of 1998-2001 forced 1.4 million Afghans and an unknown number of Tajiks to flee into exile during Central Asia's warmest winter on record. Soviet climatologists counted the disappearance of more than a thousand glaciers in the Pamir-Altai range of what was then the Kyrgyz SSR between 1959 and 1988, victims of a 0.9 to 2.7 degree warm-up over the last half-century. (A single degree increase is extremely significant.) Glacier melt has resulted in higher rivers and more frequent flooding.

Global warming isn't linear. Because it pumps more energy into the atmosphere, it can create colder winters as well as hotter summers. Warming has had a perverse effect on Lake Issyk-Kul in Kyrgyzstan, reversing a historical trend of dropping water levels at the expense of melting glaciers. Issyk-Kul has risen nearly a foot since 1998. Radzimir Romanovskiy, head of laboratory services at the Institute of Water Resources and Hydroenergy in Bishkek, says: "We think the climate has been changing here over the last thirty years, becoming warmer and wetter. We're getting more rain and snow here now, and that's showing up in the lake. We've also found temperature changes deep in the lake. It's risen from 3.7 to 4.2 degrees Celsius in parts."

Because Central Asia's authoritarian regimes are defined by a combustible mix of incompetence, corruption and poverty, they couldn't be less prepared for the challenges posed by global warming. They also couldn't be any more vulnerable to being toppled once something—drought, mass poisoning, an epic flood—goes terribly wrong.

Kyzylart-Pass
4280
6613
5821
Pik Lenin
7134
6048
6030
Karakul
3914
5588
6220
5358
Rangkul
3782
4655
Akbajtal-Pass
6128
5060
5946
6025
Pik Ismail Somoni
7495
Pik Garmo
6601
Muzkol sanctuary
6233
Kuna Kurgan
Murgab
3630
Aksu
5138
Pik Revolution
6974
5731
3000
Khudara
5981
5989
5879
Roshorv
Barchadiv
Sarez
4314
Najzatash-Pass
5194
5617
Pik Vudor
6132
5931
Basid
5349
5179
Alichur
Bartang
5558

Tajikistan 2002

Roshtkala
5049
6723
Vrang
Lyangar
2810
Barogil Pass
3882
4812
Sindev
Vrang
Kala-i-Pandzh
Wakhan
Garm-Chashma
6105
6872
Yamchun
Pik Mayakovskij
6095
6535
6518

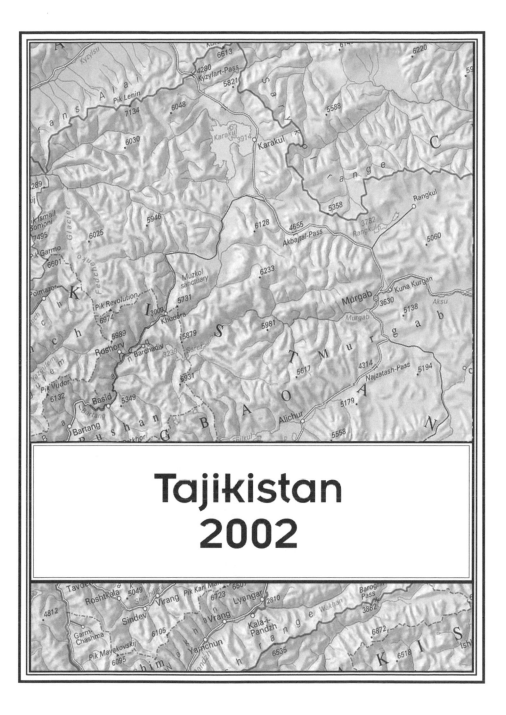

I wrote about my experiences covering the American invasion of Afghanistan for The Village Voice *and* KFI *in my graphic travelogue "To Afghanistan and Back." While passing through Tajikistan en route to the Afghan border that fall my fixer mentioned that the biggest international tournament of buzkashi—the most violent sport on earth—would be held the following spring, in conjunction with the festival of Navruz in and around Dushanbe. I returned in March 2002 to cover the meet for* Gear *magazine.*

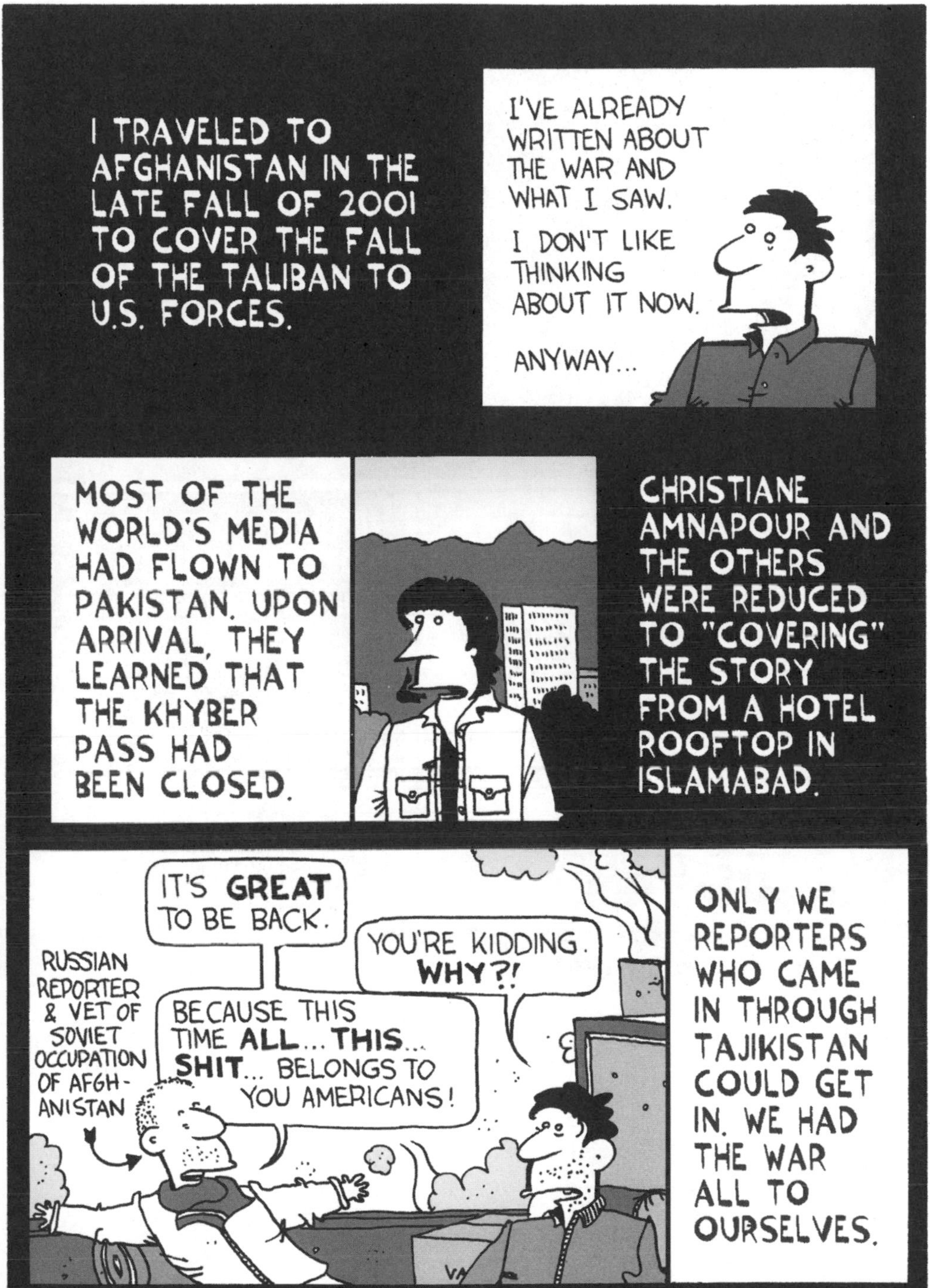
I TRAVELED TO AFGHANISTAN IN THE LATE FALL OF 2001 TO COVER THE FALL OF THE TALIBAN TO U.S. FORCES.
I'VE ALREADY WRITTEN ABOUT THE WAR AND WHAT I SAW.
I DON'T LIKE THINKING ABOUT IT NOW.
ANYWAY...
MOST OF THE WORLD'S MEDIA HAD FLOWN TO PAKISTAN. UPON ARRIVAL, THEY LEARNED THAT THE KHYBER PASS HAD BEEN CLOSED.
CHRISTIANE AMNAPOUR AND THE OTHERS WERE REDUCED TO "COVERING" THE STORY FROM A HOTEL ROOFTOP IN ISLAMABAD.
IT'S GREAT TO BE BACK.
YOU'RE KIDDING. WHY?!
RUSSIAN REPORTER & VET OF SOVIET OCCUPATION OF AFGHANISTAN
BECAUSE THIS TIME ALL... THIS... SHIT... BELONGS TO YOU AMERICANS!
ONLY WE REPORTERS WHO CAME IN THROUGH TAJIKISTAN COULD GET IN. WE HAD THE WAR ALL TO OURSELVES.

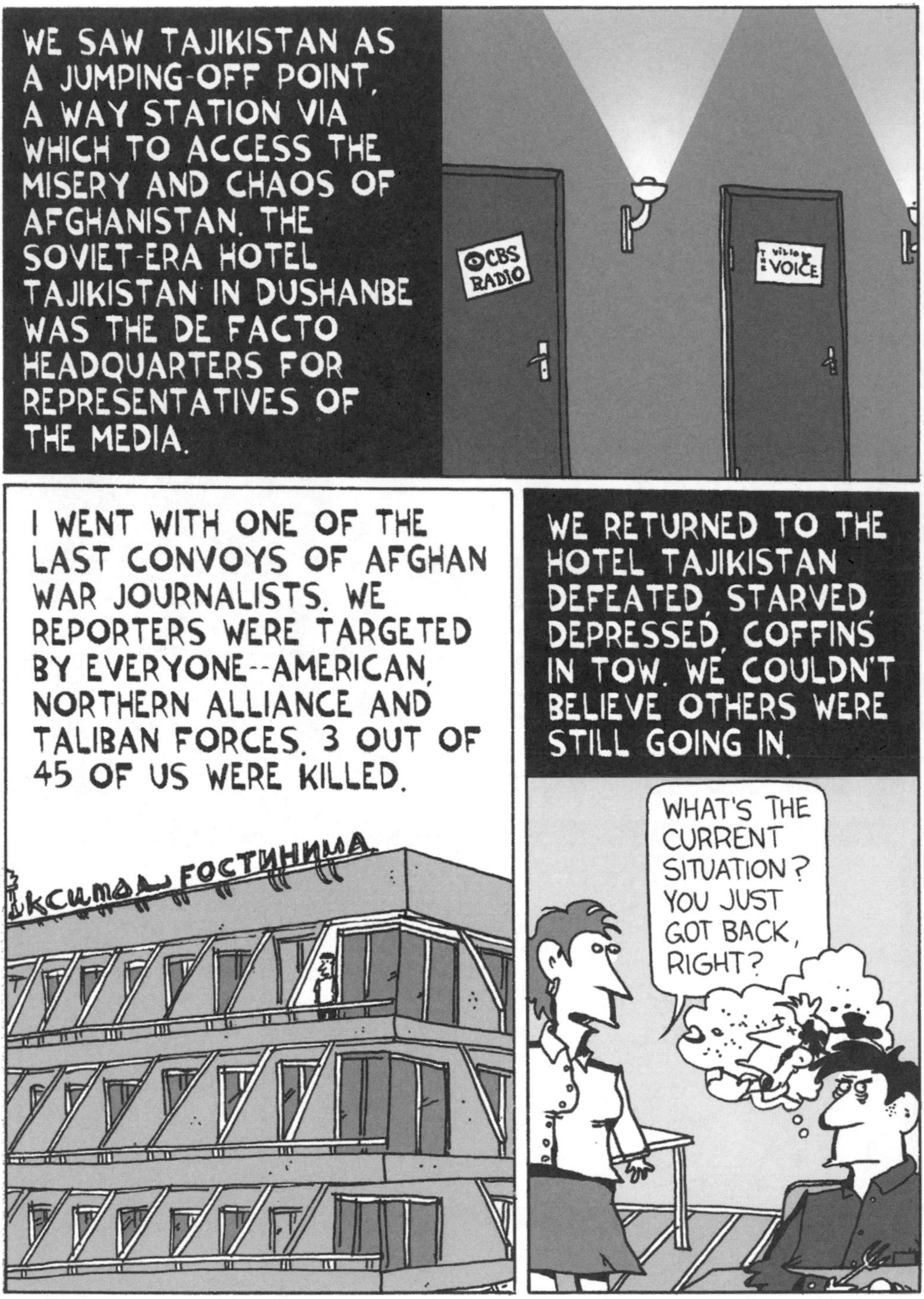
WE SAW TAJIKISTAN AS A JUMPING-OFF POINT, A WAY STATION VIA WHICH TO ACCESS THE MISERY AND CHAOS OF AFGHANISTAN. THE SOVIET-ERA HOTEL TAJIKISTAN IN DUSHANBE WAS THE DE FACTO HEADQUARTERS FOR REPRESENTATIVES OF THE MEDIA.
CBS RADIO
VOICE
I WENT WITH ONE OF THE LAST CONVOYS OF AFGHAN WAR JOURNALISTS. WE REPORTERS WERE TARGETED BY EVERYONE--AMERICAN, NORTHERN ALLIANCE AND TALIBAN FORCES. 3 OUT OF 45 OF US WERE KILLED.
WE RETURNED TO THE HOTEL TAJIKISTAN DEFEATED, STARVED, DEPRESSED, COFFINS IN TOW. WE COULDN'T BELIEVE OTHERS WERE STILL GOING IN.
WHAT'S THE CURRENT SITUATION? YOU JUST GOT BACK, RIGHT?

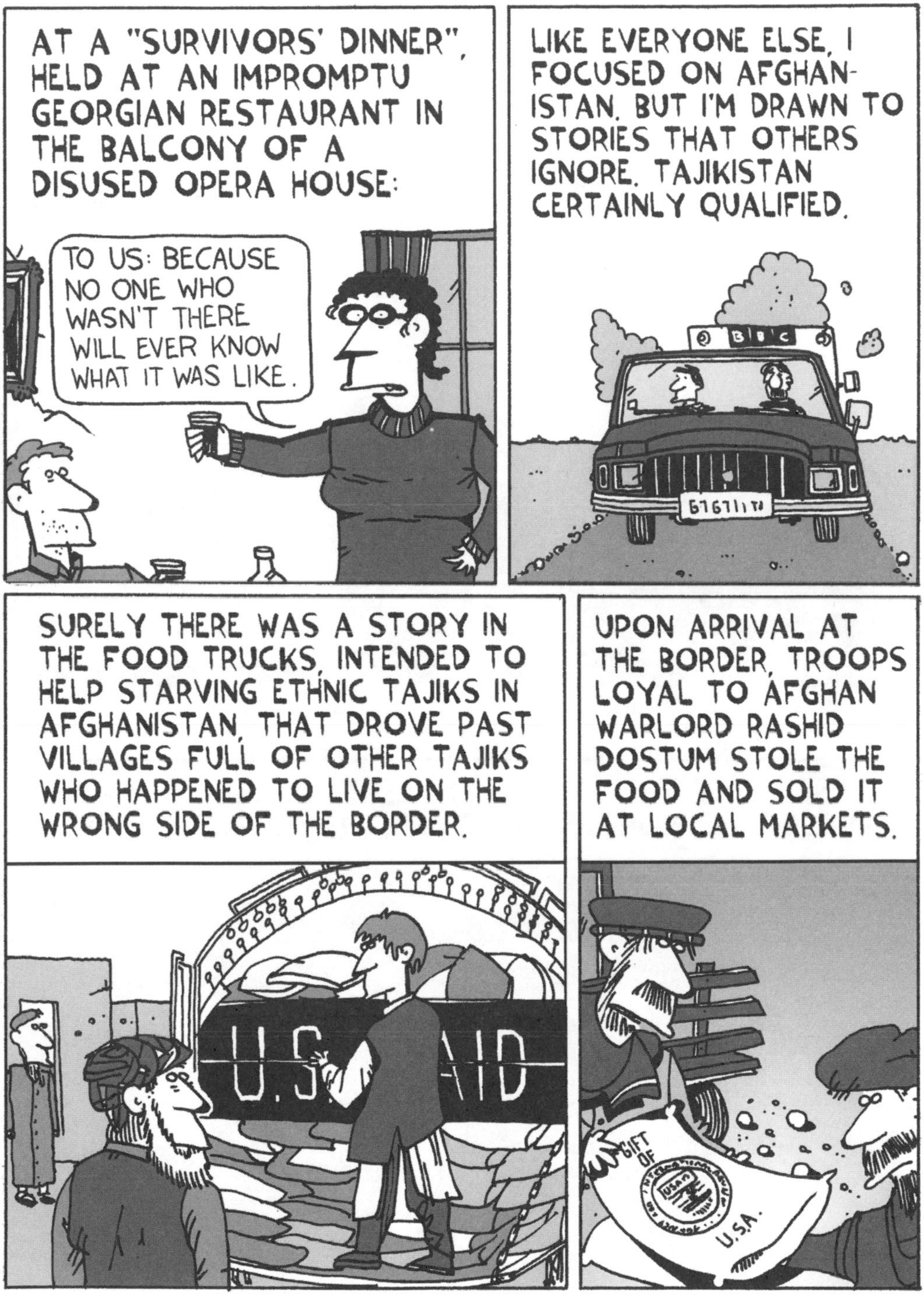
AT A "SURVIVORS' DINNER", HELD AT AN IMPROMPTU GEORGIAN RESTAURANT IN THE BALCONY OF A DISUSED OPERA HOUSE:
TO US: BECAUSE NO ONE WHO WASN'T THERE WILL EVER KNOW WHAT IT WAS LIKE.
LIKE EVERYONE ELSE, I FOCUSED ON AFGHANISTAN. BUT I'M DRAWN TO STORIES THAT OTHERS IGNORE. TAJIKISTAN CERTAINLY QUALIFIED.
BBC
SURELY THERE WAS A STORY IN THE FOOD TRUCKS, INTENDED TO HELP STARVING ETHNIC TAJIKS IN AFGHANISTAN, THAT DROVE PAST VILLAGES FULL OF OTHER TAJIKS WHO HAPPENED TO LIVE ON THE WRONG SIDE OF THE BORDER.
U.S. AID
UPON ARRIVAL AT THE BORDER, TROOPS LOYAL TO AFGHAN WARLORD RASHID DOSTUM STOLE THE FOOD AND SOLD IT AT LOCAL MARKETS.
GIFT OF
U.S.A.

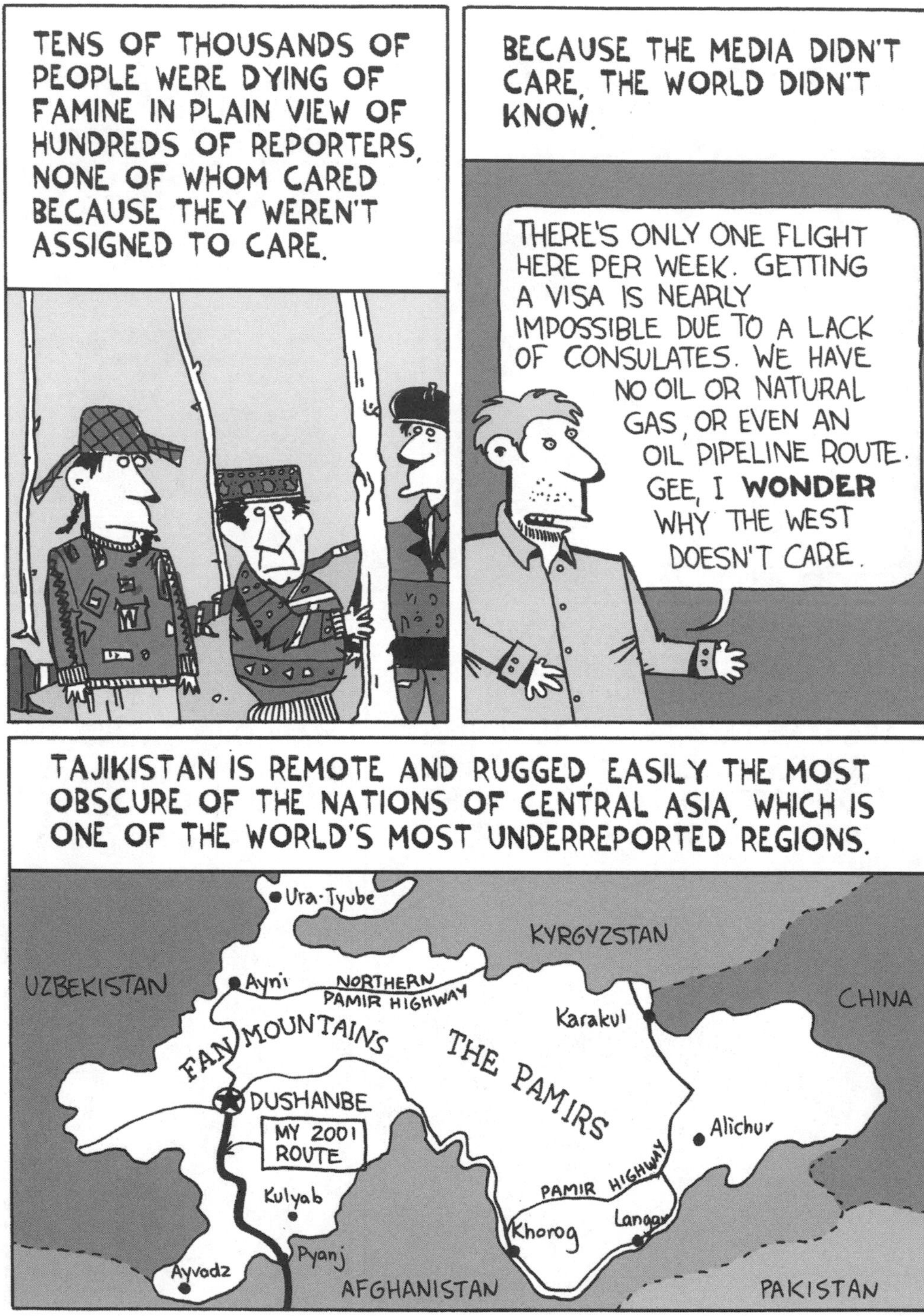
TENS OF THOUSANDS OF PEOPLE WERE DYING OF FAMINE IN PLAIN VIEW OF HUNDREDS OF REPORTERS, NONE OF WHOM CARED BECAUSE THEY WEREN'T ASSIGNED TO CARE.
BECAUSE THE MEDIA DIDN'T CARE, THE WORLD DIDN'T KNOW.
THERE'S ONLY ONE FLIGHT HERE PER WEEK. GETTING A VISA IS NEARLY IMPOSSIBLE DUE TO A LACK OF CONSULATES. WE HAVE NO OIL OR NATURAL GAS, OR EVEN AN OIL PIPELINE ROUTE. GEE, I **WONDER** WHY THE WEST DOESN'T CARE.
TAJIKISTAN IS REMOTE AND RUGGED, EASILY THE MOST OBSCURE OF THE NATIONS OF CENTRAL ASIA, WHICH IS ONE OF THE WORLD'S MOST UNDERREPORTED REGIONS.
Ura-Tyube
KYRGYZSTAN
UZBEKISTAN
Ayni
NORTHERN PAMIR HIGHWAY
CHINA
Karakul
FAN MOUNTAINS
THE PAMIRS
DUSHANBE
MY 2001 ROUTE
Alichur
PAMIR HIGHWAY
Kulyab
Langar
Khorog
Pyanj
Ayvadz
AFGHANISTAN
PAKISTAN

FOR INSTANCE, CHILDREN IN DUSHANBE OFTEN APPROACH VISITORS BEARING A MYSTERIOUS VESSEL...WHAT DOES IT MEAN? THAT FOUL SMELL COMES FROM BURNING THE HERB

ASPAND

THE CUSTOM OF CIRCLING BURNING ASPAND LEAVES AROUND A PERSON'S HEAD STEMS FROM AN ANCIENT ZOROASTRIAN RITE. ALTHOUGH ZOROASTRIANISM WANED SIGNIFICANTLY AFTER THE MUSLIM CONQUEST OF THE PERSIAN WORLD, ITS CULTURAL AND SOCIAL PRACTICES CONTINUE IN PLACES LIKE TAJIKISTAN, ONCE THE EASTERN OUTPOST OF THE PERSIAN EMPIRE AND NOW THE ONLY NON-TURKIC STATE IN CENTRAL ASIA.

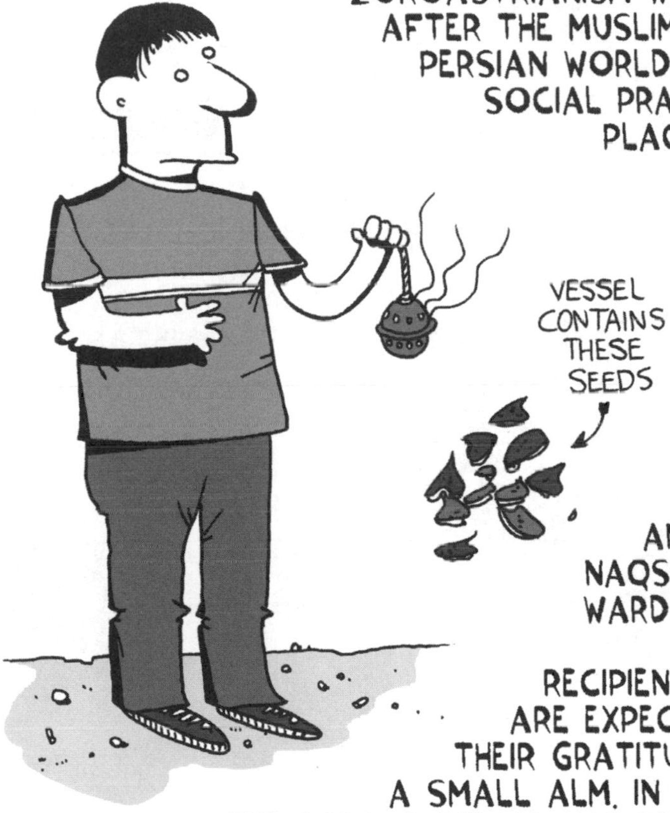
VESSEL CONTAINS THESE SEEDS

THE ASPAND RITE, DEDICATED TO THE ANCIENT PERSIAN KING NAQSHBAND, SUPPOSEDLY WARDS OFF THE EVIL EYE.

RECIPIENTS OF THE BLESSING ARE EXPECTED TO SHOW THEIR THEIR GRATITUDE IN THE FORM OF A SMALL ALM. IN PRACTICE, HOWEVER, THE ASPAND RITUAL HAS BECOME AN ANNOYING MEANS OF BEGGING. VISITORS ARE ACCOSTED SO OFTEN, BY SO MANY CHILDREN, THAT THEY HAVE TROUBLE DISTINGUISHING THEM FROM THE *MILITSIA*. THERE IS NO GRACIOUS WAY OF FENDING OFF THESE KIDS: EVEN YELLING "NE" DOESN'T WORK.

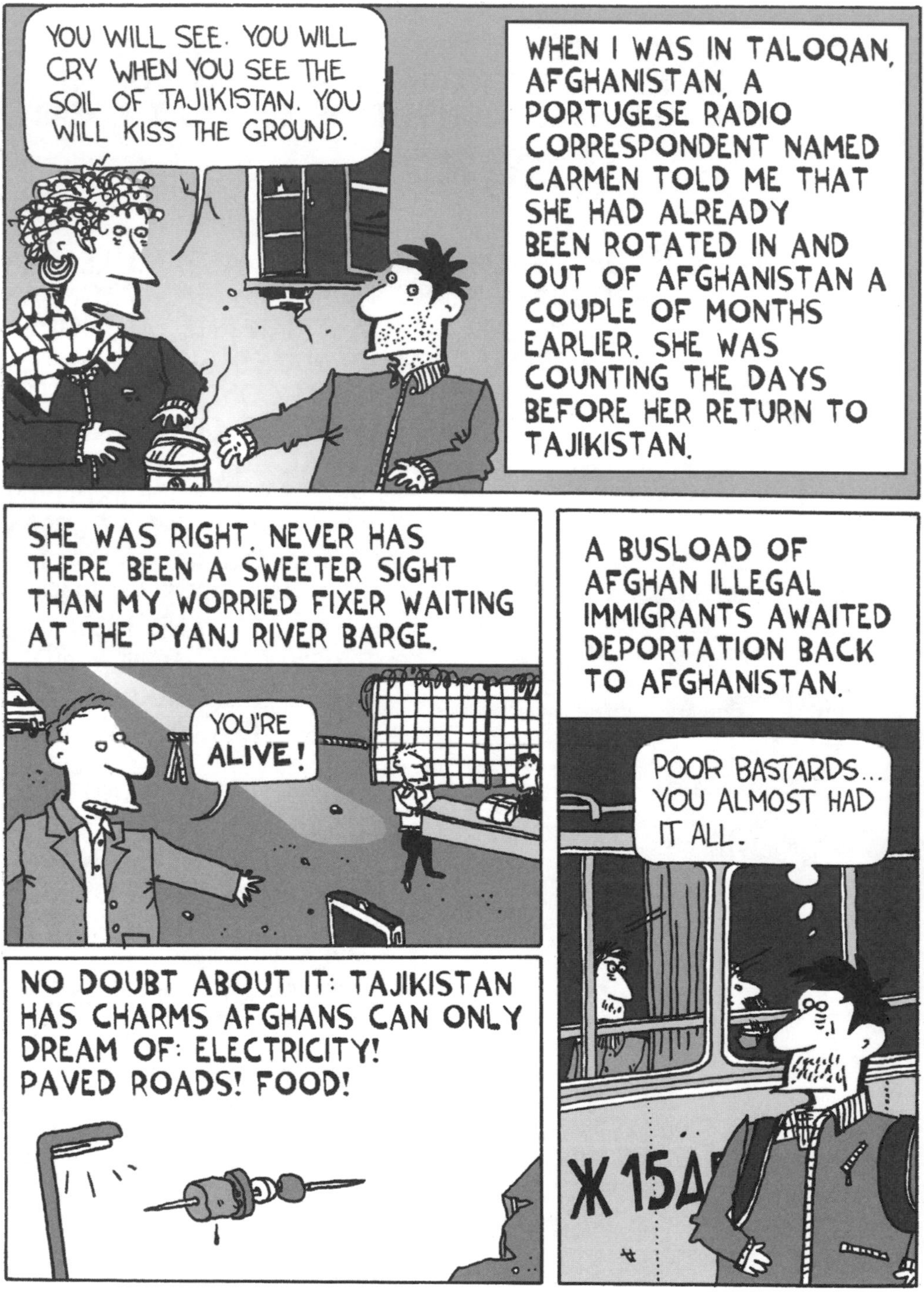
YOU WILL SEE. YOU WILL CRY WHEN YOU SEE THE SOIL OF TAJIKISTAN. YOU WILL KISS THE GROUND.
WHEN I WAS IN TALOQAN, AFGHANISTAN, A PORTUGESE RADIO CORRESPONDENT NAMED CARMEN TOLD ME THAT SHE HAD ALREADY BEEN ROTATED IN AND OUT OF AFGHANISTAN A COUPLE OF MONTHS EARLIER. SHE WAS COUNTING THE DAYS BEFORE HER RETURN TO TAJIKISTAN.
SHE WAS RIGHT. NEVER HAS THERE BEEN A SWEETER SIGHT THAN MY WORRIED FIXER WAITING AT THE PYANJ RIVER BARGE.
YOU'RE ALIVE!
NO DOUBT ABOUT IT: TAJIKISTAN HAS CHARMS AFGHANS CAN ONLY DREAM OF: ELECTRICITY! PAVED ROADS! FOOD!
A BUSLOAD OF AFGHAN ILLEGAL IMMIGRANTS AWAITED DEPORTATION BACK TO AFGHANISTAN.
POOR BASTARDS... YOU ALMOST HAD IT ALL.

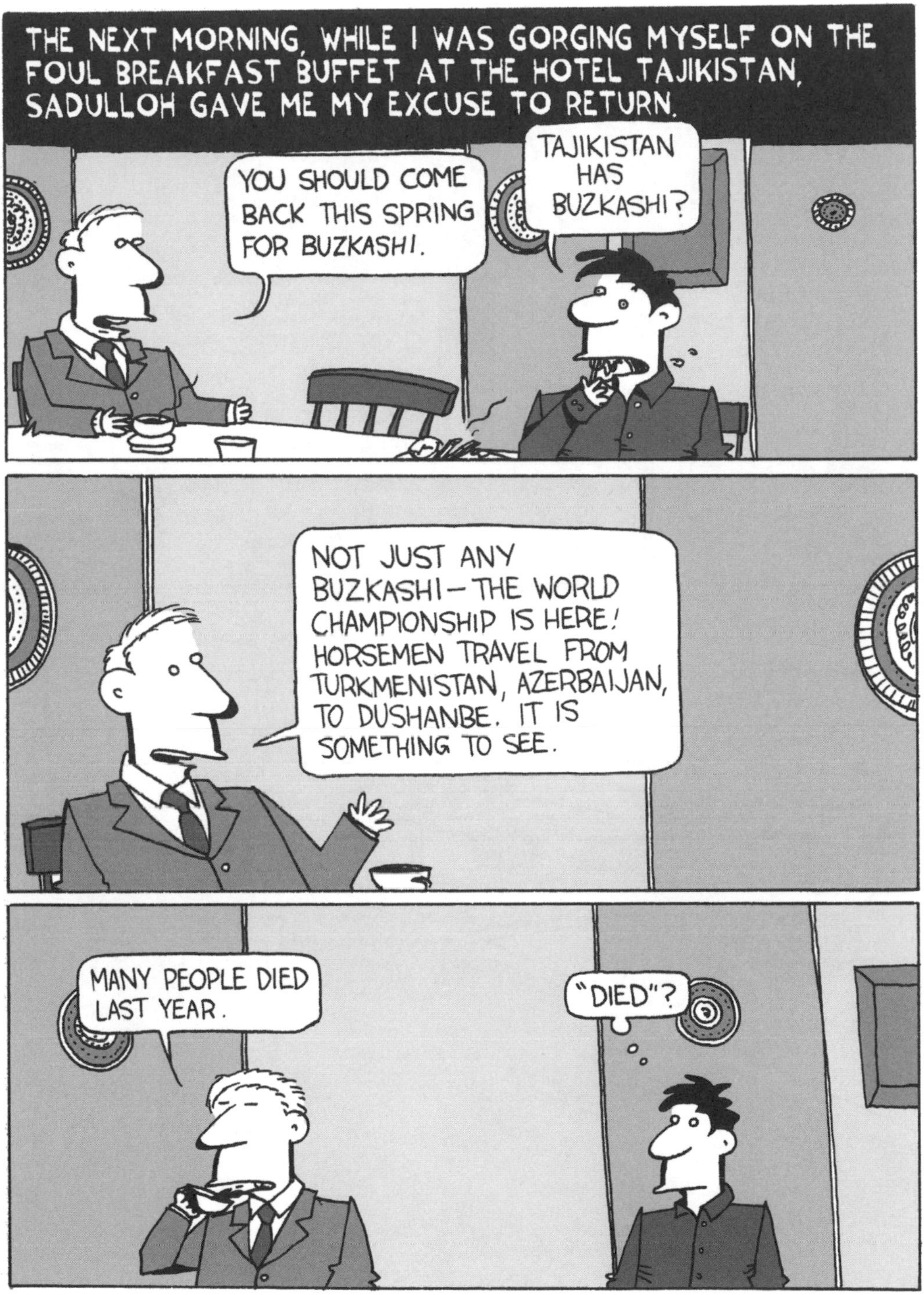
THE NEXT MORNING, WHILE I WAS GORGING MYSELF ON THE FOUL BREAKFAST BUFFET AT THE HOTEL TAJIKISTAN, SADULLOH GAVE ME MY EXCUSE TO RETURN.
YOU SHOULD COME BACK THIS SPRING FOR BUZKASHI.
TAJIKISTAN HAS BUZKASHI?
NOT JUST ANY BUZKASHI—THE WORLD CHAMPIONSHIP IS HERE! HORSEMEN TRAVEL FROM TURKMENISTAN, AZERBAIJAN, TO DUSHANBE. IT IS SOMETHING TO SEE.
MANY PEOPLE DIED LAST YEAR.
"DIED"?

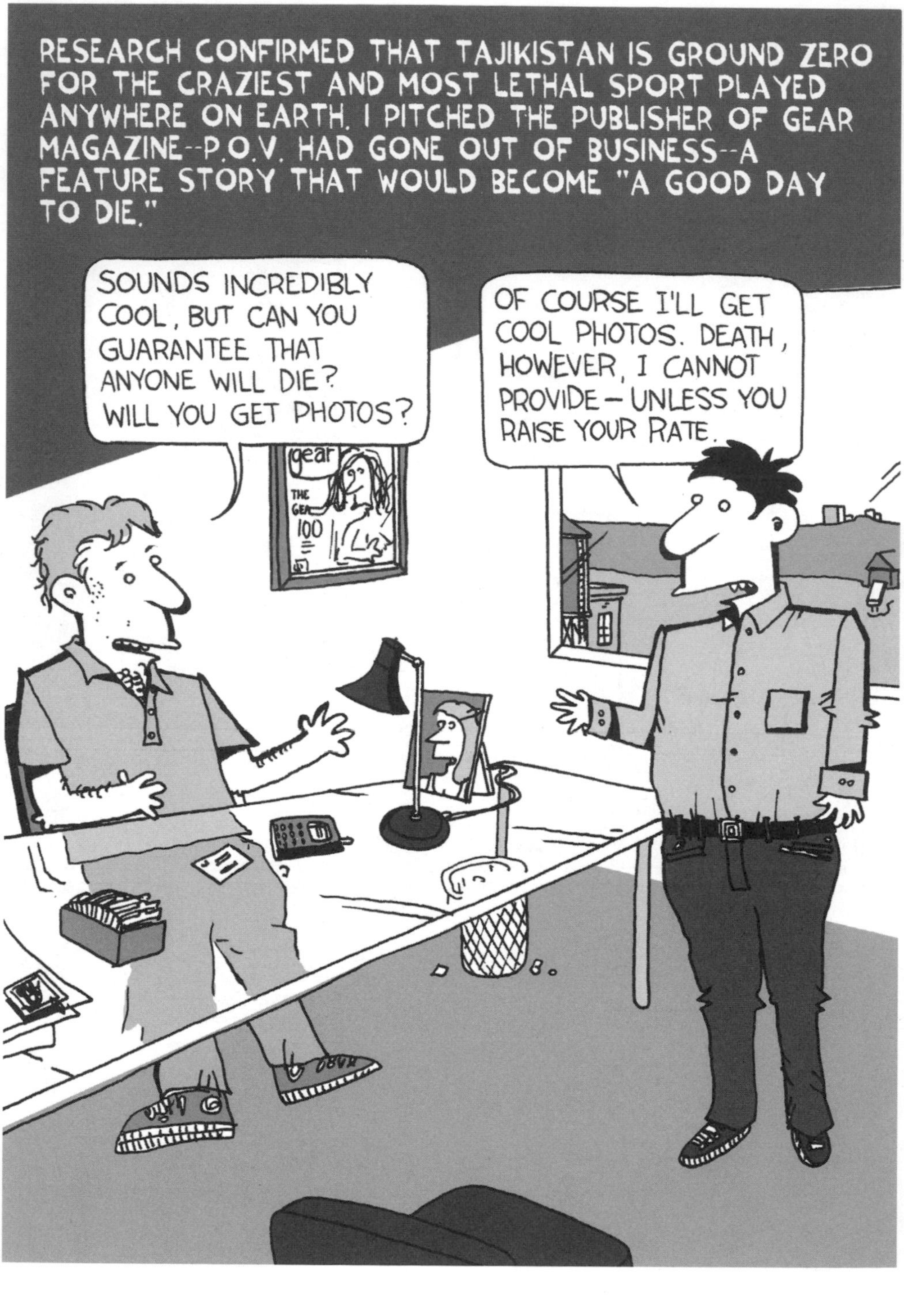
RESEARCH CONFIRMED THAT TAJIKISTAN IS GROUND ZERO FOR THE CRAZIEST AND MOST LETHAL SPORT PLAYED ANYWHERE ON EARTH. I PITCHED THE PUBLISHER OF GEAR MAGAZINE--P.O.V. HAD GONE OUT OF BUSINESS--A FEATURE STORY THAT WOULD BECOME "A GOOD DAY TO DIE."
SOUNDS INCREDIBLY COOL, BUT CAN YOU GUARANTEE THAT ANYONE WILL DIE? WILL YOU GET PHOTOS?
OF COURSE I'LL GET COOL PHOTOS. DEATH, HOWEVER, I CANNOT PROVIDE—UNLESS YOU RAISE YOUR RATE.
gear
THE GEAR 100

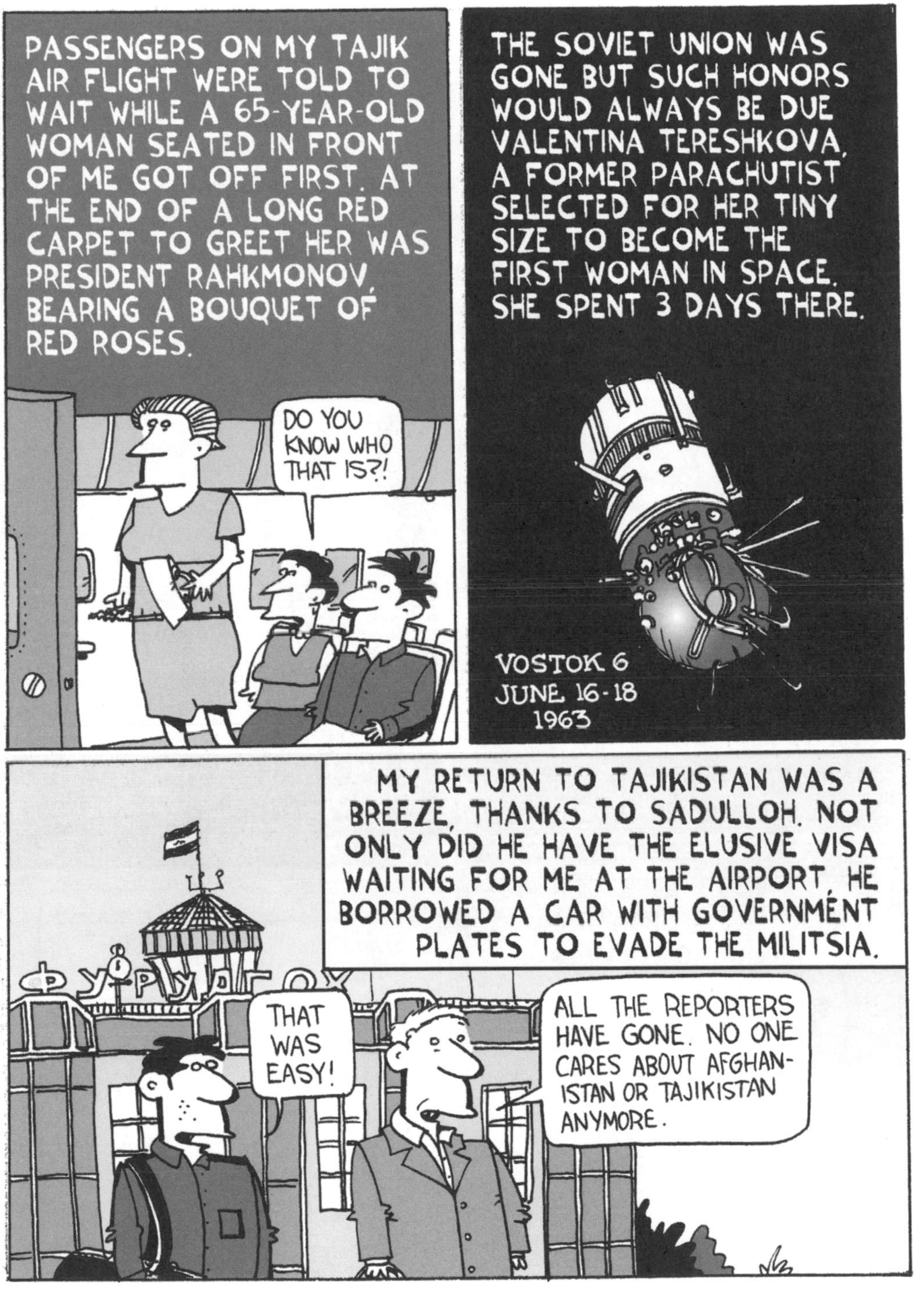
PASSENGERS ON MY TAJIK AIR FLIGHT WERE TOLD TO WAIT WHILE A 65-YEAR-OLD WOMAN SEATED IN FRONT OF ME GOT OFF FIRST. AT THE END OF A LONG RED CARPET TO GREET HER WAS PRESIDENT RAHKMONOV, BEARING A BOUQUET OF RED ROSES.
DO YOU KNOW WHO THAT IS?!
THE SOVIET UNION WAS GONE BUT SUCH HONORS WOULD ALWAYS BE DUE VALENTINA TERESHKOVA, A FORMER PARACHUTIST SELECTED FOR HER TINY SIZE TO BECOME THE FIRST WOMAN IN SPACE. SHE SPENT 3 DAYS THERE.
VOSTOK 6 JUNE 16-18 1963
MY RETURN TO TAJIKISTAN WAS A BREEZE, THANKS TO SADULLOH. NOT ONLY DID HE HAVE THE ELUSIVE VISA WAITING FOR ME AT THE AIRPORT, HE BORROWED A CAR WITH GOVERNMENT PLATES TO EVADE THE MILITSIA.
THAT WAS EASY!
ALL THE REPORTERS HAVE GONE. NO ONE CARES ABOUT AFGHANISTAN OR TAJIKISTAN ANYMORE.

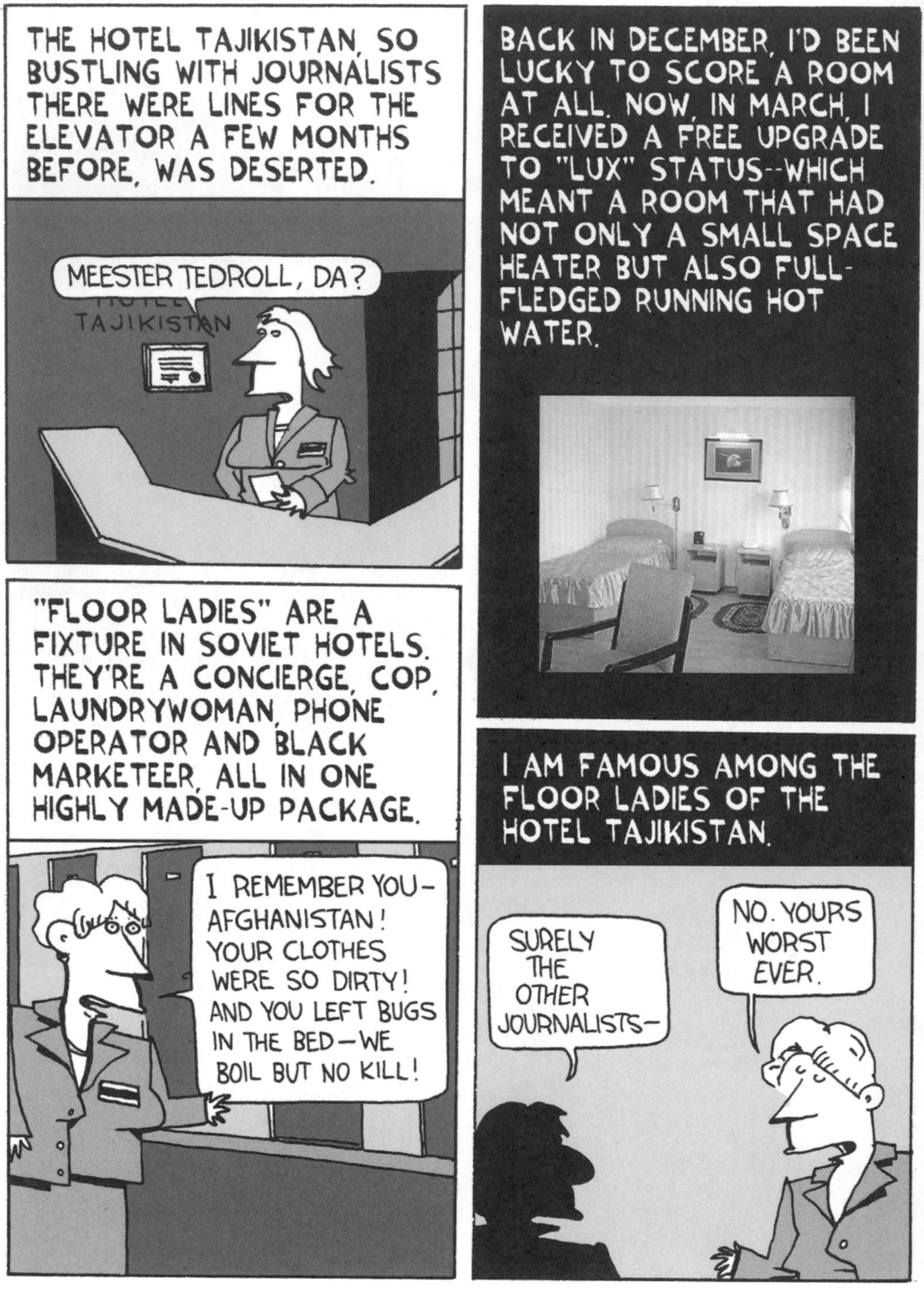
THE HOTEL TAJIKISTAN, SO BUSTLING WITH JOURNALISTS THERE WERE LINES FOR THE ELEVATOR A FEW MONTHS BEFORE, WAS DESERTED.
MEESTER TEDROLL, DA?
TAJIKISTAN
BACK IN DECEMBER, I'D BEEN LUCKY TO SCORE A ROOM AT ALL. NOW, IN MARCH, I RECEIVED A FREE UPGRADE TO "LUX" STATUS--WHICH MEANT A ROOM THAT HAD NOT ONLY A SMALL SPACE HEATER BUT ALSO FULL-FLEDGED RUNNING HOT WATER.
"FLOOR LADIES" ARE A FIXTURE IN SOVIET HOTELS. THEY'RE A CONCIERGE, COP, LAUNDRYWOMAN, PHONE OPERATOR AND BLACK MARKETEER, ALL IN ONE HIGHLY MADE-UP PACKAGE.
I REMEMBER YOU-- AFGHANISTAN! YOUR CLOTHES WERE SO DIRTY! AND YOU LEFT BUGS IN THE BED--WE BOIL BUT NO KILL!
I AM FAMOUS AMONG THE FLOOR LADIES OF THE HOTEL TAJIKISTAN.
SURELY THE OTHER JOURNALISTS--
NO. YOURS WORST EVER.

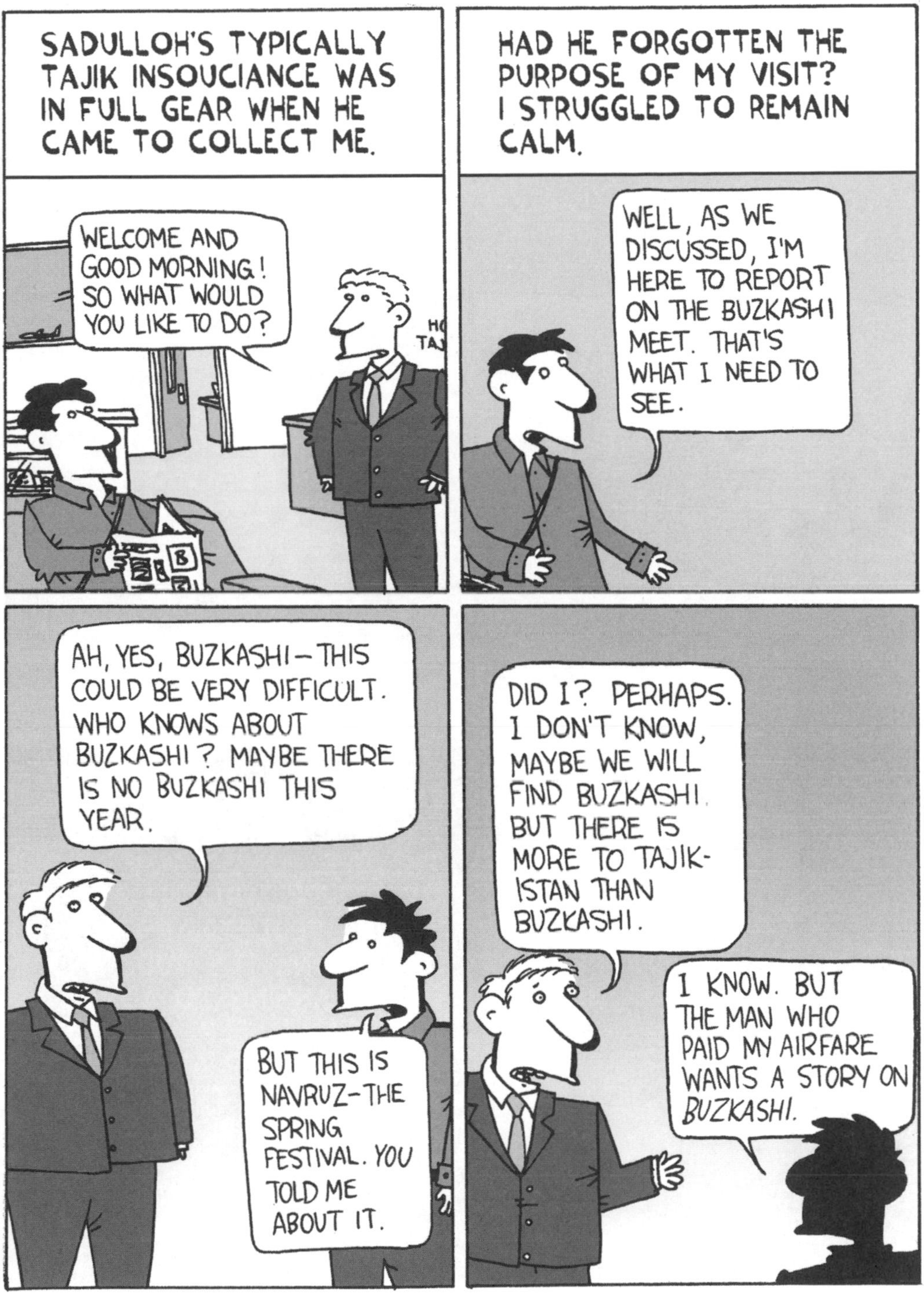
SADULLOH'S TYPICALLY TAJIK INSOUCIANCE WAS IN FULL GEAR WHEN HE CAME TO COLLECT ME.
WELCOME AND GOOD MORNING! SO WHAT WOULD YOU LIKE TO DO?
HAD HE FORGOTTEN THE PURPOSE OF MY VISIT? I STRUGGLED TO REMAIN CALM.
WELL, AS WE DISCUSSED, I'M HERE TO REPORT ON THE BUZKASHI MEET. THAT'S WHAT I NEED TO SEE.
AH, YES, BUZKASHI—THIS COULD BE VERY DIFFICULT. WHO KNOWS ABOUT BUZKASHI? MAYBE THERE IS NO BUZKASHI THIS YEAR.
BUT THIS IS NAVRUZ—THE SPRING FESTIVAL. YOU TOLD ME ABOUT IT.
DID I? PERHAPS. I DON'T KNOW, MAYBE WE WILL FIND BUZKASHI. BUT THERE IS MORE TO TAJIKISTAN THAN BUZKASHI.
I KNOW. BUT THE MAN WHO PAID MY AIRFARE WANTS A STORY ON *BUZKASHI*.

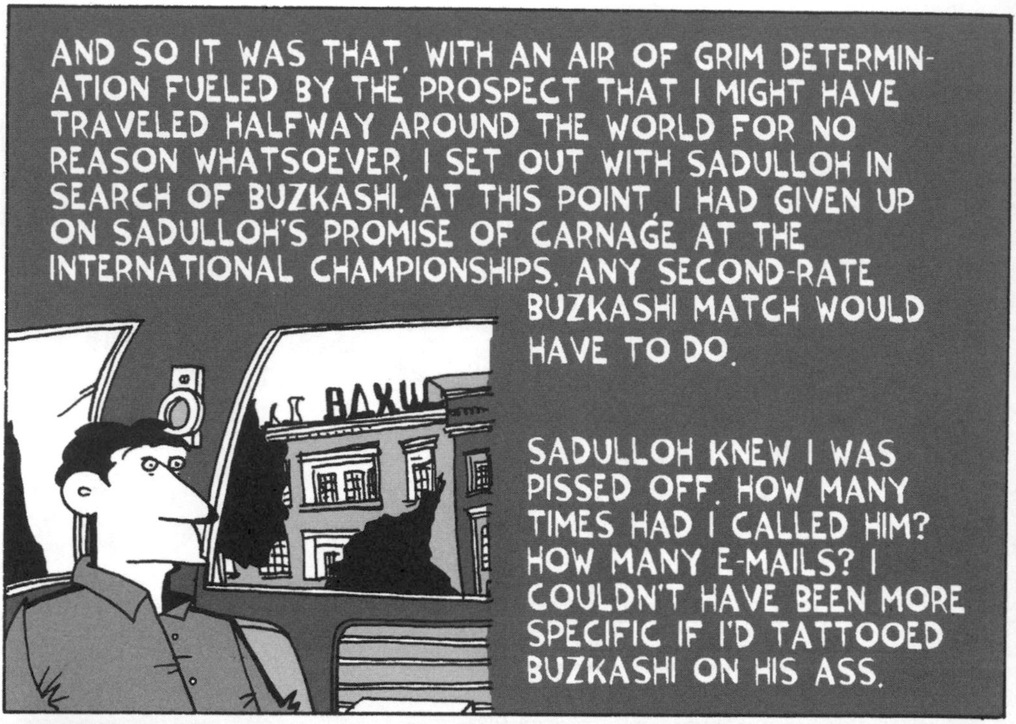
AND SO IT WAS THAT, WITH AN AIR OF GRIM DETERMINATION FUELED BY THE PROSPECT THAT I MIGHT HAVE TRAVELED HALFWAY AROUND THE WORLD FOR NO REASON WHATSOEVER, I SET OUT WITH SADULLOH IN SEARCH OF BUZKASHI. AT THIS POINT, I HAD GIVEN UP ON SADULLOH'S PROMISE OF CARNAGE AT THE INTERNATIONAL CHAMPIONSHIPS. ANY SECOND-RATE BUZKASHI MATCH WOULD HAVE TO DO.
SADULLOH KNEW I WAS PISSED OFF. HOW MANY TIMES HAD I CALLED HIM? HOW MANY E-MAILS? I COULDN'T HAVE BEEN MORE SPECIFIC IF I'D TATTOOED BUZKASHI ON HIS ASS.

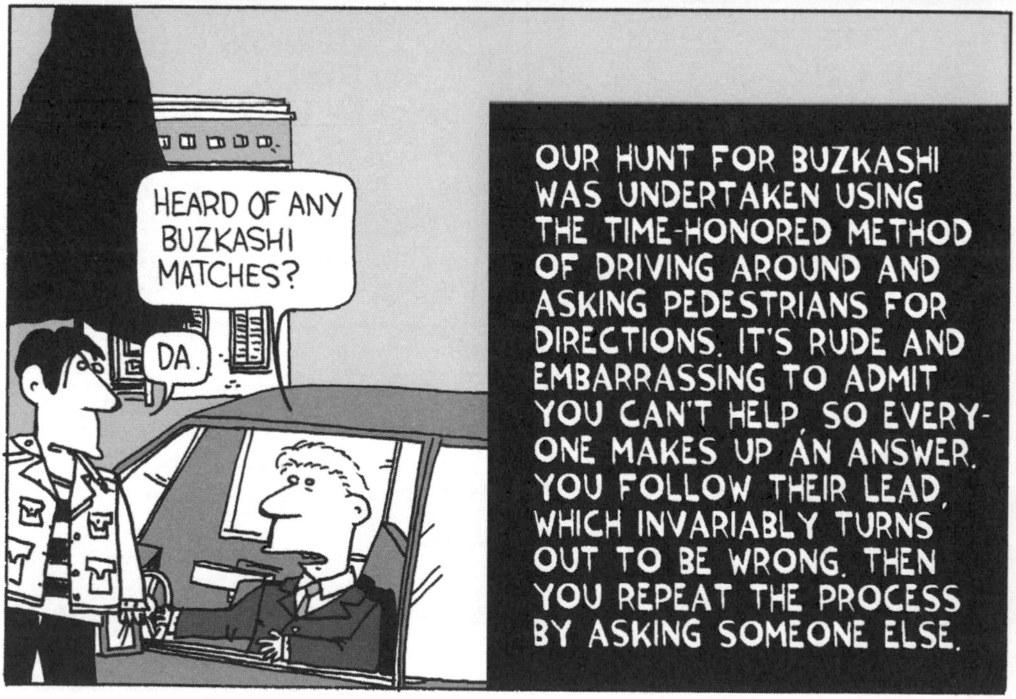
HEARD OF ANY BUZKASHI MATCHES?
DA.
OUR HUNT FOR BUZKASHI WAS UNDERTAKEN USING THE TIME-HONORED METHOD OF DRIVING AROUND AND ASKING PEDESTRIANS FOR DIRECTIONS. IT'S RUDE AND EMBARRASSING TO ADMIT YOU CAN'T HELP, SO EVERYONE MAKES UP AN ANSWER. YOU FOLLOW THEIR LEAD, WHICH INVARIABLY TURNS OUT TO BE WRONG. THEN YOU REPEAT THE PROCESS BY ASKING SOMEONE ELSE.

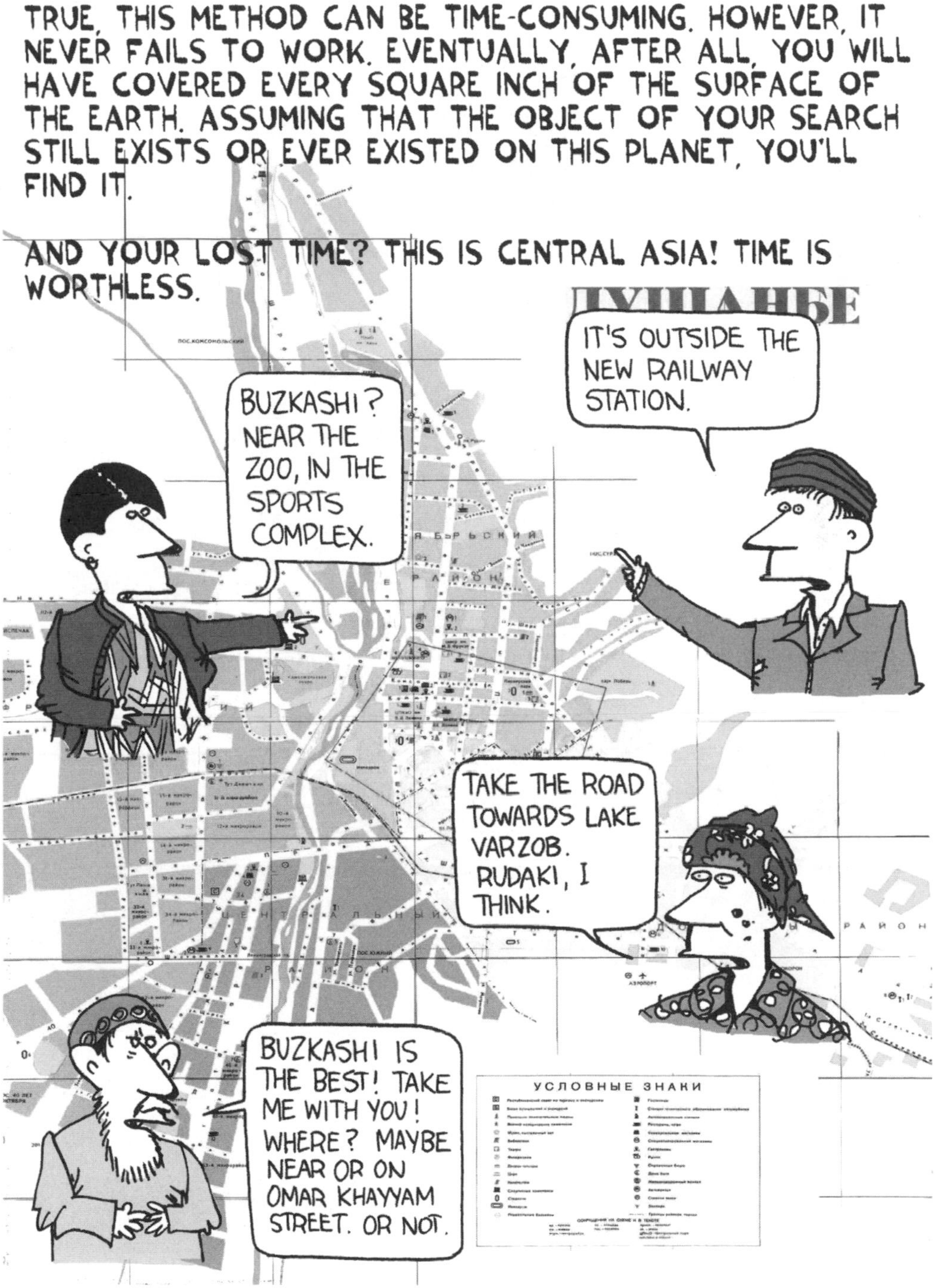
TRUE, THIS METHOD CAN BE TIME-CONSUMING. HOWEVER, IT NEVER FAILS TO WORK. EVENTUALLY, AFTER ALL, YOU WILL HAVE COVERED EVERY SQUARE INCH OF THE SURFACE OF THE EARTH. ASSUMING THAT THE OBJECT OF YOUR SEARCH STILL EXISTS OR EVER EXISTED ON THIS PLANET, YOU'LL FIND IT.
AND YOUR LOST TIME? THIS IS CENTRAL ASIA! TIME IS WORTHLESS.
BUZKASHI? NEAR THE ZOO, IN THE SPORTS COMPLEX.
IT'S OUTSIDE THE NEW RAILWAY STATION.
TAKE THE ROAD TOWARDS LAKE VARZOB. RUDAKI, I THINK.
BUZKASHI IS THE BEST! TAKE ME WITH YOU! WHERE? MAYBE NEAR OR ON OMAR KHAYYAM STREET. OR NOT.
УСЛОВНЫЕ ЗНАКИ

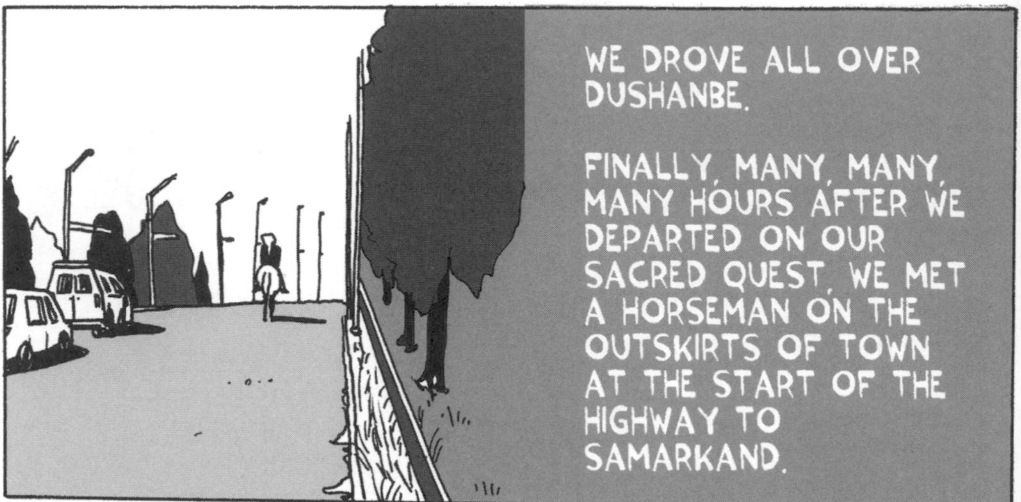
WE DROVE ALL OVER DUSHANBE.
FINALLY, MANY, MANY, MANY HOURS AFTER WE DEPARTED ON OUR SACRED QUEST, WE MET A HORSEMAN ON THE OUTSKIRTS OF TOWN AT THE START OF THE HIGHWAY TO SAMARKAND.

SADULLOH HAD NO MORE FAITH IN HIM THAN IN THE OTHERS WE HAD ASKED, BUT I HAD A GOOD FEELING. WE FOLLOWED HIS INSTRUCTIONS AND LEFT TOWN. WE ARRIVED IN THE CITY OF HISSAR, DROVE A FEW BLOCKS AND ROUNDED A CORNER, AND--THERE IT WAS! BUZKASHI! AND NOT JUST SOME PIECE-OF-SHIT BUZKASHI, EITHER. THERE WERE HUNDREDS OF CONTESTANTS, INCLUDING AFGHANS AND UYGHURS, FROM ALL OVER CENTRAL ASIA. WE'D FOUND THE SEMI-FINALS OF THE INTERNATIONAL CONTEST SADULLOH HAD PROMISED ME THAT PREVIOUS FALL.

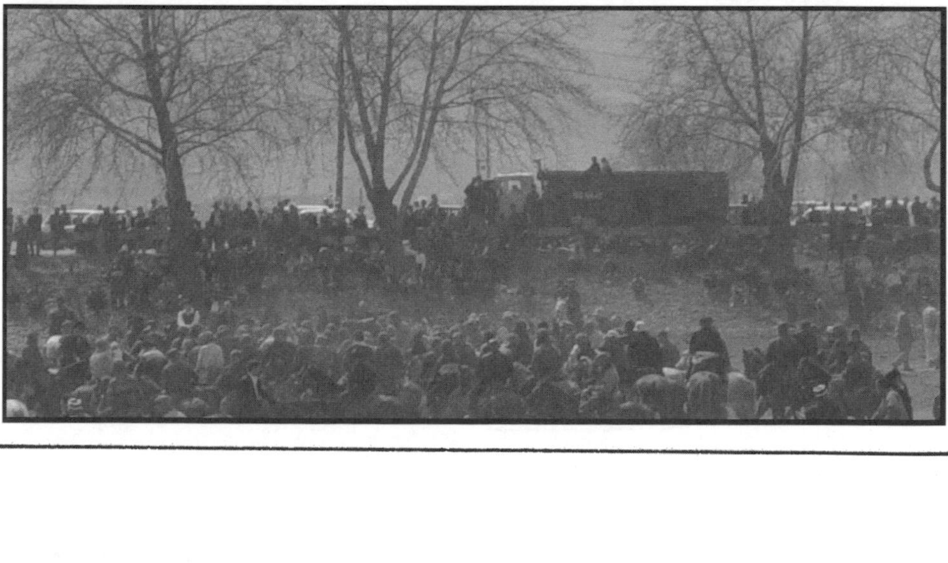

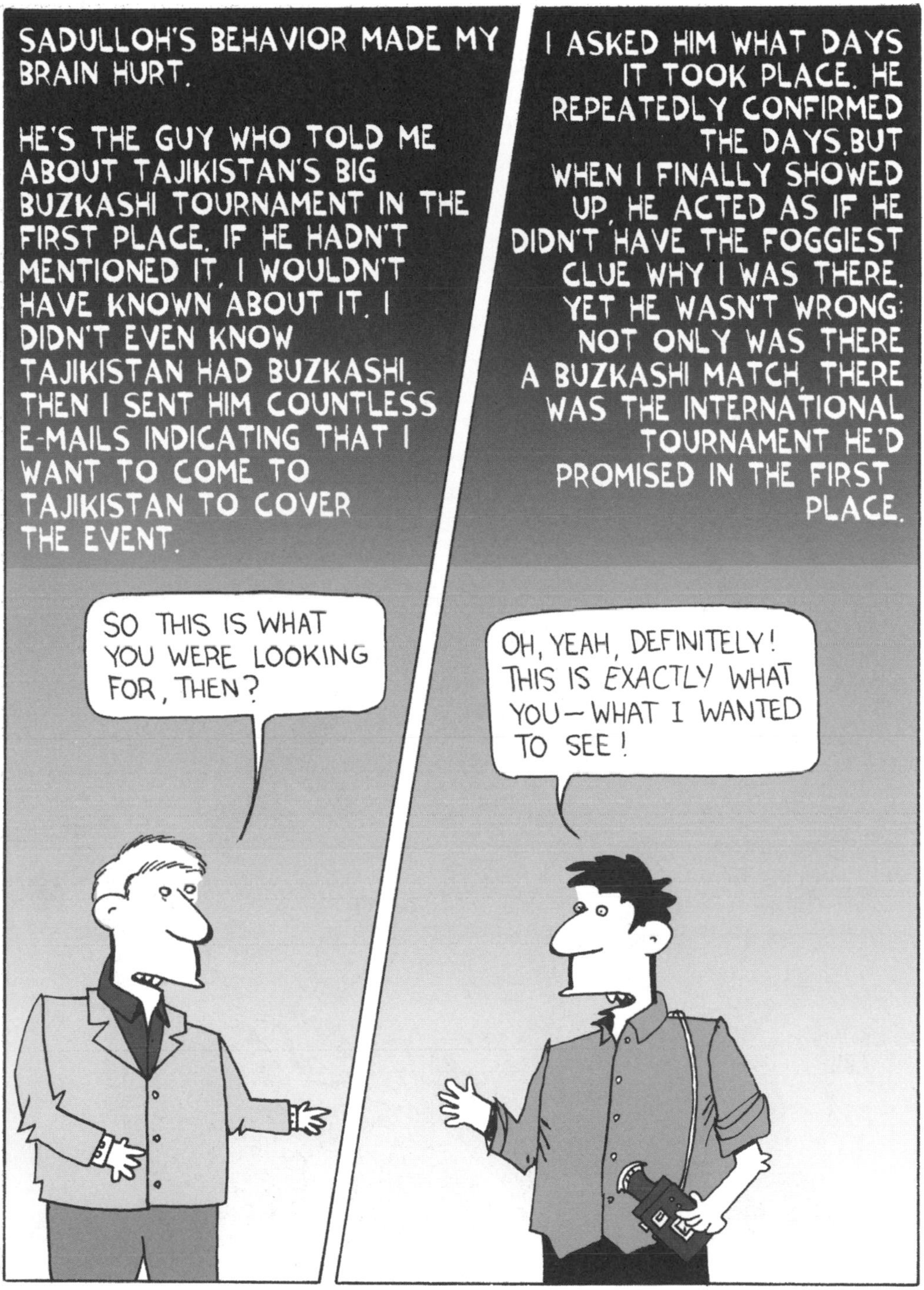
SADULLOH'S BEHAVIOR MADE MY BRAIN HURT.
HE'S THE GUY WHO TOLD ME ABOUT TAJIKISTAN'S BIG BUZKASHI TOURNAMENT IN THE FIRST PLACE. IF HE HADN'T MENTIONED IT, I WOULDN'T HAVE KNOWN ABOUT IT. I DIDN'T EVEN KNOW TAJIKISTAN HAD BUZKASHI. THEN I SENT HIM COUNTLESS E-MAILS INDICATING THAT I WANT TO COME TO TAJIKISTAN TO COVER THE EVENT.
SO THIS IS WHAT YOU WERE LOOKING FOR, THEN?
I ASKED HIM WHAT DAYS IT TOOK PLACE. HE REPEATEDLY CONFIRMED THE DAYS. BUT WHEN I FINALLY SHOWED UP, HE ACTED AS IF HE DIDN'T HAVE THE FOGGIEST CLUE WHY I WAS THERE. YET HE WASN'T WRONG: NOT ONLY WAS THERE A BUZKASHI MATCH, THERE WAS THE INTERNATIONAL TOURNAMENT HE'D PROMISED IN THE FIRST PLACE.
OH, YEAH, DEFINITELY! THIS IS *EXACTLY* WHAT YOU— WHAT I WANTED TO SEE!

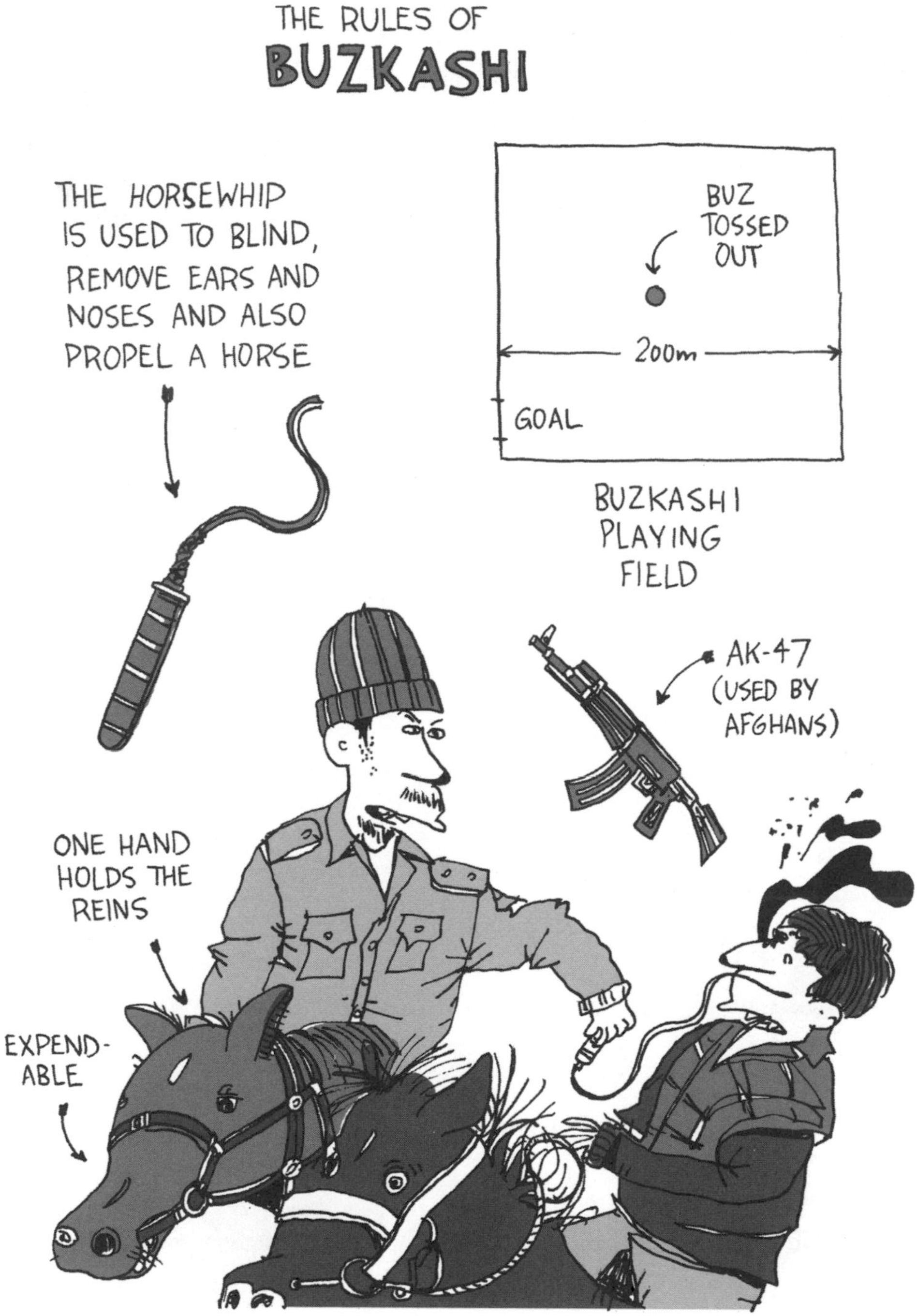
THE RULES OF
BUZKASHI
THE HORSEWHIP IS USED TO BLIND, REMOVE EARS AND NOSES AND ALSO PROPEL A HORSE
BUZ TOSSED OUT
200m
GOAL
BUZKASHI PLAYING FIELD
AK-47 (USED BY AFGHANS)
ONE HAND HOLDS THE REINS
EXPEND-ABLE

WAS SADULLOH SCREWING AROUND WITH ME? NO, HE SEEMED GENUINELY RELIEVED WHEN WE FOUND HISSAR. WAS HE SENILE? THERE WAS NO (OTHER) EVIDENCE TO SUPPORT THAT HYPOTHESIS. I STILL DON'T GET IT.

I DIDN'T TAKE MOST OF THE BUZKASHI PHOTOS.

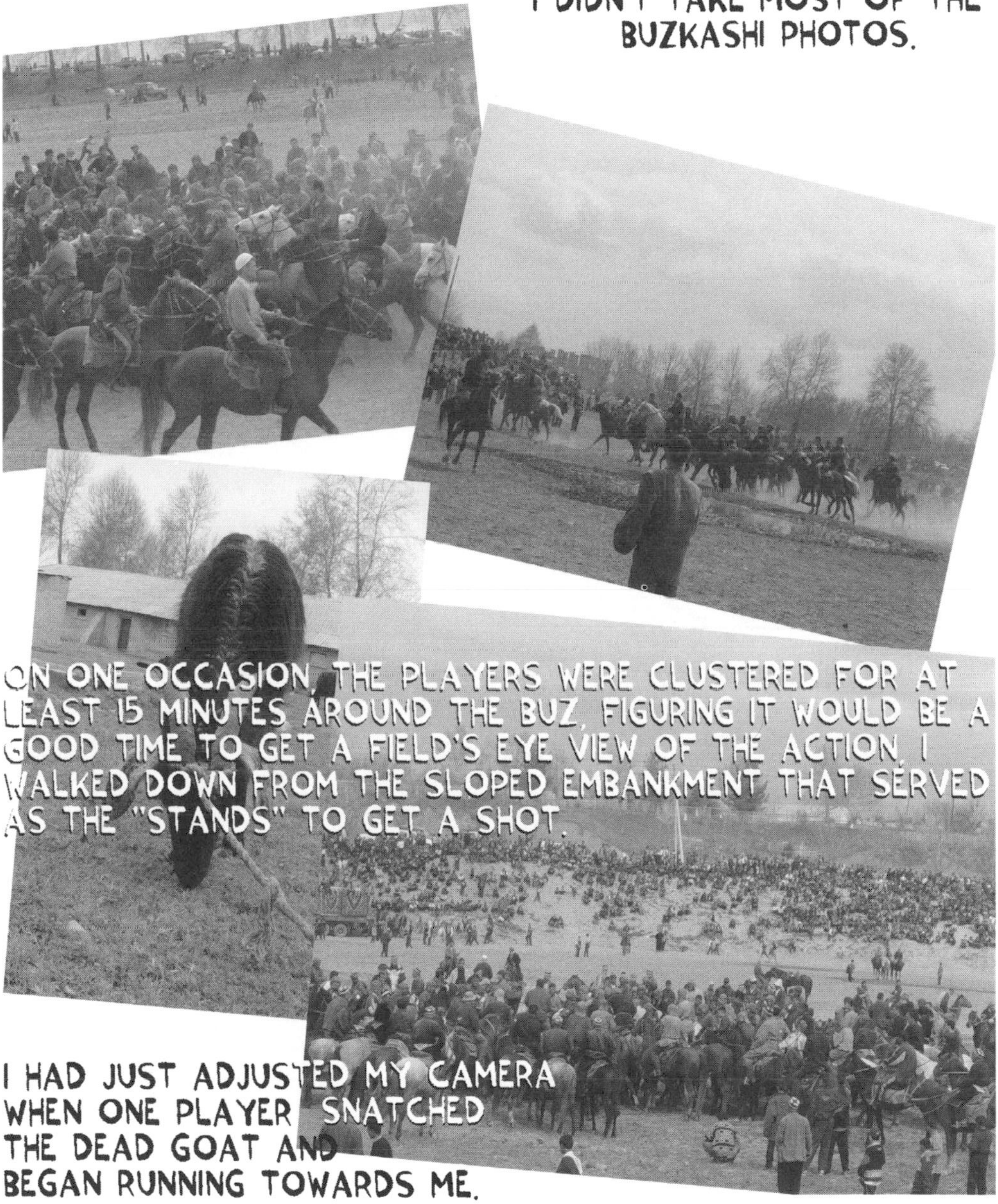

ON ONE OCCASION, THE PLAYERS WERE CLUSTERED FOR AT LEAST 15 MINUTES AROUND THE BUZ. FIGURING IT WOULD BE A GOOD TIME TO GET A FIELD'S EYE VIEW OF THE ACTION, I WALKED DOWN FROM THE SLOPED EMBANKMENT THAT SERVED AS THE "STANDS" TO GET A SHOT.

I HAD JUST ADJUSTED MY CAMERA WHEN ONE PLAYER SNATCHED THE DEAD GOAT AND BEGAN RUNNING TOWARDS ME.

RIGHT BEHIND HIM WERE SEVERAL STAMPEDING HORSES RACING TOWARDS ME AT TOP SPEED. I SNAPPED THE PHOTO, TURNED AROUND AND RAN.

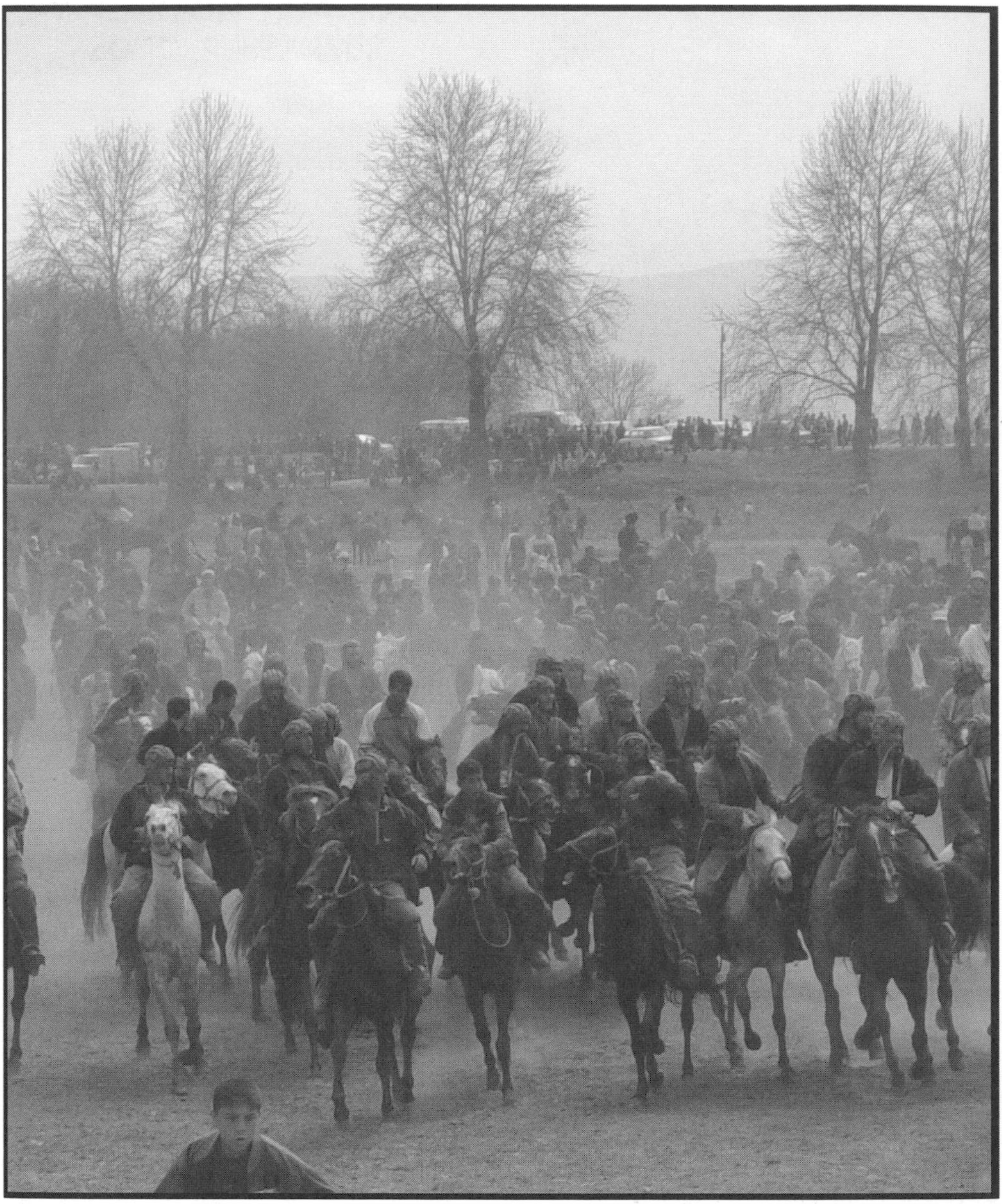

YOU KNOW HOW, IN HORROR MOVIES, PEOPLE WHO ARE
CHASED ALWAYS TURN AROUND TO SEE THEIR PURSUER?
THAT'S FICTION. YOU DON'T DARE TAKE THE CHANCE OF
STUMBLING. YOU RUN AS QUICKLY AND EFFICIENTLY AS
YOU CAN.

I COULD HAVE DIED FOR THAT SHOT. I WOULD DO IT AGAIN.

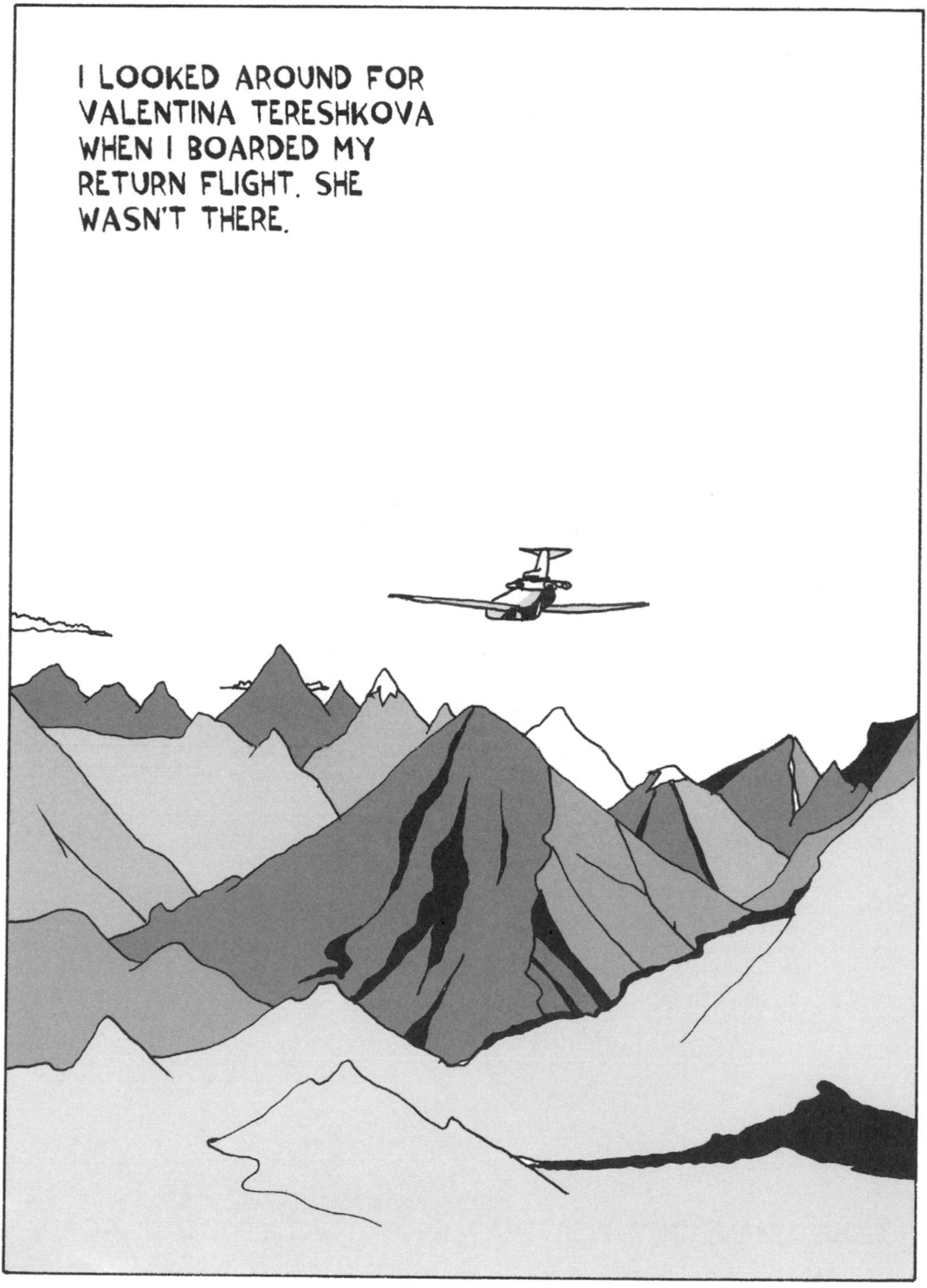
I LOOKED AROUND FOR VALENTINA TERESHKOVA WHEN I BOARDED MY RETURN FLIGHT. SHE WASN'T THERE.

What Is To Be Done?

Until September 2001, the United States, and the West in general, paid little attention to the region. They merely mentioned its huge energy potential and were not too active in defending the few local dissidents. Until recently, Washington's economic and defense cooperation with these countries was based on unilateral advantage and minimal costs. The United States is pursuing its [current] strategy on several levels. It is flirting with the top echelons of local power, promising to help them solve their major domestic problems, and making some moves to the West-oriented local opposition, funding it through various non-governmental organizations as a potential "reserve." The United States is stepping up its economic influence in the region, relying on its new military bases.

—Andrei Grozin, United Press International, April 5, 2006

The United States claims that encouraging the protection of human rights is a top priority in its dealings with other countries. "A central goal of U.S. foreign policy has been the promotion of respect for human rights, as embodied in the Universal Declaration of Human Rights," reads the mission statement of the State Department of the U.S. "The United States understands that the existence of human rights helps secure the peace, deter aggression, promote the rule of law, combat crime and corruption, strengthen democracies, and prevent humanitarian crises." The American government repeatedly issues reports calling for economic sanctions against and even "regime change" in countries that it claims violate the rights of their citizens to speak, worship or vote freely. Yet, after he personally supervised the massacre of hundreds of protesters in Andijon, American officials were falling all over themselves to watch Uzbek dictator Islam Karimov's back.

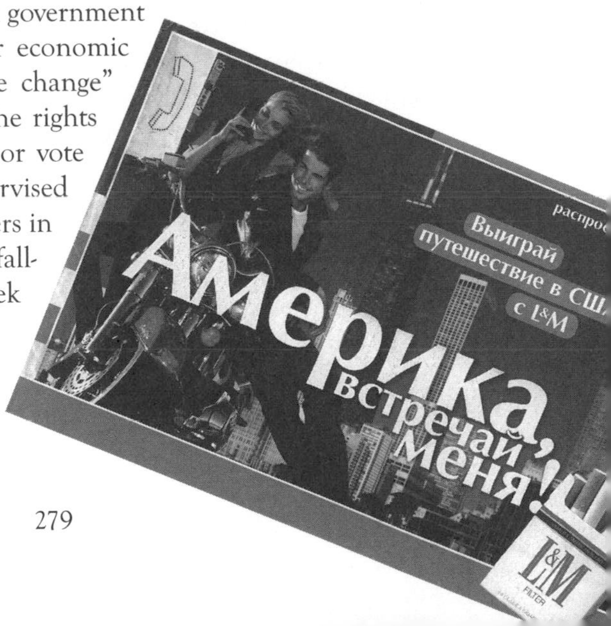
Выиграй
путешествие в
с L&M
Америка,
встречай
меня!
L&M

Karimov had already retaliated against earlier pro forma Bush Administration criticism by

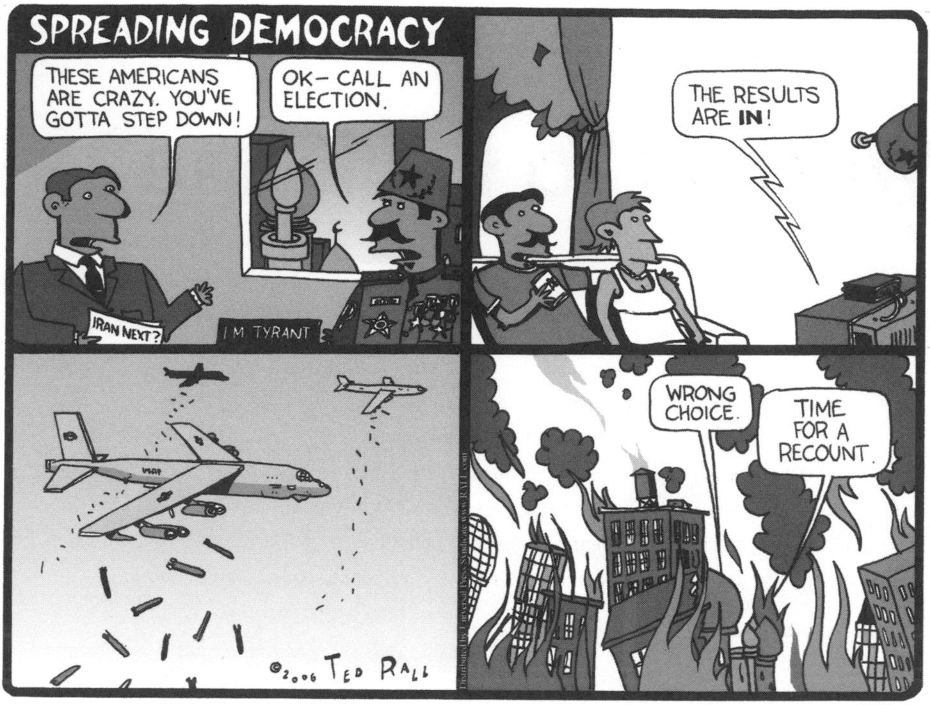
SPREADING DEMOCRACY
THESE AMERICANS ARE CRAZY. YOU'VE GOTTA STEP DOWN!
OK– CALL AN ELECTION.
IRAN NEXT?
I M TYRANT
THE RESULTS ARE IN!
WRONG CHOICE.
TIME FOR A RECOUNT.
©2006 TED RALL

curtailing the number of American flights allowed into the United States' Karshi-Khanabad (K-2) airbase. Uzbek-American relations continued to cool over the next few months, culminating with America's eviction from K-2. In the interim, however, America's initial response to the most notorious act of state-sponsored genocide since Rwanda revealed its true priorities. "The Pentagon wants to avoid upsetting the Uzbekistan government," *The Washington Post* quoted a senior diplomat on July 15, 2005. So what if Uzbekistan, long a notorious violator of human rights, had ruthlessly slaughtered civilians, including women and children? As long as Central Asia retained its geopolitical importance, America would want continued access to K-2 and Uzbekistan would remain a crucial ally in its war on Islam, er, terror.

So when "British and other European officials...pushed to include language calling for an independent investigation [into Andijon] in a communiqué issued by defense ministers of NATO countries and Russia," U.S. defense officials used their veto to block it. "At the private general meeting...of all NATO alliance ministers...[Defense Secretary Donald] Rumsfeld's remarks on the issue emphasized the risks of provoking Uzbekistan," the *Post* reported. "Rumsfeld said the ministers needed to know that the Uzbekistan situation had direct implications on NATO operations in the region. He mentioned the tons of humanitarian aid that pass through the Karshi-Khanabad air base and warned that alternatives to the base would be more difficult and expensive."

The Pentagon demanded that the Uzbek government that carried out the murders be held accountable...to itself. "The United States has repeatedly urged

Uzbekistan to undertake a full and transparent inquiry into the Andijon incident," spokesman Bryan Whitman said, apparently with a straight face.

One year after Uzbekistan's Tiananmen Square, neither the United States nor its Western allies had made any meaningful attempt to hold its repressive regime accountable. Germany refused a Human Rights Watch request to investigate former Uzbek interior minister Zokirjon Almatov for crimes against humanity when he traveled there for medical treatment in April 2006 because, according to Radio Free Europe, "prosecutor Kay Nehm... did not expect cooperation from Uzbekistan and the case would likely fail as a result."

Perhaps more surprising is the United States' willingness to overlook Andijon even after the Uzbeks evicted its troops from K-2. RAND Corporation pundit Olga Oliker summarized the Bush Administration's position in a *Baltimore Sun* opinion column authored shortly after the expulsion. "Cutting all ties between the two nations would be a mistake," Oliker wrote, because "the country remains a way station for illegal and dangerous trafficking in drugs, weapons and fighters. This has made the Uzbek government a valuable partner in combating those problems." True, the weapons and the insurgents who carry them drew much of their strength from Karimov's campaign of anti-Muslim repression. But let's not forget the United States' primary policy motivation: Uzbekistan has some of the world's largest reserves of natural gas.

So while U.S.-Uzbek relations have cooled, they remain solid. No ambassadors have been recalled. American subsidies remain at pre-Andijon levels. Uzbek soldiers fight and die under the American flag in occupied Iraq. In the end, despite

Uzbek schoolchildren in Samarkand. One shows off his "Tom and Jerry" backpack.

PHOTO COURTESY OF DEPARTMENT OF DEFENSE

A U.S. Marine Corps FA-18D Hornet taxies by French Mirage fighters on arrival at Manas Airport, Kyrgyzstan.

it all, Islam Karimov knows that the U.S. government will keep propping up his regime. After him, after all, comes chaos. "Internal developments in Uzbekistan are really worrisome," points out Royal Institute of International Affairs analyst Yury Federov. "The ruling regime keeps itself in power through repression, and many people in Uzbekistan believe that repression in the final end cannot save the current regime from the crash, which may lead, in turn, to a general destabilization of the situation in the country and in the neighboring region."

It's the same insane mindset that led Jimmy Carter to disaster in Iran. We're propping up a dictator because he's easier to deal with than the presumed religious nuts at whom his oppression is directed. Everyone knows that, in the not-so-long run, Karimov's regime is as doomed as the Shah's. An Islamic regime, or civil war followed by one or several Islamic regimes, is almost certainly inevitable. When the Hizb-ut-Tahrir or its equivalent rises to power in Uzbekistan, the new Islamic government will seek revenge on the U.S. for its years of pro-Karimov suckuppery. It will align itself with Russia or China. It may build training camps for anti-Western jihadis. The U.S. it putting its chips on the evil past while passing up a chance to invest in a dubious but inevitable future.

Such is the case throughout Central Asia.

When Tajikistan's state committee on religious affairs proposed legislation that would ban worship by members of unregistered religious communities, the United States government didn't issue a word of protest. Religious freedom in Iran, on the other hand, was the frequent subject of State Department broadsides.

On August 3, 2005, George W. Bush issued an open letter to Kazakh president Nursultan Nazarbayev asking him to guarantee that the upcoming presidential elections would be clean. "The latest events in the region have stressed the importance of a balanced economic growth, responsible governance and democratic development," Bush's letter said. "I urge you to make sure that economic reforms are backed up with bold democratic reforms." Four months later Nazarbayev won a Saddam-style reelection that international observers found to have been rife with fraud and intimidation. He claimed a Soviet-style ninety-one percent of the vote.

Before the balloting Kazakh government goons repeatedly beat and threatened to kill Svetlana Rychkova, editor of the key opposition newspaper *Assandi Times*. And after the "returns" came in, the dictator received news that gave him even more cause for joy: one of his most outspoken political opponents had been conveniently murdered. The bodies of former minister Altynbek Sarsenbaev and four other men, reported Radio Free Europe, "were discovered on a desolate stretch of road outside Almaty on February 13, [2006], their bodies riddled with bullets and their hands bound behind their backs." The National Security Committee (the successor agency to the KGB) pinned the blame on Erzhan Utembaev, a former deputy prime minister then serving as head of administration of the Kazakh Senate, but political opponents and some *militsia* sources say Nazarbayev personally paid sixty thousand dollars to have him silenced.

It wasn't the first time that one of Nazarbayev's enemies fell victim to an accident. Weeks before the 2005 elections Zamanbek Nurkadilov, another former Nazarbayev ally and minister who joined the opposition For a Fair Kazakhstan

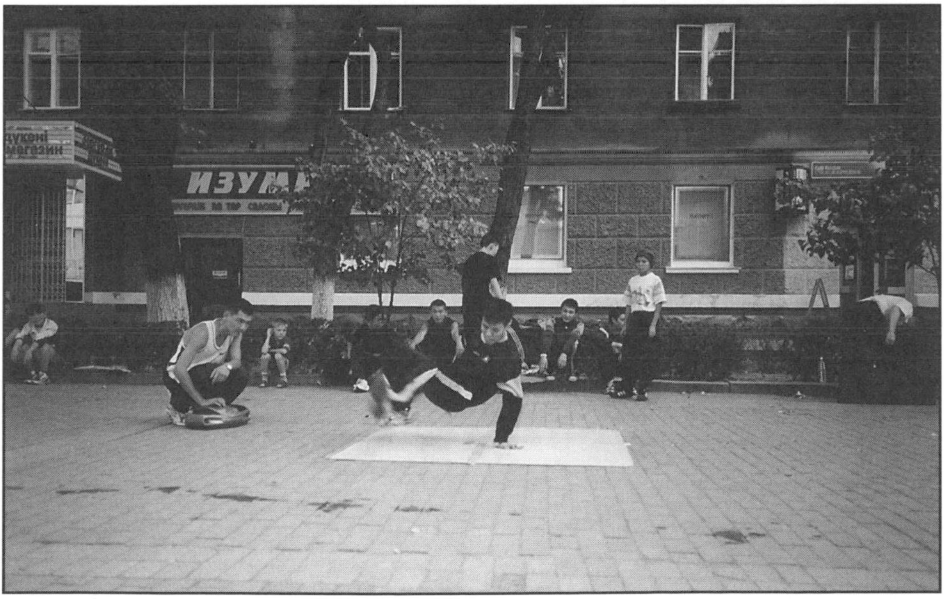
ИЗУМ

Kazakh kids breakdance on Zhibek Zholy Street in Almaty. Western influences—and companies—are everywhere in Central Asia.

movement, was found in dead at his house in Almaty, a pistol lying at his side. Although he had been shot three times—twice in the chest and once in the head—the authorities ruled Nurkadilov's death a "suicide." Oddly, Bush apparently forgot to follow up on his clean-elections letter. "The United States views Kazakhstan as a strategic partner in Central Asia," Bush gushed as Nazarbayev's opponents dropped like flies. "The stability and prosperity that your country enjoys stand as a model for other countries in the region." The two leaders planned reciprocal state visits, a courtesy later denied the president of China, for late 2006.

Turkmenistan continues to enjoy warm relations with Washington despite Saparmurat Niyazov's escalating campaign of repression. In March 2006, for instance, a Turkmen security court sentenced two correspondents for Radio Free Europe to fifteen days in prison for "hooliganism."

PHOTO COURTESY OF DEPARTMENT OF DEFENSE

Turkmen military officers in Ashkhabat.

Meret Khommadov, one of the RFE journalists, said the two fifty-four-year-old men were forced to sign a confession in order to obtain their release. "We were waiting for two hours at the police station," he recalled. "Then we were taken to the Hakimlik [the Mary provincial governor's office]. There were a lot of [village elders] there who talked to us. They were shouting, calling us traitors. They were very aggressive toward us. They promised to evict us from the village and not let us live there...We were kept in the [southern] town of Mary, in a solitary confinement cell. There are no conveniences there, only a metal bed without any mattress or sheets. There are cockroaches, lice. You have to stay together with people suffering from tuberculosis and drug abusers. There was no food except one piece of bread and at noon some kind of cereal we ate without any spoon."

After they were released, Turkmen *militsia* "told us not to speak out against government policies, saying if we did not follow what they said they would 'smash us' and they wouldn't stop with this and continue dealing with our family members and children in the same way."

U.S. officials had no comment on the incident.

Such hypocrisy has long been part and parcel of United States foreign policy. A nation's government can get away with virtually any abuse of basic human rights so long as it cooperates with American economic, political and military objectives. The instant that the ruler of a client state acts independently, however, out come angry State Department press releases and growling chatter about regime change splashed

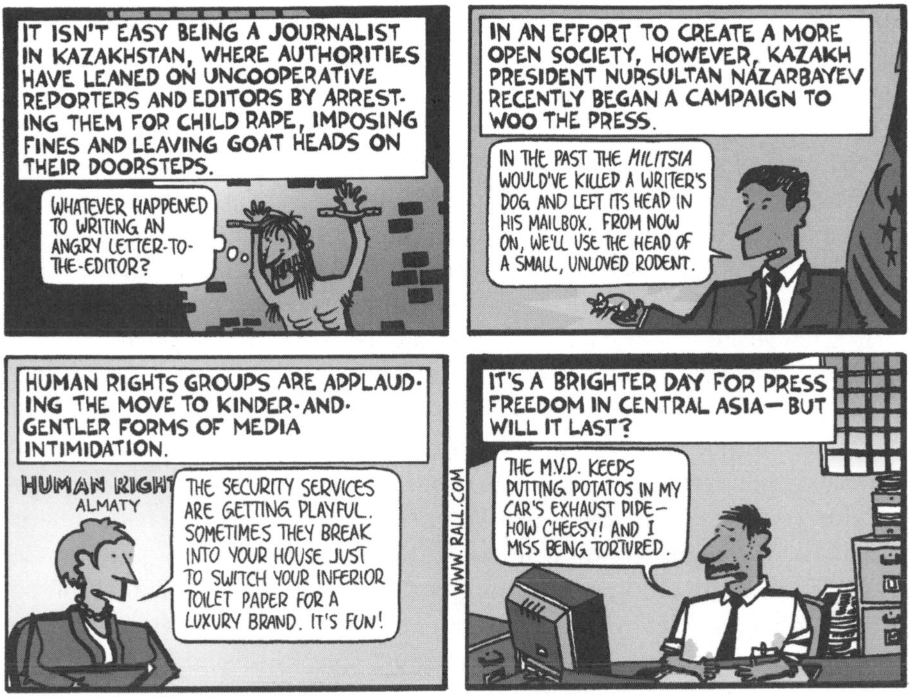
IT ISN'T EASY BEING A JOURNALIST IN KAZAKHSTAN, WHERE AUTHORITIES HAVE LEANED ON UNCOOPERATIVE REPORTERS AND EDITORS BY ARRESTING THEM FOR CHILD RAPE, IMPOSING FINES AND LEAVING GOAT HEADS ON THEIR DOORSTEPS.
WHATEVER HAPPENED TO WRITING AN ANGRY LETTER-TO-THE-EDITOR?
IN AN EFFORT TO CREATE A MORE OPEN SOCIETY, HOWEVER, KAZAKH PRESIDENT NURSULTAN NÁZARBAYEV RECENTLY BEGAN A CAMPAIGN TO WOO THE PRESS.
IN THE PAST THE MILITSIA WOULD'VE KILLED A WRITER'S DOG AND LEFT ITS HEAD IN HIS MAILBOX. FROM NOW ON, WE'LL USE THE HEAD OF A SMALL, UNLOVED RODENT.
HUMAN RIGHTS GROUPS ARE APPLAUDING THE MOVE TO KINDER-AND-GENTLER FORMS OF MEDIA INTIMIDATION.
HUMAN RIGH
ALMATY
THE SECURITY SERVICES ARE GETTING PLAYFUL. SOMETIMES THEY BREAK INTO YOUR HOUSE JUST TO SWITCH YOUR INFERIOR TOILET PAPER FOR A LUXURY BRAND. IT'S FUN!
WWW.RALL.COM
IT'S A BRIGHTER DAY FOR PRESS FREEDOM IN CENTRAL ASIA—BUT WILL IT LAST?
THE M.V.D. KEEPS PUTTING POTATOS IN MY CAR'S EXHAUST PIPE—HOW CHEESY! AND I MISS BEING TORTURED.

across the opinion pages of the *New York Times* and *Washington Post*.

The Clinton and Bush Administrations have chosen to overlook human rights abuses in the Central Asian republics because of their obvious geopolitical importance. But these nations' regimes are fragile, and the United States is setting itself up for one hell of a fall.

Kazakhstan: America's Big Opportunity, Slipping Away

The most important reason for the United States to remain engaged in Central Asia is Kazakhstan. (And the most important reason for the United States to remain engaged in Kazakhstan is oil.) Though Nazarbayev is disliked by a majority of Kazakhs his regime is stable by regional standards, improving the odds that an alliance with him will eventually pay off. Although he has not yet implemented meaningful political reform, Nazarbayev's willingness to pay lip service to economic and political liberalization is unique in the region. William Veale, executive director of the U.S.-Kazakh Business Association, believes that "Kazakhstan clearly wants to diversify its economy beyond the energy sector." Western investment bankers are bullish on Kazakhstan. They project that the nation's gross domestic product will double every seven years as more of its oil hits the market.

Since independence the U.S. has cultivated Kazakhstan because of its vast oil and gas resources. In recent years, however, as Mevlut Katik wrote for EurasiaNet, "the strategy outlined by President Nursultan Nazarbayev and other officials in effect suggests that Russia, and to a lesser degree China, are now viewed in Astana as the main facilitators of growth—not the United States. Thus, it would appear at present that the more Kazakhstan implements its development agenda, the less geopolitical and economic influence Washington stands to enjoy in Central Asia."

Like Niyazov and Karimov, Nazarbayev holds the United States responsible for the 2005 revolution in Kyrgyzstan. He also feels betrayed by the American prosecution of a lobbyist ensnared by "Kazakhgate," a kick-back scandal in which U.S. energy companies are accused of bribing Nazarbayev and other Kazakh officials for drilling rights. "Accordingly, [Kazakhstan] now seems to be counting on Russian and China, two countries that have traditionally stressed political stability over individual rights, to help act as guarantors of stable economic development," writes Katik.

As U.S. influence ebbs, so does its time-honored strategy of divide and conquer. As a result, Uzbekistan and Kazakhstan are smoothing over their long-standing rifts over border disputes, environmental issues such as the Aral Sea clean-up and pipeline politics. "Both [Nazarbayev and Karimov] fight for the leadership of the Central Asian region," said Kamoliddin Rabbimov, a Tashkent-based political analyst. "Each of them sees himself and his state as a hegemonic power in Central Asia. Kazakhstan has gained an upper hand in political, social and economic competition so far. This undoubtedly irritates President Islam Karimov a great deal." They closed their 2006 Tashkent summit meeting by announcing closer military and political cooperation. Nazarbayev went so far as to defend Karimov's role in the Andijon massacre, saying that he had "defended the peace...not only of Uzbeks, but also Kazakhs, Kyrgyz and Tajiks" by taking on "trained extremist groups."

Immediate Danger: Uzbekistan and Kyrgyzstan

Less than a year after its 2005 Tulip Revolution was described by the Western media as a triumph of pro-democracy "people power" on par with the Czech Spring, Kyrgyzstan was on the brink of being formally declared a "failed state"—a designation reserved for such totally disintegrated societies as Afghanistan during the early 1990s. It has been a shocking fall for the Kyrgyz, who under the presidency of Askar Akayev enjoyed a reputation as a peaceful and relatively transparent, if poor, country with Central Asia's only functioning democracy and free press. By December 2005 the International Crisis Group had found "a real risk that the central government will lose control of institutions and territory, and the country will drift into irreversible criminality and permanent low-level violence." Its report was titled "Kyrgyzstan: A Faltering State."

"If Kyrgyzstan is not to become a failed state whose fate reinforces the views of its neighbors that the path to stability lies not in democracy but in dictatorship," the ICG found, "the U.S., European Union and other donors need to give the shaky government more political and financial backing." Few expect this advice to be heeded.

Kyrgyzstan's current interim government, the result of its predecessor's unwill-

PHOTO COURTESY OF DEPARTMENT OF DEFENSE

U.S. Secretary of Defense Donald Rumsfeld arrives at Karshi-Khanabad (K-2) Airbase while visiting troops in December 2001. In July 2005 Uzbekistan informed the U.S. that it would be evicted from the Soviet-era facility.

ingness to maintain control through violence, faces the classic paradox of the revolutionary: The men who helped bring it to power are among its greatest threat.

One such figure is Nurlan Motuyev, an early ally of interim prime minister Felix Kulov. Motuyev seized personal control of the Kara Keche strip mines near Naryn, in the Tian Shan mountains in southern Kyrgyzstan, and aligned himself with the Kyrgyz branch of the Russian mafia. Called "a combination of Hitler, Zhirinovskii, and Mussolini" by local officials, he not only refuses to pay taxes on the coal but has effectively transformed himself into a warlord whose fiefdom is no longer subject to central government control. Motuyev, who likes to be photographed brandishing a shotgun, now calls himself the leader of the People's Patriotic Movement of Kyrgyzstan. "I have enough people, guns and hand grenades to defend myself in case Felix Kulov wants to take the mine by force," Motuyev bragged.

The Kyrgyz government has fallen into such extreme fiscal and political dysfunction that its national prison system has fallen under direct control of the mafia. "Machine guns and knives, mobile phones, and computers with Internet connection, large amounts of money in U.S. dollars and euros as well as narcotics—all are in the possession of a *vor v zakone*, or a criminal kingpin, in Kyrgyz jails," Gulnoza Saidazimova reported for EurasiaNet after prison uprisings during the fall of 2005.

Aziz Batukaev, serving time in Moldovanovka Prison No. 31, had an entire floor of the prison to himself, including a sixteen-floor suite where he kept three horses and fifteen goats, as well as his wife, daughter and a bodyguard. Meanwhile, other inmates died of disease and malnutrition. Topchubek Turgunaliev, a political dissident held at the prison, said: "Conditions are extremely harsh, firstly, because of lack of food. What they get is [called] *balanda*, which is not only not nutritious, but also kills people. In some prisons, inmates have no food at all or get it once a week. The other problem is that prisons are overcrowded. So there is simply no air. I experienced that myself. In the cells of five-to-six people, we were seventeen to eighteen inmates."

Colorful mafia kingpin Ryspek Akmatbayev, whose brother was rubbed out during a prison riot, marked the complete collapse of civil society by muscling his way into the race for parliament in April 2006. Edil Baisalov, head of the Coalition for Democracy and Civil Society, a Kyrgyz non-governmental organization, said that allowing known criminals to hold public office proved that "the legitimization of gangsterism" had arrived in Kyrgyzstan. "Incoherent steps on the part of the authorities has led people to assume that the country's leadership has become dependent on criminals," said political analyst Nur Omarov.

In a replay of Russia during the early 1990s, local strongmen are stealing public companies, *biznezmen* are forming gangs to protect themselves and assassinate their rivals and small-time entrepreneurs are being squeezed out of business. But, as bad as things became, Russia managed to keep the mob out of politics and its territory remained contiguous. Kyrgyzstan's misery has been amplified not only by mafia corruption but via the direct inclusion of mobsters in the government. If regional warlords like Motuyev continue to resist the central government in Bish-

PHOTO COURTESY OF DEPARTMENT OF DEFENSE

Secretary of State Condoleezza Rice speaks to U.S. airmen at Manas Airbase in 2005. Rice stopped at the base during a tour of Central Asian nations.

CIA Shenanigans in
Soviet Central Asia

Steve Coll's 2004 book *Ghost Wars* reviewed the history of covert actions carried out by American intelligence agencies in Central and South Asia in the years before September 11, 2001. Among its revelations is the stunner that the United States launched direct armed incursions into the Soviet Union, risking thermonuclear war at the peak of Cold War tensions.

Coll quotes Robert Gates, then CIA director William Casey's assistant and later a CIA director himself, as confirming that U.S.-backed Afghan *mujahedeen* "began cross-border operations into the Soviet Union itself" during the spring of 1985. These attacks, he says, were carried out "with Casey's encouragement."

Mohammed Yousaf, brigadier for the Pakistani ISI intelligence service at the time, recalls that "Casey said that there was a large Muslim population across the Amu Darya that could be stirred to action and could 'do a lot of damage to the Soviet Union.'" Casey, Yousaf claims, said: "We should take the [CIA translations of Korans in the Uzbek language] and try to raise the local population against them if possible."

In April 1987, the Iran-Contra scandal was raging in Washington. But the CIA was up to its old fun and games. "As the snows melted," Coll writes, "three ISI-equipped teams secretly crossed the Amu Darya into Soviet Central Asia. The first team launched a rocket strike against an airfield near Termiz in Uzbekistan. The second, a band of about twenty rebels equipped with rocket-propelled grenades and antitank mines, had been instructed by ISI to set up violent ambushes along a border road. They destroyed several Soviet vehicles. A third team hit a factory site more than ten miles inside the Soviet Union with a barrage of about thirty 107-millimeter high-explosive and incendiary rockets. The attacks took place at a time when the CIA was circulating satellite photographs in Washington showing riots on the streets of Alma-Ata [now Almaty], a Soviet Central Asian capital."

Finally, "The Soviets were fed up with the attacks on their own soil. As they counted their dead in Central Asia that April, they dispatched messengers with stark warnings to Istanbul and Washington. They threatened 'the security and integrity of Pakistan,' a euphemism for an invasion...The attacks ended."

Several of the current leaders of Central Asia were in power at the time: all held important positions in their respective Soviet republics. Their memory of the United States' ultimately successful campaign to bring about the collapse of the Soviet system cannot have faded much.

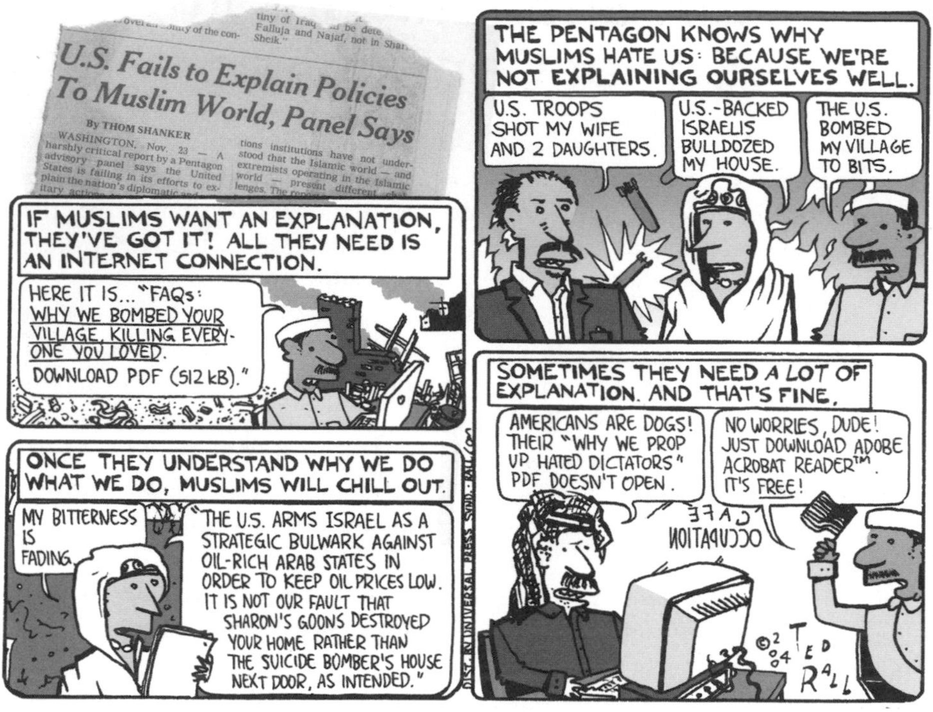
U.S. Fails to Explain Policies To Muslim World, Panel Says
By THOM SHANKER
THE PENTAGON KNOWS WHY MUSLIMS HATE US: BECAUSE WE'RE NOT EXPLAINING OURSELVES WELL.
U.S. TROOPS SHOT MY WIFE AND 2 DAUGHTERS.
U.S.-BACKED ISRAELIS BULLDOZED MY HOUSE.
THE U.S. BOMBED MY VILLAGE TO BITS.
IF MUSLIMS WANT AN EXPLANATION, THEY'VE GOT IT! ALL THEY NEED IS AN INTERNET CONNECTION.
HERE IT IS... "FAQs: WHY WE BOMBED YOUR VILLAGE, KILLING EVERYONE YOU LOVED. DOWNLOAD PDF (512 kB)."
SOMETIMES THEY NEED A LOT OF EXPLANATION. AND THAT'S FINE.
AMERICANS ARE DOGS! THEIR "WHY WE PROP UP HATED DICTATORS" PDF DOESN'T OPEN.
NO WORRIES, DUDE! JUST DOWNLOAD ADOBE ACROBAT READER™. IT'S FREE!
ONCE THEY UNDERSTAND WHY WE DO WHAT WE DO, MUSLIMS WILL CHILL OUT.
MY BITTERNESS IS FADING.
"THE U.S. ARMS ISRAEL AS A STRATEGIC BULWARK AGAINST OIL-RICH ARAB STATES IN ORDER TO KEEP OIL PRICES LOW. IT IS NOT OUR FAULT THAT SHARON'S GOONS DESTROYED YOUR HOME RATHER THAN THE SUICIDE BOMBER'S HOUSE NEXT DOOR, AS INTENDED."
DIST. BY UNIVERSAL PRESS SYND.
©2004 TED RALL

kek, the republic could become a fractured wasteland like Somalia. Radical guerilla groups such as the Islamic Movement of Turkestan have already seized villages in Kyrgyzstan but could increase their presence by building permanent bases in the southern Ferghana Valley, which may in turn become staging areas for invasions of other Central Asian states, most likely Uzbekistan.

Former European Union external affairs commissioner Chris Patten believes that the government of Islam Karimov, widely considered "the epicenter of instability" in Central Asia, is destined to topple. Civil war in this ethnically and culturally fractured state would then be virtually inevitable. The only thing the world can do to prepare is to batten down the hatches. "Uzbek neighbors Kyrgyzstan, Tajikistan, and Kazakhstan," Patten counsels, "should get foreign assistance to strengthen their borders and, at the same time, to prepare in advance for possible refugee flows from Uzbekistan."

Everyone agrees that Uzbekistan has a date with disaster. The Karimov dictatorship, perceiving itself as under siege since the Tashkent bombings, has jailed and tortured thousands of Muslims accused of affiliation with anti-government Islamist groups. Radical organizations such as Hizb-ut-Tahrir, meanwhile, are gathering thousands of new recruits among secular and moderate Uzbeks disgusted by the crackdown. "Not only is the number of those who join the group growing, so is the number of those who support its ideas," an Uzbek woman whose two sons are serving jail terms for membership in HUT says. "Why? Because people want a just system. They want to live in a just and fair society with good governance. Nowadays, there is no justice. Corruption and bribery are everywhere. Unemployment is the people's biggest problem. That's why they read the word of God. Since the seventh century, when Prophet Muhammad, may peace be upon him, lived, there was a caliphate for fourteen centuries. It was a just system. I also believe that if people learn these things, they will become more just."

As a previously minor threat grows, so does official repression. Yevgeny Zhovtis, head of Kazakhstan's International Bureau for Human Rights, predicts that "Uzbekistan is rapidly moving toward a Turkmen-type of dictatorship, not necessarily in terms of a personality cult, but in terms of control and of the violation of political and civil rights." Karimov has even resorted to one of the most despised tactics of official repression used by the Soviet Union: committing political dissidents to insane asylums. Human rights activist Yelena Urlaeva has been imprisoned, tortured, and injected with psychotropic drugs in mental hospitals three times.

Jahongir Mamatov, chairman of the dissident Congress of Democratic Uzbekistan, said that Uzbek officials deliberately provoke large gatherings of government opponents. "Terrible repressions start after every big event. [President] Islam Karimov arranges [a demonstration or uprising] in order to suppress growing opposition. He then eliminates the society's leading opposition forces. It's his policy."

As Uzbekistan goes, so does Central Asia. Not only does the vast nation have immense reserves of natural gas, it borders all of the other Central Asian republics as well as Afghanistan. It also controls Central Asia's most modern infrastructure of international air links, military facilities and hardware. Were areas dominated by Tajiks to rise up in open rebellion, a rump Uzbek Tajikistan might declare autonomy and demand unification with Tajikistan. The Islamic Movement of Turkestan could seize power in Tashkent and establish a base for its longed-for caliphate. Pipelines and refineries could be bombed or held hostage. The United States and its Western allies, facing skyrocketing fuel prices, might be tempted to launch a full-scale invasion that would make Iraq look like a police action by comparison.

Hedging Our Bets

No one trusts the United States.

HUT, IMT, the Uyghur ETIM and other groups that seek to overthrow Central Asia's autocratic rulers have seen themselves officially designated as terrorist organizations and their members deported to the Guantánamo Bay concentration camp for torture and indefinite imprisonment. A 2002 Treasury Department announcement cites "terrorists and terrorist supporters associated with Osama bin Laden and his al Qaeda network the Eastern Turkistan [sic] Islamic Movement (ETIM)" and pledges "greater cooperation in Central Asia against common terrorist threats and the instability and horror that they sow." In this clash of ideological visions, the United States has made clear which side it's on—and it's not that of the Muslims.

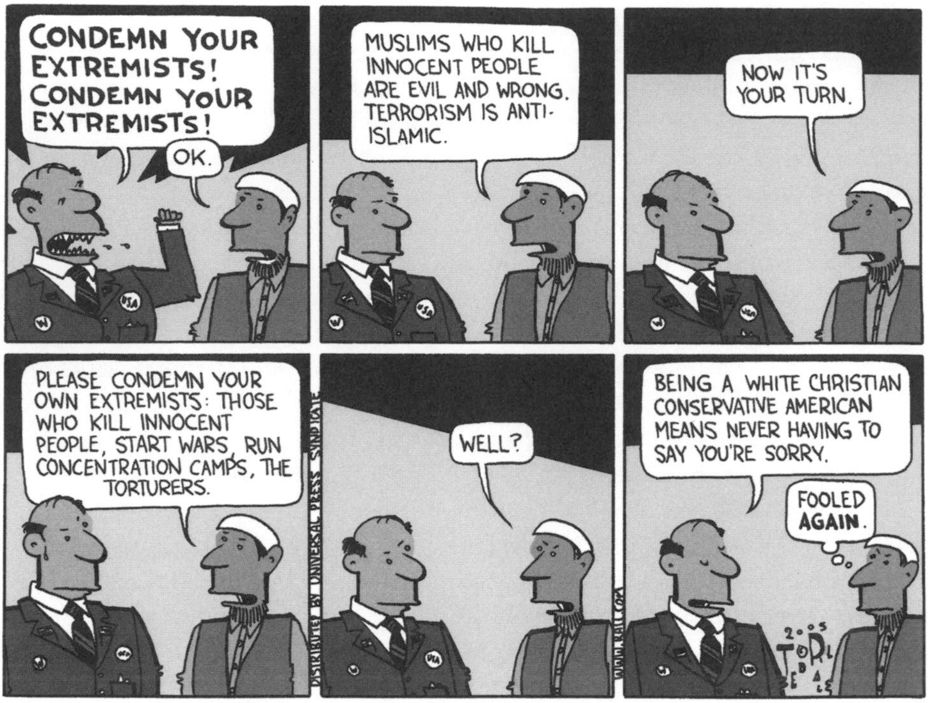
CONDEMN YOUR EXTREMISTS! CONDEMN YOUR EXTREMISTS!
OK.
MUSLIMS WHO KILL INNOCENT PEOPLE ARE EVIL AND WRONG. TERRORISM IS ANTI-ISLAMIC.
NOW IT'S YOUR TURN.
PLEASE CONDEMN YOUR OWN EXTREMISTS: THOSE WHO KILL INNOCENT PEOPLE, START WARS, RUN CONCENTRATION CAMPS, THE TORTURERS.
WELL?
BEING A WHITE CHRISTIAN CONSERVATIVE AMERICAN MEANS NEVER HAVING TO SAY YOU'RE SORRY.
FOOLED AGAIN.
DISTRIBUTED BY UNIVERSAL PRESS SYNDICATE

Nevertheless, the secular dictators have good cause to doubt American intentions. The U.S. and its right-wing proxies funnel money and logistical support to such Central Asian-based non-governmental organizations as Freedom House, a spin-off of the Central Intelligence Agency. The right-wing Freedom House financed an opposition press that helped bring down the relatively liberal regime of Askar Akayev. Uzbekistan's Karimov, taking no chances, then kicked FH out of Tashkent. On the other side of the ideological divide progressive-minded NGOs like the Open Society Institute, funded by George Soros, encourage the development of a free press and democratization. (OSI got its walking papers a few weeks before FH.) Some of Central Asia's U.S. embassies further muddy the waters by meeting with anti-government activists and conducting programs like the one I attended in Ashkhabat in 2000 in order to educate Turkmen college students about independent journalism. That message is clear as well. The United States supports you for now—but we're hedging our bets in case things change. Attempting to play Central Asia's autocrats both ways—mostly propping them up even while we undermine them using low-impact means—is pushing them into the arms of the Russians and Chinese.

U.S. policy might stand some chance at long-term success if there were viable moderate opposition groups to support. After all, members of Uzbekistan's Birlik (Unity) and Erk (Freedom) parties haven't been deported to Gitmo or declared to be terrorists; members of the Party of Democratic Development of Turkmenistan have little direct reason to dislike the United States. The problem for U.S. practitioners of *realpolitik* is that neither the Turkmen nor Uzbek governments tolerate any organized political party; indeed, none are officially registered. Because they are unable to publish newspapers or campaign in public, their membership rolls are tiny. Because they are certain to be arrested and possibly tortured or even murdered, outspoken sympathizers usually choose to live underground or in exile overseas. "Those opposition figures who remained in Turkmenistan are either in prison or under house arrest," Radio Free Europe's Bruce Pannier reports. In 2005 the leaders of Birlik, Erk, Ozod Dehkonlar (Free Peasants), and the human rights group Ezgulik met at a summit near Washington in an attempt to unify the Uzbek opposition. Exiled Erk leader Mohammad Solih reported that the factions had been unable to resolve their differences. The total turnout: between ten and twelve people.

Tajikistan is the only Central Asian republic with an opposition party permitted to hold seats in parliament.

The Choice: Total Engagement or Total Withdrawal

While it's tempting to cherry-pick the Stans, it is impossible for the U.S. to dominate Kazakhstan without similarly controlling Uzbekistan to the west or Kyrgyzstan to the south. Central Asia's republics are intertwined by history, tribal ethnicity, economics and transportation infrastructure. The last two are ignored at our peril, for the truth of the Silk Road is that it will always be a place through which goods manufactured elsewhere pass. Commerce and trade are more than merely essential in a place that produces nothing but fossil fuels. They are all that there is. If a superpower is to control Central Asia—whether America, Russia or China—it must own all of it or nothing at all.

A neocolonialist approach would be extremely expensive, both in terms of money and manpower as well as in harm to the dominant power's international prestige. Secondary mini-superpowers such as the member states of the European Union would probably retaliate, justifiably seeing such a policy as a ploy to corner the oil market. It is therefore likely that the New Great Game will continue, with the three big powers and possibly India and a few others, vying for access to the Stans.

Of course, it's possible to imagine a total control scenario: Uzbekistan or Turkmenistan disintegrates into ethnic violence and the threat rises of an Islamist regime coming to power in Tashkent or Ashkhabat. The United States would be tempted to lead a "peacekeeping" operation or police action to restore order and the continued delivery of oil to its refineries in the Mediterranean Sea and Indian Ocean. But it's virtually inconceivable that it would ever conquer the Stans as completely as Russia did during the late 1800s and early 1900s. Alternatively it's possible to imagine an American presence that makes a sincere effort to ensure that it was perceived in a positive light. Funding a solution to the Lake Sarez threat, for example, would earn the United States a (new) reputation for caring about ordi-

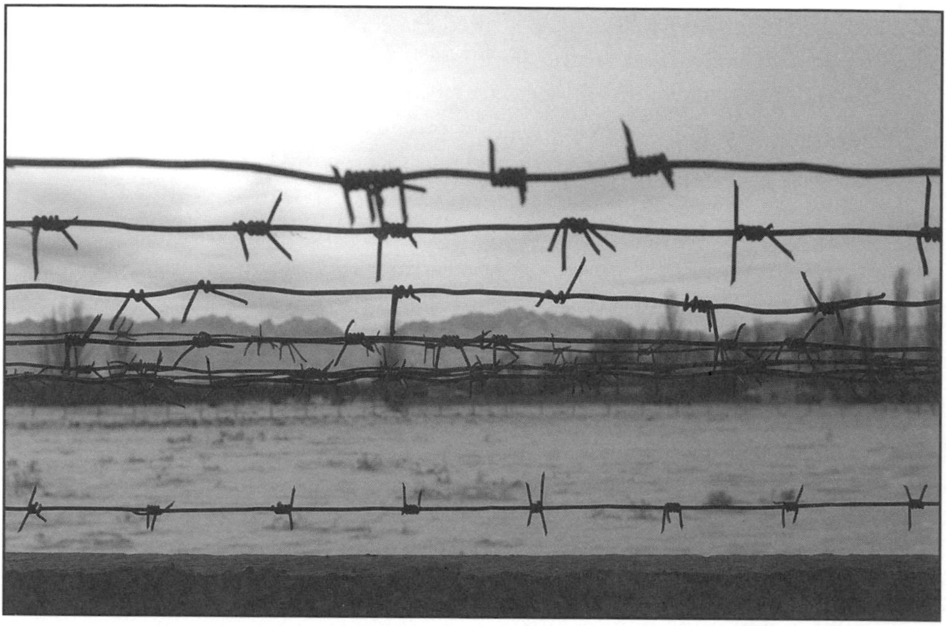
PHOTO COURTESY OF DEPARTMENT OF DEFENSE

A mountain range near Manas International Airport seen through a perimeter fence.

nary people. Alternatively it could leave the people of Central Asia to determine their own destinies, even if that meant overthrowing the men who have ruled them since the Soviet period.

Blissful Ignorance

By far the most likely, and most wrongheaded, level of American involvement would be the mild escalation, ad hoc priorities and cobbled-together responses to breaking events that characterize the current U.S. approach. As things stand, the United States is sufficiently attached to its pet dictators to breed resentment among their long-suffering subjects but not so fully vested in them that the U.S. is positioned to induce them to reject advances by China and Russia. The U.S. is interested in Kazakh oil and Uzbek gas but not in Kyrgyzstan because it has neither. What it doesn't fully understand is that an unstable Kyrgyzstan threatens both.

What it doesn't fully understand: it's a phrase that perfectly captures the American relationship with Central Asia. Robert Baer, a retired CIA field officer who wrote about his twenty-one years at The Company in *See No Evil*, recalls his posting to Tajikistan during the early 1990s. Thousands of Afghan refugees were pouring over the border into Tajikistan, but the CIA couldn't debrief a single one of them because it didn't employ an employee who spoke Dari or Pashto. When Baer was transferred out of Dushanbe in 1992, the Tajik desk lost its only speaker of the Tajik language—and human intelligence gathering there came to a halt.

The September 11th attacks were supposed to change all that. The United States invaded Afghanistan—a nation where Turkmen, Uzbek, Kyrgyz, Kazakh, Tajik and Uyghur are spoken in significant numbers—and is fighting a fierce counterinsurgency against troops of the deposed Taliban government. But when the Modern Language Association conducted a survey of which classes students were taking on American college campuses three years after 9/11, they found that the number studying Central Asian languages was statistically insignificant. Out of 1.4 million students studying a foreign language, a miniscule twenty-three were studying Uzbek, the language spoken by the most populous of the Central Asian states. (The number studying Turkmen, Kyrgyz, Kazakh and Uyghur totaled zero.)

If our government were serious about getting to know Central Asia it wouldn't have to wait for college students to become fluent in their languages. After all, New York City is home to thousands of Uzbeks. One of them cuts my hair on the Upper West Side of Manhattan; I'm sure he'd love a raise, not to mention health benefits.

Media coverage of Central Asia, briefly in the spotlight after 2001, has reverted to thin-to-nonexistent levels. To most Americans, Kazakhstan is pronounced "Kazakastan" and Turkmenistan gets truncated to "Turkistan," which the U.S. government routinely misspells while they call Uzbeks "Uzbekis" and Afghans "Afghanis" (*afghanis* are the currency, not the people). Kyrgyzstan is the I'd-like-buy-a-vowel Stan, not a real country whose millions of citizens have been profoundly impacted by, and are now deeply resentful of, American foreign policy.

It is perfectly fine for the American public and its government not to take any interest in Central Asia and its problems, tribes, languages and politics—but only if they consciously decide to disengage from the region. As long as the U.S. continues to promote some regimes while toppling others, however, it is not entitled to enjoy the sublime luxury of ignorance. Owning an empire entails the responsibility of basic maintenance. And a major part of maintenance is awareness. For we are creating new enemies. They are learning to hate us and eventually will seek revenge against us later—perhaps not much later—in this century. We are neglecting problems that will worsen as a result—and cause us terrible harm. Worst of all, we are pretending that the two hundred billion barrels of oil estimated to lie beneath Central Asia are of greater importance than the eighty million people who live in its cities, villages, deserts, steppes and mountains.

Ryan Eddings, one of those twenty-three American college students in 2004, explained why he chose to study Uzbek. "We're all convinced that Central Asia is going to be the next hot spot, the governments are so repressive there," he said. "It might be stable now, but it doesn't mean they're going to be stable in five to ten years."

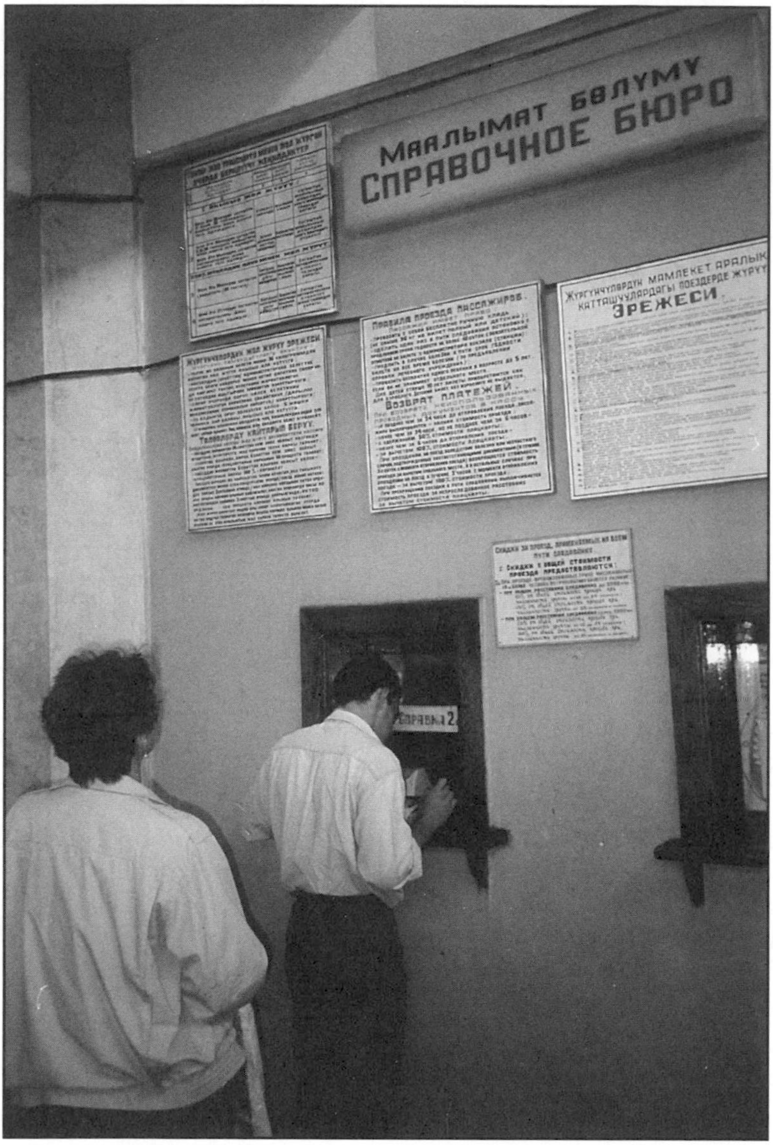
Маалымат бөлүмү
СПРАВОЧНОЕ БЮРО
Правила проезда пассажиров
Возврат платежей
ЭРЕЖЕСИ

Purchasing train tickets in Central Asia is easy! Simply follow the instructions on the signs.

If You Go

If your visa ends June 26, don't show up at the airport on June 27. You will be arrested, robbed and deported ... many traveler Web sites and guidebooks still tell cheapskates that they can save a few hundred bucks by talking their way past the border guards. People who follow this advice will be arrested, robbed and deported.

– Ted Rall

Think you've got what it takes to fend off voracious *militsia*, IMU guerillas and intestinal parasites? Shifting political and military situations can change the best advice on how to get into the Central Asian republics in a heartbeat, but here's the scoop as of the date of publication of this volume:

First and foremost, *you must have a valid visa* for each country you wish to visit. Central Asia's post-Soviet bureaucracy works the same way as the classic test of how well you follow instructions—you know, the one that begins, "do not answer any question before you have first read the entire test." The *militsia* try to shake down everyone, but as you will soon discover, it's a psychological game best played against those whose documents are in less than perfect order. Ninety-nine times out of a hundred, valid papers will prompt a corrupt cop to hand back your passport with a dull grumble. Don't think you can avoid contact with the authorities in this land of police states. And don't show up at the border hoping for the best. Casual backpacker types accustomed to talking their way into an airport-issued entry visa in other countries find that three things happen when they try the same shit in, say, Uzbekistan. First, they are arrested. Second, the *militsia* rob them. (Strip searches, virtually unheard of elsewhere, are the norm in this situation.) Third, they are deported.

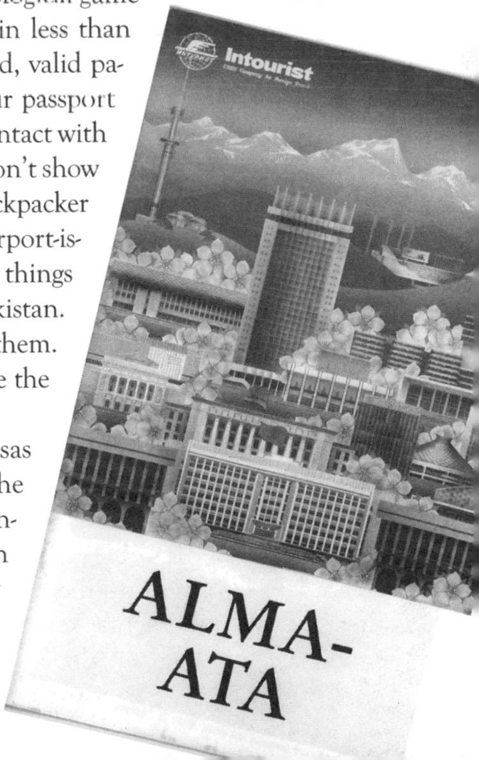
Intourist
ALMA-
ATA

Do not overstay your visa. Although exit visas have been officially eliminated throughout the Commonwealth of Independent States, your entrance visa becomes your de facto exit visa upon departure. If your visa ends June 26, don't show up at the airport on June 27. You will be arrested, robbed and deported. Some of the Stans allow you to extend your visa for a modest fee but it usually takes several days and can only be done at the main office of the Ministry of Foreign Affairs, in each nation's capital. If you overstay in the hinterlands, you'll be picked up by the *militsia* before you can get back to the capital, so don't.

Get the right kind of visa. Are you planning to fly to Tashkent, take the bus to Almaty and stop in Bishkek on the way back to Tashkent? You need a double-entry visa for Uzbekistan, but only a single-entry for Kazakhstan. That's because, although the Tashkent-Bishkek highway passes through Kazakhstan, you're considered "in transit" between Uzbekistan and the Kyrgyz Republic. Taking a cab instead of a bus? You need the double-entry visa for Kazakhstan too. Ask a local, but if you're not sure what to do get the double-entry visa.

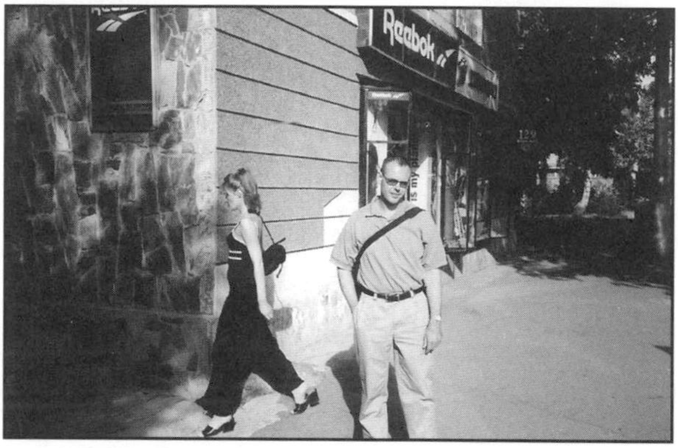
Reebok
Cole seeing the sights in Almaty in 1997. Quick tip: Always apply for visas to Central Asian countries as a tourist.

Get special permissions and city visas in advance. Most Central Asian republics ask which cities you plan to visit during your trip. It's tempting to ignore this question. Don't. Enter every city, town and two-bit burg you're thinking of possibly visiting on your application, and indicate that you want these noted on your visa. City-specific visas are nearly *militsia*-proof because they show you know what you're doing. Visits to militarily sensitive places—the Baikonur Cosmodrome, the Uzbek city of Termiz on the Afghan border, Tajikistan's Badakhshan Autonomous Zone, the Torugart Pass between Kyrgyzstan and China—require "special permissions." Your best bet is to arrange special permissions through a travel agency before traveling or at or the Ministry of Foreign Affairs, if you're in country.

The three-day rule is dead. I was detained by the Turkmen border police while trying to take advantage of a CIS rule that allows travelers to use a valid CIS state visa to pass through any other CIS state so long as they leave within seventy-two hours. The rule was still in effect in 1997. It is now effectively dead, but many traveler Web sites and guidebooks still tell cheapskates that they can save a few hundred bucks by talking their way past the border guards. People who follow this outdated advice will be arrested, robbed and deported.

Don't travel on an old passport. Most Central Asian states have a visa rule that is arcane, yet so obvious to their governments that they don't bother to list them on their list of requirements: Your passport must not expire in more than six months from any date of travel. If your passport is less than a year from expiration, get a new one.

Don't freak out if you don't know anyone in Ashkhabat. Many former Soviet republics demand a "letter of invitation." (Turkmenistan, for example, requires a "letter of invitation from the person or company to be visited certified by the State Foreign Citizens Registration Service of Turkmenistan.") The LOI, as it's called, is necessary but anyone can get one through a local travel agency for a modest fee.

Get the easiest visa first. CIS consulates tend to feel more comfortable about letting you in if their neighbors think you're OK. If you're going to Uzbekistan and Kyrgyzstan, for example, apply first for the Kyrgyz visa. Ranked in general order of ease, Kyrgyzstan is looser than Kazakhstan, which is more relaxed than Uzbekistan, which is difficult but not nearly as much of an ordeal as Tajikistan or Turkmenistan, which has become virtually impossible to enter legally. Afghanistan and China are comparative visa sluts, with the caveat that travel to Xinjiang tends to draw more scrutiny than in years past.

Obtain your visas in the West. With the exception of Tajikistan's limited consular representation, it is much simpler and less time-consuming to arrange visas before you leave the United States or other Western country. Local consulates may be closed during national holidays and processing is so slow that you can easily get stuck for days or even weeks at a time.

You're a tourist. Even—especially—if you're a journalist writing a book about Central Asia, apply as a tourist. At land crossings, however, journalists find that press ID cards make malicious *militsia* quake.

You can't always do it alone. Most visa applications are fairly straightforward. As long as you're polite, concise and aren't the author of a treatise bashing the president, your visa will be approved. That said, even repeat travelers to Central Asia use fixers and local travel agents at times. They're especially necessary during periods of political tension. Turkmenistan, for example, is currently not issuing visas to journalists because Turkmenbashi feels slighted by unfavorable coverage in the West. But if anyone can grease the skids, it's Stan Tours or another reputable outfit.

Don't ask how they do it; you already know.

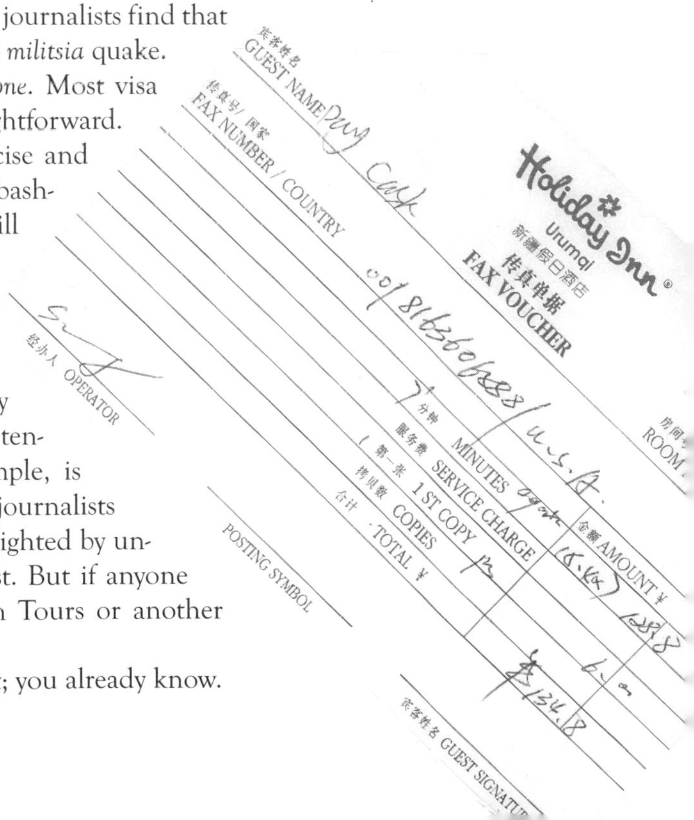
Holiday Inn
Urumqi
新疆假日酒店
传真单据
FAX VOUCHER
宾客姓名 GUEST NAME
传真号/国家 FAX NUMBER / COUNTRY
经办人 OPERATOR
分钟 MINUTES
服务费 SERVICE CHARGE
第一张 1 ST COPY
拷贝数 COPIES
合计 TOTAL ¥
金额 AMOUNT ¥
POSTING SYMBOL
宾客姓名 GUEST SIGNATU

Before you leave for Central Asia

The following relates specifically to citizens of the United States. To obtain a tourist visa you will be required to submit your original passport, an application (sometimes in duplicate), passport photo (ditto), and a fee depending on how much time you give them to process your application, the length of your stay and the number of entries into the given nation. Also include a self-addressed stamped envelope. Turkmenistan, Uzbekistan and Tajikistan require a LOI. Kyrgyzstan and Kazakhstan do not, unless you plan to stay over a month. Afghanistan requests a sponsorship letter from your employer if you're on business.

Embassy of **TURKMENISTAN**
2207 Massachusetts Avenue, NW
Washington DC 20008
Phone: (202) 588-1500
Fax: (202) 588-0697
www.turkmenistanembassy.org

If you live in the South ...
Embassy of **UZBEKISTAN**
1746 Massachusetts Avenue, NW
Washington DC 20036-1903
Phone: (202) 887-5300
Fax: (202) 293-6804
www.uzbekistan.org

... if you don't:
Consulate General of the
Republic of Uzbekistan
801 Second Avenue
20th Floor
New York NY 10017
Phone: (212) 754-7403
Fax: (212) 838-9812
www.uzbekconsulny.org

Embassy of the **KYRGYZ REPUBLIC**
1001 Pennsylvania Avenue, NW
Suite 600
Washington DC 20004
Phone: (202) 338-5141
Fax: (202) 742-6501
www.kyrgyzembassy.org

If you live in the South ...
Embassy of **KAZAKHSTAN**
1401 16th Street, NW
Washington DC 20036
Phone: (202) 232-5488
Fax: (202) 232-5845
www.kazakhembus.com

...if you don't:
Consulate of the Republic of Kazakhstan
866 UN Plaza, Suite 586A
New York NY 10017
Phone: (212) 888-3024
Fax: (212) 888-3025
www.kazconsulny.org

Embassy of the Republic of **TAJIKISTAN**
1005 New Hampshire Avenue
Washington DC 20037
Phone: (202) 223-6090
Fax: (202) 223-6091
www.tjus.org

Embassy of **AFGHANISTAN**
Consular Office
2233 Wisconsin Avenue, NW
Suite 216
Washington DC 20007
Phone: (202) 298-9125
Fax: (202) 483-6488
www.embassyofafghanistan.org

Visitors to **XINJIANG PROVINCE** need a visa from
China. Check www.china-embassy.org/eng for requirements
and to learn which of the People's Republic's six U.S. consulates serves your state.

Selected Bibliography

Coll, Steve, *Ghost Wars: The Secret History of the CIA, Afghanistan, and bin Laden, from the Soviet Invasion to September 10, 2001*. New York: The Penguin Press, 2004.

Curtis, Glenn E., editor, *Kazakstan, Kyrgyzstan, Tajikistan, Turkmenistan, and Uzbekistan: Country Studies*. Headquarters, Department of the Army, 1997.

Fisk, Robert, *The Great War for Civilisation: The Conquest of the Middle East*. New York: Alfred A. Knopf, 2005.

Fletcher, Arnold, *Afghanistan: Highway of Conquest*. Ithaca, New York: Cornell University Press, 1965.

French, Patrick, *Younghusband: The Last Great Imperial Adventurer*. London: Flamingo, 1995.

Frye, Richard N., *The Heritage of Central Asia: From Antiquity to the Turkish Expansion*. Princeton: Markus Wiener Publishers, 1996.

Griffin, Michael, *Reaping the Whirlwind: The Taliban Movement in Afghanistan*. London: Pluto Press, 1996.

Grousset, René, *The Empire of the Steppes: A History of Central Asia*. New Brunswick, New Jersey: Rutgers University Press, 1970.

Hopkirk, Peter, *Foreign Devils on the Silk Road*. Amherst: The University of Massachusetts Press, 1980.

Hopkirk, Poeter, *The Great Game: The Struggle for Empire in Central Asia*. New York: Kodansha International, 1992.

Kaplan, Edward H. & Whisenhut, Donald W., editors, *Opuscula Atlaica: Essays Presented in Honor of Henry Schwartz*. Bellingham, Washington: Western Washington University, Center for East Asian Studies, 1994.

Macrory, Patrick, *Signal Catastrophe: The Retreat from Kabul 1842*. London: The History Book Club, 1963.

Magnus, Ralph H. & Naby, Eden, *Afghanistan: Mullah, Marx, and Mujahid*. Oxford: Westview Press, 2002.

Margolis, Eric S., *War at the Top of the World: The Struggle for Afghanistan, Kashmir, and Tibet*. New York: Routledge, 2002.

May, Walter, translator, *Manas: The Great Campaign*. Bishkek: Kyrgyz Branch of the International Centre for Traditional Cultures and Environments, 1999.

Meyer, Karl E. & Brysac, Shareen Blair, *Tournament of Shadows: The Great Game and the Race for Empire in Central Asia*. Washington: Counterpoint, 1999.

Myrdal, Jan & Kessle, Gun, *Gates to Asia: A Diary from a Long Journey*. New York: Pantheon Books, 1971.

Rashid, Ahmed, *Jihad: The Rise of Militant Islam in Central Asia*. New Haven: Yale University Press, 2002.

Rashid, Ahmed, *Taliban: Militant Islam, Oil and Fundamentalism in Central Asia*. New Haven: Yale University Press, 2000.

Rashid, Ahmed, *The Resurgence of Central Asia: Islam or Nationalism?* Karachi: Oxford University Press, 1994

Roux, Jean-Paul, *l'Asie Centrale: Histoire et civilisations*. Paris: Librarie Arthème Fayard, 1997.

Schofield, Victoria, *Afghan Frontier: Feuding and Fighting in Central Asia*. London: Tauris Parke, 2003.

Waller, John H., *Beyond the Khyber Pass: The Road to British Disaster in the First Afghan War*. New York: Random House, 1960.

Whitlock, Monica, *Land Beyond the River: The Untold Story of Central Asia*. New York: St. Martin's Press, 2002.

Wood, Frances, *The Silk Road: Two Thousand Years in the Heart of Asia*. Berkeley: University of California Press, 2002.

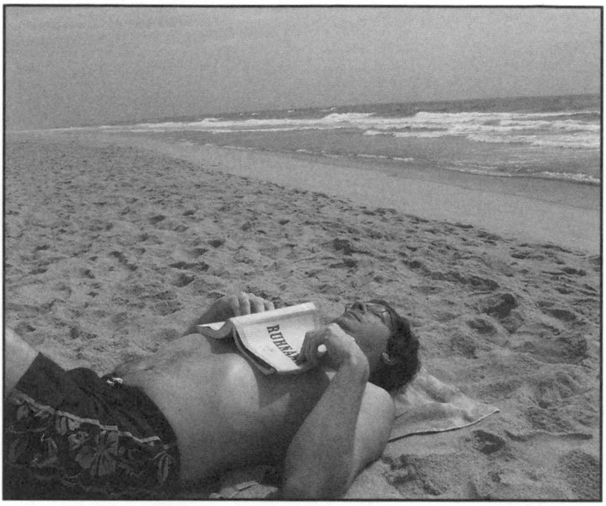

RUKHNAMA

Soaking in the wisdom of Turkmenbashi from the supreme ruler's best-selling book *Rukhnama*.

About the Author

Ted Rall, forty-three, is an editorial cartoonist and columnist for Universal Press Syndicate. A graduate with honors in History from Columbia University, he has been writing and drawing cartoons about Central Asia since 1997. Highlights of his previous work on the region include his exclusive reporting on Taliban incursions into Pakistani Kashmir in 1999, a "Stan Watch" Central Asian news segment that was featured on National Public Radio and the BBC, and an award-winning graphic travelogue about his stint as a war correspondent during the 2001 American invasion, *To Afghanistan and Back*. Rall was a Pulitzer Prize finalist in 1996 and has twice won the Robert F. Kennedy Journalism Award.

DATE DUE

PN
6727
.R35
S56
2006

Rall, Ted.

Silk road to ruin

SCHEME
OF TASHKENT METRO

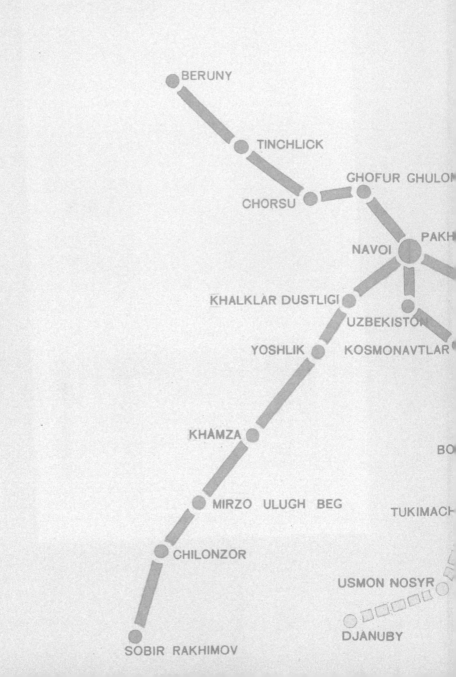

BERUNY

TINCHLICK

GHOFUR GHULO[M]

CHORSU

PAKH

NAVOI

KHALKLAR DUSTLIGI

UZBEKISTON

YOSHLIK

KOSMONAVTLAR

KHAMZA

BO

MIRZO ULUGH BEG

TUKIMACH

CHILONZOR

USMON NOSYR

DJANUBY

SOBIR RAKHIMOV